D1437567

18.95

This book is to be returned on or before the last date stamped below.

W

g

0 6 JUN 2005

2 2 MAR 2002

2 5 MAY 2007
1 6 DEC 2009
2 1 DEC 2009

2 7 FEB 2017

1 1 APR 2003

1 3 JUN 2003

16/4/2012

8 NOV 2010

2 7 APR 2015

LIBREX
28103

© Oxford Centre for Staff Development 1994

Published by
THE OXFORD CENTRE FOR STAFF DEVELOPMENT
Oxford Brookes University
Gipsy Lane
Headington
Oxford
OX3 0BP

Improving Student Learning - Theory and Practice
ISBN 1 873576 36 6
British Library Cataloguing-in-Publication Data.
A catalogue record for this book is available from the
British Library.

Designed and Typeset in Palatino and Helvetica
by Ann Trew

Printed in Great Britain by
Oxonian Rewley Press Ltd
Oxford

Printed on paper produced from sustainable forests.

The Oxford Centre for Staff Development

Improving Student Learning

Theory and Practice

Editor Graham Gibbs

Preface

This volume contains papers from the 1st International Improving Student Learning Symposium: 'Theory and Practice', held at Warwick University in September 1993. It was an event which differed markedly from past conferences on research into student learning. At such events in the late 70's a small group of researchers used to talk to each other, and to no-one else, and had very little impact on practice. I was one of those researchers and many of the other members of that small group were also present at this Symposium nearly twenty years later. In contrast to the events in the 70's 180 people came to this Symposium and over 90% of them were lecturers and educational developers, not researchers. Many of the papers reported here are by lecturers who were using research frameworks and research tools to make sense of their own teaching and their own courses. This represents a sea change in attitudes and behaviour and is a remarkable testimony to the development of what Boyer has termed the 'scholarship of teaching'. It is, in this country at least, in part due to the Improving Student Learning project after which this Symposium was named, funded by the Council for National Academic Awards (CNAA). In this project lecturers were supported by funds and expertise to study changes in their courses designed to increase the extent to which students took a deep approach in their learning. It made use of a well articulated framework based on existing research and applied this research to a wide variety of sometimes unpromising contexts. It was disseminated through leaflets to 30,000 people and through two national conferences, a book and more than 30 workshops. It aroused considerable interest and stimulated much research. Other research frameworks, especially concerning experiential learning theory, were also in evidence at the Symposium and a number of papers have proposed new ways of interpreting student learning, but the framework used in the CNAA Improving Student Learning project was clearly dominant.

This framework, based originally on work in the 70's by Ferenc Marton in Sweden and John Biggs in Australia, is founded on four key observations. First, students go about learning in qualitatively different ways. The approach students take to their studies can be seen to involve either an intention to make sense (a deep approach) or an attempt to reproduce (a surface approach). Second, the outcomes of student learning are not just quantitatively different, they are also qualitatively different - students understand different kinds of things, structured in different ways, not just more or less. Third, students understand what learning itself is, what knowledge is, and what they are doing when learning, in profoundly different ways, seeming to develop over time in the sophistication of their conceptions of learning. Fourth, teachers understand what teaching and learning to consist of, and therefore what 'good teaching' should consist of, in qualitatively different ways. These factors interact (as described in John Biggs introductory paper) so that all learning phenomena can be seen to take place in a context mediated by the perceptions of students and their teachers involving their conceptions and approaches.

The most important research tools associated with this framework are first, categories of description of approach, conception of learning and conception of teaching, allowing interview data to be categorised reliably and meaningfully. Second, the SOLO taxonomy, enabling the easy categorisation of the structural qualities of learning outcomes. Third, questionnaires (such as the ASI or Approaches to Studying Inventory) allowing easy measurement of the extent to which students generally take a surface and deep approach. And fourth, questionnaires (such as the CEQ or Course Experience Questionnaire) allowing easy measurement of students' perceptions of key features of courses which are known to influence students' approach.

The following extremely brief summary of the main research findings from within this framework provided the context for many of the the studies reported at the Symposium.

- Students vary in their approach from context to context. Most students take a surface or deep approach depending on the context. A few students always take a surface approach. Most courses have students taking both approaches to some extent. A surface approach is very prevalent.

- A surface approach nearly always leads to poorer quality learning outcomes: little understanding and only short-term recall of information. It also leads to poor marks and degrees when the assessment system rewards the outcomes of a deep approach. A deep approach can lead to good understanding, good long term recall and better marks and degrees.

- Students develop in their conceptions of learning and in their conceptions of knowledge. Students who almost always take a surface approach will tend also to have an unsophisticated conception of learning.

- Students' conceptions of good teaching are closely related to their conceptions of learning - those who have crude conceptions of learning believe teaching should be teacher-centred.

- Study skills can be used to implement either a surface or a deep approach. Crude conceptions of learning constrain approach. So the appropriate focus of learning-to-learn courses is on conception of learning, knowledge and tasks, rather than on techniques.

- Students tend to take a surface approach when the workload is perceived to be heavy, where the assessment system is perceived to demand, reward or tolerate memorisation and in a number of other known circumstances.

- Students tend to take a deep approach where they are motivated to understand, where they are active, where they discuss what is to be understood, and where they encounter knowledge in well structured ways.

• It is possible to change students' approach and the quality of their learning outcomes by manipulating those features of the context which the research has identified as crucial and especially by changing the assessment system.

This research framework and these research tools have been used in a wide variety of ways in the papers presented at the symposium. Six of the main types of use are identified here and one example given of each.

1 **Monitoring entire degree programmes**
Gregory, Thorley and Harland studied 20 degree and other courses (involving nearly 1,000 students) in a large Engineering School using the Course Experience Questionnaire. They identified several degree programmes with low scores on most of the crucial scales (such as good teaching, appropriate workload, appropriate assessment). This has led to workshops with appropriate staff and study of student workload and assessment tasks in the courses concerned in order to identify more clearly what is causing the problems. The CEQ enabled them to identify and diagnose problems in a way which conventional evaluation would not.

2 **Monitoring changes in modules**
Blackmore and Harries-Jenkins report a study, involving the use of the ASI, of several very large business and accountancy modules into which open learning materials had been introduced and where teaching had been greatly reduced. In one module student performance had markedly declined The ASI showed that student motivation had progressively declined, a surface approach had progressively increased and a deep approach had progressively declined. The conceptual framework helped to diagnose the causes of the problems and this had led to a range of specific changes.

3 **Monitoring changes within modules**
Tang studied the introduction of longer assignments alongside traditional short-answer tests in a context where short-answer tests and a surface approach were common. It was found that students took a surface approach to preparation for the short tests but a deeper approach to the longer assignments. However inexperienced students inappropriately retained a surface approach to the longer assignments highlighting the need to introduce new methods with an eye on how students will respond.

4 **Diagnosing individual student problems**
Meyer and Parsons used the ASI and other devices to identify at risk students early on in their studies and enable early intervention to reduce the likelihood of failure. In contrast Leitch, reports several attempts to identify at risk students using an atheoretical statistical method (discriminant analysis) which had not been successful. The clear implication is that you need a theoretical framework and that purely statistical approaches are unlikely to be successful.

5   **Designing curricula and assessment criteria**
     Jackson describes the structure and operation of a degree programme in
     Graphic Information Design designed around fundamental principles from
     student learning research, including conceptions of learning and the SOLO
     taxonomy, to define goals and levels of achievement which translate into
     project briefs and assessment criteria.

6   **Rewarding excellence in teaching**
     Lublin and Prosser recast their institution's evaluation and promotion
     mechanisms around a definition of good teaching derived from student
     learning research:

     *"Good teaching is teaching which helps students to learn. It discourages the
     superficial approach to learning and encourages active engagement with the
     subject matter ..... it encourages in the learner motivation to learn, desire to
     understand, perseverance, independence, a respect for the truth and a desire
     to pursue learning"*

The participants at the symposium fell into three main categories:

(i)   professional researchers concentrating on fundamental research developing
      theory, principles and research tools, with the aim of empowering teachers;

(ii) teachers doing research on their own courses and teaching, using these
      theories and tools. This theory-based research is distinct from 'grounded'
      action research which tends to hold out the promise of eventually
      rediscovering the wheel, and from student feedback collection which,
      without a theoretical underpinning, provides little basis for understanding
      what is going on.

(iii) educational developers, undertaking four main roles: supporting teachers'
      research, disseminating research findings, undertaking institution-wide
      research and using research to direct institutional policy on issues such as
      course review, evaluation and promotion.

What is needed to link these three groups is an agency concerned not with
undertaking research but with making existing research accessible to teachers and
policy makers. In the absense of such an agency this Improving Student Learning
Symposium will continue to provide a valuable forum for those wishing to
research student learning and apply findings in order to improve their learning.

Graham Gibbs
Oxford Centre for Staff Development
September 1993.

Contents

Chapter 1   The research context

Student Learning Research and Theory where do we currently stand?

John Biggs, University of Hong Kong

"There is nothing so practical as good theory"

Lewin is as right today about the relation of theory and practice as he was over fifty years ago when he first wrote the above words. However, the message has still not got across. Teachers, as Liz Beaty points out at this conference, "are only interested in practical solutions to problems", and with the lack of a common meeting place between researchers and teachers, teachers do not see that researchers can in fact offer practical solutions. My role here is to argue that some theories of learning and teaching are indeed eminently practical.

But there is a deeper, ideological, issue I would like to address first. That is the perception by many teachers and by the movers and shakers in education that interest-driven, non technological, research in educational issues has no worthwhile flow-on as far as practice is concerned. This is alarmingly evidenced in the current determination to shift the locus of teacher education from the university faculties of education to the schools. The academic input to teacher education will thus be diminished, that of the apprentice/master teacher enhanced.

This is a highly retrograde move for many reasons. What concerns me most is the underlying assumption that theory has little or no place in the practical mater of teaching; teacher training, that is to say, is best left to those who can teach. But even to say that is to assume a theory: the theory of osmotic learning. That is, place a novice in close contact with an expert, and by a process of osmosis expertise will flow from expert to novice. And of course osmosis is so much cheaper than proper professional education.

Yet this act of academic vandalism is not entirely undeserved. If educational psychologists had delivered the goods they had long been promising, the politicians would not have been able to carry through such a radical proposal. Since Thorndike (1992) underwrote arithmetic teaching with the theory of conncectionism, every decade or so someone had bemoaned the lack of impact on practice that can be traced to advances in our understanding of the psychology of learning. The problem was invariably thought to be that the wrong theory had been applied, the solution of course being to apply the theory we now know in our latter-day wisdom to be the correct one. We have thus seen a passing parade of the Now-atlast-the-One-Correct-Theory-of Learning: behaviourism,

Piagetianism, Maslovian then Rogerian humanism, cognitive psychology with information processing being the current academically correct version in some quarters, phenomenography (Marton, 1988) in others.

Some theories were more applicable to education than others, but the strategy of top down application of the One Correct Theory is simply misguided, essentially because psychologically-based theories are derived to explain the data emerging from laboratory contexts, and they are stretched to snapping point when applied to classroom and institutional contexts.

In this paper, I want to review the kinds of theories that have been developed to explain educational, and particularly tertiary, learning contexts. First, I shall start with the basic implicit and informal theories of learning and teaching held by educators, and then elaborate the more formal theories that are in current use.

Making implicit theory explicit

Any deliberate act is founded on some sort of theory, a coherent set of assumptions. You do this rather than that because you think it will work, and it will work because . . . of this, or the other. Argyris' (1976) distinction between espoused theory and theory-in-use is useful to capture what I am saying. The espoused theory is the "official" theory one holds of educational or other processes, the theory-in-use the implicitly held theory that drives action. The process of professionalisation involves matching the two; that is, where the espouses theory becomes the theory-in use. The osmotic theory of learning is a theory-in-use, but one that is far removed from the espoused theories of educational psychologists.

However, the problem is that much espoused theory remain declarative and self-referential: a public body of knowledge, supported by ingenious experimentation, and concerned with consistency within itself, all according to the academic rules, but not unfortunately easily translated into action. It is this aspect of theory that makes honest practitioners groan with impatience, while politicians delightedly sharpen their knives.

A student's or a teachers conception of what learning is, or what teaching is, become an implicit theory-in-use learning and teaching; as a theory-in use, it directs the way the students learns or the teacher teaches. Common conceptions of learning are described in Gibbs (1992), and I imagine that these will be familiar to you. Following Cole (1990), I would make just two distinctions: quantitative and qualitative implicit theories of learning and teaching, which I would more simply call "outlooks" on learning.

The quantative outlook

In the quantatitive outlook, learning is conceived as the aggregation of content: to be a good learner is to know more. The context of learning are treated as discrete quanta of declarative or of procedural knowledge: bits of knowings, any one bit being independent of any other bit. Thus, the curriculum becomes discrete units of content, such as facts, skills and competencies. The competency movement, and the current concern with performance indicators, stem from the same tradition, but as elaborated later, they need not maintain that tradition.

The process of learning is this quantatitive view is to aggregate more and more bits, internalise them, and be able to reproduce them accurately. Teaching is conceived as transmitting knowledge, or conveying knowledge from one head to another. In tertiary institutions, the most common method of teaching is of course by lecture and of learning by note-taking. The teacher's task is too expound, the student's to incorporate; hence, possibly, the learning-as-eating metaphor with which this conception seems to be obsessed: "assimilate", "absorb", "digest", regurgitate:, "spoon-feed", "chew over", "get you teeth into". Thus, once the teacher knows the content well, and can talk about it coherently, any failure in learning becomes the student's fault.

The quantitative outlook sees assessment as involving test situations that reliably indicate whether or not the student can reproduce correctly and speedily the taught item. It is assumed that the context is knowledge are learned in binary units, correct or incorrect, and that the correct units may be summed to give an aggregate or total score that is an index of competence in what is learned. Multiple choice tests, for example, represent learning as a total score of all items correct with or without guessing penalties), any one item being "worth" the same as any other. In standard methods of test construction and item analysis, items are selected on the extent to which they correlate with the total test score, not in terms of their intrinsic content. even essay marking is likely to have a quantatitive bias in practice. The most common procedure in marking open-ended essay responses is to award a mark for each relevant point made, and convert the ratio of actual marks to possible marks into some kind of number, which the teacher may then adjust for overall quality. The final grade (A, B, or D; Pass, Fail, or Distinction) is thus essentially arrived at quantitatively.

In the quantitative outlook assumptions are made about the nature and the acquisition of knowledge, that are untenable in the light of what is now know about human learning. However, the related test technology of item analysis, test construction, and establishing reliability and validity is sophisticated and in wide-spread use, so that conceptual deficiencies are masked by technocracy.

The qualitative outlook

In the qualitative outlook, it is assumed that students learn cumulatively, interpreting and incorporating new material with what they already know, their understanding progressively changing as they learn. Thus, learners' comprehension of taught content is gradual and cumulative, more like climbing a spiral staircase than dropping chips into a bag, with qualitative changes taking place in the nature both of what is learned, and how it is structured, at each level in the spiral. The curriculum question is to decide what meaning or levels of understanding are "reasonable" at the stage of learning in question.

As regards teaching method, the teacher's task is not to transmit correct understandings, but to help students construct understandings that are more rather than less acceptable. Content thus envolves cumulatively over the long term, having "horizontal" interconnections with other topics and subjects, and "vertical" interconnections with previous and subsequent learning in the same topic. The process of teaching is to help the learner undertake activities that involve progressive understanding of the meanings. The process is multidimensional, not linear: it is to intrigue the gourmet, not to sate the glutton.

Teaching here then engages the learning in constructive, in addition to receptive, learning activities. Typically, these activities involve (Biggs, 1989):

- a positive motivational context, hopefully intrinsic but at least one involving a felt need-to-know and a aware emotional climate.

- a high degree of learner activity, both task-related and reflective

- interaction with others, birth at the peer level with other students, and hierarchically, within "scaffolding" provided by an expert tutor.

- a well-structured knowledge base, that provides the longitude or depth for conceptual development and the breadth, for conceptual enrichment

How each of these dimensions may be utilised in tertiary contexts is well illustrated in the action research studies reported in Gibbs (1992).

Whereas the logic of assessment from a quantatitive point of view implies aggregating units of earning, that from the qualitative tradition implies charting longitudinal growth. The outcomes of learning become the constructions the learner has made at any given stage, so the aim of the developmental model of qualitative assessment is to discover where students currently are in their understanding or competence in the concept or skill in question. It is thus necessary to first chart the course of development of a concept or principle, so that the stages of development can be defined. This may be done by establishing a hierarchy of conceptions of understanding on a topic by topic basis (Marton, 1988; Ramsden, (1988), or by using a general taxonomy that applies over a range of topics or of subjects as in the SOLO taxonomy (Biggs & Collis, 1982), as discussed later. In the ecological model of assessment, applied or procedural knowledge is applied to test situations that are "authentic" or ecologically valid. The question in this last case is procedural; can the students solve a problem involving instructed knowledge in a real context? This means that the test has to be situated in an "authentic" setting. In a sense, this is simply saying that tests should be valid, yet so detached and quantitative has assessment become that authentic testing has become a recent catch-cry, and testing problem-solving by giving students the sort of problem they would meet in real life, rather than giving them an exam in the declarative knowledge prerequisite to problem solving, a major innovation (Master & Hill, 1989; Wiggins, 1989).

I have presented the quantitative and qualitative outlooks as implicit theories of learning, but they are more than that; they also describe a person's whole orientation towards learning and teaching, affecting a very wide range of academic decisions. I once heard an academic remark at a Higher Degree Committee meeting that as a student's M. Phil. proposal mooted a sample size of over 2,000 subjects: "But that's enough subjects for a PH.D.!" Now there's a quantitative outlook on the academic world.

Unfortunately, such outlooks are hard to modify, but a qualitative outlook is probably a necessary conditions for the more desirable ways of teaching and learning. To effect that change is a major challenge to staff developers. An even greater challenge is when staff developers and educators try to drive teaching-related decisions with a qualitative outlook, when the parameters within which they are forced to work are quantitative. Precisely this is happening at the moment with the performance indicators and competency based accountability drive.

I turn next to the question of formal theories of student learning, as opposed to informal outlooks on learning.

Explicit theories of student learning

Viable theories of students learning are, like any other form of intellectual construction, formed in situ, using one or more of the basic components in the tertiary context: the student, the teaching context, the ways of engaging or processing the task, the outcome of learning, and the institutional context. Each group of theories has its uses, but some are much more useful than others.

1   Student-based
This family of theories comes from individual differences psychology, the focus being on qualities inherent in the student that have a powerful effect on educability.

Figure 1 Student-based theories of learning

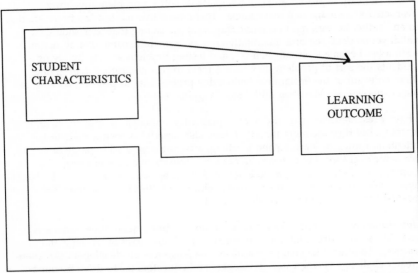

Such factors would include abilities, prior knowledge, motivation, personality facts that promote or lessen student teachability, quantatitive or qualitative outlook on learning, learning styles, stabilised learning approach, and so forth.

Most of these factors focus on stable individual traits, such as ability or learning style, that are thought to affect the nature of the outcome, independently or particular learning contexts domains. Learning style once had a considerable vogue under the name of cognitive style, instances of which had proliferated to what can only be described as a silly extent. Styles have been usefully synthesised by riding and Cheema 91991), who find two generic styles: wholist-analytic, and verbaliser-imager. But the essence of these student based factors is that, like ability or socio-economic status, they are thought t be far more important than "educational" factors in determining educational outcomes, a view given inaccurate but influential support in the famous Coleman Report (Coleman et al., 1966)

There are two problems with the individual differences approach. First the lack of research demonstrating that styles and abilities do interact with teaching methods in ways that are practicable and usable. Second, it is another variant of the blame-the-student model, that is, when learning is inadequate it is because the students are unmotivated, of low ability, have poor backgrounds, and so on.

The teacher is let off the hook.
However, good teaching involves helping students learn; it should not involve finding reasons that conveniently inhere in the student to explain when teaching fails. Thus, the student-focused model isn't about teaching at all; it may help teachers to find fault with their students more effectively, but it doesn't help them find fault with their own teaching, which is what being reflective practitioner means (Bowden, 1988; Schon, 1987).

2   *Teacher-based*
This family of theories might be called the traditional staff-development model, where the focus is on the teacher and on the development of teaching skills. This too is a blame model, in this case blame-the-teacher.

Figure 2 Teaching-based theories of learning

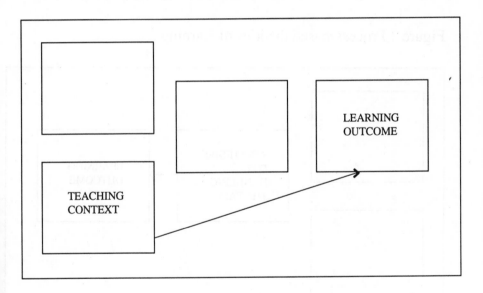

Blaming the teacher is precisely what the accountability movement is about; it sees the teacher as the prime actor, who should dazzle with a fine display of mastery of teaching skills, and other performance indicators of good teaching. Many staff developers still work on the assumption that their function is to increase the range and efficiency of an individual's teaching skills, and the linking of staff development with A/V or ed tech centres, which have the corresponding function of increasing the range of teaching related hardware, thus reinforcing the teaching skills model of staff development. The model appears eminently reasonable on the surface, but teaching skills are teaching skills only if students learn, otherwise teaching is a spectator sport.

3   *Process-based*
This family of theories derives from information processing psychology; the interest is in the efficiency with which basic cognitive strategies are deployed. The emphasis here is not upon individual characteristics, but upon the "on-line" cognitive strategies that students may be trained to use when handling tasks.

Figure 3 Process-based theories of learning

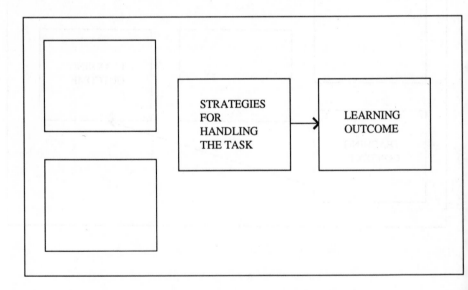

The information processing model is similar to learning style in that information processing strategies are conceived as being context-free or detached; elaboration, imaging, reversal, and the like (Weinstein and Mayer 1984). These strategies operate in much the same way whether the material being elaborated or rehearsed is being prepared for an examination or for a laboratory experiment. Study skills training, and heuristics training deriving from Polay's (1945) How to Solve it, also derives from this model. Students are trained to use appropriate strategies or study skills in one context (the training sessions) and are then required to carry them into actual work settings. There is an element of the blame-the-student deficit model in this approach in that the students are thought to lack something, in this case study skills, which of course may well be the case but it leaves the teacher out of the picture.

The evidence on strategy training is equivocal (Garner, 1990). In the case of study skills, given appropriate contextual and motivational backup there is some evidence that skills training can work (Biggs, 1988) but under other circumstances such training can even be counterproductive, Ramsden, Beswick, and Bowden 91986), for example, found that after a study skills course for first year students, the only noticeable result was an increase in surface approaches not deep as intended. The reason turned out to be that students perceived from the messages signalled from course structure, work loads, and assessment, that accurate reproduction of facts and study skills was what was required for success in first year, over several subject departments; accordingly, the study skills course was used selectively, those aspects seen to lead to better reproducing were taken on board, those leading to better understanding were seen as at best irrelevant. Whatever their real intentions, it is clear that the teachers concerned had a massive selling job to do first, before study skill training could bear fruit. This study should however not be seen as evidence against study skills training, but as argued more fully below as evidence for the need to integrate both teaching-based, student-based, and process-based, approaches to improving learning.

All the model discussed so far are deficit model; poor learning is seen to be due to lack of something, either in the student, the teaching, or in something the student a be trained to do. To improve learning, all you have to do is to add something. It may occasionally be the case that such an assumption does result in improvements, but it is avoiding the real situation; that you are dealing with a complex system of events, in which the parts interact, which brings me to the next model.

4   *Classroom-based*
This model sees, student, teaching method, learning approaches and outcome as interactively related:

Figure 4 Classroom-based theories of learning

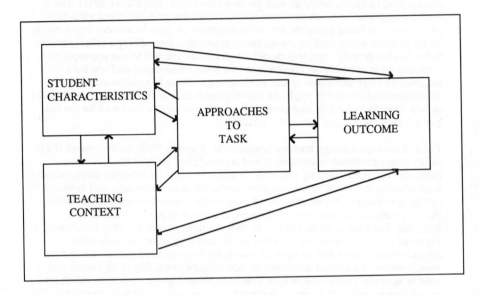

This model derives from Dunkin and Biddle's (1974) presage-process-product classroom teaching model, who saw a linear progression from presage (teaching context) through process (teaching acts) to product (class achievement). The present version (Biggs, 1993b) differs in two main ways:

- we are talking about student learning, not teaching
- all factors should mutually affect each other

Thus, student do not blunder on with their initial intentions or expectations regardless; they get a feel for the course and for the teacher once it is underway, and continually revise. Likewise, good teachers are sensitive to student feedback, even at the most informal, inter-ocular, level and revise their teaching and assessment conditions.

Thus, too task processing is tuned (a) to students' expectations, prior relevant knowledge, preferred or stabilised approaches to learning, and so on, and (b) to their perceptions of task demands arising from the teaching context requirements. Feedback from the task processing from the student's point of view involves metacognition, deliverbate awareness and control over task processing; it is not something that the student runs of on cue, but which is planned, monitored, and if necessary revised according to progress and to perceptions of task requirements. This is why teaching detached skills, when ignoring both context and students' changing expectations and intentions, can be hit or miss. Task feedback also affects teaching decisions, if the teacher is sufficiently aware to take them on board.

Task processing determines the outcome in ways that are now very clear: surface processing leads to bitty, unstructured outcomes, deep processing to well-structured outcomes (Biggs, 1979; Marton & Saljo 1976; Trigwell & Prosser, 1991; Watkins, 1983). Again, however, metacognitive monitoring of the outcome enables optimising the link between process and product; and at the presage level, adjustment by student and by teacher.

The open-ended, recursive feature of this model means that there is a tendency for the parts to attain equilibrium, in other words, it has the essential features of a system in balance (Von Bertalanffy, 1968). What this means is that any change will be absorbed into the existing balance, unless it is drastic, in which case a new system will be created, as happens so readily in the case of eco-system. The classroom is just such an eco-system; for example, the presence or absence of one or two key players can make a huge difference to, say, a group discussion in which all nevertheless participate.

Thus, teaching students how to study more effectively in a system in which surface learning is perceived as the adaptive way to go will result in more effective surface learning, as Martin, Ramsden and Bowden found. The answer is not to target the student, but to target the system of teaching and assessing that made the unwanted learning approach ecologically valid. Students tend to stabilise their approaches to learning according both to their ongoing experience of the teaching context, and to their own motivational and other predisposition, so that an individual's preferred or stabilised approaches are ones that work for that person, in that teaching context. If the context is perceived to change, then the individual would readjust. Questionnaire assessments of approaches to learning, such as the ASI (Entwistle & Ramsden, 1983) or the SPQ (Biggs, 1987), thus reflect a current state of affairs in a student's institutional adaptation, and if averaged over a large class would give and index of the quality of teaching in that class (Biggs, 1993a). Approaches to learning are thus sensitive to individual differences, and to teaching contexts, in a way that is not the case with learning styles.

5   *The phenomenographic model*
Phenomenography is a highly influential methodology in the student learning literature (Marton, 1988), with Marton and Saljo's (1976) study of surface and deep approaches to learning, and their relationship to the quality of the outcome, a much-quoted source. Learning is studied from the perspective of the learner, not that of teacher or researcher, the object being to see how students construe the content, expressed as the form of the relationship the knower sets up with the

known. Usually such constructions, or conceptions, can be expressed in a limited number of hierarchically ordered ways, some learners having partial or distorted conceptions of the intended topic, others sophisticated ones. Learners may "comprehend", more or less, the teacher's perspective, but they genuinely learn only what they construct from their own perspective. Their approach to learning is how they go about that construction.

In many respects phenomenography has much in common with the classroom level systems model, but it differs in other respects. In view of the popularity of this view of student learning, it would be appropriate to devote some time to a compare-and-constrast with the systems model.

The starting point of each is the student's perspective. This is quite explicit in phenomenography, but it is also clear in the systems model: it is the student's perceptions of the task demands, the student's construction of meaning that is important. This element is absent in the teaching skills model, where it is what the teachers does that is the important thing, not what the student does.

Learning (and teaching) are context dependent, an important difference from both the student- and teacher-based models. Learning takes place with respect to content and context; you learn something somewhere. Indeed, Marton is reluctant to talk about learning as an independent process at all; learning and outcome are as it were two sides of the same sphere. Thus, it is conceptually OK to view the elements in the learning situation separately in the systems model, but it is not OK in phenomenography.

A major difference between the models is on the question of generality. Phenomenography derives from phenomenlogy, which takes as the only reality the student's immediate perception of the task; questions of overlap with other student's perceptions, let alone the teacher's perceptions, are ruled out of order. There are two consequences. First, individual personality factors are rules out; they may affect the immediate phenomenal space of the student, but how they do so is not relevant. A bright student will see things differently from a dumb student; the importance is the perception itself in each case, not the brightness or the dumbness which may affect the perception. This position necessarily follows from adopting the student's perspective as the only reality: brighteness is a category used by an outsider, not by the experiencer. However, there is considerable evidence that perceptions are altered by "personality" factors (see Figure 4), and that is worth knowing, studying, and taking into account, as would be the case in the systems model.

The second consequence is that it becomes impossible to generalise across teaching/learning situations. If each individual's perspective is unique, you are left with an infinite number of perspectives. Thus, find it difficult to see where pjhenomenography can lead to action. On the other hand, Bowden (1988; 1989) has adapted what he calls "phenomenography pedagogy", which he sharply distinguishes from phenomenography itself, as a basis for staff development. Teachers are faced with hard evidence that their students' understandings of taught concepts are in fact miserably below the expected level, and then "reflect on the the learning experiences most likely to bring about conceptual change in teachers, ie. the shift in student understanding" (1989: 10). This work certainly brings about conceptual change in teachers, ie. the shift to a qualitative outlook mentioned earlier, but the answer to the procedural question "But what can I do to improve my teaching?" does not appear to be forthcoming from phenomenography. Ramsden (1992), in addressing that questions, goes well beyond phenomenography itself.

Phenomenography and the systems model have in common, along with constructivist theories in general, the assumption that students learning cumulatively and in clear stages; assessment of learning, as stated in the qualitative outlook, aims to nominate the stage at which a student is presently at in the understanding of a concept. This may be done on a topic by topic basis, as is the case in phenomenography, or by using a general taxonomy, such as the SOLO taxonomy (Biggs & Collis, 1982) that applies over a range of topics or even subjects. The topic-by-topic approach is more sensitive, but it requires considerable research and development for each topic addressed. The SOLO taxonomy assumes a general sequence in the development of many concepts and skills, and that sequence may be used to guide the formulation of specific targets or the assessment of specific outcomes, and can be used in a conventional letter grade scheme (Biggs, 1992).

Finally, in phenomenography there is a hint of a prescriptive return to the One-Correct-Theory: that this is the way to construe learning and that any other way is simply wrong. Systems thinking, on the other hand, is not so much a theory as a way of generating ideas about how a complex of variables may interact, when the predictability of relations between subsets of variable is low. As such, system thing is applicable to a variety of disciplines and situations, such as physics, biology, mathematics, cybernetics, management, or economics; it is not a theory belonging to any one discipline (von Vertanlanffy, 1968).

In short, there are many aspects that henomenography and systems thinking have in common. Where they differ, is on the focus of interest: on the conceptions that people carry around in their heads, or on the complex factors that link thinking, action, and context.

6   The institutional model
An elaboration of the systems model brings institutional considerations into focus; recent events have rammed home the fact that systems thinking does not stop at the classroom. Teachers may have a certain degree of autonomy, but basically they have to work within the framework and structures dictated by the

institution (which in turn has to operate within nationally dictated policies and resourcing limitations).

Figure 5 The Institutional System

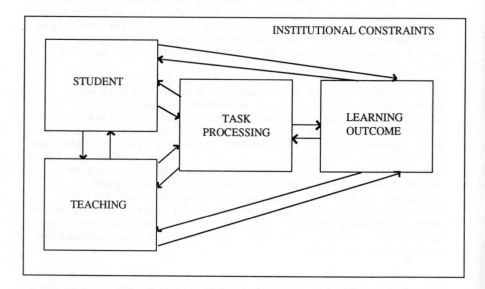

Reid (1987) distinguishes three major components in the institutional system: the rhetoric, the technology, and the social system, with the social system setting the terms of equilibrium for the others, the "technology", or teaching know-how, mainly belongs in the classroom, to serve institutional rhetoric, but its effective application depends on the social system of the institution, which has two aspects;

i   the formal requirements established on a collegian basis;
ii   the formal requirements of bureaucracy

Institutions vary in the extent to which deviance at the classroom level is tolerated.

One example that illustrates both formal and informal requirements comes from one university in Hong Kong, which like UK universities 20 years ago, has regulations preventing the release of examination results to students, obviously not on educational grounds, but on grounds of institutional and collegian convenience. On one occasion an academic claimed the right to use his own judgment on releasing marks, only to be told by a senior academic: "But if you do it, students will put pressure on al of us to follow suit. That's just not cricket!" And he was in this case able to add institutional support: "Anyway, you can't. It's against the regulations."

The use of external examiners may constrain the nature of the assessment tasks to ones that an outsider to the teaching process can handle. Feedback is written as much with an eye to the external's anticipated comments as to informing the student. The use is personalised assessment tasks such as portfolios, diaries, etc., or tasks involving self-assessment and peer assessment, despite the relevance of these modes of assessment to teaching objectives and to higher order learning processes (Harris & Bell, 1986; Masters & Hill, 1991), are discouraged.

Most institutions require that the gradings obtained in course units are combined in order, inter alia, to determine levels of Honours or Distinction/Pass levels in the total programme. This puts almost irresistible pressure on markers to use quantative marking schemes. It need not do so, as profiling or other qualitative schemes can be used, but as in practice teachers are required to come up with a grade that can be quantified in a common metric, they too easily mark quantitatively in the first place. This provides them with a frequently inappropriate mind-set when marking: "so many marks for this, so many for that ...". In an extended piece of writing, the shapes of the total argument becomes lost, the shape of the argument figuring minimally as just another thing to be tallied when arriving at the final grade.

A quite recent phenomenon in the concerns about assessment in tertiary institutions has to do with quality control, performance indicators, and their accountability to governments, as part of the market rationalism that had come to obsess the Western world.

There is nothing wrong with monitoring the effectiveness of one's operations. In the case of individual performance it's called being metacognitive. Now institutions are required to be metacognitive, but there are two problems. The first is translating self-monitoring into operational terms; what aspects are you monitoring, qualitative ones or quantatitive? Economic rationalists think quantatively to a person, so that raises problems problems when you bring in issues that go beyond immediate cost-effectiveness. The second problem is that of accountability. If institutions are being held in true metocognitive fashion to be accountable to themselves, that's one thing. But if governments who attempt to define the currency in which accountability is transacted, we are back again to a quantatitive mind-set.

"Performance indicators" is the leading term given to this currency, and at its lowest would define output in relation to input, and the higher that ratio the better: the more graduates out for fewer dollars in, the more effective the institution. The real danger is that such indicators are usually but not necessarily quantatitive, which have their own backwash, in exactly the same way a teacher's assessment techniques have their backwash on student learning. If we want quantitative approaches to assessment at the classroom level, the organisational climate of the institution as a whole is implicated, as discussed by Lublin and Prosser at this conference. It is very difficult for teachers to construct a qualitative framework for their students to operate within, when they themselves have to operate within a framework of quantatively defined performance indicators.

Conclusion

I have tried to give an overview of the state of play in theories of student learning. In summary, several features strike me.

1 Theory is at last being derived from the context to which it is to be applied, as opposed to attempting to applying psychological theories from a distance.

2 We are beginning to move away from deficit models, according to which you find out what's wrong and fix it. Education is not like that. Rather, education is as Schon (1987:3) describes it: "a soft, slimy swamp of real-life problems" to which adding or subtracting things will either have to measurable effect, or worse, will destroy the swamp's eco-system.

3 The palmy days of high degrees of autonomy for the individual teacher appear to be over. Independently of the colour of particular governments, a quantatitive mind-set seems to be setting constraints not only on resourcing, hence on the numbers of students in a given class which itself of course suggests mass methods of teaching and assessing, but on the structure of degree programmes and how they are to be delivered and accounted for institutionally. The classrooms quite evidently a subsystem within the larger institutional systems, which is something that realistic theories of teaching need to take into account.

References

Argyris, C. (1976) Theories of action that inhibit individual learning. *American Psychologist, 31,* 638-654

Biggs, J B (1979). Individual differences in study processes and the quality of learning outcomes. *Higher Education, 8* 381-394.

Biggs J. B (1987). *Student approaches to learning and studying.* Australian Council for Educational Research, Hawthorn, Victoria.

Biggs, J. B (1988). The role of the metacognition in enhancing learning. *Australian Journal of Education, 32,* 127-138.

Biggs, J. B (1989). Approaches to the enhancement of tertiary teaching. *Higher Education research and Development. 8,* 7 -25.

Biggs, J. B (1992). A qualitative approach to grading students. *HERDSA News, 14* (3), 3-6.

Biggs, (1993a). What do learning process inventories really measure? A theoretical review and clarification. *British Journal of Educational Psychology, 63,* 3-19.

Biggs, J. B (1993b). From theory to practice: A cognitive systems approach. *Higher education Research and Development 12,* 73-86.

Biggs, J.B & Collis, K F. (1982). *Evaluating the Quality of Learning: The SOLO Taxonomy.* New York Academic Press.

Biggs, J.B & Collis, K.F (1989) Towards a model of school-based curriculum development and assessment: using the SOLO Taxonomy. *Australian Journal of Education, 33,* 149-161.

Bowden, J.A. (1988). Achieving change in teaching practices. In P. Ramsden (ED.) *Improving learning: new perspectives.* London: Kogan Page.

Bowden, J.A (1989. Curriculum development for conceptual change learning: A phenomenographic pedagogy. Paper presented to 6th Annual Conference, Hong Kong Educational Research Association.

Cole, N.S. (1990). Conceptions of educational achievement. *Educational Researcher, 19*(3), 2-7.

Coleman, J.S., Campbell, E., Hobson, C., Partland, J., Mood, A., Weinfeld, F., and York, R. (1966). *Equality of educational opportunity.* Washington, DC: Officer of Education, US Department of Health, Education, and Welfare.

Dunkin, M.J., & Biddle, B.J. (1974). *The Study of Teaching.* New York: Holt, Rinehard & Winston.

Entwistle N. & Ramsden P. (1983). *Understanding Student Learning.* London: Croom Helm.

Garner, R. (1990). When children and adults do not use learning strategies: Towards a theory of settings. *Review of Educational Research, 60,* 517-529.

Gibbs, G. (1992). *Improving the quality of student learning*. Bristol: Technical & Educational Services Ltd.

Harris, D. & Bell, C. (1986). *Evaluating and assessing for learning*. London: Kogan Page.
Marton, F. (1988). Describing and improving learning. In R.R. Schmeck (ed.), *Learning strategies and learning styles*. New York: Plenum.

Marton, F., & Saljo, R. (1976). On qualitative differences in learning - I: Outcome and process. *British Journal of Educational Psychology, 46,* 4-11.

Masters, G,N., & Hill, P.W. (1988). Reforming the assessment of student achievement in the senior secondary school. *Australian Journal of Education, 32,* 247-286.

Polya, G. (1945). *How to solve it.* Princeton: Pinceton University Press.

Ramsden, P. (Ed.) (1998). *Improving Learning: New Perspectives.* London: Kogan Page.

Ramsden, P. (1992). *Learning to teach in higher education.* London: Routledge.

Ramsden, P., Beswick, D., & Bowden, J (1986). Effects of learning skills interventions on first year university students' learning. *Human Learning, 5,* 151-164.

Reid, W.A (1987). Institutions and practices: Professional education reports and the language of reform. *Educational Researcher, 16* (8), 10-15.

Riding, R & Cheema, I (191) Cognitive styles - An overview and integration. *Educational Psychology, 11* 193-215.

Schon, D.A (1987) *Educating the Reflective Practitioner.* San Francisco: Jossey-Bass.

Trigwell, K. & Prosser, M. (191). Improving the quality of student learning: The influence of learning context and student approaches to learning on learning outcomes. *Higher Education, 22,* 251-266.

Von Bertalanffy, L. (1968). *General systems theory.* New York: Braziller.

Watkins, D.A (1983). Depth of processing and the quality of learning outcomes. *Instructional Science, 12,* 49-58.

Weinstein, C., & Mayer, R (1984). The teaching of learning strategies. In M.C. Wittrock (Ed.), *Handbook of Research on Teaching.* New York: Macmillan.

Wiggins, G. (1989). Teaching to the (authentic) test. *Educational Leadership, 46,* 41-47.

Using research on student learning to enhance educational quality

Paul Ramsden

A few years ago David Minton published a book about teaching skills in adult education (Minton 1991). To introduce an idea about the importance of the teacher's experience as a key factor in the quality of learning and teaching, he described his own experience of eating a delicious dish of garlic mushrooms in a restaurant in the Beaujolais. Madame served, and her husband did the cooking. But Minton made a mistake. He asked Madame for the recipe. "Monsieur," came the withering reply, "It is not what, it is who."

Minton had asked the wrong question. The difference between one dish of garlic mushrooms and another does not depend on the recipe, but on the person who cooks it.

Much the same is true of the quality of university teaching and university courses. There are no certain prescriptions for good teaching. There are no foolproof techniques for guaranteeing quality. There are only teachers, and educational effectiveness depends on their professionalism, their experience, and their commitment. We must ask the right questions in the search for quality. We must emphasise the importance of the "who" on in order to achieve quality.

What does it take to improve the quality of learning and teaching in higher education? What will help teachers to achieve it? In this chapter I would like to illustrate how some of the ideas from student learning research might be used to improve the quality of university education. There are three areas I want to apply these lessons: helping the novice lecturer to become more expert; providing appropriate academic leadership; and using methods of evaluating teaching and courses which combine the need to assure quality with the principal purpose of enhancing it.

Lessons from student learning research

The main lessons from the last fifteen years of research into student learning will have an everyday ring to most readers. The ideas of a formerly obscure group of academics from Britain and Sweden have become accepted into the discourse of quality in higher education. Powerful people and statutory bodies now use phrases from what used to be a comfortably private area of educational research as part of their lingua franca.

It seems now generally accepted that we need to look at students' learning in the natural environment in which it takes place. University students' experiences of teaching and assessment matter more than particular teaching methods in determining the effectiveness of their learning. Perhaps less embedded in academic culture, though it follows directly, is the idea that "teaching" means more than instructing and performing and extends more broadly to providing a context in which students engage productively with subject matter. There is now a widespread view in academic development circles, derived directly from the student learning research, that we should concentrate on learning, on what the learner does and why the learner thinks he or she is doing it, rather than what the teacher does (Shuell, 1986: Biggs, 1990,1993). And, if teaching is about helping to make learning possible, assessment becomes defined as being about understanding students and what they have learnt. Effective assessment helps students develop the skills of self-assessment.

I want to go beyond this, however. These examples can be translated into another set related to improving educational quality. University teaching takes place in a context, and understanding the academic's experience of academic work is a key to understanding how to improve it. Improving teaching is about helping to make teacher learning possible; evaluating teaching is about getting to know teachers and their teaching; effective teaching is professional, self-evaluating teaching – and effective evaluation helps develop the skills of self-evaluation.

Improving teaching: Helping novices become experts

One reason for the impact of the research on student learning is that it reflects, in a special way, how accomplished teachers go about their work. The great body of research on teaching expertise makes it clear that the experts focus primarily about what their students are doing and thinking. Expert teachers look at teaching from the point of view of the learner, not the teacher. There is a strong association between this way of teaching and the quality and quantity of student learning.

Novices as well as experts use models or theories of teaching when they teach. Experts and novices express different conceptions of teaching, and different intentions underlie the strategies they use (see Bain, 1993: Trigwell and Prosser, 1990. Cushing, Sabers and Berliner, 1992). For novice teachers, the immediate reality of class management, lecture notes, teaching materials, and numbers of students looms large. They want to do what I did when I gave my first lecture – to fit into the existing environment. How did my predecessor teach this class? How can I do the same? They see teaching primarily as telling or transmitting knowledge, and organising is to that it can be efficiently transferred from teacher to learner. Events in the classroom are interpreted from the teacher's point of view alone, and their implications for students' learning are rarely perceived. Novices typically believe that reflection on the effects of teaching on student learning is "only theory": they sharply distinguish educational theory from "reality".

The expert differs not only in terms of strategies and the effectiveness of his or her students' learning, but also in terms of conceptions and intentions. Naturally the expert teacher often does the things that a novice does. But something like class management, for example, does not usually occupy the foreground of his or her thinking, any more than declutching and hear changing occupied Juan Fangio. The expert thinks about teaching as interacting with students and monitoring their learning. This may involve some presentation of information, but that is only a step on the way; it is not what an expert thinks teaching is. He or she intends to make the educational environment, not simply respond to it, and sets the ground rules by making explicit what is expected from students as far as he or she is concerned, not by reference to other teachers. The expert is very alert to classroom events, and fully understands the value of reflection on practice as a way of adapting and improving.

Although you can tell teachers about effective strategies, this is not enough to improve their students' learning, since they will often not use them, or will misuse them, unless they also change their intentions and their conceptions. Failure to understand these relationships remains one the serious errors of conventional staff development, just as it remains the fundamental misconceptions of conventional study skills courses. The mistake has been repeated in many texts on teaching methods in higher education. Too often, the lecturer's education in teaching methods has stopped at the strategies. Sometimes it encourages a spilt between conception and strategy by marginalising theory "So much for the theory about how rats learn to run mazes. Now on to the real world of teaching large classes in a converted cigarette factor". It is interesting that this dualist ontology – quite different from modern views of how professionals learn and practice – has been recently formalised in an unfavourable contrast between "practical strategies" and "theoretical ideas about teaching" in universities (see Bligh, 1993). The dualist conception embodies the novice's error.[1]

The results of ignoring the importance of teachers' conceptions in staff development are familiar to every staff developer. If you understand teaching as information transmission, and intend so to teach, how will you react to the suggestion that you should use buzz groups in lectures? Probably by saying that you don't have time for student activity; you won't be able to get through all the content. If you try a student-centred strategy, you will probably take it very seriously, and when it doesn't work, you will probably abandon it rather than try to make it work; you may use it superficially in a way contrary to its purpose. Teaching strategies are important, and teachers must learn them; but they must learn them and change their understanding if the strategies are to lead to better student learning (see Trigwell, Prosser and Taylor, 1994).

---

[1] *It also makes the nature of the error invisible to those who have the conception, an effect that has been noted in phenomenographic studies of learning.*

These ideas about how university teachers learn to teach are expressed in the best of the programmes for new staff and accredited courses for lecturers in Australia and the UK (Bain, 1993; Anderson, 1994; SEDA, 1994). SEDA's scheme in particular represents exemplary practice in professional teacher education. We are seeing a change from a dualist model to a unified one, where ideas about how students learn and how assessment and teaching affect their learning are integrated with the experience of teaching. In these programmes, "classroom strategies" and "theory" are in constant dependence with each other, each taking its meaning from the other. The new pattern is similar to the general movement towards more problem-based and experience-driven professional education (Schon, 1987). It reflects today's understanding of how students and teachers learn.

A recent study of Australian new academic staff programmes provides support for the proposition that courses of this type lead to more effective teaching than the traditional ones (Martin and Ramsden, 1994). It also confirms the conclusions of a long-term investigation of American courses for new faculty (Boice, 1992). The naive dualism of foundational theory versus teaching practice in university staff development is not longer tenable.

The best courses involve staff in a lengthy programme, related to their special needs alone, in which there are many opportunities for inter-colleague interaction. Even the most carefully designed course, however, may have little impact on teaching quality unless the much more powerful effect of the

academic's normal environment – the department, school or faculty – is taken into account. There is no point in having great ideas about new ways to help students to learn if the departmental environment is hostile to their application. New academics soon abandon their innovatory strategies if their colleagues give them no encouragement to use them. They adapt to the context they find themselves in. This is another commonplace of student learning research that we must apply to educational development.

The context of teaching: Leadership that enables

Recently I was discussing the problem of how to recognise and reward good university teaching with the Deputy Vice Chancellor (Staffing) of an Australian university. The talk went through the usual topics: perceptions that good teaching went unrewarded in comparison with research; the issues of how to measure good teaching; the ways of altering promotion systems to take more account of teaching; the use of portfolios and the pitfalls of student ratings. Then he said, "Do you know the single most important thing that would lead to better teaching, and a feeling that good teaching is properly rewarded? Appoint the right Vice Chancellor".

He is right of course. Promotions are a necessary but small part of recognising and rewarding the effort put into teaching. The problem is much more fundamental. It is a problem of environment and leadership. Its solution requires creating the conditions in which staff feel empowered to help their students. It involves helping them feel that their work is valued, and praising and supporting their efforts to assist their students, not ignoring or criticising them. It implies the time and the resources and the behaviour that helps teachers learn. It means helping them to learn from each other.

There is a remarkable analogy between what student learning research says about the effect of the context of learning on approaches to learning and the effects of the academic environment on approaches to teaching. Just as good teaching can encourage active engagement with academic content, so good leadership can encourage staff to give their best to their students. Good leadership helps create an environment for teacher learning and collaborative problem-solving.

Studies of secondary school effectiveness demonstrate this point so faithfully that I am surprised at how little attention is still paid to academic leadership by educational developers. The nature of the principal's leadership is the crucial variable in determining the satisfaction and success of the staff. In a good school, where the children learn a lot and enjoy their work, the principal is typically someone who knows what he or she wants the school to achieve and helps teachers to work together towards shared goals. He or she is primarily interested in solving educational problems rather than administrative ones. These principals provide leadership that enables staff to operate as a team. They monitor the effects of their management strategies, striving continuously to improve them. They use consistent delegation policies. They model risk-taking in teaching. They emphasise educational values. They focus on the value of caring about students as a critical aspect of what the school does. They actively use knowledge and ideas from outside the school to improve what goes on within it (Donaldson, 1991).

To push this analogy even further, the findings of studies of secondary school teachers' perceptions of what a good principal does reflect those of studies of students' perceptions of good teaching (Louis, 1993; Ramsden, 1992, chapter 6). The student learning research tells us about the importance of intellectual challenge, clear goals, creating an environment where they take responsibility for their own learning, encouraging co-operation between students, concern and respect for students as learners and people, understand what students have learnt and what they still need to learn, giving a lot of feedback on learning, continuously monitoring the effects of one's teaching in order to improve it, seeing teaching as a conversation or dialogue rather than a transmission process, and understanding teaching as a process of enabling learners, rather than a set of recipes.

Each of these factors in good teaching has a counterpart in effective academic leadership. If teaching is helping to make learning possible, educational leadership is helping to make effective teaching possible. Proficient academic leadership involves building a shared vision through establishing clear goals, improving communication, and creating challenge in an environment of collaborative decision making and teamwork where each individual feels a responsibility for achieving excellence in teaching and learning. It involves engaging in a conversation or dialogue with teacher. It implies encouraging staff to become involved in the process of evaluating improving their teaching as a normal part of their work. Very importantly, it also implies putting ideas into practice through observable action – nothing is more disheartening than rhetoric about supporting good teaching that is not backed up by appropriate management behaviour that recognises the value of good teaching.

Viewed like this, leadership is indeed a process analogous to good teaching; and like good teaching, its highest aims is to achieve redundancy. Of the best teachers the students say "We learned it all without you". Of the best academic leaders the academics say "We did it all ourselves".

Investigations of research productivity generally support the argument that leadership and the academic context are important determinants of individual research output. Co-operatively-managed academic units with participative, goal-directed governance lead to higher productivity (Bland and Ruffin, 1992). When researchers move from more supportive environments to less supportive ones, their productivity declines: and vice-versa. The context of research affects the researcher's activity and output.

Is this true about university teaching? How does the context of teaching affect the quality of teaching? Mike Prosser, Keith Trigwell, Elaine Martin and I have just started to look at the associations between the academic environment and lecturers' approaches to teaching. Trigwell and Prosser have identified different approaches to university teaching among science lecturers which are similar to the "knowledge transmission" versus "facilitating learning" conceptions of teaching which others have previously described (see for example Samuelowicz and Bain, 1992). The different approaches are empirically connected to the use of different teaching strategies and, moreover, they appear to elicit different approaches to learning among students. Our hypothesis now is that these approaches to teaching, like students' approaches to learning, are related to the perceived academic environment. We hope to be able to trace a path from departmental management to the quality of student learning (see Figure 1). Present indications are that perceptions of so-called transformational leadership "The head motivates you to do more in your teaching than you ever thought you could", participatory management "The head of this department listens to what you have to say" and teacher involvement "People discuss their teaching problems with each other here" may well form a link between academic management and good teaching.

Assessing educational quality: taking control of evaluation

According to the student learning research, assessment gives messages about the kind of learning required. If so, then evaluation gives messages about the kind of teaching required. The third area where student learning research impacts on educational quality is evaluation. Any credible scheme for evaluation has to take account of two apparently conflicting goals: the need to provide publicly-verifiable information for purposes of accountability purposes. If enhancing the quality of student learning is the primary goal, it is imperative to prevent the task of collecting and demonstrating from overwhelming the process of reflection and change. It is no use simply ignoring the need for rigorous reporting of good data, but is is no use either pretending that perceptions of the assessment process will not determine its effectiveness. Luckily, if we get the improvement part right, the accountability part is generally sure to follow. Good evidence of improvement is automatic evidence of accountability.[2]

If Minton is right about the importance of the "who" in teaching, then the methodology must build a sense of ownership in and responsibility for the process among teachers. Like a good student assessment regime, it should provide plenty of feedback and encourage openness and cooperative activity. It should minimise anxiety and the sense of being continually inspected. It should be valid, generous, and fair. It should be the subject of a dialogue between assessors and assessed. It should not do anything that discourages people from trying to criticise their performance candidly, and from trying to use the information they gather about their performance to enrich what they subsequently do. It should encourage responsible self-assessment. It should be integral to teaching and learning, rather than additional to teaching and learning. It must lead to trustworthy judgements about academic performance.

It is interesting that the process of quality assessment of Australian universities has, for all its other faults, used an evaluation model that is surprisingly up to date and congruent with the student learning research findings about the effects of assessment on the quality of learning. Instead of using an expensive and clumsy inspection model, the Australian system has approached the problem by requiring sound self-evaluation linked to institutional objectives, followed by external audit of the results of this process. The message that this system is trying to convey is that outcomes and evidence of improvement matter more than the existence of quality management processes in themselves; and that the responsibility for demonstrating excellence lies with the institution. The external assessment is an attempt to verify the university's claims. the results of the assessment are linked directly to funding incentives. There are immediate parallels with systems of student self-assessment.

---

[2] *I am indebted to Lee Harvey for this way of expressing the association.*

Unfortunately the internal quality management processes of Australian universities have not always reached the same standard. The analogy is again appropriate: even the best assessment is sometimes interpreted by the students in a way different from the intentions of the teacher. In many cases far too much emphasis has been placed on quite trivial (but often costly) processes (such as the existence of compulsory student ratings of lecturers) which may have damaging side-effects on teacher morale and student goodwill, and too little on evidence of improvements in the quality of student learning outcomes. to use a geological time scale, millennia seem to have been spent on devising "objective" quantitative indicators, a day on what the indicators are supposed to indicate, an hour or two on whether the indications show that students are learning well, and seconds on whether their learning has improved.

My conversations with quality managers in large corporations have convinced me of what I had never thought I would be convinced of – that universities have a lot to learn from the best industry practice on quality. Their approach to quality, unlike many of the universities', is closely aligned with the student learning research findings. Excellence in products and services requires a focus on cooperation (even between competitors in the same market, in benchmarking best practice, for example), commitment, rigour, ownership of processes and vision, value-added, and above all an environment where improvement is normal and support for improvement is freely given. In contrast the universities' approach to quality in learning and teaching often still reeks of unskilful assessment practice, especially a conception that high standards are the almost automatic consequence of high quality inputs (good students, good researchers, lots of money), high pressure to perform, and high levels of secrecy and competition. No wonder that ICI Australia, Eastman Kodak and the rest are sceptical about the pretensions of higher education to claim a special rate at the table of quality management.

I have been involved in two schemes at Australian universities which have tried to grapple with the problem in a more adroit way. Both schemes draw in part on the excellent work of the Scottish Office Education Department in devising qualitative performance indicators for secondary schools (SOED, 1992), as well as on the lessons from student learning research, and the valuable work that has been done on student self-assessment in the past few years. It is absolutely necessary to provide course teams and departments with models on which they can base their self-evaluations, and suggested criteria which might be used. It is equally important to ensure that teaching staff develop ownership over the process, and that they find it useful.

The Griffith University scheme (Figure 2) is based on the principle that good universities, like good learners and good teachers, are constantly learning about how they can improve their performance. Quality improvement and the development of students are primary purposes. Separation is made between the process of evaluating individual teaching (column 3) and the process of evaluating courses and faculties (columns 1 and 2).

Examples of excellent performance, phrased generally, are provided initially to help course teams to evaluate different aspects of their work (see Figure 3, which uses material from the SOED secondary school project). New examples related to particular disciplines are constantly being created from actual practice. Principles that guide the process are listed in Figure 4.[3]

Out of the process of self-evaluation, which will have identified strengths to build upon and weaknesses that need to be addressed, groups of teachers devise development plans to improve the quality of their courses and their students' learning. These plans then become performance objectives against which they and external auditors can evaluate progress made. This evaluation process is facilitated by the use of quantitative indicators of effectiveness such as the results of the Course Experience Questionnaire, results from employer surveys, and data about student completion and progression. These quantitative indicators are useful for confirming strengths and weaknesses, assessing improvement, and assisting inter-university cooperation and sharing of good practice.

The RMIT scheme makes similar use of descriptions of criteria and examples of different levels of performance, and again emphasises the importance of developing ownership of evaluation process through dialogue. An example of the results of this work – showing the development of self-assessment criteria – appears in Figure 5. The RMIT procedures involve individual lecturers' reports to course coordinators and course coordinators' reports to "Directors of Teaching".

Both these schemes imply the need for leadership development programmes, since so much of the effectiveness of a rigorous self-evaluation process depends on strong support from senior staff. Both also involve the support of designated leadership positions which the senior management. RMIT has its "Directors of Teaching" and Griffith has its Deputy Deans (Learning and Teaching). The importance attached to these posts is reflected in the emoluments they attract and the heavy responsibilities they demand. The function of their incumbents is to educate, enable, introduce new ideas, model best practice, and remove impediments to excellent teaching and learning. They signify a conception that the quality of learning and teaching is an issue that should be tackled by the smallest academic units that can deliver it, a view entirely compatible with the quality movement beyond higher education.

---

[3]*I am not able to go into the evaluation of individual teaching performance in this chapter, but the development of criteria and the use of individual portfolios in order to help recognise and reward good teaching is part of the wider scheme.*

Contrasting models of learning and teaching

The main ideas about improving teaching, educational leadership in universities, and evaluation I have been trying to express may be placed in their wider context by reference to the two different models shown in Figure 6.[4]

We are seeing a shift from the first model to the second, as undergraduate education becomes more like a mass system and focuses more on developing lifelong learning competence, including generic employment-related skills, rather than on preparing a research elite. This changing social context of university education is presumably the reason why research on student learning now seems to be so relevant. The transit to a more student-centred view of undergraduate education has been foreshadowed before, of course, notably at the time of the Hale Report and the founding of the "new" universities in the 1960s; but the momentum was never as great as it has today. It is now, surely, and unstoppable phenomenon.

Model I is essentially a lecturer- and discipline-dominated view of undergraduate teaching and learning. Lecturers teach (or more likely lecture); students do the learning. Its conception of learning is foundationalist: first learn the basics before you go and use your knowledge. It emphasises the idea that learning is a profoundly individual phenomenon. Assessment is largely about marking and classifying and competition. Teaching is improved through practice alone. Evaluation is about "objective" numbers.

The second model is focused on learning and students rather than on teaching. The problem is how to engage people with the things they learn. Its implications are consonant with the findings from student learning research; but more . significantly, it reflects the changed environment in which universities in the UK and Australia now find themselves. Model II recognises the importance of the social context of learning and the need in undergraduate education to integrate knowledge with its practical use. It focuses on assessment as part of learning. It stresses the similarities between how experts work and how students should learn to be experts. It embraces views of academic leadership and evaluation such as those I have tried to describe above.

Of course we must not interpret Figure 6 in trivial dualist terms. Knowledge is often cumulative. Good teaching generally does involve good presentation. Effective leadership almost invariably requires transactional strategies as well as transformational insights. Quantitative indicators of performance can marry happily with qualitative ones. Grading students is not a bar to giving good

---

[4] *I am most grateful to John Bain for allowing me to adapt his original ideas and table into the*

feedback and focusing on formative processes. Producing publicity-verifiable data on educational performance should go hand in hand with self-evaluation. It is a matter of emphasis and not of simply dualities; it is a matter of balancing and integrating apparent opposites in an educationally valid way.

Remembering Minton's conclusions about the right questions and what makes the difference between quality and mediocrity, and understanding of the last row of Figure 6 is the one that matters most. We will continue to return to same issues as we try to improve our students' learning, our management of university teaching, and our evaluation of the effectiveness of higher education. In approaching these issues the search for right answers is a snare and a delusion. "Many of the issues facing teachers are not problems to be solved" says Welker (1992). "They are dilemmas to be repeatedly encountered. Dilemmas don't require answers; they require enduring human responsibility".

References

Anderson, L. (1994). *Many roads to one place: Which place? Which roads? Paper presented to the Invitational Symposium on the Experience of Quality in Higher Education,* Griffith Institute for Higher education, Griffith University, 3-5 July.

Bain, J. (1993). *Towards a framework for more effective teaching in higher education: Some experiences based on a new Graduate Certificate in Higher Education.* Invited presentation, Swinburne University of Technology.

Biggs, J. B. (1990). Teaching: Design for learning. In B. Ross (ed.), *Teaching for Effective Learning.* Sydney: HERDSA.

Biggs, J. B. (1993). From theory to practice: a cognitive systems approach. *Higher Education Research and Development,* 12, 73–85.

Bland, C. J. and Ruffin, M. T. (1992). Characteristics of a productive research environment: Literature review. *Academic Medicine,* 67, 385–397.

Blight, D. (1993). Review article: (P Ramsden) 'Learning to Teach in Higher Education'. *Studies in Higher Education,* 18, 105–111.

Boice, R. (1992). *The New Faculty Member: Supporting and Fostering Professional Development.* San Francisco: Jossey-Bass.

Cushing, K. S., Sabers, D. S. and Berliner, D. C. (1992). *Olympic gold: Investigations of Expertise in Teaching. Education Horizons,* Spring, 108–113.

Donaldson, G. A. (1991). *Learning to Lead: The Dynamics of the High School Principalship.* New York: Greenwood Press.

Louis, k. (1993). *Keynote Address Presented at the International Congress on School Effectiveness and Improvement*, Norrkoping.

Martin, E. and Ramsden, P. (1994). *Evaluation of the Performance of Courses in Teaching Methods for Recently Appointed Academic Staff*. Canberra: Australian Government Publishing Service.

Minton, D. (1991). *Teaching Skills in Further and Adult Education*. Basingstoke: Macmillan.

Ramsden, P. (1992). *Learning to Teaching in Higher Education*. London: Routledge.

Samualowicz, K. and Bain, J. D (1992). Conceptions of teaching held by academic teachers. *Higher Education*, 24, 93–111.

Schön, D. A. (1987). *Educating the Reflective Practitioner*. San Francisco: Jossey-Bass.

Scottish Office Education Department (SOED) (1992). *Using Performance Indicators in Secondary School Self-Evaluation*. Edinburgh: SOED.

Shuell, T. J (1986). Cognitive conceptions of learning. *Review of Educational Research*, 56, 411–436.

Staff and Education Development Association (SEDA) (1994). *The Accreditation of Teachers in Higher Education*. Birmingham: SEDA.

Trigwell, K. and Prosser, M. (1993). Approaches adopted by teachers of first year university science courses. In a Viskovic. (ed.), Towards 2000: Trends in tertiary teaching. *Research and Development in Higher Education 14,*. Sydney: HERDSA, 223–228.

Trigwell, K., Prosser, M. and Taylor, P. (1994). Qualitative differences in approaches to teaching first year science courses. *Higher Education*, 27, 75–84.

Welker, R. (1992). Reversing the claim on professional status: What educators can teach experts. *Educational Horizons*, Spring, 115–119.

Figure 1. Leadership and the quality of student learning

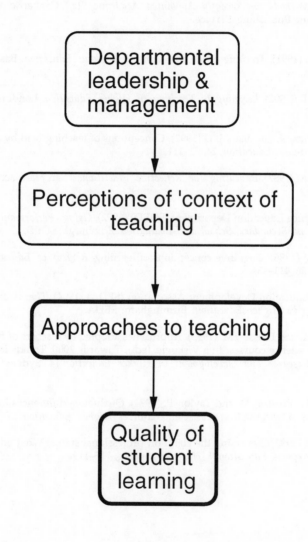

Figure 2. Evaluating and improving the quality of teaching and learning at Griffith University

Basic principles: The process of audit and improvement should be systematic, flexible, empowering, developed, collaborative, and rigorous. A variety of different sources of evidence should be used. The process should consume thr minimum amount of time and resources consistent with demonstrating accountability and genuine improvement. The process of rewarding and recognising individual teachers' performance should be kept distinct, as far as practicable, from the process of reviewing courses.

For each of the three columns: Publicise definitions of effective teaching and learning; agree criteria; list appropriate sources of evidence; undertake development exercises (eg. workshops on how to evaluate a course); set up trustworthy reporting processes.

Audit and improvement of the teaching and learning environment (University/Faculty level)	Audit and improvement of courses (Faculty/School level)	Recognising and rewarding teaching (Individual level)
Academic staff profile analysis (eg. qualifications)	Quality of learning and teaching (eg. quality of teaching process; staff-student relationships and course ethos)	Planning and preparationfor teaching (eg. teaching sessions have clear goals for learning)
staff professional activities (eg. teaching grants secured)	Quality and relevance of subjects and courses (eg. expert review, including external stakeholders; links between subjects)	Processes of teaching (eg, explanations, and questions are clear and at appropriate level)
Staff development (eg. participation in seminars and courses)	Student progress and achievement (eg. quality of learning outcomes; responsiveness to particular needs)	Assessment of students and their learning outcomes (eg. students obtain high quality, regular feedback on their progress)
Faculty management: leadership and planning (eg. effectiveness of Dean's leadership in shaping the learning and teaching environment)	Management for excellence in teaching and learning; leadership and planning (eg. effectiveness of Head's leadership in promoting successful learning and teaching)	Evaluating and improving teaching (eg. information from assessment used to modify teaching)
Evaluation processes (eg surveys of student experiences and their effects)	Evaluation processes (eg. existence of effective methods for monitoring student progress)	Subject/course coordination and leadership in teaching (eg. models good practice and inovation in teaching)
		Scholarship in teaching (eg. publications on teaching)

Figure 3.   A qualitative performance indicator for a undergraduate course

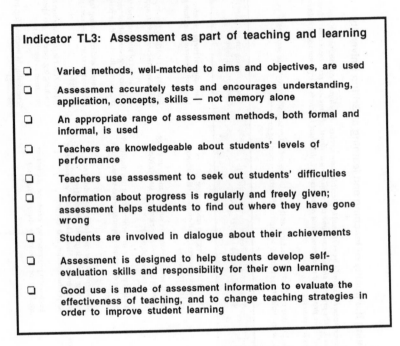

Indicator TL3: Assessment as part of teaching and learning

❑   Varied methods, well-matched to aims and objectives, are used

❑   Assessment accurately tests and encourages understanding, application, concepts, skills — not memory alone

❑   An appropriate range of assessment methods, both formal and informal, is used

❑   Teachers are knowledgeable about students' levels of performance

❑   Teachers use assessment to seek out students' difficulties

❑   Information about progress is regularly and freely given; assessment helps students to find out where they have gone wrong

❑   Students are involved in dialogue about their achievements

❑   Assessment is designed to help students develop self-evaluation skills and responsibility for their own learning

❑   Good use is made of assessment information to evaluate the effectiveness of teaching, and to change teaching strategies in order to improve student learning

(Based on material in SOED, 1992)

Figure 4. Griffith Institute for Higher Education: Principles of Quality Management for Teaching and Learning

- Quality improvement is a primary purpose

- Evaluation should seek to empower staff, not impose on them

- Focus on the quality of learning rather than the teaching process

- Quality outcomes matter more than the existence of quality procedures

- The distinctive mission of the University is vital

- Self-evaluation with stakeholder input should precede external audit

- International referencing is expected

- Excessive use of student questionnaires must be avoided

- Course evaluation is separate from subject and teaching evaluation

- Good teaching should be recognised and rewarded by appropriate behaviours rather than symbolic gestures

- Leadership in teaching and learning is crucial

Figure 5. Levels of performance for 'Quality of the Teaching Process' (sub theme 'Clarity of questions/explanations and linking topics')

(Two levels of performance written by a group of social science lecturers to evaluate their own teaching)

Excellent performance:

"Teachers clearly introduce concepts, stress key ones, and make links between them. They use language that most students find comprehensible. Concepts and explanations are demonstrated in examples that are relevant to the experience of most students. Learning is centred around the application of ideas, not the repetition of words. Concepts are introduced in steps, moving from simple to complicated; teachers check at each stage that students understand. Topics are introduced in logical sequence. Classes are well presented and handled. As a result, most students can recognise and use explanations and theories in new cases."

Performance showing more weaknesses than strengths:

"Teachers present concepts and explanations unsystematically. There is little attempt to link them to the experiences and understandings that students already possess. Concepts , explanations and topics are not connected logically, and teachers do not always ensure that students understand at each stage. Expositions are not satisfactory; there is evidence that materials such as visuals and handouts are not well prepared and not closely linked to presentations. As a result, many students can echo the teachers' words but not use the concepts in new situations."

Figure 6. Contrasting models of teaching, educational leadership, and evaluation in higher education

	Model I: 'Disseminating knowledge'	Model II: 'Making learning possible'
Epistemological assumptions	Knowledge exists separately from the people who possess it. Knowledge can be conveyed. Concepts and facts are prerequisites for problem-solving in a field of study. Theory and practice are separate domains.	Knowledge doesn't exist apart from people. Knowledge must be reconstructed by learners. Facts and concepts are learned as they are used. Problem-solving, concepts and facts are mutually dependent, in learning as well as in expert practice.
Academic and social environment	Of little importance: knowledge is created through a social system but is learned through individual study and practice; other students provide competition but are otherwise marginal to learning.	Of central significance: effective learning occurs in an environment that mimics social systems of inquiry; social interaction and cooperation are essential to the negotiation of understanding.
Student learning	Teacher focused – practise procedures, produce correct answers, reproduce knowledge accurately. Infer methods of inquiry from knowledge organisation and texts.	Learner focused – responsibly regulate inquiry, construct personal understanding, and emulate experts' methods. Abstract concepts and principles from experiences.
Teacher's role	Ensure that the ever-expanding content is covered. Organise and present knowledge well. Arrange suitable teaching activities, including lectures, tutorials and labs as appropriate. Rely on students to understand and absorb presented knowledge and procedures.	Limit the content to essentials. Model the methods of practice and scholarship in the field. Design diverse tasks strongly related to learning goals. Challenge misconceptions and build understanding through dialogue. Constantly monitor student understanding and intervene whenever necessary.

Figure 6 continued.

	Model I: 'Disseminating knowledge'	Model II: 'Making learning possible'
Desirable learning and assessment tasks	Well-structured problems and standard exercises with high reliability. 'Decontextualised practice': parts are studied separately and only brought together towards the end of the course. Tasks provide feedback at end of unit, or not at all.	Loosely structured problems and realistic tasks requiring student decision making. 'Situated practice': tasks of increasing complexity that incorporate essential skills and knowledge. Tasks provide continuous feedback.
How is teaching improved?	Mainly through practice; driven by extrinsic rewards.	Mainly through repeated cycles of reflection and action; driven by intrinsic interest.
Approach to management and leadership of teaching	Essentially transactional: assigning tasks and rewarding their successful completion.	Essentially transformational: creating an enabling environment and pursuing a moral vision.
Evaluation and audit	Measurement focused, externally directed and value-free. Preferred indicators are quantitative, such as pass rates and student ratings.	Process focused, user directed and permeated by values. Preferred indicators are qualitative, such as student comments and evidence of changes in conceptions.
Educational effectiveness	Essentially technical: a problem to be solved.	Essentially problematic: an enduring human dilemma.

Based on Bain, J.D. (1993).

Implications of Recent Research on Student Learning for Institutional Practices of Evaluation of Teaching

Jackie Lublin and Michael Prosser, University of Sydney

Introduction

The fundamental issue for teaching in higher education is the improvement of the quality of the processes and outcomes of student learning. There has been a substantial amount of research in recent years into the processes, outcomes and context of student learning. This research has shown that students approach their studies in fundamentally different ways, depending to a large extent on the context, with the result being that they learn fundamentally different things (Marton, Hounsell and Entwistle, 1984; Ramsden, 1992). This research has been applied, to some extent at least, at the individual student level, and at the classroom level (Ramsden, 1988). There has been little application, however, at the institutional level. This paper focusses on some experiences of applying the ideas from this research at the institutional policy level in a large, well-established, research-based metropolitan university.

Research on student learning has shown that students adopt qualitatively different approaches to their studies depending upon their prior experiences of studying and the particular context in which they find themselves. These different approaches lead to qualitatively different learning outcomes. Surface approaches, in which students focus on reproducing the content and processes they are studying, seem to be associated with perceptions of high workload and of assessment demands being able to be met by rote learning. Deep approaches, on the other hand, seem to be associated with perceptions by students that the teaching is good, that the goals are clear, and that they have some freedom and choice in how and what they learn. Deep approaches to study are in turn associated with an understanding of the subject matter which can broadly be described as relational, while in surface approaches the understanding can be described as multi-structural (Biggs and Collis, 1982). That is, students can understand the outcomes of the course and what the course was about in terms of a coherent or of an unrelated set of ideas and procedures. Student approaches to study are not stable aspects of cognitive structure, but are conceived of as relations between the student and the context (see Biggs, 1993, for a recent discussion of this issue). The way institutions structure the teaching and learning contexts of students has an important impact on what and how students learn.

A model describing the results of much of this recent research on student learning is shown in Figure 1.

Figure 1: Model of Student Learning

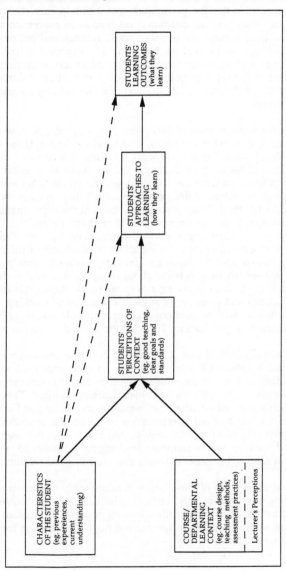

It shows that students' perceptions of teaching and learning contexts are a function of both their prior experiences of teaching and learning and the present context. It is in relation to these perceptions that they approach their studies. In order to improve their learning outcomes, we need to be concerned about both the context and their perceptions of that context. Institutional policies and practices of student evaluation of teaching would be expected to have substantial effects on the way staff approach their teaching and structure the teaching and learning context. If the focus of evaluation is on presentation and not on student learning, then staff will structure the context of their teaching around presentation issues.

Very recently, the focus of some of this research has changed to how teachers conceive of and approach their teaching, and how such conceptions and approaches affect student learning. Broadly speaking, it seems that university teachers conceive of teaching on the one hand as transmitting information to students, with a focus on what the teacher does, and on the other as helping students develop an understanding, with the focus being on what the students do as a result of the teaching. There is some evidence, at the departmental level at least, that these conceptions and approaches to teaching are associated with students' approaches to learning in a way that would be expected. That is, a department which sees teaching as being about transmission of information is more likely to have students adopting surface approaches to learning, while departments that see teaching as being about changing students' understanding is more likely to have students adopting a deep approach. Again, it is expected that institutional policies and practices of student evaluation of teaching would have a substantial effect on staff conceptions and approaches to teaching (Prosser and Trigwell, submitted for publication; Trigwell, Prosserand Taylor, in press).

What are the implications of such a view of student learning and teaching for institutional policy makers? If institutions wish to encourage students to focus on understanding and not reproduction, then they need to establish their policies and practices with an explicit view of student learning in mind. They need to have an explicit statement on what the institution means by good teaching. Then issues such as the institutional interpretation of the results of student evaluation of teaching, their way of using such results, and distinctions between competent teaching, good teaching and outstanding teaching for purposes of appointment and promotion need to be consistent with that view of good teaching.

This paper addresses some of these issues in relationship to current research on student learning and describes and critically discusses how one university is attempting to institutionalise these ideas into its practices. But before describing these practices, some comment on the current Australian context for higher education are warranted.

The Australian Context

Traditionally institutions refer to their major academic activities as "teaching and research". Until quite recently in Australia university teaching remained relatively unexamined. There was no pre-service or in-service requirement of new academic staff that they study teaching or have any formal qualification in teaching. Little evidence was required that a tenurable staff member had thought about, evaluated or taken steps to improve their teaching. Consequently, in spite of the research evidence that has emerged in the last 20 years which questions the usefulness of traditional teacher-centred, information transmission approaches to teaching, little was done at the institutional level.

However, things are changing in this respect in Australia, and several streams are starting to merge which are encouraging institutions to examine and revise their view of teaching and thus the approach to its evaluation. The first is the growing visibility and respectability of that stream of research activity already mentioned which takes Galileo's precept as its basis: "You cannot teach a man anything, you can only help him learn." With a conceptual basis in the experiences of students' learning, enlightened staff development has begun to focus on assisting interested staff to redefine teaching in terms of student learning. Such a paradigm change of thinking has profound implications for the way the curriculum is mediated and for what is meant by "good teaching". But while such changes may be occurring at the level of the individual academic, the reality is that innovative approaches to the facilitation of student learning are unlikely to survive if those individuals move on and their innovations have not become institutionalised.

The second issue, however, which may have the potential to effect such changes at a more fundamental level is the current emphasis on quality management and quality assurance. For our purposes this has two aspects:

(a) the obligation of institutions to focus on the outcomes of the undergraduate education they provide (Higher Education Council,1992). With such a focus, it soon becomes apparent that undergraduate education involves more than the transmission of a body of knowledge and that conventional teaching will not facilitate outcomes such as independence, the ability to work in a team, the desire to continue to learn and the ability to justify decisions.

So an obligation arises for an institution to define what it means by good teaching. If teaching is defined in terms of student learning, then good teaching is teaching which most effectively does this, i.e., which encourages high quality student learning, or, to restate this, which "discourages the superficial approach to learning and encourages active engagement with the subject matter" (Ramsden, 1992).

(b)   the obligation on institutions to monitor, evaluate and work towards improving what they do.

This leads directly to the third issue, which also has the potential to contribute to the re-examination and redefinition of teaching. The Commonwealth government took over complete financial responsibility for funding Australian universities in 1972. In its subsequent reports the importance of teaching was continually asserted, but it was not until the late 1980s that the Commonwealth itself earmarked money for the improvement of teaching via the National Staff Development Fund, the National Priority (Reserve) Fund, and most recently the Committee for the Advancement of University Teaching, which disbursed $5 million in 1992 on teaching development grants. Good teaching now had some explicit rewards, and with it went the gradual move to procedures to formalise the evaluation of teaching for individual and department purposes.
So in the early 1990s, as an activity, the evaluation of teaching has become transformed from something done sporadically by individual staff via a feedback questionnaire to students, to something done routinely by a department as part of the monitoring and review processes which are now becoming institutionalised in Australian universities in response to accountability and quality assurance pressures.

Institutional incorporation of these ideas about teaching has resulted in the need to develop or rewrite policies to direct or reflect practice. We are particularly interested in the way in which our own institution has been brought to the point where its policies are being amended to incorporate conceptions of good teaching which rely on the concerns of this conference, i.e., the promotion of high quality student learning.

Institutional Policies Designed to Encourage High Quality Student Learning

The institution described here is the University of Sydney. It is Australia's oldest university, having been founded in 1850. It is big (30,000 students), well established, with a pre-eminent research record, and its faculties cover the entire span of mainstream professional and generalist education. It has had a small academic development unit since 1981, the Centre for Teaching and Learning, established in the teeth of conservative opposition. Until quite recently research was the sine qua non for promotion.

This would not seem to be a promising institutional context for the dissemination and application of advanced theories of student learning. Nevertheless, the institution has responded to the pressures referred to by adopting a specific definition of good teaching, by developing a student evaluation of teaching questionnaire and means of interpreting it for formative and summative purposes, and by revising its criteria for promotion and tenure in ways consistent with the research on student learning.

Institutional definition of good teaching

In 1992, in response to a perceived need by the Chair of Academic Board, the centre presented a paper on the evaluation of teaching which was accepted by the board and thus became university policy. It included the following:

> Good teaching is teaching which helps students to learn. But more than that, "Good teaching encourages high quality student learning. It discourages the superficial approach to learning and encourages active engagement in the subject matter" (Ramsden, 1992). This does not imply that good teaching will always result in high quality student learning, but that it is designed to do so, and that it is practised in a way likely to lead to high quality learning. Indeed, it would be foolish to assume a direct relationship between teaching and the results of student assessment – the processes of learning are complex, and the effects of motivation, personality and preference on the learning process are not well understood. This means that we cannot be precise in behavioural definition of good teaching, and that the personal style of the teacher is important. But it can be assumed that good teaching is that which encourages in the learner no matter what the subject content, motivation to learn, desire to understand, perseverance, independence, a respect for truth and a desire to pursue learning.

> If good teaching can be seen from this perspective, then the evaluation of teaching should not focus on attempts to make judgments about the quality of teaching which are based upon absolute professional standards, but rather to make judgments on the quality of the professional approach taken to improve the quality of student learning. What is important is that the processes used for the evaluation of teaching be consistent with the goal of improving student learning, and this mandates that respect, concern and attention be paid also to the students' perspective on the experience of the teaching they perceive.

This definition incorporates much of what has been learnt about good teaching and its relation to student learning. Its focus is on student learning and formative evaluation of teaching aiming at improving the quality of student learning. This statement forms the basis of the policy and practices associated with student evaluation of teaching.

Institutional policy on student evaluation of teaching

Given this institutional policy on what constitutes good teaching, it was necessary to have a form of student evaluation of teaching consistent with the policy, both in terms of the instrument used and the interpretation and use results of the administration of the instrument for both formative and summative purposes.

Student evaluation questionnaire

Over recent years there has been a growing demand for the use of student evaluation of teaching and courses questionnaires in the university. In many institutions this has resulted in the development of standardised forms of student evaluation questionnaires often focussing substantially, but not exclusively, on presentation techniques for both formative and summative purposes. These questionnaires are often interpreted in terms of students making judgements on performance, with little or no theoretical view of what constitutes good teaching.

Based upon this recent research in student learning, the Centre for Teaching and Learning has developed a questionnaire which

1. is explicitly formative in nature;
2. is non-standardised;
3. has a view that good teaching is about developing high quality student learning;
4. focusses on student perceptions of the teaching and learning context, rather than on students making judgements about a staff member's performance.

The questionnaire has been developed to help staff obtain information about how their students perceive their teaching. The questionnaire is based conceptually upon the Course Experience Questionnaire (Ramsden, 1991). It is composed of a number of sub-scales, and a bank of items. Staff members construct their own questionnaire from the sub-scales and the item-bank. No two questionnaires need be similar, although we strongly recommend that staff select most of the items from the first sub-scale – the general scale – which contains items focussing on clear goals, inappropriate workload, inappropriate assessment, help in study and organisation. The second sub-scale focusses on students' approaches to study (surface or deep). The third focusses on good teaching in lectures and the fourth good teaching in tutorials. The fifth sub-scale includes the three open-ended questions – best thing about the course, worst thing about the course, and how to improve the course.

The in᪄᪄ questionnaire included 21 separate courses with a total of ᪄᪄ m of the trial was to ensure that the items in the general ᪄᪄hing scale were relating to approaches to study as expected ᪄᪄evious research on student learning. Using the individual ᪄᪄alysis, the factor analysis shown in Table 1 shows that ᪄᪄ived the teaching to be good, saw clear goals for the ᪄᪄ing help in studying and thought the course was well ᪄᪄pting a deep approach to their studies. On the other hand, students who perceived the workload to be too high and saw assessment in terms of reproduction and not understanding reported adopting a surface approach to their studies.

Table 1 Rotated Factor Analysis of the Course Perceptions and Approaches to Study Sub-scales, Using the Student as the Unit of Analysis

Sub-scale	Factor	
	1	2
Good teaching (L1-L7)	.74	
Clear goals (G1, G3)	.78	
Inappropriate workload (G2, G8)		.64
Inappropriate assessment (G5, G7)		.64
Help in study (G4, G6)	.61	
Organisation (G9, G10)	.70	
Surface approach (S1, S2, S7, S9)		.74
Deep approach (S3, S4, S5, S6, S8)	.37	.30

Loadings less than .30 deleted
n=1,794

A second factor analysis, shown in Table 2 using the individual student as the unit of analysis, showed that students who rated the teaching and course highly reported adopting deep and non-surface approaches to study.

Table 2 Rotated Factor Analysis of Overall Evaluation Items and the Approaches to Study

Sub-scales

Evaluation Items/Sub-scale	Factor 1
Overall course evaluation (G)	.83
Overall teaching evaluation (L)	.71
Surface approach (S1, S2, S7, S9)	.50
Deep approach (S3, S4, S5, S6, S8)	.55

Finally, a correlational analysis shown in Table 3, using the course as the unit of analysis, showed that students reported adopting deep approaches to their study in those courses in which they perceived that the goals were clear and they received help in their study, and which were well organised. They reported adopting surface approaches in those courses in which they perceived that the goals were not clear, workload was too high, assessment measured reproduction rather than understanding and they did not get help in their study and which were not well organised. They also rated highly those courses in which they reported adopting a deep approach, and lowly those courses in which they reported adopting a surface approach.

Table 3 Pearson Correlation Coefficients for Course Perception Sub-scales and Approach to Study Sub-scales, Using the Course as the Unit of Analysis

Course perceptions	Approaches to Study	
	Surface	Deep
Good teaching (L1-L7)	.02	.13
Clear goals (G1, G3)	.50	.66
Inappropriate workload (G2, G8)	.56	.22
Inappropriate assessment (G5, G7)	.59	.19
Help in study (G4, G6)	.68	.61
Organisation (G9, G10)	.53	.41
Overall course (G)	.62	.63
Overall teaching (L)	.04	.08

n=21
r=.43, p<.05; r=.55, p<.01

These results are consistent with those of the research on student learning (Prosser and Trigwell, 1990; Prosser and Trigwell, 1991; Trigwell and Prosser, 1991), and so we judge that the questionnaire was working as intended. The results of the administration of the questionnaire are consistent with the definition of good teaching adopted by the university.

Since the initial trial, the questionnaire has been used in 339 courses , with 19,430 students.

Policy on interpretation of questionnaire results
As noted above, the centre's questionnaire was designed for formative purposes, that is, it was designed to provide feedback in order to improve teaching and thus it should be different to one designed to make judgements about performance. For the latter purpose, staff would wish to collect data that highlight their best aspects, while for the former staff would wish to collect data that identify areas which are not necessarily their best aspects and in which improvement is possible.

The centre's own policy precludes it from being involved in processes which provide information for personnel decisions, such as summative student evaluation questionnaires. Inevitably, however, staff applying for promotion need to provide evidence from students about the quality of their teaching. The following extract from "The Evaluation of Teaching" policy document explains how the results of the formative questionnaire can be used for summative purposes such as a promotion application:

> Evidence from formatively based questionnaires can be used constructively by promotions committees in certain ways: when results from a formatively based questionnaire are tendered in a promotion application then it is strongly recommended that promotion committees, rather than taking note of the actual results, should ensure that applicants provide information about and be prepared to discuss their reflections on the survey results, and on the steps they have taken to effect change in their teaching on the basis of these results. This is consistent with the argument presented earlier that the evaluation of teaching should focus on the quality of the approaches taken to improve learning rather than on a comparison with absolute standards.

This view on the evaluation of teaching for promotion and tenure is being consistently reinforced by the Deputy Vice-Chancellor responsible for the administration of the promotion and tenure system.

Institutional definitions of competent, good and outstanding teaching
Given that the university, through its academic board, has accepted a particular view of good teaching, that the University has developed a student evaluation questionnaire consistent with this view, and has adopted a policy for the use of student evaluation data for promotion and tenure decisions, it is presently considering the criteria to be used for judging competent, good and meritorious teaching for tenure and promotion. Competent teaching is to be judged in terms of performance-based criteria, while good teaching will be judged by criteria known to be associated with high quality student learning, and meritorious teaching will focus on presentation, student learning and scholarship in teaching. Each of these sets of criteria are described in more detail below.

Competent teaching (satisfactory performance)
All members of the teaching staff would be expected to meet this criterion. It is a performance-based criterion which, if met, would require positive responses to questions such as:

1. are the objectives of the applicant's teaching made clear to students and other relevant staff?
2. does the applicant attempt to explain course requirements and assessment procedures to students?
3. are the applicant's assessment procedures fair and reliable?
4. is the applicant punctual in his/her teaching duties?
5. does the applicant provide timely feedback to students on their progress in the course?

6.   is the academic quality of the content of the applicant's teaching satisfactory?
7.   does the applicant engage in course development, examining and administration of the teaching programme?
8.   is the applicant available to students outside class?

Good teaching (superior performance)

As discussed earlier, good teaching has been defined by the university's academic board to be teaching which encourages high quality student learning. It is not just a matter of completing teaching duties satisfactorily (although this would be necessary), but that there is evidence that the teaching is likely to, or does result in, high quality student learning.

Questions such as the following would require a positive response. Does the applicant:

1.   systematically review *how* students learn in his/her course, and subsequently adjust his/her teaching?
2.   systematically review *what* students learn in his/her course, and subsequently adjust his/her teaching?
3.   systematically collect, and act upon the results of, student evaluations of his/her teaching?
4.   periodically review the way the students see the aims of his/her teaching, the workload, and what and how the course is assessed and adjust such aspects in the light of the review?

Meritorious teaching (outstanding performance)

The criterion for meritorious teaching goes beyond that of good teaching. In this case, the applicant provides evidence of scholarship in teaching by having made a contribution to the development of teaching in his/her discipline which is recognised beyond the institution. To meet this criterion, positive responses would need to be given to questions such as the following. Has the applicant:

1.   led professional development activities, e.g., seminars,workshops and professional meetings intended to improve teaching and learning?
2.   contributed to the literature on teaching and learning in higher education, including professional journals in the applicant's field?
3.   been invited to teach courses at other institutions?
4.   contributed to the literature on teaching?
5.   engaged in research into aspects of his/her own teaching?
6.   held leadership positions in professional associations associated with the improvement of teaching and learning?

These judgements of teaching performance are related to the criteria for promotion as shown in Table 4.

Table 4: Relation Between Criteria for Promotion and Judgements of Performance

Criteria for Promotion[1]	Judgements of teaching performance		
	Acceptable Teaching (Satisfactory performance)	Good Teaching (Superior performance)	Metitorious Teaching (Outstanding performance)
from Associate Lecturer to Lecturer			
(a Satisfactory in teaching, satisfactory in research or	Clear evidence	Continuing development	
b) Exceptional in teaching	Clear evidence	Clear evidence	
from Lecturer to Senior Lecturer			
a) Satisfactory in teaching, outstanding in research or	Clear evidence	Clear evidence	
b) Superior in teaching and research or	Clear evidence	Clear evidence	
c) Outstanding teaching, satisfactory in research or	Clear evidence	Clear evidence	Clear evidence
d) Exceptional in teaching	Clear evidence	Clear evidence	Clear and sustained evidence[2]
from Senior Lecturer to Associate Professor			
a) Outstanding in teaching, exceptional in research or	Clear evidence	Clear evidence	Clear evidence
b) Exceptional in teaching, outstanding in research	Clear evidence	Clear evidence	Clear and sustained evidence[2]

[1]Taken from Information to Applicants

[2]For Exceptional Teaching, the required level of performance must have been maintained over several years.

The implication of Table 4 is that, in virtually all cases, promotion depends on staff producing evidence showing that their focus is not just on their classroom performance but on their students' learning.

Discussions and conclusions

In this paper we have shown how some of the implications of the research into student learning is being applied in one institution and incorporated into its policy documents. The institution has accepted a definition of good teaching consistent with this research, and has developed a system of student evaluation of teaching consistent also with the research. It is reconsidering its teaching criteria for promotion in ways which are consistent with this research. So it would appear that it is indeed possible to realign an institution's policy on teaching to make it consistent with current research into student learning. Unfortunately, this is not enough of itself to effect change in practice.

There are two issues which must be considered in any discussion of institutional policies:

1.   what actually happens, i.e., does anything really change as a result of a change of policy?
2.   what are staff perceptions of how things are?

Both these issues point to the vital importance of the need for educating and developing all staff in the institution. For instance, there is evidence of quite a deal of confusion among staff about these developments. Many remain unaware of them, and still consider teaching in terms of classroom performance and not in terms of student learning. Promotion procedures are conducted at two levels – firstly at the faculty, and then centrally. We suspect that, while these ideas have been accepted at the central level, there continues to be misunderstanding at the faculty level. Many staff believe that it is the results of student evaluation, i.e., the figures themselves, which are important for promotion, not the staff member's reflections on these in terms of student learning, as set out in the policy document.

We are not aware of what faculty promotions committees are actually accepting as evidence of teaching, or of whether they have in fact taken on board this new learner-centred approach to the definition of teaching. As such committees are usually comprised of older staff members it is quite likely that individual long-held personal conceptions of a traditional definition of teaching still hold sway among many members. Thus the need for development for attitude change in this respect is pressing – it is of little use for an enlightened staff member to present evidence in the new mould if it is going to be judged by traditional criteria. Fortunately the institution has agreed to a series of development activities being offered in 1994 to faculty promotions committee members by the

university's academic development unit.

The other area where education is needed is of course for academic teachers themselves. Unless staff are aware of the changes and accept them, they will continue to teach in ways inconsistent with the research. What we hope for in the longer term is that the effects of the research and its incorporation into the university's policies will be understood, valued and practised by academic teachers. For this to happen we believe it is necessary for both a top-down approach and a bottom-up approach to be implemented in order to improve teaching and learning, i.e., policy must lead the way, and be overtly supported by senior people, but persuasion and education must be offered to staff to change their perceptions of good teaching. The latter may well be a more difficult task than the former, depending as it does on the relative standing of teaching vis-à-vis research in the institution, the amount of resources able and willing to be devoted by the institution to the improvement of teaching, and the effects of prior experiences and beliefs of staff themselves concerning teaching.

References

Biggs, J. (1993). What do inventories of students' learning processes really measure? A theoretical review and clarification? *British Journal of Educational Psychology*, 63, 3–19.

Biggs, J. B. and Collis, K.F. (1982). Evaluating the Quality of Learning: the SOLO Taxonomy. New York: Academic Press.

Higher Education Council, National Board of Employment, Education and Training (1992). *Higher Education: Achieving Quality* Canberra: Australian Government Publishing Service.

Marton, F., Hounsell, D.J. and Entwistle, N.J. (eds) (1984). *The Experience of Learning*. Edinburgh: Scottish Academic Press.

Prosser, M. and Trigwell, K. (1990). Student evaluation of teaching and courses: student study strategies as a criterion of validity. *Higher Education*, 20, 135–142.

Prosser, M. and Trigwell, K. (1991). Student evaluations of teaching and courses: student learning approaches and outcomes as a criterion of validity, *Contemporary Educational Psychology*, 16, 293–301.

Prosser, M. and Trigwell, K. (submitted for publication). *A Phenomenographic Study of Academics' Conceptions of Science Learning and Teaching.*

Ramsden, P. (1988). Studying learning: improving teaching. In P. Ramsden (ed.), *Improving Learning: New Perspectives* . London: Kogan Page.

Ramsden, P. (1991). A performance indicator of teaching quality in higher education. *Studies in Higher Education*, 16, 129–150.

Ramsden, P. (1992). Learning to Teach in Higher Education. London: Routledge.

Trigwell, K. and Prosser, M. (1991). Relating learning approaches, perceptions of context and learning outcomes *Higher Education* [special edition on student learning), 22, 251–266.

Trigwell, K., Prosser, M. and Taylor, P. (in press). Qualitative differences in approaches to teaching first year university science. *Higher Education*.

Chapter 2   Identifying st approaches to

Conceptually at Risk Students: Diagnostic and Intei based on Individual Differences

J.H.F. Meyer and P.G. Parsons, Student Learning Research Group, University of Cape Town

Part 1 Diagnostic Strategies

Introduction

The work described here flows from the proposition that research on student learning has something substantial to feed back into the context within which it is undertaken. At the very least it opens a window that illuminates how the context and content of learning is being perceived by students, and in a form that permits an evaluation in qualitative terms that can be acted upon. The strategic relevance to educational practice of how students perceive their own learning actions, the context within which these occur, and to which their actions may be a response, are thus held to be a focus that can be subjected to conceptual interpretation and value judgement.

Student learning is a complex multivariate phenomenon. And yet, it is also apparently amenable to understanding, at least at the level of a first order approximation to perceptual task engagement, within relatively simple conceptual models that exhibit varying degrees of redundancy in terms of explanatory variables. To the extent that conceptual models can be 'fitted' to observational data via instrumentation in a plausibly valid manner, the models can also be used for inferential purposes; ideally they can inform expectations and consequences, inferred from the modelled data, that would not otherwise be possible from a purely empirical analysis of the source variables.

At the heart of any attempt to model student learning within the 'student experience of learning' framework lies the need to address manifestations of intra- and inter-individual variation. It is the variation attributable to the existence of qualitative individual differences in learning engagement that needs to be explained, and this is commonly attempted in terms of concepts such as 'deep', 'surface', 'strategic', or others such as 'meaning', 'reproducing' and 'achieving' that have similar semantic connotations. It follows that any instrumentation employed in quantitative research must be sensitive to sources qualitative variation, and the extent to which this is possible is clearly a function of the complexity of the model the instrumentation represents. It is not the purpose here to review in detail the attributes of the various current models of student learning, and their associated instrumentation, which have emerged from a variety of research perspectives. The emphasis here is rather to position an argument within the 'student experience of learning' framework,and discuss the extent to which the essential features of some of the models that represent this framework have been explored in practical settings by the present authors.

Sources of qualitative variation

It has been argued that contrasting forms of strategy constitute one primary source of variation in student learning. As such, this concept deserves a brief and appropriate historical introduction from at least one relevant research perspective, albeit an information processing one.

In their proposal for an alternative framework to multistore models of memory, Craik and Lockhart (1972) proposed a conceptual framework grounded on levels of perceptual processing. Within this framework, and drawing on earlier research in this field, concepts such as 'intention to learn', 'intentional strategy', 'extraction of meaning', 'depth of processing' and 'level of processing required by the orientating task' were used to posit theoretical relationships between memory function and levels of processing. The basic proposition was that the degree of 'depth' invoked in processing information had a correspondence in the degree of associated semantic or cognitive analysis, and was a function of 'the orienting task'. The instruction 'to learn', as they put it, 'facilitates performance only insofar as it leads the subject to process the material in a manner which is more effective than the processing induced by the orienting task in the incidental condition' (Craik and Lockhart, 1972, p.677).

Transported and extrapolated into the receptive framework representing 'students' experiences of learning', resultant actions involving strategy and the other related concepts (which technically now have different framework-dependent meanings) are readily discernible in the contemporary models of student learning advocated by Biggs (1993) and Entwistle (Entwistle and Ramsden, 1983). The general dynamics of their models, in keeping with the evidence and conclusions of phenomenographic research (Marton and Säljö, 1976a, 1976b; Ramsden, 1987), emphasize that the outcome of learning is a function of strategy, especially strategy in tandem with motivational influences. The resultant actions are then further purposefully shaped by contextual perceptions, and especially those related to perceived task requirements.

Conceptually coherent patterns of strategy, motivation and contextual perceptions thus represent primary sources of variation between students. In self-reported phraseology these patterns map the contextual locus of purposeful action in terms of 'here', 'why' and 'how' that can be interpreted within the models. However, it has been argued that there are also other sources of variation that should be accommodated in these patterns.

In Entwistle's model (Entwistle and Ramsden, 1983), and in its associated instrumentation (the Approaches to Studying Inventory: ASI), these sources are represented by additional deep-level study processes, learning styles and pathologies (Pask, 1976) as well as other study behaviours and characteristics. It is a variant of this model, in conjunction with a set of contextual variables, that has been used by the present authors as a basis for exploring manifestations of student learning at an individual level (Meyer, 1991).

Background research
A range of earlier studies have explored manifestations of student learning using an individual-difference statistical model (multi-dimensional unfolding analysis) that is independent of correlational assumptions. Unfolding analysis is a particularly appropriate procedure for analysing individual differences, for it enables an individual response to be located within the underlying empirical data structure. The location of an individual response, thus indicated, can be used as a basis for inter-individual comparison within the data structure. To the extent that a conceptual model also 'fits' the empirical data structure, an individual location can be evaluated in qualitative (and model-dependent) terms; some locations, for example, might be proximate to 'deep' aspects of the data structure while others might be proximate to 'surface' aspects (Meyer, 1991).

In other individual-difference studies of failing students, an interesting phenomenon has been reported that does not fit neatly into any model-dependent conceptualization of student learning: subgroups of failing students manifest what appears to be a fragmented association (or conceptually disjointed individual-similarity preference structure) of source variables that do not assume the form of any recognizable, or previously reported, study behaviour pattern (Meyer and Muller, 1990). Verification of this phenomenon, based on factor analysis of failing student data collected in Edinburgh, has also been reported by Entwistle, Meyer and Tait (1991).

Subsequent investigation, coupled with a review of previously reported work undertaken in Cape Town and elsewhere, led to the conclusion that this phenomenon might be further investigated in terms of model-independent categorizations of self-reported, and apparently disintegrated, forms of deep-level study behaviour patterns. Extensions, or mutations, of surface-level patterns are then simply admitted as special cases. There were basically two reasons behind this exploratory course of action.

There was, firstly, a consistent body of incrementally obtained evidence that the phenomenon was not an isolated statistical artefact and that its empirically manifested features were amenable to independent verification through interviews, even to the extent of co-existent and contrasting learning style pathologies (Meyer, 1991). It has also been observed more recently that some plausible insights into this phenomenon can obtained by 'fitting' a locus of control model to empirical data structures corresponding to varying degrees of disintegrated response patterns (Meyer, 1993). Secondly, difficulty had been experienced in interpreting aspects of many empirical individual-difference data structures in terms of 'pure' fixed-dimensional models of student learning or their arguable variants, and especially so in terms of surface-level interpretations. It is generally acknowledged that surface-level strategy is a difficult construct to quantify reliably. A recent conclusion of Richardson (forthcoming), based on an extensive review of quantitative studies of student learning carried out across various disciplines, cultures and languages, also contrasts the robustness of deep-level patterns of study behaviour relative to surface-level patterns.

Approaches to categorization

Given the reasonable assumption that students are validly able to externalize the basic character of their learning actions via self-reported inventory (or interview) response patterns to appropriate stimuli, the proposition is that the dominant attributes of such patterns are amenable to ordinal classification. This can occur within a model-dependent framework, some chosen continuum such as 'understanding', or a set of externally defined criteria.

An early attempt to classify response patterns within a synthetic model of student learning has been described by Meyer, Parsons and Dunne (1990). This essentially involved recognizing the degree to which an observed response pattern conforms to a model-dependent stereotype or variant, for example, a 'deep' approach (which is ordinally 'better' than a 'surface' approach on a continuum of 'understanding'). One can similarly select an alternative continuum (and interpretive framework), such as the one based on 'conceptions of learning' (Säljö, 1979), and subject (interview) responses to the question 'What do you actually mean by learning?' to an ordinal classification procedure (Martin and Ramsden, 1987). In another (quantitative) variation on this theme Biggs (1985, 1988) advocates a procedure whereby inventory subscale scores obtained from his Study Process Questionnaire (SPQ) are symbolically graded, in terms of magnitude, as above average (+), average (0) or below average (−). To the extent that the resultant symbol sequences in an individual response indicate interpretable, or admissible, congruency between motives and strategies, a model-dependent classification is also possible.

Ordinal classification of student inventory responses can also be attempted by assessing their relative positional values within an empirical data structure to which a conceptual model has been 'fitted', and an example of this approach can be found in Meyer (1991). Using the empirical data structure as the principal frame of reference, some locations are 'better' or 'worse' than others. It should be noted, though, that there is subjectivity in the process of location assessment as well, partially as a result of spatial interpretation and individual location precision. However, in cases involving the disintegrated patterns of specific interest here, the condition of 'worst location' can be objectively determined as one of empirical non-conformity.

A problem with the above approaches is that the resultant categorization is conceptually constrained to the interpretive framework. If the framework conceptually precludes 'disintegrated' response patterns, it is not of much value in categorizing them. A third approach, and the one of interest here, involves relaxing conceptual constraints and logically examining the structure of the observed response pattern for additional model-independent embedded features that can serve as a basis for ordinal classification on an extended continuum of (in this case) 'understanding'. To the extent that the embedded features may also be amenable to alteration through external intervention, there is a sense in which the diagnosis may (for some individuals) also be the cure.

Risk categorization using programmable logic
Full details of an approach to model-independent 'at risk' categorization has been described in Meyer (1994). In essence, an individual response to a set of source variables (substantively derived from the ASI in this case, and supplemented with contextual perception variables) is treated as a preference structure with detectable embedded features. Such a preference structure is represented in the first (left hand) column of Table 1.

Table 1. A response pattern exhibiting two embedded masks

Obs CZ	mask1	mask2	variable
sb			
wl		wl	workload
Ol			
ds AD		ds	disorganized studying
cs			
eM rs Am			
ip	ip		improvidence
DA	DA	DA	deep approach
ls			
fa	fa		fragmentation
St gL RE	gL		globetrotting
LD			
ff			
BD ma		ma	memorizing
UE RI RD CL	UE RI	UE RI	using evidence/relating ideas

The second and third columns in Table 1 represent examples of embedded features of interest that empirically give rise to manifestations of 'disintegrated' patterns in individual-similarity subgroups. The second column represents a pathological compromise of the 'deep' strategy variable, while the third column similarly represents a non-pathological compromise of the same variable as indicated.

More generally, the empirically indicated defining features of 'disintegrated' response patterns (of 'deep' level study strategy) can be represented as a conceptually discontinuous lattice as shown in Table 2. Each column in Table 2 represents a numbered set of discrete conditions under which the core of 'deep' strategy and supporting processes, defined here by deep approach (DA), use of evidence (UE) and relating ideas (RI), is compromised by a set of conceptually incompatible variables (the asterisks). These discrete numbered sets are referred to as mask values. Values that correspond to pathological compromises are referred to as mask1 values while those corresponding to non-pathological compromises are referred to as mask2 values. Sets of mask values are experimentally aggregated into mask groups that are intended to exhibit notionally ordinal properties as the lattice in Table 2 is traversed from left to right. Five such mask1 groups are indicated in Table 2. Combinations of mask1 and mask2 groups yield, in turn, conceptually ordinal risk categories that can be expanded or contracted quite easily for exploratory modelling purposes.

It is thus possible to examine unambiguously an individual response pattern for embedded features, as represented by the mask sets, on a true/false basis. Any particular feature detected corresponds to its mask value – an index that ranges from 1 to 19. (A value of 20 indicates the absence of any of the features.) In the example shown in Table 1, and in terms of the conditions set out in Table 2, the second column indicates a (pathological) mask1 value of 4, while the third column indicates a (non-pathological) mask2 value of 2.

Of further interest are empirical explorations of factor structures controlled by mask1 groups, and the extent to which conceptual models of student learning 'fit' them. Table 3 (taken from Meyer (1994)) summarizes attempts to fit a congruent motive/strategy model of the form advocated by Biggs, as well as a fuller model of the form advocated by Entwistle. The four mask1 groups are labelled pathological suppression, infiltration, progression and recession respectively and are composed of the mask sets shown in Table 2. The results speak for themselves and point to the dangers of ignoring underlying and contrasting individual-similarity patterns in the data that, when detected, violate the fundamental assumption that group-level analyses adequately represent all the individuals in the group.

Table 2. Discontinuous conceptual lattice

Mask Set No.	Group 1			Group 2				Group 3					Group 4				Group 5		
	01	02	03	04	05	06	07	08	09	10	11	12	13	14	15	16	17	18	19
	*																		
	*	*	*					*											
	*	*	*	*	*	*		*	*	*				*					
	da	da	da	da	da	da	da	da	da	da	da	da	da	da	da	da	da	da	da
		*		*	*	*	*				*	*	*	*		*			
				*			*				*	*							
							*												
	ue	ue	ue	ue	ue	ue	ue	ue	ue	ue	ue	ue	ue	ue	ue	ue	ue	ue	ue
			*	*				*	*	*			*	*			*	*	*
								*					*				*	*	
																	*		
	ri	ri	ri	ri	ri	ri	ri	ri	ri	ri	ri	ri	ri	ri	ri	ri	ri	ri	ri
		*		*				*		*	*	*	*	*	*		*	*	
													*	*					*

Note:
1. Each column in Table 2 constitutes a single mask against which an individual response pattern can be compared.

2. Each mask represents a preference structure in terms of two conceptually incompatible sets of three constructs each; one set of 'pure' meaning constructs in the form of deep approach (DA), use of evidence (UE) and relating ideas (RI), and another set of constructs (the asterisks) which, in the first phase of the categorization procedure described in the present study, represent the pathologies of improvidence (ip), globetrotting (gl) and fragmentation (fa).

3. For the sake of visual simplicity, each mask represents only one of the set of permutation sequences that can occur by independently permuting the two sets of incompatible constructs within the mask. In the categorization of 'at risk' forms of study behaviour, all such permutations within each mask are considered to be conceptually equivalent. Thus, for example, in any column in the lattice the sequence DA UE RI can be permuted independently of the asterisks to yield the equivalent sequences DA RI UE / UE DA RI / UE RI DA / RI DA UE / RI UE DA.

There is a clear warning against the indiscriminate use of instrumentation that represents such models, and especially reduced versions of them, in monitoring or evaluating student learning – an argument that is independently supported (in the case of the 'short form' of the ASI) on purely psychometric grounds by Richardson (1992), and also on conceptual grounds by Entwistle and Tait (1993).

Clearly if a response pattern contains no embedded mask1 or mask2 features it can be further explored for embedded contextual perception and study behaviour features that are of interest– in this case contrasting forms of what have been referred to as study orchestrations (Meyer, 1991). This has in fact been attempted via a third experimental mask intended to capture ordinally conceptually distinguishable states of holistically contextualized, deep-level learning strategy. The distinguishable states essentially capture degrees of perceptual contextualization, versatility and motivational support. This aspect of risk categorization is not further discussed here as it is not relevant to the intervention strategies discussed in Part II.

Table 3. 'Fitting' of conceptual models to mask structures

| | | 'Fit' | |
| | | Model 1: Entwistle Full Model1 | Model 2: Biggs Simpler Model2 |
Mask 1 groups	n		
Group 1: Pathological suppression[3]	59	no	yes
Group 2: Pathological infiltration[4]	64	no	no
Group 3: Pathological progression[5]	66	no	no
Group 4: Pathological recession[6]	62	partial	partial

Notes:

1, 2 The variables employed in the study by Meyer (1994) substantively approximate the conceptual models advocated by Entwistle and Biggs respectively.

3 'Fit' of the simpler model contradicts failure to 'fit' the full model. See Appendix in Meyer (1994) for a full discussion of this case.

4 No correspondence between conceptual and empirical structures.

5 There is limited 'fit' in both models in terms of a 'strategic' component.

6 Simpler model does not do justice to the complexity of the data structure evidenced in the full model.

Table 4. Frequency table of September by April categories and outcomes corresponding to the risk distributions

April

Freq	1	2	3	4	5	Total	%Mark	n	s.d
S 1	25	11	3	3	0	42	46.7	40	13.9
e 2	16	24	11	8	1	60	50.3	56	12.8
p 3	7	14	25	13	0	59	57.1	59	15.2
t 4	1	4	13	26	9	53	64.1	52	16.8
5	0	2	1	5	6	14	66.9	13	18.5
Total	49	55	53	55	16	228			
%Mark	48.8	52.0	55.6	60.8	71.6				
n	48	51	51	54	16				
s.d	16.6	14.1	14.7	15.9	14.6				

Summary statistics of ordinal assn:	Value	ASE
Gamma	0.679	0.047
Kendall's Tau-b	0.546	0.042
Stuart's Tau-c	0.529	0.042
Somers' D C|R	0.549	0.042
Somers' D R|C	0.544	0.042
Spearman Correlation	0.631	0.045

McNemar's Chi Square 7.70 (p>0.05)

Note: 1. Due to missing data, there are fluctuations in the sample sizes used in calculating the overall percentage mark for each of the April and September risk-categories.

2. Asymmetry about the diagonal is not significant as indicated by the McNemar statistic. It appears that such shifts as do occur are mostly in terms of one category as indicated in the cell entries on the adjacent sub-diagonals. Cell entries on the diagonal indicate stable subgroup categories, while improved and deteriorated subgroups correspond to the cell entries in the lower and upper triangles respectively.

For the sake of completeness, however, Table 4 (taken from Meyer and Sass (in press) provides empirical support for the risk categorization approach outlined above. It also further confirms earlier conclusions about the general stability of such risk categorizations within a course of study and their association with learning outcome. The sample in this case (n=228), and the context (a first year course in applied mechanics), comes from the Faculty of Engineering at the University of Cape Town. Risk categorization is in terms of five ordinal categorization on a scale of 1 to 5 (1 representing 'high' risk, and 5 'low' risk). An individual risk categorisation was determined twice during the course (in April and September) based on a self-reported inventory response pattern. The September by April contingency table (Table 4) clearly indicates the stability of the risk categorization as evidenced in the general statistical measures of ordinal association. The risk distributions for April and September are indicated, respectively, by the cell entry totals that appear at the bottom and on the right-hand side of the table. Each cell total represents a categorical subgroup of students, and is flanked by the corresponding outcome measure for that sub-group–in this case, the mean raw percentage obtained in the mid- and final-year examinations. The expected correspondence between risk category and outcome is evident for both risk distributions in spite of the variation in outcome within the subgroups–a correspondence that has a random probability of less than 1 per cent in either case.

It is the high risk category (category 1) that is of especial interest here. Students who manifest apparently stable forms of 'disintegrated' study behaviour have been observed to fail or generally do very poorly in their courses and are an obvious (if extreme) target for intervention strategies.

Part II Intervention Strategies

Introduction

The strategic relevance to educational practice of students' perceptions of their own learning actions, and their perceptions of the context within which these occur, has been recognized from the outset. Entwistle and Ramsden (1983), in particular, formulated a captivating argument that 'approaches' to learning, and resultant outcomes, are a function of the context and could, therefore, be altered by contextually directed intervention. In its simplest form, they framed such intervention against the posited linkages between context, approach and outcome.

In initially setting out to explore the viability of contextually based intervention strategies, the present authors first reconciled an apparent gap in the evidence supporting the underlying argument, namely, empirical verification of the posited linkages between contextual perceptions and learning actions that had been gleaned from qualitative analyses of interview data (Ramsden, 1988). Since intervention, by definition, was to be directed at individual students, and given that the dynamics of the linkages are essentially non-linear, there was a considerably more stringent requirement to demonstrate such linkages within an individual-difference statistical model that was independent of correlational assumptions. Several studies thus directly addressed the linkage between perceptions of key contextual variables, and 'approaches' to studying at an individual level as a precursor to subsequent intervention attempts.

Contextual variables

Since a set of contextual variables would initially form the basis of intervention strategies, their selection was approached with considerable caution. Empirical attempts to verify the existence of sufficiently robust associations between the source variables of the ASI and those of the Course Perceptions Questionnaire (CPQ) described by Entwistle and Ramsden (1983) generally yielded unsatisfactory results, with the exception of the workload subscale that was subsequently retained (Meyer and Parsons, 1989). An alternative set of exploratory contextual variables developed independently by Meyer (1988) proved more satisfactory and evidenced the required association with the source variables of the ASI using an individual-difference statistical model (Meyer and Muller, 1990).

These contextual variables originated from teachers' and students' conceptualizations of learning contexts, solicited and interpreted within a general system theory framework; teachers were asked to describe teaching and learning processes in terms of the attributes of the constituent elements of a system, as well as the functional relationships that existed between the elements. This analytical methodology yielded a pool of contextual perception variables which was subsequently refined (and extended by the inclusion of the workload subscale of the CPQ) that could serve as a basis for intervention strategies in a plausibly valid manner: the variables emanated essentially from teachers' own experiences and were also demonstrably empirically associated in the minds of students with their learning actions. This raised the possibility of using individually self-reported inventory response patterns for diagnostic and intervention purposes.

Before the first pilot intervention was initiated, a number of studies were undertaken to explore the validity and interpretability of students' individual study response patterns. Through interviews with staff (concerning individual students), and with students (concerning themselves), it was confirmed that these response patterns sufficiently accurately approximated individuals' study approaches, and that students could readily interpret them.

Pilot interventions

Intervention has thus been attempted based on active student engagement (by way of explication, reflection and discussion) with such individual response patterns. It was hypothesized that some students exhibiting at risk response patterns might be assisted by focussing on their apparent inability to perceive adequately the context within which they were functioning. Specific intervention strategies have thus centred on methods of sufficiently developing students' perceptions to enable them to adopt more (theoretically) desirable congruences of strategy, motive and process (Parsons and Meyer, 1990; Parsons, 1993).

A first attempt at a model-dependent categorization of individual study response patterns located individuals on a continuum from 'deep' to 'surface' learning approach concomitantly with 'deep' and 'surface' perceptions of the learning context. Students considered to be 'at risk' (in this case, those apparently manifesting an extreme 'surface' approach and associated 'surface' contextual perceptions) were invited to participate in a pilot intervention programme.

This intervention was conducted on a limited scale with four groups of first-year and two groups of second-year electrical engineering students at the Cape Technikon during 1989 and 1990. The intervention was conducted within the discipline-specific context of electronics, a major subject for all students during their first and second year.

On both occasions the intervention was conducted in small groups (of typically four to six students) in the presence of both the subject lecturer and the programme facilitator (the second author). The intervention, conducted during the first eight weeks of the semester, involved a reflective dialogue with students about their contrasting perceptions of elements of the learning context and their associated approach to studying within that perceived context. No guidance was given in terms of specific study skills. The only notable difference between the two pilot programmes lay in the manner in which guidance on how to interpret the individual response patterns was given to students (verbal in the first programme, and written in the second).

Several high risk students expressed the benefit of the programme in terms such as 'I won't say I've worked harder; I've thought more about what I was doing', and, 'It made you more aware ... I use textbooks more and more effectively now'. Contrastingly, a low risk student who evidenced a conceptually 'deep' approach, and who asked to attend the intervention, expressed his attitude in these terms: 'It wasn't something new to me – I did know about these things. For me, I was hoping to get out of the course some form of study methods, like rigid study methods that I could perhaps apply. That's the main reason I attended. And that I didn't get from the course. ... It just highlighted some of the aspects which I could have used and which I wasn't using to the full.'

Second-year students appeared to express themselves better: 'Study-wise it didn't change things but reading-wise it did. Before, I used to study, you know, that and that. I used to think that was important and that was important and I studied that I saw from the piece of paper you gave me (his individual study response pattern) that I liked strategic-type studying, but that changed because I did more reading. In other words I spent more time trying to understand it rather than trying to learn something that was just there.' Another student commented that, 'I became aware that I had completely the wrong conception of what was expected in terms of how I had to approach the work, and I realized I must not only work harder, pay more attention to what the lecturer was saying and also do more personal research by looking things up in the book. I applied it to all my subjects. I worked harder, asked more questions of the lecturer in connection with the work if I didn't understand something. In general, my marks improved in all my subjects.'

The effects of the intervention with first-year students were equivocal. Two conclusions were reached: it was apparent from the observed results of the intervention, and from interviews with students, that the intervention had generally succeeded in developing positive shifts in perceptions and study approaches. In terms of academic achievement, however, this improvement was not sufficient, nor sustained enough, to enable some students to pass the course (Parsons, 1993).

By contrast, second-year students who participated in the same form of intervention demonstrated statistically significant and sustained improvements; their final examination performance reflected observed improvements (attributed to the intervention) in the preceding tests. This was not generally the case for the first-year groups (Parsons, 1993).

An overall conclusion was that the pilot interventions, focussed only on contextual perceptions and based on limited model-dependent individual differences, were beneficial for some students. In addition, students' ability to engage their self-reported response patterns, by way of individual and small group dialogue, supported the basic intervention methodology.

Extended interventions
Two subsequent studies reported by Meyer, Cliff and Dunne (forthcoming) have extended the basic intervention strategy as outlined. categorizations of progressively disintegrated forms of deep-level response patterns (with conceptually ordinal properties) have replaced the previous and more simplistic model-dependent categorizations. Specific attempts have been made to address students' metalearning capacity as part of the intervention strategy (Biggs, 1985). Other related perspectives emerging from interventions taking place outside the 'student experience of learning' framework have also been incorporated into the intervention strategy, namely, 'self-regulated learning' (Vermunt and Van Rijswijk, 1988) and 'attributional retraining' (Van Overwalle, Segebarth and Goldschtein, 1989).

The first study was conducted with 49 students in the first year academic support programme in engineering at the University of Cape Town. These students are predominantly African Black students from educationally disadvantaged backgrounds who are admitted to their first year of study through special admissions procedures. The intervention was applied specifically in the context of applied mechanics, one of the major subjects in the first-year study of engineering.

Upon registration, all students retrospectively self-reported on how they had approached the studying of science in their final secondary-school year. All students were subsequently interviewed to confirm their inventory response patterns. There was complete congruence between categorization of inventory response patterns and interview data, and students were subsequently aggregated into 'low risk' and 'high risk' subgroups. Students were told that the information obtained concerning their learning experiences would be used in the course as the basis of an on-going learning dialogue which would form an integral component of the course. Some students subsequently reported that this opportunity to discuss in depth their study behaviour had been a powerful stimulus for reflecting on their school learning history. In fact individual study counselling was available for all students on the intervention programme, and was perceived to be a particularly beneficial aspect of their experience.

A second (inventory-based) categorization of self-reported learning behaviour was performed shortly before the mid-year examinations (now specifically in the context of studying applied mechanics). Students were presented with a copy of their response patterns (again, with no indication of the categorization) and invited to interpret it against a given theoretically desirable study response pattern. On the basis of this interpretation, they were given a choice as free agents to participate in an on-going programme of intervention workshops.

The first of these dealt with contextual variables (such as methods of assessment and the use of textbooks) in a similar manner to the pilot programmes. The second workshop, in smaller groups, discussed concepts such as 'understanding' and specific processes that might be employed in studying applied mechanics. A third workshop took the form of a discussion by five senior students who had participated in the same academic support programme in engineering as to how they had prepared to write examinations in their first year. An objective of this third workshop was to convey to students a sense that some factors affecting their academic progress were under their own control.

On the basis of quantitative and extensive qualitative data (see Cliff, 1992) it was concluded that five out of the nine students categorized as being 'high risk' (those students for whom the intervention was specifically intended) showed a qualitative improvement in their study behaviour and passed the final Applied Mechanics examination. Viewed as an extension of the basic intervention methodology for students at risk initiated by Parsons and Meyer (1990), this study provided further incremental support for the viability of monitoring risk categorization and consequential intervention via sustained individual and group interaction.

This strategy, however, is impossible to implement fully on a large scale in a conventional course operating under uncompromising constraints. A second exploratory study, also undertaken in 1992, examined the effects of implementing a reduced version of the intervention described above (Meyer,

Cliff and Dunne, forthcoming).

A large, second semester, first-year course in introductory statistics was selected for this purpose, in which in excess of one hundred at risk students were targeted on the basis of a single inventory response snapshot about three weeks into the course. The stability of the individual response patterns could not be confirmed in this case, either through interviews or instrumentation. Individual profiles, as before, served as the basis for initiating the intervention. In this case, however, targeted students were invited, on two separate occasions, to a workshop on 'study methods' at which they were presented with their response patterns, an explanation of what they meant, and a specially written 'learning guide' (Dunne, 1992) that explained the epistemology of statistics and contrasting approaches on how to study it. The remainder of the intervention centred on voluntary attendance at tutorial meetings intended, in part, to promote self-reliance in achieving understanding of concepts covered in the course.

Significant aspects of the earlier intervention strategy were thus compressed into a single event, namely, the presentation of the profiles, the invitation to engage them further, and the explication of discipline-specific contextual perception variables within a 'student experience of learning' framework. At the same time, however, new intervention material was introduced in the form of the 'learning guide' which attempted to clarify for students the meaning of 'deep-level' learning in statistics. (In another context use of such material has been advocated by Coles (1990) to help students with learning difficulties.)

The results were very disappointing; only a quarter of the targeted students initially responded voluntarily and participated. Eventually the number of participants increased but was still fewer than half the target. Using examination marks as the outcome measure criterion, no effects attributable to the intervention could be statistically determined. A sobering conclusion was that scale-induced, impersonal and group-level interventions of this form, however well intentioned, are not a viable option.

Concluding discussion
The diagnostic strategies described in Part I and the development of more sophisticated model-independent methods to facilitate the categorization procedures emanating from self-reported perception response patterns have proved their worth in a variety of disparate settings. The appropriateness of the instrumentation employed to naturalistic settings in higher education, and the diagnostic methods applied to the individual response patterns by way of categorization, have enabled the early identification of at risk students. It has been possible, on a regular basis and across a number of different courses in higher education institutions, to integrate this procedure into the regular teaching programme and to use the results thus obtained for a variety of purposes.

The individual level interventions described in Part II collectively constitute a set of strategies that, within the parameters set, give rise to cautious optimism with regard to integrating such strategies as have proved successful into the regular teaching programme. To date these interventions have been directed at the most extreme cases of students manifesting disintegrated response patterns associated with academic failure. There is incremental evidence that these interventions have been at least partially successful in effecting qualitative learning improvement and attendant improvement in outcome performance. It is difficult to make comparisons with other reported interventions. Reported studies describing intervention programmes or proposed strategies, such as those by Martin and Ramsden (1987), Biggs (1987), Schmeck (1988), Weinstein (1988) and Coles (1990), not only differ from the work described here; they also differ considerably from one another in terms of interpretive framework, methodology, and most notably in their diversity in terms of 'target' groups.

Thus, while limited success has been observed with at risk students in the work reported here, interest must also focus on other identified categories, especially those categories of students who are not conceptually at risk but who have been observed to fail. The authors are not aware of any interventions aimed at failing students with apparently conceptually integrated response patterns. However, Biggs (1987) has reported considerable success with highly motivated students who were not at risk of failing but who were underachieving. This could indicate that intervention targeted at such students may, in fact, be more successful in improving outcome performance than strategies aimed at high risk groups. Research is currently under way to investigate appropriate intervention strategies for such low risk individuals who, nevertheless, indicate early in-course signs of failure.

Student-based course evaluation, at least in South African higher education, is an established regular, if not compulsory, phenomenon. Insofar as the instrumentation and analytic techniques described here provide an alternative and complementary window to monitor student perceptions of the content and context of learning, as well as the effect of these on the learning strategies that they adopt, they represent potentially powerful ways of evaluating the quality of the learning experience provided by any course. It has proved possible, in a number of courses, to put this complementary evaluation method in place as an additional source of diagnostic information with which both staff and students can readily engage.

It is the experience of the present authors that such information can be provided to practitioners in higher education, despite its apparent (and genuine) complexity, in a readily accessible and interpretable form that is plausibly valid in terms of their own teaching experience. Benefit is not necessarily limited to the context of intervention strategies. Indeed, there is every reason to believe that the qualitative monitoring of student learning has a key role to play in areas such as staff development and tutor training, where the conceptual framework employed,and the information provided, at the level of both the individual and the group, acts as a powerful vehicle for engaging those aspects of the learning experience that are most amenable to reflection and qualitative improvement.

References

Biggs, J. B. (1985). The role of metalearning in study processes *British Journal of Educational Psychology*, 55, 185–212.

Biggs, J. B. (1987). *Student Approaches to Learning and Studying*. Hawthorne: Australian Council for Educational Research.

Biggs, J. B. (1988). Assessing student approaches to learning *Australian Psychologist*, 23, 197–206.

Biggs, J. B. (1993). What do inventories of students' learning processes really measure? A theoretical review and clarification *British Journal of Educational Psychology*, 63, 3–19.

Cliff, A. F. (1992). *The 'Educational Disadvantaged'Student: Impacting upon Conceptions of Learning and Perceptions of Learning Contexts,* Unpublished M.Ed. Thesis, University of Cape Town.

Coles, C. R. (1990). Helping students with learning difficulties in medical and health-care education *Medical Education*, 24, 300–312.

Craik, F. I. M. and Lockhart, R. S. (1972). Levels of processing: a framework for memory research *Journal of Verbal Learning and Verbal Behaviour*, 11, 671–684.

Dunne, T. T. (1992). *Learning Statistics: a Guide for First Year Students* Mimeograph, Department of Statistical Sciences, University of Cape Town.

Entwistle, N. J., Meyer, J. H. F. and Tait, H. (1991). Student failure: disintegrated patterns of study strategies and perceptions of the learning environment *Higher Education*, 21, 249–261.

Entwistle, N. and Tait, H. (1993). *Identifying Students at Risk through Ineffective Study Strategies*. Paper presented at the 5th European Conference for Research on Learning and Instruction, Aix-en-Provence, France, 31 August–5 September.

Entwistle N. J. and Ramsden, P. (1983). *Understanding Student Learning*.

London: Croom Helm.

Martin, E. and Ramsden, P. (1987). Learning skills, or skill in learning? In Richardson, J. T. E., Eysenck, M. W. and Warren Piper, D. (Eds), *Student Learning*. Milton Keynes: SRHE. and Open University Press.

Marton, F. and Säljö, R. (1976a). On qualitative differences in learning: I: outcome and process *British Journal of Educational Psychology*, 46, 4–11.

Marton, F. and Säljö, R. (1976b). On qualitative differences in learning: II: outcome as a function of the learner's conception of the task *British Journal of Educational Psychology*, 46, 115–127.

Meyer, J. H. F. (1988). Student perceptions of learning context and approaches to studying *South African Journal of Higher Education*, 2, 73–82.

Meyer, J. H. F. (1991). Study Orchestration: the manifestation, interpretation and consequences of contextualised approaches to studying. *Higher Education*, 22, 297–316.

Meyer, J. H. F (1993). *The Individual-Difference Modelling of Student Learning*. Paper presented at the 5th European Conference for Research on Learning and Instruction, Aix-en-Provence, France, 31 August–5 September .

Meyer, J. H. F. (1994). Academically at risk study behaviour: a categorization procedure and an empirical exploration based on programmable logic *South African Journal of Higher Education*, 8 in press.

Meyer, J. H. F. and Parsons, P. (1989). Approaches of studying and course perceptions using the Lancaster Inventory - a comparative study *Studies in Higher Education*, 14, 137–153.

Meyer, J. H. F. and Sass, A. (in press). The impact of the first year on the study behaviour of engineering students *International Journal of Engineering Education*, 0, 000–000.

Meyer, J. H. F. and Muller, M. W. (1990). Evaluating the Quality of Student Learning I: an unfolding analysis of the association between perceptions of learning context and approaches to studying at an individual level *Studies in Higher Education*, 15, 131–154.

Meyer, J. H. F., Parsons, P. and Dunne, T. T. (1990). Individual study orchestrations and their association with learning outcome *Higher Education*, 20, 67–89.

Parsons, P. G. (1993). The student at risk: the successful integration of intervention into the regular teaching programme *South African Journal of Higher Education,* 7 , 000–000.

Parsons, P G. and Meyer, J. H. F. (1990). The academically 'at risk' student: a pilot intervention programme and its observed effects on learning outcome *Higher Education,* 20 3, 323–334.

Pask, G. (1976). Styles and strategies of learning *British Journal of Educational Psychology,* 46, 128–148.

Ramsden, P. (1987). Improving teaching and learning in higher education: the case for a relational perspective *Studies in Higher Education,* 12 3, 275–286.

Ramsden, P. (1988). Context and strategy: situational influences on learning. In Schmeck, R. R. (ed.), *Learning Strategies and Learning Styles.* New York: Plenum Press.

Richardson, J. T. E. (1992). A critical evaluation of a short form of the approaches to studying inventory *Psychology Teaching Review,* 1, 34–44.

Richardson, J. T. E (forthcoming). *Cultural specificity of approaches to studying in higher education,* I: a literature survey.

Säljö, R. (1979). *Learning in the Learner's Perspective, I: Some Commonsense Conceptions.* Reports from the Institute of Education, University of Gothenburg, No. 77.

Schmeck, R. R. (Ed.) (1988). *Learning strategies and learning styles.* New York: Plenum Press.

Van Overwalle, F. Segebarth, K. and Goldschtein, M. (1989). Improving performance of freshmen through attributional testimonies from fellow students *British Journal of Educational Psychology,* 59, 75–85.

Vermunt, J. D. H. M. and Van Rijswijk, F. A. W. M. (1988). Analysis and development of students' skill in self regulated learning *Higher Education,* 17, 647–682.

Weinstein, C. E. (1988). Assessment and training of student learning strategies. In Schmeck, R. R. (ed.) Learning Strategies and Learning Styles. New York: Plenum Press.

Acknowledgement

The financial assistence of the Centre for Science development towards some aspects of this reserach is hereby acknowledged. Opinions expressed inthis paper, and conclusions arrived at , are those of the authors and are not necessarily to be attributed to the Centre for Science Development.

Using Questionnaires to Evaluate Student Learning: Some Health Warnings

John T.E.Richardson, Brunel University,

Introduction

There is a general consensus in the research literature that students in higher education manifest a number of different approaches to learning that are dependent upon the context, the content, and the demands of the learning task (see, e.g., Marton, Hounsell, and Entwistle, 1984; Richardson, Eysenck, and Warren Piper, 1987). In particular, they may adopt a "deep" approach insofar as they acknowledge the more abstract forms of learning that are demanded in higher education and are motivated by the relevance of the syllabus to their own personal needs and interests; they adopt a "surface" approach insofar as they encounter an overloaded curriculum and methods of assessment which emphasise the superficial properties of the material that is to be learned; and they adopt a "strategic" approach to the extent that they receive cues about their assessment schemes from members of teaching staff. The defining characteristics of these three different approaches to learning are summarised in Table 1.

Table 1. Defining Features of Three Approaches to Learning

Deep approach
-     Intention to understand
-     Vigorous interaction with content
-     Relate new ideas to previous knowledge
-     Relate concepts to everyday experience
-     Relate evidence to conclusions
-     Examine the logic of the argument

Surface approach
-     Intention to complete task requirements
-     Memorise information needed for assessments
-     Failure to distinguish principles from examples
-     Treat task as an external imposition
-     Focus on discrete elements without integration
-     Unreflectiveness about purpose or strategies

Strategic approach
-     Intention to obtain highest possible grades
-     Organise time and distribute effort to greatest effect
-     Ensure conditions and materials for studying appropriate
-     Use previous exam papers to predict questions
-     Be alert to cues about marking schemes

Source: adapted from Entwistle (1987, p. 16).

Most of the original research which gave rise to this categorisation of approaches to studying used a qualitative, interview-based methodology that has been variously described as "experiential", "introspective" and "phenomenographic". This has been claimed to be much more sensitive to the different meanings that individuals ascribe to learning in different academic situations, and yet the precise research procedures used in these studies are typically not specified in any detail. In particular, Fleming (1986) criticised this work for neglecting "the essentially social nature of the interview" (p. 560), and he argued that students' accounts of their approaches to learning had been reduced to the level of the stories told to tourists by their couriers. Fleming commented: "It may be tempting to consider the perspective of the culture which the tourist can develop through conducted tours to be limited, partial, biased or in other ways inadequate compared to the perspectives of the indigenous population in the routine, mundane activities of their everyday life" (p. 559).

In fact, the only piece of phenomenographic research that I have come across in which the researchers even begin to specify their methodology is a study by Morgan, Taylor and Gibbs (1982), who interviewed 29 British students on an introductory social science course at the Open University. Morgan et al. stated that transcripts of their interviews were analysed according to the methods of "grounded theory", and that this analysis revealed deep-level and surface-level approaches to studying that were broadly similar to those which had been described previously by Marton and Säljö (1976) in Sweden (see also Morgan, Gibbs, and Taylor, 1980).

Now, grounded theory is a methodology developed by Glaser and Strauss (1967) for the analysis of qualitative data, in which specific themes are derived from the respondents' accounts without regard to the researcher's own preconceptions. According to this general approach, "it makes no sense to start with 'received' theories or variables (categories) because these are likely to inhibit or impede the development of new theoretical formulations" (Strauss and Corbin, 1990, p. 50). However, Morgan et al. began their account by asserting that Marton and Säljö's (1976) contrast between deep-level and surface-level approaches to studying marked "a crucial aspect of understanding how students handle learning materials" (p. 107), and it is clear that a fundamental goal of their work was to identify the same distinction in the accounts given by Open University students. A sceptic might therefore argue that their analysis was rather more a case of reading things into the facts than a genuine instance of grounded theory.

Other researchers who follow in the phenomenographic tradition are quite prepared to use "chats at the foot of the stairs" with students as well as informal discussions "over a beer" with their teachers (Eizenberg, 1986, p. 21). As a result, the context of their research is often poorly structured, so that (intended or unintended) aspects of the researchers' behaviour may well prompt the participants to respond in a way that tends to confirm the researchers' own expectations. This process of behaviour confirmation in social interactions (commonly described as the idea of a "self-fulfilling prophecy") has been well documented (Snyder and Swann, 1978). Of course, I would not want to claim that research carried out by people who are properly trained and supervised in the use of qualitative methods is vulnerable to the same flaws (at any rate, not to this extent). However, since there are very few opportunities for research training in this area, and none (to my knowledge) that is professionally accredited, the validity of most of the phenomenographic research that is carried out must be open to question.

The availability of training is important not simply as a scientific issue, but also as an ethical one. The aim of qualitative research is to reveal personal meanings, and it follows that much of the material that is uncovered in an interview can be of considerable personal significance to the informant and emotionally very highly loaded. Occasionally, indeed, the encounter may slip from a research interview to a counselling session. This will obviously make considerable emotional demands on the researcher, and yet few people who embark upon qualitative research have the personal skills, professional training, and competent supervision to handle those demands. So, although the phenomenographic approach is often held up as a model to be followed by those who wish to understand student learning, and indeed has been proposed as a device for enhancing the professional skills of teachers themselves, I would personally counsel against the use of such an approach in the absence of appropriate training and supervision.

These ethical issues can be avoided (some might say, "evaded") by the use of standardised instruments that do not depend on any direct personal interaction between the researcher and the informants, such as checklists, inventories or questionnaires administered to individuals in large groups. This also tends to reduce the possibility of the informants being prompted by intended or unintended aspects of the researcher's behaviour. A number of attempts have been made to operationalise the distinctions among different approaches to learning in terms of the students' responses to different subscales of particular questionnaires. The rest of this paper will therefore be concerned with evidence obtained from the use of three of these instruments.

The Study Processes Questionnaire

This instrument was developed by Biggs (1978, 1985) in Australia and Canada. It contains seven items on each of six scales that are intended to measure the respondents' motives and strategies on three approaches to learning ("surface", "deep" and "achieving"). Unfortunately, studies in Australia and other countries have failed to reproduce this constituent structure.

Instead, the scales appear to define merely two factors: one is a generalised deep approach to studying, measured by deep and achieving motives and strategies; the other is a generalised surface approach to
studying, measured by surface and achieving motives and surface strategy (Biggs, 1987, p. 16; Biggs and Rihn, 1984; Watkins and Akande, 1992; Watkins and Regmi, 1990; cf. Hattie and Watkins, 1981; O'Neil and Child, 1984). There is also concern about the item composition of the scales intended to measure a surface approach to studying (see Christensen, Massey, and Isaacs, 1991; Kember and Gow, 1990, 1991; O'Neil and Child, 1984).

The Inventory of Learning Processes

This was developed in the United States by Schmeck, Ribich and Ramanaiah (1977) on the basis of contemporary theoretical developments in experimental research into human learning and memory. It contains a total of 62 true-false items intended to measure four different scales. These were explained by Schmeck and Grove (1979) in the following manner:

synthesis-analysis: assessing deep, as opposed to superficial, information processing; study methods: assessing repetitive, drill-and-practice habits of processing information;
fact retention: assessing attention to details and specifics as opposed to generalities; and
elaborative processing: assessing elaborative, as opposed to verbatim, information processing.

Recently, Schmeck, Geisler-Brenstein and Cercy (1991) supplemented these scales with seven other scales examining broader aspects of self-concept and personality to produce a Revised Inventory of Learning Processes in which the respondents indicate the extent of agreement or disagreement along a six-point scale with each of 160 statements.

While the Inventory of Learning Processes was originally validated using factor analysis and other techniques, subsequent studies both in the United States and elsewhere have failed to replicate its intended factor structure (Schmeck and Geisler-Brenstein, 1989; Speth and Brown, 1988; Watkins and Hattie, 1981). Moreover, the original scales were supposed to be independent of each other, but more recent studies have found them to be correlated, sometimes extremely so (Henson and Schmeck, 1993; Schmeck et al., 1991). Finally, the "levels-of-processing" framework which motivated this Inventory is no longer seen as providing an adequate rationale for understanding and investigating human memory (Baddeley, 1990, pp. 160-172; Eysenck and Keane, 1990, pp. 148-155). Hence, the instrument has no special advantages over other inventories for research purposes by virtue of its supposed theoretical underpinning.

The Approaches to Studying Inventory

Without doubt, the most widely used questionnaire on student learning in higher education is the Approaches to Studying Inventory (ASI) devised by Entwistle and his colleagues (Entwistle, Hanley, and Hounsell, 1979; Entwistle and Ramsden, 1983, pp. 35-55; Ramsden and Entwistle, 1981). The ASI incorporates a variety of constructs taken from interview-based work on student learning, and in its final version consists of 64 items in 16 subscales, grouped in turn under four general headings (see Table 2). The specific distinction between "deep", "surface" and "strategic" approaches is subsumed within a somewhat broader classification in terms of a "meaning orientation", a "reproducing orientation" and an "achieving orientation", and supplemented by a fourth domain representing various learning styles and pathologies described by Pask (1976).

Table 2. Subscales Contained in the Approaches to Studying Inventory

Subscale	Meaning
Meaning orientation	
Deep approach	Active questioning in learning
Inter-relating ideas	Relating to other parts of the course
Use of evidence and logic	Relating evidence to conclusions
Intrinsic motivation	Interest in learning for learning's sake
Reproducing orientation	
Surface approach	Preoccupation with memorisation
Syllabus-boundness	Relying on staff to define learning tasks
Fear of failure	Pessimism and anxiety about academic outcomes
Extrinsic motivation	Interest in courses for the qualifications they offer
Achieving orientation	
Strategic approach	Awareness of implications of academic demands made by staff
Disorganised study methods	Unable to work regularly and effectively
Negative attitudes to studying	Lack of interest and application
Achievement motivation	Competitive and confident
Styles and pathologies	
Comprehension learning	Readiness to map out subject area and think divergently
Globetrotting	Over-ready to jump to conclusions
Operation learning	Emphasis on facts and logical analysis
Improvidence	Over-cautious reliance on details

Source: Ramsden and Entwistle (1981, p. 371).

Unfortunately, research studies have consistently failed to reproduce the intended constituent structure of this instrument (for reviews, see Harper and Kember, 1989; Meyer and Parsons, 1989b). Most of these obtained clear evidence for two major factors:

(a)   a "meaning orientation" factor indexed by the subscales concerned with deep approach, inter-relating ideas, the use of evidence and logic, intrinsic motivation and comprehension learning; and

(b)   a "reproducing orientation" factor indexed by the subscales concerned with surface approach, syllabus-boundness, fear of failure, disorganised study methods, negative attitudes to studying, globe trotting and improvidence.

In addition, some studies (though by no means all) have produced evidence for two additional factors:

(c)   a "narrow orientation" factor indexed by the subscales concerned with operation learning and strategic approach; and

(d)   a "goal orientation" factor indexed by the subscales concerned with extrinsic motivation and achievement motivation.

Moreover, a few studies have reported factor analyses of the responses to the individual items, and these have often failed to reproduce many of the subscales (Entwistle and Ramsden, 1983, pp. 50-52; Entwistle and Waterston, 1988; Meyer and Parsons, 1989a, 1989b; Schmeck, 1988; Speth and Brown, 1988).

Given the somewhat doubtful status of certain of the subscales of the full ASI, it might be thought useful to develop an abbreviated inventory which focussed upon these two fundamental study orientations. Entwistle (1981, pp. 57-60, 100-103) devised a version for use with sixth-formers in which 30 items defined seven subscales which could be combined in various ways to yield eight indices of studying, including meaning orientation, reproducing orientation and achieving orientation (see also Entwistle and Ramsden, 1983, pp. 53-55). Gibbs, Habeshaw and Habeshaw (1988) proposed that this version could be shortened further to produce an inventory of just the 18 items concerned with the different orientations to studying. This was used to evaluate innovative forms of course design and delivery in the CNAA project on "Improving Student Learning" (Gibbs, 1992).

However, these shortened versions of the ASI are inadequate because their subscales lack sufficient internal consistency (see Watkins, 1984). There is also evidence that they measure fairly specific aspects of study behaviour rather than more global study orientations (Richardson, 1992; but cf. Newstead, 1992). I have argued instead (Richardson, 1990) that it would be more appropriate to abbreviate the original ASI by focussing upon the eight subscales which had been consistently identified with meaning orientation and with reproducing orientation across the different academic disciplines studied by Entwistle and Ramsden (1983, p. 52). This yields an inventory of 32 items with the following structure:

Meaning orientation:	Reproducing orientation:
deep approach	surface approach
comprehension learning	improvidence
inter-relating ideas	fear of failure
use of evidence and logic	syllabus-boundness

I was able to show that these eight subscales and the two principal study orientations could be successfully reproduced by means of factor analysis.

Cultural Specificity of Approaches to Studying

The three instruments that have just been discussed were originally developed in three different countries (Australia, the United States and the United Kingdom, respectively). Marton and his colleagues originally argued that the different approaches to studying were cultural phenomena which were socially constructed (see Dahlgren, 1984; Marton, 1981; Säljö, 1984, 1987), and this suggests that they may well be culture-relative and culture-specific (Marton, 1976). Be that as it may, these questionnaires tend to be employed by researchers and practitioners in various countries in a relatively indiscriminate manner. Is this in fact warranted?

Most of the relevant evidence has come from the use of the ASI. In factor analyses of the subscale scores, similar solutions have been found in studies carried out in the United Kingdom, Australia, South Africa, the United States, Nepal, Venezuela and Hong Kong. This indicates that the ASI is fairly "portable" from one system of higher education to another. However, factor analyses of the responses to individual items have failed to confirm the integrity of some of the subscales in the United Kingdom, in South Africa, and especially in the United States. I have carried out a study using the 32-item version of the ASI at a university in the United States, and have come to the conclusion that the basic study orientations are interpreted in a manner that is distinctive to each cultural context. Similar research at the University of the South Pacific using the 18-item version of the ASI has led to broadly the same conclusion. It is unclear at present whether this conclusion applies equally to cultural or ethnic groups within the same country.

Variations with Educational Level

These questionnaires have also been employed with students at different educational levels. Most specifically, the Study Processes Questionnaire and the ASI have both been adapted for use with secondary schoolchildren. Whether it is legitimate to employ the same constructs in such diverse educational settings has not, however, been rigorously tested. There is some evidence from South Africa that black students from disadvantaged educational backgrounds are more likely to show a fragmented pattern of study orientations (Meyer, Dunne, and Sass, 1992). Another study carried out in the United States using the Inventory of Learning Processes came to essentially the same conclusion in the case of students who entered higher education through community colleges rather than directly to universities (Henson and Schmeck, 1993). At Brunel University we have been exploring the approaches to studying of mature students taking "Access" courses and have similarly failed to find any coherent factor solution from their responses to the ASI. Nevertheless, other mature students who enter then University directly (with or without conventional entrance qualifications) manifest the same general pattern as younger students coming straight from school. This suggests that something odd may happen to students' study approaches as the result of following an "Access" course into higher education.

Individual Differences in Approaches to Studying

Previous research has tended to focus upon the aggregated responses given by groups of students in reporting how they engage with academic learning, rather than the responses of individual students who make up those groups. Meyer and his colleagues (Meyer and Muller, 1990a, 1990b; Meyer, Parsons, and Dunne, 1990) have advocated the use of different methodologies to compare the patterns of responses that are given by individual students. However, their analyses are based upon the subscale scores generated by particular students, and hence have taken for granted the integrity of the subscales themselves (cf. also Meyer and Parsons, 1989b).

Most research into student learning has failed to investigate whether there are systematic qualitative differences between individual students. In fact, typically no information is provided about the students' personal characteristics at all. This is true even of the earlier phenomenographic studies, in spite of their avowed concern to give a proper account of the personal meanings ascribed to learning by individual students. Such basic information as the gender and age of the participants in these studies was left wholly unspecified. Subsequently, however, Entwistle (1981, p. 75) reported that all of the participants in Marton's original experiment were women. So, are there systematic qualitative differences between older and younger students or between men and women in their approaches to studying?

The variable of age is of some interest because British institutions of higher education are currently having to recruit from the older sectors of the population, and yet it seems to be widely held that mature students lack the basic skills needed for effective study in higher education. The totality of research evidence does not support this stereotype, however: mature students are more likely than younger students to adopt a meaning orientation to their studying and are less likely to adopt a reproducing orientation (Richardson, in press). Their academic attainment is also at least as good as that of younger students (Richardson, in preparation). Perhaps most crucially, there is no sign of any difference at all between the factor solutions generated by older and younger students from their responses to the 32-item ASI (Richardson, in preparation).

The effects of gender are more complicated. In the United States there has developed a very influential tradition based upon the use of qualitative methods which maintains that women demonstrate conceptions of knowledge, truth and learning in their intellectual development that are qualitatively different from those of male students (see Belenky, Clinchy, Goldberger, and Tarule, 1986; Clinchy and Zimmerman, 1982; Gilligan, 1982; Gilligan, Ward, McLean Taylor, and Bardige, 1988). Nevertheless, research using formal inventories or questionnaires to quantify students' use of different approaches or orientations has failed to produce any consistent evidence for differences between men and women in their responses (see Richardson and King, 1991). This seems to apply even to the constituent structure of their responses across different items (Richardson, 1993).

This might be taken to support the view expressed by Perry (1981) and others that quantitative methods cannot provide an adequate account of the cognitive structures and social meanings of students in higher education. However, it might be that gender differences in approaches to studying do influence students' responses to questionnaires in specific contexts. In my own investigation of university students in the United States and in a previous study by Miller, Finley and McKinley (1990), male students were found to produce higher scores on meaning orientation and lower scores on reproducing orientation than female students. I attributed this to the widespread use in North America of multiple-choice tests, which are known to favour male students over female ones (Murphy, 1982).

Recent interview-based research by Thomas (1988, 1990) in the United Kingdom suggests that differences between male and female students will vary across different academic subjects, and will be especially apparent in science courses, since these tend to challenge the personal identity and confidence of female students. In support of this idea, Meyer, Dunne and I have found qualitative differences between men and women taking a first-year service course in statistics at one South African university. However, consistent with the views of Marton and his colleagues, I and my colleagues at Brunel University have also found evidence for a three-way interrelationship between gender, subject, and learning context in a study of men and women at three Oxbridge colleges. In particular, women taking science courses obtained higher scores on meaning orientation if they were in a more male environment (a college that was formerly exclusively male), whereas women taking arts courses obtained higher scores if they were in a more female environment (a college that was exclusively female).

Conclusions

For both ethical and practical reasons, I would suggest that both researchers and practitioners should use quantitative devices such as inventories and questionnaires if they wish to monitor and evaluate the approaches to studying of their students. My first "health warning" is that qualitative research methods should only be employed by people who have the proper skills, training and supervision.

Three different inventories have been employed in previous research on student learning, but none of these devices measures what it claims in the sense that its constituent structure can be empirically confirmed on participants similar to those on whom it was originally developed. So my second "health warning" is that these questionnaires should be used only with great care, if at all. The same observation applies to the 30-item and 18-item versions of the ASI. I would personally commend the 32-item version of the ASI as the only instrument for monitoring student learning whose constituent structure has been successfully replicated.

These questionnaires serve to operationalise constructs whose value in describing individual differences in student learning has been clearly documented. Nevertheless, the generalisability of these constructs from their original domain of application should not be taken for granted. My third "health warning" is that problems of interpretation may well arise in seeking to use these instruments with students from different cultures or from different educational levels.

Finally, I have criticised previous research into student learning, including that motivated by the phenomenographic tradition, for paying insufficient attention to differences between individual students based upon obvious demographic characteristics such as age and gender. I have argued elsewhere that an insensitivity to such variables merely helps to maintain the manifest inequalities that already exist in higher education (Richardson, in press; Richardson and King, 1991). Thus, my fourth "health warning" is to urge researchers and practitioners alike to be attentive to the needs, aspirations and achievements of all of the students with whom their investigations are concerned.

References

Baddeley, A. D. (1990). *Human Memory: Theory and Practice.* Hove: Erlbaum.

Belenky, M., Clinchy, B., Goldberger, N. and Tarule, J. (1986). *Women's Ways of Knowing: The Development of Self, Voice, and Mind.* New York: Basic Books.

Biggs, J. B. (1978). Individual and group differences in study processes. *British Journal of Educational Psychology,* 48, 266–279.

Biggs, J. B. (1985). The role of metalearning in study processes. British Journal of Educational Psychology, 55, 185–212.

Biggs, J. B. (1987). *Student Approaches to Learning and Studying.* Melbourne: Australian Council for Educational Research.

Biggs, J. B., and Rihn, B. A. (1984). The effects of intervention on deep and surface approaches to learning. In J. R. Kirby (ed.), *Cognitive Strategies and Educational Performance* (pp. 279–293). Orlando, FL: Academic Press.

Christensen, C. A., Massey, D. R., and Isaacs, P. J. (1991). Cognitive strategies and study habits: An analysis of the measurement of tertiary students' learning. *British Journal of Educational Psychology,* 61, 290–299.

Clinchy, B. M. and Zimmerman, C. (1982). Epistemology and agency in the development of undergraduate women. In P. Perun (ed.), *The Undergraduate Women: Issues in Educational Equity* (pp. 161–182). Lexington, MA: D. C. Heath.

Dahlgren, L.-O. (1984). Outcomes of learning. In F. Marton, D. Hounsell, and N. Entwistle (eds), *The Experience of Learning* (pp. 19–35). Edinburgh: Scottish Academic Press.

Eizenberg, N. (1986). Applying student learning research to practice. In J. A. Bowden (ed.), *Student Learning: Research into Practice. The Marysville Symposium* (pp. 21–60). Parkville: Centre for the Study of Higher Education, University of Melbourne.

Entwistle, N. (1981). *Styles of Learning and Teaching: An Integrated Outline of Educational Psychology for Students, Teachers, and Lecturers.* Chichester: Wiley.

Entwistle, N. (1987). A model of the teaching-learning process. In J. T. E. Richardson, M. W. Eysenck, and D. Warren Piper (eds), *Student Learning: Research in Education and Cognitive Psychology* (pp. 13–28). Milton Keynes: SRHE & Open University Press.

Entwistle, N., Hanley, M., and Hounsell, D. (1979). Identifying distinctive approaches to studying. *Higher Education*, 8, 365–380.

Entwistle, N. J., and Ramsden, P. (1983). *Understanding Student Learning*. London: Croom Helm.

Entwistle, N., &andWaterston, S. (1988). Approaches to studying and levels of processing in university students. *British Journal of Educational Psychology*, 58, 258–265.

Eysenck, M. W., and Keane, M. T. (1990). *Cognitive Psychology: A Student's Handbook. Hove:* Erlbaum.

Fleming, W. G. (1986). The interview: a neglected issue in research on student learning. *Higher Education*, 15, 547–563.

Gibbs, G. (1992). *Improving the Quality of Student Learning*. Bristol: Technical & Educational Services.

Gibbs, G., Habeshaw, S., and Habeshaw, T. (1988). *53 Interesting Ways to Appraise Your Teaching*. Bristol: Technical & Educational Services.

Gilligan, C. (1982). *In a Different Voice: Psychological Theory and Women's Development.* Cambridge, MA: Harvard University Press.

Gilligan, C., Ward, J. V., McLean Taylor, J., and Bardige, B. (1988). *Mapping the Moral Domain*. Cambridge, MA: Harvard University Press.

Glaser, B. G., and Strauss, A. L. (1967). *The Discovery of Grounded Theory: Strategies for Qualitative Research*. Chicago: Aldine.

Harper, G., and Kember, D. (1989). Interpretation of factor analyses from the Approaches to Studying Inventory. *British Journal of Educational Psychology*, 59, 66–74.

Hattie, J., and Watkins, D. (1981). Australian and Filipino investigations of the internal structure of Biggs' new Study Process Questionnaire. *British Journal of Educational Psychology*, 51, 241–244.

Henson, M., and Schmeck, R. R. (1993). Learning styles of community college versus university students. *Perceptual and Motor Skills*, 76, 118.

Kember, D., and Gow, L. (1990). Cultural specificity of approaches to study. *British Journal of Educational Psychology*, 60, 356–363.

Kember, D., and Gow, L. (1991). A challenge to the anecdotal stereotype of the Asian student. *Studies in Higher Education,* 16, 117–128.

Marton, F. (1976). What does it take to learn? Some implications of an alternative view of learning. In N. Entwistle (ed.), *Strategies for Research and Development in Higher Education* (pp. 32–43). Amsterdam: Swets & Zeitlinger.

Marton, F. (1981). Phenomenography: describing conceptions of the world around us. *Instructional Science,* 10, 177–200.

Marton, F., Hounsell, D. and Entwistle, N. (eds) (1984). *The Experience of Learning.* Edinburgh: Scottish Academic Press.

Marton, F. and Säljö, R. (1976) On qualitative differences in learning: II. Outcome as a function of the learner's conception of the task. *British Journal of Educational Psychology,* 46, 115–127.

Meyer, J. H. F., Dunne, T. T., and Sass, A. R. (1992). Impressions of disadvantage: I. School versus university study orchestration and consequences for academic support. *Higher Education,* 24, 291–316.

Meyer, J. H. F., and Muller, M. W. (1990a). An unfolding analysis of the association between perceptions of learning context and approaches to studying. *South African Journal of Higher Education,* 4, 46–58.

Meyer, J. H. F., and Muller, M. W. (1990b). Evaluating the quality of student learning: I. An unfolding analysis of the association between perceptions of learning context and approaches to studying at an individual level. *Studies in Higher Education,* 15, 131–154.

Meyer, J. H. F., and Parsons, P. (1989a). An empirical study of English- and Afrikaans-speaking students' approaches to studying. *South African Journal of Higher Education,* 3, 109–114.

Meyer, J. H. F., and Parsons, P. (1989b). Approaches to studying and course perceptions using the Lancaster Inventory: a comparative study. *Studies in Higher Education,* 14, 137–153.

Meyer, J. H. F., Parsons, P., and Dunne, T. T. (1990). Study orchestration and learning outcome: Evidence of association over time among disadvantaged students. *Higher Education,* 20, 245–269.

Miller, C. D., Finley, J., and McKinley, D. L. (1990). Learning approaches and motives: Male and female differences and implications for learning assistance programs. *Journal of College Student Development,* 31, 147–154.

Morgan, A., Gibbs, G., and Taylor, E. (1980). *Students' Approaches to Studying the Social Science and Technology Foundation Courses: Preliminary Studies* (Study Methods Group Report No. 4). Milton Keynes: Open University.

Morgan, A., Taylor, E., and Gibbs, G. (1982). Variations in students' approaches to studying. *British Journal of Educational Technology*, 13, 107–113.

Murphy, R. J. L. (1982). Sex differences in objective test performance. *British Journal of Educational Psychology*, 52, 213–219.

Newstead, S. (1992). A study of two "quick-and-easy" methods of assessing individual differences in student learning. *British Journal of Educational Psychology*, 62, 299–312.

O'Neil, M. J., and Child, D. (1984). Biggs' SPQ: a British study of its internal structure. *British Journal of Educational Psychology*, 54, 228–234.

Pask, G. (1976). Styles and strategies of learning. *British Journal of Educational Psychology*, 46, 128–148.

Perry, W. G., Jr. (1981). Cognitive and ethical growth: the making of meaning. In A. W. Chickering & Associates, *The Modern American College: Responding to the New Realities of Diverse Students and a Changing Society* (pp. 76–116). San Francisco: Jossey-Bass.

Ramsden, P., and Entwistle, N. J. (1981). Effects of academic departments on students' approaches to studying. *British Journal of Educational Psychology*, 51, 368–383.

Richardson, J. T. E. (1990). Reliability and replicability of the Approaches to Studying Questionnaire. *Studies in Higher Education*, 15, 155–168.

Richardson, J. T. E. (1992). A critical evaluation of a short form of the Approaches to Studying Inventory. *Psychology Teaching Review*, 1, 34–45.

Richardson, J. T. E. (1993). Gender differences in responses to the Approaches to Studying Inventory. *Studies in Higher Education*, 18, 3–13.

Richardson, J. T. E. (in press). Mature students in higher education: I. A literature survey on approaches to studying. *Studies in Higher Education*.

Richardson, J. T. E. (in preparation). Mature students in higher education: academic performance and intellectual ability.

Richardson, J. T. E., Eysenck, M. W., and Warren Piper, D. (eds) (1987). *Student Learning: Research in Education and Cognitive Psychology.* Milton Keynes: SRHE & Open University Press.

Richardson, J. T. E., and King, E. (1991). Gender differences in the experience of higher education: Quantitative and qualitative approaches. *Educational Psychology,* 11, 363–382.

Säljö, R. (1984). Learning from reading. In F. Marton, D. Hounsell, and N. Entwistle (eds), *The Experience of Learning* (pp. 71–89). Edinburgh: Scottish Academic Press.

Säljö, R. (1987). The educational construction of learning. In J. T. E. Richardson, M. W. Eysenck, and D. Warren Piper (eds), *Student Learning: Research in Education and Cognitive Psychology* (pp. 101–108. Milton Keynes: SRHE and Open University Press.

Schmeck, R. R. (1988). Individual differences and learning strategies. In C. E. Weinstein, E. T. Goetz, and P. A. Alexander (eds), *Learning and Study Strategies: Issues in Assessment, Instruction, and Evaluation* (pp. 171–191). San Diego: Academic Press.

Schmeck, R. R., and Geisler-Brenstein, E. (1989). Individual differences that affect the way students approach learning. *Learning and Individual Differences,* 1, 85–124.

Schmeck, R. R., Geisler-Brenstein, E., and Cercy, S. P. (1991). Self-concept and learning: The Revised Inventory of Learning Processes. *Educational Psychology,* 11, 343–362.

Schmeck, R. R., and Grove, E. (1979). Academic achievement and individual differences in learning processes. *Applied Psychological Measurement,* 3, 43–49.

Schmeck, R. R., Ribich, F., and Ramanaiah, N. (1977). Development of a self-report inventory for assessing individual differences in learning processes. *Applied Psychological Measurement,* 1, 413–431.

Snyder, M., and Swann, W. B., Jr. (1978). Behavioral confirmation in social interaction: from social perception to social reality. *Journal of Experimental Social Psychology,* 14, 148–162.

Speth, C., and Brown, R. (1988). Study approaches, processes and strategies: are three perspectives better than one? *British Journal of Educational Psychology,* 58, 247–257.

Strauss, A., and Corbin, J. (1990). *Basics of Qualitative Research: Grounded*

Theory Procedures and Techniques. Newbury Park, CA: Sage.

Thomas, K. (1988). Gender and the arts/science divide in higher education. *Studies in Higher Education,* 13, 123–137.

Thomas, K. (1990). *Gender and Subject in Higher Education.* Buckingham: SRHE & Open University Press.

Watkins, D. (1984). Student learning processes: an exploratory study in the Philippines. *Human Learning,* 3, 33–42.

Watkins, D., and Akande, A. (1992). Assessing the approaches to learning of Nigerian students. *Assessment and Evaluation in Higher Education,* 17, 11–20.

Watkins, D., and Hattie, J. (1981). The internal structure and predictive validity of the Inventory of Learning Processes: some Australian and Filipino data. *Educational and Psychological Measurement,* 41, 511–514.

Watkins, D., and Regmi, M. (1990). An investigation of the approach to learning of Nepalese tertiary students. *Higher Education,* 20, 459–469.

Chapter 3 Student learning research and educational development

A distance Programme for Resource-based Training of Academic Staff

Pat Cryer and Lewis Elton

Introduction

The changing learning environment in universities requires academic staff to acquire new knowledge, skills and attitudes, while the finances and staffing for training are becoming increasingly strained. This paper will discuss how a programme in the distance mode, which uses self-development methods, self-instructional resources and action research, can provide a cost-effective means for such training and lead to accredited qualifications. If the programme proves effective, it will be possible to extend it to other categories of staff, e.g., academic staff developers, academic staff with educational management tasks, academic related and support staff.

At a time of financial stringency and steadily increasing class size (Cryer and Elton, 1993) it is particularly important to invest in the improvement of student learning. In order to improve student learning, three things need to come together:

- research on student learning has to produce usable results;
- teachers in higher education have to have a knowledge and understanding of these results;
- teachers in higher education have to use that knowledge and understanding to develop and practise appropriate teaching.

Most of this conference is devoted to the first of these items, of which much indeed is known (Bonwell and Eison, 1991; Entwistle, 1992); this paper is devoted to the second and third. These relate to the needs of teachers to acquire appropriate knowledge, skills and attitudes, all of which are usually met by staff development, interpreted in the widest sense. That this is a crucially important method to improve the student learning environment has been known for a long time (see, e.g., Seldin, 1977); more recently it has been one of the main conclusions of Academic Audit (Academic Audit Unit, 1991). Unfortunately, neither the resources nor the staffing exist at present can provide the necessary staff training through orthodox face-to-face methods, and it is this that has led us to consider the possibility of a distance programme for the resource-based training of academic staff, in which local staff developers (see, e.g., Cryer, 1981) act in support and as facilitators. It is based on research into the identification of training needs (Cryer, 1991) and the experience with earlier work on staff training at a distance (Elton et al. 1988). This earlier work provided substantially more learner autonomy (Elton, 1988) than is normal in distance courses, with their frequently very rigid course materials, in that assessment was based on assignments and a project which allowed much negotiation and freedom to course members, but it was still based on a set of structured course materials and to that extent was content oriented. It did teach us, however, that there were some real advantages in the distance mode over more conventional modes and that many of the normally perceived disadvantages could be overcome.

There were two outstanding advantages. The first was that course members were embedded in their work while taking the course (this was in fact a condition for participation), which enabled them to integrate theory and practice unusually well. The second was that they were inevitably less able to contact their tutors and thus were thrown back much more on their individual resources, so that autonomy became a guiding principle. Of course, this second advantage has a corresponding disadvantage, i.e. some course members could not cope with such autonomy and wanted more contact with tutors – perhaps more than they really needed. Finally, it was necessary to replace the ready-made support of fellow students in face-to-face courses by support from colleagues who may or may not have been on the same course. There are obvious disadvantages in this; what is less easily appreciated is that this different kind of support has compensating advantages.

The present proposal has taken note of all the lessons learnt. It is for a problem oriented approach, which adapts the methods developed originally in the medical curriculum (Barrows and Tamblyn, 1980) to academic staff training and development. Instead of a set of course materials, course members identify problems in a number of problem areas, negotiate their validity and appropriateness with their course tutors and then, with the help of their tutors, proceed towards tackling them, mostly probably along action research lines (Zuber-Skerritt, 1991). The reports by the course members on their problem-solving work constitute the assignments and eventually a synoptic project on which they are assessed at the postgraduate diploma level. Progression to MPhil and PhD will depend on successful performance at diploma level. In all their work, course members will be helped by available resource materials such as, for instance, the "Effective Learning and Teaching in Higher Education" self-instructional materials (Cryer, 1992; Cryer 1993); the main support materials specifically provided will be (a) An Introduction to the Programme, (b) Advice on Assignments and Project and (c) a Portfolio pro forma (see below). Other self-instructional materials for staff development can be created as required (Cryer and Elton, 1992).

It may be conjectured that this method is appropriate for the "knowledge and understanding" part of the distance approach to staff development which we wish to establish, but that it cannot significantly lead to the development of appropriate skills and attitudes. That this is too facile a conclusion was amply demonstrated by the earlier distance course (Elton et al., 1988), where the revelations that new knowledge engendered and the close interaction between course member and tutor, similar to that in research supervision (Elton et al., 1992), in the development of the assignment and the project led also to very significant attitudinal changes. Even skills were developed, since academics can learn much in the way of skills through self- and peer-evaluation, so that classroom observation by experienced tutors became less important.

All this is very relevant to another recent development in staff training, the accreditation by the Staff and Educational Development Association (formerly SCED) (Baume, 1992). This requires course members to carry out certain activities within a training programme, and these can be documented and assessed through a portfolio, similar to the one that the Open University, under the Enterprise in Higher Education Programme, has developed for students and is at present developing for academic staff (Maher, 1993).

A draft programme along the lines indicated above was discussed at a SCED workshop in May 1993. The discussion question was quite deliberately phrased in the most orthodox way, i.e. in terms of the concept of "distance delivery", (see Appendix 1). The result was first a revolt and then a proposal that matched exactly our own ideas, i.e. that of a problem oriented training, in which course members held the initiative and owned their learning throughout.

We next used a questionnaire (Appendix 2) with a group of 46 staff who had attended a conference on "The Management of the Teaching Task in Higher Education" at Salford University. Of the 13 who returned the questionnaire, only one seemed to have any doubts about the value and timeliness of such a programme. The results for the first two questions were:

1. I am interested in taking this programme up to the following levels:

	Yes	No
Diploma	7	3
MEd	5	4
PhD	6	4
SCED accreditation	7	3

2. The total number of colleagues who might also be interested were:

0, 0, many, 15 (wild guess), 2, 5, 3, 0, 0, 2, 3, 2, 415 (approx).
The third and last responses came from staff developers, who may have engaged in some wishful thinking! The open responses to the other questions were both

constructive and encouraging, and as a result we felt sufficiently confident to formulate a draft scheme for the programme (Appendix 3), which the Open University Validation Service has declared it is willing to validate. This scheme is now up for discussion and evaluation at this conference. After that all that is needed is a fairy godmother to provide the necessary pump-priming resources; the programme, once started, should be self-supporting on the basis of course members' fees.

Our thanks are due to Paddy Maher and Liz Beaty for many helpful discussions and good ideas.

References

Academic Audit Unit (1991) *Annual Report of the Director 1990/91*. London: Committee of Vice Chancellors and Principals.

Barrows, H. S. and Tamblyn, R. (1980) *Problem based learning: an approach to medical education*. New York: Office of the Director of Medical Study.

Baume, C. (ed.) (1992) *SCED Teacher Accreditation: Year Book*, Vol. 1 Birmingham: Standing Conference for Educational Development.

Bonwell, C. C. and Eison, J. A. (1991) *Active Learning: Creative Excitement in the Classroom*. ASHE-ERIC Higher Education Report No 1, Washington: George Washington University.

Cryer, P. (1981) Who are the staff developers in UK universities and polytechnics? *Higher Education* 10, 425–436

Cryer, P. (1991) *Checklist for identifying training needs*. Sheffield: Universities' Staff Development Unit

Cryer, P. ed.) (1992) *Effective Learning and Teaching in Higher Education – a Compendium of Resources*. Sheffield: Universities' Staff Development Unit.

Cryer, P. (1993) *Effective Learning and Teaching in Higher Education – a Compendium of Resources: Overview* Sheffield: Universities' Staff Development Unit.

Cryer, P. and Elton, L. (1992) Preparing self-instructional materials. In P. Cryer, (ed.)(1992), Module 8, Block B

Cryer, P. and Elton, L. (1993) Active learning in large classes and with increasing student numbers. In Cryer, P (ed)(1992), Module 4, 2nd edition.
Elton, L. (1988) Conditions for learner autonomy at a distance. *PLET* **25** 215–224.

Elton, L., Oliver, E. and Wray, M. (1988) Academic staff training at a distance: a case study. *PLET* **23**, 29–40.

Elton, L. Wort, M. and Oliver, E. (1992) Research supervision at a distance. In O. Zuber-Skerritt, (ed.), *Starting research: Supervision and Training*, Tertiary Education Institute, University of Queensland

Entwistle, N. (1992) *The Impact of Teaching on Learning Outcomes in Higher Education*. Sheffield: Universities' Staff Development Unit.

Maher, P. (1993) private communication.

Seldin, P. (1977) *Teaching Professors to Teach*. Croton-on-Hudson, NY: Blythe-Pennington.

Zuber-Skerritt, O. (ed.) (1991) *Action Research for Change and development* Aldershot: Avebury.

Appendix 1

Extract from the handout for the SCED Conference workshop on "Academic Staff Training and Development through Distance Learning"

Purpose of the workshop

To explore the effectiveness of different modes of distance delivery for the different domains and target audiences:

Domains	Target audiences
Knowledge and understanding	New staff
Skills and competences	Experienced staff
Attitudes and values	Staff developers

Questions for group discussions:

Each group should **create a list of different modes of distance delivery** that might be appropriate for the three different domains, and then **answer the questions** below for these modes.

1. How far can the objectives of staff development in the three domains be achieved through the different modes at a distance?

2. What kind of face-to-face contact may be needed to supplement the distance modes?

3. What kind of support at a distance should be available?

Appendix 2

Teaching for Active Learning in Higher Education: a Staff Development Programme Largely at a Distance.
[The preamble to the questionnaire was an early version of what became Appendix 3 below.]

1. I am interested in taking this programme up to the following levels:

	Yes	No
Diploma		
MEd		
PhD		
SCED accreditation		

2. I know of . . . of my colleagues who might also be interested.

3. I have the following comments on the nature of the proposed programme:

   (a) The programme, which will have the title "Teaching for Active Learning in Higher Education", will be based on a structured series of projects carried out by course members, which will be rooted largely in their developing practice.

   (b) Participants will work with a distance tutor and with locally appointed mentors.

   (c) Participants will be able to build up their own course, in line with their projects, using the many relevant resource materials available (e.g. the "Effective Learning and Teaching in Higher Education" modules) and will build up their skills and attitudes in conjunction with a local interest group.

   (d) The programme will be modular, allowing for different interests, specialisations, etc. It will minimally lead to a postgraduate diploma and SCED accreditation.

   (e) Assessment will be based on a learning outcomes approach. For the Diploma it will be on the basis of a number of project reports and for the MEd and PhD by dissertation/thesis, all validated by the Open University Validation Service. SCED accreditation will be based on a portfolio.

   (f) I have the following additional comments:

Appendix 3

Teaching for Active Learning in Higher Education
[A proposal for a distance programme for resource based training of academic staff]

1. Title
Teaching for active learning in higher education.

2. Aims
2.1 To provide a theoretical introduction to teaching for active learning in higher education.

2.2 To link theory to practice.

2.3 To develop appropriate skills and attitudes.

3. Target audience and likely uptake
The target audience are practising teachers in higher education. Because of the nature of the programme, it will not be possible for the programme to be taken by anyone who is not concurrently a practising teacher, but the concept of "practising teache" will be flexible and may include people for whom teaching is only a comparatively minor part of their work, e.g. librarians. A questionnaire enquiry has revealed definite interest in the proposal and it was favourably received at a recent SCED annual conference.

Note: It is intended in due course to provide similar distance programmes for

     (a) academic staff developers.
     (b) academic staff with educational management tasks
     (c) academic related and support staff.

4. Standard
The programme will be at the level of a postgraduate diploma and will provide SEDA (formerly SCED) teacher accreditation. It may be possible to accredit prior learning.

Note: The question of possibly meeting NCVQ requirements will be investigated in collaboration with SEDA.

5. Progression
Holders of the Postgraduate Diploma may apply for progression to MPhil and PhD. Direct entry to MPhil and PhD will not be possible.

6. Form of programme
6.1 The Programme will be problem oriented. It will take course members

through a progression of problem areas, in each of which course members will negotiate a problem that is of interest and relevance to them and on which they will present an assignment. The areas to be covered will be decided by the programme board (still to be appointed), but they are likely to include:

- teaching and learning (theory and practice)
- course planning and design
- student assessment
- the development of personal and professional skills
- evaluation of the student learning environment
- the management of learning

6.2 There will be a final major project which will build on the assignments.

6.3 Members will carry out appropriate activities to meet the requirements of SEDA accreditation and record these in a portfolio.

6.4 Learning support will be provided through:
(a) tutorial support at a distance through correspondence, fax, E mail and telephone.
(b) local mentoring by a local staff developer or trained colleague. Short courses for mentors will be provided. Mentors will be nominated by the course member and approved by the programme board. Depending on the wishes of the course member, their strength could be mainly pedagogic or mainly disciplinary.
(c) resource materials. [See next section.]

In addition, course members will be encouraged to develop local interest groups from among their colleagues, to provide on-going support. The form that such local interest groups will take will depend very much on the people involved, but it is not necessary for all the members of such a group to be course members who take part in the programme.

7. Resource materials
7.1 Members will be advised on the appropriateness of materials to meet their specific needs. Many of these are commercially available and it is envisaged that a high proportion of the needs will be met by the series on "Effective Learning and Teaching in Higher Education", published by the Universities' Staff Development Unit.

7.2 The following materials will be specially prepared for the programme:
- introduction to the programme
- advice on assignments and project
- the pro forma portfolio.

8. Assessment

Assessment for the postgraduate diploma will be based on the assignments and the project. There will be no written examination. Assessment for SEDA accreditation will be based on the completed portfolio. The assignments and project, which assess the academic aspects of the programme, will be closely integrated with the portfolio, which assess the aspects of the programme that relate to skills and attitudes.

The Role of the Developer in Linking Research on Learning to Teaching Practice

Liz Beaty, University of Brighton

Introduction

Research which is published in journals is read only by other researchers. Teachers are interested only in practical solutions to problems. These two statements may be contentious but in my experience they are mostly true, Yet there are many ways in which research on learning could improve practice. It is not that researchers are researching the wrong things nor that their findings are not applicable, and it is not that teachers are disinterested or unable to learn from research on learning. Rather it is the lack of a common meeting place in the literature, conferences, etc. This paper discusses the role of educational and staff developers as a conduit between research on learning and teaching practice. The paper asks what is the role of the developer in linking research to teaching and what strategies and approaches work? What types of publication, workshops, staff development events, etc., produce an effective strategy for linking research into practice?

In this paper I outline my own development as an educational and staff developer in some depth. The reason for this approach is that I have gone from being a full-time researcher to being a full-time educational developer and a full-time teacher and am now working half time on staff development and half time as director of a management research programme. My ambition has always been to improve student learning and this chequered career has provided me with much to reflect on.

An Abridged Autobiography of a Development Agent.

Full-time research

From an undergraduate degree in sociology I went to study at IET Surrey University and spent an interesting three years researching student orientations to study towards a PhD. The institute was a small but thriving unit full of research students from around the world, many working on aspects of technology in the curriculum, including early work on computers and learning. The concentration at this time seemed to be moving away from the idea that technology held the answers to effective learning – e.g., the teaching machines towards technology used for diagnosis and support for learning – and as my three years went on increasingly the interest was on the learner and their approach, style, orientation towards and feelings about their learning context. Concepts of individual difference were very much to the fore. The view that approaches to teaching would affect all students in the same way was strongly questioned. What we learnt in those times from the strong research groupings at Surrey, in Lancaster and in Göteborg, Sweden, was how to research student learning from the point of view of the student.

How far our growing understanding affected teaching practice is questionable. The researchers were not teachers, nor were we on the whole concerned with staff development of teachers. Rather, we wrote articles in journals and talked to each other at conferences about learning. There were one or two notable exceptions to this. Professor John Cowan, then at Herriot Watt University, was eagerly transforming the first-year engineering course to encourage deep learning and intrinsic motivations for his students. He was loved by most of his students but sometimes misunderstood by his colleagues. There were also the beginnings of small-scale training courses for new teachers into higher education. Professor Lewis Elton's teaching and learning week course at Surrey University has been running since 1975 and by 1977 had a distance-learning version used by teachers as far away as Japan. Apart from these few areas, however, research into student learning and staff development were on the whole separate activities. Staff development, to most staff in HE, meant going to conferences in the area of your academic speciality.

In 1979 I became a research assistant at the Open University. The work was in two parts. Primarily I was to continue and extend my research on student learning to look at how far the concepts drawn from the recent research could be applied to mature Open University students studying at a distance. Secondly we were to help with the evaluation of a foundation course and the development of the next generation course. The study methods group comprising Alistair Morgan, Graham Gibbs and myself worked intensively with longitudinal interview data from a small group of students which eventually became a set of eight-year long-case studies. The focus on students' development was stronger now as was a wish to influence the course design of the new course from an understanding of how students learn.

This focus had been one that was deeply underpinning the work of the IET at the Open University. There were at that time two groups within the institute. One part was research made up of a number of discrete research groups concentrating on an aspect of educational technology in order to feed ideas into courses. The second was a course development group very much concerned with the development of material in a form which would be useful to students. Technically the ideas from the research groups found their way into courses through the course development groups. True to form however, the research was rarely applied enough or timed to have any direct bearing on course design except over a long time period. The Open University has been very successful in making its course materials accessible, and some of this is due to a concentration on the process of development of materials in a form and style to suit distance learners. So research on learning has had some impact, but to me and to the group the impact felt so indirect and so tenuous. We still spent most of our time talking to other researchers about our research. There was still an enormous gulf between our research work and the development of courses. There was still a credibility gap between our work and its being used by course teams. The impact we had on the new course was visible but marginal.

Full-time educational development
In 1980 Graham nailed his colours firmly to the mast of development by moving to Oxford Polytechnic Educational Development Unit, from where great things have come, including the work with Trevor and Sue Habeshaw on 53 interesting things . . . and OCSD. I followed his lead a number of years later by moving out of research and joining the Educational Development Service at Newcastle Polytechnic. This shift was a rude awakening into the busy world of the developer. Incidentally the person who had the job before me was Paul Ramsden, so I took over a firm foundation in the use of research on learning. I took over Paul's Diploma in Educational Development and produced a masters level course.

I discovered the power of courses in harnessing resources for development. Universities understand that courses need staff and other resources. It is a mode of operation that can fit the system and make staff development a mainstream activity. The second discovery was hard won - through the route of frustrating mistakes. The one-off workshop or seminar series put on by a central organisation for the institution as a whole is a poor use of time and resources. If this 'central place' happens to be the back end of beyond in a lunch-time slot when it rains then it is likely that very few people will come. One vivid picture of this reality was drawn by Graham at a SCED conference a year or two ago - it showed a very full desk with memos and books all over it and an advert for a seminar pinned on the over-full notice board. The implication was that with all these pressures the priority will rarely be to attend a workshop of something neither urgent nor perceived to be central to today's concerns.

There were also some positive discoveries. I learnt that to work at the policy level was a powerful thing to do. An example was working on a group to address the issue of student feedback, and we designed a policy to ensure that all courses each year gathered student feedback in a way which would allow each individual student their say. The policy allowed for great flexibility of approach while ensuring that all course teams did collect and use the information. Without this policy workshops on collecting and using student feedback were poorly attended. After the policy there was a rash of requests for such information and support. The research can be used when there is a perceived need for it and the motivation to take it seriously.

The second important discovery was that, instead of spreading thinly across the whole institution, it was very much more powerful and also fulfilling to work with groups of staff, course teams, interest groups departments on things that they were concerned about and developing at the time. My work become much more responding to needs and much less stabbing in the dark with things I imagined people wanted. It also targeted my work. There were down sides to this. I expect that I was invisible to some parts, indeed whole faculties, of the university, while other groups used a great deal of my time, in accessing both my research library and my knowledge of other educational services they could use. The results were tangible. When a group of librarians asked me to join their team meeting I was able to introduce ideas on student learning that influenced their choice of teaching methods. They knew they wanted to change things, but without the ideas from the research they would not have had a rationale for the changes. Some of the lecturers even read some of the research papers on the subject. People are interested in their own concerns. Researchers have to meet them halfway and provide the ideas and information at the right time and in the right form to be usable.

So the move to educational development felt good to me. At last I felt that my research training had been of some practical benefit to students. Where I felt inadequate was in how to present this efficiently. It seemed to me then that I had to be there, in person, to talk people through my understanding of the research on learning: I was the translator. There were few books that were of a practical nature to give to lecturers who wanted to develop courses. This has changed, and with SCED publications, USDU materials, Enterprise and RSA work on capability and the 53 series, we have an increasing library of useful and informative work which is practically oriented. This is an important way in which research can help to inform practice without every teacher needing a translator in tow.

Full-time teaching

My next move was into a teaching post. This was a side step that was almost accidental in that I didn't intend to make this kind of a career move, but when it happened I became intrigued by what I was learning. The set of courses I worked on were BTEC, HND and HNC for those aspiring to management within the public sector. The courses were all about learning skills, including transferable skills of teamwork and communication. The course team was innovative and a challenging group within which to work and I found myself learning about learning in a different way. What I found out was that many lecturers are interested in teaching and learning and are very concerned about the development of their students. "Development" was a new word for learning and it included much more about the development of the whole person and not just intellectual development. The work took me into a whole new area of research on learning to do with personal development and management development. Was it coincidental that many other researchers from the students learning world were also taking this road? David Boud and John Heron spring to mind. I was very surprised to find that a whole new literature of practical developmental work was available to me from the management development field – a lot of it American and much of it transferable easily into the staff development in higher education. I broadened my vision to encompass the development of the lecturer as a whole person. Stress and time management became part of what I recognised as useful to the lecturer, alongside a new focus on the development of skills for students and skills that went a good deal beyond the original focus of researchers on study skills.

The impact that this time had on my staff development work was profound. For example, I realised that staff development encompassed all staff and not just lecturers, that staff development was distinct from educational development in that it was about a focus on the development of the person. I learnt that research must have a personal dimension to be of use. Creating a knowledge base may not be the best way to disseminate research - rather research needs to link into teaching and curriculum design through the skill of the developing teacher practitioner. Researchers themselves or developers on their behalf must translate their work into highly practical and targeted publications.

Later, in working more centrally in management development, I began to focus on experiential learning through a concentration on working with part-time students – or rather full-time managers who were studying part time. I have spent the last three years using and developing approaches to action learning. This process with its heavy emphasis on learning through reflection on practice has provided a potent force for the development of professional staff in higher education. Action learning draws together the need for action and practical approaches to development of courses and methods of teaching with a method for linking this action to ideas, theories and knowledge gained from research. People develop through learning from an informed approach to actions. Learning follows from experience informed by ideas. The action learning sets are not enough on their own but, with workshops to display and discuss the ideas and with experience gained from practice, the circle between research and practice is joined.

Half and half
In this half-and-half capacity I run two programmes: one is an action-learning part-time MPhil programme for managers and the other also uses action learning and is a programme for our new staff at the University of Brighton. This programme has workshops on different aspects of teaching and learning and includes a good dose of learning theory, albeit in the context of practical implications for teaching. We make good use of basic texts on helping students to learn and on learning how to teach (e.g., Ramsden, 1992; Morgan, 1993; Gibbs, Habeshaw and Habeshaw , 1987-93; and SCED publications). The regular action learning sets help the new staff to solve problems encountered during their everyday teaching and to reflect and learn from practice and from each other. I have learnt to respect the care and effort that new staff give to their new jobs and to understand the nature of the stress that the swift changes in higher education have caused.

I also learnt that I had become used to working as a teacher and that the normal day to day of it all caused me little stress. I found that direct empathy with the new lecturer was harder as I grew more experienced. The physical stress symptoms of shaking or nausea before sessions was a thing of dim memory. That is, until I had to do a presentation for a press launch of a new venture with 90 people in the audience, including Vice Chancellors and members of the press. For the first time in years I suffered the stress of a sleepless night and anxiety attacks the day before the presentation. This showed me in a very direct way what some new staff face as they begin their career. It also demonstrated the need for me as a developer to continue to develop myself; to be open to new challenges in order to understand the situation of those I want to help and to mitigate the danger of complacency and cynicism. I learnt again the importance of the individual orientation – I felt like I did because it mattered a great deal to me that the event was well received. It emphasised the emotional content of individual development. Individual staff development involves commitment to the focus of the development. Development involves risks - it may go well or it may not. Just doing what I have done before is not the best way to develop me or the programme. But the risks taken must be measured: they need to be acceptable risks or I will not develop, only fail. Reflection is crucial for development. It is through analysis of what happened and how I would have liked to do it differently, etc., that helps to foster learning from the experience. I also needed the challenge of a new type of event and the support of my colleagues in planning and designing as well as in dealing with my anxieties. Challenge and support are important props on the road to development.

The current context
Staff development is now a higher priority for institutions because of the need to change and because without help for staff the pace of change would involve a deterioration in standards. The new challenge for researchers on student learning is to gain access to change agents, and to make an impact where there is now opportunity to do so. Working in a faculty as well as at the 'centre' of the institution has shown me that the way to have an impact is through a constant awareness of where change is happening - in curriculum, in course design and in teaching and learning processes. It is also necessary to have the time to help inform those changes. Having a split job gives me little room to manoeuvre or to focus attention where I know it would be most useful.

The latest synthesis for me has been working with SCED – now SEDA – to develop a national accreditation scheme for teachers in higher education. This scheme is a set of objectives and values. Programmes of staff development which can show that they assess against the scheme are given recognised status and individual staff who successfully complete the programmes are awarded accreditation. This scheme is a flexible approach to development. It provides a framework which is clear and yet allows very different modes of delivery and practice in each institution. It feeds off current issues of quality and competence and it provides an opportunity for learning from shared practice nationally. The scheme aims to produce the reflective practitioner. To gain accreditation teachers must demonstrate how their practice is informed by values including :

- an understanding of how students learn
- recognition of individual differences
- concern for students' development
- commitment to scholarship
- team working
- practising equal opportunities
- continued reflection on professional practice.

In setting the agenda the SEDA scheme makes staff development an assertive activity and not merely a responsive one. The scheme demands that staff are given the support and training to do their work as teachers. The aim is that in demanding this reflective practice in early training the habit will be formed which produces in teaching staff a willingness to learn from research on student learning thereafter.

Conclusions

In reflecting on my career I have presented some views about where research, development and practice meet. I want now to make a small number of concluding statements by way of summary.

1. As a full-time researcher there was little opportunity to ensure that research informed practice.

2. Working with course teams while researching is unlikely to produce much change since the research takes longer than the development of the course.

3. Research on learning is a very useful form of training for a staff and educational developer.

4. Development needs to follow the needs of staff/departments.

5. Development is more likely when linked to policy.

6. Development is easier to fund when linked to course provision.

7. Concentration of effort where it is wanted is better than a thin spread evenly across the institution.

8. Staff development is not the same as educational development; it involves a holistic approach at the individual level.

9. Research needs to be translated to inform the practitioner.

10. The emotional content of development must not be ignored.

11. Development of staff involves a blend of challenge and support within a context of an acceptable level of risk.

12. For learning to take place, reflection is crucial. It is the link between research and practice and between experience and practice.

13. It is easier to gain resources and commitment for staff development in a time of institutional/sector change.

14. Staff and educational development must be assertive and not merely responsive.

15. In order to be credible and to empathise with those they support, educational and staff developers must continue to develop themselves.

The role of the developer in linking research on learning into teaching practice is crucial. In order to be able to do this a research training is extremely valuable. This is not to say that only ex-researchers on learning can be effective developers of academic staff. More crucial than doing the research is scholarship – keeping up to date with theory and practice as it evolves throughout the system. This implies an academic type of job – one which has the academic terms and conditions which allow time for this scholarship.

Secondly the statements above point to the role of experience in learning how to design and deliver staff development events. This, for me, points to the importance of training for the staff development role. New staff and educational developers should learn their professional role with help from their more experienced peers. This may point to the need for specific training courses or mentorship. It also shows the background need to specify the nature and responsibilities of the role. The SEDA accreditation scheme for teachers is being followed by a similar scheme for the accreditation of staff and educational developers. This could prove to be the emergence of a new professional group within higher education.

The third link is in the encouragement of staff in the crucial activity of reflecting on their teaching practice. The support given to staff in designing new programmes and through action research in developing them is an important and effective approach to staff development. Academics in the new universities are being encouraged to become researchers. Research does not need to be a competitor for attention with teaching. We need, rather, to reinforce the value of the teaching role through researching the **process** of teaching as well as its content.

Finally, if research on learning is to have an impact on how we teach and how students learn we must above all else ensure that research on learning continues to happen. Whether or not they are active researchers themselves, staff and educational developers have a responsibility to point out where further research is required.

References

Gibbs, G.(1992). *Improving the Quality of Student Learning* Bristol: Technical & Educational Services.

Gibbs, G., Habeshaw , T. and Habeshaw , S. (1987-93) *53 Interesting Ways Series* .

Morgan, A.R.(1993).*Improving your Student's Learning* . London: Kogan Page.

Ramsden, P.(1992).*Learning to Teach in Higher Education.* London: Routledge.

Chapter 4 Limits on improving student learning

Dilemmas? Focus on Some Potentially Contending Forces Underlying the Process of Improving the Quality of Student Learning

Sylvia M.Rhys, The Open University in Wales

Introduction

It is the dynamics of the process of facilitating learning, with particular attention to "deep learning", which is the focus of attention in this paper. It is a process which is subject to the influence of a wide variety of variables of which the selection and strength in a given situation cannot necessarily be known in advance. If a tutor wants to facilitate deep learning effectively then, it seems to me, he or she needs to be aware of the types of variables likely to play a part, to be able to recognise them if and when they manifest themselves, and to have, as far as is possible, a range of skills for coping. Juggling with a number of variables , which may or may not be complementary, may not be easy, hence the title "Dilemmas?".

Included in this discussion are three sources of variables. These are, first, the nature of the ideology associated with deep learning. Secondly, there are the frameworks within which the process of facilitating deep learning takes place, both at the national level and the local institutional level. And the third source is the human factor; any one teaching/learning situation involves interaction between two or more unique individuals, each of whom brings to bear on the processes which take place his or her personal resources and characteristics. These three sources are not discrete, but overlap and interact in a variety of ways. There will be brief consideration of each, leading on to a series of questions which, I suggest, it is important for tutors to reflect upon in relation to themselves and their work.

Ideology and Some Implications for the Process of Facilitating Learning

An important initial question is "what is meant by learning?" It is a process which is not as easy to define as might at first appear; it means different things to different people, and precisely how we learn we do not as yet fully understand. Some people think of learning in terms of process, others concentrate primarily on outcome, and yet others have both aspects in mind. To some people the process of learning is primarily about the accumulation of information. To others it is a far more complex activity which involves the learner as a whole person who acts and feels and perceives as well as thinks, and who brings to any learning situation attitudes, assumptions and values which stem from experiences of past situations and from present circumstances, and which are influenced by motivations and hopes for the future. This more complex conception of the process is about changes in knowledge, skills, attitudes, motivation, and so on, a rewriting of personal scripts, or, in the terminology of Mezirow (1983), "perspective transformation". I believe that if we wish to promote deep learning it is the complex conception of the learning process which is relevant.

In the light of the complexities, it is not surprising that a wide variety of theories have been advanced about the nature of the process of learning. I will mention just a few by way of illustration. There is, for example, the behaviourist tradition. Skinner (1971) saw learning in terms of changes in behaviour, and emphasised the importance of the stimulus/response process as a person interacts with the environment. Kolb (1984) has put forward a multi-dimensional model of the modes of interaction between the person and the environment. He has developed a circular idealised pattern of the learning process in which an individual moves from concrete experience to reflection on that experience, to abstract propositional knowledge; he then goes on to apply this in active experimentation, which in turn creates a new experience, and so the process starts again. Another approach, often labelled the personal growth and developmental approach, emphasises the importance of interpersonal transactions and the significant role played by feelings. One exponent, Freire (1972), regards education as liberating because it enables people to see links between their thoughts and actions, and to develop a critical consciousness of cultural and psychological assumptions; it thus opens up to them the possibility of exerting influence over their environments and changing the way in which things happen. Another exponent, Rogers (1961, 1983), has stressed the importance of the sharing and re-creation of values, and this school of thought lays particular emphasis on learning as the development of individual identity.

The path of learning is not necessarily easy. Most individuals desire constancy, and tend to resist interference from competing information which disturbs their internal "set" or filing system, the chains of association which over time they have built up inside themselves, and which help to give order and stability to their lives. The processes of reflecting and questioning highlight the uncertainties of knowledge, and in turn this can give rise to feelings of internal conflict and personal insecurity. More (1974) suggests that there is first of all a stage of intellectual awareness of new knowledge. This is followed by emotional responses, and then ever-increasing awareness of these responses as they are brought to the level of the intellect. The intellectual and emotional interplay which follows may last just a few minutes, or perhaps days, weeks, months or even years, and operates against the background of the learner's life situation. Sometimes the conflict remains unresolved and ways have to be found of tolerating it. Most learners, however, according to More, bring themselves through to the final stage, the resolution of learning conflict. The learning has then truly become part of themselves, and they are ready for more learning. Kolb and Rogers have shown in their theories of the learning process how much they too recognise that conflict and tension are an integral part of the process.

Another way of seeking to understand conflicts which may accompany learning is by looking at the process in terms of movement between levels. For example, Perry (1970) has outlined a nine-stage scheme. Students initially have absolutist conceptions of knowledge, the tutor is seen as the authority figure, and students concentrate on the accumulation of information. They may move to a more contextual relativistic conception of knowledge and reasoning, and there is deepening appreciation of the relationship between data and opinion. And then students may go on to appreciate the relevance of this way of thinking to their everyday lives. Perry points out that emotional conflicts may be involved, arising, he believes, from a recognition of the uncertainty of explanations of human values and actions. Marton and Säljö (1984) similarly have identified different conceptions of learning. Their first three steps are concerned with accumulating and reproducing information, that is, with a quantitative increase in knowledge associated with memorising and the acquisition of facts, methods, and so on, which can be retained and used as necessary. A learner who moves to the next two steps goes beyond the information given, and is concerned with abstraction and the construction of meaning, and learning becomes an interpretative process aimed at the understanding of concepts, ideas and reality.

Deep learning is usually conceived of in the kind of terms used by Perry and Marton and Säljö to describe their more advanced steps. This type of learning is not reserved just for the library or tutorial, but becomes integral to the process of living. Beaty and Morgan (1992) have investigated how a group of OU students have developed as learners. This is a quotation from a student in the fifth year of study who is moving towards deeper levels of learning and is explaining the process:

> Real learning is something personal and it's also something that is continuous; once it's started, it carries on and on and it might lead to other things. So much learning is learned for a particular purpose, and, when you have achieved whatever it was learned for, then that's it, it can go away, it's disposable, you can get rid of it. But with real learning hopefully the unit of work you are given is only the catalyst; really it is only one hundredth of the learning and the test goes on once you put the book down. And the next time you talk to someone or read something in the newspaper, that's when the test happens because it's been started and you carry it on for yourself because you want to, and you get something lasting from it.

Study skills are often thought of in terms of strategies and tactics associated with reading, note-taking, essay writing, and so on, that is, in terms of handling information. It is necessary for a learner to be conversant with a range of such devices, but a much wider and deeper range of skills is important for students entering the realms of deep learning, a journey which requires an increasing awareness of, and ability to analyse, personal thoughts, feelings, attitudes and skills, and an increase in the inter-related characteristics of confidence, competence and control (Beaty and Morgan, 1992).

In the light to the complexities of the learning process, it is not surprising if the rate of progress along the path of learning for any one person varies over time. Sometimes the journey runs relatively smoothly, but at other times it may be very difficult for many different reasons. To persist requires not only motivation, but also courage to carry on journeying into the unknown, and it requires the development of skills to cope with problems which may arise, plus the ability to utilise constructively knowledge, skills and insights which are gained along the way.

What implications do the complexities of the learning process have for the work of the tutor? How can we who are tutors play as constructive a role as possible in facilitating deep learning? I suggest that we cannot effectively help others to develop skills which we ourselves do not possess, nor encourage them to pass through processes from which we shy away. I think we have to ask ourselves some searching questions, which can be grouped under two main headings.

First, how well do we know ourselves as thinking, feeling and doing beings? How aware are we of the values and assumptions on which we base our personal approach to the process of learning? We need to know our subject in cognitive terms, but how do we rate our ability to make explanations clearly so that the material becomes comprehensible to others. How competent are we when it comes to handling information, and do we have a range of strategies and tactics which we can offer as suggestions to others? Deep learning for us, as for students, goes beyond the accumulation of information. To what extent do we question and reflect? Do we have the motivation and confidence to carry on journeying into the unknown, or do we tend to cling to the familiar? Do we recognise the experience of perspective transformation in ourselves? Have we developed our own range of strategies and tactics for coping with inner conflicts which may arise? The process of learning is open-ended, and constantly offers challenges.

The second group of questions is related to the first group, namely, how student orientated are we? In a learning relationship the tutor usually has the greater political power, and how it is exercised can help, or can hinder, the learning journeys of others. The better we know ourselves the more able we are to be student orientated, and to use our resources constructively. For example, we are more able to recognise when our own interpretations, beliefs, actions, feelings and thoughts are getting in the way of the progress of others, and when we are imposing our personal agenda on a learning situation rather than paying attention to the needs of others. It is important to recognise that we can try to do too much, as well as too little, to help others, and so prevent them from developing for themselves methods appropriate to them personally of extending their knowledge, increasing their confidence and competence, as so on. How willing are we to reflect on the ways in which we seek to facilitate the learning of others, and to understand them better, to learn from experience how to fulfil our roles more effectively.

Frameworks, and Some Implications for the Process of Facilitating Learning

So far in this paper it has been taken for granted that deep learning is a desirable aim. It is generally fashionable in academic circles to believe that the well-educated person is one who is capable of learning at various levels according to circumstances and needs; this is a sign, it is generally considered, of a healthy, mature personality. However, neither tutors nor students live all the time in an enclosed academic world, but in a wider society, the culture and beliefs of which cannot be kept separate from the learning process.

One point to note in this connection is that the concepts of learning which have been outlined are associated primarily with a Western capitalist industrial culture. As there is more movement between cultures, it becomes increasingly necessary to recognise that in different cultures what counts as useful knowledge, and also ways of understanding and doing things, are not identical.

In one respect, however, which is associated with matters political, deep learning may be a source of tension in all cultures. If deep learning is learning for freedom, as Freire (1972) suggests, those who practise thoughtful, reflective, critical appraisal and relate it to society are not necessarily welcomed, because they may challenge underlying principles and ways in which society functions. In the UK, it is politically fashionable to work for "improvement" in our society, but there are not universally agreed criteria defining what constitute improvements. For example, movements advocating greater equality in terms of gender and race, better deals for those on low incomes and those with disabilities, and so on, may be viewed in negative as well as positive terms. It took a long hard struggle, for instance, even to get women's rights in the matter of equal pay on to the political agenda, let alone the struggles since the 1970 Equal Pay Act to put it fully into practice.

In addition, most students need to earn a living, and therefore need the "correct" knowledge and skills and abilities for which other people, potential employers in particular, are currently looking. There is a movement now towards a new qualification in the public education and training system, namely, a system of national vocational qualifications which have to be assessed through demonstrations on the job, and assessed according to certain criteria – in other words, they are competency-based qualifications. While it is possible to point to positive features in this system, it has been suggested also that this type of qualification in its present form threatens to become "the new Fordism of the educational system" (Field, 1991) by attempting to define competencies with increasing precision, thereby narrowing fields of initiative and responsibility available to employees. If the emphasis is on outcome rather than on process, then deep learning would not seem to be of major importance. In a variety of ways the process of facilitating learning is bound up with power relations in society.

Policy at the national level may influence working conditions at the institutional level. For example, there are pressures to increase numbers of students and throughput, and it would appear that HEFC funding is moving towards output measures. Each institution has to find ways and means of obtaining funding, as well as at the same time being expected to serve the needs of society and of the individual student. It may be, therefore, that, for instance, larger classes, higher workloads and greater emphasis on achieving tangible results become the order of the day, and these in turn impact on the process of facilitating learning.

How competent in our work are we as tutors at identifying and coping with a range of external pressures, be they along cultural, social, economic or practical dimensions? For example, to provide learning opportunities to meet the needs of individual students we need to know something about them, but if groups are large and resources limited this raises problems. If a group includes some students who are motivated to pursue the path of deep learning and other who, for justifiable reasons, are not, how flexible can we be? How much attention do we pay to long-term process needs and how much to shorter-term output requirements? Do we reflect on the ways which we devise for coping, and, within those limitations within which we have to work, seek improvements? Do we ask ourselves if it is perhaps possible for us to modify, if only to a limited extent, the power of any of the pressures?

The Human Fact or and Implications for the Process of Facilitating Learning

The process of learning involves handling new information and coping with new thoughts and feelings and outlooks. Students are learning about topics which, to a greater or lesser degree, are new to them, and they are learning how to communicate using terminology and language which may be strange. Thoughts and feelings may aid or hinder in a variety of ways, and methods of coping have to be devised. For example, a student may feel inspired, or irritated, by the style of a writer or tutor, or perhaps excited by, or object strongly to, evidence being presented in a course, or possibly may find that thoughts or feelings associated with, say, a happy, or sad, domestic event keep intruding on studies. And at different stages along the path of learning, the process of perspective transformation may turn out to be relatively easy, or more difficult, to manage.

If students are to have the opportunity to gain as much as possible from interactions with a tutor and with one another, then a relaxed and friendly climate is necessary. If people do not feel comfortable with one another they are less likely to be willing to explore and question knowledge, share feelings, thoughts and experiences, and provide support and assistance for one another.

Some people in a group of students may be competent communicators, and others not. Learners need a range of skills to make the most of the group activities, and not all possess them to the same degree. Participation is hard work, for it involves simultaneous tasks of acquiring information, organising thoughts, making contributions, perhaps reorganising cognitive systems and/or noting the need to reflect on this later, and coping with feelings which are around. Some may feel encouraged and others inhibited when taking part in group work.

Achieving mutual understanding may be a more complex process in groups containing learners from different cultures. Class backgrounds vary; some students, for instance, may be coping with one characterised by a degree of hostility towards education (Westwood, 1984). And gender differences may be of importance. There are different expectations of men and women in society, and, as they move along the path of learning, women may perhaps find themselves struggling against stereotypes of themselves as being less capable of rational thought than men, and expected to confine themselves to a somewhat narrower range of academic subjects (Walkerdine, 1989). It has been suggested that there are entrenched attitudes which are likely to colour relationships in tutorials so that some women feel themselves at a disadvantage when trying to communicate in a group setting (Saraga, 1991).

Theorists such as Rogers, who emphasise personal growth and development as basic to learning, highlight the importance of climate and the nature of the relationship between facilitator and learner. Rogers (1961) suggests three qualities are necessary for tutors to possess if they are seeking to develop a climate in which free interchange can take place, namely, genuineness as a person, positive regard for, and trust in, learners, and empathic understanding of the points of view of learners. To develop a warm and relaxed climate, tutors need to show that they value the students as individuals; that they respect them and recognise that their thoughts, feelings and actions are important to them. But this of itself is a complex task because each learner brings different resources, knowledge, attitudes and practices, as well as different styles of learning and their own experiences and cultural baggage.

It is being assumed that active interactive learning is an essential part of the work of a tutor who subscribes to the approach to learning at the centre of attention in this paper. It demands far more of the tutor as well as the learner than does the relatively impersonal chalk and talk scenario. Questions about how well we as tutors know ourselves and how student orientated we are are again relevant. Our style of communication rests both on what we say and do and also on how we are as persons, and the resources we possess. How much thought and effort do we put into the process of active learning? For example, do we develop a range of strategies and tactics so that if one way of communicating, and encouraging others to communicate, seems not to be satisfactory we can try out another? Are we able to vary structure and pace and levels of communication as seems appropriate? Do we help students not only with understanding the part of the course on which they are presently working but also assist them when necessary to develop study skills to handle information, and also group work skills? How much effort do we make to get to know our students, and how flexible are we when faced with a group who between them possess a wide range of resources, knowledge, attitudes and practices and different learning styles? Are we alert to verbal and non-verbal indicators as to how smooth or rock-strewn students are finding their paths of learning? Are we able to empathise with those in difficulties, and enter with students into satisfactions when they are making progress? To what extent do students trust us? Are we able, when we find our feelings aroused by what learners do or say, or how they are as people, to recognise and then to put our feelings on one side, at least for the time being, and not let them get in the way of helping? Indeed, to what extent do we really apply to ourselves, and use in the process of facilitating learning, the skills necessary for entry into deep learning?

The Tutor as Facilitator

Some brief consideration has been given to three sources of variables. Reflections on ideology raise questions about the extent to which we as tutors are conversant with, and our attitudes towards, the process of learning, and in particular deep learning, and how student orientated we are. Reflections on frameworks as a source of variables draws attention to the context in which activities based on that ideology take place, and how fashions and policies current in society at large, and the aims of individuals and institutions, may push and pull in different directions and complicate the process of translating ideology into paths of learning. Reflections on people as whole persons highlights a further range of variables relevant to the task of facilitating deep learning which are associated with the characteristics of individuals and the dynamics of group processes and the characteristics of the tutor as a person.

What would be the characteristics of the "ideal" tutor? Such a person would possess all the qualities of the ideal learner, and would be a highly motivated, independent, fully functioning person, aware of personal thoughts, feelings and actions, and able to analyse and control and use them for the benefit of personal learning. If the process generated internal conflicts, the tutor would have the skills to cope. Such a tutor would possess all the academic knowledge necessary for a particular course, and be able to communicate it through the written and spoken word in a variety of ways so that the knowledge and language of the expert became comprehensible to all learners. They would be not only adept at handling information but also able to help others to become equally adept.

In contacts with students, this ideal tutor would be not only a fluent communicator but also an active listener and a perceptive and accurate observer of non-verbal communications at an individual and group level, and adept at identifying, and empathising with, meaning perspectives. This tutor would be skilled at generating a warm and relaxed climate and winning the trust of students. This tutor would be ready to offer to learners help at cognitive, practical and affective levels, on an individual and group basis, and with whatever problems and queries learners might raise, be they related to academic, personal or group matters. At the same time the amount and type of help offered would be skilfully adjusted so that it did not appear patronising or overwhelming. Long- and short-term needs would both be kept in view, and attention paid to them according to the needs of group participants. In addition, the ideal tutor would be skilled at helping learners to adjust to the culture and language of the institution of which they were a part, and to cope effectively with external influences which might affect the process of learning. Finally, such a tutor would be constantly on the look-out for ways of deepening understanding of the learning process, and of improving the process of facilitating learning.

It must be clear that such a paragon of all the virtues does not exist. Even if he or she did, that person could only offer help, and could not promise success to others, for each student has responsibility for making personal decisions about how to proceed along the path of learning. And it is difficult to imagine how even a paragon could find the time and energy to be all things at all times to all learners, given the range and variety of cultures, personal backgrounds, skills and resources, degrees of confidence and competence, and motivation likely to be found within even a small group of students. And a tutor cannot banish extraneous factors which hinder the learning process, be they difficulties in a learner's personal circumstances, institutional roles, or decisions at a national level.

This quick sketch, however, has a purpose. It helps to highlight how complex is the process of facilitating learning, and particularly learning at deep levels, and the wide range of skills which are involved, and which different tutors are likely to possess to different degrees. There is one skill, however, which all tutors need if they are encouraging active learning, and that is the ability to cope with uncertainty. This is because an active learning session cannot be planned neatly and tidily in advance in the same way as can a lecture. While outline plans can be made, more detailed decisions are taken in cooperation with participants in the course of a session, and it may seem advisable at times to modify, or even to put on one side, the outline plans themselves.

It is possible to conceive of the role of the tutor in terms of a series of decisions needed to cope with the many influences on the process of facilitating learning. But these decisions are not always easy to make. This is not only because pressures may push in different directions, but it may also be because of the nature of the evidence on which decisions are based – for example, how accurate are a tutor's diagnoses of needs of students. It is partly because of the uncertainty of outcomes in a situation in which neat and tidy cause and effect patterns do not exist; it is difficult, for instance, to assess the extent to which others are incorporating critical thinking into their lives, and judgements in any case are based on short-term evidence, for we are usually in contact with individual students for only a limited amount of time. And decisions are not always easy to make because tutors are less than perfect; no person is the complete exponent of every skill which might be required, and sometimes, however well intentioned, a tutor makes mistakes.

Dilemmas do inevitably arise. We who are tutors have to make compromises. We may seek to express through our work our personal ideology and beliefs, but the universalism of the wider institutional and national systems may help or hinder, and attention must be paid at the same time to the particularism of the individual student. Paradoxically, the more we are aware of variables in play, the more frequent the dilemmas are likely to be. But the better we know ourselves, and the more sensitive we are to people and situations, the more likely we are to be able to offer constructive help, and the less likely we are to hinder others as they move along their paths of learning. Helping is a risky game, for it can be all too easy to confuse and frustrate, even though intentions are worthy.

If we enter into the process of deep learning and its facilitation as fully as we can, then we shall find it hard and demanding work. We might decide it is not worth the pain and frustration and effort. On the other hand, however, we might view it as a very interesting and absorbing on-going challenge which offers many satisfactions as well as difficulties, and we continue to embrace it again and again because it becomes integral to our way of living.

References

Beaty, E. and Morgan, A.(1992). Developing skill in learning. *Open Learning* 7, 3, 3–11.

Edwards, R., Seminsky, S. and Zeldin, D. (eds) (1993). *Adult Learners, Education and Training* London: Routledge.
Field, J. (1991). Competency and the pedagogy of labour *Studies in the Education of Adults*, 23, 1, 41–52.

Freire, P. (1972). *Pedagogy of the Oppressed* Harmondsworth: Penguin.

Gibbs, G. (1992). *Improving the Quality of Student Learning* Bristol: Technical & Educational Services.

Kolb, D. (1984). *Experiential Learning* Hemel Hempstead: Prentice-Hall.

Learning Through Life: *Education and Training Beyond School* (1993). Course EH266 Milton Keynes: Open University, Press.

Marton, F. and Säljö, R. (1984). *Approaches to learning* in F. Marton, D. Hounsell, and N. Entwistle, (eds), *The Experience of Learning*, Edinburgh: Scottish Academic Press.

Mezirow, J. (1983). A critical theory of adult learning and education In M.Tight, (ed.), *Adult Learning and Education* London: Croom Helm.

More, W. S. (1974). *Emotions and Adult Learning* Farnborough: Gower.

Northedge, A. (1990). *The Good Study Guide* Milton Keynes: Open University Press.

Parsons, S. F. (1990). Feminist challenges to curriculum design *Studies in the Education of Adults* 22, 1, 49–58.

Perry, W. G. (1970). *Intellectual and Ethical Development in the College Years* New York: Holt, Rinehart & Winston.

Rhys, S. M. and Lambert, C. (1983). Tutorials styles and tutor assumptions *Teaching at a Distance* 53, 63–69.

Rogers, C. R. (1961). *On Becoming a Person* London: Constable.

Rogers, C. R. (1983). *Freedom to Learn for the 80s* Columbus: Charles E. Merrill.

Saraga, J. (1991). *Women in tutorial situations* Open D-bate, no.9 Milton Keynes: Open University Press.

Skinner, B. F. (1971). *Beyond Freedom and Dignity* Harmondsworth: Penguin.

Thorpe, M. Edwards, R. and Hanson, A. (eds) (1993). *Culture and Processes of Adult Learning* London: Routledge.

Walkerdine, C. (1989). Femininity as performance *Oxford Review of Education* 15, 3, 267–279 [quoted in *Learning Through Life* (op.cit.) Learning Experience Module, Unit 2].

Weil, S. W. (1989). Access: towards education or miseducation? Adults imagine the future In Thorpe et al. (eds), *Culture and Processes of Adult Learning* (op.cit.), 159–177.

Westwood, S. (1984). Learning and working: a study of women on the shop floor *Studies in the Education of Adults*, 16, 3–19 [quoted in *Learning Through Life* (op.cit.), Learning Experience Module, Unit 2].

Woolfe, R. Murgatroyd, S. and Rhys, S. (1987). *Guidance and Counselling in Adult and Continuing Education* Milton Keynes: Open University Press.

Constraints on Student-Centred Learning Practices

Isis Brook, Jane Hunt, and Peter Hughes, Lancaster University

Introduction

In this paper we reflect on the various constraints that affect the School of Independent Studies' Part 1 course. This highly innovative course, which aims at maximising student-centredness in its practice, is prey to many of the problems which arise with any movement from passive learning to student empowerment. Our primary task is set out in our student's and tutor's handbook, which states:

> Based in a supportive small group environment, Independent Studies Part I empowers students to take responsibility for their own learning, and explore and develop their academic and personal potential, through flexible learning practices.

> The course aims to achieve this by offering the students the opportunity to:
> * benefit from participating in small learning groups;
> * gain academic and personal confidence, by developing existing and new skills;
> * pursue individual interests and utilise a variety of creative approaches;
> * learn through active educational experiences;
> * engage in collaborative study.

The course operates through weekly two-hour meetings of usually eight students and one tutor. Over the course of 25 weeks the students will learn to work as a group and have fulfilled their assessment obligations (currently six pieces of work). They will participate in study skills workshops and exploration of a topic area, loosely defined prior to the course and related to the tutor's expertise, but subject to revision and negotiation within the group. Assessed work can be in a variety of formats and has included sculpture, music, poetry and drama, as well as more conventional essays and reports. Students are encouraged to participate in a group project. Assessment can be undertaken by the tutors, the group or an individual student.

It can be seen from this outline that we offer a flexible programme providing substantial student choice and power. However, this freedom brings it into conflict with more traditional methods of teaching and learning. The conflict largely forms the constraints under which we operate, although there are also inherent conflicts within the course which also operate as constraints. We have divided our analysis of these constraints into two categories: institutional constraints and peer pressure. Before embarking on consideration of these, we offer the following comments on our research methods.

Research Methods

Our approach to research has developed alongside the course and shares its aims and ethos; it is essentially practical and experiential. The course as a whole undergoes a process of constant reflection. At their weekly sessions the students are encouraged to reflect on their progress both as individuals and as members of the group. The tutors also meet weekly: this is a peer support and learning group. The emphasis on group processes and self-development is reflected in the way in which this group works. Its non-competitive spirit allows tutors to discuss difficulties freely, share solutions and develop their expertise as a group. This non-formalised method – the "how was it for you" approach – is valued by the tutors and students, but it does not yield tidy quantifiable results. Our other research activity of a slightly more structured nature is to conduct half yearly and yearly assessments of the course from student feedback. The half yearly feedback which the students discuss in their learning groups often facilitates positive changes in the group as well as giving us valuable information. At the end of the year all the students are encouraged to give feedback, for which we have a very open questionnaire. This is used by the tutors prior to their yearly training week to discuss and implement any changes that might be necessary to respond to the expressed needs of the students.

Although that is the model, our formal evaluation procedures could certainly be improved. One of the constraining factors here is the students' dislike of evaluation. We put a lot of energy into persuading the students of the usefulness of self-evaluation as we see this as fundamental to deep learning. Evaluation of themselves as a group they begin to see as fruitful towards the end of the course, but evaluating the course itself is less attractive especially when there is revision for other courses to be done.

Our course ethos dictates qualitative methods and we would like to develop further the very germinal practices mentioned or find an approach which takes into account the innovative nature of our practices. Our main constraint in the area of research is funding: a comprehensive and penetrating yearly review with all the tutors taking part would be our ideal, but financial considerations prevent this.

Institutional Constraints

The first set of institutional constraints can be considered as functional. The most obvious of these, and one which underlies all other considerations, is again financial. This operates mainly as a limitation on the time we can spend with students. The ground we would ideally like to cover takes more than 50 over 25 weeks to encompass. This has implications for prioritising content of sessions (e.g., should time be devoted to group building and resolving group problems, or should student work be addressed?) The university system is coming under increasing pressure: the sector as a whole is underfunded yet at the same time is expected to cope with increased student numbers. Our system of teaching is relatively labour intensive, yet we must operate under strict financial restrictions. This is an integral constraint in that to achieve the potential depths of learning and personal development ideally requires more contact time than we can afford or the students can commit. In addition, the limitation on time can affect the way students perceive the course; one student suggested that more contact hours may make the students take the course more seriously and attend more regularly.

Independent Studies (IS) Part 1 is only one of three courses that students undertake in their first year. This has various implications. Firstly, timetable constraints dictate that students cannot necessarily sign up for the group topic of their choice, which can pose problems for the students and for the group in which they find themselves. Secondly, IS Part 1 will be the intended major for only around 20% of participants, meaning that motivation among students may be at widely varying levels. Thirdly, as other courses have strict deadlines and formally structured workloads, even well-motivated students may find themselves postponing their IS work in favour of that which they are under more (external) pressure to submit. IS can find itself relegated to the bottom of the student's list. Students have thus failed to take responsibility for their own learning in a highly pressured situation.

Another functional constraint is that of space. With small group teaching and learning the space used by the group is tremendously important. The group must be able to feel comfortable and relaxed: this is not easy in a standard university teaching room with bare floors and walls. Particular requirements of our course include a space suitable for doing warm-ups – a carpet helps – and wall space to display student work. Usually we are subject to the vagaries of the university timetabling system. For the first year of the course we were allocated a standard, bare room. Whilst we did put students' work on the walls we were asked to remove it as other people using that particular room felt that we were invading each other's space. We did eventually get our own room (with a carpet!) and this made a great difference to the groups. However, this room was obtained only by "bending" the university rules – the point being that this type of teaching is not catered for within the university's system of academic practice, and can often be facilitated only through a "creative" approach.

The university requirements for marks dictates the formal aspects for our assessment procedures. Each department must award one overall mark for each student at the end of the year, and communicate that mark to the university administration. This mark must fit into the overall grading system and be seen to be comparable with marks on other courses. How we arrive at a mark is up to us, but arrive at a mark we must. It became apparent to us that this requirement for marks conflicted with our aims of empowering students and enabling them to determine their own values, but here we are bound by university regulation.

However, it also became apparent, when we raised this issue with students, that they wanted marks. This leads us to consideration of the second set of institutional constraints which we here label structural. We are operating within a traditional education system, and, more importantly, most of the students who sign up for the course have emerged from such a system, and continue to be exposed to such a system through their other university courses. Students are used to being told what to do and what to learn. They are taught (largely) to accept the knowledge that their teacher imparts to them. This "passive" system of acquiring knowledge is the antitheses to the Independent Studies approach. The difficulty we face is getting students to accept, and get used to, a new way of learning. This means that we have to devote a lot of time and energy, especially at the beginning of the course, to preparing students for a new style of learning. This both puts pressure on the limited time available, and can cause resentment among students who are expecting to engage in, and be "taught" about, a subject area straight away. As one student said:

> The course in a way hasn't got enough push behind it for me. I
> know it's all supposed to be independent but it's difficult for some of
> us who have had a "normal education" to adjust to this.

The problem, as we understand it, is essentially one of power. Our efforts are directed towards empowering students, resisting the power which is structurally located with the tutor and the institution by enabling students to take on responsibility and choice themselves, within a relatively free and safe context. However, this can be threatening, sometimes for the student and often for the institution. The university expectations of academic education do not encompass this remit. In our circumstance, this is best exemplified by the Senate perspective of our course. The initial requirement was for us to teach science-policy related studies in which the tutors have expertise. We interpreted this broadly to allow the formulation of topic areas such as "alternative medicine", "environment and society", "religion and science", and "green thinking and green action".Although the science policy requirement was softened at the first annual review of the course, it was replaced by the Senate viewing our course as "a living experiment". This is both a positive description with which we can concur, but also, importantly, a relegation of our work to the realms of the preliminary and probationary.

To conclude this section, we can see from the the above that institutional constraints range from the functional to the structural, reflecting wider social commitments and embedded positions which reproduce established teaching practices.

Peer Pressure as a Constraint on Student-Centred Learning Practices

Peer pressure can be classified as operating in two main categories, pressure on tutors (including the wider pressure on IS as a whole) and pressure on students.

Taking students first, it is apparent from student evaluation of the course and formal and informal discussion with the students that the main pressure they face from their peers, both those who are not taking IS and sometimes those on the course, is that IS is seen as a soft option. Students, it appears, "read" a course (at least on one level) in terms of its formal requirements, i.e., contact time, coursework and examination requirements. Because there is no formal syllabus in terms of the information content and the assessment practices are wide-ranging including self-assessment, it can be interpreted as meaning that it is not a "proper" course, and that, in the words of one student, it is "below the salt". By the time of their final evaluation students generally recognise and appreciate the freedom of the course and that they have acquired transferable skills – that thy have "learned how to learn", and that this requires self-motivation and self-discipline – outsiders continue to think that IS Part 1 is an easy option. One student summed this up:

> Rumours of [a] soft option spread by other departments and students and cries of "but where does it lead" [are] totally unfounded, but it is a prevalent attitude – even more than Educational Studies.

The consequences of this appear to be twofold. Firstly, well-motivated students on the course have their achievements undervalued by their peers. This can reinforce their own uncertainties and insecurities (although it does not appear to be a major problem as most students express very positive responses at the conclusion of the course). The second consequence is more problematic. IS attracts a certain proportion of students who take it because they believe that it is an easy option (the 'easy option' label also puts off some good students). While any course is likely to have some students who are poorly motivated and will do the bare minimum required to pass, on IS Part 1, with its emphasis on working in small learning groups, this represents particular problems. A poorly motivated student can fail to participate in group activities, can undermine other students' enthusiasm by making critical comments and can fail to attend group sessions. When the group is undertaking work on the group project such absences are a problem. Students have expressed disappointment in attendance at particular sessions, notably those when presentations are being made. The problem of attendance is being addressed by offering marks specifically for attendance and contribution to the group to emphasise the importance of this part of the course. Marks, it seems, are a language all students understand. Moreover, they see what is valued as that which attracts marks. Although this conflicts with the tutors' perspective, it does appear to be a workable compromise. The option of making attendance compulsory conflicted with one of the aims of the course, which is to develop students' responsibility for their own learning practices. This raises a more fundamental issue: that of how the aims of the course constrain its practice. Because freedom, flexibility and student responsibility are touchstones of the course, our commitment to these principles limits the options available to deal with problems such as attendance or poor motivation.

In addition, the poorly motivated student can create conflict and bad feeling. One student suggested that:

> with no hard and fast rules, students who feel they can manipulate the system fail and become aggrieved.

In effect, this means that a student who has interpreted IS as meaning that they can submit any piece of work (including those which have been prepared for other courses), fail to participate in the groups and still pass the course, can get quite aggressive when their "work" is deemed to be unacceptable. This does not help a positive group dynamic, especially when reinterpreted and related by the student in question as a form of unfairness or dishonesty. However, well-motivated students tend to make the same assessment of their peers as the tutor and can themselves be very critical of students who are thought to be "not pulling their weight", thus producing divisions in the group. Nonetheless, the problems are more of a practical nature than any serious undermining of the principles of the course. The ideal solution is of course to assist a student to become motivated by helping them to find a topic in which they have a genuine interest, and to acknowledge what they can gain from the opportunities the course offers them. Several students have reported joining the course thinking that it was a soft option and being surprised by their positive experiences and development.

The other form of peer pressure is that of other academic staff, largely related to tutors, but with some effects on students. Taking students first, some (by no means all, or even a majority) confront the attitude among staff that IS is a nebulous, undirected and somewhat worthless undertaking. This means that students can be actively discouraged from taking the course, or have work undervalued. The self-confidence and self-value which we attempt to build up in our students thus faces a lack of reinforcement. However, our students in general express their loyalty to the IS approach, and their response is to be critical to staff who express such views. It does, however, restrict their access to other members of staff who could help them with their work. This is not an integral part of Part 1(as it is in Part 2), and is thus not a major problem, but certainly does not adhere to any model of learning based on open sharing of intellectual pursuits across the university. Students effectively learn some of the limitations of university education and to some extent, confronting criticism of what they are doing from outside IS teaches them both something about the ways the university operates (a valuable experience for any student) and how to deal with criticism (another valuable skill).

It is for tutors on the course that the insecurity and reduction of confidence engendered by external criticism (or even derision) is most problematic. Working in a radical, experimental form, there are inevitably uncertainties among tutors about what we are doing, how we do it and why. In addition, as the majority of tutors are postgraduate or junior members of staff, this compounds the uncertainties to some extent. Although support from our peers in the rest of the university is forthcoming on many occasions, often in very positive ways, it is the criticism which tends to be remembered, and felt. For example, during a tutor training exercise involving the way we related to other groups in the university, it was apparent that we saw ourselves as isolated, marginalised, misunderstood and undervalued. The most obvious consequence of this is that, when problems on the course are identified, traditional remedies are raised as possible responses (such as setting hard deadlines with penalties), but the experience of working through the criticism of such remedies and the development of alternatives is itself a solution.

The problem of insecurity is addressed by affirmation practices (this also applies to student groups as an integral part of the course). The weekly tutor group meetings provide support, problem solving and a sharing of experience. More experienced tutors often recognise particular problems and the insecurities of new tutors, and have suggestions for resolution. The act of owning and sharing insecurities and criticisms or negative experiences and having these acknowledged in itself offers support. Constant attention to the ethos of the course, as well as the sharing of positive experiences, helps to focus affirmation.

In addition, the tutor training week operates as an affirming practice; in the final rounds of the course tutors often express their inspiration and excitement at the prospect of another year's teaching, having been given new skills and ideas to work with and realising the range of possibilities open to them. Enthusiasm and commitment, it seems, can be as infectious as insecurity.

The third form of affirmation comes from the students: students' comments are largely positive and on some occasions euphoric, and the experience of seeing a student develop confidence, skills and empowerment is very positive. The basic test of our practice is the student response, and here we have, on the whole, a positive experience.

Although affirmation can be a useful supportive tool it can sometimes prevent groups from listening to their critics or maintaining their own critical faculties. This is important because of the danger – inherent in strongly focussed innovative groups – of becoming exclusive and defensive. In such situations affirmation merely perpetuates a false group consciousness of self-congratulatory ambience which deflects criticism with its claims of radicalness rather than demonstrations of its effectiveness.

To conclude, the main form of constraint from peer pressure is in the form of its devaluation of the course through its being seen by some students and staff as lacking validity as a teaching and learning practice. On occasion, it has operated to restrict the external expertise available, although to date this has been overcome. Devaluation can affect motivation and commitment on the part of students and tutors but can be addressed by explicitly valuing those parts of the course which engender criticism, and by the careful use of affirmation practices.

Conclusion

Independent Studies is bound by a variety of constraints. Some of the more practical ones we can address by creative interpretation of the rules and reliance on allies, but the more pervasive constraints of the structural conditions which frame both institutional and student predispositions can be addressed only by the tutors' long-term commitment to the course ethos.

Chapter 5   Understanding adult learning

Adult Change and Development:
The Interactions of Learning with People's Lives

Alistair Morgan and Lesley Holly, Institute of Educational Technology Open University,

Background

This paper describes preliminary findings of research currently in progress which sets out to explore the outcomes of learning and how students change and develop when the experience of learning is viewed from the learner's perspective. The outcomes of learning can be conceptualised under three closely related levels of change, as follows: (i) changes in conceptual understandings, (ii) changes in study patterns and skill in learning, and (iii) adult change and development -- change in a social context. The present research focusses on the broader issues of adult change and development and the interactions of learning with people's lives. The work has adopted an interview-based longitudinal study of student learning, and is currently in progress with Open University (OU) students.

Introduction

The aim of this research is to contribute to developing a holistic understanding of student learning in a social context. The work builds on other studies of student learning in the OU (see, for example, Gibbs, Morgan and Taylor, 1984; Beaty and Morgan, 1992) and follows in the tradition of qualitative-illuminative research in student of learning, as elaborated by Parlett and Hamilton (1977), and the approach of illuminative evaluation. There is a range of researchers and theorists stressing how the human and cultural dimensions are crucial if we are to gain a complete understanding of learning. For example, Roger Säljö (1991) makes the point clearly in the way the academic division of labour between the disciplines has resulted in a reification of our understandings of learning, as follows:

"One path to further the understanding of human learning is to recognise and take seriously the assumption that human beings live in a world that is cultural in nature and that is constituted through our shared cultural practices. Culture is thus not an entity that can be introduced as a separate variable and, as it were, be added on to an acultural conception of human activities...The division of academic labour which construes culture as contents (and the responsibility of the anthropologist) and cognition as generalities (and the territory of the psychologist) is untenable if we are going to be able to understand human growth and change."(Säljö, 1991, p. 180)

In a similar way Bruner (1990), in 'Acts of Meaning', is critical of the boundaries which define much of psychology and sets out a cultural psychology which emphasises the nature and cultural shaping of meaning-making and the central place which this plays in human action. He reminds us of the power of humans to reflect on experience in a social and cultural context; although they are constrained by a structure and history which is not of their own making, they are reciprocally human agents within this structure. Entwistle (1993) stresses the need for 'research studies which explore learning holistically in context' if research is going to have relevance to inform practice.

In terms of improving student learning, and the relationship between research and practice, the aim is to generate rich descriptions of the experience of learning, which provide a 'recognisable reality' as a basis for critical reflection on practice as the starting point for change in practice.

The present research sets out to look at the wider issues of human change with OU students. It is generally acknowledged that adult students studying with the OU (and mature students participating in conventional universities) are seeking some form of change in their lives. Of course there is a diversity in the nature of these changes --- some students are seeking to increase their chance of promotion, to gain employment, or to change their jobs; some are seeking to broaden their minds, some who feel they have been unfairly judged by the educational system in the past want to prove to themselves they are capable of academic study; some are taking up something new after redundancy or some other personal crisis. This diversity in 'how students come to be engaged in study' has been termed 'orientation to education' (Taylor, 1983) --- a sort of holistic motivation which acknowledges learners' conscious control over their study -- a personal context of study. This framework has already been elaborated with OU students and related through case-studies to the more detailed processes of how students tackled particular learning activities (Gibbs, Morgan and Taylor, 1984).

For many students there are other changes which come about from the interactions of studying with their lives as adults. Some of these changes may be unanticipated, such as the realisation of the limitations of a current job, the shortcomings of a peer group of friends or the constraints of a relationship. Being an OU student is thus inextricably connected with 'human change'. Similarly, as the student population of conventional universities is changing with efforts to widen access and to increase the participation of mature students, as well as part-time students, we need to take a fuller account of the interactions of studying and learning with people's lives. With this premise that change is fundamental for student learning, it is important that research and evaluation studies of student learning are designed to explore the nature of these changes. Although it is generally recognised that OU study involves far more than the understanding of bodies of knowledge and the development of particular skills, relatively little research and evaluation has attempted to explore issues of human change. Even fewer studies have adopted a longitudinal approach to making sense of the learner's experience.

Method

Twenty-eight students who were starting a foundation course (the Social Science or Technology Foundation Course) and were in their first year of study with OU in 1990 were asked in detailed individual open-ended interviews a series of questions about how they came to be studying, what they hoped to gain from study, how it interacted with their lives and how they tackled their studies and coped with the demands of the course. (The sample of students was drawn from one OU Region, and students were chosen who would not have gained entry to a conventional university based on their formal educational backgrounds.) Students are also being interviewed again during 1993–94 about how they are experiencing study with the OU. The research sets out to generate a series of longitudinal case studies. Interviews were tape-recorded and key sections from them transcribed.

Theoretical Background

As soon as we look at the realities of adults learning in context a wide range of theoretical perspectives can be drawn upon to contribute to the analysis of the data.

Historically, the current research develops from a longitudinal study of student learning in the OU (Beaty and Morgan, 1992). This study identified the key issues of confidence, competence and control as the crucial dimensions for how students developed as learners. Although this particular piece of work was influenced by the longitudinal studies of Perry (1970), other aspects of learning and change were identified. A further analysis of some of the data identified a sixth conception of learning, 'changing as a person' (Marton, Dall'Alba and Beaty, 1993), which extends the framework of five conceptions of learning described by Säljö (1982).

This work on 'changing as a person' can be seen as the point of departure for the present research. The aim is to extend this earlier work by looking at the contextual nature of 'changing as a person' and what this means for how students tackle their work and the interactions with their lives as adults. The research can relate the concept of 'orientation to education', a sort of 'holistic motivation' (Taylor, 1983), to the more detailed processes of approach to study, and with broader issues of the interactions of studying with adults' lives.The work of Mezirow (1981) on adult learning and perspective transformation also contributes to the theoretical background. Finally, the work on social theory and the relationship of structure and agency (Giddens, 1984) provides theoretical insights for understanding students' experiences of learning in the broader social and economic context.

Emerging Themes and Issues

A preliminary analysis of the first phase of interviews has identified key themes of confidence and self-esteem, an awareness of self in society, a move towards 'empowerment', and change in relation to social and domestic context. Although these changes are described separately, they are closely inter-related. Many of these changes appear to be particularly important for the experience of women students.

Confidence and Self-Esteem

From an analysis of the interviews, gains in confidence and self-esteem stand out as a substantial dimension of experience of being a student. The following case will serve to illustrate this issue.

Pat had left school at 18 with two pass-grade A-levels, then worked in various clerical jobs. She had married and had a family, although as she explained 'always had at the back of her mind to get a degree sometime', and now, ten years later, she was studying the Technology Foundation Course. She described how she came to be engaged in OU study as improving her chances of getting work sometime in the future, building on her interest in using computers, which again she saw as building on her best school subject, mathematics. In terms of orientations to education, there are some aspects of both vocational intrinsic and extrinsic orientations, and a suggestion of an academic interest 'building on her best subject at school'.

The broader gains of confidence stand out as significant for this student beyond the subject matter understanding which is formally covered through the continuous assessment and the exam. As she explained,

> "I've done quite well really on this course – it has boosted my confidence. Most of the things you do as housewife, and doing a bit of part-time work at home, you don't get any feedback --- and people don't really notice you.

Summer school was good in the respect that having done something on my own, which I haven't done before. I haven't been anywhere on my own before for a week. I was very homesick for my husband for the first few days, but once I got over that, I really enjoyed it. I had the chance to be me and not mother or wife. And managing to hold your own for a week and get on quite well does boast your confidence a bit -- and having conversations about other things than children".

This type of comment is similar to findings in other studies with OU students on their perceptions of gains from studying (Taylor, Morgan and Gibbs, 1982) and about how students see themselves differently. For example, their changing views about the media and developing a more critical appraisal about how material is presented in the tabloid newspapers.

Change of Awareness

Another dimension of the interaction of study with people's lives is how a course structured around contemporary issues in technology can relate to an individual student's life and work experience and thus contribute to change. One of the technology students, John, made reference in the interview to the 'issue focussed' curriculum and how it initiated further reflections for him.

"I found the issues approach in the course very relevant to life --- it did make me consider all aspects of life really. In the block on 'health', it made me consider how you relate to doctors and nurses, but also other ways of tackling problems. I look at things completely differently now".
John had worked for News International at Wapping and the events in 1986 began his politicisation. He described how he had changed as follows:

"Until '86 I virtually believed what was in the papers and on TV, until I saw the mismatch at Wapping and what was reported. I can relate that now to every other news item and the half-truths. I think OU study has reinforced and developed this. I have become more political --- an awareness of how individuals and groups are used and I suppose manipulated....everybody should have the opportunity to see the issues from a more critical 'OU angle".

John had left school at the first opportunity with CSEs in the 1970s. At his school there was no expectation that people would continue to study and, as he explained, 'he just wanted to get out'. So he ended up in the printing industry as an apprentice. He did some FE study and gained City and Guild in printing, but did not pursue his education any further.

"I found technical college difficult and could not see the point in studying. Now I can see it as beneficial, whereas previously I could not...I can see it now as my big regret....The schools were not very good in the area, and I didn't see the importance of further education".

In fact it was a period of unemployment which had convinced him of the need to have further qualifications and this had led him enrol with the OU.

The broader gains and interactions from study are often more significant than the material actually studied to meet the formal requirement of the course. It is also interesting how this student made specific reference to the "issues focussed" curriculum design as important for him to engage in and consolidate this change of awareness. These changes can be understood as 'empowerment' in the sense of a 'perspective transformation' as described by Mezirow (1981), and the ideas of empowerment by Freire of how adults come to see the structural inequalities in society and how individuals (and groups) as human agents can work to challenge such domination in society.

Studying and the Social Context

One of major themes which comes out from the interviews is how OU study interacts with people's social and domestic lives. Many students do not perceive themselves as 'students'; rather they are adults with busy lives who are fitting in part-time study as just one relatively small part of that life.

The impact and response from partners, wives and husbands, and the support, or lack it, which is offered is crucial for many students. As teachers and course designers, we sometimes ignore the realities of students' wider social contexts and assume that they have ideal settings in which to pursue their studies. This is far from reality for many students, as they experience it. For some students, to be engaged in studying was almost like a clandestine relationship; their studying had to be concealed from their partners and almost carried out in secret (Holly and Morgan, 1993).

For some women students, as they described their experiences of study and their relationships with husbands, these experiences can be seen as influenced by historical factors which shape the social structures of how they are subordinated. Three women stand out clearly within this perspective. Their studying can be described as 'education without consent'.

These students were from working-class backgrounds, with little expectation or encouragement to go into higher education. Although they studied A-levels none of them gained sufficient grades for university entrance. There was also peer-group pressure on them to leave school (and education) when their friends were out working with an income, and also not to be seen wearing school uniform.

In terms of orientation to education, these students can be seen as having mainly 'personal intrinsic orientations' – a general desire to return to study to broaden and enhance their lives. One student saw the changes in her own son, who was at university, and she wanted to do the same thing. Another started an A-level evening class, abandoned that, then applied to the OU.

The way these students described their study patterns provided powerful insights into their social contexts. They worked on their OU course during the daytime when their husbands were out at work or only in the evenings if they were out then.

"If he is here, we sit and watch TV or whatever together. I'd rather not leave him on his own and go and study but if he is out, then I'll work in the evenings. He said he would be supportive, but he hasn't taken over anything on the domestic side. And I don't feel inclined to ask him if I can fit it all in".

It seems that some women students experience a 'double day', as they return to study with the OU combined with their domestic roles. Besides all the traditional expectations of gender roles, study has to be fitted in around these domestic labours. With the lack of support from husbands, these students chose to study in the daytime, or in various ways which concealed their study from their partners. This is vividly portrayed by the student who concealed her books when she was notionally watching television.

"Sometimes I slide the book inside a magazine. He thinks I'm reading 'Cosmopolitan'! He doesn't seem to mind that".

It would appear that, for some women students, to be engaged in OU study is perceived as a threat by their husbands. Studying is seen as changing the identity of the partner from being subservient and domesticated. There is almost a dilemma between a relationship with the husband and intellectual development available through study. Some women students have to contend with study under constraints of this nature.

Conclusions

This preliminary analysis has identified some of the realities of the experiences of studying in the OU. The aim is to generate rich descriptions of people's lives and how these interact with study and to theorise the various forms of change. So how can this sort of research contribute to improving practice and improving learning? In looking at the relationship between research and practice, it is important to recognise the limits to what Schon (1983) calls a 'technical' rationality for understanding how professionals operate in practice. In contrast, he identifies 'reflection in action' as the basis for understanding professional practice. Research which serves to describe the students' realities of studying can provide the basis for us to theorise our practice and subsequently change it (Morgan, 1993). Case-study research of the student experience cannot claim statistical generalisability, but this is not the aim of research within the qualitative-illuminative paradigm. It does provide a 'recognisable reality' of students learning as a foundation for theorising practice. In terms of improving student learning -- i.e. to foster a 'deep approach' to learning (Marton and Säljö, 1976) we need models of the learner which mirror their realities and experiences of studying.

Lesley Holly was a Research Consultant on this project. She is now Senior Lecturer in Sociology at Nene College in Northampton.

References

Beaty, E. and Morgan, A. R. (1992). Developing skill in learning *Open Learning*, 7, 3, 3–11.

Bruner, J. (1990). *Acts of Meaning* Cambridge, MA: Harvard University Press.

Gibbs, G. Morgan, A. and Taylor, E. (1984). The world of the learner. In F.Marton, D. Hounsell, and N. Entwistle, (eds), *The Experience of Learning* Edinburgh: Scottish Academic Press.

Giddens, A. (1984). *The Constitution of Society* Cambridge: Polity Press.

Entwistle, N. (1993). *Research on learning and instruction: contrasting methods and knowledge structures.* Presidential address, European Association for Research in Learning and Instruction Conference, Aix-en-Provence.

Holly, L. and Morgan, A. (1993). Education without consent *Student Research Centre Report*, No. 73, Institute of Educational Technology Milton Keynes: Open University.

Marton, F. Dall'Alba, G. and Beaty, E. (1993). Conceptions of learning, *International Journal of Educational Research* (in press).

Marton, F. and Säljö, R. (1976). On qualitative differences in learning: outcome and process *British Journal of Educational Psychology*, 46, 4–11.

Mezirow, J. (1981). A critical theory of adult learning and education. *Adult Education*, 32, 1, 3–27.

Morgan A. (1993). *Improving your Students' learning: Reflections on the Experience of Study* London: Kogan Page.

Parlett, M. and Hamilton, D. (1977). Evaluation as Illumination. In D. Hamilton, D. Jenkins, C. King, B.MacDonald, and M. Parlett, (eds), *Beyond the Numbers Game* London: Macmillan.

Säljö, R. (1982). Learning and understanding *Goteborg Studies in Educational Sciences*, 41 Gothenburg: Acta Universitatis Gothoburgensis.

Säljö, R. (1991). Culture and learning *Learning and Instruction*, 1, 3, 180.

Schön, D. (1983). *The Reflective Practitioner: How Professionals Think in Action.* London: Temple Smith.

Taylor, E. (1983). Orientations to Study. PhD Thesis, Guildford: University of Surrey [Taylor is now named Beaty].

Taylor, E. Morgan, A. and Gibbs, G. (1982). Students' perceptions of gains from studying the Social Science Foundation Course *Study Methods Group Report*, No. 11, Institute of Educational Technology Milton Keynes: Open University.

An Investigation into the Learning Experiences of Mature Students Entering Higher Education

Estelle King, Brunel University

Background to the Study

In recent years, there has been a marked increase in those who are mature (i.e., over 21) and returning to study (see Table 1). While approximately 40% of all mature students are registered with the Open University (studying part time by distance-learning packages), full-time mature undergraduates now comprise a significant minority, particularly in the former polytechnic and higher education college sectors. Women are now approaching half of the mature student population, for both full-time and part-time courses. Mature full-time students (particularly those aged 25 or over) embarking on first degree courses are much less likely to hold two or more Advanced Levels (or equivalent) than their younger counterparts. For 1990 entry, this comprised 35% of the university and 27% of the polytechnic and college mature entrants (DFE Statistical Bulletin, 1992).

The pursuit of access populism by the government and its client agencies has facilitated a steady trickle of research and discussion papers, but those that have been formally published have been predominantly reliant upon quantitative methodology. While there is now a substantial amount of published material on qualitative methods in educational settings (see Delamont, 1992, for a review), research concerned with the construction of meaning about mature student learners and, by implication, non-traditional students (although this category is not defined by age alone) is still in its infancy. Traditional models of intellectual development have merely attempted to accommodate women and men within pre-existing theoretical frameworks and age has usually been ignored as an important social constituent. An over-dependence on concepts, models and methods that seek to 'objectify' the research process and the nature of knowledge can result in a distorted and very inadequate representation of what people experience.

Qualitative methodology is seen as being sensitive to the needs of individuals because such an approach does not pre define learners' experience in terms of existing theoretical frameworks; it can contribute to a language of experience that reflects differences in individuals' perspectives. Looking at the 'why' and the 'how' rather than simply the 'what' facilitates the intellectual processes of interpretation, conceptualisation and analysis by recognising that alternative experiences and views may be equally valid and rational. A plethora of influences inevitably contributed to the conception of this study, the gradual formulation of the research questions and the resultant research design. Two to note here are the researcher's former responsibility for designing and implementing an access to higher education scheme in a further education college and the innovative work by Weil (1988).

Operating within new paradigm research or post-positivism, Weil sought to expand a way of thinking about the situation of adult learners and influences of their life-long learning upon their expectations and experiences of returning to formal learning contexts. She analysed her data relating to the development of learner identity around the key emergent themes of 'disjunction' and 'integration' with formal learning at school. The former relates to individuals feeling vulnerable or 'at risk' in formal learning and to those who convey a fragmented sense of learner identity. The notion of integration was applied to individuals who had not encountered painful negative experiences (in or outside of school). Life-long learning is recognised as a basic human need, made explicit, for example, in the theories of Maslow, Murphy, Rogers and Fromm (Long, 1974). Indeed the recent emphasis on access and continuing education has resulted in specific departments being established to meet that need in most, if not all, higher education institutions.

The motivations for returning to study have been expressed in different ways (e.g., by Brandenberg 1974). In general, it appears that enrolment in higher education in adulthood may be construed as a life event which stimulates change in self-conception, or is a change made when the individual is already re-evaluating his or her commitments. Such individuals are altering their roles and routines, their relationships at home and in the community at large, as well as developing those in the educational setting. Schlossberg et al. (1989), in their discussions of learning transitions, argue that the needs of such individuals differ depending on what stage of the transition process they are in, i.e., whether they are moving in, moving through or moving on. How adults negotiate and manage this transitional phase is a major focus of the present paper.

This study is fundamentally different from others in this area in a number of ways. Principally all individuals approached to participate in the study were already known to the researcher in a small group teaching situation, with a previously established level of rapport. This recognises, as does Oakley (1981), that the interviewer elicits, receives and provides information and, where the two parties have an existing relationship in which open communication is prioritised, a greater mutual reciprocity of roles and less of a power differential between the two parties may well be possible in the interview setting. This is important, because if 'hearing the voice' (Merriam, 1988) is of central value, any successful attempt to span the boundaries and reduce conflicting perceptions between the two parties, combined with the processes associated with reflexivity, will heighten the interviewer's ability to get closer to presenting and analysing the complex dimensions of genuine lived experience. Including the researcher's experience can lead to research that is insightful, stimulating and intellectually rigorous, and can also serve to reduce the vulnerability and open up the inequality prevalent in conventional research.

Aims of the Study

In essence, this paper aims:

to investigate mature students' (over 21 at point of entry to higher education) prior experience of learning and how this relates to their experiences in the initial stages of a degree or diploma course;

to explore how different dimensions of personal identity may interact with particular learning conditions to curtail or enhance learner identity and possibility.

The Conduct of the Inquiry

The first cycle of the research - the life-story interview
In order to study how non-traditional adults negotiate and manage the transitional life-event of entering higher education, only adults over the age of 21 in the first term of their current course, already known to the interviewer, were approached. Despite this latter a priori condition, some spread across most discipline areas was obtained. Figures 1–4 indicate the basic descriptors of the sample.

Prospective participants were approached by personal contact or letter, as appropriate. One chose not to participate, one was unobtainable and four who had agreed to participate in the study left higher education before interviewing commenced. (Such individuals who leave their course shortly after entry will be the focus of a further study.) Of those interviewed, close to the end of their first term in higher education, four were male, 21 female, four self-identified as black, 21 white and five were born outside the United Kingdom. Just over half identified themselves as coming from a working-class background, although a number felt that by virtue of their education and career path there had been some class drift, mostly, but not always, in an upward direction. Some time prior to interview, all interviewees were given a description of the study, its aims and objectives and the proposed interview format.

The in-depth life-story interviews, which lasted from one and a half to four hours, were tape recorded. In some cases, they were supplemented by individuals providing written material. Viewed as a joint social interaction, factual background information was collected before proceeding to the life-story interview covering the broad areas of:

childhood and learning during school years

leaving school, employment and becoming an adult

anticipating and becoming a mature student

experiences of informal and formal adult learning to date.

Each of these areas was introduced and explained in a general sense and each had a number of prompts to guide the interview. These were used as necessary, with the emphasis placed on gaining access to participants' understanding of their experiences and conceptions of themselves as a learner from their own frame of reference.

In order to facilitate the continuity of the interview and the discourse, some interviews were inevitably more closely directed by the interviewer, while in others participants offered very detailed in-depth accounts and explanations with minimum prompting. Techniques such as paraphrasing and seeking clarification were employed by the interviewer to facilitate comprehension of the narrative from the participant's perspective. Generally, participants seemed very willing to talk about their experiences and to communicate their ideas and perceptions, although sensitive and emotionally painful material was often disclosed. Narratives of past events were often commented on from participants' current understanding and interpretation, and it was clear that, for some, earlier traumas had not been resolved or worked through. At the end of the interview, participants were therefore encouraged to reflect and comment on the interview process and given the opportunity to talk through any current feelings about material they had raised as part of the 'de-briefing' procedure. In some instances, this was pursued in subsequent discussions. The intricate, sticky web of power relations and the stressors for both the researcher and the researched have led me to consider the range and level of interviewing skills required by the interviewer in such situations and to draw a parallel between research and counselling interviews (see King, 1993).

Follow-up interviews were carried out (N=19) close to the end of the second year. In addition to ideographic updating, individuals were invited to respond to the patterns and themes arising from the transcript of their first interview.

Preliminary interpretative analysis

Adopting a constructivist epistemology, the research process is viewed as a form of social process concerned with explicating the processes by which people come to describe, explain or otherwise account for their worlds (including the researcher's) and which openly acknowledges the power relationship between researcher and participant. Explicit in such an approach is that no-one has access to direct experience, for all experience is mediated through the mind and the constructions we put on it. Therefore, in the interview context, what is often referred to as 'direct' experience is a 'ragbag' of events, persons and speech acts in which many 'indirect' experiences are involved. This needs to be borne in mind when developing the analysis.

Analysis of the interview transcripts and associated notes has commenced, using a cross-case, cross-contextual approach. Adopting a 'grounded' approach, low-level categories were initially generated from the transcripts to move, as advocated by Glaser and Strauss (1967) towards a 'data descriptive' language to generate 'knowledge' from the trajectory of participants' accounts from within their own ideographic world. The interactive context of the interview and the wider socio-cultural systems are also under consideration, but not discussed here, in order to illustrate the range of dimensions of learner experience.
The core analysis and constant comparative analysis are currently ongoing in order to highlight similarities and differences between categories and concepts to explore fully the diversity and complexity of the data. From these processes, further cycles to be carried out in the study have been identified.

The core category emerging from the narratives as affecting all but two of the participants' developing sense of self may be summarised as discontinuity/conflict in childhood as indicated by a number of constituents relating to parental characteristics, personal and family trauma and environmental changes (see Table 2).

Participants' accounts offer meaningful interpretations and examples of how these constituents were inextricably bound up with their learner identity as part of their developing self-conception. Loss through separation, death or divorce affected ten of the sample during their primary schooling. Often the effects lasted until the present. These constituents were often expressed in terms of loss or denial, resulting in a stunted inner drive.

Conflict between parent and child, particularly with the onset of adolescence, frequently arose. The divergence of parent–child attitudes or educational standards attained was often articulated. Furthermore, a number voiced strongly that they had been thwarted or disadvantaged/discriminated against while at school.

Sally: When I went to the school in Kent, I didn't have any friends at all, because I had this awful [Glaswegian] accent, and no one could understand me. So I got badly bullied. I'd missed a lot of school so I was quite behind a lot of them . . . and I think they (the teachers) saw me as not being an achiever and having a funny accent and sort of, uh, I don't know.

In all such cases, the school's response and its timing (relating to teachers and occasionally pupils) may be construed as crucial contributors to the individual's sense of self and resultant learner identity.

In the majority of instances, it was most apparent that participants felt they had lacked appropriate guidance from both educators and parents. When ambition and hopes went unfulfilled the frustration experienced was described as having been immense. Some felt their attempts to do well were not rewarded, and other participants 'gave up' at school around adolescence as an act of rebellion against parental pressure from unrealistic expectation of high educational attainment.

Enid: . . . and I remember on one occasion, I got 100 out of 100 for geography and history, and came bounding home, only to be sort of stopped dead in my tracks by my father, saying, 'But you should've got 101 out of 100.' And that was my childhood, whatever I did, I could always've done better. I was doing my best, it was never enough, there was never any praise. At all.

Parental attitude towards learning, compounded by a feeling of alienation from the (white) middle-class educational system, resulted in a strong disjunction between life in and outside of school. Several narratives adopted a 'victim syndrome'; these individuals felt retrospectively they had had no control over their lives, and often blamed others for their low self-esteem and lack of achievement.

Two accounts were given of happy, non-stressful childhoods. One who described herself as "having come from a delightful, stable family" proceeded from school to university. However, the majority of the sample saw adolescence as a period fraught with inner and/or outer turmoil, and as often damaging to their vulnerable self-identity. This was often related to a desire to leave school at the earliest opportunity. Where participants told of teachers having recognised hidden potential, it had proved too late: the individual had disengaged from learning. To sum, all but two narratives may be organised around the emergent theme of disjunction with formal education. This may well be related to the fact that, having a fragmented and vulnerable sense of learner identity, most participants chose to prepare for higher education via an access course.

Many themes interweave to provide a complex pattern of interlocking and overlapping processes and experiences associated with the gradual and often very painful sense of learning to negotiate a move towards a formal learning context. Learning assumed a variety of meanings for those interviewed. Discovery experiences, often relating to issues of class, gender, relationships and race were frequently, but not always, viewed as gradually promoting a positive sense of self. Such experiences were also often pertinent to the more recent experience of higher education.

Anne: I suppose I brought my gender to college anyway, so I've probably noticed things that substantiate what I thought a bit more anyway. I'm still finding out more about it, I'm probably a bit in between at the moment, and all the opinions and views I had before are still there, even stronger. They are just either supplemented in different ways, or supplemented more strongly by things going on.

Occasionally, participants linked such experiences with their decision to enter higher education. Learning outside formal education, including the experience of child rearing, was viewed as being qualitatively and quantitatively different from formal learning, and was not positively related to self-achievement and success.

In anticipating and making the move to higher education, determination and commitment to succeed often seem to have been related to a desire to realise one's own intellectual potential, moreover to prove oneself to oneself. Echoes from the past, however, were often voiced as interfering with the struggle to reach out for an altered learner identity.

Lauren: so as a result, certainly academically, it has spread to other aspects of my life. I've got a very low opinion of my capabilities, which is why, even now, I still sort of have a tendency to pinch myself that I'm actually on the law course.
A gradual dawning of the need to assume control or responsibility for one's own learning/development was often expressed, sometimes through the use of extended metaphor.

Carl: I really saw access as my last chance. I had a feeling it could be a door (shut) new in my face again. Probably a door I was gradually closing on myself, rather than someone else. I needed to push and to motivate myself rather than expect or need someone else to do it for me.

Most participants entered higher education via an access course, although the small-scale, supportive environment of such courses did not necessarily prepare individuals for induction into higher education, which was often experienced as impersonal and chaotic.

Nancy: It [the course] was pretty awful to begin with, but the second semester wasn't so bad. With, er, just culture shock . . . I don't think any access course can actually prepare you for that. I think you all have to go through it.

At the time of the first interview, accounts of participants' current situations differed considerably. Some were fired with enthusiasm and determination to succeed, others talked more about experiencing struggle, confusion and some disillusionment. All had experienced a mixture of anxiety, apprehension and excitement at commencing their course. A need to connect knowledge with disciplines and for more guidance was voiced. Six participants had already used the counselling service. At the second interview, a further three mentioned having used this as a resource.

Early integration appears to be strongly related to the quality of the interpersonal interface between students and staff. However, when high anxiety was voiced during the interview about one's potential, this did not appear to have been markedly reduced by supportive tutoring and high grade attainment. At this early stage, support and positive feedback were not successful in enabling the individual to overcome a negative learner identity. In other instances, where the interpersonal element between the institution and the individual was lacking, support and encouragement from one's peers were crucial in gradually fostering a more positive learner identity.

Seven participants had not proceeded to Year 2, although all but one had completed Year 1 (see Table 3). Important consideration is to be given elsewhere to the specific and interconnecting processes contributing to this. Briefly, the predominant factors appear to relate to difficulties with exam technique and unmanageable levels of anxiety (as opposed to the acquisition of knowledge), spiralling family pressures and an unrealistic expectation of, or inability to meet, the demands of the institution.

The individual who did not re-sit the necessary component had become alienated by what she experienced as a rather hostile, disorganised institution with poor channels of communication. The institution had failed to actively engage her in the learning process, and with no support or encouragement she did not have the confidence to prepare for and re-sit the examination. This resulted in her already vulnerable self-identity and frail learner identity becoming severely knocked and damaged. It is worth noting that she went from higher education to an untrained social care post.

The over-arching category of integration/disjunction with the educational institution applies to the majority of narratives. For most close to the end of their second year, a far more positive learner identity was stressed, especially in terms of increased confidence and assertiveness and an awareness of developing abilities and strengths. In this sense, experience of higher education was strongly related to feelings of self-worth and esteem, connecting and extending to areas outside academic life, thereby promoting a positive self-image.

Jane: I've gained self-esteem, um . . . confidence and become more assertive. I feel I've got the me back, the me of 17 years ago.

This was not gender-specific, but several women narrated how their recently acquired powers of cogency had been used successfully with (male) authority figures outside of an educational context.

For those women in long-term relationships, the support of their partner was usually seen as paramount in enabling them to straddle the greedy demands of home and higher education. (See Edwards, 1993, for an in-depth analysis of how these public and private spheres interact and impinge on one another.) For the woman who left during Year 2, the claims of competing roles and positions were omnivorous. However, while a change in the power balance in the women's relationships with their partners was often articulated, this had only occasionally proved problematic. Considerable effort was sometimes put into involving one's partner with the perceived personal changes associated with studying for a degree, to prevent or minimise his feeling threatened or 'left behind'.

Other negative experiences were narrated in varying ways. The power of the institution and inequality of experience (and feeling oneself to be disadvantaged or discriminated against) were voiced by some in terms of gender, age, race and class. The experiences and skills of older students (interestingly, not on social science courses) were not necessarily seen as 'valuable assets' by the institution.

Lauren: They are very I find unsympathetic towards anything to do with needs of the children . . . it's a question of, 'Well, you made the choice to come here, deal with the problems when they come, if you can't cope with it, then it's your problem' . . . you just get, you hit a blank wall really.

Support and encouragement from one's peers, often valued, was seen as crucial during periods of self-doubt and at times of conflict, within or outside of the institution. However, by the second year, lack of support from the institution was often related to a developing sense of positive learner identity in terms of autonomous learning and a determination to succeed. To attain the latter, a high level of individual sacrifice and organisation to make the necessary commitment to the course was seen as vital.

Linda . . . it is really just basically trying to get myself enough time without doing damage to the family life. Um, to be selfish and to be able to say, 'Look, I've got study to do, I've got to fit this in'. I can't do any more during the day here. There isn't another minute during the day that I can use.

A number, like Linda, who talked about setting themselves very high goals, had not yet come to terms with their not being able to do as well as they would like, to strive towards attaining their potential. Yet, by the end of Year 2, less emphasis was placed on later career prospects than in the first interview; more was placed on the importance of individual growth or development.

Various interpretations relating to learning and the acquisition of knowledge were given. However, it is extremely difficult to ascertain the effects of gender. In their review of research into student learning, Richardson and King (1991) indicate that questionnaire studies do not show consistent gender differences, while qualitative studies (usually interview based) maintain that women's experiences of their world, including their conception of knowledge and learning, are qualitatively different from male students.

Many of the women in the current study on social science and humanities courses 'connected knowing' (a term from Gilligan, 1982) in their second narratives, especially with regard to race, gender or class.

Julie: I'm more discriminate in my learning now, I'm choosing where to channel my energies. The work placement system has been extremely important in being able to link up theory with practical application. It makes it all come so, so alive, knowledge then seems for real. Myself is coming through in my studies, especially with regard to race and prejudice and discrimination, I can now express myself as myself.

In this sense, life experience was important and was combined with academic knowledge to provide a broader understanding of a `topic'. Relationships with other students were also valued in this context, enabling these individuals to engage actively in intellectual discourse. Interestingly, this was often seen as taking place outside of the formal learning context.

Addressing Issues of Relevance

It is difficult to convey a language of experience in a paper of this nature. Only the predominant themes have been expressed, with minimal reference to the individuals who participated in the study. However, their narratives clearly demonstrate that nearly all did not attain the academic qualifications for higher education at school age for good reason. Their early painful experiences associated with their resultant learner identity had often impeded their intellectual development and damaged their more general sense of self. From this seemed to come an inner drive to prove oneself with higher education as the external validator.

A framework for analysing their experiences is still being developed, one which can take account of differences, both from one another and my own, and one which will also pay attention to factors which extend beyond individual lives, from the personal to the political.

Research of the type introduced here raises many questions. Until recently, higher education was not noted for its examination of learning. That position has changed dramatically. The aims of the teaching process in higher education are now very much under consideration, but the conceptualising of learning is perhaps only the start of a question-raising process. Academic values and assumptions, which are of course not independent of social conditions, are now being challenged in a variety of ways.

While higher education institutions are not known for their vertical and horizontal integration, curriculum design and delivery have and are being influenced by initiatives orchestrated at national level. Yet, a number of studies indicate that the pattern of inequality that is prevalent in our society is especially apparent in the institutions of higher education. This pattern will persist until it is acknowledged by those in positions of power and authority and until deliberate and concerted attempts are made to bring about change.

There are many consequences to be faced as a result of the recent overall increase in the student population, a number of which may be specific to the needs of mature and other non-traditional students. Maturational theories associated with life-long learning are part of a new developing paradigm that is both complex and challenging. If wider access to higher education is really to be implemented successfully, it will be crucial to listen closely to non-traditional students' accounts of the processes, boundaries and struggles involved in developing a positive sense of learner identity. While some disciplines obviously lend themselves more readily to this suggestion than others, inter-relating life experience with formal learning contexts could well be part of a process which would add richness to what should, after all, be part of an enabling, empowering experience.

References

Brandenburg, J.B. (1974). The needs of women returning to school *Personnel and Guidance Journal*, 1, 11–18.

Delamont, S. (1992). *Fieldwork in Educational Settings: Methods, Pitfalls and Perspectives* London: Falmer Press.

Department for Education (1992). Statistical Bulletin, August 1992: Mature Students in Higher Education – Great Britain, 1980–1990.

Edwards, R. (1993). *Mature Women Students: Separating or Connecting Family and Education* London: Taylor & Francis.

Gilligan, C. (1982). *In a Different Voice; Psychological Theory and Women's Development* Cambridge, MA: Harvard University Press.

Glaser, P. and Strauss, A. (1967). *The Discovery of Grounded Theory* New York: Aldine.

King, E. (1993). Power versus empowerment as part of the research process *Psychology of Women Newsletter*, No. 11.

Long, H. B. (1974). Life-long learning, pressures for acceptance *Journal of Research and Development in Education*, 7, 4, 2–12.

Merriam, S. J. (1988). *Case Study Research in Education: A Qualitative Approach* San Francisco: Jossey-Bass.

Oakley, A. (1981). *Subject Women* Bath: Pitman Press.

Richardson, J. T. E. and King, E. (1991). Gender differences in the experience of higher education: quantitative and qualitative approaches *Educational Psychology*, 11, 363–382.

Schlossberg, N. K. Lynch, A. Q. and Chickering, A. W. (1989). *Improving Higher Education Environments for Adults* San Francisco: Jossey-Bass.

Weil, S. W. (1988). From a language of observation to a language of experience: studying the perspectives of diverse adults in higher education *Journal of Access Studies*, 1, 17–43.

Table 1 Higher Education: Young and Mature First Year Undergraduate Home Students in Academic Year 1990–1991 (excluding Open University)

	Thousands	%Change	Thousands	%Change
University	Full-time	1980–1990	Part-time	1980–1990
Young	74.2	8	0.1	-57
Mature	10.6	40	2.0	136
Polytechnic & college				
Young	67.2	93	1.6	218
Mature	24.1	152	12.6	100

Table 2 Discontinuity/Conflict in Childhood as indicated by

Parental characteristics	Family trauma	Personal trauma	Environmental changes
age	separation	sexual abuse	school
culture	death	illness	address
langage	mental illness		culture
education	/handicap		country
income			language
temperament			

Figure 1

Qualifications upon Leaving School
The majority (N=19) left school at the earliest opportunity, at 15 or 16 years of age, most obtaining minimal or no qualifications. A number had become alientated from formal learning, while some had hoped to do much better, or had suffered illness during their final year. Two of the three who obtained Advanced Levels (or equivalent) at appropriate grades had entered higher education at degree level, one withdrew and one completed the course.

Figure 2

Entry to Higher Education
The majority (N=18, or 72%) prepared for entry to higher education via an access course, usually full time over one year's duration. One person had obtained a degree abroad 24 years earlier, two had obtained Advanced Levels at appropriate grades at school age, and three of the younger participants had studied for Advaned Levels on a part-time basis. One person entered higher education with a nursing qualification and a module from a university foundation course.

Figure 3

Current Higher Education Course
At the time of the first interview, 24 participants were registered for a degree course, and one for a diploma in higher education, in four institutions in the Greater London area. All but two participants were on full-time courses of three or four years duration. The remaining two were studying part time under a credit accumulation transfer scheme. Participants were primarily registered for courses in social sciences, with some representation in most other areas typical of mature students.

Figure 4

Current Domestic Situation
Most of those in the study (15, or 60%) had considerable domestic responsibilities, including children of or below school age. The younger participants were all single (although one was a single parent), and two were ,living in their parental home due to financial considerations. Only two of the (younger) participants had moved to student accommodation; the rest, apart from one, had a reasonable distance to commute. Four of those interviewed had three children of or below school age, including one of the single parents. The geographical location of the educational institution was therefore an overall priority.

Chapter 6   Assessment and student learning

Effects of Modes of Assessment on Students' Preparation Strategies

Catherine Tang, Hong Kong Polytechnic

Introduction

Within an educational context, assessment takes up a considerable proportion of time, effort and resources. It occupies a central part in the lives of the students and can amount to up to 15% or more of their time (Crooks, 1988). As the students recognise assessment, especially the summative function as a continuous and important component of their learning process, they consciously or subconsciously vary their attitudes and strategies of learning in order to cope with the assessment system (Harris and Bell, 1986).

Study approaches
Studies have demonstrated that students engage in different learning approaches when attempting to accomplish a learning task. Each of the different approaches to learning encompasses a motive for learning and a set of appropriate strategies to accomplish the task. From both qualitative (Marton and Säljö, 1976) and quantitative (Biggs, 1987a) studies, two general approaches of learning have been identified: surface and deep.

Students adopting a surface approach have an extrinsic motive to carry out the task for some external achievements other than the present task itself. This approach aims at avoiding failure but with investing minimum effort. The accompanying strategy is to learn by rote (inappropriately) and try to memorise what is perceived as important. These students focus on isolated facts and fail to see the relation among the information. Rote learning here is used for the purpose of reproducing content, not of understanding it.

Students engaging a deep approach have an intrinsic motivation of felt need based on interest in the task. The strategies thus adopted are task specific and aim at seeking and understanding the meaning of what is being learnet. Not only do these students relate the different aspects of the information with one another, they also relate them to their previous learning and their personal experiences.

Apart from these two mutually exclusive learning approaches, Biggs (1987a) has also identified an achieving approach which is rooted in attaining motivation in competing and gaining high grades. The strategies used are context oriented, aiming at maximising the chances of obtaining high marks, and involving systematic organisation and cost-effective use of time and effort.

Although surface and deep approaches are mutually exclusive in any given instance, the achieving approach can be associated with either the surface or the deep approach. A student can either learn the information systematically by rote in order to get high grades, or to get the meaning of the content, thus constituting a "surface-achieving" or "deep-achieving" approach respectively.

The "3P" systems model of teaching and learning identified three components of student learning – presage, process and product – which interact to form a stable equilibrium (Biggs, in press). Students' approach to learning is in this view a function both of student-related factors such as prior knowledge and experience, ability, preferred learning style and expectations, and of the teaching environment, including assessment. Thus, when exposed to a particular context, the students are differentially responsive to the teaching context factors such as curriculum, teaching and assessment methods, and institutional provisions and restraints, according to their perceptions of the teaching context (Biggs, 1987a; Entwistle, 1988; Meyer and Muller, 1990; Meyer, Parsons and Dunne, 1990; Ramsden, 1984, 1988). Hence, in the actual learning situation, students develop a context-specific "study orchestration" in response to the perception of the requirements of the learning context (Meyer et al., 1990). Among all the contextual factors, assessment has been demonstrated to have a powerful effect on the learning process (Boud, 1990; Crooks, 1988; Entwistle and Marton, 1984; Entwistle and Ramsden, 1983; Heywood, 1989; Newble and Jaeger, 1983).

Backwash of assessment
The backwash of assessment on learning is closely related to the students' perceptions of the demands of the assessment rather than to what the teacher intends to assess. If a particular assessment is perceived to be requiring just passive acquisition and accurate reproduction of details, students will then adopt a surface approach and employ low level cognitive strategy such as rote learning and concentrate on facts and details while preparing for the assessment. When assessment is perceived to require a high level cognitive processing to demonstrate a thorough understanding, integration and application of the context knowledge, then the students are more likely to engage a deep approach in order to accomplish the task. This backwash of assessment affects particularly "cue seeking" students, who are constantly on the alert for cues that will help them prepare for assessment (Miller and Parlett, 1974).

The assessment dilemma
Given the effects of assessment on learning and understanding, what mode of assessment should one use to assess student performance in a given course or

unit? A short essay test to ensure coverage (and maximal "security")? Or an assignment to maximise depth of engagement? Tertiary teachers are continually faced with such questions, and at present there is little more than intuition to help formulate the answers. This question is the point of interest of the present paper, which aims at exploring the effects of students' perceptions of two assessment modes, written test and assignment, on their subsequent adoption of preparation strategies and on the assessment outcomes.

Method

The context of the study

The study was conducted in the Physiotherapy Section at the Hong Kong Polytechnic. The Professional Diploma course in Physiotherapy (PDPT) is a three-year programme, and its aim is to develop within the students the knowledge, skills and attitudes in the professional practice of physiotherapy, which include the ability to analyse and evaluate the practice in the context of the local health care system (Physiotherapy Section, 1990). The philosophy of the course is to enable the students to develop their potential as self-directed and motivated learners through questioning and a critical approach to learning. At the Hong Kong Polytechnic the medium of instruction is English, although the mother tongue of all the students and most of the teaching staff is Chinese.

During the course, the students have to learn both basic preclinical science subjects and specialised professional therapeutic procedures. The integration of theory to practice is reinforced in the subject of "Integrated Professional Studies" (IPS), which requires the students to synthesise and integrate the theory and professional skills acquired in individual subject areas in a holistic perspective for the treatment and management of patients. This training prepares the students for clinical education, when they have to apply theory to practice and treat patients under supervision in various hospitals and centres. To achieve the objectives of IPS, students are expected to develop high level cognitive strategies such as critical and analytical thinking, relating, integrating, synthesising and application of knowledge.

The assessment of IPS has traditionally been by written tests consisting of short essay questions. Recently, course assignments have been introduced as an alternative mode of assessment on the assumption that assignments draw on higher level cognitive preparation strategies. However, teaching staff are worried that, as each assignment covers only one topic area, the coverage of the assessment syllabus will be very narrow, and a large amount of content will remain unassessed. On the other hand, short essay tests will be able to cover more areas, but there is the worry that they may encourage the students to adopt low level preparation strategies. Hence the present study was conducted to ascertain the effects of these two modes of assessment on the students' adoption of different preparation strategies.

Subjects

The subjects for the study were 158 Hong Kong tertiary students attending the first year of a physiotherapy programme. The first-year students were chosen as subjects because they have not been exposed to the assessment system of the course, and so any subsequent changes in their study approaches measured after the different modes of assessment might be attributed more confidently to their perceptions of the demands of these assessments, and their adaptation in study strategies in response to the respective mode of assessment.

Design of the study

The study was divided into two parts, the quantitative and qualitative studies.

The quantitative study

The quantitative study involved the examination of the students' general study approaches at the beginning of the academic year by the Study Process Questionnaire (SPQ) (Biggs, 1987b). The SPQ contains 42 self-report items operationalising the three study approaches, surface, deep and achieving, with their respective motives and strategies components with respect to the students' general orientation to learning. In the present study, a bilingual Chinese–English version of the SPQ was used. This version of SPQ has been widely used in local Hong Kong tertiary institutions and its translation has been found to be accurate (see Biggs, 1992).

A task-specific Assessment Preparation Strategies (APS) questionnaire was developed. The items of the APS questionnaire were based on the surface, deep and achieving approach items of the SPQ and were designed to explore the strategies which the students employed when preparing for the two modes of assessment under study. After a pilot study and factor analysis, the final version of the ASP questionnaire contains 30 items constituting five factors for each assessment with six items per factor. The internal consistency using the Cronbach's å varies from .55 to .60 (test) and .54 to .62 (assignment). Because of the different nature of the two modes of assessment, there were two versions of the APS questionnaire, one for the test and one for the assignment, each being specific to the particular mode of assessment. After each assessment, the students were asked to answer the APS questionnaire to indicate their strategies in preparing for that particular assessment. The five factors of the APS questionnaire are summarised below.

Factor 1 –   This factor examines the sources of study materials and the processing of the information.

                Test APST1: syllabus-bound and memorising

                Assignment APSA1: broad-focussing and summarising

Factor 2 –   This factor describes the focus of studying and whether or not the students are consciously aware of and seeking cues.

                Test APST2: narrow-focussing and cue-seeking

                Assignment APSA2: cue-seeking

Factor 3 –   This factor describes whether or not the students relate what they are studying to patients' conditions in clinical practice.

                Test APST3: deep-professional

                Assignment APSA3: deep-professional

Factor 4 –   This factor describes whether or not the students relate what they are studying to other subjects.

                Test APST4: deep-academic

                Assignment APSA4: deep-academic

Factor 5 –   This factor describes the students' organisation of work and study time.

                Test APST5: organising

                Assignment APSA5: organising

The students' performance in the assessments was indicated by three sets of assessment scores, one for the test (ASSTS), which was the total scores of the four short essay questions, and two for the assignment: (1) the scores awarded for the assignment (ASSAS) based on the relevance to the question requirements, the quality of the discussion, argument and presentation of the content, and (2) a score (ASSASOLO) based on the qualitative interpretation of the structural complexity of the assignment according to the SOLO taxonomy (Biggs and Collis, 1982). One mark was awarded for a multi-structural level, while two to five marks were awarded for various degrees of relational level assignments.

Unistructural and extended abstract levels were not expected and were indeed not observed.

Path analyses of these quantitative data were carried out to explore the effects of the students' general study approaches, their actual preparation strategies for each assessment mode and their assessment performance. The causal model of the path analyses were based on the "3 P" model. The presage domain consisted of the scores of the six subscales of the SPQ: surface motive (SM), surface strategy (SS), deep motive (DM), deep strategy (DS), achieving motive (AM) and achieving strategy (AS). The process domain consisted of the students' scores in the two APS questionnaire (test and assignment). The product domain consisted of the three sets of performance scores (ASSTS, ASSAS and ASSASOLO).

The qualitative Ssudy

The qualitative study consisted of interviews of 39 randomly selected students from the sample to explore their perceptions of assessment demands and effects on the adoption of preparation strategies. Each student was interviewed twice, once after the test, and once after the assignment. The students' perceptions of the demands of these models of assessment were obtained through open-ended questions about what they thought they had to do in order to do well in the assessments, and the problems that they encountered during preparation. The interviews were then transcribed and the data analysed.

Results and Discussion

Quantitative analysis

Path analysis for test
The results of the path analysis for the test is shown in Figure 1.

Figure 1: Path analysis for test

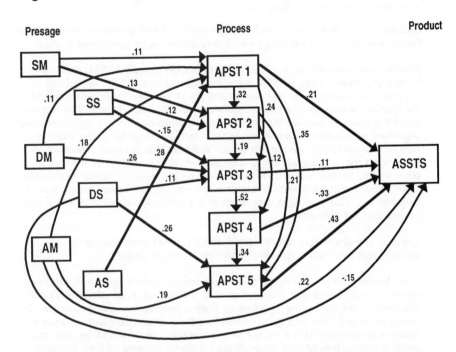

The results of these path relations demonstrated congruence between the presage general study approaches and the process assessment preparation strategies. On the whole, those students who were surface-oriented were more likely to employ low level strategies when studying for the test, while those who were normally deep-oriented had a higher tendency to employ high level preparation strategies. As for those students who were achievement motivated, their choice of strategies seemed to depend on what they perceived as the requirements of the assessment, and hence they responded accordingly.

Three specific assessment preparation strategies were demonstrated as effective for the test: focussed memorising, deep-professional and organising, that is, surface and surface-achieving strategies. The only exception to the general trend of surface dominance is that APST1: syllabus-bound and memorising was also directly influence by deep-motive DM. The explanation of this unexpected relation was clarified by the qualitative data. Some students reported in the interviews that they were basically intrinsically motivated to understand the content when studying for the test, but at the same time perceived that the test required them to memorise certain parts of the content, so they would do just that: memorise those facts after having understood them. This specific strategy is here called "deep-memorisation", which illustrates very strongly study orchestration in response to students' perception of task demands: deep-oriented students go deep with a strategy which may otherwise be considered surface.

Positive relations existing between test scores (ASSTS) and APST1: syllabus-bound and memorising, APST3: deep-professional and APST5: organising suggest that students who just memorised the physiotherapy aspects taught in the syllabus, especially in an organised way, were likely to do well. The fact that APST5: organising showed the strongest direct effect on ASSTS suggests that to be organised is important when studying for a test. The negative direct effect of APST4: deep-academic on the test results indicates that students who tried to relate what they were studying to other subjects do not do well in the test. In other words, the test was not only not assessing the students' ability to relate to other subjects, but those who did inter-relate actually performed worse than if they had not. This finding is significant as it signifies a mismatch between the subject and test objectives.

The only presage factors which related directly to test performance are achievement motivation (positive) and deep strategy (negative).

These findings thus indicate (a) that an organising surface approach, involving systematic rote learning of focussed parts of the content, is an effective way of studying for the test, while (b) adopting deep strategies is counterproductive. It would seem to follow that deep-oriented students would be disadvantaged in this mode of assessment. This does not seem to be the case, however, because the indirect effects showed that deep-oriented students adapted to their perceived quantitative demands of the test and orchestrated their study approach by adopting the "deep-memorising" strategy, and hence were able to do well in the test.

Path analyses for assignment
Two path analyses were carried out for the model of doing assessment, one concerning the assignment as marked, and the other concerning the SOLO scores of the assignments. The results of these path analyses are shown in Figures 2 and 3.

Figure 2: Path analysis for assignment scores

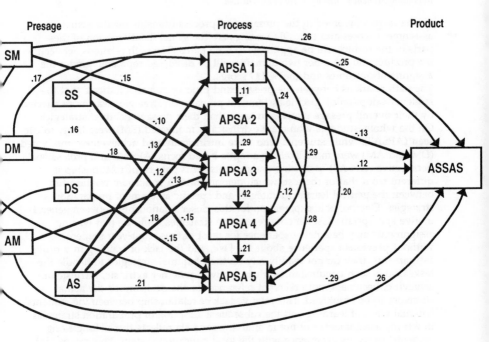

Figure 3: Path analysis for assignment SOLO

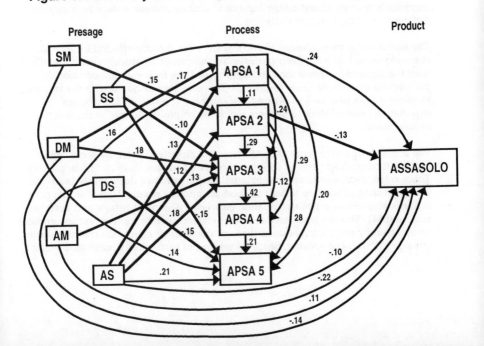

As the factors involved in the presage and process domains for the actual assignment scores and the SOLO ratings are the same, the discussion of these parts of the results will be applicable to both paths. The path relations between the product and the other two domains will be discussed separately under the assignment outcomes and the SOLO scores.

The path relations between the presage and process domains indicate that the students' adoption of specific assignment preparation strategies was more affected by their overall presage motives to learn than their presage habitual strategies. On the whole, students who were extrinsically motivated (SM) were likely to cue-seek (APSA2), while students who were intrinsically and achievement motivated (DM and AM) were more likely to adopt a broad focus (APSA1) and professional perspective (APSA3) in writing assignments. This pattern of relationship is different from that of the test, which demonstrates a congruent relationship between the general learning strategies and specific assessment preparation strategies. One possible explanation for this closer relationship between general motive and specific assessment preparation strategies could be that writing assignments may be a new experience for most of these first-year students. Without previous experience about the task, and the lack of training in writing assignments, they cannot readily rely on their habitual strategies to handle the task. Under such circumstances, their motives, whether extrinsic, intrinsic or achieving, become a more relevant reference for the decision for the actual strategies to be employed. This relative lack of relationship between the students' habitual ways of learning and the subsequent adoption of preparation strategies in writing assignments but not in studying for tests reflects these Hong Kong students' previous experience with the local education system. This places high value on examination success (Hau and Salili, 1991), and hence the students are specifically trained in test-taking but not in writing assignments, which requires a different set of preparation strategies.

The actual assignment scores (ASSAS) which were directly affected by APSA2: cue-seeking and APSA3: deep-professional indicates that students who identified with the lecturers' expectations and approached the task with a professional perspective were more likely to do well. This may be associated with the fact that, in attempting a new task of writing assignments, cue-seeking on lectures' expectations and relating to patients would be helpful to adhere to the task requirements.

The actual assignment score (ASSAS) was also directly affected by some of the presage factors: deep strategy (DS) positively, and surface strategy (SS) negatively. These relationships indicate that habitual employment of deep rather than surface strategies is likely to lead to good assignment results. However, the path analysis also shows a positive relation between assignment results and surface motive (SM). This contradictory relation between surface motive and assignment results could have been mediated through the indirect effects via the preparation strategy APSA2: cue-seeking. Students who were extrinsically motivated might resolve by identifying with the lectures' expectations about the assignment, which in turn led to good assignment results.

The assignment SOLO scores (ASSASOLO) were only directly but negatively affected by APSA2: cue-seeking, indicating that students who were too concerned with trying to identify with the lecturers' expectations when writing the assignment might actually lose out on the quality of the structure of the assignment. However, this result is opposite to the positive effects of APSA2: cue-seeking on the actual assignment scores (ASSAS). This seems to suggest that the marking of the assignment emphasised mainly the relevance of the content rather than the overall structural complexity. The ASSASOLO scores were also related to five presage factors, positively to DS, and negatively to SS, DM, AM and AS. These two sets of path coefficients seem to indicate that the ability to structure an assignment is more related to the personal orientations of the students rather than the actual preparation strategies.

The finding that presage factors predict the assignment results better than they predict test results is in keeping with the fact that writing assignments is a new experience to most of these first-year students. In the absence of previous experience and knowledge of appropriate coping strategies, these students rely on their general approach to learning to guide them in accomplishing the task.

The qualitative interview analysis
The results of the path analyses provide a framework of the backwash effects of assessment. However, they fail to illuminate the details of the students' perceptions of the task demands of these two modes of assessment and the actual process of preparation. These gaps in the information were bridged by interviews of the 39 randomly selected students after each assessment.

Perceptions of test demands
Students tended to have either a quantitative or a qualitative perception of test demand, each encompassing a set of cognitive strategies and other attribution factors, as shown in Table 1.

Table 1 *Quantitative and qualitative perceptions of test demands*

Quantitative perceptions	Qualitative perceptions
Rote learning	Understanding
Memorising and reproduction	Relate information to: other subjects previous knowledge
More effort and time in repeated studying to improve memory	Application of knowledge
Luck	Deep memorisation
Special skills and techiques	More effort and time to understand
	Good command of English for understanding and expressing ideas
	Special skills and techniques

Quantitative perceptions see testing as assessing the quantity of information, and hence requiring low level cognitive strategies such as rote learning, memorising and reproducing. Success is also perceived as requiring effort and time, and by some as requiring external factor such as luck.

Qualitative perceptions see testing as assessing the understanding, integration and application of the content knowledge through processing with high level cognitive strategies. These students also perceived that they had an active control of the process through effort in systematic organised studying.

However, a group of students emerged whose perceptions of test demands did not seem to be totally identifiable with either the quantitative or the qualitative orientation. These students perceived the test required other understanding and memorising, a combination of both quantitative and qualitative demands. To these students, the main objective in studying for the test was to understand the learning materials. However, they also perceived the need to memorise some of the factual information after they had understood in order to do the test. This memorisation, here called "deep-memorisation", is achieved with understanding rather than just rote learning. The following comment helps to illustrate this perception that tests require a deep-memorisation strategy.

You may understand the principles, but you still have to memorise the points so that you can present all of them in the test, as this is the way marking is done – by the points, so you cannot miss any.

Other perceived test demands included good command of English, and some special skills and techniques such as organisation of study time and materials. These perceived demands could be associated with either a quantitative or a qualitative perception, depending on whether they were considered to be necessary for rote learning or for understanding.

Perceptions of assignment demands
The perceived assignment demands are shown in Table 2.

Table 2 *Quantitative and qualitative perceptions of assignment demands*

Quantitative perceptions	Qualitative perceptions
Copying from journals	Large content base
	Understand question requirements
	Understand reading materials
	Have own opinions and support with evidence from journals
	Elaborate on points
	Organise information
	Relate to: previous knowledge other subjects physiotherapy
	Effort and time
	Have group discussion
	Good English for understanding

Unclassified

Extraction and selection
of information

Summarise reading material

Lecturers' expectations

Quantitative perceptions of assignment demands are concerned mainly with the need to copy from journals owing to poor command of English.

Various qualitative perceptions have been identified by the students, and these included understanding the question and the content through high level cognitive strategies such as analysing, interpreting, thinking and reasoning, having one's own opinion and supporting them with evidence from journals, and relating to previous knowledge, to other subjects, to physiotherapy and to clinical practice.

Other perceptions of assignment demands included effort and time in establishing a large and organised knowledge base, good command of English, and the ability to work within the constraint of a word limit.

During the interviews, the majority of the students identified the perceived importance of group discussion, especially when doing assignments. This form of collaborative learning was perceived as a mutual support system when students were faced with a new and unfamiliar task. Interview data also revealed the engagement of deep preparation strategies during group discussion such as relating, integrating and application of knowledge. This form of collaborative learning, which was the spontaneous effort of the students is here called "Spontaneous Collaborative Learning" (SCOLL), and has been discussed in detail elsewhere (Tang, in press).

Comparing the different perceptions of the two modes of assessment, some demands were perceived to be relevant to both test and assignment, while others were specific to only one of the two assessment modes. These different perceptions of assessment demands influence the students' ways of preparing for the assessment. Students with a quantitative perception will very likely adopt surface strategies while those with a qualitative perception will engage in deep strategies. For cognitive strategies, high level strategies such as understanding, application of information, relating to other subjects and previous knowledge are requirements perceived to be necessary for both the test and the assignment. However, low level strategies such as rote learning, memorisation and reproduction were perceived to be relevant only to the test. Hence it may appear that there is a greater possibility for students to adopt a surface approach when studying for a test.

These 39 students were classified into surface and deep groups on the basis of the quality and cognitive level of the preparation strategies reported in the interviews for each mode of assessment, and the relationship between the process and assessment performance of the two subgroups was explored. Students who could not be clearly classified into either the surface or the deep approach were excluded from this part of the study. The differences between the surface and deep subgroups for the three sets of assessments scores are shown in

Table 3 *The difference in the means of assessment scores between the surface and deep groups*

	Mean scores		
	Test	Assignment	
	(ASSTS)	(ASSAS)	(ASSASOLO)
Surface	54.94	59.10	2.29
Deep	52.14	71.07	3.67
p	NS	<.005	<.005

For the test, 17 students were classified as being in the surface group and 21 as deep, and there was no difference in the test performance scores ($p > .05$). For the assignment, 21 students were classified as being in the surface group and 15 as deep. The difference between the actual assignment scores and SOLO scores were both significant and in favour of the deep subgroup ($p < .005$). Thus, as deep strategies were perceived by the majority of students as being required for the assignment, students adopting appropriate deep strategies clearly achieved a better performance in writing assignments, as is also indicated in the path analyses.

Implications for Teaching

To return to the tertiary teachers' dilemma, the present results tend to confirm that the short essay test does provide a wider coverage of the test syllabus, but also that it tends to encourage the adoption of surface strategies owing to the students' quantitative perceptions of test demands. On the other hand, assignment, although narrower in coverage, tends to encourage engagement using deep strategies. However, it is not quite as simple at this.

Students' perceptions of task demands strongly influences their actual study approach when handling a particular learning task. Provided that they have the appropriate learning strategies at their disposal, students will orchestrate their study to accomplish the task. However, in the absence of previous experience and lack of a suitable repertory of coping strategies, students will have to rely on their presage study orientation or develop new coping strategies.

To facilitate the adoption of desirable preparation strategies, several practical implications for teaching can be drawn from the results of the present study.

Explicit and clear task demands

Evidence from the present study shows that learning context, especially the students' perceptions of the assessment demands, exerts a strong influence on the learning process and hence the learning outcomes. It is thus important that teachers should make these demands as clear as possible so that students can accurately perceive the intended task demands, and hence respond appropriately. In the education context, it is highly possible that these demands are not made explicit to the students, as Thomas and Rohwer (1986: 30) put it: "In the academic arena, ambiguity of purpose is more often the rule than the exception." In the content of the present study, the demands of test and assignment do not appear to have been explicitly explained, and the students are identifying the assessment demands based on their previous experience. Coming from an education system which places heavy emphasis on examinations, some of these first-year students may be prone to perceive tests as requiring low level strategies of rote learning and memorising, and they respond appropriately by adopting a surface approach. When writing assignments, in the absence of previous experience, students will have to rely more on their general study orientations when deciding on the preparation strategies, although many students who are surface-oriented will stand a greater chance of inaccurately perceiving these demands, and hence adopting surface strategies. Apart from clearly explaining to the students the requirements of writing assignments, Clanchy's (1985) suggestion of providing an accessible "bank" of good, medium and poor student assignment samples would be one of the ways of providing students with better guidelines for the new task.

Congruency of course objectives and assessment demands

The results of test performance outcomes showed that a surface approach was associated with high marks. On analysis of the test questions by the author and another staff member who is familiar with the philosophy and content of the subject IPS, it was found that most of these test questions were indeed assessing the students' recall of the knowledge taught in lectures. Hence students who had chosen the appropriate surface approach did well.

The setting of low level questions is contradictory to the objectives of the subject IPS, which emphasises a deep integrative learning. Boud (1990), Crooks (1988), and Synder (1971) have warned against this possible incongruence between the espoused high academic objectives and the actual assessment requirements-in-use. As students are sensitive to this hidden curriculum embedded in the assessment requirements, they will adapt and tune their learning according to the perceived demands.

Hence to facilitate the achievement of espoused (high level) course objectives, academics should be careful in the setting and implementing of objectives-in-use. Apart from employing appropriate teaching methods, another way to help ensure the consistency of the two would be to have a moderating system of course assessments so that any assessment activity set would be monitored against the espoused course objectives to ensure that what is being assessed is what should be assessed.

Coverage versus depth
One of the questions facing the teaching staff of the Physiotherapy Section, and in fact many tertiary teachers, is the dilemma whether assessment should aim at maximum coverage of syllabus (for "security" reasons) or at depth of understanding. By nature of the assessment method, tests will be able to cover a depth of understanding. By nature of the assessment method, tests will be able to cover a large part of the syllabus, but may appear to encourage a surface approach. The employment of any particular mode of assessment may seem to depend on the objective and content of the assessment syllabus. The question of the assessment dilemma may be more appropriately concerned with the design of a suitable assessment system rather than one assessment method versus the other.

As the results of the present study demonstrate that, although assignment may be concerned just with one topic area, its potential in inducing deep preparation strategies may imply that this mode of assessment could be introduced to the students at an early stage in the course so as to facilitate the development of deep preparation strategies. The students can then apply these to subsequent assessment by tests. The administration of assignment before test is also supported by the high percentage of students involved in collaborative learning when preparing for the assignment who developed high level preparation strategies. This timing of administration of different modes of assessment can be one way of arriving at a better designed assessment system.

Conclusions

The present study on Hong Kong tertiary students attending a professional education programme demonstrates the effects of different modes of assessment on student learning. At one end of the spectrum of research on student learning, theorists such as Riding and Cheema (1991) have emphasised the importance of trait-like and habitual learning styles in determining an approach to learning tasks. At the other end, straight phenomenography is based entirely on student perceptions of the context (see for example Marton and Säljö, 1976). The results of the present study do not only support the two ends of the spectrum, they also go beyond to indicate an interactive model between the presage personological and contextual influences on learning. For the test, the linear effects of presage factors (surface orientation and quantitative perceptions of task demands) on test performance is true up to a certain point. However, deep-oriented individuals orchestrated a deep-memorisation strategy which demonstrated the interaction between the study orientation and perception of the context. For the assignment, the path analysis indicated that presage orientation to learning better predicted the assignment outcomes than the process APSs themselves. Perception of task demands was overwhelming deep, yet many students did not adopt deep strategies, presumably because they did not have the requisite procedural knowledge of strategy to bring to the situation. In this circumstance, these students devised a coping strategy of spontaneous collaborative learning, and formed discussion groups. All these findings illustrate the interaction between the personal orientation and perceptions of task demands and their effects on learning. Given this interactive effect, and in view of the "stable" personal orientation to learning, effort should be put into curriculum design, and especially with teaching and assessment methods, so that a constructive and desirable learning context is created to facilitate a positive study orchestration.

References

Biggs, J. B. (1987a). *Student Approaches to Learning and Studying* Melbourne: Australian Council for educational Research.

Biggs, J. B. (1987b). *Study Process Questionnaire Manual* Melbourne: Australian Council for Education Research.

Biggs, J. B. (1992). *Education Papers 14: Why and How Do Hong Kong Students Learn? Using the Learning and Study Process Questionnaires* Faculty of Education, University of Hong Kong.

Biggs, J. B. (in press). From theory to practice: a cognitive system model *Higher Education Research and Development*.

Biggs, J. B. and Collis, K. F. (1982). *Evaluating the Quality of Learning: the SOLO Taxonomy* New York: Academic Press.

Boud, D. (1990). Assessment and the promotion of academic values *Studies in Higher Education*, 15, 1, 101–111.

Clanchy, J. (1985). Improving student learning *HERDSA News*, 7, 3, 3–5.

Crooks, T. J. (1988). The impact of classroom evaluation practices on students *Review of Educational Research* , 58, 4, 438–481.

Entwistle, N. J. (1988). Motivational factors in students: approaches to learning. In R.R. Schmeck (ed.), *Learning Strategies and Learning Styles* New York and London: Plenum Press.

Entwistle, N. J and Marton, F. (1984). Changing conceptions of learning and research. In F. Marton, D. Hounsell and N. Entwistle (eds), *The Experience of Learning*. Edinburgh: Scottish Academic Press.

Entwistle, N. J and Ramsden, P. (1983). *Understanding Student Learning* London: Croom Helm.

Harris, D. and Bell, C. (1986). *Evaluating and Assessing for Learning* London: Kogan Page.

Hau, K. T. and Salili, F. (1991). Structure and semantic differential placement of specific causes: academic causal attributions by Chinese students in Hong Kong *International Journal of Psychology*, 26, 2, 175–193.

Heywood, J. (1989). *Assessment in Higher Education* New York: John Wiley & Sons.

Marton, F. and Säljö, R. (1976). On qualitative differences inlearning, I: Outcome and process *British Journal of Educational Psychology*, 46, 4–11.

Meyer, J. H. F. and Muller, M. W. (1990). Evaluating the quality of student learning, I: An unfolding analysis of the association between perceptions of the learning context and approaches to studying at an individual level. *Studies in Higher Education*, 15, 2, 131–154.

Meyer, J. H. F. Parsons, P. and Dunne, T. T. (1990). Individual study orchestration and their association with outcome *Higher Education*, 20, 1, 67–89.

Miller, C. M. L. and Parlett, M. (1974). Up to the Mark. Guildford: SRHE.

Newble, D. I. and Jaeger, K. (1983). The effects of assessment and examinations on the learning of medical students *Medical Education*, 20, 162–175.

Physiotheraphy Section (1990). *Submission Document for the Bachelor of Science in Physiotheraphy, Part One: General Information*. Physiotherapy Section, Department of Rehabilitation Sciences, Hong Kong Polytechnic.

Ramsden, P. (1984). The context of learning. In F. Marton, D. J. Hounsell and N. J. Entwistle (eds), *The Experience of Learning* Edinburgh: Scottish Academic Press.

Ramsden, P. (1988). Context and strategy: situational influences of learning. In R. R. Schmeck (ed.), *Learning Strategies and Learning Styles* New York and London: Plenum Press.

Riding, R. and Cheema, I. (1991). Cognitive styles: an overview and integration *Educational Psychology*, 11, 193–215.

Snyder, B. R. (1971). *The Hidden Curriculum* Cambridge, MA: M. I. T. Press.

Tang, K. C. C. (in press). Spontaneous collaborative learning: a new dimension in student learning experience? *Higher Education Research and Development*.

Thomas, J. W. and Rohwer, W. D. Jr. (1986). Academic studying: the role of learning strategies *Educational Psychologist*, 21, 1–2, 19–41.

Marking Changes: Innovation in the Design and Assessment of a Post-Graduate Diploma in Youth and Community Work

Sue Bloxham and Mike Heathfield, St Martin's College, Lancaster

The research documented here is the first part of an action research programme which is attempting to incorporate some current ideas about promoting student learning into a one-year professional diploma in youth and community work. The innovation focusses on elements of course design which are considered to promote "deep" learning. However, design considerations also drew on tutors' working knowledge about the assessment-driven nature of most students - or at least the messages that students read into the assessment programmes for the different courses. In short, we were trying to integrate theory with our experience of practice and assessment seemed to be the key to this.

Theoretical Background

We are not going to repeat here the main areas of research on which we have drawn because they are a fundamental backdrop to the conference in general. Suffice it to say for the purpose of this paper that we have drawn on the notion of "deep learning" as a necessary condition of high quality outcomes (Ramsden, 1992).

The deep approach "focusses on underlying meaning rather than on literal aspects, and seeks integration between components and with other tasks" (Biggs, 1989, p. 26). It has become clear that we require further work in relation to what deep-learning approaches to our subject area (youth and community work) involve and that work is in hand as the second stage of this research project. However, this initial attempt to explore improved learning in Y & C training has rested on the generic ideas regarding depth of understanding as conceptualised in the SOLO taxonomy. On this basis, we have sought to provide the context for students to develop relational and extended abstract learning. That is learning which is integrated into a structure (relational) and then generalised to a new domain of knowedge or understanding (extended abstract)(Biggs, 1989).

For professional trainers in the human services perhaps, learning which is "extended abstract" is the point where students are able to relate and link concepts and ideas introduced through college-based learning (relational), but can also relate those ideas to professional practice; they can identify or suggest the implications for work in the field, and actually show the learning in their practice. So, for example, where supervision skills are concerned, a student who had achieved extended abstract would clearly understand the cycle of experiential learning and the theoretical basis behind the various skills and stages that might be incorporated into supervision. However, they would also be able to demonstrate this learning, firstly in formal supervision, but also in their ability to apply their learning in their response to a range of situations and activities as and when they arose.

Design for learning: creating appropriate teaching contexts
A student's approach to learning (Gibbs, 1992a) is clearly fundamental in how they encounter a given course and we have attempted to explore the approaches that students arrived with and any changes that took place during the year (see part 2 below). However, in planning the course units, we tried, at least, to design them so that they would foster deep learning (Biggs, 1989). In effect, the interplay between the approaches to learning that students arrived with and the learning context that we provided produced some interesting outcomes, particularly for students hot off the 2.1 trail:

> I was like a totally different person to what I was last year when it was the difference of getting a 2:1 or a 2:2 or something like that. But this year, straight pass or fail and 40%, it's hardly going to push you is it, I don't think. I haven't failed anything yet. (No. 6)

However, before considering these results, we shall outline the basis for our course design.

Biggs and Telfer (1987) showed in their review of relevant research that "teaching that gave evidence of deep learning contained in sharp form one or more of the following :

- an appropriate motivational context
- a high degree of learner activity
- interaction with others, both peers and teachers
- a well-structured knowledge base.

These, therefore, were our guiding principles in designing the course.

Making it happen in practice
Ramsden (1992) says, "We cannot train students to use deep approaches when the educational environment is giving them the message that surface ones are rewarded"(p. 64), and Boud (1989) points to the "number of notable studies over the years which have demonstrated that assessment methods and requirements probably have a greater influence on how and what students learn than any other single factor"(p. 35).

Anyone working in HE will know that, except for a very small minority, it is students' perception of the how the assessment works for any given course that affects the amount and type of work they do, and what they prioritise. For example, if attendance isn't assessed, then students will make very clear decisions about whether attendance at a given lecture will help them write the essay or pass the exam! In other words, assessment provides the strongest external motivation to work. What we wanted to do was to ensure that the assessment tasks themselves encouraged and developed a study culture dependent on learning of a relational and extended abstract nature. We wanted them to engage with the subject matter in an involved way; one that would require them to understand and link ideas, relate them to their own experience and apply them to their professional work. Given our working knowledge of students' fixed relationship with assessment, it became apparent that we should reconceptualise assessment not as the process by which we check the quality of learning, but as the tool which drives that learning. This has happened in a hidden form for many years as staff have recognised that most students only do the required reading (and learning?) when it is needed for an essay or exam.

Therefore we reassessed what our learning outcomes were for each unit that we were redesigning and planned assessment tasks that would require the students to undergo a range of learning activities. In other words, the design of the assessment drove the pedagogy rather than the alternative, and usual, order. Two examples of these tasks provided the focus for our research and are described here.

a)The matrix
We wanted students to explore values and philosophies that underpin different forms of youth and community work practice through locating them in the history of the work and related social changes, such as industrialisation, the emergence of adolescence as a concept, and female emancipation. We wished them to use that understanding of history and philosophy to consider current practice, including a development of their own professional ideology and values. In the past, such a curriculum might have been covered by a short course on the history of youth services, alongside a parallel course (from someone in the history department) on social history, alongside a course on principles and practice of Y & C work where students would explore their previous practice and the value-base of different organisations.

Our solution to meeting these learning outcomes in a way that provided students with a clear understanding of underlying issues and the means to apply it to the professional organisations they entered was to design an assessment task (the matrix) which would drive their information collecting and learning. We let the students' engagement with the learning task steer their activity, although we supported this through placing them in groups, providing some introductory reading material and a bibliography, and offering weekly tutor support sessions including the occasional presentation of certain key ideas.

The matrix required students to work in small groups to complete a blank grid which asked them to research and then present evidence around four specific categories of youth and community work provision: statutory, voluntary, minorities and provision for women. They were asked to sort their evidence with reference to four specific categories: brief history, analysis of underpinning ideology, relationship to contemporaneous social changes and current practice and ideology. Additionally, each student had to provide an individual and personal analysis of all the data collected by the group research.

Assessment of the task required groups to submit one completed matrix - in any format they felt appropriate. Additionally each student had to submit a short analysis of the whole content of their group matrix. The group mark and individual marks were then averaged.

b) Recruitment and selection simulation
This assessment task was part of the management unit of the diploma course. The intended learning outcomes included an understanding of theories of human motivation at work, job design and enrichment, and recruitment and selections processes, particularly equal opportunities in recruitment. They also included the development of skills in job design and basic selection techniques.

This task involved small groups of students completing a two-and-a-half-day simulation, moving from an introduction to theories of human motivation and job design to the application of these ideas in the analysis of a real job, and then conducting a recruitment and selection procedure for the job, including interviewing, selecting and debriefing applicants. The latter half included the exploration and incorporation of equal opportunity practices into recruitment and selections. The simulation was intense in as much as the groups were expected to work together throughout the two and a half days, including some individual preparation in the evenings where necessary.

Assessment of the task required the groups to submit their job description, person specification, job advertisement, a short description of their interview process and evaluation forms completed by their interviewees.

These two tasks are examples of our attempt to create an assessment-driven course which related to the principles for course design listed above. The following sections indicate how we incorporated the theory into the task design.

Motivational context
Interest and intrinsic motivation in a subject matter are effected by a student's previous learning experience, but that doesn't mean that we cannot influence his or her future approaches (Ramsden), and it is in the area of assessment where the greatest influence can be exerted. Consequently our course design was based on the notion that we must build in motivation and, as mentioned above,

assessment seemed to be the most effective way to do this. Ramsden notes that assessment is traditionally seen as a way of motivating students: "The threat of failure in a competitive situation is required to stimulate them to attend lectures and practicals and to do at least some private study" (p. 183). However, he also points out that in students' eyes the assessment defines the actual curriculum - it points up what is valued, what counts, and therefore its motivational element applies only to that part of the curriculum which appears in the assessment. If a course is assessed by three questions on an exam paper, students will only be motivated to learn about, at most, five topics on the 20-topic course!

Therefore we attempted to include all the learning outcomes for the course in the assessment and make absolutely clear to students what was demanded and why; that is, the criteria on which their work would be judged. For example, we placed no value on memorisation - frequently demanded by other assessment methods – but we did require them to "demonstrate an understanding" of , for example "how concurrent social changes were reflected in the development of youth services for young women".

We also attempted to build in motivation, not only through the assessment demands, but also through group working and the use of non-prescriptive formats for the submission of assignments. Group working will be discussed more thoroughly below, but our previous experience suggested that students find working with others intrinsically satisfying, with the group often making demands of each other that encourage weaker students to work harder than normal. Likewise, many students have skills and interests in a range of artistic, photographic, video and other communication media which they enjoy using, and therefore offering a fairly free license to demonstrate their learning was intended as a further means to improving the motivational context. Ramsden's argument that choice and independence in study also foster favourable evaluations by students was seen as further enhancing the motivation in our learning design.

Learner activity
The research indicates that "independence, control and active engagement" are related to high-quality learning in so far as they allow students to choose ways to engage with the subject matter that suit them (Ramsden). Higgs (1988, in Boud) lists the active participation of learners in the learning process as a key condition of adult learning.

Gibbs (1992b) argues that the link between activity and improved learning lies in the opportunity it provides for students to make greater links with past learning and between new concepts. However, he suggests that activity alone is insufficient and it must be carefully planned to provide appropriate opportunities.

There are obviously many approaches to the active involvement of students, and one is the use of "problem solving" tasks (Frazer 1992, in Barnett). In effect, our designs drew on this notion of presenting the students with various problems to solve rather than content to be assimilated.

Thus, our course design handed over considerable responsibility for learning to the student. Lectures that we might have given in previous years were reproduced on paper, along with starter readings and specific student guidelines. Elements which had a major skill component, such as supervision, group work and one-to-one skills, were still "taught" in practical workshops with tutor guidance and feedback, but knowledge-based elements were attended to via group-based learning assignments. It was impossible for students to be anything but active in the resolution of such problems. There were virtually no lectures and the role of tutors was reconceived largely as engineers of the learning experience through carefully planned tasks for group and independent learning.

The matrix and R & S simulation were examples of these tasks. Other examples included making a bid for funding for a new project based on a choice of community scenarios. The competitive tender specification included very detailed information regarding criteria for selecting successful bids and was designed to cover a range of relevant material learning outcomes, including planning, evaluation, needs analysis, objective setting, etc. A further task involved groups in preparing cases for a "court of inquiry" to examine case-studies in professional ethics and professional boundaries. These examples indicate our clear intention to involve the students thoroughly in the learning process with clear guidance and support but no right answers!

Interaction with others, both peers and teachers

Frazer (1992) argues that students can learn more from each other than from their teachers for various reasons:

Students see their teachers also as assessors and so are reluctant to display their ignorance by making mistakes or asking elementary questions in front of the teacher. A student having difficulty with a concept can be helped by someone who has just overcome the difficulty and therefore is sympathetic and understanding of the causes of the blockage or misconception. There is a competitive element within a peer group which can motivate learning. Peer groups can work at their own pace.(p. 61-62)

Biggs (1989) also stresses the importance of interaction with teachers or responsive experts, something which is harder to provide under current funding arrangements in HE!

Therefore our designs largely involved students working in groups of different sizes, from pairs upwards. The nature of tasks ranged from those which were individually assessed but involved practising on peers with a third party as critical observer (for example, supervision skills) to group problems which generated a joint assessment (for example, recruitment and selection simulation). In-between group tasks involved a mixture of individual work and group work where, for example, members of the group would be expected to apportion out tasks, complete the research individually and then share their learning with the other group members.

Our plan to develop this high level of student interaction and autonomy did not include significant interaction with tutors, and this oversight will be discussed below.

A well-structured knowledge base

Gibbs's (1992b) argument for a well-structured knowledge base lies in the view that, "Without existing concepts, it is impossible to make sense of new concepts". Biggs (1989) discusses the difficulties students have if they face a series of piecemeal topics. There is a clear notion of frames of reference here with the development of deep learning, characterised by understanding, fostered by students being able to link ideas, information and concepts together. These concepts will be from both their past learning and their concurrent education.

Our application of this condition to our design was to try and design problems that were interdisciplinary, that linked constantly to professional practice, that encouraged students to draw on their previous experience in education and in practice, that made connections across the other units on the course, and that avoided dealing with ideas in isolation. In some respects, the other features of our design such as student activity and interaction militated against the fragmentation of the syllabus. In an attempt to offer students substantive problems to deal with, we automatically drew together related areas of understanding.

However, both the matrix and the R & S simulation are examples of tasks where we deliberately tried to organise the students' experience so that it illuminated a clearly structured curriculum.

The Reality and the Research

This, then, was our strategy. We completely replanned half the units in this one-year professional course in order to implement the principles of course design outlined above. So, what were the outcomes?

Over the course of the year, and particularly in the last term, we collected a range of data in order to evaluate the impact of our innovation. This research involved quantitative and qualitative methods. The qualitative methods are the ones we focus on here.

The qualitative approach to the research involved an independent interviewer carrying out semi-structured interviews with 12 (63%) of the students on the course. The interview schedule focussed on the matrix task and the recruitment and selection simulation in order to collect data about specific experiences rather than generalised accounts. Furthermore, they were both tasks from the first term, so students were able to discuss them with the benefit of hindsight and in relation to their subsequent experience on a 12-week professional placement. The interviews concentrated mostly on the process of the tasks (motivation, interaction, activity and structure) but they also sought examples of learning that students had retained in order to explore the depth of learning (as measured by means of the taxonomy) .

The discussion of the results is also divided in this way, with part 1 covering students experience of the process and part 2 exploring the learning outcomes in terms of both the curriculum of the course and changes in the participants' approaches to learning.

Part 1: Evaluating the Process
This evaluation of the process is derived from students' accounts of their experiences as disclosed in the interviews.

Motivation
What was fascinating was that fewer than half the students expressed internal motivation towards the work, i.e., that they were intrinsically interested in finding out and self-development. This was despite the fact that this was an intensive one-year professional course drawing only on students who had achieved substantial previous experience in the field of work, often on a voluntary basis. Only five out of the 12 expressed views such as:

> It was the first time I'd started back in. I was into education and I was very pleased to have got on the course. It was a course I wanted to do. So that was my initial motivation. (No. P2)

Students with such intrinsic motivation also stressed the wish to cover the work well:

> I'm not sort of trying to be wonderful or anything but I'm conscious that a lot of people just said: Oh let's get the bloody thing done. I remember thinking this is great. I really want to learn this. (No. 10)

However, motivation was much more likely to be attributed to external factors, and these were usually integral to the course design. For example, eight students indicated that their motivation emerged from aspects of the task, including the type of activity, its "newness", and its experiential nature:

> The exercise was nice because I like doing experiential things. It was like a real exercise, it was the real thing. And that gave me a little bit of a kick. And the people were sharing this excitement with me. So we were all highly motivated because it was designed . . . and we typed some of these things up on the computer so it looked like the real thing. It looked like a real advert in the Guardian which we photocopied in, and everybody could see - yes, this looks good, this is brilliant, and we were getting charged from what we'd done. (No. 5)

One particular motivating feature of the matrix task was the freedom to demonstrate their learning through a choice of media:

> We didn't want to hand in A4 paper because there's nothing more boring, and I didn't want to write A4 paper . . . something where you're more . . . it's up to you how you present it, I'd say. There isn't a set style of presentation. I prefer that - which there wasn't a set style of presentation with that, whereas an essay, it's set. (No. 7)

However, one student attributed lack of motivation to the design of the matrix task:

> I think the enormity of it was for me demotivating, because it seemed like an enormous thing for me. I felt like [another group] knew what they were doing, I was the only one who didn't really. That was a bit demotivating. I suppose time slipping away was a motivating factor. (No 4)

The notion of motivation emerging from 'excitement' with the experience is reflected in the interviews of half the students:

> You're speaking to someone who got a buzz out of the whole process. (No. 2)

> I'd be really pumped up when I got home at tea-time that night, pumped up because of what had happened through the day. I mean motivation not necessarily as a positive motivation but motivation. Emotional motivation and engagement was very very high. (No. 10)

For a number of students this buzz was clearly a feature of working in a group:

> As I say, we worked very well as a group so the motivation came from the energy within the group. (No. P2)

> I was motivated because I liked the group, and we had a good laugh while we were doing it, and everybody worked really hard, no hassles. (No. 8)

But the group-based nature of the course design was also a motivator for other reasons, particularly the enjoyment of working well with others:

> Being in a group definitely, definitely, because it was something which gelled really well and everyone . . . I don't know . . . we just really wanted to do it and do it well and it sort of happened. It was very good. (No. P1)

> I think that everybody . . . there was team spirit. Everybody wanted to get it done. Well, not . . . we wanted to get it done, but it wasn't let's hurry up, let's get it done. It was a thing, we've got to do it, so, come on, let's do it the best we can, and it was a team effort then that got it done. (No. 7)

In fact three-quarters of the students attributed motivation to their group in one form or another and an additional two students saw the group as a source of motivation, but from a more negative stance such as peer group pressure, to do the work.Motivation came from:

> Probably the fact that we were in a group, because there was a responsibility to that group. Maybe if it had just been me on my own, it would have been longer and longer. (No. 4)

> I feel committed to the group, which is probably quite important. Because I know the girls have put in effort, I would take time to read. (No. 2)

Consequently, the vast majority of students, while not necessarily commencing these tasks with a strong desire to learn, achieved a high level of motivation through the learning design. The involvement in new activities with groups of people were a source of interest and enjoyment.

Nevertheless a minority of students continued to struggle with motivation and were limited to an approach based on instrumentalism. In other words, the source of motivation was independent from active involvement in the task and linked to meeting deadlines and passing the course:

> My motivation has been pretty low because there's no exams at the end of the course and it's a straight pass or fail. And with 40% (pass mark) you have to try pretty hard to fail I think. (No. 6)

Such an excessively "achieving approach" (Biggs, 1989) was expressed by only one student but five students commented on the difficulty of maintaining motivation and indicated that they tended to cover the work in a hurried, last-minute way because the deadline was too distant in the early stages.

Interestingly, some students found motivation no difficulty with the condensed (and fairly directed) R & S simulation but struggled with the autonomy offered by the matrix.

Consequently, our efforts to build motivation into the course structure through use of the assessment procedure appeared justified in the majority of cases, but we need to examine ways to improve the motivation of some students, particularly those who have difficulty structuring their own work without some clear and short-term boundaries. Indeed, the interviews themselves produced a number of helpful suggestions from the students about ways in which group progress could be monitored to help them.

> I think signposts . . . today it must be presented in short form and then it must be presented in its whole form later on. I think that kind of thing is helpful. And if it's well structured it can be an awful lot more use, I think. Not to say here's the whole product, but here's where we're going and why, why we're going. Because a lot of people just said: oh my goodness we must get the matrix done, you know, and it didn't happen. (No. 10)

Gibbs (1992c) discusses the balance between "independence" and "control" strategies in motivating students, and it appears to be the case that we either have to increase the intrinsic motivation by building on aspects of our design that were very successful, or we have to reduce the autonomy somewhat to provide more regular extrinsic motivation for students who need it. Students' approaches to learning may be an important factor in this development and we are probably expecting too much from those hailing from a very achieving prior educational experience.

Learner activity
The discussion above indicates that our design made it difficult for students to avoid activity and still complete the various units of study. There was little opportunity for students to be passive recipients of tutor-prepared material. Therefore it is not surprising that this strategy in the design was borne out in practice. In effect, students described a wide range of independent learning activity, including the traditional use of library resources:

> Well I asked people - my contacts in the other voluntary services, annual reports - have you got a history on this service? Contacting agencies, the library here. (No. 5)

It is interesting that, despite the emphasis on group working, many students (five) saw their individual research as the main source of their learning

> A lot of personal reading that I was doing, that was important to me to

clarify in my own mind what my understanding of the area of work we were undertaking. I think that's probably the main thing. (No..2)

And in the best cases, the nature of the activity was certainly characterised by "Independence, control and active engagement":

> Well, I had the papers. You just look under . . . what is it, Home Office? You look under author, you go to the computers, go into the banks and then you ask around. You find out more stuff. It's the process of going through the key words, the buzz words. That's right, that's what I did - went to the....had a bibliography for the Government Acts that Sue had given me that said Milson. So I looked up Milson and you see Fred Milson, community worker in the 70s . . . see what he had written. (No. 10)

> The personal reading was more intense [than sharing in group] I think, because it was also researching. It was like following a detective trail. You'd get a bit of information here, and have to follow up some report here. So you began to piece together your sector in your mind, fill the gaps.(No. 5)

However, there was a minority that limited their research activity to material provided by or suggested by the tutors:

> I didn't do much reading on . . . well, I didn't really do any reading for my section, but we did have handouts and stuff in our files and the Butters thing. We had, you know, these sort of theory books that you could go to. I don't think we did read that much to be honest - no books in the library as such. (No. 1)

> He gave us this model which was in incredibly complicated English - this Butters model - and I really couldn't stand it because it was written in really weird complex language . . . Then Mike sort of explained it a little bit and I went away and I had a couple of books that have it in English. And I actually understood it a lot better when I'd finished . . . My understanding was much better when I'd read around it a little bit in English rather than complex language. (No. 9)

or were able to draw on previous study:

> It wasn't really too bad for me, that wasn't, because coming from a sociology/psychology background, I just looked at a load of past notes, 3rd-year and 2nd-year notes. (No. 6)

And two students (including the highly instrumental student mentioned under motivation above) revealed considerable difficulty with the notion of student directed activity:

> As far as the exercise . . . as it goes, it was a non-starter, as far as I'm concerned. There is no way in my eyes that you're going to get students to do that sort of thing. It is just expecting too much to keep on meeting once a week . . . you know, people just . . . you do a bit at the start and it just all gets packed in at the end. (No. 6)

> I would have preferred someone to say: this is the right way and this is the wrong way, but of course that's not how this course works. But because when I was on sort of dodgy ground, you'd rather somebody said well there's a right way of doing it and there's a wrong way of doing it. When you're a bit more skilled in an area, I think you can probably accept somebody saying there are no right or wrong answers. (No. 4)

However, such concerns were rarely expressed in the interviews and, in addition to library research, students reported visiting youth and community work resource centres, contacting various agencies for information, talking to professionals, other tutors and students on other courses, and reading each other's work. Interaction with other members of their groups was mentioned by the vast majority of the students as a key element of their activity. They also reported considerable activity devising ways to demonstrate their learning, and this included making board games, collages, training exercises, posters, and a newsletter as well as the more traditional prose report.

The link between active engagement and learning is thoroughly supported by our student interviews. The greater the individual's participation in the process, the more likely they were to feel that they had developed their understanding. Participation was frequently linked to motivation, and therefore the importance of engendering that characteristic in learners is further strengthened by this research.

The challenge is not so much to devise interesting ways to facilitate student, activity for which there are an increasingly useful number of sources, but to engage *all* the students in that activity. One solution is to increase the link between the activity and the assessment, and not only assess the results of the activity, but also reward the activity itself to some extent. An approach to this is to assess an individual's contribution to the group process. This is seen as a means to provide greater support to groups as a key motivator of students, and the nature of this support will be discussed in the next section on interaction.

Interaction with others, both peers and teachers
In designing our interviews with the students, we were concerned to discover their perceptions of working in groups: how it had helped and hindered them,

what were the benefits and what were the disadvantages of group-based learning. The two exercises we focussed on made very different demands on the groups. One (matrix) required the group to programme its own work over a ten-week period, whereas the other (R & S simulation) involved the groups in an intensive two-and-a-half-day experience with little room for manoeuvre, at least regarding decisions about when they would meet or how long they could spend on different elements of the exercise.

The interviews produced some fairly emotive responses to the questions regarding groups, both negative and positive. However, every student interviewed described the way in which working with others had contributed to their learning. This happened through the sharing of information:

> So we all sort of brought along all our material and went back and fed through what we felt was the important things. So we shared all the information and then from that we formed our own opinion. (No. P1)

> We focussed on our reading then coming together and discussing what were the issues here for each of the sections. So it was really pooling our resources. (No. 5)

> That was my greatest learning because then I had to share what we'd put in our boxes and what we thought the key boxes were. So I knew what other people had put in the other two boxes. They'd pulled out the important bits. That was the biggest part. (No. 7)

It also involved the opportunity to negotiate and clarify ideas:

> I mean, on the sharing experience, it's like . . . I couldn't have done it on my own. I didn't have enough information to do it on my own. I think other than sharing experiences, I think it's bouncing the ideas around. You know, everyone's coming up with ideas and discussing things. It's leading you down different avenues and you're sort of exploring different ways of thinking, your views on things . . . And you tend to - you sort of take that on board. (No. 9)

And take into account different approaches to the material:

> Reading the others' essays [helped my learning] because they have a different perspective. We all had a different perspective . . . We got a really good mark for that and I'm sure it's because we actually pooled our knowledge and that sort of thing. (No. 1)

Another strong theme emerging from the interview material is the opportunity that group work gave to build on others' previous experience and learning:

It was actually because people in that group had got different skills, and it was really interesting to listen to those talking about the skills. (No. 3)

There was one person who was more familiar with social theory than I was, so that was really useful. (No. 4)

Well to share, pool ideas. I learnt from other people who'd been in the job so they could contribute things I couldn't contribute. (No. 7)

The quotations above all refer to the contribution of group work to students learning outcomes, but many other responses indicated the benefits of groups in relation to the process of learning, the fun, the motivation, the team work, and the support received and given.

One of the people in our group is dyslexic so we had to work with him on actually writing his out, spell-checking. (No. 8)

That particular exercise - recruitment and selection - because I was interested and because I was motivated and I liked being in the group, I probably learnt the most of any of the other exercises. You know, this pulling together in the same direction, you weren't too concerned with conflicts because there weren't really any. (No. 5)

And so everyone was busy writing up their information and everyone was being creative, and I was enjoying that. It was good. So that was the major thing because we were really working as a group. We had been very isolated before collecting information. (No. 1)

Overall, therefore, the research indicated a very strong positive reaction to working in groups for the benefits to both learning outcomes and the learning process. This was slightly surprising to the course tutors, who expected a more negative reaction to the frustrations of trying to coordinate with others, deal with difficult and dominating personalities and cope with the diversions of chatting, procrastinating and poor attendance by group members. References to the problems of working in groups were far fewer than positive reports, but about three-quarters of the students did make comments regarding difficulties. These included feeling frustrated and let down:

It probably wasn't worth some of the frustrations I had over it which were . . . but it's like I said I'm a bit task orientated and I tend to get a bit het up about these sort of things. (No. 1)

Pulling our hair out, pulling our hair out by the end of it. And the other two were pulling their hair out as well. It was dreadful. It was really, really dreadful. It was the most stressful thing I've been through on the whole course. Especially when one person at the end of it starts crying, you know, and starts saying that it's this problem that they have. (No. 4)

Although it's a nice idea that people will manage their time and come in when they're meant to . . . to save all that hassle and people nagging people to come in, I think they should have like the sessions allotted or days allotted when people come in. (No. 9)

They also expressed concern that groups were only successful when the participants worked well together, and a couple of students felt that their learning had been limited by the poor contribution of others in their group:

It means that your learning for a whole big section of the matrix is dependent on someone else's research . . . I remember thinking: you know, this could be so much broader and so much better. So I think they need more accountability in that exercise to each other - what are you doing about my learning here? (No. 10)

In some cases, it appears that groups were reduced to a forum for the delegation of work rather than a positive source of learning:

It was like, we've got to get it done, go away and do a bit, we'll trust you, we'll trust you to do it because you obviously know a bit about it, which wasn't the point of the exercise at all. Normally . . . share all the information, you get a general grounding in these areas, but we didn't really do that. I'm not going to pretend we did. I certainly didn't anyway. (No. 9)

On balance, students appeared to gain significantly from working in groups, but there are clearly some unresolved problems in this approach to increased student interaction. The student responses to the highly structured R & S simulation were more consistently positive than for the matrix with its greater autonomy, although the latter produced the greater independent learning activity for the majority of the students. In dealing with the problems of group working, it would be essential not to lose the benefits of learning autonomy offered by open-ended problem-solving tasks like the matrix. One clear response, then, is to recognise the need for clearer directions for students who flounder when confronted with self-organisation. In order to maintain the advantages of autonomy for students, the direction needs to be built into the process rather than the content.

Higgs, (1989) makes the point that some learners are more ready than others for independent learning and that their past experiences, often of dependent learning, present problems for them when they are required to act autonomously. She suggests that learning should be planned in such a way that students gradually develop greater ability to learn autonomously and this is helped by the experience of enjoyable and successful learning activities. She says, "Another point of discussion was the need to monitor the learner's ability and progress as a self-directed learner during the course in order to provide feedback, encouragement and guidance as needed" (p. 45).

One argument about this course may be that it was Gibbs's interaction with teachers that was insufficient or not directed at the real probems. The need to monitor, review and support the interlinked characteristics of motivation, activity and interaction are indicated in order to improve the experience of those students less ready for independent learning – that is, to improve the balance between independence and control. This control could be in the form of group learning contracts, timetabled group meeting times, tutor-led review of group process, breaking the assignment up into smaller, more manageable tasks in the early stages, intermediate deadlines, and peer assessment of individuals' contributions to their groups. Higgs emphasises the "value of the learners reflecting on, and verbalising about, their own learning behaviour and 'thinking out loud' about their ideas as they deepened their understanding of the topic area" (p. 48) and, on this basis, we must direct our attention to monitoring and supporting the process for students. This research seems to indicate that, to a large extent, if you get the process right, the content will take care of itself.

A well-structured knowledge base
Our research was also concerned to test whether students perceived their studies to be linked together in a clear structure which built on both previous and concurrent learning.

The vast majority of students reported that they were able to see clear links between the different elements within each task.

> I would be the only one who had been working on that particular subject. But it all came together fairly well in the end. We had a fairly good idea of where the links were. (No. 4)

> Like where's this coming from - it wasn't like that. It wasn't hung out on a limb. It was quite integrated. (No. 7)

> I think it brought out diversity of the youth service and all the gender stuff and that. You were looking at so many different things - you know, the Sports Council and homelessness and things - and I think the way we had to look at it was quite well structured. It was sort of history and . . . history and philosophy, that sort of thing. (No. P1)

Indeed, all students said that they could see the links between different elements by the end, even if it required a period of reflection. A number of students also made unprompted references to how their work on these tasks had linked with other units of their course:

> The whole collage, the whole picture of work that's being undertaken within the country by both statutory and voluntary agencies, that made me aware of that. Not specifically the matrix. It was a means to an end doing the project at the end of the day. You know, it was: you've got to do it, so we're going to do it and do it best we can. (No. 2)

> One thing that was quite convenient about being at the end of term, handing it in, was that we'd done things in other courses that linked up really well, and so we could use that information, which was quite convenient. (No. 9)

Furthermore, several students made reference to the links between the tasks and their previous learning and experience.

> A couple of us in the group have had a bit to do with like recruitment and selection. I think we based what we did on those experiences really. Taking the best out of each bit and trying to see where those personal experiences had pitfalls and trying to improve on them. (No. 4)

It is not surprising that students found a clear structure in the content of each task, as they had been very consciously designed in this way. It is a greater achievement that they were able to link it to past learning and learning across other units. However, even within the tasks, some students continued to express difficulties with the lack of explicit structure:

> Well you could [make links], but you didn't know whether you were doing the right thing. I mean you start off with the history and then I can't remember what was next. But we did the history of it first - of each provision. We just took a line. And then there was something else and you didn't know . . . if you got the history wrong, you didn't know whether you were doing the next bit right did you? You know what I'm trying to say? You know, you needed some yardstick to keep going whether you were doing the right thing. (No. 6)

It is interesting to note that students' perceptions about lack of structure are as much concerns about getting the right answers, the right links, than they are about the overall coherence of their study. It is not surprising that the same students who struggled with independent learning also appeared to lack confidence in their ability to make links in their work without being directed to them by a tutor. Clearly the need for confirmation of their work and reassurance in the validity of their findings was missing for these students.

> Interviewer: Did you feel you got the whole picture?

> Student: No because you only concentrate on . . . like I did women so I looked at the Girls Brigade. So I only saw that. You couldn't have got the whole picture because you could have gone on forever and ever and ever.

> Int: It's such a big task?

> Student: Yes and there was no word limits on it. So . . . I don't know...could you have done 300 words and passed it? I don't know. You didn't know in how much depth does this have to be in.

> Int: So you would have really welcomed more guidelines?

> Student: Oh yes. You could write a whole dissertation on provision for young women, but what did they want? (No. 7)

This section analysing the student's perception of the knowledge base that they were tackling tends to complement the earlier discussion in illuminating our failure to take into account students' readiness for this form of study. It is as though the learning design was very able to provide the right conditions for deep learning (motivational context, activity, interaction, well-structured knowledge base) but only if the students were able to take advantage of it. This research indicates that approximately a quarter of the respondents' approach to learning prevented them from benefiting fully. Our task now is to take the results from this experience and try to devise ways to change students' approach to learning early in the programme. Our next programme will therefore incorporate the various suggested changes to process that have been mentioned in the foregoing sections.

However, this first part has concentrated only on meeting the suggested conditions for deep learning. The second test of our design is to look at the actual outcomes of the process, particularly for that majority of students who were motivated, highly active, fully participating members of groups. What did they learn and how can we measure the quality of this learning? Were there any changes in the way in which they approached their learning tasks? Part 2 will explore these issues.

Part 2: Evaluating the Changes in Student Approaches to Learning and the Quality of Learning on Two Specific Exercises

The SOLO taxonomy (Biggs and Collis, 1982) was used to attempt to locate the level of student responses to specific cues given in interview about curriculum content. In this way we could attempt to measure the quality of the learning outcomes around our two chosen curriculum areas.

In the interview schedule we constructed a number of questions, both on the matrix and the recruitment and selection simulation exercise, that we felt contained "cues" to encourage respondents to talk about their understanding of issues relevant to the concept of oppression.

The purpose of the matrix exercise was for students to have explored debates about the purpose of youth and community work and the values that underpin it and considered how different approaches to youth and community work are given expression in curriculum practice. Through this process it was intended that the students firstly identify and develop their own personal philosophy of work and, secondly, be able to relate this to both the current field of work and its historical development. If we were successful in this students would be able to integrate all these various strands and locate them within their own professional practice.

The purpose of the recruitment and selection simulation was to understand theories of human motivation, job design and recruitment and to practise these with particular reference to equality of opportunity. A crucial measure of quality for this exercise was how the learning related to real professional contexts.

Learning outcomes measured by the SOLO taxonomy
Data gained from interviews was used to attempt to measure at what level students were operating when given specific cues about their understanding of the curriculum content areas identified previously for both the matrix and recruitment and selection exercises. Clearly students did not enter the course as empty vessels and therefore learning outcomes identified may be a summation of various influences. However, the questions attempted to distinguish outcomes accertained from the course, or the interplay of course activity with previous experience and understanding.

Responses were measured against the intended objectives of the exercises in the light of the five levels of the taxonomy. As stated at the outset of this paper, our intention was to engineer learning experiences that encouraged students to operate at relational or extended abstract levels. The previously outlined generic code of the concept of oppression was used here to attempt to measure the quality of outcomes. Responses related to this generic Code were intended to be elicited during the questions relating to equal opportunities in the recruitment and selection simulation. In a number of cases interview respondents also provided data that could be measured in this way during responses given about their understanding of the content areas of the matrix exercise.

Although classifying responses in this way can be questionable on grounds of reliability, we tried to minimise this problem in our content analysis by two researchers independently and separately analysing the data before conferring. They each classified the responses, seeking examples of multi-structural, relational and extended abstract thinking. In classifying responses, students' ability to deduce and generalise beyond the given experience was crucial in allocation to the extended abstract category. At the highest level we would be expecting students to integrate their knowledge and understanding and make it their own – that is, develop a fully integrated professional identity.

This content analysis indicated that all the sample were operating at least at a multi-structural level, with five at a relational level and six at the extended abstract level. It would be fair to say that a large number of those operating at the relational level may also have been offering responses that could be classified as extended abstract, but the interview data here is not as clear-cut as in the six most obvious cases. The following examples show the level of understanding gained from students who undertook the matrix exercise successfully. It is important to remember that these students ostensibly followed a group and independent study programme to acquire their knowledge and understanding of this curriculum. The following examples show how students achieved the objectives of the exercise by identifying a personal philosophy and value-base derived from an analysis of youth and community work practice both now and in the past.

> I've got a feeling of where I now sit in there which is my personal philosophy. Where I'm most comfortable. So I think I take that away. That was part of the matrix . . . I would say I sit . . . I wouldn't be extreme as like a radical paradigm, whatever they call it. I'd sit somewhere like social reform stage of it. I think things certainly need to be changed. It's no good just like fixing things up. I think things actually need to be changed, but I'd say it's more of an evolutionary process than a revolutionary process. (No. 9)

> I've never been motivated towards history and things that happened even in this century. So it's given me a knowledge of what's happened. But then the analytical part - why did these things happen? And then you get the why and then you get some policies coming from this . . . some reports coming from this. For me, coming from the science and technology angle, I'm 100% more clued up.

This student concludes discussion of the matrix with:

[I'm] more political, because for many years I've been convincing myself that I'm not political and I'm not really interested in that sort of thing. But I think you have to be now. And not . . . the matrix has shown us because it's part of the overall course, so the matrix has been one step in. (No. 5)

The evidence here suggests that the exercise has provided a clear opportunity for students to relate historical knowledge and understanding into a professional identity for their future practice.

This desire to develop a methodology for measuring learning outcomes led us to focus in detail on the qualitative outcomes provided by the interview data from four students. In this section of the paper we concentrate on these four specific students. Two students were chosen because, by their own admission, they struggled with the nature of the exercises they were given (expressly the matrix) and this is borne out by many of their interview responses about process which have been covered in Part One. A further two students are used here because they responded well to the exercises, did not have motivational problems and were not daunted by the apparent non-prescriptive nature of the matrix exercise in particular.

In analysing responses relating to the matrix and the recruitment and selection exercises there are some key questions that help identify the knowledge base that the students have gained and their level of understanding about the curriculum areas the exercises were designed to cover. A number of these questions are also clearly useful in helping to locate the students' responses within the framework of the taxonomy. The questions you see outlined here were formulated to analyse the data and were not necessarily the questions used by the interviewer. They are the means by which we can assess the quality of the responses, not necessarily the cues by which the responses were elicited.

The matrix exercise
In looking for evidence of learning at an extended abstract level, we looked for links, coherence, integration and deduction. The following quotations provide evidence for this as taken from interview responses.

1. Did the students make links, were they able to generalise and deduce across the whole curriculum span covered by the exercise?

. . . that was a bit disjointed. But we felt we wanted to do it that way to give us all an insight into a bit of each section. Instead of one person doing the whole of the minorities, like I would have been the only one working on that subject. But it all came together fairly well in the end. We had a fairly good idea of where the links were. (No. 4)

Yes I can see where it's coming from. Definitely, yes that part of it. But, like

I say, there was just too much to take it on board. You could see where it was going but with no direction or anything like that, it's difficult to focus.

Could you make links?

Well you could, but you didn't know whether you were doing the right thing. I mean you start off with the history and then I can't remember what was next. But we did the history of it first, the history of each provision . . . if you got the history wrong, you didn't know whether you were doing the next bit right, did you? You know what I'm trying to say? (No. 6)

Yes, yes, it was quite easy to make links across the sections. In fact, in some ways we felt there was a lot of repetition. I wondered, but I didn't give that a lot of thought - but I wondered if it could have been organised in a different way. (No. 8)

Yes, yes. I think if you have an understanding of oppression in the broader sense and a political structure and realities in a broader sense, you can see those patterns again and again in the statutory and the voluntary and the minority with women and black people, with all the rest. You can make links across the board. (No. 10)

Only one student here responds about the content (No. 10) of the learning; the other is fixed within the process of the exercise. However, at other points in their interviews, all students indicate that their learning spreads across the curriculum and links have been made. Responses to the following analysis question give evidence to this effect.

2. Did they understand the inter-relationships and the diversity of provision both historically and currently?

I think probably the most important thing for me was that it hasn't been a recent thing. The youth and community service hasn't been a recent thing, and some of the ideology behind it these days isn't a recent thing either. That there have always been theories about how to help as such, do you know what I mean? What to do with people. That was interesting for me, looking at like the sort of philanthropy aspect, you know, because I've never really thought about that before, because I was very much in the present day, stuck in the present day. And I always wondered sort of how . . . . I always felt the youth and community service was just sort of there, and it had just been plonked on the 1990s and the 1980s or something, and I never knew anything about that. I always felt that was missing. I didn't know what the background was to any of it. (No. 4)

> I suppose the philosophy sort of like Boy's Brigade stuff and things like that, sort of Scoutish things, like developing the individual to get . . . because I've always looked at it from an anti-establishment point of view . . . I suppose I've learnt something like that. Learnt how not to do youth and community work on that sort of score. I didn't really like it and you've got to know it haven't you? And when you start looking at those sort of things, you know like charities and things and things like that. I didn't have a clue but that's opened my eyes a little bit. Those are the two main things. Wasn't impressed but I've learnt something. (No. 6)

> Well I think . . . well, it's . . . looking at the girls' work bit, which was the bit I did, there was the issue of young girls working as servants and so on . . . and the mill girls . . . and lack of education. And it was more like preparing them for marriage - stopping them from going on to a life of prostitution in a way . . . keeping them good girls . . . well I'd like to think that the attitude is different now. (No. 8)

> But that exercise provided an opportunity for really getting to grips with the undermining stuff behind it all, the political theory behind it, the historical context, the understanding of institutions. I just saw it as a real opportunity for actually coming to an understanding of what . . . for me what the statutory sector is, where it's come from, why it came from there, what influences it, the political sort of parallels and that, and government interest in the statutory sector. It was just brilliant to give you political awareness behind your . . . behind why you want to work as a community worker . . . For me I feel equipped now to look back and ask them and say: look it's a big political agenda and it's rooted in a lot of old stuff which we want to be getting rid of I suppose. (No. 10)

Here we see evidence of a diversity and range of understanding that has a historical perspective that is leading students to a more focussed sense of professional identity, and this applied across all four students.

As a professional training course we need to be able to monitor the development of some sense that students can deduce professional implications for their learning.

3. Were there any indications that this new knowledge and understanding would inform their future practice?

> Because I think the youth and community service often doesn't locate itself within other structures. Do you know what I mean? I think it does see itself as a bit of an island, and that it is important for me to locate itself in society rather than just be this insular blob that gets on with its own thing, because I think we negate our responsibilities if we do that. (No. 4)

If anything, that there are lots of points of view about how to do youth and community work. That would be the thing for me. Because I thought when I started we'd all be like trendy lefty sort of things. And we're not . . . I thought we'd all be coming from the same background but we don't, which is good for me. I mean, like it's more experience. But that shocked me. That's probably what I've learnt off the matrix the most. I didn't realise that there were so many angles that people approach youth and community work. (No. 6)

Well it's made me more aware of . . . I can . . . so if I look at . . . You see I've done a lot of work in the past, and I miss that gut feeling that that's good, that's good stuff and that's not, that's not so good. I like working this way, I don't like working that way. But if somebody asked me what I was doing, I couldn't really say - I'm doing this and I'm doing this because . . . And I'd no historical background or theory at all and I used to get really worried if people asked me what I did because . . . I'd have to actually describe what I did rather than telling them, you know I'm doing this and it's called social education and I'm doing it because . . . So learning about that and putting it into a historical context and seeing this stuff about character building, where that fitted into the matrix, and when and why the different style of work started to emerge, social education, and how that sort of developed was really useful. (No. 8)

It's going to be different for me because at the forefront of my mind it's the oppression of different peoples. Practice - my greatest fear is how on earth can I come to the understanding that I have now of the position of gay people in society . . . how on earth do I put that into practice? How on earth do I make an LGG group in Northern Ireland? . . . But you know, how on earth do you really shake the apple cart like that? I mean that's for certain what I am challenged to do, but I do fear I think . . because with learning and with change and development comes the fear and the realities . . . Oh OK it's great that you've learnt and great that everything's changed, but then the ball's in your court to do something about it. (No. 10)

Obviously a great deal of learning took place during this exercise. These students all developed a stronger sense of their personal identity and how their understanding of the history and ideology of practice would hopefully inform their future professional practice. Responses here also indicate a surprising depth of understanding which within the terms of the taxonomy learning was being transformed and integrated into a coherent professional identity. Of course there must obviously be many influences from the rest of the course and outside it, but the matrix exercise had been important in initiating and generating a bed-rock of understanding. This important function of the matrix is confirmed by other students.

> I suppose doing the matrix and work before the matrix we did in the sessions was useful in sort of like positioning yourself within the provision - your beliefs anyway, your values. (No. 9)

It is significant to note that these students were talking of an exercise they had completed a full six months before the interviews took place. In conclusion, the most effusive student (and one of the least practically experienced) had this to say:

> – I've changed incredibly as a person.
> – Really?
> – Oh, unbelievable. But how do I get away from all that stuff which I can look at and which I can represent and relate to . . . But how do I get it to be in a place where I'd like it to be? That for me is the crux of the challenge. (No. 10)

The evidence here is encouraging in that all four students achieved high levels of learning from this exercise despite differences in their ability to cope with the process. It confirms the value of independent and group learning. Indeed, rather than pull back from these innovations, we need to continue but with increased process support for the more instrumental students.

The recruitment and selection simulation

Again on this exercise there are a number of crucial questions that are useful in ascertaining the level of understanding around the curriculum areas the exercise was designed to meet. Within these questions it is also possible to see the particular "cues" designed to elicit data useful in positioning responses within the taxonomy. The interview question asked about "equal opportunities" in job recruitment procedures. This was an intended cue to elicit responses primarily around the concept of oppression and anti-oppressive practice.

1. Was the exercise practically relevant, could students see how it could inform or change their future practice?

> I think it probably already has actually. I mean when I've looked at job descriptions and personal specs now I think . . . You know as far as I'm concerned, you know what I mean, there shouldn't . . .they can't state things like that. That's discriminatory. (No. 4)

> Minimal probably. I'll always try and . . . if those sort of things come up, I'll always try and pass the buck sort of thing. I'd much rather get on with face-to-face work rather than the bureaucracy side of youth and community

work. When it comes to that sort of thing, I'd always like someone else to do it. But I know I've got to do it sooner or later, but . . . probably something I'm trying to avoid I should think. (No. 6)

Well I think it would have done anyway. But just the thing about making interviews more realistic, and I think that you can be rigorous in your aims and objectives for a post, and the job spec and the personal specification . . . And I still think you can be warm and friendly and non-threatening during the interview procedure . . . I feel quite confident about going through all the stages. And I don't think . . . I think we slipped up in our group with some of them . . . So you know I've learnt from our mistakes as well. (No. 8)

Yes. All I can say almost as a radification of that exercise - I went to London on placement, I observed a selection process. They were looking for a new families worker - and it was almost a carbon copy. Incredible. I couldn't believe it. I was watching their process. Their advert, their personal specification, their job specification, their interview, their short-listing, their selection of the candidate. And it was almost a carbon copy. I just felt as though I'd lifted it out of my file. And I watched the whole process over a couple of months of selection of a worker. It was great. (No. 10)

The practical usefulness of the exercise is very evident here and was a major feature in most interview responses.

2. Was there an understanding of the need for equality of opportunity?

Yes it was, certainly. I think because it was so simple and yet very effective. I mean we all sort of . . . when we saw the sheet of all the sort of things that are often used on application forms, why they shouldn't be used and alternatives for them. it was like really simple but mind blowing at the same time. (No. 4)

No, that's one thing I didn't take on board, no. I can't remember thinking of that at the time anyway. But that is always at the forefront of my mind . . . equal opportunities are always at the forefront of my work, but I didn't consciously think about it then. (No. 6)

Well, I think by using the sort of very basic application forms that don't ask your age and don't ask your sex and don't ask how many children you've got and don't ask where you were born - that sort of thing. (No. 8)

I believe in positive action. I believe that if there is inequality in society, that that must be reflected in how you go about selecting a worker and I believe in a free market thing about staff because if you have free market recruitment procedures - i.e., the best person gets the job–it will invariably be the best man who gets the job. Or the best white man or the best white heterosexual able-bodied man. I think because of the way society and structures and institutions are, those people invariably make it to the top. (No. 10)

3. Could they translate or generalise their learning into other contexts?

I can't remember whether it was actually given out or not. Talking about childcare and things. That it's really dodgy to start asking about childcare because obviously you're not going to ask . . . well you might not ask a male about childcare. (No. 4)

So I am conscious now that it's not just the Protestants and Catholics fighting one an other. There are so many other issues which divide - gender issues, race issues, not just Protestants and Catholics. (No. 10)

The data as analysed by questions 2 and 3 indicates that three of these four students had difficulty stepping beyond the specifics of the exercise and translating their learning into other contexts. With particular reference to equality of opportunity and anti-oppressive practice it would seem that learning here was operating at a lower level. Students seemed fixed in the detail and specifics of the exercise (which they all recalled accurately) and had difficulty moving beyond this. The concentrated time span and task-driven agenda seems to have played a part in this. As one student noted, more reflective and evaluative time after the exercise may have been useful in moving understanding beyond the specific bounds of the exercise to encourage a deeper understanding of the generic code around the concept of oppression. It is interesting that,although all the students were comfortable with the more tutor-directed experience of this recruitment and selection simulation, the results were weaker in terms of depth of learning. In fact, only one of the four provides clear evidence of translating the learning from the specifics of the exercise into wider and more universal contexts. Therefore, this research confirms the notion that greater student autonomy leads to a better quality of learning. The challenge is to help students become more comfortable with that autonomy.

Conclusion
At the outset of this paper our intention was to detail the specific and theoretically grounded changes we had made to two particular learning experiences on our Post-Graduate Course in Youth and Community Work.

We feel that we were considerably more successful in devising learning experiences which fostered a deep approach to learning, but as yet we have not developed the methodology to measure these changes in a quantitative way. The research has given us greater confidence in the direction of our innovation and pleasure in the tremendous developments made by individual students.

Overall, this research has shown conclusively that assessment that is concomitant with the learning experience and desired learning outcomes of a course can be used successfully to improve the quality of students' learning. Perhaps the most important learning point for us has been the realisation that, as engineers of the learning experience, our focus in this pilot study has been a little one-sided. We may well be using some very good techniques, designing well, but our basic materials - the students themselves - need more accurate and structured support and monitoring before they can all capitalise more fully on the experiences we have devised.

References

Biggs, J. B. and Telfer, R. (1987). *The Process of Learning*. Englewood Cliffs, NJ: Prentice-Hall.

Biggs, J. B. (1989). Does learning about learning help teachers with teaching? Psychology and the tertiary teacher. *In Supplement to the Gazette*, 36, 1.

Boud, D. (1989). Moving towards autonomy. In *Developing Student Autonomy in Learning*, 2nd edn. London: Kogan Page.

Frazer, M. (1992). Promoting learning. In R. Bartlett, *Learning to Effect*. Milton Keynes: Open University Press

Gibbs, G. (1992a). *Improving the Quality of Student Learning*. Bristol: Technical & Education Services.

Gibbs, G. (1992b). Improving the quality of student learning through course design. In R. Bartlett, *Learning to Effect*. Milton Keynes: Open University Press

Gibbs, G. (1992c). *Problems and Course Design Strategies (Teaching More Students 1)*. Oxford: Centre for Staff Development.

Higgs, J. (1989). Planning learning experiences to promote autonomous learning. In D. Boud (ed.), *Developing Student Autonomy in Learning*, 2nd edn. London: Kogan Page.

Ramsden, P. (1992). *Learning to Teach in Higher Education*. London: Routledge

Richardson, J. T. E. (1990). Reliability and replicability of the approaches to studying questionnaire. *Studies in Higher Education*, 15, 2, 155–168.

Chapter 7   Writing and learning

The "Pedagogic Relation" in Accounts of Student Writers' Needs and Difficulties

Mary Scott, University of London Institute of Education

The central focus of this paper reflects the paradoxical fact that, although published accounts of student writers' needs or difficulties are usually intended to prompt new, more soundly based pedagogic practices, such accounts pay scant attention to the "pedagogic relation" (Bernstein, 1990). As Bernstein points out, that relation – between teacher and taught – is "essentially and intrinsically asymmetrical" but its realisation is often "very complex", since strategies may be used for "disguising, masking, hiding the asymmetry". However, in the published literature about student difficulties in academic writing in higher education the asymmetry between tutor and student, as explicitly or implicitly represented, tends to take on an idealised form remote from the complexities of actual contexts and resting on hidden ambiguities. Thus there is silence or contradiction at the very point where, in view of the practice-oriented tenor of the texts, tutors might justifiably expect developed insights; in other words, the pedagogic relation is un – or under-examined so that finally the texts do not do justice to their declared or implicit emphasis on improved pedagogic practice as their ultimate aim.

Nevertheless it is perhaps attention to those very silences and contradictions that may raise most sharply issues of central importance to more effective practice. My aim in this paper is to take a step in that direction. To that end I examine representations of the pedagogic relation in a selection of texts about student writers' needs or difficulties. Bernstein (1990) and Kress ([1985] 1989 and [1982] 1993) provide a foundation of insights on which I develop analytical readings of the chosen texts. I follow Bernstein in treating the pedagogic relation as fundamentally about the kind and degree of authority exercised by those who teach – or to borrow Bernstein's own words – as about "patterns of subordination and super ordination". Kress's ([1982] 1993) reference to the importance in learning to write of power-differences not only between teacher and student but also between discipline and teacher and discipline and student has also helped to shape my analyses. Kress's focus is, however, developed within the context of young children's writing. In applying it to texts about student writing in higher education I have had to extend it slightly to indicate the interdependence of the power-differences that Kress lists. As will be demonstrated, the implied or stated power-difference between tutor and student is most clearly visible in the texts selected for discussion when it is viewed as a function of, and thus secondary to, the relation to academic discourse (rather than, in this instance, a discipline) of the tutor and of the student. In other words, perceptions of the asymmetry between tutor and student turn in each case on perceived differences regarding the nature, extent and relevance of particular kinds of knowledge or skills. Those differences are reflected in the social identities offered in the texts to tutors and students, or as Bernstein (1990) puts it: in "the rules of social order, character and manner which are held to be the `condition for appropriate conduct".

The social identities constructed in the texts are not, however, to be seen as simply the individual creations of the writers of the texts. They rather represent widely held competing views within education. In short they are discourses in the sense that Kress (2/1989) ascribes to the word when, following Foucault, he glosses it as the linguistic expression of an institution's meanings and values. However, as Kress ([1985] 1989) also points out, each individual's history is composed of the experience of a range of discourses. As tutor to students from many countries with markedly different cultures I have observed that there can be considerable differences in tutors' and students' discourses concerning the pedagogic relation. "Student" and "tutor" are words that trail the memories, both individual and collective, of their use in other concrete contexts. Bakhtin ([1926] 1984) expresses that aspect of language clearly:

> The life of the word is contained in its transfer from one mouth
> to another, from one context to another, from one social
> collective to another, from one generation to another
> generation. In this process, the word does not forget its own path
> and completely free itself from the power of those concrete
> contexts into which it has entered.

It is the meeting of different memories that helps to create the complexities of the asymmetry between teacher and taught in any particular academic context. I therefore include in this paper a few brief examples of student reactions to the kinds of pedagogic relation presented in the texts to be discussed. The inclusion of such data is in keeping with my primary intention which is to draw attention to a neglected but important area in the literature about student writing and to the issues and problems associated with it. Finally, while offering no easy solutions, I do suggest that a way forward in both teaching and research might be found in a stance currently being emphasised in both anthropology and psychoanalysis.

Readings of Selected Texts

The texts to be discussed are grouped into four broad categories. Each category has been formed to accommodate a particular view of the tutor–student relation that a number of texts explicitly or implicitly endorse. On the basis of that principle of categorisation the patterns of authority constructed within the texts appear respectively as:

1. hierarchical
2. oppositional
3. collaborative
4. problematic.

It is not my intention to suggest that the categories cover all texts concerning student difficulties in academic writing though that may be the case, nor is the categorisation meant as a denial of the subtle differences between texts in any one category or of a match between a text and the criteria for more than one category; rather it is intended to provide a sharp focus on issues concerning the pedagogic relation.

1. *Hierarchical pedagogic relation*
This view of the pedagogic relation tends to reflect a concern with the precise scientific description of academic discourse as comprising structures, moves, strategies or genre. However, whatever the particular form of the description, academic discourse is perceived as a largely unproblematic given. The asymmetry between tutor and student is consequently explicitly or implicitly presented as marked: tutors are, by and large, the owners of the knowledge that counts and their role is to transmit that knowledge to the students, who in their turn are expected to receive the knowledge and master it by practice.

The conception of the pedagogic relation as hierarchical is illustrated by several versions of the genre approach to the teaching of writing. Although a great deal of the literature about that approach is concerned with the teaching of writing in schools, in practice the approach has been shown to be easily transferable, in one form or another, to higher education. Among those regarded as pioneers of the approach is J. R. Martin. Martin ([1985] 1989) views genre as "staged structures" that reflect their social purposes in their form. Reports, for example, are defined as describing "how things get done and what things are like", i.e., they are factual texts. In keeping with that definition Martin characterises reports as comprising a general classification that locates the phenomena (natural, social or technical) which are the subject of the report and several stages (e.g., types, parts and functions, uses) that contribute to the description of the phenomena.

Martin links his concern with genre to a social aim. He states that the inability to read and write "powerful texts" is serious since:

> it excludes people from social processes at just those points
> where it matters most – at beginnings (where people might try
> and join) and at ends (where decisions are made).

Thus Martin regards the pedagogic relation as necessarily hierarchical. Teaching means passing on the knowledge and skills that the society regards as important so that students are not "disempowered". That view of the teacher's authority has, however, provoked intense criticism and debate. Thread gold (1993), for example, accuses Martin and his followers of "taking their knowledge for granted . . . teaching the limits of what they have seen as what there is to see". In other words, their endorsement of a hierarchical pedagogic relation can be said to turn on an unsubstantiated claim to an objective body of knowledge that matches an external social reality. Kress's ([1982] 1993) criticism is essentially similar to Threadgold's. He points to Martin's tendency to reduce the nature of academic discourse to a set of transmissible "generic models or exegeses of schematic structure", which inevitably has as its corollary a pedagogic relation that is markedly asymmetrical.

Cope and Kalantzis (1993) write about the genre approach within the context of the criticisms of the pedagogic relation that it is held to trail in its wake. Their attempt to silence the criticisms seems to me, however, to side-step what is at issue since their position is based on the assertion that the pedagogic relation is always asymmetrical but that that asymmetry is to the students' benefit provided only that the teacher minimises managerial discourse and positions the students as active learners. Peters (1966), however, leads me to question that neat separation of issues of control or management from issues of knowledge. Firstly, like Bernstein ([1975] 1977), though from a very different perspective, Peters refers to the conflation in teaching of being "in authority" and being "an authority". He then points to the importance of a particular epistemological stance to the avoidance of authoritarianism. Conceding that "authority" presupposes the "notion that something is right or correct" he emphasises that that notion must be regarded as a "provisional expedient"; in other words, those who teach "need both to be an authority and to teach in such a way that students become capable of showing him [sic] where he is wrong". That is a view of knowledge on which Cope and Kalantzis are silent. Indeed, their examples of teaching methods could serve as an illustration of "strong framing" joined to the "strong classification" of knowledge (Bernstein, [1975] 1977). Control of the sequencing, pacing and timing (i.e., framing) of the curriculum are firmly placed in the hands of the teacher whose final objective is that the students master the "theoretical knowledges" in which their teachers are already expert. Cope and Kalantzis attempt to temper that goal by asserting that the means to that end should involve the students in developing transferable cognitive skills. However, they inadvertently introduce a contradiction into their text: on the one hand they stress the significance of social contexts, but on the other they treat processes such as generalisation and evaluation not as manifesting themselves in a range of socially embedded concrete forms but as universally applicable cognitive skills that are highly valued in society.

An example of the hierarchical version of the pedagogic relation which is drawn directly from higher education is provided by Davies (1988). She is concerned with designing a writing syllabus in English for university students. She recommends a genre approach as the basis for such a syllabus. However, where Martin and, in their very different way, Cope and Kalantzis insist on a marked asymmetry between teacher and taught with respect to knowledge, Davies does point to gaps in the language tutor's expertise; those gaps relate to the student's academic subject area; a degree of collaboration between student and tutor is thus necessary for the purpose of identifying the genre that the student needs, which makes a "tidy" syllabus impossible. Furthermore, once the target genres have been identified, open-minded analyses of them, with tutor and student working together, are required since:

> neither subject tutors nor language tutors are yet able to make explicit the features which distinguish one type of writing from another.

Davies refers to the potential power of such collaboration to develop self-monitoring strategies in the student and to enable the tutor to learn "content" from the student, but, as the "yet" in the quotation above suggests, with its note of regret, the primary tenor of Davies's paper leads us in a very different direction from "collaboration". The verb that occurs most frequently in relation to the student's role is "acquire" (or some grammatical form of it). Within the context of Davies's paper it means that once the textual realisations of the genre have been identified it is the student's task to master them by practice. The view offered of the pedagogic relation is finally unambiguously hierarchical.

Martin, Cope and Kalantzis, and Davies all share a basically similar view of academic discourse and thus of the pedagogic relation. To them meanings come with forms attached; those forms are identifiable (or potentially identifiable) and teachable. The asymmetry between tutor and student is thus portrayed as necessarily marked with the tutor playing the role of expert in the areas of language and pedagogy and the student representing a deficit or lack. Strong criticism of the approach therefore seems justified. However, as I shall suggest later, there may be circumstances in which the hierarchical approach is precisely what students need at a particular moment in their development as writers.

2. Oppositional pedagogic relation

The oppositional view of the pedagogic relation assumes that the dominant form of that relation is hierarchical. From that perspective the conventions of academic discourse are seen as reflections of marked patterns of subordination and superordination. However, in the texts that fall into the oppositional as distinct from the hierarchical category, such patterns are regarded as a threat to the students' personhoods in one way or another. The appropriate student response is thus considered to be either resistance or a conformity that is perceived as that, but is deliberately chosen in the light of the students' assessments of their priorities.

A paper jointly written by Ivanic and Roach (1990) demonstrates the oppositional pedagogic relation. Ivanic, a lecturer, and Roach, a mature student, together analyse a selection of Roach's essays in order to reveal a conflict between "privilege power" and "personal power", terms which Roach coins and which are explained in the following way:

> Privilege power is what people acquire from joining the club: conforming to the discourse conventions in order to gain qualifications, status and credibility. Personal power is the result of gaining control over our own lives, being in a position to exercise choice and know the consequences.

That opposition between "privilege power" and "personal power" is basically an opposition between the institution and the individual. It is that opposition that serves to structure the discourse of Ivanic and Roach's text. Roach identifies those conventions in her writing which are "disguises" or, in other words, indications that she is simply "playing the academic game", and contrasts them with other forms and strategies that she likes and feels a personal commitment to. It is Roach's ambition ultimately to abandon disguises and "a bought-in identity, an off-the-peg set of clothes" to use her own metaphors. She concludes the paper with the following words:

> I will have personal power when my skeleton is wearing all its own clothes, has flesh on its bones, and can walk upright with its head up high and no gust of wind could knock it over.

The opposition between the institutional and the personal is presented in a more developed form in another and later paper which Ivanic also wrote with a student (Ivanic and Simpson, 1992). In that paper the emphasis on the personal is stated even more strongly: a central concept in the paper is "I-essays", which denote "commitment" and "realising that everything you write says something about you, and making sure as far as possible that you are showing yourself as the sort of person you want to be". That focus on academic writing leads Ivanic and Simpson to conclude their paper with the following celebration of the self:

> We can't guarantee that "I-essays" will get good marks, because marks are an issue in themselves. The only thing we can say is that if you put the "I" into your writing, it will definitely have you in there and no matter what anyone else thinks, that YOU is important.

The pedagogic relation is also viewed as oppositional by Clark, Cottey, Constantinou and Yeoh (1990). Clark, a lecturer, and Cottey, Constantinou and Yeoh, three MA students, comment on the effectiveness of the "critical language awareness" course that Clark offered in a department of politics and international relations. The course involved the students in adopting a particular focus derived by Clark from a number of sources but emphasising two themes: firstly, that there are ideological presuppositions embedded in texts, and secondly, following Fairclough (1989), that the analysis of the linguistic forms and conventions in texts thus requires attention both to the socio-cognitive processes involved and to the socio-historical context.

In recounting what they have learnt in reflecting on academic discourse and writing practices in the light of those themes the students use a discourse that is in common currency in education. For example, they use expressions such as "to show my commitment"; "to be in control"; "to take responsibility". Similar phrases occur in each of the two papers that Ivanic writes together with a student: "taking responsibility commits you to truthfulness"; "in control of the self they create"; "finding your own voice". Behind such expressions lies a particular view of the self as an autonomous, authentic and morally committed agent. Also present, particularly in Ivanic's paper, is the Romantic image of the writer as as an original, creative spirit seeking to escape the constraints of convention. In the light of Harvey's definition of modernism (1989) the focus is modernist: the self is viewed as unitary and social constraints are seen as leading to the alienation of the inherently creative individual.

A number of criticisms can be made of that focus. A post-modernist would probably argue that Clark and Ivanic mispresent and idealise the writing process. For example, can we really write without "disguise" or be fully in control of our meanings or freely choose our identities? Furthermore, in the papers I have referred to, the central values, "truthfulness", "responsibility" and "commitment", are presented as incompatible with linguistic expressions of qualification (which are termed examples of "hedging") and are thus implicitly reduced to a directness of manner that excludes subtlety or tentativeness and shows no concern for cultural differences among students regarding appropriacy of tone.

The questions and comments above are not intended to deny the sense of involvement that the students gained from working in the manner in which they did with Ivanic and Clark. It would seem that the discourse with which they were presented matched their current needs. However, Clark and Ivanic seem to believe that that discourse is the only or primary discourse that students need, which assumes that students' writing problems have their main source in a conflict between self and institution. That assumption overlooks the fact that students carry with them many different views of academic discourse and thus of the pedagogic relation. Those differences introduce complexities into actual academic contexts which, I shall argue later, make any one theory more or less appropriate at any one moment in the individual student's history.

3. *Collaborative pedagogic relation*

The collaborative version of the pedagogic relation assumes a partnership between student and tutor. It thus obscures the tutor–student asymmetry.

The papers discussed above, Ivanic and Roach (1990); Ivanic and Simpson (1992); and Clark, Cottey, Constantinou and Yeoh (1990), demonstrate a masking of the language tutor's authority in their accounts of actual collaboration. In their encouragement to students to resist the conventions of academic discourse Ivanic and Clark adopt an outsider role vis-à-vis the institution of higher education and place themselves on the side of the students. However, despite their challenging of certain conventions by, for example, using first names to refer to themselves and to the students and presenting the students as their co-researchers, their institutionally derived authority is clearly visible in their texts. The theoretical framework is provided in each instance by them and in each paper the students' primary role is to provide endorsement of that framework.

The failure to recognise where they are actually placed in the university as a knowledge-institution, coupled with their deliberate use of the vocabulary of personal opinion (e.g., "believe", "think", "assumptions"), creates an ironic effect. Instead of representing the relinquishing of authority their personal stance begins to appear like the imposition of a new orthodoxy. Although in a later paper Clark (1992) defends herself against the possible accusation of "prescriptiveness", she is trapped within the polarity she has established between the personal and the institution and can thus only state that, while she would want a student consciously to reject the conventions of academic discourse, apart from a minimal set of norms (e.g., avoidance of plagiarism), which she justifies largely on the moral grounds of personal integrity and responsibility, she would respect a student's decision not to challenge other of the norms, provided that such a decision did not represent a lack of "critical language awareness". In short, issues of authority are narrowly confined to conformity to Clark's alternative approach on the one hand, and, on the other, to tolerance, within broad, tutor-defined limits, of difference and of individual choice. In both instances authority remains at the disposal of the tutor. Thus while Clark's call for a critical awareness on the part of students of the academic practices they have to engage in is in itself unproblematic, the particularities of that call disguise the extent of the tutor's assumption of authority.

Hounsell's paper (1987) on the problem of providing students with feedback about their essays that they will find helpful also contains an image of collaboration, but Hounsell's focus is very different from that of Ivanic and Clark. He draws on the work of the linguist Rommetveit, and in particular on Rommetveit's concept of inter-subjectivity which "presupposes complementarity and reciprocal role-taking". The focus he derives from Rommetveit shapes Hounsell's interpretations of the consequences of the gap his research revealed in some instances between tutors' and students' conceptions of essay-writing:

> Where students' conceptions of essay-writing are qualitatively
> different from those of their tutors, communication cannot
> readily take place because the premises underlying the two
> disparate conceptions are not shared or understood.

Hounsell therefore concludes that:

> Attempts to improve the quality of students' essays . . . must
> spring from and turn upon dialogue about the nature of
> academic discourse.

Hounsell makes the further claim that, if such dialogue is effective, students will
experience the "kind of intellectual revolution charted in Perry's developmental
scheme". In other words, they will move from simple styles of right–wrong
thinking to a relativistic view of knowledge. It is, however, at that point that a
contradiction becomes visible in Hounsell's text. That contradiction centres on
the question of authority. As I have argued elsewhere (Scott, 1992):

> Hounsell recommends "dialogue" between tutors and students
> and a relativistic approach to knowledge. Yet there is an implicit
> and marked asymmetry between tutor and student in his text.
> The tutor is presented as an authority on essay-writing. Students
> are thus pupils like those in the Socratic academy: they are to be
> led towards the competencies the tutor already has.

Furthermore, and ironically, in view of his emphasis on the pedagogic relation as
ideally characterised by dialogue, Hounsell analyses student comments only in
terms of the extent to which their implicit conception of essay-writing meets his
principal criterion: a "meaning-making" that reflects an interpretive focus. The
following statement, for example, which surely refers primarily to the pedagogic
relation and the student's personal history, is dismissed as "literalistic": "I wasn't
going to get aggressive in an essay." Hounsell thus, and in unintentional
contradiction of his emphasis on "complementarity" and "reciprocal role-
taking", reduces "dialogue" to tutor assessment of the degree of match between
students' and tutors' conceptions in order that mismatches may be corrected.
Nevertheless, to tutors in search of improved pedagogic practice, Hounsell offers
a reminder of the importance of listening to students and trying to understand
their meanings. Later I shall suggest how that general view of a primary aspect of
the pedagogic relation might be differently elaborated in order to accommodate a
more complex perception of the tutor–student asymmetry.

4. *Problematic pedagogic relation*
In terms of the categories I use in this paper the view of the pedagogic relation as
problematic is characterised by an emphasis on the paradoxical implications of

the tutor–student asymmetry. It is, however, a view that is under-represented in the literature about student writers' needs and difficulties.

One writer who has made it explicit is Bartholomae (1985). He describes the paradoxical situation of the student in the following way:

> I think that all writers, in order to write must imagine for themselves the privilege of being "insiders" . . . The student, in effect, has to assume privilege without having any.

In other words, students have to create a necessary fiction; they have to "invent the university . . . or a branch of it, like history or anthropology or economics or English". Elaborating that statement Bartholomae adds:

> The student has to learn to speak our language, to speak as we do, to try on the peculiar ways of knowing, selecting, evaluating, reporting, concluding and arguing that define the discourse of our community.

In short, "our students are our students".

Such statements might seem to indicate a hierarchical view of the pedagogic relation. That is, however, not the case. The difference between Bartholomae and writers such as Martin and Davies lies in his different conception of the nature of academic discourse, which in turn leads to a difference in his perception of the pedagogic relation. Bartholomae is concerned not with forms as attached to particular meanings but with the positioning of the writer within the range of discourses within a discipline. In that way he accommodates flexibility within the conventions of academic writing. For example, he presents students at an advanced stage as those who:

> claim their authority . . . by placing themselves both within and against a discourse, or within and against competing discourses, and by working self-consciously to claim an interpretive project of their own, one that grants them their privilege to speak.

Such a perspective differs from that associated with the oppositional focus on the pedagogic relation in that, while it emphasises the involvement of the writer in making choices, that emphasis on agency is based not on Romantic ideas of the self or on the moral discourse of personal responsibility but on a particular view of texts which matches Kress's ([1985] 1989) statement that texts are "the manifestations of discourses and the meanings of discourses and the sites of attempts to resolve particular problems". Bartholomae thus focuses on the writer as located "on a page . . . in a text and a style and in . . .codes or conventions".

Doris Lessing's novel The Golden Notebook ([1962] 1989) can be read in such a way as to provide an elaboration of Bartholomae's emphasis on the need for student writers to locate themselves in the midst of competing discourses. Within the context of this paper that novel suggests the following meanings to me. Anna, the principal character, is a writer who is faced in that role with the choice of placing herself outside the conflicting discourses that beset her, which in the novel is represented by the metaphor of going permanently mad, or of locating herself inside the dominant literary conventions of her time, as she does in the novel "Free Women" that forms the outer frame of the book. Instead, however, Anna works in and against those conventions to write The Golden Notebook, which represents, and derives its rich complexity from, her paradoxical position as insider and outsider.

I would argue that, of the different views of academic discourse with their correlative patterns of authority that I have discussed in this paper, it is the paradox constituted by the insider–outsider position (which carries as its corollary the student's need both to learn and to experiment) that offers the most subtle and comprehensive view of text and of the asymmetry between tutor and student. However, I would not deny a place in higher education to those other views of text and the pedagogic relation that I have examined. In short, as a tutor I am confronted with the paradox that what I prefer at the level of theory may not be what is most appropriate in practice. In my experience each of the approaches referred to in this paper can be either helpful or unhelpful in a particular situation. For example, highly anxious but potentially able students who are blocked by fear may be able to get started if provided with structures and forms such as Martin and Davies suggest. Students new to academic writing may also benefit, provided that the structures are not presented as inviolable sets of rules or schema. On the other hand, I would estimate that there are as many students again for whom such an approach is unhelpful. It may in fact even reinforce existing problems, for example, in the case of those students who view academic discourse as a teachable formula which they should master by practice. Such students need to be encouraged to view academic discourse as characterised by fluidity as well as stability (Kress, 1993), which inevitably involves a narrowing of the asymmetry between tutor and student.

The oppositional focus also holds value for individual students in particular circumstances. It can help some, as Ivanic and Clark have demonstrated, to free themselves of any attempt to achieve a slavish conformity and may thus encourage a risk-taking that carries forward their thinking. Other students, however, may find the manner it recommends uncongenial or may experience a conflict between its particular moral emphases and their own culture's values. Furthermore, my own experience as a tutor has shown me that some students can in fact be prevented from achieving a personal stance vis-à-vis the topic they are discussing because the discourses of originality and the creative self are such powerfully controlling memories that the students do not move beyond a simple "I agree" or "I disagree" into a personal position within the academic discourse of their discipline.

Students tend to be very aware of the asymmetry between the tutor as representative of the institution's authority and themselves, and so to be either puzzled or cynical when tutors talk of "dialogue" or use metaphors in common currency such as "negotiation" (e.g., negotiation of a position in relation to the conventions of academic discourse). I quote:

> Where I come from staff are staff and students are students. In British universities there's a fine rhetoric about our all being learners together but that just masks the reality. After all they finally pass or fail my dissertation.
>
> I like the friendly attitude but negotiation suggests an interaction between equals. Students and tutors are not equals. We may be able to teach them some things but final approval of what we do rests with them.
>
> It's hardly a dialogue when the tutors want you to take on their ideas; however hard the tutors try to understand your problems there isn't a true mutuality. It all sounds cosier has it can really be.

The quotations above show the power of words to prompt discourses of differing strength and meaning in different individuals and to reflect those individuals' personal and academic biographies. Nonetheless, Hounsell's (1987) emphasis on the need for tutors and students to listen to each other is very valuable, as I stated earlier, even though he finally offers an idealised image of the pedagogic relation that edits out its complexities.

There is available, furthermore, an alternative conception of "dialogue" that matches the insider–outsider perspective suggested by Bartholomae and Lessing. It is to be found in recent developments in anthropology and psychoanalysis. In criticising the research stance of the objective observer, some anthropologists have discovered value in those new directions in psychoanalysis that have refocussed Freud's concept of counter transference, reinterpreting it as primarily a means to an enlarged awareness of one's reaction to the words of the other. As Ewing (1992) puts it:

> Psycho-analytic technique is essentially the process of observing one's own participation in dialogue with another.

In ways that are reminiscent of Bakhtin's emphasis on words as memories, which I quoted earlier, such a view of dialogic interaction stresses awareness of one's own history and its bequest of memories as a means to an enhanced awareness of the other. The memories do not have to be either disclosed or suppressed. What is important is that they be treated as a source of tentative understandings that need to be carefully assessed for their relevance to particular situations and contexts. If applied in pedagogic practice, such a stance would not represent a denial of the asymmetry that always exists between tutor and student, but would indicate a consciousness of the constantly shifting nature of that asymmetry when it is used to the student's advantage. I would suggest that it would thus encompass Peters's paradoxical statement (to which I have already referred) that teachers should exercise authority in such a way as to enable students to show them where they are wrong. Peters's paradox implies that in their different ways, determined by their different roles, tutors and students should come to be engaged in the same process, which, to return to the subject of writing, I would describe as the construction of texts that would represent a crisis in the students' and the tutors' relation to language as discourse, in that the texts would denote an unsettling of the "consistency of their tastes, values and memories" (Barthes, 1976); or, to let Doris Lessing have the final word in relation to the conception of dialogue that I have offered above, both students and tutors would become involved in writing their own Golden Notebooks.

References

Bakhtin, M. (1929). *Problems of Dostoevsky's Poetics.* Minneapolis: University of Minneapolis Press, 1984.

Barthes, R. (1976). *The Pleasure of the Text.* London: Jonathan Cape.

Bartholomae, D. (1985). Inventing the university. In M. Rose, *When a Writer Can't Write.* New York & London: Guilford Press.

Bernstein, B. (1975). *Class, Codes, and Control,* 3. London: Routledge & Kegan Paul. 2nd edition, 1977.

Bernstein, B. (1990). *The Structuring of Pedagogic Discourse: Class, Codes and Control,* 4. London: Routledge.

Clark, R. (1992). Principles and practice of CLA in the classroom. In N. Fairclough, (ed.), *Critical Language Awareness.* London: Longman.

Clark, R. Cottey, A. Constantinou, C. and Yeoh, D. C. (1990). Rights and obligations in student writing. In *Language and Power.* British Studies in Applied Linguistics 5 (Papers from the Twenty-Second Meeting of the British Association for Applied Linguistics at Lancaster University, Sept.,1989). London: CILT

Cope, B. and Kalantzis, M. (eds), (1993). *The Power of Literacy: A Genre Approach to the Teaching of Writing.* London: Falmer Press.

Davies, F. (1988). Designing a writing syllabus in English for academic purposes: process and product. In P. Robinson, (ed.), *Academic Writing: Process and Product.* ELT Documents 129. London: Modern English Publications with the British Council.

Ewing, K. (1992). Is psycho-analysis relevant for anthropology? In T. Schwartz, G. M. White, and C. A. Lutz, (eds), *New Directions in Psychological Anthropology.* Cambridge: Cambridge University Press.

Fairclough, N. (1989). *Language and Power.* London: Longman.

Harvey, D. (1989). *The Condition of Postmodernity: an Enquiry into the Origins of Cultural Change.* Oxford: Blackwell.

Hounsell, D. (1987). Essay writing and the quality of feedback. In J. T. E. Richardson, M. Eysenck, and D. Warren Piper, (eds), *Student Learning: Research in Education and Cognitive Psychology.* Milton Keynes: SHRE & Open University Press.

Ivanic, R. and Roach, D. (1990). Academic writing, power and disguise. In *Language and Power.* British Studies in Applied Linguistics 5. London: CILT.

Ivanic, R. and Simpson, J. (1992). Who's who in academic writing. In N. Fairclough, (ed.), *Critical Language Awareness.* London: Longman.

Kress, G. (1982). *Learning to Write.* London: Routledge. 2nd edition, 1993.

Kress, G. (1985). *Linguistic Processes in Socio-Cultural Practices.* Oxford: Oxford University Press. 2nd edition, 1989.

Kress, G. (1993). Genre as social process. In B. Cope, and M. Kalantzis, (eds), *The Power of Literacy: A Genre Approach to the Teaching of Writing.* London: Falmer Press.

Lessing, D. (1962). *The Golden Notebook.* London: Paladin, 1989.

Martin, J. R. (1985). *Factual Writing: Exploring and Challenging Social Reality.* Oxford: Oxford University Press. 2nd edition, 1989.

Peters, R. S. (1966). *Ethics and Education.* London: Allen & Unwin.

Scott, M. (1992). Reading academic writing. *Australian Journal of Teacher Education*, 17, 1.

Threadgold, T. (1993). Performing genre: violence, the making of protected subjects, and the discourses of critical literacy and radical pedagogy. *Changing English*, 1, 1.

"I Thought I Could Write until I Came Here": Student Writing in Higher Education

Mary Lea, University of North London

Research methodology

This research has been carried out among university undergraduates, many of whom are mature students from non-traditional educational backgrounds. Some come from diverse ethnic backgrounds and Standard English is not always their primary dialect. Students have self selected to attend a "Writing and Language Centre" in order to consider their own problem areas of writing and language use in higher education. During consultation with a writing researcher, students work on their own written assignments to tackle the difficulties that both they and their tutors experience with their written work. The research has considered writing practices in terms of three perspectives:

- students' written assignments
- students' self-commentaries on their own writing
- staff comments on marked assignments.

The rationale behind the research is to develop a methodology which will enable both staff and students to develop a clearer understanding of the processes that are at work when students are writing in an academic environment. This methodology could be considered when developing materials for use with students, either in conjunction with staff, or as self-study materials. The research also hopes to move away from the traditional study skills approach to student writing, which generally regards writing skills as those obtained elsewhere and then brought back to be used in subject areas.

Social context

Various authors have referred to the importance of social context in the consideration of linguistic practices. Street (1984) suggests that literacy practices are not autonomous and are related to specific cultural contexts, which themselves are associated with relations of power and ideology. Ballard and Clanchy (1988) consider context in respect of academic literacy and suggest that "becoming literate involves becoming acculturated: learning to read and write the culture." They pay particular attention to the function of language within the university culture and define literacy as "a student's capacity to use written language to perform those functions required by the culture in ways and at a level judged acceptable by the reader"(p. 8.) Sheeran and Barnes (1991), with reference to school literacy, talk about the academic "ground rules" which pupils need to identify within any one subject and the fact that such "ground rules" are frequently "unclear, changeable, and open to interpretation" (p. 1.) Fairclough (1989) suggests that any examination of texts needs to consider the relationship between texts, the processes of their production and interpretation, and the social conditions of their production and interpretation. Following from these authors, it would seem that any useful analysis of student writing would necessarily have to take account of the social context in which it had been produced.

When considering academic writing practices within the social context of an institute of higher education, I would like to suggest that it is possible to identify four different frameworks within which we can examine student writing; at any point in time there seems to be a permanent process of interplay between these frameworks. The frameworks can be identified as follows:

- language structure and form
- features of subject specific discourses
- an academic discourse of an ideological nature
- students' other language experiences.

Language structure and form

This is the traditional category that most staff and students refer to when they express concern about writing. Staff frequently make reference to students' difficulties with grammar, syntax and punctuation; students themselves suggest that if they had a more efficient grasp of some of these concepts they would be more effective writers:

> I haven't got a knowledge of grammar that I think maybe should have. I have been sitting down and thinking this is what I want to say. How do I say it?

> . . . . And trying out different sentences. It drives me mad but I think it's probably a good thing to do. And try to play around with say short sentences and long sentences and try to make it a bit more interesting and things.

> Well I mean I find it hard to know what a verb is. Well, in poetry the other day we were doing adjuncts and I don't know what they are. And I keep promising myself. I've got one of those grammar books and I'll sit there and learn it all but I never have the time.

> My sentences are inclined to be very long, they're long because I'm not sure where commas and that should be going.

These comments came from students who strongly believed that their writing could be enhanced by the application of a better knowledge of grammar in their assignments.

Comments by academic staff about a student's lack of knowledge of grammar are frequently coupled with comments regarding the inability to structure written work appropriately:

> Use of language skills need to be developed. Arguments are sometimes rendered ineffective because of weaknesses in this area.

> You must make sure that any quotations fit in syntactically.

> You are being held back by a lack of care and thought in relation to your grammar, spelling and overall essay construction. In terms of your sentence construction you need to be careful about your use of words for expressing your ideas. Your essay structure starts off well but about half way through it starts to read like a shopping list of points and we have no conclusion.

The difficulty with such comments is that they give students no explicit knowledge as to how to acquire the skills that are being alluded to or even what these skills are.

Features of subject specific academic discourses

Each discipline and each subject within each discipline has specific ways of ordering and presenting knowledge . What is regarded as appropriate in one subject may be regarded as inappropriate in another. Bazerman (1981) suggests that the way in which language is used in different academic contexts creates different assumptions about the body of knowledge that the writer and reader shares and this creates contrasting methods of representing information in academic discourses. My research with undergraduates has shown that personal experience may be valued in some subject areas when carefully matched with reference to another work; in another subject personal experience may have no place, and be dismissed as being purely anecdotal. Evidence from other authorities may be given more weight in one subject area than in another.Peter Elbow (1991) has outlined the very disparate nature of the different discourses within English studies alone: the contrast between the rhetorical tradition of C. S. Lewis with today's psychoanalytic theorists and these two with post-structuralist, continental discourse. Susan Peck McDonald (1991) has identified the lengthy nominal style of literary critics in academic literary writing and the use of non-standardized terminology and referentially vague terms. Students' commentaries on their own writing frequently make reference to new vocabulary and

terminology; yet in order to become a successful writer in the university the
student has to incorporate these features of subject specific discourses into his or
her own writing:

> I don't think that I can say things in a more complicated way until
> I've got the vocabulary.

> That's one thing I'm trying to do as well . . . like to increase my
> vocabulary, but then spelling is so difficult. One can know lots of
> new words and then not know how to spell them and I think
> that's a problem with being self-educated as well which I think I
> am in a sense. For me you often read new words and you don't
> have the faintest idea how to say them.

> There are quite a lot of words in the English course, for instance
> semiotics, deixis, which I haven't come across before and have
> difficulty understanding what they mean.

> I wasn't sure whether I was required to write about the structure
> of the actual poem.

At the same time, emulating academic discourses can result in an
incomprehensible written style as students try to negotiate this new language:

> Franco's regime had been able to formulate a language to
> produce a total mentality which seemingly conditioned the
> minds of his country men with one ideological homogoneous
> conglomerate and thus successfully repressing the spirit of
> Spain for four decades.

Students also make reference to distancing themselves from their own academic
writing. The following student seemed to be attempting to emulate particular
subject discourses and this is a process with which she felt uncomfortable. When
asked why she used so many inverted commas:

> Cortes "pulled" on every superstition that surround his men in
> an attempt to "mentally manipulate" the Indians,

she replied:

> This isn't me speaking . This is a term that has been put on it and
> it's surrounded by connotations that aren't necessarily mine. If
> you're not sure of something then just put inverted commas
> round it.

All too often emulating these academic discourses and focussing on using new terminology is the way in which students try to convince their tutors that they have a grasp of the subject. The result is frequently an incomprehensible written style as students try to negotiate this new language and integrate it with more familiar ways of writing.

Additionally, tutors' comments frequently refer to an inappropriacy of language use within a particular discourse and may make elusive reference to the way in which written work is expected to be organised within a discipline:

> You've done a lot of work on this and I'm glad to see an appropriate bibliography. However, you have not linked the first part of the question to the second. As I told you after your seminar the first part of the question is theoretical, to be answered with reference to Kuznets, summarized by Ghatak and Ingersent, as I presented them in class.

> I think this assignment faces problems of form and content, as well as language. In terms of form, it is closer to an essay rather than a first assignment format, e.g., your lengthy discussion of the Law and Order sequence could have benefited from the use of a shot analysis. In terms of content, you didn't always draw out the differences between the two extracts, e.g., you initially failed to mention the narrator and then said there was one in a later comment. Finally your sentence structure and grammar is shaky.

An academic discourse of an ideological nature

The third framework may be considered as a super-ordinate category which in some senses embraces the other categories. Following from Fairclough (1989), I have suggested that any examination of student writing should take account of the context of the text's production: students within the university write for their tutors. Their writing reflects the students' understanding of what is required of them and this interpretation to a large part will be conditioned by feedback on previous written assignments. Unfortunately academic conventions generally remain implicit and students have difficulty accessing what is required from the tutors' feedback. In addition to trying to understand features of subject specific discourses, students seem to be trying to access some ideological notion of what is required in their writing through an interpretation of the tutors' comments. Fairclough (1992) writing on ideology helps an understanding of how these implicit conventions become embedded as the "common sense" way of writing assignments:

> I shall understand ideologies to be significations/constructions

of reality (the physical world, social relations, social identities), which are built into various dimensions of the forms/meanings of discursive practices . . . The ideologies embedded in discursive practices are most effective when they become naturalized, and achieve the status of common sense. (Fairclough, 1992, p. 87)

Although students are able to access particular features of subject specific discourse they still seem to be trying to grasp some other notion of what is, and what is not, acceptable or appropriate in their writing at the university and their comments frequently allude to this ideological notion:

> . . . that's probably what I need to focus on. Having more of an argument maybe as well, because I often find it easy to write an essay if you've got a definite point of view that you really want to put across. There are wording of essays that open themselves to that and I often find it easier if I've got a definite point of view that I can swing everything around.
> Another important point is finding out what the tutor wants, like for some tutors they would allow that, some tutors are very hung up about the narrator and the narrator is never the author, and other tutors say that's not like a bug of theirs.

> I don't really know, is one allowed to say that?

> Whereas, for example, some tutors are quite happy for you to use "I" whereas others I think maybe still wouldn't be. I wouldn't like to use "I" because it's been drilled into me that you don't unless they say you can, I think on my Access course. You'd never use "I",you'd never be that personal and it annoys me because it would be a lot more helpful often to use "I" and you read a lot of books, critics and they always seem to use "I".

Tutors' comments on students' written work also seem to echo this ideological notion of appropriacy:

> Try to use quotes to back up your argument.

> Could you develop this?

> You need to back this up more firmly.

> This seems like an added point but you haven't really argued this.

> Your grasp of Bazin's general argument is good and your

criticisms well made. This is at a conceptual level, but your textual analysis doesn't quite drive home the points you have raised, usually falling short of explaining how such and such a feature does not fit with Bazin's idea.

Why? You need to put this into context.

Have you argued this?

Such comments make reference to developing particular ways of ordering written knowledge without any explicit reference as to how students are meant to accomplish this. To be able to understand how to develop an argument, create structure, or "drive home points", students need a clearer understanding of the processes that are involved and the ways that these are manifest in writing. The tutors' comments give no indication of this but make allusion to the "common sense" way of presenting written knowledge in higher education.

Students' other language experiences

The final framework concerns other language experiences, other discourses within which the student participates, features of which may contrast, compete and conflict with discourses within the environment of higher education. Most obviously students may be more used to oral discourses, and strategies from these may be directly transferred to writing. In matters of language form, tutors may be inclined to identify the influence of dialect in writing as being ungrammatical, and have difficulties identifying influences from more commonly used spoken language forms. A student struggling with an unfamiliar subject area may have problems finding the most appropriate register and they may slide into a "journalese" which contains some elements of the formal style they are trying to emulate. They may be aware that previous language experiences do not equip them for the requirements of higher education but they still have difficulty making the transition from one discourse to another:

It's like learning a different language here. I speak differently than I do at home. It is a new language that you use here. It's something that has to be learnt. It is a tool that has to be learnt. You're using words like didactic and when you are outside it doesn't mean anything.

You have to write about things in a different way. For example, in film I've always just seen a film and had particular reactions but now I have to write about it in a particular way and I can't see it that way. It's as if all the ways I've used before don't seem to matter here.

I think it's with working twenty-odd years in industry and that . . .
it needs to get things done by the end of the day so therefore you
can have one point and then you can jump to number five but
you can always come back to number two ...but it doesn't work
like that in academic writing.

Students seem to find it difficult to draw on previous experiences of language use
and incorporate them into their writing practices at the university. They
frequently conceptualise previous skills as being inappropriate - or even invalid -
in the present context but cannot find new ways of filling the gap. The comments
on their written work may also imply inappropriacy, but students are probably
already aware of the contrasts between these academic discourses and those more
familiar to them. Feedback does not give explicit direction as to how to move
from one discourse to another:

Avoid this kind of journalistic non-sentence.

You are clearly longing to slide off into a psychoanalytic analysis
of film - but are right to resist it! It's not appropriate to the
question in hand, or to the word limit imposed.

In certain cases you need to be careful about your use of words
for expressing your ideas.

The experience of the following student seems to illustrate the interplay between
the different frameworks as she explains her struggle to make sense of writing in
higher education.

Following an initial session she had spent working with me on "Analysing the
Assignment", Alice worked with a fellow student on developing the ideas that
she had begun to discover :

Well, when we sat down what she said to me was to look at the questions.
I mean what I really discovered is that I hadn't been looking at the
questions properly. And she even explained to me about this "critical".
Critical needs to have sort of like two or three theories. Now I didn't really
understand about that either. So that was like . . .oh, right. And the we did
. . . she told me about drawing like a spider diagram and putting a question
in the middle. So we did that and then we left, which I thought was quite
interesting to me, the intro blank, whereas before I always thought I had to
start with an introduction, start at the beginning. So we left that blank and
then we looked at like sort of putting the areas that would em . . into
paragraphs that would lead off from these. So we looked at sort of em . .
the social area and the impact that would have socially and then the

> political area and then the moral . . . ethical area and then we looked at the conclusion. And then she said to me how you write the introduction. You look at all these and you say well, what are you going to do? First of all look at the social . . . and it all start to make sense to me. You can have a flowing, moving chart to help with the paragraphs to bring them out a bit more. So that was OK.

Alice then went on to talk about a seen examination paper that she was given:

> When they gave us the paper we didn't have any sort of . . this is the way, you know when you get your questions, this is the way you should do it. I could have gone in totally not knowing that a plan would have helped.

Then talking in more general terms about writing her assignments:

> My ideas were starting to come out about what I had read but I had actually got confused about how I was putting them on paper. Before when I was writing my essays it seemed to be very jumbled in terms of me never having a structured introduction. And never having one paragraph that deals with this area . . . because my line of thought is very sort of . . . I think it's with working twenty years in industry and that . . it needs to get things done by the end of the day. So therefore you can have one point and then you can jump to number five but you can always come back to number two . . . but it doesn't' work like that in academic writing. I just wasn't really aware of . . . I mean I'd probably look at the word critical but not realise that I had to use two or three theories about the same thing. I think that was important as well. And yet it's like the assignment in my film studies. I wasn't told that it would have been good to have done it in a "shot analysis" form in that respect and I didn't understand the difference between an essay and an assignment. I assumed that everything had to be done as an essay. I mean OK we were told that wasn't the case but there was nothing in the library to look at to say this is different either.

Alice makes reference to her difficulty constructing paragraphs, specifically the content of a paragraph; this makes direct reference to the first category of structure and form. Her reference to "shot analysis" can be regarded as part of a subject specific discourse: the discourse of film studies. Alice's assumption that everything had to be done as an essay fits in with the ideological schema and she refers to other language experiences in relation to the previous twenty years of her working life.

Conclusion

Identifying these four different frameworks, and considering the social context in which students are writing, should give us a clearer picture of the difficulties that students in higher education begin to write are facing when they for the first time. If difficulties with writing are perceived by academic staff as existing within only one framework, language structure and form, independently of all other, then students will have difficulty benefiting from their tutors' comments on their written assignments. It is useful for staff to be able to see that, for example, apparent grammatical problems cannot be considered outside an understanding of the overuse of terminology within a particular discipline. In the same way the inability to structure written work effectively may be a process of interplay between students' ideological notions of academic discourse and influences from other more dominant discourses. Using these frameworks may enable us to understand how constraining writing in higher education can appear to students, and consider the processes that would have to be set in place in order to make writing practices more explicit. Work in critical linguistics, carried out at Lancaster University by Clark and Ivanic (1991), would suggest that students can be helped to understand their own practices as writers in higher education through the development of a critical language awareness. A corollary to this approach with students could be the explicit identification by academic staff of the ways in which knowledge is expected to be ordered and processed in the written form within their own subject areas. It seems clear that the gap between students' and staff expectations needs to be closed; looking at writing practices in context with this multi-dimensional methodology and considering the influences of the different frameworks should hopefully go some way towards closing the gap between staff and student perceptions of writing in higher education.

References

Ballard, B. and Clanchy, J. (1988). Literacy in the university: an anthropological approach. In R. Gordon et al. (eds). *Literacy by Degrees*. Milton Keynes: Open University Press.

Bazerman, C. (1981). What written knowledge does: three examples of academic discourse. *Philosophy of the Social Sciences,*11, 361–387.

Clark, R. and Ivanic, R. (1991). Consciousness-raising about the writing process. In C. James, and P. Garrett, (eds). *Language Awareness in the Classroom*. London: Longman.

Elbow, P. (1991). Reflections on academic discourse: how it relates to freshman and colleagues. *College English,* 53. 2.

Fairclough, N. (1989). *Language and Power*. London: Longman.

Fairclough, N. (1992). *Discourse and Social Change*. Cambridge: Polity.

Peck MacDonald, S. (1990). The literary argument and its discursive conventions. In W. Nash, *The Writing Scholar*. Newbury Park, CA: Sage.

Sheeran, Y. and Barnes, D. (1991). *School Writing: Discovering the Ground Rules*. Milton Keynes: Open University Press.

Street, B. V. (1984). *Literacy in Theory and Practice*. Cambridge: Cambridge University Press.

Chapter 8 The role of metacognition and metalearning

Enhancing Student Learning in Higher Education Through the Development and Use of Cognitive Process Strategies

Diane Montgomery, Middlesex University

Introduction

Studies of the promotion and enhancement of student learning in higher education have appeared to become a major focus for research attention only in the last ten years in this country. Much more attention has been given to the needs of schoolchildren than to students. In relation to pupils in schools this attention has been directed to the lower attainers, the slower learners and those with specific learning difficulties. It is only in the last few years since the Education Reform Act (1988) has been implemented that it has been realised that the National Curriculum, geared to meet the needs of average learners, was not extending the development of able learners sufficiently nor meeting the needs of lower attaining but potentially able pupils (HMI, 1992).

In other countries, consideration for the more able student of all ages has been vigorously pursued. Failure to address the needs of able learners is difficult to understand, for promoting their achievement has high economic value for a country. Students in higher education represent in the large majority the more able people in the population. The AH5 and 6 (Alice Heim) Tests for intelligence during the norming processes demonstrated an inverted U-shape distribution of this higher ability in the upper half of the normal distribution. However, high ability as measured by intelligence tests is not always associated in a consistent manner with attainment. Other factors come into play. Good memorising ability or a near photographic memory can lead to high achievement in some degree subjects in some types of programme. Neither good memory nor a first-class degree may signify future achievement, intellectual high quality or ability. Temperamental factors such as perseverance and stability within the highly able group also contribute to later achievement in a consistent fashion (Terman, 1946). If we examine the research in "gifted education" or the area of "high ability and talent" at student level, it is found that most of the work has taken place in the USA in recent years.

Analysis of this area of the literature reveals that many of the problems which we currently identify in higher education have been investigated at least in part and can provide a useful context to the research which is currently taking place. Both school and college education research have useful contributions to make in this respect.

Researchers in the area of high ability and talent seem to agree that intelligence is a multi-layered and multi-factorial concept (Necka, 1991) and as the century ends the broadest view of intelligence has been adopted. It began with a narrow test-defined conception and has ended with an acceptance that high achievement or potential in any area of endeavour with at least average ability on tests of intelligence may signify a person with potential high ability or talent. Research and general experience of educators has shown that intelligence tests and scholastic achievements in schools may not identify able individuals (Passow, 1990).

Intelligence itself has come to be regarded as not only the capacity to acquire knowledge and concepts but also the ability to use these flexibly in a range of cognitive and intellectual processes. McClelland's (1958) work was widely influential in teacher education in Britain in the 1960s and 1970s. He argued that intelligence was a widespread characteristic transformed into talented performance by various of the *right sorts of education*. Even at that stage he said we should stop refining tests and concentrate more upon defining learning environments which link learning opportunities with identification.

In 1965, having reviewed 176 research studies on gifted education, Goldberg came to the conclusion that there were two great research needs. To find:

- what would stimulate a love of learning among able children;

and

- what kinds of assignment would most effectively develop independence of thinking and independence of effort.

The one thing Goldberg was really sure about was that we did *not* need more tests. What was less clear was whether able children needed acceleration through some programmes or depth in others.

Twenty-five years after Goldberg's research Passow (1990), in his review of research on gifted education, was able to state that the two major areas for research and development were still:

- what kinds of educational and social opportunities are needed to promote high ability?

and

- how can we identify and nurture giftedness in disadvantaged

228

populations?

These key questions have remained the same for the whole of this century. How much we have achieved remains to be determined. These are currently the questions we need to address in our higher education programmes for the promotion of high ability in our courses is not widespread and the widening of access increases our need to help students from disadvantaged groups to succeed. Goldberg (1965) was unsure whether *acceleration* through studies or study in *depth* was appropriate for able learners. *Differentiation* of some kind was considered to be a priority. These three – acceleration, depth and differentiation – have become major issues in education in England over the last few years, first in special education and now in mainstream. It has also often been raised as an issue by students in higher education and originally by CNAA at validations to encourage programme leaders to "take account of students' prior learning and experience".

Acceleration
Evidence has been accumulating which shows it is often appropriate for highly able individuals to proceed through easy and lower levels of subjects when they have the knowledge and ability to do so. This appears to be particularly important for gifted mathematicians and musicians. In some school systems "skipping" grades can be beneficial, but it is not at all clear that acceleration is essential in higher education or across other curriculum areas and may prove unnecessary if the teaching and learning environment is *flexible*. One key concern is that acceleration should not just be accelerated content, where five year olds learn the curriculum of twelve year olds or first-year undergraduates work on third-year or postgraduate contents. It is much more important for them to learn to use their knowledge and be developing their intellectual skills instead of just learning more information. Accelerated content for able learners is, however, the most common provision observed (Montgomery, 1991) and will be promoted by modular systems permitting accreditation of prior learning and the study of multiple modules by rapid learners.

Depth
Goldberg suggested that some aspects of the curriculum should be followed in depth while others could be followed at a more superficial level. As there is always limited learning time this is reasonable, but care needs to be taken that what is learned "in depth" is not merely in terms of quantity and still at superficial or surface levels (Gibbs, 1990). It needs also to be absorbed at deep levels so that it can be used in real problem solving at a later date if and when required.

Differentiation
The issues in differentiation are critical. If we set work for different levels of

ability – *differentiation by inputs* (a) – then we have to decide at the outset who is able and who is not, with all the attendant problems of identification. Teachers often differentiate without test information and can of course choose wrongly (Painter, 1983). If they give the same work and *differentiate by outputs* (b), then the work may fail to be sufficiently challenging for the able and they may under function. This method is a variant of teaching to the middle and using tests and assessment questions to stretch the able upon which the rest perform poorly. Neither strategy is adequate and a different form of differentiation is proposed in the following (c). At college level it is rare to find any form of differentiation provided. All undergraduates are subject to the same diet and teaching programme, although they may "vote with their feet" or negotiate other studies. Students frequently complain of the need for differentiated provision. However, there is an increasing attempt to take account of students' prior learning in some programmes.

Differentiation
(a) The setting of different tasks at different levels of difficulty suitable for different levels of achievement
(b) The setting of common tasks that can be responded to in a positive way by all pupils/students
(c) The setting of common tasks to which all pupils/students can contribute their own knowledge and understanding in collaborative activities and so structure their experiences and progress from surface to deep learning and thus be enabled to achieve more advanced learning outcomes.

It is believed by many people that segregating able and highly able students in separate programmes in colleges and schools is socially and politically divisive (Barton and Tomlinson, 1984). It sets the students and the outside world to think that they are an elite. As they are only likely ever to be a small proportion of an intellectual elite, this is unfair and also unwise. The fact of putting them in a special school or university for the most able may have far more to do with later success than their actual ability. We see this in the "public school" to Oxbridge system. Their pupils make up 7% of the school population and they hold over 45% of all the highest-paid jobs. Ability to pay rather than intellectual ability is the criterion for entry into this sector.

If we could provide a differentiated curriculum and a flexible approach which could be shared with teachers in schools and tutors in higher education, we could improve the quality of education of all our students. This means we must ask questions about quality in teaching and learning and try to identify what is good and how it can be transferred from one situation to another. In the course of this research a review of statements on the nature of "good" teaching was undertaken, and they ranged from "arrives at lectures on time", to "is inspirational" and "gives good feedback". Very few statements gave any clear guidance on precisely how to recognise it or how to do it. The three cited may well be associated with both good and poor teaching, as became apparent in appraisal research (Montgomery and Hadfield, 1989).

What then constitutes good teaching? In my view "good" teaching is *occurring* where:-

"Students want to learn rather than have to be made to, where they continue discussing and thinking about the subject long after the lesson ends." (Montgomery, 1988)

This may seem a roundabout approach but it is an important one. Getting students to want to learn or to be motivated to learn is probably the most important attribute of the good teacher or product of good teaching. We know able students can learn easily and more quickly, but that they can also become bored equally as easily and quickly by the pace of learning in schools and colleges. Learning information is on the whole easy for able students but learning large quantities of information does not necessarily promote intelligence. Some able students have the capacity to memorise prodigious quantities of information and may become dissatisfied with education which does not offer them plenty of it. Others may have grown tired of an "education" which only offers this or more of the same diet which they may have experienced at school. The needs of the learner may often be lost sight of in the attempts by first-year tutors to teach all that aspect of the "A"-Level programme which was "missed out on" at school using the didactics of higher education. The key issue it seems is to identify those practices in which tutors engage that are highly motivating, causing the drive which energises student learning and keeping them on task despite other would-be distractions. Cognitively challenging or "brain-engaging" work maintains the student on task, involving the intrinsic motivation which Gibbs (1990) describes as the essence of "good" teaching and which we might prefer to regard as the attribute of the good learner. However, it can be induced in learners by tutors using appropriate teaching methods and/or intrinsically interesting contents. But we have to appreciate that much content in academic programmes of itself is not intrinsically interesting to many learners. Where it is so this can be regarded as a bonus.

When 500 university undergraduates were asked how they had behaved at school and if they were model students, few had been attentive and well behaved, indicating low levels of intrinsic motivation. The following is a list typically produced from each cohort (Montgomery, 1991).

What did you do at school today?
  Day-dreamed
  Nothing

> Propelled things
> Displacement activities
> Damaged property
> Absented self
> Distracted teacher
> Sat resentfully
> Discredited others or subject
> Recruited others
> Exited to loo
> Wandered
> Volunteered
> Avoided
> Kept head down and chatted
> Clowned
> Continuously talked
> Disrupted
> Continuously queued
> Persistently refused to work.

In other words, present methods were patently not working. These students were obviously not motivated by their earlier classroom experiences, suggesting they had been exposed to much indifferent teaching. In addressing the problem of how to promote intelligence and ability in able students through good teaching and make quite sure that under-functioning and disadvantaged able students are stimulated to achieve higher levels of functioning, we have to consider what can possibly be the 'right sorts' of education highlighted by McClelland (1958) which will motivate them. It is puzzling to discover that after three and a half decades this question is still relevant. How can these styles of activity have remained hidden for all this time? Presumably good practice is widespread. Perhaps what has been lacking is definition and research to underpin it. This may have arisen because so often there is a separation of research from educational practice, in that expert practitioners do not have the opportunity or the training to engage in research and researchers do not always have the practical experience in the profession to inform their methodologies. A significant number of studies have, however, shown success in promoting the abilities and scholastic achievements of disadvantaged groups (Feuerstein et al., 1980; Weinstein, Goetz and Alexander, 1988) but there would seem to be insufficient attention paid to promoting the abilities of able but non-disadvantaged samples which this conference has set out to address.

This paper presents a summary of the results of more than twelve years' work with in-service graduates and undergraduate teacher education students defining teaching strategies to try to promote learning and to enable them to unlock their own abilities and talents as well as those of their pupils. A research grant has recently been obtained from the university to enable more exploratory work to take place. The research has developed at two levels – developing a theory and practice of teaching and learning to use with students in schools and colleges and developing a set of strategies from this same theory and practice to enable teachers in training to promote their pupils' learning. It became necessary to analyse the teaching process itself and then examine the implications of this in practice. A key concept was put forward by the philosopher Hirst (1968) in which he argues that, if we teach, this carries with it the implication that during the process the learner learns. Lecturing carries with it no such implications. The lecturer tells the students information or demonstrates skills but the students do not automatically learn them as a result. Teachers therefore do not teach subjects, *they teach students to learn subjects.* Teaching is thus a more complex activity than dictionary definitions can lead us to suppose. Some lecturers of course may well be teaching some or all of the time, but it would be a mistake to think that all lecturers do or would even wish to.

For the purposes of transmission of teaching methodology to the teacher education students, *two central objectives in teaching* were defined as:

> 1. to enable pupils to think efficiently
>
> *and*
> 2. to communicate those thoughts succinctly through a variety of modes and media. (Montgomery, 1981, 1982).

These two objectives were to override all concern for subjects and skills which were to be secondary or subordinate. Students preoccupied with subject or content learning found this hard to follow. They too often confused strategies geared to memorising with those geared to developing thinking or cognitive skills which would result in the remembering of content. This attitude is evident also in recent government and DFE pronouncements on teaching in schools, where content and testing is vigorously promoted, whereas the opposite view seems to be promulgated by the same sources in relation to higher education.

By a process of grounded research a set of six *cognitive-process pedagogues* (Montgomery, 1990) were defined by which students' thinking processes could be engaged during learning whether they were children in school or undergraduates at university.

Cognitive-Process Pedagogues

> 1. Investigative and problem solving and resolving strategies, particularly in *real* problem-solving situations;
> 2. Cognitive study skills (requiring higher order reading and study skills);
> 3. Collaborative learning, in which pairs and small group discussion was an integral part of the student learning activity;

4. Experiential learning experience-based learning;
5. Language experience methods in which students' own experience is used as a major part of the study and resource material for learning;
6. Games and simulations.

The teacher students were taught to design their lesson strategies and contents so that there was an element of the unknown, a puzzle for their pupils to think about, resolve and make closure upon. By these means natural curiosity and motivation were to be harnessed and used in the learning process (Kelly, 1955).

The learning process was also the subject of study and the following aspects were incorporated into the theoretical framework for developing teaching and learning strategies – the Piagetian (1952) framework describing intellectual development and Vigotsky's (1968) and Donaldson's (1978) critiques, together with more recent perspectives from Kolb (1984) and Gibbs (1990). It was emphasised that in order for secure or deep learning (Gibbs, 1990) to occur, the learner should be an active participant in the learning process not just as a child but throughout life. Gibbs contrasts *deep learning* (accommodation in Piagetian terms) with what he describes as *surface* or superficial learning.

The characteristics of surface learning are said to be:

1. a heavy workload;
2. relatively high class contact hours;
3. an excessive amount of course material;
4. a lack of opportunity to pursue subjects in depth;
5. a lack of choice over subjects;
6. a lack of choice over methods of study;
7. a threatening and anxiety-provoking assessment system.

Fostering a deep learning approach rests on the obverse of surface approaches:

1. relatively low class contact hours;
2. intrinsic interest in the subject;
3. freedom in learning in content and method or scope for intellectual independence;
4. experience perceived as "good" teaching. (Gibbs, 1990)

Kolb's (1984) contribution was on the value of active participation in the learning process and his proposal of a learning cycle in effective learning. His research showed that active participation by the learner in itself was not enough, but that it must be followed by reflection upon the activity if learning was to take place.

> Learning occurs not in the doing but in the reflection
> and conceptualisation that takes place during and after

the event (Kolb, 1984).

It was felt, however, that this definition needed some elaboration if it was successfully to meet the needs of learners engaged in higher cognitive activities, and so the learning process became described as a *cognitive process learning spiral* (see Figure 1)to provide a model for the processes which the teacher needed to allow the students to go through if, for example, they were to be able to operate at the higher levels of intellectual processing described in Bloom's (1956) Taxonomy of Educational Objectives, such as analysis, synthesis and evaluation.

Figure 1: COGNITIVE - PROCESS LEARNING SPIRAL

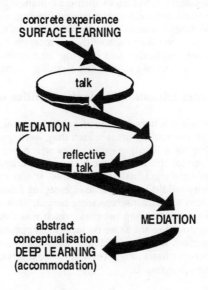

concrete experience
SURFACE LEARNING

talk

MEDIATION

reflective talk

MEDIATION

abstract conceptualisation
DEEP LEARNING
(accommodation)

The model indicates that learners can progress from surface to deep learning by a variety of experiential learning methods mediated by the teacher and encouraged by reflective talk. This process of learning does not return them to the same position as before. Through the learning process cognitive structures and strategies are developed and changed. In this paper *two* cycles of reflective talk are proposed as necessary for full cognitive growth which the tutor can enhance through judicious questioning indicated by the term *mediation*. The first cycle of reflective talk should centre on that which has been or is being learnt so that an appropriate structure for understanding is developed. The second cycle, which may at times interact or overlay the first, is that in which the students reflect upon the process of learning itself or *h o w* they learned the material, the meta-cognitive level. Meta-cognition is regarded as a highly important contribution to higher order learning. It is defined as:

> The processes whereby we think about our cognitive machinery and processing mechanisms. (Flavell, 1979)

Meta-cognitive activities contribute to the development of self-regulatory and self-management skills as well as a sense of personal agency. Self-monitoring in particular has been found by Wang and Lindvall (1984) to contribute not only to improved acquisition but also to improved generalisation and transfer of knowledge and skills. Brown, Bransford, Ferrara and Campione (1983) have defined self-regulatory activities as including planning (predicting outcomes, scheduling time and resources), monitoring (testing, revising, rescheduling) and checking (evaluating outcomes). We included not only these in our studies but also reflective talk upon how each of these processes had been undertaken or achieved, with the emphasis upon learning from mistakes, how to reschedule, reconstruct, replace and re-evaluate the learning outcomes.

How the Teacher Education Students' Abilities were Promoted

In order to produce teachers capable of generating real problem-solving approaches in all curriculum areas which they were going to teach, it was found necessary to give them learning experiences which paralleled those they needed to develop for school children. These learning experiences needed to be developed within their graduate programmes. It was found that, unless this was done, the majority would be incapable of escaping from, or regressing to, the methods by which they themselves were taught. This information was obtained through the in-service training network which was developed with teachers who were being introduced to the same pedagogical approaches attending in-service courses. The teachers with responsibility for student support and supervision reported an over-emphasis and reversion to didactic expository methods as the teaching practices progressed.

The teacher education students represented those in the top 20% of the ability range in the population. Many were intellectually highly able. Some were often lower attainers in the able group. Some of them were creatively intelligent with poorer memorising abilities. Thirty per cent were married women returners and mature students who had left school sometimes before "A" Levels. A few had had dyslexic difficulties in school. Despite gaining access to higher education each cohort seemed to be made up of a large proportion of under-functioning able who, despite all the advantages of higher education, remained disappointed by their achievements or disappointing to their tutors as their initial motivation declined. School education did not appear to have prepared the majority of them for academic studies. It appeared that the intellectual skills they needed to pursue higher education had developed only by the end of their four-year course, when they frequently said, "I now realise what I needed to know and how to study", "I wish I was beginning the programme now". This information was elicited when they were asked to write their own final-year reports. In the 1970s teacher education students participated in the Reading to Learn Project (Thomas and Harri-Augstein, 1975). These researchers found that 50% of teacher education students and other undergraduates on BA and BSc programmes had insufficiently developed higher-order reading skills in their first year to benefit from their higher education programmes. They concluded it was a widespread phenomenon, indicating schools had not prepared their pupils adequately. Meek and Thomson (1987) came to a similar view, arguing that study skills training should be made an integral part of school education. It should not be an additional study, for few transfer effects were to be seen.

In order to try to break this cycle of disadvantage and unrealised potential, the whole teaching programme in the psychology/special needs area was redesigned. The emphasis was moved from expository teaching and lecturing to *learner-orientated independent study methods.* The course was scheduled to occupy four hours "contact" teaching time per week for the final year. The typical schedule consisted of a one-hour lecture followed by a 1.5-hour tutor-led workshop and a 1.5-hour seminar. The new plan had to cater for a 50% reduction in staff because of cuts in teacher education as well as the development of the new learning structure. The concept of structured student learning time or directed study was developed in which the programme ran as follows: a one-hour lecture followed by a two-hour student self-directed workshop and feedback session and a one-hour seminar with the tutor on alternate weeks. The seminars on alternate weeks and student-led workshops enabled the reduction in staff time to be accommodated in the programme without increasing the size of the seminar groups (12–15 students per member of staff). In another part of the BEd course, where tutors maintained their original type of programme and incorporated staff cuts by doubling seminar group sizes, deleterious examination results were obtained. In addition there were numerous complaints from students about the programme and its lack of relevance to their perceived needs, especially where seminars deteriorated into mini-lectures related to the main lecture content. In the structured student learning programme reports became increasingly favourable.

The first problem which was discovered under the new regime was that most of the students lacked any form of self-organising strategy and study skills for the learner-managed learning sections. For example, after a lecture on test construction, test standardisation and norming, including details of testing for reliability and validity, they were given the workshop brief to "Determine if test

X is a 'Good' test for use by the classroom teacher. Examine the three attainment tests set out and select one to study in detail and upon which to write a brief report." The in-service teachers were given the same lecture and the brief "Your head teacher has been to a conference where the virtues of test X were promoted. Examine the test carefully and write a brief report clarifying whether or not it is a good test."

In both cases the problem set was "real". It was not an easy task to do and 1.5 hours was set aside for completion. It was with some amazement that tutors saw many of the undergraduates leaving the workshops after 20 minutes quite sure they had completed the task. After questioning about what they had done they were asked to hand in their report and were permitted to leave. Each seminar following the workshop had been designed so that the first 15 minutes was for feedback from and on the workshop. The rest was for discussion of the relevant research papers. It will not be surprising to find that very few of the undergraduates gained more than C– grades for their test evaluations. Most of the practising teachers gained at least C. The more effective undergraduates had formed working groups of two and three persons to discuss and plan their evaluation. Others worked individually or in loose association and at a superficial level. They made no systematic analysis of the lecture content and its application to test evaluation. The feedback session took an hour, since the first half was spent in the students showering blame on the task, the tutors and the poor quality of the instructions in coming to terms with their failure. Their dignity was upset. They listened to and reflected upon their strategies or lack of them and began to see how they might easily have accomplished the task. They also learnt that they had to enter into a detailed and concentrated interaction with each other and the material. They needed to interrogate text, tests, learning strategies and solutions. They would then begin the process of operating at higher-order intellectual levels. It was agreed they should repeat the whole workshop again the following week, not as a punishment but to prove to themselves they could actually do the work. The repetition was the subject of some discussion by the tutors, several of whom thought that the feedback on the failure would be enough. However, in the long term the complete repetition of the whole event was of both immediate and long-term benefit. The students could complete the task successfully and gain satisfaction and closure. They also learnt the need to link lecture content and theory with the workshop activities and practice. In the process they learnt to plan, organise and evaluate learning and the contents of their own learning in relation to external and internal criteria, all highly useful cognitive and meta-cognitive skills. A full cognitive learning spiral had been completed and they had operated at Bloom's (1956) highest level – *evaluation*. Each student could exit at the point where they were satisfied they had successfully completed the tasks.

These experiences for staff and students alike confirmed that we learn most from having to repeat a task we have already completed unsuccessfully, when we have

> to reflect upon the process of learning as well as the contents of that learning. It is only after one has solved a problem that one can learn most effectively how one should have solved it. (Larkin et al., 1980)

On the second occasion all the groups worked systematically throughout the workshop period unsupervised, and many stayed during the lunch period practising their new found appraisal techniques on several other tests. None of the groups scored lower than B+ for their analysis, and the grasp of the concepts of norming, reliability, validity and correlation were remarkably sound. From that period they were able to give a professional and succinct evaluation of any test within 20 minutes. Their success was accompanied by a new feeling of vigour. From that moment they became alert for any new challenge the tutors might issue. Each group would discuss tactics and tutors' designs and motives as part of their task organisation strategies. At examination time little revision was required and a high standard of answer was achieved. In lectures a higher level of attention was observed, for they continually expected to be asked to apply what had been explained to some new area. The level of questioning by students was noticeably more penetrating.

The seminar which accompanied the test assessment, lecture and workshop was to discuss a research paper on early screening techniques by Leach (1983). Ten numbered copies of the paper were held in the library, complying with copyright conditions. The 80 students could make their own copy for study, use the library copy in the library or consult the journal article itself. They had to organise and complete their review within a week. The task set was that the article should be read and a *flow chart of key concepts* (see Figure 2) should be completed and handed in at the start of the seminar.

It was explained that the top box should hold the key concept, which was central to and underpinned the rest of the sense of the paper. The other boxes should reflect the major concepts and issues which were discussed in the paper and followed from the key concept, the subordinate concepts. An introduction to flow charting and other cognitive study skills had already been part of an earlier study programme based upon the work of Thomas and Harri-Augstein (1975), Royce-Adams (1977) and Schools Council (1981). Whereas previously reading a research paper and making notes for the seminar might take an hour or so, the problem posed by the empty boxes in the flow chart caused much lengthier independent study and preparation periods. Each student took time according to individual need. The constant searching of the text for deeper structures complied with the demands of complex written material for *reflective* reading (Schools Council, 1981) as opposed to *receptive* reading which most had engaged in previously. The capacity to remember the papers' structure and contents and give an accurate summary of them after this form of directed study was very good and continued for a very long period. The seminar strategy was also modified to promote the

Figure 2

Early Screening Procedures Flow Chart

From Leach (1983)

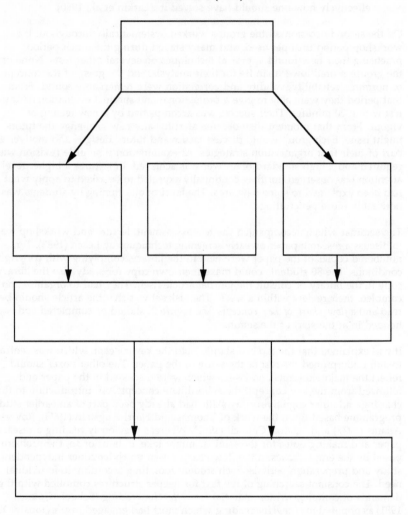

Name: ....

Date: ....

development and use of cognitive processes. In traditional seminar, groups of 12–15 students are assigned to a tutor. The students read and prepare notes on one or two of several research papers and then two of them are asked to present each paper to the rest of the group. Quite often only those who present the papers read them and their presentation is in the lecture form. It was realised very early on that very little learning for the majority could be taking place through this strategy. The students who had presented the papers were the ones for whom the learning had been most successful and this was evidenced in their examination papers. It was therefore essential to replicate the conditions under which they had worked with all the students.

The seminar strategy had to be changed and the following format is the one which was evolved and found to be the most effective. It was also the one which tutors would often fail to follow and would lapse back into the mini-lectures mode. The new strategy required the tutor to have read the paper, analysed it and hold back in releasing that knowledge. Continuous staff team support was necessary to keep seminar mode going.

The Directed Seminar Mode

- All students are required to read at least one of the two seminar papers for the session;

- Students were asked to make personal notes on the paper for discussion at the seminar;

- At the outset of the seminar they were asked:
  a) "how does the paper begin?" The required response was: title, author(s), date, journal and page references;
  b) to explain key words in the title.

It was perhaps not surprising to find at this first "demonstration" seminar that most had disregarded the title and other bibliographic information and had not considered the meaning of the key concepts. Some titles had not been understood at all.

- At this point all students who had not had time to read the paper were asked quite pleasantly to leave the seminar and go and read the paper, because they would be unable to contribute anything further to the group or their own learning.

This also proved difficult for some tutors to develop the confidence to do. At the beginning of such a programme it might be expected that two or three students will withdraw. In subsequent weeks there will be no withdrawals. Those who have not read the paper do not turn up and will often report in giving a genuine excuse and go to the library. One or two may opt out and need to be followed up carefully.

In general, if the tutor is working efficiently and well the seminar group is well attended. If not, as is recognised on in-service courses, the students "vote with their feet". Student response, both formal and informal, was built into the programme from the outset using questionnaires, rating scales, plenary sessions and nominal group techniques.

- The seminar exposition began with the tutor asking the students to identify the key point of the paper. Various points might be put forward and discussed – they were *not* permitted to refer to their notes
- The students were asked to put forward any aspects of the paper which they could remember. In 1970s parlance this is called "brain-storming" and has the effect of bringing the material into consciousness and demonstrated that they remembered more than they at first thought. It also encouraged the less communicatively advantaged to dare to participate. They were still not permitted to consult their notes and a "games" atmosphere often developed.
- The real analysis of the paper now began. Students were permitted to consult their notes and then the paper was taken in sections, even line by line systematically, to analyse and expose the author's intent and the paper's meaning, structure, research methodology, errors and conclusions.

The first seminar was regarded as a training session, showing the students how to work over the paper. It demonstrated to them whether their research paper study skills were adequate. It is likely that the study of just one paper in this way will take the whole hour, whereas in later seminars there would be time to work on two, for certain of the phases such as the brain-storming section can be curtailed or omitted.

On some occasions concept mapping strategies were used to structure seminar discussion and the evaluation of papers. This activity has emerged at various times as mapping, spidergrams, memory nets and brain-storming.

Concept Mapping Task

1. The students were shown how to draw a concept map which would illustrate their thoughts about a particular topic. The concept RUN was used as the example (Figure 3(a)).
2. The students then took the key concep, e.g.. Giftedness (talent or high ability), and before reading or studying anything were asked to draw a concept map expressing the knowledge, links and concepts which came to mind when

thinking of the key concept.
3. The students were then given readings or lectures and practicals around the topic and were asked to complete another concept map on the same subject. This would take them through the first cycle of reflection upon the area.
4. The final stage, however, was to ask them to write ten ways in which their pre-and post-readings concepts maps were different. This moves them through the second round of reflection in the learning spiral and is not only difficult for them to do but brings their cognitive processing to a higher level of awareness and operation.

Figure 3a   Note examples of the Concept Map of RUN below

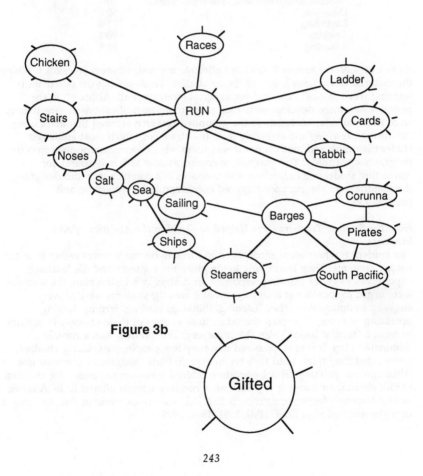

Figure 3b

A range of techniques such as these were used to bring the students to a higher level of cognitive functioning. Other examples were to set them to write a book review of a text they had just read according to review criteria, to design a short answer examination paper based upon the contents of these research papers, and so on.

The research quoted by Race (1992) later showed the extent of undergraduate learning through different methods and materials as follows:

Lecture	5%
Books	10%
Audio-visual presentation	20%
Dramatic lecture with audio-visual presentation	30%
Discussing	50%
Explaining	75%
Teaching	90%
Assessing	95%

As can be seen the lecture is the least effective method, whereas students teaching the material to students is one of the most effective. Assessing the outcomes of learning was the most powerful pedagogical strategy of all. Although in the period when these developments took place these quantifications of effectiveness were not available, nevertheless the grounded research showed that *discussing, explaining, teaching* and *assessing* were the strategies which most enhanced student learning and motivation. It was these which were incorporated into the programmes of study. This was not, of course, as easy as it may sound, for converting students into teachers and assessors is a complex task and designing the materials for the purpose required considerable inventiveness and preparation.

How the Student Teachers were Helped to Develop the Abilities of Able Students.

The student teachers were encouraged to focus upon the learners rather than the subject contents. They learnt how to structure the contents and the learning experiences to evoke learning responses. In designing a lesson plan, the teachers were urged to consider at each stage what it was the students were actively engaged in doing. Were they listening, thinking, reading, writing, talking, operating or doing? The plan should include a series of these changes in activity to form a "tactical lesson" plan (Montgomery, 1989) rather than a content, dominated plan. It was emphasised that very few people, particularly children, know what they think until they try to explain their thoughts to someone else. Although our primary school education offered some opportunities for children to talk about their learning experiences, secondary schools offered little. A range of Her Majesty's Inspectorate reports had indicated weaknesses in this area over a considerable period of time (HMI, 1981, 1986, 1989).

For key phases of the lessons, teachers were shown how the curriculum task should be designed so that it promoted talk about the work in hand. This was in contrast to the observations made by Bennett (1986), who showed that most talk in "collaborative" groups in classrooms was of a social nature and rarely about the work in progress.

An example of a problem-solving type lesson is exemplified in the following. The purpose was for the students to understand a history topic about why castles were built and the type of site which would be likely to be chosen. Students at the ages of 12–13 years would be likely already to have a range of experiences and knowledge about castles which could usefully be drawn upon before new information was presented. An exercise similar to that described would use their knowledge but also help them organise and share it with each other. Their group discussions would be the first subject input, with the second round led by the teacher amounting to the reflective talk stage.

A pictorial map of an area with mountains, marshes, villages, woods, rivers and so on was given to each group of five students. Six sites were identified on the map, some with good castle-building potential, others with varied attributes. Each group was assigned a site and told to produce a site agent's selling brief focussing on the advantages to the potential lord and lady if the castle were built on their site. The six groups were given 10–15 minutes to prepare their brief and asked to discuss this in independent leaderless groups. At the end of the preparation period, the teacher asked one or two representatives from each group to make their presentation. Great fun and humour resulted as the groups vied with each other. At the end of the presentations the class was asked to decide which would really be the best site and to identify the pros and cons for each of the six (analysis). The class were then asked to select castles of their own choosing from pictures; books and other resources were also made available. They were asked to use these to write an introduction to a class book on why that castle was built where it was and what was its purpose (application and analysis). It might be thought that it would be quicker for the teacher to question the pupils at the outset and elicit the information from them, shaping it into pros and cons and the written introduction. It would be marginally quicker but would be a far less powerful strategy for student learning. Such learning by expository and didactic methods may result in only superficial levels of learning for even the able students, and far less motivation would be evident. The able can easily become bored and the less able fail to grasp even the main ideas in didactic approaches. This collaborative problem-solving approach resembles *"real"* problem-solving which is so essential for highly able students according to Freeman (1991).

The two histograms in Figure 4 show *post hoc* the results of cohorts of teacher education students following a psychology/special needs programme leading to a three hour examination paper as part of their final fourth-year assessment programme.

(NB: The columns of the distributed scores are based upon standard deviations.)

Figure 4. Degree "Classifications" before aggregation with other grades

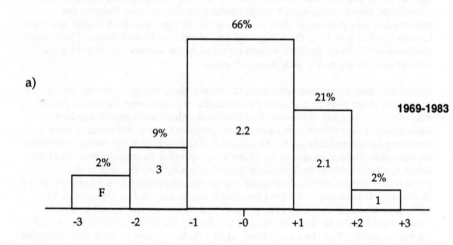

a)   1969-1983

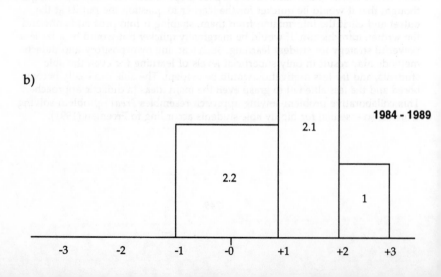

b)   1984 - 1989

There is a distinct improvement in examination grades appearing after 1984. Before this the grades had been more normally distributed. The negative skew seen after 1984 appeared on a consistent basis; the pattern shown is a typical one. Year cohorts increased from 20 to 85 students over the period. There are of course a number of factors which might bear upon the changes seen in the two histograms. For example, questions set in the examinations might have become easier; intake ability might have increased; the range of topics might have been set within narrower limits; tutors might have fed more clues to the examinees. For those engaged in the work there was a constant change in the programmes over a 15-year period, but the students' scores on the final examination tended to be distributed normally until there was a critical change in delivery of the programme in the "class of '84".

The students were also asked to write their own reports on their learning in lectures, seminars and workshops. These reports were most detailed, reflective and informative and helped keep the programme on course in its new form. This was important, for the tutors often became the ones who felt insecure. They became worried that they were not feeding out information in lectures to the students and had constantly to be weaned from not providing the answers, crib sheets and summaries. Immediately they did provide answers many students felt more secure and regressed to waiting to be told the correct answers and strategies. It was a continual battle to keep some of the students thinking. Their reflective reports, however, showed that important changes had taken place. An excerpt from two of these follows in the final section of the paper.

Summary

The subject of this paper is the enhancing of student learning in higher education through the development and use of cognitive process strategies. The strategies and contents of cognitive process method teaching programmes for students in schools and their teachers in training have been outlined. The general results of these programmes have been reported. Direct statements from the learners were common, such as:

It was interesting and made you think.	10 year old
Much better than the usual boring stuff we get.	11 year old
At last we are being treated as adults.	18 year old
We feel like real students at last.	24 year old
I know I have really developed intellectually in the last year.	29 year old
It's the first time since I've been here I have really had to use my brain. It's quite hard, thinking.	25 year old
Using these materials has rekindled my interest and motivation to teach which I thought was dead.	35 year old

This has been real "engage brain" stuff. 40 year old
Course evaluations were very positive and the marked increase in the number of
examination grades in the B+, A–, A range was noted, as well as the general
improvement through the grades. What has been lacking until now is an
opportunity to provide hard evidence that these strategies have promoted high
ability and talent. In the next few years there will be the opportunity to produce
this evidence from studies of teachers on the MA distance learning programmes,
and a teacher-researcher has been appointed and has set up a research evaluation
study with undergraduates.

Thus far the results from the programmes have shown that a love of learning
can be rekindled in the wider range of students in classrooms and universities. It
has also been shown that it is possible to design assignments which will most
effectively develop independence of thinking and effort based upon cognitive-
process principles. These techniques would appear genuinely to induce intrinsic
motivation in the learner, and it is this which energises the learning and engages
the students' attention, counteracting and over-riding the effects of competing
stimuli and other distractions. It appears that the nature of learning, especially in
its collaborative mode, is emotionally satisfying as also is satisfaction deriving
from completing the task. In other expository and didactic modes the learners'
emotional needs tend to be suppressed. These emotional needs for self-
expression, self-fulfilment and self-esteem can be met through the cognitive
process methodologies by making provision for the learners to contribute from
their own experience to the task in hand. Learning mediated in this way
promotes deeper learning in which new material becomes part of the cognitive
structure of the learner.

Teachers and tutors, however, need help to move them from their traditional
lecture mode strategies to become managers of learning, facilitators and
collaborators with students, and their emotional needs also have to be met.

Examples of Student Self-Assessment, Reflective Reports

Julie C. , Year 4

Lectures
My note-taking is more effective than in earlier years. I have more confidence to
write my own interpretation of the information received, rather than attempting
to form copious notes of everything mentioned. I feel I have acquired a basic
understanding of the content of the lectures so far, but need to read much more
to enhance my superficial understanding.

Workshop
I like the design of the day's programme in the sense that the workshop sessions

enable me to internalise the content of the lectures; to discuss with other people apparent uncertainties. The intensity of the whole day, during which we explore an aspect of the course, means that I have time to consolidate ideas and, consequently, generally leave the college feeling that I have learnt something.

Seminars

I feel I participate far more in these seminars than I have done in those during previous years. However, I am still often reluctant to offer verbal comment, despite my good intentions! The seminars clarify and extend my understanding of the papers we are required to read. Listening to other people's ideas and experiences makes the papers appear more relevant and meaningful. I am very aware of the fact that the more I put into this course the more I will receive from it. Thus, greater reading on my part is necessary. I question my ability in terms of identifying children with learning difficulties and implementing suggested intervention techniques. Yet I am (happily) aware of my interest in the subject, e.g., when I go into school and definitely sense "problem areas" and feel myself wanting to respond to them.

Kerry O., Year 4

Course evaluation

I find the course particularly useful and relevant for work in school. We are provided with strategies for dealing with and identifying children with learning difficulties and gifted/able pupils and we have been given useful schemes, addresses, etc. which can be referred to in future years. The seminars and workshops are of great use.

Self-ealuation

I am particularly interested in this course and wish that what I have learnt, I had learnt earlier, as it would have been very useful for past experiences in school. I need to read up on the issues more frequently rather than leaving it to the end of the year! (Hopefully this will be done over Christmas.) I also enjoy the readings, believe it or not, and find the ensuing discussions stimulating; I feel I need to jot down more notes on the papers while reading them, trying to pick out main and subsidiary points rather than taking an overall view. However, I do find that I am applying ideas and skills into my teaching which I have gained from this course, which I feel shows I am interested and also understand. I need to contribute more to discussions as I tend to listen to other ideas but do not share my own!

Attendance

One one-hour seminar missed.

References

Barton, L. and Tomlinson, S. (1984). *Special Education and Social Interests.* London: Croom Helm.

Becker, H. S. Madsen, C. H. et al., (1969). *The contingent use of teacher reinforcement and praise in reducing classroom problem Journal of Special Educ,* 1, 287–307.

Bennett, N. (1986). *Collaborative Learning Children: Do it in Groups or Do They?* Conference paper published by the J. Educ Child Psychology.

Bernstein, B. (1970). Education cannot compensate for society. InA. Cashton and E. Grugeon (Eds), *Language in Education.* London: Routledge & Kegan Paul.

Brown, A. L., Bransford, J. D., Ferrara, R. A. and Campione, J. C. (1983). Learning, remembering and understanding. In J. Flavell and E. Markman (eds), *Carmichael's Manual of Child Psychology,* I. New York: Wiley.

Donaldson, M. (1978). *Children's Minds.* London: Panther.

Feuerstein, R. et al. (1980) *Instrumental Enrichment: an Intervention Programme for Cognitive Modifiability.* Baltimore: University Park Press.

Flavell, J. H.(1979). Metacognition and cognitive monitoring. *American Psychologist,* 34, 906–911.

Freeman, J. (1991). *Gifted Children Grow Up.* London: Cassell.

Gibbs, G. (1990). *Learning through Action.* London: FEU.

Goldberg, M. L. (1956). *Research on the Talented.* New York: Teachers College Press.

Good, T. L. and Brophy, J. E. (1982). *Educational Psychology: a Realistic Approach,* 2nd edn. London: Holt Rinehart and Winston.

Hirst, P. (1968). The contribution of philosophy to the study of the curriculum. In J. R. Kerr (ed.), *Changing the Curriculum.* London: University of London Press.

HMI (1981). *The School Curriculum.* London: HMSO.

HMI (1986). *Lower Attaining Pupils Project Report.* London: HMSO.

HMI (1989). Discipline in Schools: *The Elton Report.* London: HMSO.

HMI (1992). *Provision for Highly Able Pupils in Maintained Schools.* London: HMSO.

Kelly, G. A. (1955). The Psychology of Personal Constructs, 2 vols. New York: Norton.

Kolb, D. A. (1984). Experiential Learning: *Experiences as a Source of Learning and Development.* New York: Prentice-Hall.

Leach, D. (1983). Early screening techniques. *School Psychology Internat,* 4, 47–56.

Lockhead, J. and Clement, J. (1979). *Cognitive Process Instruction* Philadelphia: Franklin Inst Press.

McClelland, D. C., Baldwin, A. L., Bronfenbrenner, U. and Strodtbeck, F. L. (1958). *Talent and Society: New Perspectives in the Identification of Talent.* Princeton, NJ: Van Nostrand.

MacDonald, W. Scott (1971). *Battle in the Classroom.* Brighton: In Text.

Meek, M., and Thomson, B. (1987). *Study Skills in the Secondary School.* London: Routledge.

Montgomery, D. (198). Teaching thinking skills in the school curriculum. *School Psychology Internat* 3, 105–112.

Montgomery, D. (1984). *Evaluation and Enhancement of Teaching Performance* [Learning Difficulties Research Project]. London: Middlesex University.

Montgomery, D. (1985). *The Special Needs of Able Pupils in Ordinary Classrooms.* London: Middlesex University.

Montgomery, D. (1988). Appraisal. *New Era Journal,* 68, 3, 85–90.

Montgomery, D. (1989). *Managing Behaviour Problems.* Sevenoaks: Hodder & Stoughton.

Montgomery, D. (1990). *Children with Learning Difficulties.* London: Cassell.

Montgomery, D. (1991). *The Special Needs of Able Pupils in Ordinary Classrooms [Learning Difficulties Research Project].* London: Middlesex University.

Montgomery, D. (in preparation). *The Implications and Applications of Using*

Cognitive Process Methodologies in Higher Education Programmes.

Montgomery, D. and Hadfield, N. (1989). *Practical Teacher Appraisal.* London: Kogan Page.

Necka, E. (1991). Levels of Mind: a multilevel model of intellect and its implications for identification of the gifted. *European Journal for High Ability,* 2, 12–17.

Painter, F. (1982). Gifted secondary pupils in England: research on identification and characteristics. *School Psychology Internat,* 3, 4, 237–244.

Passow, A. H. (1990). Needed research and development in educating high ability children. *Eur J High Ability,* 1, 15–24.

Piaget, J. (1952). *Origins of Intelligence in the Child.* London: Routledge & Kegan Paul.

Race, P. (1992). Developing competence. *Professorial Inaugural Lectures.* University of Glamorgan.

Roberts, M. (1986). *Capabilities of the Young Child.* Kingston Polytechnic, New Era in Education Conference.

Rosenthal, R. and Jacobsen (eds), (1968). Pygmalion in the Classroom. New York: Holt Rinehart & Winston.

Royce-Adams, R. (1977). *Developing Reading Versatility,* 2nd edn. New York: Holt Rinehart & Winston.

Rutter, M., Maughan, B., Mortimore, P. and Ousten, J. (1979). *15,000 hours.* London: Open Books.

Schools Council (1981). *Study Skills in the Secondary School.* London: Schools Council.

Thomas, L. and Harri-Augstein, S. (1975). *Reading to Learn.* London: Centre for Studies of Human Learning, Brunel University.

Thomas, L., Harri-Augstein, S. and Smith, M. (1984). *Reading to Learn.* London: Methuen.

Vigotsky, L. S. (1978). *Mind in Society.* Cambridge MA: Harvard University Press.

Wang, M. C. and Lindvall, C. M. (1984). Individual differences and school learning environments. In E. W. Gordon, (ed.), *Review of Research in Education*, II. Washington, DC: Amer Educ Res Association.

Weinstein, C. E., Goetz, E. T. and Alexander, P. A. (1988). *Learning and Study Strategies*. London: Academic Press.

Improving Study Skills: an Experimental Approach

Ann Leitch, Glasgow Caledonian University

Introduction

Over the last 30 years, the non-completion rate for students entering higher education has remained at approximately 14%. The rate varies in different institutions, the problem being more acute in Scotland, where the rate is 4 to 5% higher on average than in the rest of United Kingdom (Johnes and Taylor, 1989; Woodley, Thompson and Cowan, 1992). Attempts to analyse the causes of failure to complete degree courses have focussed on two areas: the academic background of entrants to higher education and factors affecting academic performance within higher education.

The relationship between previous academic attainment and performance in higher education, as assessed by correlation studies, is unclear. The coefficients vary in magnitude and direction and have generally been less than 0.5. Thus, less than 25% of the variance in university examination results is explained by school performance. Woodley et al. (1992) demonstrated a strong inverse relationship between non-completion rates and school examination scores. However, analysis of the data in this study reveals that, for relatively high school examination scores, the non-completion rate is still pronounced. For example, the non-completion rate for a Scottish Highers score of 16 points, the equivalent of four B passes, varied from 21% for females to 29% for males. Thus, selection procedures, based solely on the use of national examination results, cannot provide a solution to the problem of high non-completion rates, unless a large proportion of the population is excluded from higher education.

Students' background knowledge accounts for a small and inconsistent proportion of the variance in performance in higher education. In addition, the ability to select and apply appropriate approaches to learning in a new educational setting has been shown to be important. Entwistle, Wall, Macaulay, Tait and Entwistle (1991) presented evidence from interviews that many students, particularly those from the Scottish school system, felt unprepared in terms of the study skills required at university.

Four study orientations have been identified by factor analysis: meaning orientation,reproducing orientation, achievement orientation, and non-academic orientation and the characteristics of these have been summarised (Entwistle and Tait, 1990). Various studies have examined the relationship between approaches to learning and performance. For example, positive correlations between the tendency to adopt a deep approach and academic performance have been found (e.g., Entwistle, 1987). In addition, it has been found that the approaches to learning which students adopt are influenced by their perception of the course (Entwistle and Ramsden, 1983).

The present study consisted of an action research project designed to develop a model of student performance which could be refined throughout the project according to its predictive validity; at the same time, an intervention programme was undertaken to help to foster more appropriate approaches to learning among students identified by the model as potentially "at risk". The rationale was to develop a model based on explanatory variables including students' background knowledge, their approaches to learning and their perceptions of the course. Variables explaining the greatest proportion of the variance in student performance were incorporated into a model, and manipulation of these variables formed the basis of the "treatment" applied to the students.

Method

The subjects in the study were three first-year student cohorts of the BSc Applied Biosciences at Glasgow Caledonian University. Explanatory variables included background data (age, gender and school performance indicators which were collected at enrolment to the course), and assessment of study skills by the "Experiences of Studying and Higher Education" inventory (Entwistle et al., 1991) at the sixth week of the first semester. The criterion variable consisted of a four-point ordinal scale indicating student performance at the first final examination diet. From this large data set from students that had completed the first year of the course, a model consisting of a small number of explanatory variables was developed; this model was applied to subsequent cohorts near the start of the course.

In the first year of the study, questionnaire responses of students who had completed the first year of the course were read carefully and extreme scores which might be associated with failure were noted for each student. This was carried out in order to elucidate patterns of student failure. The data was then entered into Statview 512+™ on the Apple Macintosh LC and a correlation analysis was performed both at individual item level and using groups of items or dimensions, in the case of the study skills variables. Stepwise regression was performed in order to identify groups of variables which would explain the greatest proportion of variance in the criterion variable.

Several groupings of variables were thus identified. For every group of explanatory variables, a median value on the chosen variables was found for each student. The median of the students' median values was calculated for the whole class. Students with median values falling below a fixed point less than the class median value were identified as potentially "at risk". This procedure was repeated for each group of variables until eleven explanatory variables providing the most accurate prediction of failure were found.

The class was subsequently divided into two random halves with an equal number of passing and failing students in each half. Data on the eleven explanatory variables and the criterion variable was entered into Minitab 8 for one half and a predictive model was set up by means of discriminant analysis. The predictive ability of the model was tested on the remaining half of the class. With the second cohort of students, data on the explanatory variables was collected as before and the likelihood of students passing or failing was estimated using the model set up by discriminant analysis. Twenty-four students were identified as most likely to be "at risk". This group of students were divided into an experimental and a control group using a matched pairs design with the matching based on gender, age and the probability of failure derived from the model. Students in this cohort were made aware of the purpose of the questionnaire and the rationale behind the selection of the experimental group; the existence of a control group was not revealed.

For the remainder of the academic year, students in the experimental group were given additional guidance on an individual basis. The programme was standardised for all the students in the group and was designed to manipulate the variables applied in the predictive model and to develop aspects of study behaviour. The latter had been identified from the literature and were incorporated into the programme in order to enhance students' awareness of a variety of approaches to learning and improve their academic self-confidence. The control group were given no additional tutorials. The final results of the two groups were compared after the first examination diet by means of the Wilcoxon signed-ranks test (one-tailed).

In advance of the enrolment of the third cohort of students, the model was improved to take account of weaknesses identified in its predictive ability. At the sixth week of the first semester, 28 potentially weak students were identified and experimental and control groups were formed as before. Students within the experimental group were provided with a more intensive study skills programme than the rest of the cohort. This took place within the tutorial sessions of three of the first-year modules. On this occasion, a group approach was used, employing methods suggested by Gibbs (1981), again designed to manipulate variables utilised in the predictive models. Students were not informed of the rationale for selection of the experimental group. The first diet examination results of the experimental and control groups were again compared by means of the Wilcoxon signed-ranks test.

Results

Detailed examination of the questionnaire responses which was undertaken for the first cohort of students indicated that there was a lack of uniformity in responses among the weak students. No single pattern of failure could be identified.

For most of the explanatory variables, both the magnitude and direction of the correlation with the criterion variable, first-year examination performance, varied considerably between the three cohorts of students. The results for gender and the variables within the achievement orientation dimension were the most stable over the three years: females performed better than males and the achievement orientation correlated positively with performance. A similar trend was observed when study skills variables were examined as dimensions: the magnitude and sign of the correlation coefficients varied for the three cohorts, with the exception of the achievement orientation dimension where the relationships were more consistent, particularly for female students. Values for Spearman Rank correlation coefficients for six dimensions of study behaviour are shown in Table 1.

Table 1

Dimension	Number of explanatory variables	Cohort 1 rs	(n)	Cohort 2 rs	(n)	Cohort 3 rs	(n)
ASC	2	.04	(53)	-.08	(59)	.05	(40)
AO	7	.18	(49)	.07	(59)	.12	(40)
MO	7	.10	(53)	-.04	(59)	.00	(40)
RO	5	.01	(50)	-.02	(59)	-.01	(40)
NAO	5	-.12	(51)	.10	(59)	.01	(40)
CO	2	-.27	(53)	.37**	(59)	-.11	(40)

Table 1 Spearman Rank correlation coefficients (rs) for three cohorts of BSc Applied Biosciences students, indicating the relationship between first-year final examination diet results and six dimensions of study behaviour :academic self-confidence (ASC), achievement orientation (AO) meaning orientation (MO), reproducing orientation (RO), non-academic orientation (NAO), and career orientation (CO); n is the number of students completing items relating to each dimension on the questionnaire.
** significant at P = .01

The eleven explanatory variables which were selected as the best group of predictors and which were entered into the discriminant analysis procedure were as follows:

- gender
- school performance in chemistry and biology
- two items on the achievement orientation dimension (organisation and ability to "get down to work")*
- three items on the non-academic orientation dimension (difficulty in concentrating, ability to see relevance of work, finding work boring)*
- one item on the meaning orientation dimension (understanding course material)*
- one item on the reproducing orientation dimension (tendency to memorise information)*
- number of hours of study*.

* individual items from Entwistle's "Experiences of Studying and Higher Education" inventory. When the model established with these eleven variables was tested in a split-half procedure, it yielded 78.6% and 80% accuracies for the "likely to pass" and "likely to fail" groups of students respectively.

The predictive validity for the above model was tested on the second cohort of students (experimental group excluded) and it was found that only 50% of the weak students were correctly identified. Only one of the seven "fails" among the female students had been successfully identified, and hence attempts were made to incorporate predictor variables into the model to provide a more effective means of predicting females most likely to be "at risk". The modified model was tested on the third cohort of students (experimental group excluded), when an accuracy of 50% was again observed in predicting fails. Eight students in the third cohort failed to complete the questionnaire; all of these students scored 1 or 2 on the criterion variable and were thus unlikely to proceed to Year 2 of the course.

For each of the two years of the intervention programme, the mean aggregate marks for seven of the eight modules of the Year 1 syllabus were higher amongst students in the experimental groups than in the control groups. However, when the aggregate marks of the pairs were examined, none of the differences were significant in terms of the Wilcoxon signed ranks test (P=.05). The differences in means are shown in Table 2.

Table 2

Module	First year	Second year
	Mean x-y (n=8)	Mean x-y (n=13)
The Cell	0.38	2.70
The Gene	–2.13	0.15
Organic Chemistry	2.00	2.17
Mathematics/Statistics	4.63	–3.00
Whole Organism Biology	0.63	1.46
Microbiology A	5.00	4.69
Physical Chemistry	3.50	2.54
Physics	7.88	0.23

Table 2 Difference in mean scores for the experimental (X) and control (Y) groups for two successive cohorts of first-year students in the BSc Applied Biosciences (where N is the number of matched pairs continuing to the end of the programme)

The difference in final results between members of the matched pairs is expressed in terms of the four-point ordinal variable, which was the main criterion variable used in the study, in Table 3.

Table 3

Cohort 1, experimental group	4 4 4 3 4 4 4 3	
Cohort 1, control group	2 3 3 4 3 2 4 4	
Cohort 2, experimental group	4 4 4 3 4 4 4 4 4 4 4 4 3	
Cohort 2, control group	4 2 3 3 4 4 3 4 2 4 4 3 4	

Table 3 Comparison of scores on the criterion variable (where 4 represents no resits, 3 is 1 to 2 resits, 2 is 3 to 4 resits, 1 is 5+ resits) for experimental and control groups for two cohorts of B Sc Applied Biosciences students

For five of the matched pairs in each cohort, the results of the experimental group were better than those of the control group. In the second cohort, a control group member performed better than an experimental group member in only one case. However, the results just failed to reach a significant level (P=.05) on the Wilcoxon signed-ranks test.

Discussion

Detailed examination of the questionnaire responses, although based on only one cohort of students, indicated that the quest for a simple model of student failure is unlikely to be fruitful. Several patterns emerged: the anxious student, the disorganised student, the disinterested student, but the numbers of student failures examined were too low to permit useful categorisation. Analysis of additional questionnaires and interviews with students who have failed may enable different patterns of responses associated with weakness to be clearly identified.

The low correlation between questionnaire items and performance can be explained in terms of variability in individual student responses at this level. However, the relationship at the level of dimension was no more robust. This could be explained in part by the small numbers of students involved in the study. There was some evidence from the preliminary examination of the questionnaires that there may have been some interaction between variables. For example, anxiety combined with low academic self-confidence could have a negative effect on performance whereas anxiety combined with high intrinsic motivation could have a positive effect on performance. Further study employing a more qualitative approach may provide greater insight into such interaction and lead to the development of a variety of models of failure.

The low correlation coefficients and, indeed, some negative coefficients between the meaning orientation and performance were unexpected. Analysis of first-year examination questions reveals that many of the questions could be answered effectively by simple recall of lecture material. In order to examine the effects of the changing pattern of assessment throughout the course, the approaches to learning employed by the students and student performance will be studied longitudinally. Although such an explanation of the correlation coefficients between the meaning orientation and performance appears logical, it would have been expected that this argument would have been supported by strong positive correlations between the reproducing orientation and performance; this is not the case and it may be that the effect of low numbers in the study and possible interaction of variables underlie the unexplained pattern of responses.

Although the predictive validity of the model was high in the initial split-half test, the value of the model as a predictive tool did not persist between cohorts. This may be related to the existence of various patterns of responses among weak students. If the distribution of such patterns varied between cohorts, a model developed on the basis of data from one cohort may not be applicable to subsequent cohorts.

Various difficulties were associated with the first year of the experimental programme. Students were aware of the rationale of the programme and a number of them indicated that their questionnaire responses had been influenced by their desire not to be selected for the experimental programme. In addition, several students appeared to be adversely affected by difficulties associated with work with the tutor on a one-to-one basis and by some degree of ridicule from their peers due to their selection for remedial work. The second year of the programme, which employed a group approach and avoided identifying those students receiving the remedial programme, was accepted enthusiastically by the students. Sharing of experiences among students encouraged group members to consider their own patterns of study behaviour in the light of group discussions.

The difference between the performance of the experimental and control groups just failed to reach the level of significance (P=0.05). This may have been due to imperfect matching of the groups at the outset of the programme or to the influence of uncontrolled variables throughout the programme. These factors are being investigated by means of interviews to be conducted with the experimental and control group members. It is also likely that the amount of additional time spent with the experimental group, about four hours per semester, was inadequate to produce a significant effect.

Conclusions

A more elaborate model of student failure is required. A more qualitative approach designed to identify patterns of responses among weak students may yield data which can be tested quantitatively with the subsequent development of a variety of models. The success of the intervention programme may be improved by the application of a model of greater predictive validity but, in addition, a more rigorous programme may be needed to produce significant effects.

With recognition and help in funding from Dr Ken Richardson, School of Education, Open University, and Professor John T. Knowler, Department of Biological Sciences, Glasgow Caledonian University.

References

Entwistle, N. J. (1987). A model of the teaching-learning process. in J. T. E. Richardson, M. W. Eysenck, and D. W. Piper, (eds), *Student Learning: Research in Education and Cognitive Psychology*. Milton Keynes: Open University Press, 13–28.

Entwistle, N. J. and Ramsden, P. (1983). *Understanding Student Learning*. London: Croom Helm.

Entwistle, N. J. and Tait, H. (1990). Approaches to learning, evaluations of teaching and preferences for contrasting academic environments. *Higher Education*, 19, 169–194.

Entwistle, N. J., Wall, D., Macaulay, C., Tait, H. and Entwistle, D. (1991). School to Higher Education: Bridging the Gap. *Interchange*, 2, SOED.

Gibbs, G. (1981). *Teaching students to Learn: a Student-Centred Approach.* Milton Keynes: Open University Press.

Johnes, J. and Taylor, J. (1989). Undergraduate non-completion rates: differences between UK universities. *Higher Education*, 18, 209–225.

Woodley, A., Thompson, M. and Cowan, J. (1992). *Factors Affecting Non-Completion Rates in Scottish Universities.* SRC Report No. 69, Institute of Educational Technology, Open University.

Chapter 9   Students' understanding about learning

Assessing students knowledge of learning: a comparison of data collection methods

Gillian M. Boulton-Lewis and Barry C. Dart, Queensland University of Technology

Both authors, who jointly taught this class and undertook the research, believe that learning is relational (cf. Ramsden, 1988), that prior knowledge plays a crucial part in subsequent learning, and that if deep learning is to occur students must construct their own cognitive links by reflecting on new information and relating that to what they already know and believe. If lecturers are to facilitate this process for students we posit that they must have some idea of students' beginning knowledge of a discipline area and the structural organisation of that knowledge. The purpose of the research was to find out, using a variety of methods, what the students in this sample knew about learning, and adult learning in particular, and to compare the methods and the results obtained from them.

Open Statements, Written Assignments and the SOLO Taxonomy

Students' knowledge of learning can be classified according to the level of structure evidenced in written responses. Students wrote open statements about learning at the beginning of the semester and written assignments focussing on an aspect of adult learning at the conclusion of the subject. Both the open statements and the end-of-semester assignments were categorised according to the SOLO taxonomy (cf. Biggs and Collis, 1982; 1989; Biggs, 1991). Biggs and Collis described five levels of the structure of observed learning outcomes (SOLO) in a range of secondary school content areas, from incompetence to expertise, as follows: prestructural (incompetence), unistructural (one relevant aspect is known), multistructural (several relevant independent aspects are known), relational (aspects integrated into a structure), extended abstract (knowledge generalised to a new domain). The levels occur in a cyclical fashion for increasingly more formal modes of learning from sensori- motor to formal-2. Such a taxonomy can be used as a model to assess and describe students entering and changing knowledge as they progress through courses. Students at the tertiary level ideally should develop knowledge in their discipline areas at the relational level in the formal-1 mode (Biggs and Collis, 1989; Biggs, 1991). In this case the discipline was learning and that of adults in particular, and almost all the students were experienced educators of some kind. Boulton-Lewis (submitted) proposed a version of the SOLO taxonomy as it applied to knowledge of learning. The levels of the SOLO taxonomy as they apply to learning, expressed in general terms, are summarised in Table 1, and examples of these are given in Table 2 (Boulton-Lewis, 1993).

Table 1 Levels of the SOLO Taxonomy at the Formal-1 level as they Might Apply to Knowledge of Learning

Taxonomy level	Description
Prestructural	There is no evidence of any knowledge of the processes involved in learning.
Unistructural	One relevant aspect of learning is understood and focussed on.
Multistructural	Several relevant independent aspects of learning are presented. These are not integrated into an overall structure.
Relational	Relevant aspects of learning are integrated into an overall structure. Typically these responses include references to one or more of the following beliefs: learning is a life-long process that changes the quality of existence; learning involves understanding; the application of learning is important.
Extended abstract	The integrated knowledge of learning is generalised to a new domain.

Table 2 Example Responses for Levels of the SOLO Taxonomy for Learning

---

Prestructural

No idea

Unistructural

Real learning is what you remember, that is important values and lessons, even information you remember from schooling in the years after it. That is how I have found it. You remember it and in your later years it is amazing the data you can recall.

Multistructural

Learning is to have real understanding about a particular subject whether through actual experience or through other sources such as textbooks, etc.

This belief was probably acquired through the conservative thinking of the education system I was brought up with. I know that I can learn easily and quickly if there is a teacher who teaches in a methodological planned way; where I can see the plan and know where I am heading. I usually go about learning by reading, memorising, by applying to my actual experiences or knowing about other people's experiences. By applying it to reality it becomes simpler. Other people's espoused opinions and beliefs and values influence how I learn, and sometimes make it difficult to learn. By this I mean I sometimes want to hold my own opinion but other people try to sway me to their belief. I know that I have learnt something when I feel satisfied. I also know when I use the knowledge years later.

Relational

Learning involves the sharing of knowledge to facilitate personal growth and a greater understanding of the world around me. This perception learning is based entirely on my own subjective value judgement and could not be considered a view that I have acquired within the education system, which, in the most part, focusses on a relatively utilitarian approach, producing skilled people for the workforce. Learning for me is facilitated by my being able to gain further insight into why I am here, how I fit into the society I live in, and why certain attitude and belief systems exist in that society. I know I have learnt something when I reach a greater understanding of myself as a person and the complex inter-relationships that mould the society in which I live.

In preliminary research with a small sample of students enrolled in a master's degree in education (Boulton-Lewis, 1992) it was found that the majority of statements were multistructural. This, despite the fact that they were experienced educators studying at the postgraduate level. In subsequent research (Boulton-Lewis 1993), with a sample of tertiary students in a range of courses and discipline areas, the majority of statements were also multistructural in their knowledge of learning, although their knowledge of specific aspects of learning was not as great generally as was that of the educators in the previous study. In this second study lecturers responses were also analysed and the majority of their responses, across all disciplines, were also multistructural, although almost as many of this group gave relational responses as multistructural ones.

The majority of responses at the multistructural level in both these studies indicated that generally students and lecturers could describe some or many relevant aspects of the learning process. However, they had not organised the information sufficiently to view it as a whole and from the perspective of an over-arching structure that they could apply selectively to different aspects of learning or teaching. A small percentage of students and an even smaller percentage of lecturers gave responses at the unistructural level, indicating that they were aware of only one way of learning. At the upper end of the Taxonomy the small percentage of students and the larger percentage of lecturers who gave relational responses indicated that they perceive learning from an organized structural perspective. The only response that was categorised as extended abstract came from a postgraduate student. In the study described above the data were used to describe the students' knowledge to lecturers and the lecturers' knowledge was taken into account in discussing their teaching strategies with them. In the study described in this paper the students' written responses were used by the authors to inform their teaching and to compare the information that they provided about students' knowledge of learning with that obtained from the other methods of data collection described below.

Concept Mapping

Concept mapping is a process by which conceptual knowledge and change can be identified. It has been used in a number of studies in teacher education (Beyerbach, 1988; special issue of the *Journal of Research on Science Teaching*, 1990; Morine-Dershimer, 1989, 1993). It is a meta-learning strategy developed by Novak and Gowin (1984) and its use in teacher education programmess may have pay-offs in three ways. First, it may help student teachers and in-service teachers in their understanding of course material by requiring them to identify key concepts, arrange them in a way that reflects a movement from general to specific, and relate them to each other in a meaningful way. Second, it may lead to them adopting more reflective and meaningful approaches to their practices in that they will look for ways by which their students can form a conceptual understanding of the subject matter. Thirdly, their experience with it and other meta-cognitive tools may increase the likelihood of their becoming more skilful in the use of these tools and therefore cause them to be more likely to use them with their own students. Novak (1990, p.943) states that the studies by Beyerbach and Smith (1990) and Hoz, Tomer and Tamir (1990) " . . . point to the need for empowering teachers to learn meaningfully so that they can be more successful in helping their own students learn meaningfully."

In this study students' concept maps were evaluated both quantitatively and qualitatively at the beginning and the end of the semester's course of study on adult learning. Quantitative evaluation was considered necessary to provide a comparison of structural characteristics including hierarchy, relationships, branching and cross-links. Qualitative evaluation was undertaken to determine the change in level of structure (according to the SOLO taxonomy) and to compare this with the other measures of structure described previously.

Method

Sample

The original sample consisted of 28 students enrolled in a subject in adult learning at a fourth-year level. Most were experienced educators in primary, secondary or TAFE education, two were overseas tertiary educators and three were preservice graduate diploma students. There are complete data for 23 of these students.

Procedures

Written statements and assignments

In response to the following instructions students were asked to write an open statement under the heading "Your beliefs about learning".

> Please write about a page or so on your ideas about learning. In that, you may consider such things as a description of what you think learning is, how you think you acquired that belief, what you know about your own learning, how you actually go about learning, what factors you think influence your learning and how they influence it, and how you know that you have learnt something.

Students undertook an assignment at the end of semester which required them to negotiate a learning contract with their lecturers where they applied their knowledge of adult learning to an aspect of their own practice. Some students chose to present the main part of their work in an alternative form, such as video, but they all provided an explanation of learning or adult learning and its relation to their work.

267

Concept maps

At the first meeting of class, after administrative tasks had been completed and the structure of the subject and subject demands had been discussed, students were introduced to concept maps. Their purpose and development were described and they were shown how to construct these by one of the authors. They were then given a number of concepts relating to everyday phenomena, of which they were expected to have some understanding, and were asked to draw concept maps showing this understanding. After each student had completed a map, these were discussed by the group and various examples were analysed and discussed. When student concerns had been addressed they were asked to draw a concept map showing their understanding of the important aspects of learning. At the last class meeting at the end of the semester students were again asked to draw a concept map depicting their view of the important elements of learning.

Analysis

Open statements and assignments

The open statements were analysed by two trained researchers and checked by one of the authors. Any contentious examples were referred to John Biggs, one of the authors of the SOLO taxonomy. The inter-rater reliability was greater than 80%. The statements were categorized as prestructural, unistructural, multistructural, relational or extended abstract as described above and in accordance with the framework in Table 1. Minus and plus were used to modify categories to indicate greater or lesser conetent knowledge.

The end of semester assignments were analysed and assessed according to the content knowledge of adult learning and its application as well as for their structural and therefore SOLO levels. The latter levels are included as data in this study.

Concept maps

The concept maps were analysed quantitatively using a method developed by Vargas and Alvarez (1992) which is a modified form of the concept-map scheme developed by Novak, Gowin and Johansen (1983) that provides a consistent syntax and grading system for concept maps. The grading scheme allocates points as follows:

(a)   hierarchy – one point is allocated for the number of hierarchical levels that are correct;

(b)   relationships – one point is allocated for each relationship drawn between two concepts that is described correctly by an explicit proposition;

(c)   branching – a branch is a relationship formed between one concept and two or more concepts at the next hierarchical level; one point is allocated for the first level of branching and three points for any branching that occurs at subsequent levels;

(d)   cross-links – a cross-link connects relationships and shows integration between two relationships. One point is allocated for each cross-link.

The qualitative analysis of the concept maps was undertaken with a method devised by the second author. SOLO levels for the concept maps were determined according to the following principles:

(a)   unistructural – a linear map with no branching;
(b)   multistructural – at least three levels with appropriate branches;
(c)   relational – as for multistructural plus evidence of appropriate cross-links.

As well, these categories were established in terms of the number of levels, branches and cross-links use. For example, for the multistructural level, M+ indicated a relatively high number of levels and branches, whereas M - indicated fewer levels (at least three) and branches.

These methods of analysis are exemplified in the concept map drawn by a student at the end of semester (see Figure 1).

Figure 1: Example of a concept map and its evaluation

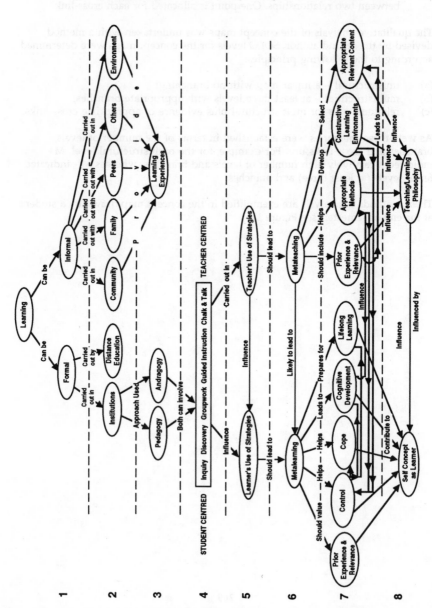

Results

Open statements and assignments
The SOLO levels for open statements at the beginning of the semester and for assignments at the end of semester were as shown in Table 3.

Table 3 SOLO Levels for Written Statements at the Beginning and End of the Semester

Level	Statement	Assignment
Unistructual	2 (9%)	0 (0%)
Multistructual	19 (74%)	19 (74%)
Regional	4 (17%)	6 (26%)
Total	25 (100%)	25 (100%)

The summary shown in Table 3 indicates that the general move was upwards in terms of levels. At the end of the semester there were no unistructural responses and a greater percentage of relational responses. Individual students moved as follows: 14 upwards, that is, from minus to that level or to plus, or to the next level; four students stayed at the same level and six submitted final assignments where they were down a level or part of a level respectively from multistructural(M) to M - and from M+ to M. This shows a general improvement in the structure of the knowledge of learning, although the majority were multistructural at the beginning and end of the course, as were the majority of students in both the earlier studies described above. This means that this group also knew more at the end of the course about a range of aspects of the learning process but had not organised them into a structure that they could apply at the relational level.

Content analysis of open statements
The content of the open statements included some discussion of aspects of learning as an adult, although there was little mention of some characteristics identified by research in the area (Knowles, 1990; Brookfield, 1986) such as independence, use of prior experience and knowledge, intrinsic motivation, desire to be self-directed and there was no explicit mention of others such as the need to be treated as an adult, a problem-focussed orientation, or of being personally responsible for learning. There were more statements about students' own learning styles generally, about desire for relevance and immediate usage, of like or dislike for collaborative learning, and of critical reflection on their own learning.

There was also a range of statements made about learning generally, including definitions of learning, factors influencing learning, learning strategies, motivation and kinds of learning outcomes.

In general most aspects of learning that are of current concern were included in student responses However, individual students varied greatly, even at this level, in the range of aspects that they discussed and in the level of structural organisation of the information that they possessed.

Concept maps
At the beginning of the semester concept map scores ranged from 7 to 42 with a mean of 16. Scores at the end of the semester ranged from 9 to 74 with a mean of 23. Individually, 16 students increased their scores, five decreased and one remained constant. The change resulted from increases in the number of levels and appropriate branches in the final maps. This is reflected in the increase of major categories and of sub-categories used to develop the main categories. As well, there was greater understanding of the inter-relatedness of the concepts employed as evidenced by the use of more precise linking phrases between the concepts. This indicates not only a more comprehensive knowledge of important factors related to learning but also a better understanding of how these are related to their identifying components. There was little change in the number of cross-links used.

SOLO levels for concept maps at the beginning and the end of the semester are shown in Table 4.

Table 4 SOLO Levels for Concept Maps at the Beginning and the End of the Semester

Level	Beginning	End
Unistructural	2	0
Multistructural	19	19
Relational	2	4

Although this table suggests relatively little change in terms of levels, inspection of results for individuals shows that nine students moved upwards from minus to that level or to plus, or to the next level; 12 students stayed at the same level and two went down a level (1 from M+ to M and the other from M to M -. These results are similar to the results for the open statements and assignments in that most students were multistructural at both the beginning and the end of the course.

There was a high level of consistency on SOLO levels for the written statements and concept maps at the beginning (70%) and at the end (74%)of the semester, as shown in Table 5. The differences that did occur could perhaps be explained by the differing ability of students to express their ideas in written form or in figures. Nevertheless we believe that the consistency is high enough for one or other of the procedures to be used confidently as a measure on its own or for students to be given the choice as to which procedure they would like to use to make their knowledge of learning explicit.

The analysis of the content of the written statements and of the concept maps presented us with a daunting range of beliefs and knowledge about learning which we knew it would be difficult to affect in a 13-week semester subject. We attempted to facilitate changes in knowledge and beliefs by trying to help students to make their knowledge of learning explicit in such statements and concept maps, to discuss it with others, to write about it in learning logs, to apply it to an aspect of their practice and therefore to be meta-cognitive about making links between new ideas and their prior knowledge. The results show that some change occurred. However, not many students changed in their level of structure of knowledge; most of them merely acquired more information and demonstrated greater skill in applying it.

Table 5 Comparison of SOLO Levels on Open Statements and Concept Maps

Beginning of semester

Concept map

		Uni	Multi	Rel	Row total
Written statement	Uni		2		2
	Multi	2	15		17
	Rel	3	1		4
Column total		2	20	1	23

End of semester

Concept map

		Multi	Rel	Row total
Written assignment	Multi	17	2	19
	Rel	3	1	4
Column total		20	3	23

Taken together, the quantitative and qualitative results suggest that students came into the course with knowledge of a number of factors influencing the learning process that were generally unrelated to one another. By the end of the course they had increased their knowledge of influencing factors as well as their understanding of how main categories were related to their subordinate categories. However, most of them had not integrated these to provide a concept relational structure (as shown by little increase in the number of cross-links in the final maps).

Discussion
The value of the written statements was that they provided us at the beginning and the end of the semester with an idea of the aspects of knowledge that the students possessed individually and as a group. They also provided information about the level of structural organisation of that knowledge. We believe that analysis of the structure of students' written responses, as well as the content of those responses, is an effective way of measuring students' knowledge of a content area for assessment purposes, as proposed by Biggs (1992), as well as, in this case, providing information to guide teaching.

The study also indicates that concept mapping is a useful procedure for measuring changes in students' knowledge, understanding and structure of subject matter. It has shown that concept mapping can provide evidence of students' elaboration of the conceptual understanding they already possess, as well as the extent to which these concepts are integrated into a coherent body of knowledge.

In this case the results of the analyses of the concept maps confirmed the findings from the open-ended statements and assignments, namely that most teachers have some knowledge about various aspects of the learning process but do not appear to have synthesised this into a meaningful gestalt. The consequence of this would most likely be that their approach to teaching includes a number of strategies designed to focus on different elements of the learning process, without any organising thread to coordinate their application and effects. It would be most unlikely that students in their classrooms would adopt a deep approach to learning.

Conclusion

On the basis of this study we would suggest that both written statements and concept maps are effective ways of obtaining data about students' knowledge of a discipline area, and in this case knowledge of learning. The results suggest that confidence can be placed in either measure to provide the required information about individual students and a group generally. However, the two measures used together will give a fuller description of their knowledge.

References

Beyerbach, B. (1988). Developing a technical vocabulary on teacher planning: preservice teachers' concept maps. *Teaching and Teacher Education,* 4, 339-347.

Beyerbach, B. and Smith, J. (1990). Using a computerized concept mapping program to assess preservice teachers' thinking about effective teaching. *Journal of Research in Science Teaching,* 27,10, 961-972.

Biggs, J. B. (1992). A qualitative approach to grading students. *HERDSA News,* 14,3, 3-6.

Biggs, J. B. (Ed.) (1991). *Teaching for Learning: the View from Cognitive Psychology.* Hawthorn, Vic.:ACER.

Biggs, J. B. and Collis, K. F. (1989). Towards a model of school-based curriculum development and assessment: Using the SOLO taxonomy. *Australian Journal of Education,* 33, 149-161.

Biggs, J. B. and Collis, K. F. (1982). Evaluating the Quality of Learning: *The SOLO Taxonomy.* New York: Academic Press.

Boulton-Lewis, G. M. (1992). *The SOLO Taxonomy and Levels of Knowledge of Learning.* Paper at the HERDSA 1992 Conference, 7-10 July, Monash University College Gippsland, Churchill, Australia.

Boulton-Lewis, G. M. (1993). *Tertiary Students' Knowledge of their own Learning and a SOLO Taxonomy.* Paper at the 5th Conference Research on Learning and Instruction (EARLI), Aix-en- Provence, France, 31 August – 5 September.

Brookfield, S. (1986). *Understanding and Facilitating Adult Learning.* Buckingham: Open University Press.

Hoz, R., Tomer, Y. and Tamir, P. (1990). The relations between disciplinary and pedagogical knowledge and the length of teaching experience of biology and geography teachers. *Journal of Research in Science Teaching,* 27,10, 973-986. *Journal of Research in Science Teaching,* (1990). Special Issue: *Perspectives on Concept Mapping.* 27,10.

Knowles, M. S. (1990). *The Adult Learner: aNeglected Species,* 4th edn. Houston: Gulf.

Morine-Dershimer, G. (1989). Preservice teachers' conceptions of content and pedagogy: measuring growth in reflective, pedagogical decision-making. *Journal of Teacher Education*, 40, 46-52.

Morine-Dershimer, G. (1993). Tracing conceptual change in preservice teachers. *Teaching and Teacher Education*, 9, 15-26.

Novak, J. (1990). Concept mapping: a useful tool for science education. *Journal of Research in Science Teaching*, 27,10, 937-950.

Novak, J. and Gowin, D. (1984). *Learning How to Learn*. New York: Cambridge University Press.

Novak, J, Gowin, D. and Johansen, G. (1983). *The Use of Concept Mapping and Gowin's Vee Mapping Iinstructional Strategies in Junior High School Science*. ERIC Documentation Reproduction Service No.ED200437.

Ramsden, P. (1988). Studying learning: improving teaching. In P. Ramsden (ed.), *Improving Learning: New Perspectives*. London: Kogan Page.

Vargas, E. and Alvarez, H. (1992). Mapping out students' abilities. *Science Scope*, 15,6, 41-43.

Know the Formula and Hit the Jackpot! First-year Students on Learning

Rob Hyland, Bedford College of Higher Education

Introduction

The research has its origins in formal and informal discussions with a group of students throughout the first semester about learning and coping with the demands of the modular course. Its immediate prompt was a specific statement from a student outside the group studied: "I haven't seemed to learn much: I've done a lot of assignments." More deep-seated reasons for the research lie in my involvement in writing course aims and modules for course submissions, and in Enterprise in Higher Education initiatives to foster student-centred learning. The approach shares Morgan's "basic tenet . . . that understanding learning from the learners' perspective is the crucial starting point for our work as teachers, trainers and course designers . . ." (Morgan, 1993, p. 11), though I would emphasise the plural nature of learners' perspectives.

There have been many studies of student learning. Two, however, Perry (1970, 1988) and Säljö (1982), have provided frameworks and categories which can broadly summarise the learner's approach to learning. It is possible from such models at least to consider individuals' development and to raise questions about the way specific courses may contribute to the development of learning. Such models do have inherent normative implications, whether explicit or implicit, and research into learning must necessarily disclose some wider view of the purposes of education. "Improving student learning" would seem to be both logically underpinned by and practically dependent upon some consideration of students' perceptions of both the processes and the ends of learning in higher education.

Context

The college has a modular scheme leading to a BA/BSc or BEd (Primary). The extent of integration between the routes to different degrees varies across the subject "pathways".

The college documentation for courses is very explicit about the need to develop students' learning in its broadest sense. Fundamental to the modular scheme structure is that all students take "supporting studies", which is, the students are informed, "designed to ensure that your chosen programme of study meets your academic, personal development and vocational needs" (BCHE, 1992, p. 5.)

Supporting studies has three strands: professional tutor groups; skills courses;

and Ccreers orientation. The skills courses in Semester 1 are essentially subject related study skills for each pathway.

The professional tutor group has wide-ranging functions. The professional tutor (who in other institutions might be described as "personal tutor") has a general responsibility for the students and their progress, but may in fact teach none of them. The tutor acts as an administrative and personal link with the students but also has a role in the promotion of learning. The list of the professional tutor's responsibilities includes: "to encourage an active approach to learning" and "to support you in developing a reflective approach to learning, life planning and personal development'" (BCHE, 1992, p. 6).

The handbook includes an outline suggested programme for tutors to work with their group. It also includes a range of reflection and analysis exercises for students to consider their skill, progress and aspirations. In practice, however, students do tend to see professional tutors in terms of a fairly traditional model of a personal tutor.

The college has an interest in a number of initiatives which focus on the development of teaching and learning. In particular, it is a member of ERTEC, the Eastern Region Teacher Education Consortium, an Enterprise in Higher Education project which has influencing pedagogy as an explicit objective.

Methodology

The students who were the immediate focus of the study constituted a first-year 'professional tutor group'. The group was simply selected by its being the professional tutor group of the researching tutor. The method of research was necessarily kept simple as it was important that the research process did not conflict with the needs of the students in relationship to me as professional tutor. The group itself was a mixture of BA and BEd students and drawn from a range of subject pathways and including 18+ entrants and mature students.

The principal source of data is individual interviews. Eleven of the 13 students in the group were individually interviewed using a semi-structured approach, early in the second semester. The interviews were recorded, transcribed and analysed for key concepts and illuminative comments. Participation was voluntary; the two students not interviewed were simply missing at the time.

Most of the group were then interviewed more briefly and informally towards the end of the second semester. Some significant elements of the first interview were discussed and clarification sought where appropriate. One of the students missing from the original sample was interviewed at the end of the year.

In addition there are notes of comments and conversations accumulated during the year from group and individual discussions and activities.

Students' responses were often personal and specific. Responses related to concepts of "learning" were compared with the categories and "exemplars" given by Säljö (1982). Säljö's framework of conceptions of learning has five categories:

1   learning as the increase of knowledge;
2   learning as memorising.;
3   learning as the acquisition of facts, procedures, etc.,
    which can be retained and/or utilised in practice;
4.   learning as the abstraction of meaning;
5.   learning as an interpretative process aimed at the understanding of
    reality. (Säljö, 1982, p. 182)

The first two categories are associated with a "surface approach" to learning. The last two are central to a "deep approach" to learning. More general responses on the nature of the personal and intellectual enterprise represented by being a learner in higher education were also considered in the light of Perry's "Scheme of ethical and cognitive development" (Perry, 1970, 1988), though only brief reference will be made to this here.

Learning and Non-Learning in Year 1: the View from the Students

The interviewees were relatively relaxed, even when being recorded, and expressed themselves freely. It is important to record at the outset how overwhelmingly positive they were about their total experience of a first year of higher education, though their most incisive comments tended to focus on problems. The following is no more than a selective summary of some of the key themes illustrated with the words of the students.

Knowledge to be remembered
After the first semester, when asked indirect questions about their concepts of "learning", the answers varied in sophistication and reflectiveness. There were many references to knowledge:

> and I think doing a degree is just gaining knowledge, probably more
> knowledge than others, or more knowledge in the things I am
> interested in than others . . .

Such a statement might well be seen in terms of Säljö's first category, "learning as the increase of knowledge". There seems also to be a prevalent idea that the knowledge lies with the institution or tutor and is to be transferred to the learner. At the end of the year one student defined learning as:

It's being able to remember something you've been told, I guess.

However, after a long pause, this student added:

And to understand it.

"Learning as memorising", Säljö's second category, is closely associated with this view of learning as the gathering of information. The following account (of which there will be more to say) is a very explicit illustration of memorising as an approach:

One of the modules . . . I found the work really really hard. I went to all the lectures, and all the seminars and everything. I usually go to most of them anyway, but I made a point of going to all of them, and I still didn't understand it, and it was the general consensus that not many people did, but I like spent the whole weekend just continuously learning it, parrot-fashion, and I came out with 64%, something like that, and I was so pleased with that, 'cos I really worked hard for that, and I was really pleased. It's difficult sometimes, you know.

There were other references to the ability to recall information as a key aspect of learning.

Articulating and ordering knowledge
Non-learning is associated with several factors; key among these is the inability to order knowledge because of information overload and inadequate explanation:

. . . just too much information rammed down our throats. Too many long words not explained, just like thick information.

So how does that make you feel when you do it?

Thick!

The image of "thick information" and the play on "thick" is an apt summary of how several students felt when they clearly lacked the conceptual framework to sort out lecture and seminar material.

For some students the order desired is a relatively unsophisticated order. There is still a great emphasis on the completeness and comprehensiveness of notes.

One student was clear at the mid-year point where she learnt most:

> . . . in the seminars, that's when I take most in. Because that's when
> any ideas I might have grasped in the lectures or might have
> grasped when reading set texts or whatever will actually start to
> form some sort of pattern in my mind. They have to because I have
> to talk on it. Because I have to try my ideas out.

Creating this "pattern in my mind" clearly involves some abstraction of meaning
(Säljö) and the reordering of previous thoughts. For all the students learning is
associated with bringing order. The question really is as to the level of
conceptualisation which goes into the making of that order. There are degrees of
"abstraction of meaning".

Encountering different perspectives
A more subtle approach to learning seems fundamentally bound up with an
appreciation of the plural nature of perspectives and a more relativist concept of
what counts as knowledge.

> You don't sort of learn things so much, you just sort of broaden
> your ideas, I mean it's not like, when you do maths you think "Oh,
> I've solved a problem", you can think "Yeah I've got a definite
> answer to that", cos you can't get a definite answer to anything. It
> bugs me a bit, because I like having a definite answer, but you can't.

> Give me some examples, what you say you've been thinking about
> and you can't have a definite answer to.

> Well say I think something about a book and the tutor thinks
> something totally different, they say, "No you're wrong", and you
> think, "Well how can I be wrong? I've got my own ideas on it", and
> I wish I knew what is right.

For several of the group this coming to terms with different perspectives is a key
point in their learning. Its relationship with Säljö's fifth category was illustrated
at the end of the year when one student described how satisfying but disturbing it
had been to write a sustained feminist critique of a novel while personally
distancing herself from this perspective. She was beginning to wrestle with the
implications of seeing learning as an "interpretative process", and construing
reality as disconcertingly multiple.

Encountering different perspectives seems a key experience for developing more
complex ordering skills. It does not in itself guarantee their development. There
is certainly a paradox in the student memorising perspectives for a test on
"critical theory".

The students are clearly at different stages in coming to see learning as "an interpretative process" (Säljö). They all appreciate there are different views about issues, but they differ in their understanding of the way points of view assemble into more or less coherent perspectives.

Assessment: the dominant goal

For all the students assessment is a dominant concern. Initially modes of assessment are an issue in the selection of modules. Once the first semester grades are returned the search for marks is the underlying concern in their discussion of their learning experiences.

Assessment also structures the perception of what is relevant to pay attention to:

> Clear assignments. I want to know what to expect, what I'm
> learning for, so if I'm sitting in a lecture not learning that this is
> going to be the content of an assignment, I'm obviously not that
> eager to take notes and you just don't take it in as much.

One student well illustrated the mystifying power of numerical assessments. In a comment in a profile folder against a module for which she got 71% (70+ = first-class band) she wrote:

> V happy with the mark, though not entirely sure why I got it.

Her reply on being asked 'why?' was illuminating:

> In some ways it's more frustrating to get a good mark and not know
> why than to get a bad mark and not know why.

> Why?

> Because you want to know what the formula is, because then you
> hit the jackpot.

Knowing the formula neatly expresses the goal for many of the students. Most students expressed the concept of "formula" at some point, albeit in different words.

Untheorised learning

> I don't know. It's not something I will specifically sit down and
> think about. I'm here to learn. That's why I've come here, to do a
> degree, and therefore the learning process is something I take for
> granted and don't tend to analyse. In every lecture I will come out

> having learnt something, but that will just get filed away. You
> know, I won't sit dwelling on that.

Students have some difficulty in articulating their developing conception of
learning; the disjunctions and apparent contradictions in their accounts make
this clear. They also make it clear that the students are working on these
thoughts, but arguably in a private and scarcely conceptualised way:

> What's satisfying about doing an assignment then?

> Understanding it. If you actually understand the question, and then,
> I'd just say, when you finish it, you read through it, and you think,
> "Mm, I've actually done that", and if you've understood it as well,
> because sometimes, you've done it, and you read through it and
> you think "Well, OK, I've done it and it's in the book", but if you
> actually understand it as well, because sometimes you do just, well,
> read the book and although you understand what they're saying,
> you haven't actually grasped the theory of what they're saying.

In the following exchange about learning the interviewee goes from an apt simile
for the illumination which occurs when ideas fall into place to a more basic
model associated with the gathering of notes and the taking in of information:

> Things seem to come together, seem to make more sense. Like a
> little light being switched on. You know you were in a dark room
> before and everything is tidy and in order, which is nice. It doesn't
> happen that often, but when it does it's good.

> Do you get any feeling much about learning at other times than
> doing an assignment?

> I think in the first few weeks, when you are actually putting your
> notes together, then I think you're actually learning more then than
> when you actually write the assignment, because you're taking it all
> in at that point, whereas when you're writing the assignment,
> you're just trying to put it all out, put it in some sort of order.

The promotion of learning

There is widespread agreement that learning is associated with good feelings and
non-learning with negative feelings. One student spoke of "an incredible high
when you take an idea on board". Non-learning is associated with disorder, and
material being "over my head" on the one hand, and with over familiarity and
boredom on the other.

Learning is associated with knowing or being able to do new things. The students
expressed it in different ways, but there is general agreement that learning is best

promoted by being just at the edge of one's existing understanding. This may be an unsurprising conclusion, but it needs remembering.

Discussion: the students' understanding of learning

The mature students and those who had some other experience between school and college generally gave more considered and coherent accounts of their own aims in learning and their motivation for study. Their accounts of learning processes were, however, not significantly different in any conceptual sense from those of younger students.

It is hardly insignificant that nobody gave an account of their own learning which drew upon theoretical perspectives. This is not a criticism of the students concerned, but an observation. If asked to give an account for various forms of overt behaviour, students typically draw upon a range of moral, social and psychological explanations (however popularised and simplified); but "learning" is treated as unproblematic common sense until the question is pressed. The student who commented, "the learning process is something I take for granted and don't tend to analyse". might have spoken for the group as a whole. This is not to say that students never reflect upon the nature of their learning experiences (and the volume of data gathered in this study suggests no reluctance to discuss the topic) but this reflection may, arguably, be limited by the conceptual tools to hand. The implications of this are worth exploring.

Whatever the overall aims of the course, and the many specific module objectives which explicitly or implicitly suppose a "deep" rather than a "surface" approach to learning, learners necessarily respond to the powerful messages communicated by assessments. To "know what the formula is" and "hit the jackpot" expresses neatly what many of the interviewed students had come to see as the principal task by the end of the first year. Some expressed it with more understanding, cynicism and regret than others. Student instrumentalism may often be narrow and uncritical, but it may also be a rational adaptation to the welter of bunching modular assessments. The volume of assessment which has come to be associated particularly with modular courses certainly can encourage a certain volume of work. It would be facile to suggest this can have no positive bearing on the volume of learning, but there must be a point at which more means less. "Surface learning" may well lie in the unsophistication or superficiality of the individual student's approach to ideas, but it may also be an adaptive response, the retreat to a short-term but known technique. The fully conscious "parrot learning" illustrated earlier was adopted to cope with uncertainty about content against the threat of a one-hour test. Some of the strategies employed by the students interviewed might be described as rational but maladaptive: they help the student through the immediate assessment, the module, the semester or the year, but they may slow or positively impair the development of more powerful approaches to learning.

In contrast and in tension with the prevailing instrumentalism with regard to assessment, most of the students did also have a broader view of themselves as learners. Almost all expressed some view of the intrinsic value of learning. One mature student expressed it most clearly:

> I think it's all a very necessary part of the continuous growth of
> myself as a person and how I relate to society. I don't actually see a
> degree as being the end of learning, and hopefully, once I've got a
> degree I'll carry on. It's not something I want to give up, relinquish.
> I think education is a very necessary driving force. It fulfils
> something in each person. It fulfils something in me, and I find it a
> very satisfactory experience.

The value of undertaking such a relatively prolonged course as a degree is also seen in terms of challenge. "Learning" at this level represents a conflation of Samuel Smiles and the labours of Hercules – a simultaneous improving and proving of oneself.

From the perspectives of the students, many of the barriers to learning seem to be described as practical rather than cognitive. However, in different ways according to the pathways they were following, these first-year students were coming to terms with seeing learning as presenting epistemological problems. The gradual shifting of perspectives on the nature of knowledge, of which Perry has written so extensively, was evident. The relationship between this and their specific concepts of learning requires a longer study. A tentative conclusion, however, might be that some of the difficulties in learning experienced at this stage are part of the broader intellectual problem posed by coming to terms with multiple interpretative paradigms.

Improving Student Learning: Course Development

Improving students' learning is both an unexceptional and unexceptionable educational goal, and as a fully conscious objective at least as old as Socrates. That a formal education process seeks to "improve" learners is self-evident; what that involves is not entirely self-evident. Improving students' learning (or at least the explicit intention to do so) necessarily rests upon some view of educational purpose. The normative implications of "promoting learning" cannot be escaped: they must always be examined; for the means by which learning might be improved must necessarily relate practical method to desirable aims. If, as Zuber-Skerritt (1992, p. 23) claims, "many academics do not share the implicit assumption in the research literature that a surface approach to learning is bad and should be discouraged", then the basis for asserting the superiority of deep approaches to learning must be constantly clarified in terms of the purposes of education.

There may also be some mismatch between the impeccable higher level objectives of many courses and the realities of assessment as seen by students. For some the search for the "formula" seems more akin to initiation into some mysterious (and somewhat arbitrary) rite than an understandable process. Students' understanding of their own learning cannot be ignored if the mismatches are to be overcome. The question remains as to how we best make use of the insights generated through research into students' concepts of their own learning.

The task for researchers is not just to find out, but to communicate, key findings in such a way as to influence the majority of teachers in higher education to give all students a realistic opportunity (and doubtless the odd firm prompt) to develop effective strategies of learning. Effective strategies must necessarily equip students to meet assessment requirements which, equally necessarily, act as the public verification of learning. These assessment requirements must, however, more closely reflect appropriate overall educational purposes. These need to be clarified not just for students but with students. But, beyond this, learners must be made more capable and (let us not shun the word) more inspired to challenge, to think, and to stay near the cutting edge of their own learning wherever they may find themselves. "Deep approaches" to learning are not simply techniques for improving grades, but fundamental to any sense of higher education as a critical activity.

References

Bedford College of Higher Education (1992). BA/BSc and BEd *(Primary) Student and Professional Tutor Handbook* (1992). BCHE.

Morgan, A. (1993). *Improving Your Students' Learning: Reflections of the Experience of Study*. London: Kogan Page.

Perry, W. (1970). *Forms of Intellectual and Ethical Development in the College Years:* A Scheme. New York: Holt, Rinehart and Winston.

Perry, W. (1988). Different worlds in the same classroom. In P. Ramsden, (eds.), *Improving Learning: New Perspectives*. London: Kogan Page.

Säljö, R. (1982). *Learning and Understanding: A Study of Differences in Constructing Meaning from a Text*. Göteborg: Acta Universitatis Gothoburgensis.
Zuber-Skerritt, O. (1992). *Action Research in Higher Education: Examples and Reflections*. London: Kogan Page.

Chapter 10 Changing students' approach to learning

Course Design for Learning: Towards Improving Student Learning in New Courses

Barry Jackson, Falmouth School of Art and Design

Background and Context

Falmouth School of Art and Design is a monotechnic, a higher education corporation which specialises in education in the areas of art, design and communication. Its courses are predominantly studio-based, practical courses, for which it has a high reputation. It is the descendant of and natural successor to the "Art School", but it has adapted successfully to a radically changed higher education context.

Although the school recognises the value of credit accumulation and transfer and of unitisation, its current provision takes the form of discrete, continuous courses. Modularity, and the flexibility of choice which that provides, are not of great relevance in the monotechnic environment. This is an important characteristic to note in the context of this paper: discrete courses have advantages and disadvantages when compared with modular structures. One of the disadvantages is the comparative lack of choice which is offered to students over what they study. This is one of the issues which the course development team hoped to address in designing new courses.

The school's portfolio of courses up to now has remained largely within the traditional areas of art and design. The staff have consequently developed considerable experience in the practical, project-based teaching which has been a feature of art and design education. However, to date this has not been a feature of the theoretical aspects of courses in the school.

The school provided a case study for the Improving the Quality of Student Learning project, funded by CNAA and organised by OCSD. This was the only art and design case study in the project. It provided a valuable learning experience for the Falmouth staff directly involved, Allan Davies and Barry Jackson, giving the opportunity to develop further their understanding of the concepts of deep and surface approaches to learning and the work of Biggs, Marton, Entwistle et al.

The need and rationale for new courses
Changes to the funding strategies in higher education in 1992-93 made it
necessary for the school to change its strategic plan at short notice and to bring
forward its plans to broaden the range of the courses it offers at degree level.

The school sought to develop a range of theoretical courses in areas associated
with its existing portfolio, that is, courses associated with communication or
media studies. Unlike most of the existing courses in the school the new courses
were to be concerned with critical and theoretical approaches rather than practice.
It was implicit in the development brief that the high levels of staff contact and
the provision of permanent student studio workspaces which are associated with
art and design should be avoided. It was also envisaged that the new courses
would seek efficiency and interaction wherever possible: for example, in the
sharing of staff or common units of study.

Proposals for courses were sought, and were found from within the information
studies area, a department in which the school's postgraduate courses in
broadcast journalism and history of modern art and design are located. Both
these courses provided an academic background which could nourish
undergraduate courses. It was decided that two courses should be developed and
validated with a view to starting in September 1993, with a further two starting in
September 1994. The first two courses, BA(Hons) Visual Culture and BA(Hons)
Broadcasting Studies, were successfully validated in April 1993.

The course development process
The normal procedures for the development and progression of course proposals
allows time for reflection and consideration of the implications of following one
or another route. The proposals are subject to review by a number of groups until
they are presented to the Academic Board for approval to progress to validation.

In the light of the urgency of the requirement for new courses, a decision was
made to set up course development groups for each course, chaired by a senior
academic working in a subject related to the course in question, and made up of
academics from a range of other courses. Both course development groups took
an individual direction which reflected the conceptions of their respective chairs.
Their initial proposals not only shared little in the way of structure, but both also
demonstrated a very traditional approach to the delivery of their subject matter.
The proposals could be characterised as "content led", that is to say they started
from a view that there was a body of knowledge ("stuff") which had to be "given"
to students. In this model the course planning process was merely the planning
of the sequence in which parcels of "stuff" were to be handed out.

The development process for both courses was halted and restarted with the
formation of a new development team, to attempt to develop a stucture and

delivery strategy which could be common to both courses and to the courses to be developed during the following year. This potential set of courses became known as "cognate courses".

It was a deliberate strategy of the new development team to plan "off-the-shelf" structures and strategies that could be adapted, with fine tuning, to any of the planned cognate courses, or indeed, any future courses sharing similar critical and theoretical concerns. This reflected the development group's view that course development should not be "content-led". The acquisition of prespecified knowledge about the subject of the course is only one, and a limited one, of the course aims. The course aims and objectives rightly stress, above all, the importance of students gaining a critical understanding of the subject, and of the appropriate theories and methodologies. The skills of analysis, argument, communication and cooperation are also stressed. A course development strategy which allowed for the encouragement of these skills and abilities was required.

In this context the development group sought to design a course which would take account of lessons learned from the Improving Student Learning project – one which would encourage students to take a deep approach and one which avoided the worst of the features identified as promoting a surface approach.

Identification of Pedagogic Features, Derived from the ISL Project

The ISL project drew attention to the results and implications of educational research from a wide range of sources over recent years. These were effectively summarised in the project report book (Gibbs, 1992). In the context of this symposium I have assumed that the significant features of this research, undertaken by Biggs, Marton, Ramsden, Entwistle, Säljö, Gibbs et al., are familiar to most participants, and it is not my intention to go over them in detail.

It is useful, however, to use as a reminder the lists of course features which encourage deep or surface approaches to study, which appeared in Gibbs, since these acted as a checklist for the course development group at FSAD in designing the courses in question.

Features encouraging a deep approach
Gibbs drew attention to four features associated with encouraging a deep approach, features which were identified originally by Biggs (1989):

Motivational context
Students are more likely to take a deep approach to learning when the motivation to learn is internal, coming from the student's own needs and desires. A positive climate, in which students "own" their learning, can be established by involving students in the selection and planning of what is learnt

and how learning takes place. A good motivational context may be a necessary condition for deep learning.

Learner activity
Deep learning is associated with activity. Students are more likely to make connections between what is being learnt and past learning if they are active rather than passive.

Interaction with others
Talking and discussing ideas and concepts with others is a powerful way of reflecting on and testing learning. It provides a means of negotiating and structuring meaning which is more effective than solitary reflection alone.

Well-structured knowledge base
New learning can be approached deeply only if the student can relate it to their existing knowledge and experience. The growing sense of a visible structure which the subject matter acquires if it is presented in an integrated way provides the student with a model of the knowledge they are acquiring, which can then be more easily manipulated and related to other knowledge. Interdisciplinary approaches can encourage a well-structured knowledge base.

Features associated with a surface approach

Heavy workload
A heavy workload allows no time for reflection and discussion: there is limited opportunity to consolidate the structure of knowledge or to relate it to existing knowledge. The actual workload which is imposed on students may often be heavier than lecturers think. The expectations of various lecturers associated with a course or programme may mean that students have to commit substantial extra time to writing assignments, reading set texts and preparing presentations.

Relatively high levels of contact time
Students need to be independent and active in their learning, and to have opportunities to discuss their learning with peers. A high level of contact time may not leave sufficient time for these important activities. It may also encourage the view that learning is passive, which is likely to encourage a surface approach.

Excessive amount of course material
In addition to contributing to a heavy workload, excessive amounts of course material reduce the student's chances of being able to relate meaningfully the various components of their learning, and to build a well-structured knowledge base.

Lack of opportunity to study subjects in depth
If students have no opportunity to develop their learning in depth in any particular area, their "ownership" and their ability to make personally meaningful sense of it are likely to be diminished.

Lack of choice in what is studied, and how
Lack of choice may reduce the positive emotional climate which encourages good motivation.

Threatening or anxiety-provoking assessment methods
A sense of anxiety or threat may be conditions which are in themselves sufficient for surface learning. Assessment is the main anxiety-inducing part of any educational experience.

A Brief Description of the Courses

The features identified above were those which the course development team chose to take into account in designing the set of new courses. Other needs, determined as important by the institution, were also necessarily addressed. These included resource and staffing limitations. None of the imposed needs were felt to conflict with course strategies which encouraged a deep approach.

Cognate courses
One of the first decisions was to design the set of "cognate" courses with a common structure and delivery strategy, as described above. The courses all have close links in terms of subjects, and indeed when all four become operational there will be some obvious overlaps. (see Figure 1) The four proposed course subjects are: visual culture, broadcasting studies, media studies and publishing studies. All four are concerned with a theoretical and critical understanding of particular aspects of communication in the contemporary world. The development team saw in this possibilities for encouraging a deep approach:

Greater breadth/choice available for students through electives –
Each course in the set offers a number of electives - small-scale elements of study, which address particular aspects of the main course subject, or issues around the main subject. Students are required to choose three electives per term for the first five terms of the course. Their choice can include a maximum of two electives from another course. In fact the course design even allows for a student on Course A to take elements of the main study of Course B as an elective. On the basis of this experience students could apply to transfer on to the cognate course at the end of the first year. Electives can therefore be seen as a means of offering the student an opportunity to choose a broadening or deepening of their understanding of the main study.

Opportunities to structure knowledge base to individual needs –
By means of shared electives, which map out a network of connected concepts
and ideas across the range of media and communication studies, students have
more freedom to construct a more personally meaningful knowledge base, and to
see how ideas and issues from one area can be connected to those in another.

Increased student interaction in shared first term –
The common structure of the courses provides for a first term which explores
and addresses students' conceptions of the subject and their approaches to
learning. Since the work of this term is driven largely by the exploration of what
students already know, understand and expect, it lends itself very well for
activities which can be undertaken by mixed groups from different courses. The
range of peers with whom discussion and reflection can take place is thereby
extended in an early critical stage of the course.

Other outcomes of having a common design for the courses were identified,
which, though not contributing directly to the promotion of a deep approach to
learning, could nonetheless be seen as beneficial:
- increased staff interaction between course teams could be expected,
  encouraging cross-course initiatives;
- more efficient use could be made of staff expertise and experience by
  contributing across courses, and by developing common teaching strategies;
- course development, administration and documentation would be eased.

A Brief Outline of One Course

To illustrate the main features of the course design by which the development
team hoped to improve student approaches to learning it will be helpful to take
one course as an example: BA(Hons) Broadcasting Studies (see Figure 2).

Significant features of the course structure

Foundation for learning term
Previous experience indicated to the development team that self - and peer
assessment, self-managed study, and other features promoting student
responsibility and independence could not be successfully introduced into a
course without addressing students' expectations and conceptions of learning.
Students whose expectations and conceptions of learning are oriented towards
"teacher-active, learner-passive" modes of teaching are likely to take a surface
approach in their learning, and, in addition, for these students the teaching
strategies implicit in the course are likely to be anxiety-provoking. The
foundation term is designed principally to give students an opportunity to
become more aware of their own learning approaches and those of others, to
explore alternatives and to understand the teaching strategies used on the course.

The decision to allocate a full term to "foundation studies" reflects the team's view of the importance of questioning and exploring not only students' conceptions of learning, but also their knowledge and assumptions about the subject of study. The exploration of learning takes place firmly in the context of the subject, students being encouraged to reflect on what they think the subject is and what they know about it already.

The work of the foundation term takes place through a series of group and individual projects and finishes with an exercise in which each student designs their own individual ideal course, which they then compare with the course on offer. The views of students are taken into account by the course team at this point and can be used to check the closeness of match between the course plans and students' aspirations. Although the course has a curriculum defined in its validated document, there is scope within this for minor changes to be made if it seems appropriate.

Electives
Following the foundation term the course content consists of the main study and electives (see Figure 2). The main study is a mandatory core study, which addresses the subject by means of themes. Electives are smaller scale theme studies which relate to the main study in one of two ways: they may explore some aspect of the main study in more depth; or they may explore issues which are more marginal and contextual to the main study (as has been noted above, electives from other cognate courses can be taken). Students have a choice from the electives on offer, and can thus choose to take a deeper or broader approach to their understanding of the main study.

Case-studies
The sixth term of the course is given over to a case-study, identified, managed and presented by the student. The case-study is an opportunity to bring together and apply all the learning of the first two years. Students will be using the theoretical models, research approaches and critical analysis which they have acquired to examine an identified aspect of, in the case of this course, broadcasting practice. Carrying out the case-study requires students to plan and manage their own progress, which may involve spending considerable time off-site, visiting relevant institutions. The case-study marks a boundary between the earlier part of the course, in which the curriculum, though flexible, is determined by the course team, and the final year, in which students determine the subject of study for themselves.

Independent study in the final year
The work of the final year is entirely identified and managed by the student: there is no longer any identified input of "content" from the course. Students select and specify the outcomes for a major study and a limited number of minor studies. Their proposals are negotiated and agreed with the course team. The

constraints are provided by the curriculum objectives for the final year, which are in effect the course objectives: students' proposals must satisfy the course team that these objectives could be satisfactorily addressed by their projects. (Some flexibility is maintained in that modifications to the proposals are allowed, by negotiation, in response to what students learn as the projects progress.)
The students' progress is continually monitored by their learning teams, in which presentation and discussion of work in progress is a central feature. In the final term there are formal presentations by students to their entire cohort, in which some sharing of knowledge can take place. The main activity of this term is the assessment of project outcomes for determination of the degree award. The usual outcome is expected to be written, but other forms are not precluded – the appropriate form would be determined as part of the initial proposal. Assessment is undertaken against the objectives agreed by students in their proposals, and student's self- and peer assessments are taken into account by the staff assessment team. (It is hoped that student involvement in the final assessment may eventually become more formalised, in the way in which it occurs throughout the body of the course. Current practice within the school does not permit this development at present.)

Clearly identified curriculum objectives
Each component of the course has an identified set of curriculum objectives. These are detailed lists of what students are expected to be able to do, know or understand as outcomes of the course component. They form the basis for assessment throughout the course and they are discussed with students at the outset of each year and of each course component. They are subject to annual review and updating in response to staff and student feedback.

In planning the delivery of a course component the lecturer responsible will be planning a set of learning experiences which will allow for all the curriculum objectives to be addressed. The particular objectives addressed by an individual student within each project of a component will be negotiated by the student him/herself: the requirement is merely that the student address all objectives within the component, in whichever way suits them best.

The curriculum objectives approach is an attempt to focus on outcomes and to make them explicit for staff and students. It is intended to allow flexibility in the teaching strategy for staff and to encourage ownership of their learning by students.

Significant features of course delivery and assessment

Project work
Teaching on the course is predominantly by means of project, an approach which is common practice within art and design, and which involves students in

activities. Projects may be small or large, lasting only one day, or, in the case of the final year's self-determined projects, extending over two terms.

Lectures and seminars may be used within projects, but they will have clearly identified purposes related to the students' own active learning. Lectures, for example, are used within projects as initial orientations or "scene-setters"; there may be later lectures within a long project, arranged in response to student-identified needs.

Wherever possible and appropriate students are encouraged to undertake practical activity: the projects concerned with understanding audiences, for example, may include making and testing simple audio and video "programmes". Projects encourage students to be active, to work collaboratively (this is sometimes a requirement) and to explore resources outside of the school.

Learning teams

Students work in learning teams, meeting regularly for structured discussion of the course component in which they are currently involved, the progress of their own project work and the development of their learning. The team meetings are all facilitated initially by course team members, but their role becomes increasingly less significant as students grow in experience. As the course progresses it is expected that the teams will operate effectively with reduced staff presence. Students are prepared for the responsibility required for self-managed groups during the foundation term. Learning teams provide the principal form of tutorial monitoring. Individual tutorials with a member of staff are undertaken once a term, as an 'insurance' that the system is working well.

Student involvement with assessment

The assessment methods adopted by the course development team include a number of strategies intended to reduce anxiety and increase ownership for students. All assessments are made using a common set of criteria which are defined and discussed with students at the start of the course. The criteria are grouped into domains covering conceptual, critical, communication abilities, etc. They are expressed as a series of statements of level of achievement in the various domains. Using these criteria allows a student to gain a profile of their performance in each project, indicating where their strengths and weaknesses lie. A set of common criteria facilitates the process of self- and peer assessment which is used throughout the course. In this process the staff input is limited to sampling and the resolution of dispute between peers. Experience indicates that the system does not induce any loss of rigour in assessment, and considerably increases students' sense of responsibility and understanding.

As noted above, the final assessment does not yet formally allow self- and peer-assessment judgements to be the basis of making a degree award. However, they are still undertaken since they are a valuable formative experience for the student, and they are used to inform the judgement of the assessment panel.

The deployment of staff time

The resource limitations within which the course must operate have meant that it has been easy to avoid a course design which required a large proportion of contact hours. The limitations have meant that the strategic planning for the deployment of staff time has been a priority. The development team's decision was to load the majority of staff contact into the early part of the course, particularly the foundation term, in an attempt to prepare students in a planned way for greater independence right at the start. As an example the average percentage of study time spent in contact with tutors in Year 1 is approximately 18%. In Year 3 the percentage is around 5%.

The way in which the allotted staff hours are used by the individual tutor responsible for a component of the course is the responsibility of that tutor, working within guidelines set out in the course design. The contact hours must be closely targeted to ensure their relevance to the curriculum objectives and the nature of the project work. All components must have staff time allocated for feedback and evaluation of the component at its end.

The relationship of the course design to the identified features

The table illustrated in Figure 3 shows the relationship of the course design to the list of features extracted from Gibbs (1992) and Biggs(1989).

The features listed above are the principal ones built into the course to incorporate factors associated with a deep approach. None of them might be expected to work effectively unless they are used in a context which values the rationale and research behind them, and used by staff with a sympathy and understanding for that rationale. As a consequence all staff teaching on the course were required to attend a series of staff development workshops which tried to introduce and address the concepts of deep and surface approaches, their relationship to outcomes, the particular features and strategies associated with deep and surface approaches, and other related issues. This staff development exercise was seen as very important by the development team. As discussed below, the level of its success is questionable.

Issues Arising

The course design described above was successfully validated this year: the first two courses begin operation in September 1993. The success of the design in meeting its aims clearly cannot be judged before another three years! However, some issues about the course development process have been identified.

One of these is the difficulties faced when trying to validate courses having a rationale and structure which may conflict with "normal" expectations. Validation panels appear to be very uneasy about validating courses which are not described as lists of content – "stuff" to be learnt. There are also concerns about the rigour of self- and peer-assessment processes, and the levels of tutorial support needed. A number of panel members involved in the validation of the two courses described here expressed doubts that students could cope adequately with independence. The availability of research evidence and case-studies of good practice were extremely valuable to the course devlopment team in persuading validators that precedents existed for the kind of approach which was being proposed.

A greater problem is the resistance encountered within groups of staff within the school who express the same kind of considerable doubt about the course designs. Doubts about the validity of the teaching strategies proposed, the rigour of assessment schemes, the "coverage" of the "body of knowledge", even the existence of deep and surface approaches were not easily overcome. Sceptical colleagues remain sceptical, even though they are now committed to teach on the courses. It may be noted that those colleagues who expressed greatest doubts were also those whose circumstances prevented them from attending the full staff development programme which had been prepared for the course teams. Although this does not augur well for the success of the courses it is to be hoped that the doubts will be overcome as the courses progress, with those staff who are sympathetic leading the way. Our experience of students on other courses leads us to believe that the students, at least, will adapt to and meet the challenges of more responsibility for their learning.

Figure 1

Cognate courses

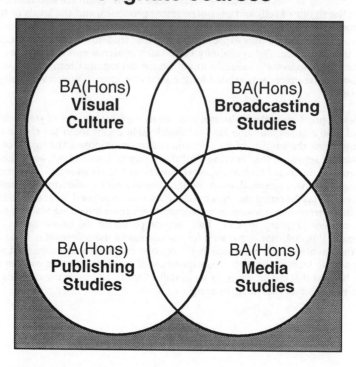

- **Greater breadth of choice available through electives**
- **Opportunities to structure the knowledge base according to individual needs**
- **Increased amount and breadth of student interaction**
- Increased interaction between staff
- More efficient use of staff time and expertise
- Facilitation of course development and administration

Figure 2

BA(Hons) Broadcasting Studies - Course Structure

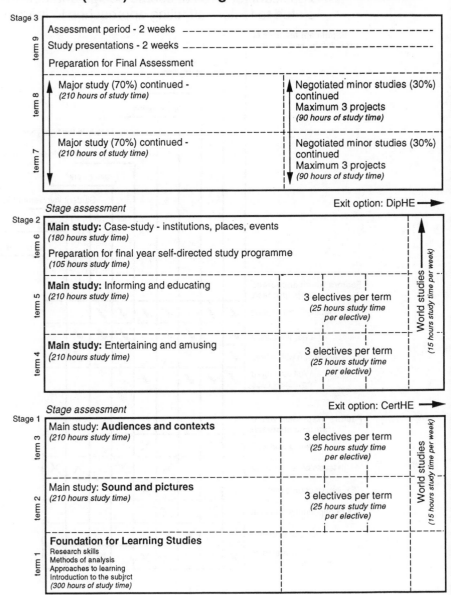

Figure 3

Significant features of course design and delivery related to factors affecting approaches to learning

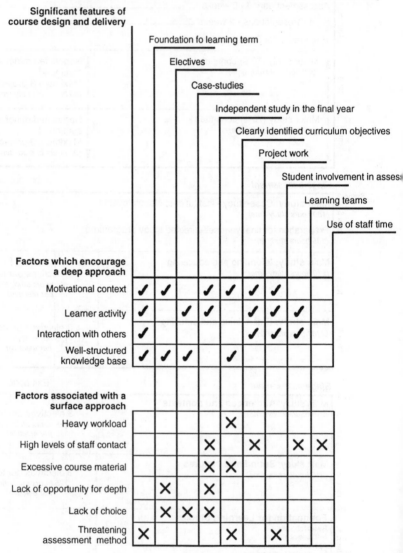

Learning in the Process of Learning

Jean Robb

Introduction

Process learning was originated to explain the contradictions and difficulties which interfere with successful models of learning.

It was developed to give a code for communication during learning which preserves the integrity of all participants in a learning situation by recognising the realities of human relationships, whether personal, professional or social. The code is embodied in the principles and guidelines of process.

Learning, whether formal or informal, has effects that are recognised and effects that are unrecognised. To be successful and positive the learner needs to look at the experience reflectively so that ambiguity in understanding is not carried forward as though it is a firm base for future learning in that field.

It is only when learning experiences provide an individual with the techniques to evaluate his or her own and other's behaviour that the excitement and richness of life experience becomes apparent and a sense of excitement for learning replaces the fear or doubt or incomprehension that weak, unchallenged understanding produces. Process learning teaches these techniques.

It has proven effective in teaching, training, management and parenting and for students' development of their true potential.

Process is a thinking skills approach but differs from other thinking tkills approaches in that it is a practical philosophy which can be used immediately in any areas of the curriculum. It can be learnt by anybody and the practitioner's performance can be evaluated by themselves. The use of the guidelines ensure feedback from the group or individual with whom the practitioner is working. process can begin to be implemented immediately but the journey of learning about learning will continue and understanding will deepen.

Process learning is a holistic and humanistic communication method enabling dialogue and reflection. Learning is interactive, dynamic, responsive and focussed to the needs of individuals and groups. Process learning seeks to utilise all of the processes which life encompasses. Students are taught to recognise these processes and use them productively. By focussing on the elements which create conditions favourable to learning, process learning overcomes barriers and rapidly transforms both individual and group learning experiences.

Process learning produces successful outcomes in all environments - work, family, school, self - as its basis is self-correction. The individual becomes autonomous, reflective and critical by developing logical and critical thinking processes. At the same time the understanding of the individual's place in the community is increased. Process has particular application to higher education because of the multiplicity of experiences students have when they arrive at the course and the wide variety of demands – financial, domestic, social and academic – which will be competing for their attention. Process enables students to prioritise and use energy effectively by teaching a simple approach to a piece of work.

What do I Know?

<table>
<tr><td>What new
questions have arisen?</td><td></td><td>What do I
need to know?</td></tr>
<tr><td>What have
I learnt?</td><td></td><td>Where can I
find out?</td></tr>
</table>

How can I organise
the information?

Using this formula students are able to apply a structure which will provide them with clarity of thought in every situation.

Some of the benefits of using process in a higher education setting

- Interaction between both students and lecturers and students and students is stimulated.

- The resource base is widened by everyone recognising that among the students there will be valuable insights into the subject matter.

- The method allows for and encourages differentiation by recognising the range of experiences within the group and ensuring that lecturers get feedback on the student's position in terms of understanding content or skills.

- The process learning method teaches students how to understand the way they think in order to develop the way they learn.

- Process learning is a thinking skills approach which ensures dynamic interaction, competent learning and a true sense of optimism in students and teachers.

- Process learning is a methodology which allows lecturers to present their material in a way which is meaningful to the students.
- Students are enabled to create supportive, intellectual environments to foster intellectual strength.

- Students are provided with a community of support where trust and honesty are protected.

- Students recognise how to get the best from their lecturers and the resources of the institution.

The Situation Today

How can lecturers teach students who are high on motivation but low on prerequisite knowledge and skills?

Now that the emphasis in higher education is on as many individuals as possible receiving university education the temptation may be to vary entrance requirements. Interest and enthusiasm may be all that is required of prospective students. Alongside this the government is asking that results show successes, failures and drop-out rates. There have for years been complaints made by lecturers about the quality of students. These complaints have been echoed by students on the quality of their lecturers.

The process learning method can respond to these complaints and turn the student – teacher relationship into a highly productive interaction.

Students and Learning - Barriers to Learning

1. The students' own barriers

The barriers to learning are the result of the effects of the physical, social, emotional, psychological and intellectual and academic processes which impinge on the individual.

In the context of the theory underlying process the definitions used are:

- Physical: Aspects include the student's state of physical health and physical comfort. There can be situations where people who have poor physical health appear to be untroubled; however, most people will find some of their learning impaired if they have any physical handicap, be it temporary or permanent.

If the student is unwell or deaf, has food allergies or problems with sight, can't cope in sunlight, is short or tall for the size of chairs provided, needs to go to the toilet more often than most, etc., then these differences, if not recognised and compensated for, can lead to problems of learning. The difficulty may be only temporary. However, if, during the time there was a physical problem, something important has been taught, the student may feel inadequate as a learner, because the effect of the illness or physical problem has not been realised.

- Social: Human being are responsive to indications of acceptance or rejection. A marginalised learner may have impaired functioning. Some marginalised students will learn despite the feeling of isolation, but most people need to feel secure in order to release energy necessary for successful learning.

If the student has no friends, or does not recognise the friends who are there, then loneliness may take up energy which could be used for learning. Sometimes the student will become introverted, sometimes the difficult member of the group, sometimes very morose, particularly at home. These negative effects could lead to students giving up the course.

- Emotional: All human being are experiencing feelings all of the time. If these engender a relaxed, purposeful learning attitude then the emotions are positive, but if they interfere with that sense of purpose and focus, they are negative.

A student may appear very emotional. Excess emotion may use up energy which will affect the supply left to concentrate on learning. This inability to concentrate could add to the stress of the student. A dialogue with an emotional student can help to unravel the causes of the stress. It is advisable to have a colleague with you if you are talking to a distressed student.

Some students explode and we notice them, but some are imploding, i.e., all their emotions are seething around on the inside. If you are concerned, check the policy of the institution on welfare provision before proceeding on your own.

Although we all experience emotions, often all we want is for them to be recognised as part of our lives in order that we can focus on work. Students whose emotional reactions are not noticed or recognised as significant may feel rejected and isolated and unable to learn.

- Psychological: What has happened in the past could be causing your student's present state. An individual's early experiences, no matter how tiny or apparently insignificant, may be affecting current performance. Past events are stored away and the individual may be reacting to them but have apparently completely forgotten that they ever happened. Our experiences is that, once the psychological barriers are overcome, learning is almost unbelievably rapid. Finding the psychological barrier will be done by the student in the course of studying a subject using process. The recognition of the barrier is natural rather than contrived and the student retains control of the rate of discovery.

- Intellectual: This is the state of reasoning ability, understanding or readiness or the pre-skills. If your student is having a problem then you need to check just what it is they can't do. A student doing complicated algebraic equations and failing may only have a problem with taking away, not the procedures for handling the equation. Never assume that you know why someone is unable to perform an intellectual activity.

- Academic: This is an understanding of how to relate to the demands of the course and the institution. Students need to know how to gain help from the resources available. They need to know how to marshal thoughts and communicate those thoughts in a way which can be assessed. Students also need to recognise how to undertake a new piece of learning and how to revise that which they already know.

If barriers to learning are allowed to remain then the individual will not achieve their true potential.

2. Barriers at the institutional level

In many situations frustration and the consequent lowering of morale and productivity can be caused when change is introduced. People's reluctance to adapt to and utilise new methods or equipment is often perceived as obduracy by the management and inadequacy by the employee. The negative effects of change become paramount and the positive reasons for change are obscured or lost altogether.

The particular principles of process enable participants in a changing situation to recognise how to ask a question, how to pursue a line of enquiry and to see the needs of others. Too often, in organisations, individuals are marginalised. Consequently large amounts of their energy has to be used to survive the sense of isolation and inadequacy this marginalisation brings. If the energy is released to facilitate change, a beneficial effect, not only on the individual but also for the institution, will occur.

Without process, or other methods which address the needs of those responsible for the introduction of change, a sense of marginalisation can occur. This will leave those members of the team feeling battle scarred and apprehensive about any future modifications they may have to implement. The tension that those feelings generate can permeate through a section, department or office, reducing the efficiency of it all.

Without process or a similar method, employees expected to absorb the new methods or equipment into their working practices are left feeling that their contribution to the organisation is misunderstood, undervalued or ignored. Process ensures this does not happen to any participant at any level in the dynamics of the organisation.

Process creates a supportive, thinking environment. This produces a staff confident in their protected right to have ideas explained in a way suitable for them and able to ask for this explanation in terms which lead to successful communication. The staff develop skills in identifying specific problem areas. This reduces inefficient use of time and energy. It increases employee flexibility, sense of responsibility and initiative.

Process identifies that there is more than one dimension to learning to cope with change and that it is important to address all the dimensions otherwise learning can appear to have failed. If learning appears to have failed to happen, correct identification of specific problems has failed to happen. The skill of correct identification of the problem can be developed by the individual, whether a manager or an individual working for a manager.

Time spent establishing the requirements of the individuals to feel supported is not only beneficial in one particular area being examined at present. It will also be beneficial in all areas of the employee's lives. This benefit will have a positive impact on productivity at work.

Because process is a holistic teaching and management method, it enables learning to be interactive, dynamic, responsive and focussed to the needs of the individual or groups. Only by investigating the way the individuals think of themselves as able to change and as members of teams, during and after change, can apprehension be overcome and new learning implemented effectively.

3. Barriers as a result of government impositions and requirements

Often the institution's preferred model for dealing with staff, students and the curriculum is superseded or undermined by external directives. This can result in an overworked and demoralised staff. The staff may be expected to take on more students with fewer resources. These resources could be the student's state of readiness for study, provision in the library, staff time, reduced budgets, inadequate lecture facilities. The effect of these changes can result in staff being resistant to the changes because they feel overloaded, under resourced and undervalued. Typically staff try very hard to ensure the quality of what they provide to students or management, but faced with a continual onslaught which undermines their sense of competence they resort to using their energies for survival rather than endless forward planning which could have no chance of being implemented.

How does the process method eliminate barriers to learning in students?

Process learning is an interactive rather than a didactic teaching, learning or management method, the crucial aspect of which involves establishing the baselines of the individual's understanding. This is done dynamically, thus identifying how the individual is thinking. The baselines may include the individual's inherent ability, their current factual or skill knowledge or emotional, physical or social state.

The Process method encourages critical thinking. Critical thinking involves identifying salient questions ad expressing them accurately. This is understood to happen incrementally. Each stage is checked. This technique allows participants of all levels of ability or experience to take a full part in the enquiry. The guidelines for process generate a safe and open atmosphere for enquiry and process allows misconceptions or assumptions by the members of the group or individuals to be explored. The baseline of each member is identified as new knowledge is gained and questions are tried to check relevance to the student's new level.

Process seeks to narrow the gap between rhetoric and practice. By setting up democratic interactions the practitioner cannot hide behind jargon to justify imposing inadequate responses to questions or situations. Individuals or groups with whom they are working will feel confident to challenge and know how to question in a positive and productive manner.

Process recognises that thinking is happening. It then draws attention to what is interfering with successful or effective thinking.

Process does not impose formulas. Rather it stimulates a desire to seek out the possible responses to any situation and modify those responses to suit particular needs.

Process requires change. It appears to be like other methods. However, participants report that it is an entirely new experience in learning. This experience can be enhanced by workshops but people who have read about process have been excited to explore as well.

Process recognises that dynamic interchange will be successful. Complacent responses may be apparently successful but will weaken the potential of any situation, for example: a meeting of managers and subordinates at work where the pretence is that the group is democratic but everyone knows that there is a hidden agenda, or an open learning session where those who guess the hidden agenda gain the reward.

When process is applied/used, each member of the group will have the opportunity to say what they see. The initial question will be a true question, i.e., the questioner will not have any preconceived idea of the answers. (Often in this type of "open" situation the facilitator or questioner has a preconceived idea of what the answers will be.)

Using any object or subject as the focus a group of any size can be introduced to this thinking skills method. By discovering how other people view a situation or an object individuals discover that the range of responses is huge. Their own resource base is widened with the possibilities for it extending further, very rapidly, becoming endless. They also become competent at observing in every situation and gathering information which can be put to effective use.

Process is a technique which gets any group to gel very quickly and turns a passive situation into one that is dynamic, exciting, challenging and relevant for all, not just those in the apparent power position. The technique can be used with any group—multi-ability, age, academic understanding or ethnic origin.

Process is minimalist and everyone engaging in a process discussion, particularly the facilitators, must have a "blank sheet" in their mind in terms of possible outcomes. This blank sheet will heighten their receptivity to the evidence of their eyes and ears. The effect of this is to deepen the attention of all the participants, creating an environment where people are confident to claim what they know, reveal what they don't know and explore methods for finding out and communicating new knowledge.

A process session instantaneously sets up a sense of intimacy. People are searching for meaning individually and together. This sense of being involved in a worthwhile pursuit unleashes energy and enthusiasm to keep commitment high. Process must not be confused with brain storming. Brain storming can encourage surface responses as there is no time for reflection. Process allows time and fosters the desire for reflection on, as well as expansion and modification of, ideas. Individuals can engage in their own process session while working alone.

Principles

Process learning works on the principle that:

- if the teacher is not learning then the student's potential to learn effectively will be limited;

- effective learning is failing to happen, effective teaching is failing to happen;

- if there is a learning block,that the teacher needs to find out where the student's point of competence is;

- assignments should only be set if pre-skills have been checked;

- the student can learn how he or she learns best;

- the student can be taught to become his or her own teacher;

- if the learner is feeling successful then huge stores of energy will be released for new learning;

- everyone has the ability to learn:

teaching potential	=	learning potential
learning	=	expanding potential
untutored	≠	stupid
tutored	≠	clever
unco-operative	≠	unteachable

- the purpose of learning is to produce reasoning thinking and thinkers;

- effective learning will produce reasoning thinkers;

- rote learning has its uses, but rote learning must change to internalised learning for the information to be used in reasoned thinking;

- learning should never remain on a plateau;

- students can become confident in their ability to use their own intellectual strength.

Guidelines

The guidelines emerge from the holistic and humanistic approach where the physical, emotional, psychological, intellectual and social dimensions of the learning experience are acknowledged and supported. The elements, apart from number 1, do not appear in hierarchical order but are interwoven.

1. Don't criticise anyone, especially yourself.
2. All members of the group are part of the democratic community of enquiry. Let people have access to each other.
3. Be optimistic, believe there will be positive outcome(s) because of the quality of the communication.
4. Honour the group. Do not have private conversations while the group is operating in total as any aside can be interpreted as a negative comment on someone else's contribution.
5. Provide a safety net for risk taking.
6. Everyone is entitled to feel comfortable physically.
7. Notice what you see, listen to what others see – every answer is valuable.
8. Check assumptions.
9. Remember that learning is intuitive, incidental and incremental.
10. Everyone has the right to have material re-presented.
11. The responsibility for communication is with the communicator.
12. You have the right to change your mind.
13. You have the right to be a minority.
14. Create a questioning environment.
15. Ten out of ten is not necessary or realistic in every situation.
16. A mistake is an opportunity to learn.
17. Practice at letting go. Don't own your ideas, they are on the table for discussion.
18. Each member of the group has an obligation to create a successful working environment, to keep the energy levels in mind.
19. Discussion must be recorded on paper and be observable in order to facilitate reflection and recall.
20. Every person has the right to request a change of direction in discussion and for that request to be debated.
21. There is an obligation to recognise that skills are necessary for the development of potential.
22. Recognise that practice is necessary for skill acquisition.
23. Complacency limits potential.

Teaching a New Concept Using Process

At the University of Hertfordshire two demonstration sessions using process were run with groups of first-year science undergraduates, who felt insecure about their competence at maths.

The students were asked to write down individually what they hoped they would get from the session. After they had written on their own for a minute they shared their ideas. Each student spoke to one other person about what they had written and then found someone else to talk to. The importance of this stage is to set the scene for the democratic community of enquiry.

Everyone knows why someone else is there and will support their efforts to feel the session had been worthwhile. It also gives the group a chance to check assumptions they were making about each other.

One group hoped to find out about logarithms while the other group wanted to learn about equations.

The students were then asked to write a definition of either logarithms or equations. At this point the lecturer finds out what is known. (A more comprehensive account of the demonstration lessons will be found in the video and notes. There is also an article describing "The process method for teaching logarithms and equations" available from Successful Learning.)

An indication of the sort of vocabulary a student would need to have in order to be able to understand logarithms – "do logs" (sic) – follows.

Algebra	Product	Express	Expression	Rule	Exponent	Root
Evaluate	Definition	Solution	Scientific notation or Standard Form			Polynomial
Degree	Reciprocal	Base	Power	Index	Natural numbers	
Positive	Negative	Denominator	Numerator	Factor	Convention	Property
Commutative law		Associative law		Monomial	Simplify	Coefficient

This is what needs to be recognised as the terminology if the student is to gain any real understanding of familiarisation with logarithms. To be able to manipulate data by using logarithms the following would be needed. How to use the rules for:

- multiplying and dividing in decimals
- natural numbers and their powers, e.g.,

  - any positive number to any power is positive
  - any negative number to an even power is positive
  - any negative number to a negative power is positive

- multiplying fractions

- indices, powers, exponents (there are seven rules or conventions).

The students had little idea of any of the vocabulary or the rules and conventions. Lecturers who were part of the group were startled to realise how little was known. Practitioners using process would not continue trying to teach content. The important concept to remember is that learning should proceed slowly (in terms of content) in order to gain mastery over concepts. This lack of speed is compensated for as understanding is deep and students are to proceed with later work more rapidly while not losing their deep understanding of novel work.

Conclusion

The process learning method is applicable to everyone in the institution. Its use will create in members of the learning community energy, enthusiasm and clear thought. The method allows people to be focussed but not blinkered, able to share views but not dictate, so that successful working practices can be followed with commitment, thus reducing the gap between rhetoric and practice for everyone.

The Language of Knowing and Learning: Bridging the Apparent Dichotomies

Reva Berman Brown, University of Essex

Introduction

The paper discusses an apparently trivial exercise which appears to make a contribution to the introduction of deep learning strategies to course participants.

The exercise is based on five pairs of words concerned with knowing and learning: (1) learn/study, (2) educate/train, (3) know/understand, (4) teach/tutor, and (5) student/pupil. They are synonyms deriving from root words in the various languages (among them, Latin, Greek, Anglo-Saxon, French and German) which have been absorbed into modern English. We make problems for ourselves as knowers, teachers and learners by treating them as though they were opposites, as two coins of differing values, rather than two sides of the same coin.

The first section of the paper discusses the theoretical framework upon which the exercise is based and from which it draws its inspiration, and the next section explains the exercise itself; the five pairs of words are explored in the third section, while the final section attempts to draw out the implications for educators and for those being educated, of the negative and positive implications of conducting the exercise.

Deep and Surface Learning

Thankfully, the approach students take to learning is not fixed, though it may well be consistent. Students are flexible enough to adapt their learning mind-set (that is to say, their way of being) to the learning task, although they will tend to use the style or approach most comfortable to them, even if this is not the most appropriate one. What is meant by the term "learning mind-set" concerns one's patterns of being or consciousness which we use as learners. In other words, my learning mind-set is the way I am as a learner rather than the ways or styles in which I do my learning. For example, I may well be an impatient human being in a given situation, and thus I would be an impatient learner/human being who could nevertheless do my learning by imposing on myself a patient learning style.

It is necessary to distinguish the learning mind-set from the term "learning style", which is a way of doing, and which has a specific meaning in the literature (see Kolb, 1984; Weil and McGill, 1989), where it forms part of the model of experiential learning.

Concepts and modes of learning, as seen by both the learner and the teacher, have been researched (for example, Knowles, 1986; Marton and Säljö, 1976 and 1984; Perry, 1970; Prideaux and Ford, 1988) and the studies and models produced range from the superficial to the sophisticated. The scheme given by Gibbs (1992) is both comprehensive and robust. This has been adapted and is illustrated in Table 1.

Table 1:	Concepts of Levels of Learning
Level 1	Learning as an additive product. The student passively receives and accumulates knowledge which is actively transmitted by the teacher. In this sense, the student doesn't have to "do" anything in order to accumulate learning.
Level 2	Learning as memorising and recalling. The student is active, and may take responsibility for learning. The knowledge acquired, however, is not transformed in any way; indeed, it need not even be understood, it being sufficient to reproduce it for assessment. The process has been somewhat crudely described as vacuuming it in and vomiting it out.
Level 3	Learning as acquiring facts, procedures or formulas, so that what is learnt are skills which enable repetition at a later date – if the student recognises that a particular fact or procedure is appropriate for the new situation.
Level 4	Learning as making sense. The student is trying not only to know but also to abstract meaning, both personal/emotional and intellectual, from the learning experience and process.
Level 5	Learning as understanding reality. The learning experience enables the student to see the world differently, in a way which is individual and meaningful.
Source:	Gibbs, 1992

Levels 1, 2 and 3 are concerned with reproduction, while levels 4 and 5 provide the student with the opportunity to make sense of both the learning experience and the learning process. Students who apply levels 4 and 5 are able to move between deep or surface approaches to their learning because they are able to perceive the demands of the learning task and can adopt the most appropriate approach. As Gibbs (1992) states:

> The connection between these underlying conceptions of learning and the approach students take to specific learning tasks is so strong that it is possible to predict the quality of learning outcomes directly from students' conceptions of learning. (p. 6)

The exercise outlined below has benefits both for my students and also for me in that it provides students with an opportunity to become aware of their learning mind-set and to explore their learning approach, and it allows me access to the prediction of the likely quality of the learning outcomes of the courses I deliver to them. The assumptions underlying the exercise are that students' conceptions of learning can be changed, that in many instances these conceptions should be changed, and that the change must be initiated by the student in order to be enduring and effective.

I designed the exercise with the theoretical concepts of deep and surface learning in mind, but initiated it without complete confidence that it would do as I hoped and activate the capacity for deep learning in my students. It is because I now have evidence that the exercise does work as a stimulus to awaken this existent, but often dormant, capacity in students that I have produced this paper.

The Exercise

Much of the substance of this paper has been provided by my students. I have found it fruitful to spend time discussing these five pairs of words with the undergraduates and masters students with whom I am involved and for whose development I am responsible. The purpose of the exercise described below is to initiate, albeit indirectly, circumstances where deep learning becomes possible.

In a sense, the exercise tends towards a Socratic teaching method, where the questioning is so poised that the students realise that they have learnt and known whatever-it-is all along, but haven't been aware of it until they hear themselves reveal their learning and knowledge as they respond to the issues which the questions raise. Simple as the exercise is, it provides a starting-point for the subsequent development of strategies which have been shown to foster a deep approach to learning (Gibbs, 1992):

- independent learning
- problem-based learning
- independent group work
- developing learning skills
- personal development
- reflection
- learning by doing
- project work.

The exercise creates an atmosphere for the practice in the use of the four factors identified by Biggs (1989) which foster a deep approach to learning:

- motivation content
- a well-structured learning base
- active learning
- discussion.

The course being taught doesn't appear to be relevant to the outcome of the exercise, and I tend to apply the exercise relatively early on in my encounter with a class or group. I present it playfully, so that the course participants are not aware that there is more to the activity than light-hearted diversion. I write the five pairs of words on slips of paper, making multiple slips to the amount needed so that each person has one, as it does no harm to the efficacy of the exercise should several of them have the same pair. I fold the slips, place them in a container, and the students take a lucky dip. Although they are forced into making a choice of a slip of paper from the container, once they have done so they feel that in some sense they have nevertheless voluntarily participated, and so they will take responsibility for their selection.

The students are then given a week to prepare what they wish to say about their pair of words. I express no expectations about what they ough" to say and I give no guidance on how they ought to approach the "researching' for information. Surface learners aren't happy about this, but the group norm – "If I have to do this (unnecessary/meaningless) project, then you aren't getting out of it for no good reason" – is sufficient to channel them into accepting the assignment with some sort of good humour.

Because the presentation of what they want to say means that they are going to be teaching and informing each other, they are required to prepare a handout to give to the others, so that each will have a record of what everyone has done. When they then present their findings to one another, without realising it, they reveal their learning mind-sets to me. (And I find this inadvertent information of great help to me as the course proceeds.) The handouts come in a variety of forms: neat columns of numbered comparisons, intricate diagrams of connection and difference, continuous narrative text. They present how they have found out at the same time as they present what they have discovered. And it seems that they enjoy the opportunity to share with one another.

The presentations themselves range through the confident and the flamboyant to mumbled, tentative offerings. There are mini-lectures with careful overheads, structured and controlled monologue-discourses, excited presentations of discoveries, shambolic incoherences, sulky and cursory rambles.

The five pairs of words, while apparently neutral, awake in the students a highly personal response. I find that discussion breaks out like measles. They seem to have found a sense of self as they communicate to one another. For some of them, it is the first time that they have reflected on the past-however-many years of formal schooling they have experienced. They appear to uncover for themselves the underlying, intimate meaning of what they are undertaking at this stage in their lives. What the discussion can produce is the posing, and sometimes the answering, of the two "big questions" at the bottom of all formal study: "why are you here?" and "what do you think you are doing?".

Of course, that is when the exercise works. It doesn't always. Success seems to depend on timing, which I don't always get right. The exercise works best when the class has managed to become some sort of group, however tentative, rather than a collection of individuals in the same place at the same time for the same reason. And I can misjudge when this happens, or indeed it may never happen. I am not the only person to have had classes which stayed a collection of strangers despite all efforts to get them to come together.

Like the girl with the curl in the middle of her forehead, when the exercise is good, it is very, very good, and when it is bad, it is horrid for all of us enduring the flat, sad experience. But it is more often good than bad, and the students aren't the only ones to gain from giving a small amount of time and a great amount of attention to the language of knowing and learning.

Exploring the Pairs

(1) Learn/study

To learn: Definitions include:

- to gain knowledge of something; to acquire a skill in; to gain by experience; to acquire by example; to be taught; to gain skill and/or knowledge by study, practice or teaching; to find out.

To study: Definitions include:

- to apply the mind to a subject; to investigate; to examine by observation or research; to scrutinise; to meditate and reflect; to apply careful and critical thought; to be engaged in learning; to consider seriously.

To learn and to study share characteristics: both are time- and goal-orientated, are different applications of a similar process of knowledge and experience, and may be concerned with committing to memory and becoming informed.

Comparisons of "learn" and "study" are given in Table 2. This illustrates how much the concepts are aspects of the same phenomenon rather than different, and contrasting, activities.

Table 2	Learn and Study
Learn	**Study**
1 Is a final goal in itself, and learning without study (e.g., by experience) is possible	The final goal is to learn, although study without learning is possible
2 Concerned to gain knowledge of a topic/subject	Concerned to apply the mind or acquire a skill in something
3 Is the result of being taught, though not always	Is a self-motivated activity
4 Not always a conscious or deliberate process	Implies conscious reflection on learning and thus tests it
5 Continues throughout life, governed by changing experience	Is a specific activity which tends to be undertaken at certain times of life, in a particular institutional environment

(2) Educate/train

To educate: Definitions include:

- to teach and discipline, so as to develop the natural powers; to develop and train for some special purpose; to instruct; to provide schooling for; to train mentally and morally; to improve; to develop.

To train: Definitions include:

- to bring to a requisite standard as of knowledge or skill; to lead into taking a particular course or direction; to draw along; to give education by instruction and discipline; to go into a course of exercise and discipline; to cause to grow in a particular way.

In Britain, these two words have a long history of controversy, which can be illustrated, for example, by the Education for Capability Manifesto issued by the RSA in 1979:

There is a serious imbalance in Britain today in the full process which is described by the two words "education" and "training". The idea of the "educated" person is that of the scholarly individual who has been neither educated nor trained to exercise useful skills, who is able to understand but not to act. Young people in secondary or higher education increasingly specialise, and do so too often in ways which mean that they are taught to practice only the skills of scholarship and science. They acquire knowledge of particular subjects, but are not equipped to use knowledge in ways which are relevant to the world outside the education system.

This imbalance is harmful to individuals, to industry and to society. . . There exists in its own right a culture which is concerned with doing, making and organising . . . [which] emphasises the day-to-day management of affairs, the formulation and solution of problems and the design, manufacture and marketing of goods and services. Educators should spend more time preparing people in this way for a life outside the education system. (Stephenson and Weil, 1992, p. xiii)

Where my own field of expertise (management) is concerned, the problematic of the apparent education and training dichotomy seems deeply embedded. It is assumed that managers require education, while non-managerial employees need training. The possibility that education might incorporate training or that training is founded on education is given lip-service but is not often specifically applied in the design of many management/business studies courses and programmes.

Table 3 provides some of the alignments and disparities between "educate" and "train".

Table 3	Educate and Train	
	Educate	**Train**
1	To provide circumstances for the accumulation of knowledge	To provide circumstances for the development of existing abilities
2	Oriented to the practical and theoretical, which need not be separated	Oriented to action (often routine repeatable operations)
3	Can be active and passive in transmission and absorption	Always active, and tends towards results
4	Development of moral and intellectual achievement	Instruction by systematic discipline and practice
5	For the sake of knowledge	To acquire skills
6	Final objectives not necessarily clear-cut	Clear-cut objectives
7	Tends to be problem-centred	Tends to be subject-centred

(3) Know/understand

The nuances between knowing and understanding are more problematic.

To know: Definitions include:

- to be familiar or acquainted with; to have a grasp of; to understand; to have knowledge of; to be aware of; to recognise; to have experience of.

To understand: Definitions include:

- to perceive the meaning of; to know and comprehend the nature of; to possess judgement and intelligence to know the origins of; to realise.

The double-sidedness of these concepts is brought out by the fact that "to know" is defined as "to have an understanding of", and "to understand" is defined as "to have knowledge of".

It is possible, however, to know without understanding, which requires greater depth of comprehension of the subject matter; to know in the sense of having a grasp of the basic facts is a step towards fully comprehending their origins and derivations. For example, a student may need to know which mathematical formulae to select in order to solve a problem. This may be achieved by past experience of similar tasks or by memorising of the formulae. A complete understanding of the meaning and origin of the formulae is unnecessary to accomplish the task; it is sufficient to know which are appropriate.

The attributes of "know" and "understand" are given in Table 4.

Table 4	Know and Understand	
	Know	**Understand**
1	Can be obtained through experience	Requires knowledge
2	Can be obtained through memorising	Greater depth of knowledge required
3	Taken as true	Requires reflection
4	To possess a range of information	To know the origins and context of

(4) Teach/tutor

To teach: Definitions include:

- to impart knowledge to by lessons; to give instruction to; to guide by precept or example; to make known; to communicate the knowledge of; to train by practice or exercise; to impart skill; to guide.

To tutor: Definitions include:

- to instruct another in one or more branches of knowledge, especially a private teacher; to be entrusted with the care of the undergraduates of a college; to teach individually or in small groups.

The activities of "teach" and "tutor" are illustrated in Table 5.

Table 5	Teach and Tutor
Teach	**Tutor**
1 To instruct groups	To guide individuals
2 To transmit prescribed content	To assist in learning
3 To communicate by means of instruction, generally to groups	To give special instruction often on a one-to-one basis
4 Takes place in a controlled and formal environment	Takes place in a relatively informal environment
5 Learning needs subsumed into application of graded levels of instruction	Learning needs individually identified and attended to
6 Graded levels of instruction, rewarded by standardised marks	Individualised levels of guidance rewarded by encouragement

Once again, the activity of teaching or tutoring tends to be dichotomised, while the concepts are synonymous. A teacher is defined as a person whose function is to give instruction, especially in school, while a tutor is defined as a person engaged by students to assist them in their studies – which enables teachers to tutor and tutors to teach where circumstances require this. Teachers are seen as being responsible for a class of students, and for what and how their students learn, while tutors tend to oversee the individual learning of their tutees. It goes without saying that the tutoring aspects of the lecturing role are currently being eroded, and emphasis is being put on teaching to increasingly larger groups.

(5) Student/pupil

Student: Definitions include:

* A person engaged in a course of study, especially an advanced scholar, as in a university; one who closely examines or investigates.

Pupil: Definitions include:

- A person of either sex or of any age under the care of a teacher; a scholar; a learner.

Table 6	Students and Pupils		
A plus/minus system is used to show whether or not the characteristics mentioned under each component are applicable to the student or pupil.			
General components		**Student**	**Pupil**
1 Learner			
	a) adult	+	-
	b) role of experience	+	-
	c) readiness to learn	+/-	+/-
	d) instrumentally motivated	+/-	+/-
	e) integrally motivated	+/-	+/-
2 Academic Institutions			
	a) school	-	+
	b) college	+	-
	c) university	+	-
3 Education			
	a) pedagogically orientated	-	+
	b) andragogically orientated	+	-
	c) compulsory	-	+
	d) free-choice	+	-
4 Learning modes			
	a) directed learning	-	+
	b) independent learning	+	-
5 Teaching modes			
	a) classroom	+	+
	b) lecture/seminar	+	+
	c) teacher as spoonfeeder	-	+
	d) teacher as facilitator	+	-

A comment voiced, sometimes inarticulately, by university students is that they are (or they are not) treated as pupils, rather than students. Those who are used to surface learning tend to want to be regarded as pupils, and it can sometimes be difficult to get them to make the transition to becoming students.

Implications of the Exercise

These pairs of words come embedded in assumptions as to their meaning and significance. Assuredly, their meaning is dynamic rather than static, and they interact with each other to fill the space they occupy in our lives. These are words trailing nuances, which make them difficult to translate into other languages.

Unpack any of the words and their scent of prejudice, stereotype and fallacy is released: for example, the learner has a willingness and ability that the student does not share; the learner runs (and even flies) while the student plods. Education is what gentlefolk experience; lesser folk get trained. Knowing requires less creativity and reflection than understanding. Teaching is more stressful than tutoring; the teacher imparts while the tutor elicits knowledge. Students are not only older but also more able than pupils.

In a sense, it all pivots around the meaning the individual lecturer gives to the verb "to learn". The lecturer can safely adopt a passive approach to student learning if this is seen as an activity undertaken only by the learner, whether student or pupil, whether for education (to provide mental and moral training) or for training (to cause to grow in a particular way). The lecturer can be passive (or lazy) because learning has become something that is up to the student, requiring little action on the part of the lecturer: "I lecture to them/tutor them; it is up to them to get on with it and learn."

And the ultimate aim of the process also makes a difference to the lecturer's approach to student learning: do we make it explicit to ourselves and our students whether we want them to know, or to understand, or to combine both of these elements in the process of studying and learning?

What I personally find valuable in the word-pair exercise is that it requires me to examine my motives, aims and intentions towards each group of students who do the exercise. It gives me a structured moment to step back and become aware of what that set of students and I are actually undertaking as we interact together during the delivery of the course.

I must admit that I hadn't realised when I tried the exercise out for the first time that it can be such an elastic tool, and that it has implications for both the students and me in my role of teacher and academic, interested in how my students learn and whether they benefit in any non-instrumental way from the knowledge that passes between us.

Even when it has worked well, however, the exercise has negative implications. It can increase the anxiety level of already stressed and anxious students. It can show them a learning mind-set that they feel unable to become. It can increase the scepticism or cynicism of those students who, because of past bad or painful educational experiences, have arrived on the course already alienated from any learning other than the instrumental and the surface. It can be interpreted as my making unacceptable intellectual and emotional demands on them – "Don't tell me I could get more out of my time here at university. All I want is an easy ride to getting my piece of paper; I don't need any of this navel-gazing stuff."

Despite this negative potential, however, by a combination of design, accident and serendipity, I now have a tool which helps me to fulfil my personal hopes for my students. The exercise provides a small step towards enabling me to broach the more profound aspects of what the students are here at Essex to achieve. In the words of the CNAA project "Improving Student Learning", I can begin the process of reaching towards the general aims of a programme of study in higher education:

> . . . the development of students' intellectual and imaginative powers; their understanding and judgment; their problem-solving skills; their ability to communicate; their ability to see relationships within what they have learned and to perceive their field of study in a broader perspective. (Gibbs, 1992, p. 1)

The main positive implication of the exercise is that it opens a beginning towards the development of the students' conceptions of learning, and, in allowing them overtly to reveal to themselves their particular learning mind-set, it makes possible a change of their conceptions.

At worst, when the exercise has not worked, it provides them with a brief glimpse of the existence of other learning mind-sets. At best, they can become less instrumental about learning in general and the course in particular; they develop a trust in themselves, a trust of me, and a confidence that makes them less likely to reject my pressure towards a course that is student- and process-centred and therefore somewhat more difficult and demanding than a course with a more surface approach. They find that it is safe to experiment with 'an enquiring, analytical and creative approach' to the course, and to develop "independent judgment and critical self-awareness." (Gibbs, 1992, p. 1)

This does not happen every time, or last all the time, but it has happened on sufficient occasions for me to offer the exercise as a simple and mainly effective way into the introduction of the existence of deep learning strategies to course participants, and to demonstrate the undoubted benefits such an approach to their studies can provide for them.

References

Biggs, J. B. (1989). Approaches to the enhancement of tertiary teaching *Higher Education Research and Development*, 8, 7, pp. 7–25.

CNAA (1990). *Improving Student Learning Project* Oxford: Oxford Centre for Staff Development.

Gibbs, G. (1992). *Improving the Quality of Student Learning* Bristol: Technical & Educational Services.

Knowles, M. (1986). *Using Learning Contracts*. San Francisco: Jossey-Bass.

Kolb, D. A. (1984). *Experiential Learning: Experience as the Source of Learning and Development*. Englewood Cliffs, N J: Prentice-Hall.

Marton, F., Hounsell, D. and Entwistle, N. (eds) (1984). *The Experience of Learning* Edinburgh: Scottish Academic Press.

Marton, F. and Säljö, R. (1976) On qualitative differences in learning, I: outcome and process. *British Journal of Educational Psychology* 46, pp. 4–11.

Marton, F. and Säljö, R. (1984). Approaches to learning. In F. Marton, D. Hounsell and N. Entwistle, (eds) *The Experience of Learning* Edinburgh: Scottish Academic Press.

Perry, W. G. (1970). *Forms of Intellectual and Ethical Development in the College Years: A Scheme* New York: Holt, Rinehart & Winston.

Prideaux, S. and Ford J. E. (1988). Management development competences: teams, learning contracts and work experience based learning *Journal of Management Development* 7, 3, pp. 13–22.

Ramsden, P. (1988). *Improving Learning: New Perspectives* London: Kogan Page.

Stephenson, J. and Weil, S. (1992). *Quality in Learning: A Capability Approach in Higher Education* London: Kogan Page.

Weil, S. W. and McGill, I. (1989). *Making Sense of Experiential Learning*, Milton Keynes: SRHE/Open University Press.

Chapter 11 The role of computers in improving student learning

Towards a Methodology for Evaluating the Quality of Student Learning in a Computer-Mediated-Conferencing Environment

Brian Webb, D. R. Newman, Clive Cochrane, Department of Information Management, The Queen's University, Belfast

1. Introduction

Computer-mediated-communication (CMC) is widely employed as a medium of education delivery both in the UK and the USA. Used primarily in the distance learning environment, it has been utilized by the Open University since 1988, and some UK institutions are now using CMC on campus as an alternative or appendage to seminars and tutorials. Research into the educational value of this medium has, however, been inhibited by concentration on analysis of activity rather than content. A natural tendency to measure that which is most easily measurable has mistaken activity for learning, interaction for collaboration (Mason, 1991).

The need for a methodology to measure the quality of learning in a CMC environment has become more pressing as the importance of the cognitive and social context to individual learning has been recognized. In particular, educational research and practice has focussed on small group work and peer assessment (Gibbs, 1992).

There is a need to bring together these two strands of research. CMC research has focussed on the medium itself, mostly print based, audio conferencing and teleconferencing. Research into social interaction and cognition has focussed on the face-to-face environment. Where the two strands have overlapped research has concentrated on one element of the learning context – the importance of social cues. We need to investigate more fully the importance of the social context in the CMC environment. In particular we need to investigate the value of CMC as an educational medium by assessing the quality of learning which takes place. Only with such research will we be able to design the computer supported cooperative learning tools that will support the best educational practice.

This paper reports early results of work being carried out by the Department of Information Management, The Queen's University Belfast.

2. Aims and Objectives

The research seeks to develop a methodology to evaluate the quality of student learning in a CMC environment.

Approach

- Develop a methodology based on work to date.
- Test this methodology in a real student learning environment.
- Assess its wider significance and utility.

Key issues

- What is the quality of student learning in a CMC environment?
- What is it about the CMC environment that influences the student approach?

3. Brief Literature Review

Increasingly student learning is seen not as an individual but as a social phenomenon. Psychologists have long believed that individual cognitive skills are developed in a social context (Resnick et al., 1991) and have cited the psychological development of children as evidence (Rogoff, 1990). The importance of the social context to learning has been emphasised by Lipman (1991), who believes that the development of a 'community of enquiry' is essential for the development of higher level, critical-thinking skills within the individual. Garrison (1992) lists five stages in critical thinking – problem identification, problem definition, problem exploration, problem applicability and problem integration – and Anderson (1993) argues that social interaction underpins each of these stages.

A clear link between critical thinking, social interaction and deep learning has emerged. Ramsden (1983) has highlighted the importance of horizontal (student–student) and vertical (student–teacher) interaction. Biggs (1985) associated deep learning approaches with 'affective involvement', which is supported by interaction, and Entwistle and Entwistle (1992) valued sustained interaction and the negotiation of shared meaning.

Research into CMC has concentrated on individual cognitive development, largely within the distance learning environment. Recently Anderson (1992) has embarked on 'the first exploration of socially shared cognition within the mediated learning environment' by studying audio conferencing in Canada.

What insights we have gained from previous research into the value of social interaction in the CMC environment have been inconclusive. Davis (1984) compared teleconferencing with face-to-face sessions and could not declare a clear winner based on course scores. Rother (1984) believed audio conferencing supports interaction but Burge and Howard (1990) reported that the majority of students they surveyed felt that interaction was inhibited by the medium. Henri (1988) warned not to mistake participation for interaction and found that on one course the percentage of interactive sequences initiated by students was relatively low and the majority of messages were independent.

A key challenge is to isolate and study the impact of CMC independently of other factors in the learning context. Clark (1985) reminds us that course design is more important than the medium used. A poor lecture is a poor lecture however given, but CMC does open up new dimensions for learning and we need to identify those components of CMC that support or inhibit critical thinking/deep learning.

4. Development of Methodology

The first stage of our research, survey analysis, used a modified version of the student perceptions questionnaire developed by Anderson for his study of audio conferencing in Canada. This was developed specifically to measure the quality of learning in this CMC environment, in particular to assess the level of critical thinking/deep learning taking place, and uses constructs both from Lipman's 'community of inquiry' and Garrison's critical thinking model. Anderson rejected both Ramsden and Entwistle's (1983) Approaches to Student Inventory and Biggs's (1987) Study Process Questionnaire because they 'deal with individual cognitive preferences with which students enter the learning environment and do not focus specifically on the social components of learning.'

Our questionnaire excluded questions based on Lipman's community of inquiry as these were less likely to produce consistent responses with Garrison's five stages, given the limited scale and scope of the survey. Of the remainder, those questions which were not relevant to our computer conferencing environment were omitted. The final questionnaire based on Garrison's five-stage critical thinking model addressed the following issues:

1. the capacity of the computer conferencing environment to arouse and sustain interest and to increase awareness of important issues;
2. problem definition: to what extent does computer conferencing clarify course objectives and make relevant personal experience?
3. problem exploration: does computer conferencing have the capacity to help the student to develop new ideas and solutions and understand issues, including those contained within study texts?
4. critical assessment of course content, possible solutions and the ideas of

others;

5. problem integration: to what extent does computer conferencing help the student to understand by applying course content to his or her own life situation?

The methodological approach to survey development and testing was based on that followed by Entwistle and Ramsden (1983). This entailed:
− validation of the survey instrument through response correlations;
− factor analysis to identify critical constructs.

The second stage of our research, context analysis, used Garrison's critical thinking model to mark up indicators of deep or surface learning in CMC messages. Indicators of learning such as importance, novelty, bringing in outside knowledge, justification, critical assessment and relevance were used to identify content statements suggesting deep learning (+) or surface learning (−). For example, relevant statements were marked R+, irrelevant statements or diversions were marked R−. This was done both for face-to-face and CMC sessions. When all the transcripts were marked, a deep to surface scale ranging from a−1 all surface to a+1 all deep was created.

5. Testing the Methodology

A major difficulty in trying to measure the quality of student learning in a computer conferencing environment is the lack of a comparator methodology for face-to-face seminars. It was therefore necessary to apply the chosen survey instrument to seminars as well as to computer conferencing sessions.

We wanted to compare the quality of student learning in computer conferencing with that in face-to-face seminars. But few people even attempt to measure whether deep learning takes place in seminars. So we surveyed attitudes and reactions to seminars as well as conferencing.

A pilot survey was administered to 35 second-year students studying the Information Society module in the Department of Information Management, Queens University, Belfast. Traditionally, these students were obliged to attend seminars each week. In the groups of 10 to 20, some of them would then discuss an issue raised in the lectures with the lecturer (others would say nothing).

For this pilot study, they were briefly shown how to use the Network Telepathy computer conferencing system, and then used it to discuss their choice of individual projects. Then for the last five weeks of the semester, each week some of the seminar groups met on the computer conferencing system instead of face to face. So conferencing was used as a seminar substitute in a module designed for face-to-face, not open or distance learning.

At the end of the semester, each student was asked to complete questionnaires relating to their studying experience with the two media. twenty-eight completed surveys were returned for seminars and 26 for computer conferencing.

Seminar questionnaires
These responses allowed us to test the relationship between Garrison's constructs. Seminar data were examined using correlation of individual variables. Emerging relationships can be seen more clearly following factor analysis. SPSS was used to carry out principal factor analysis followed by rotation to oblique simple structure. Six factors with eigen values greater than one, accounting for 73.3% of the variance, were retained.

	F1	F2	F3	F4	F5	F6
AROUSED INTEREST					.75	
TRIGGERED A DESIRE TO UNDERSTAND					.78	
AWARE OF ISSUES	.73					
CLARIFIED SUBJECT			.88			
IDENTIFY PERSONAL EXPERIENCE	.69					
EXPLORE NEW IDEAS		.86				
DEVELOP NEW SOLUTIONS		.50				
UNDERSTAND ISSUES			.77			
DISENTANGLE IDEAS				.65		
CRITICAL ASSESSMENT					.56	
JUDGE SOLUTIONS				.85		
CRITICALLY EVALUATE				.78		
ASSESS PRACTICAL UTILITY				.40		
PREVIOUS KNOWLEDGE						.54
TEST SOLUTIONS						.84
APPLY IDEAS	.82					
CONCERNS RELATED TO PROJECT			.77			

Figure 1: Seminars (highest loading on each factor for all variables)

These results support Garrison's stage model, particularly on Factor 2 (problem exploration) and Factor 4 (problem evaluation), but also Factor 5 (problem identification) and Factor 6 (problem integration).

Factor 3 relates clarification of the purpose of studying the subject with an opportunity to discuss concerns related to assignments/projects. Factor 1 incorporates problem integration (apply ideas to own life), problem identification (aware of issues) and problem exploration (relevant personal experience).

There is also support for an early approach to study inventory developed by Entwistle, Hanley and Hounsell (1979), which attempted to distinguish between deep/surface approaches and comprehension/operation learning. This model stated that all of the following four processes are used during a deep approach to learning:

1. building overall description of content area;
2. reorganising incoming information to relate to previous knowledge or experience and establish personal meaning;
3. detailed attention to evidence and steps in the argument;
4. relating evidence to conclusion and maintaining a critical, objective stance.

Computer conferencing questionnaires

When applied to the computer conferencing returns, principal factor analysis followed by rotation to oblique simple structure produced five factors with eigen values greater than one, explaining 73.2% of variance.

	F1	F2	F3	F4	F5	F6
AROUSED INTEREST					.75	
TRIGGERED A DESIRE TO UNDERSTAND					.78	
AWARE OF ISSUES	.73					
CLARIFIED SUBJECT			.88			
IDENTIFY PERSONAL EXPERIENCE	.69					
EXPLORE NEW IDEAS		.86				
DEVELOP NEW SOLUTIONS		.50				
UNDERSTAND ISSUES			.77			
DISENTANGLE IDEAS				.65		
CRITICAL ASSESSMENT					.56	
JUDGE SOLUTIONS				.85		
CRITICALLY EVALUATE				.78		
ASSESS PRACTICAL UTILITY				.40		
PREVIOUS KNOWLEDGE						.54
TEST SOLUTIONS						.84
APPLY IDEAS	.82					
CONCERNS RELATED TO PROJECT			.77			

Figure 2: Computer conferencing (highest loading on each factor for all variables)

The five factors to emerge from this survey are:

1. *Discussion of concerns related to assignments/projects*
   This factor describes an approach to studying which uses computer
   conferencing to understand course content better through discussion, to
   develop new solutions and to assess their utility through testing.

2. *Awareness of issues*
   This factor is indicative of an approach built on an initial awareness of
   important issues being discussed, the application of ideas arising out of the
   discussion to the student's own life (including previous experience and
   knowledge) and an ability to understand course texts and lectures better.

3. *Critical evaluation*
   This factor loads very highly on an opportunity to evaluate critically the
   assumptions and ideas of others, a critical assessment of discussion content
   and clarification of the purposes of studying the subject.

4. *Negative impact on motivation and interest*
   This factor has a high negative loading on both triggered a desire to
   understand more and aroused interest in the subject matter. A reverse
   association with these two constructs is at odds both with the other emerging
   factors under computer conferencing and with the results of the seminar
   questionnaire. This anomaly may be explained by a 'fear of computing'
   evident in some of the open-ended question responses received.

   > Being unfamiliar with the technology and disliking the computer
   > environment and being self-conscious of using the system, I did not
   > concentrate on the topics being discussed.

   > By the time I found the bit I was looking for, I didn't have the
   > inclination to apply information for my own purposes. I had too
   > many problems with the technology.

   > I feel learning through conferencing would be boring, as you would
   > be staring at a computer screen for a certain length of time.

The circumstances under which our study was conducted were unlikely to allay
any reticence to use computers. Less than one hour was spent on training the
students to use the system. And the telepathy system, while much easier to use
than command-line COSY, does not have an intuitive graphical user interface.
(It took 2–3 hours for a third year class in information systems to learn telepathy
in the first semester.) The computer conferencing sessions ran in the final weeks
of the spring semester and the actual survey was conducted within a few weeks
of examinations. Added to the fact that this was a trial in the use of computer

conferencing as an adjunct to seminars, the environment may not have been conducive to overcoming any fears of computers.

5. *Identify personal experience*
This factor curiously loads the identification of relevant personal experience with a negative outcome on the opportunity to explore new ideas. It remains to be explained, but we suspect it to be an artefact resulting from factor analysis of our small sample.

In contrast with the results of the face-to-face seminar survey, the use of computer conferencing returns are less supportive of the particular stages within Garrison's critical thinking model. One factor fewer emerged from the analysis of computer conferencing responses to explain the same amount of variance. Fewer identified factors directly correspond to Garrison's stages – perhaps because things other than critical thinking were occurring when telepathy was being used as a mere information transfer mechanism when selecting projects.

Of particular note with computer conferencing is the high negative loading (factor 4) against two variables (aroused interest in the subject matter and triggered a desire to understand more) which are indicative of a motivational/deep approach to learning. Contrasting high positive loadings for the same variables in the face-to-face seminar environment point to a possible explanation in the impact of the medium itself.

The simplest explanation is that the technology was hard to learn and the students were distracted from their task by remembering keystrokes and procedures. Instead of computer conferencing being a transparent window through which students interact with each other (and teachers), it became an obtrusive player itself: a player instead of a stage (Laurel, 1991). This hypothesis will be explored in future experiments, since there are indications that the third year information systems class took much more readily to computer conferencing.

We have already discussed the possible negative impact of 'fear of computing' on the development of deep approaches to learning. Research into the impact of CMC on social interaction, in particular the absence of social cues, suggests positives as well negatives. On the one hand a lack of physical presence may equalize participation and encourage rational decision making. On the other hand a lack of physical presence robs the CMC environment of much of the immediacy and spontaneity of face-to-face social interaction. Support for both positions emerged from our survey.

> With conferencing I could be selective in what I read and what I replied to. It also allowed me more time to contemplate others' comments and structure my own replies and comments.

I feel I would prefer a traditional group myself, as I like to get immediate feedback and reactions. Although I feel someone who does not like to speak out would prefer to put their views on the conferencing system.

I prefer traditional seminars because you get immediate feedback. Others' views can be clarified at the time. People say more than they would type into a computer. The discussion is less formal.

A seminar is more flexible as you have face-to-face contact if you wish to ask about something that you do not understand.

A key challenge for researchers is to isolate and measure the impact of the absence of physical presence on the development of critical thinking/deep learning. This includes the lack of social cues such as facial expression, voice intonation and body language, but must also include, when dealing with an asynchronous computer conferencing system, the lack of real time interaction among participants (except when conferencing sessions are timetabled, since messages appear on others' screens within a minute).

Early results from content analysis (thus far, only indicators of deep learning have been marked up) are encouraging. Although face-to-face seminars have more new (or fewer old) ideas and slightly more critical assessment, CMC has many more important than unimportant statements and many more statements linking ideas than mere repetition. This suggests that CMC is more supportive of the latter stages of critical thinking (exploration, applicability and integration), whereas face-to-face sessions are better in the early stages of the process (arousing interest, motivating, generating new ideas).

6. Assessment of Utility

The results of the survey suggest that computer conferencing supports deep approaches to learning by encouraging critical evaluation/assessment and understanding of content through discussion. Somewhat paradoxically, the medium itself may inhibit the development of deep approaches in other ways by closing down motivational stimuli.

Further research is needed to see whether improvements in human-computer interaction with the software, training in the tools used, or course design can overcome the single negative factor found, to permit deep learning among larger classes than can be supported face to face.

The constructs identified in this limited study will be further developed as larger numbers of students are tested over the coming year. Crucially the constructs will be further used as a basis of identifying approaches to learning in our analysis of on-line and face-to-face discussion content. As more transcripts are analysed in full, the relationship between CMC and stage of critical thinking will be explored.

The methodological approach developed here, evaluating the social (as opposed to the individual) context of CMC learning and evaluating the quality of learning in a CMC (as opposed to a face-to-face) environment, offers a useful tool to determine the educational value of CMC. Further research into learning in a computer-supported group environment – on and off campus – is needed.

References

Anderson T. (1993). *Socially Shared Cognition in Distance Learning: An Exploration of Learning in an Audio Teleconferencing Context.* Unpublished doctoral dissertation proposal, University of Calgary.

Biggs, J. B. (1987). *Student Approaches to Studying and Learning.* Melbourne: Australian Council for Educational Research.

Burge, E, and Howard, J. (1990.) Audio-conferencing in graduate education: a case study. *American Journal of Distance Education.* 4, 2,3–13

Clark, R. E. (1983). Reconsidering research on learning from media. *Review of Educational Research,* 53, 445–460.

Davis, D. (1984). *Evaluation and Comparison of Teleconference Training with Face-to-Face Training and the Effects on Attitude and Learning.* Unpublished doctoral dissertation, Drake University.
Entwistle and Entwistle (1992). Experiences of understanding in revising for degree examinations. *Learning and Instruction,* 2, 1–22.

Entwistle, N. and Ramsden, P. (1983). *Understanding Student Learning.* London: Croom Helm.

Garrison, D. R. (1992).(Critical thinking and self-directed learning in adult education: an analysis of responsibility and control issues.) *Adult Education Quarterly,* 42, 3, 136–148.

Gibbs, G. (1992). *Improving the Quality of Student Learning.* Bristol: Technical and Educational Services.

Henri, F. (1988). Distance learning and computer – mediated – communication:

interactive, quasi-interactive or monologue? In O'Malley, C. (ed.), *Computer Supported Collaborative Learning.* Heidelberg: Springer-Verlag, 1991.

Laurel, B. (1991). *Computers as Theatre. Reading,* MA; Wokingham, Addison-Wesley.

Lipman, M. (1991). *Thinking in Education.* Cambridge: Cambridge University Press.

Mason, R. (1991). Methodologies for evaluating applications of computer conferencing. In Kaye, A. R .(ed.), *Collaborative Learning through Computer Conferencing.* Heidelberg: Springer-Verlag.

Resnick, L. , Levine, J. and Teasley S. (eds), (1991). *Perspectives on Socially Shared Cognition* (384–397). Washington: American Psychological Association.

Rogoff, B. (1990). *Apprenticeship in Thinking: Cognitive Developments in Social Context.* New York: Oxford University Press.

Rother, J. P. (1985). Audio teleconferencing and distance education: towards a conceptual synthesis. *Distance Education , 6, 2,* 199–208.

A Constructivist, Technology-Enriched Learning Environment and the Claim on Students Self-Regulation

Frank P. C. M. de Jong , University of Nijmegen

Fundamental to the issue of improving student learning are the questions what is learning, what is the goal of learning and what does it mean to learn? Secondly, one can ask which problems instructors and students have in realising that learning takes place, that learning goals are reached or that learning is meaningful? In other words the difficulties educators are confronted with may be traced to the assumptions lecturers and students have about teaching and learning. Just ask lecturers what teaching or learning is and most of their responses will correlate with the metaphors 'knowledge transmittance' and 'knowledge acquisition'. These kinds of metaphors lead to the role of lecturers, instructional designers, etc., as creators of environments which allow the efficient communication of knowledge to the learner. An environment in which lectures, textbooks or computer environments are the 'sender' of the 'objective knowledge message' and the student is the 'receiver' (Cunningham, 1992). A traditional criterion of this kind of learning is that the communicated information can be remembered some time after it has been read, heard or discussed. Questions and examinations test if the message has been received. This kind of learning prepares students for tests and retention of facts and often leads to the acquisition of 'inert' knowledge (Brown and Palincsar, 1989; Bransford, Franks, Vye and Sherwood, 1989, after Whitehead 1916). Inert knowledge refers to encapsulated information which the learner accesses in a restricted set of contexts, cued for activation, for example, by an expected examination question, although the information is relevant to a variety of situations. According to Brown and Palincsar (1989), a second kind of learning requires the assimilation of new knowledge. In this way the learner establishes ownership of that knowledge, which will afford him flexible access to it and which is potentially applicable to related but novel situations. The information becomes part of the workable knowledge (Brown and Palincsar, 1989). If the emphasis in teaching and learning shifts from the functional component of understanding (e.g., being able to answer questions; Anderson and Roth, 1989) to the structural component of understanding (e.g., creating a web of links between 'exact' knowledge, other domains, personal (pre)conceptions and personal interpretations of the world), a third kind of learning is addressed. This learning involves modification, adaptation, refinement or restructuring of the already existing knowledge structures (usable knowledge) in the face of experiencing that this knowledge proves to be incompatible in solving new problems or with new perspectives. It is this experience of the relativity of the heard or read (transmitted) 'objective' knowledge, of construction of knowledge, of theory change that leads to students' cognitive flexibility, which is needed to transfer formal knowledge in solving real-life, or new, advanced problems. Questions or problems for which experts mostly just do not have one single answer or solution.

Although learning is a process of knowledge construction and not of knowledge recording or absorption (Resnick, 1989) it may be obvious that the more exact knowledge students have, the easier it may be for them to solve new, advanced problems. From expert/novice literature (Chi, Glaser and Farr, 1988) it is known that experts use both the structural components and the specific declarative knowledge of the domain. However, it will be clear from the explanation above that knowing something does not guarantee that students are able to use it in new or advanced contexts or in other contexts than those in which the specific knowledge is acquired. Illustrative for this is the study of Jacobson (1991) which revealed that students assigned to a computer-based drill design (stressing the recognition and recall of general domain information) performed better on declarative knowledge tasks than students assigned to a thematic criss-crossing design in which multiple perspectives on cases and interconnections between knowledge components were demonstrated. In idea brainstorming and in a problem-solving essay task which required a more direct application of the cognitive skills associated with transferring acquired knowledge to a new situation the thematic criss-crossing group scored higher on these higher-order knowledge transfer tasks. However, in demonstrating knowledge of critical structural knowledge elements and their inter-relationships, ability to apply knowledge in new situations flexibly (important characteristics of expert perform-ance) the thematic criss-crossing students were not in full possession of the lower-level declarative knowledge a domain expert would have.

Perhaps it is not the question what kind of learning we are aiming at which is central to the issue of improving student learning, but when and how there has to be a stage of introductory or declarative knowledge acquisition and when and how the attainment of domain expertise or advanced stage knowledge acquisi-tion (Spiro, Coulson, Feltovich and Anderson, 1988) has to take place. Jacobson (1991) posed the question: "Whether the mastery of factual knowledge would be better developed before, during or after the acquisition of a sophisticated structural appreciation of the knowledge domain?" (p. 109). Is the lack of a flexible cognitive representation of knowledge due to the emphasis in the teaching/learning process on factual knowledge acquisition actually inhibiting advanced knowledge acquisition or to a lack of instructional interventions stressing knowledge integration at the right time? Can higher-order knowledge be stressed first, emphasizing the acquisition of factual knowledge later in the learning process, or must both types of knowledge be constructed concurrently? These are questions that research and practice have to answer in order to improve student learning. But learning as interpreting and constructing higher-order knowledge is not only a matter of acquiring functional and structural components of knowledge. Learning as a knowledge construction process also depends on the contexts, elaborations, intentions, self-monitoring, self-regulation and individual concepts of learning. Successful learners not only elaborate and develop more self-explanations that extend the information in instructional contexts (Chi and Basok, 1989), but they also monitor and use many more self-regulation activities during studying information in achieving understanding than less successful students (De Jong, 1992). Research on learning styles (Schmeck, 1988; Vermunt, 1992) also shows that there are large individual differences between the learning activities students use and how this use is regulated. These differences seem to arise from students' views of learning and how they see the division of tasks between, on the one hand, lectures, teachers, books, etc., and, on the other, students. Vermunt (1992) found four learning styles: an undirected, a reproduction-directed, a meaning-directed and an application-directed learning style. He found that external regulation was not related to the use of deep and concrete learning strategies and that the use of constructive processing strategies was especially related to the mental learning models of students and to their use of self-regulation strategies for learning. Different learning styles may constrain the educational effectiveness of computer-enhanced learning environments. Jacobson (1991) distinguished two types of students. The first type views knowledge as being orderly, discrete and homogeneous and regards learning as the accumulation of externally validated facts and as a more passive and receptive process. The second type of student views knowledge as an irregular, interconnected and inter-related construct and regards learning as a process of actively constructing knowledge that is internally validated and meaningful. The first group with the simple epistemological learning preference performed at about the same overall level in both the drill and the thematic criss-crossing design, whereas the second group of students with the complex epistemological learning preference responded negatively to the highly structured and rote-oriented approach to learning embodied in the computer-based drill design. The drill design showed to be primarily effective for those subjects with a simple epistemological learning preference; the thematic criss-crossing design resulted in improvements for subjects with either simple or complex epistemological learning preference. The interaction between epistemological learning preferences or learning styles on the one hand and the different instructional strategies running from drill-oriented and externally regulated to constructivist, process-oriented and self-regulated on the other hand can lead to congruences, destructive or constructive frictions. Woods (1989) and Vermunt (1992) speak of congruences when learning styles of students and instructional strategies correspond to each other. Constructive frictions take place when students have a moderate degree of self-regulation and one is appealing to it or when they have to apply learning activities which do not spontaneously take place but have to be activated and stimulated. Destructive frictions lead to a decline of learning performances, thinking and learning abilities, as we can see in the study of Jacobson (1991). In that case, learning and thinking abilities students master are not addressed and potential abilities are not developed. It could also be the case that the situation capitalises on abilities students have not yet developed or mastered.

Designing or creating a learning environment to improve the knowledge construction learning process of students is not only a matter of implementing constructive elements like putting together situated (Resnick, 1989), relevant, realistic, contextualised, case-based, problem-solving frameworks (Bransford, Sherwood, Hasselbring, Kinzer and Williams, 1990). It is also more than offering students a thematic or cognitive landscape criss-crossing strategy environment, authentic experiences with the concepts, multiple modes of representation, incremental introduction of complexity, stressing inter-related and web-like nature of knowledge (Spiro and Jehng, 1990; Jacobson and Spiro, 1991). If learning style interferes with certain types of instructional approaches, then improving constructive learning might also be a matter of encouraging the self-awareness of the knowledge construction process (reflexivity) (Cunningham, 1992), negotiating of meaning, knowledge and strategies, and the ownership of the learner over the learning process (Bransford et al., 1990; Honebein, Duffy and Fischman, 1991; Duffy and Knuth, 1992; Simons and De Jong, 1992). Thus, despite the availability of several constructive learning environment features, as mentioned above, this does not guarantee that students actually take that opportunity. Simons and De Jong (1992), for instance, showed that after training students were able to have an effective learner control in a simple computer-based vocabulary learning environment.

Research into the possible interaction between the students' learning style and different instructional approaches goes beyond computer-based designs. The above-mentioned constructivist environment features function also in non-computer-based instructional approaches. However, the computer and the possible mult-imedia integration make it a powerful tool to realize these kinds of learning environments. That is the reason why the study makes use of a constructivist computer-based mult-imedia program. The context of the program is teacher education aiming at improving the ability to design a lesson plan and focussing on the amount and time spent on the different facilities in the program as a function of students' learning styles.

This study traces the relations between the different and combined aspects of learning styles with the number of times and actual time spent on different aspects of a constructivist computer-based enhanced learning environment. For that, several facilities are interpreted as representatives of self-regulation activities in the learning process. The research question was whether students with a "meaning directed" learning style (self-regulated) use different program facilities than students with a more undirected learning style. Which student type profits most from working with the program?

Method

Subjects
Thirty-four students of teacher training colleges and university teacher training for schools at primary and secondary level enrolled for participation in the study. They filled in a form as evidence of their promise to participate.

Students of the teacher training colleges could get some study credits for participating. All students were promised that they would receive their learning style diagnosis and a guide on how to interpret the scores and combine them with advice to improve their learning (style) (Vermunt, 1990). Furthermore, the participation was on a voluntary basis and took place in their spare time.

Seven students did not turn up at any session. Nine students let us know they were declining to participate because of study load reasons. Five students studied several parts of the program but gave up during the course of the study without letting us know why. Thus 13 students studied the complete program. From one of those 13 we had missing data because of computer failure.

Material and variables

Inventory Learning Styles (ILS)
The students' learning styles were diagnosed by the Inventory Learning Styles (ILS) (Vermunt, 1990). This diagnostic instrument contains 120 statements about which students indicated on a five-point scale whether they did or did not agree with them or whether they fitted them or not. The 120 statements of the ILS represent four dimensions: elaboration, directing, study motives and learning concept. The diagnosed learning styles differ in the degree that students indicate by their responses to the statements that they prefer a deep level, a detailed or a concrete elaboration of information. The learning styles also differ in the degree students indicate to have more self-regulated, externally regulated or undirected study behaviour. Furthermore, the ILS differentiates between different study motives and learning concepts (epistemological learning preferences). Vermunt's (1992) four learning styles (a meaning-directed, a reproduction-directed, an application-directed and an undirected learning style) are described below.

Students with a self-regulated meaning-directed style elaborate information on a deep level and try to concretise it by relating it to their own experiences and knowledge. They set much value by constructing knowledge and are more than average personally interested.

Students with a reproduction-directed learning style are highly focussed on details, facts and definitions, and do not spend a lot of attention to the relations between the parts they studied separately. Their study behaviour is regulated mainly by external educational authorities (lectures, books, computers) and exam-directed. Their study motive is to score high on tests and knowledge acquisition in the sense of knowledge absorption is an important aspect of their learning concept.

Students who are more application-directed elaborate the information in a very concrete sense. Visualisation, real-life experience and informal knowledge, seeking concrete examples and practical applications of abstract knowledge are very important. They also personalise knowledge by trying to use it in explaining or understanding phenomena they are confronted with in practice. They focus on the practical use of knowledge. They study mainly to get a degree, are not so much personally interested in the study and are test-directed. For them learning is mainly learning to apply knowledge.

A student with a non-regulated and undirected learning style does not regulate his study behaviour and is ambivalent about his study motives and his academic competence. His learning is test-or exam-directed and he sets much value by instruction that stimulates his cognitive activities. Studying together also is of much value to him.

The multi/hypermedia environment 'Rights in the mirror'
This videodisc- and hypertext-based computer program was developed by Educavideo, Amnesty International (Nolthuis, 1989). The program has been made for students at teacher training colleges for schools at primary and secondary level and for school advisory bodies. `Rights in the mirror' shows three students at a teacher trainer college who apply the ideas about human rights education and lesson planning. The overall aim of the program is that students make a lesson plan concerning a human rights theme and improve their ability to prepare a lesson. The core of the program consists of six lessons. Each lesson is a kind of model play on dramatic principles and metaphors with particular reference to the theory and practice of Greek dramatists and the `learning plays' of Brecht (Nolthuis, 1989). The students already know, or find out as they watch the lesson, the aims of the lessons. They are allowed, as it were, to sit in the back of the classroom to watch the didactic and pedagogical behaviour of their `fellow' students on the video screen. The main characters are carefully portrayed in their private lives as well to stimulate identification. All the classroom scenes are documentary. They have been derived from reality and adapted to the aims of the interactive program.

Students can do research on their own by consulting the database. Here they will find information about the lessons, articles on didactic and pedagogical aspects of human rights education and instruction in general, about Amnesty International, the Universal Declaration of Human Rights, and didactic rules. The database has a pictorial index and a topical index on subject matter. Students can just go through the program in a linear way or choose their own route by the central index card or by the schematic map of the program (Fig. 1). Both give access to all other stacks. Their icons are constantly shown on every screen which enables the students to criss-cross through the program from any point.

After each lesson students have to judge on a ten-point scale what they think about the lesson and argue their judgement. After that they can study why the lesson worked out as planned or why it went so smoothly by analysing it on didactic, pedagogical, human rights-educational and `fellow'-student motivational aspects. To each aspect students are invited to explore the particular case from different perspectives by counselling the supervisor (audio), pupils, fellow students, literature and an open discussion platform (bulletin board function). For instance, they can see the teacher and the student during the preparation of the lesson at the student's home and how the subject and lesson gets shaped during dinnner and negotiation with his housemates. In this way they find out more about his motives. During this criss-crossing students are constantly invited to give their opinions and reasons by statements or questions and are stimulated to argue and to activate deep-level processing. Concurrent with each question they can consult video, audio and textual information sources or have a (simulated) telephone call with Amnesty International to activate or support their thinking. Students can type in all their answers, reasons and arguments and choose to print them when they want to stop. Because one lesson in the program had the theme self-concept, a part of the program consisted of a set of diagnostic questions about the students' subjective competence and feedback. Students were allowed, as with other parts, to skip this.

Variables
The ILS-scores were gathered about students' learning styles and arranged according to the different scales: Elaboration: deep processing (seeking relations and structuring, critical), detailed processing (drilling and memorising, analytical), concrete processing; Regulation: self-regulation, external regulation, undirected; Motives: degree-directed, profession-directed, test-directed, personal interest, ambivalence; Learning concept: absorption of knowledge, construction of knowledge, application of knowledge, activating education, studying together.

All the activities students undertook during the program (all cards visited), consulting video or audio fragments and literature, and the time spent on the different program aspects were recorded and saved in a linear protocol. As far as possible, these computer interactions (visited hypertext cards) were clustered in categories on the basis of conceptual arguments. These categories are: Orientation ('fellow students', terminology, overall learning goal, example video scene, introductions), Directing (literature index, subject indexes, schematic map, video index), Testing (answering questions, opinions), Literature, Lesson plans, Program (model lessons), Self-concept, Help (general, functions, typing, computer mouse control), Extra Task.

Besides these frequencies and time on program segments, the frequencies and time spent on interactions not related to special hypertext cards were extracted from the linear protocols. These concern the variables Audio, Video, Printing (only frequency), Explanation, Help, Task, Introduction to the self-concept diagnosis.

All the answers and arguments students formulated during working with the program were recorded as well. Because of privacy reasons, answers to the self-concept questions were not recorded. Because of the time a qualitative analysis takes, no results will be reported in this article concerning the answers and arguments. The same is the case for analyses of the lesson plans students had to make at the end of the program. This is due to the fact that up to now only a few students have handed them in.

Procedure
First, an introductory lecture about the program took place. In this introductory students could see some introduction parts of the program and then were told that the study had the aim of shedding some light on the students' behaviour when working with multi-media programs. The students were told that they would get study credits and study advice on the basis of a diagnosis of their learning style. After this introduction students who wanted to participate filled in a form as evidence of their promise. These students filled in the ILS and received documentation on how to work with the program 'Rights in the mirror' and instructions to subscribe for participating at a planning list during the next seven weeks. Students were free to plan when they wanted to work with the program. Students were given the advice to study one of the four themes (Rules and rights (two lesson fragments), Refugees (one lesson fragment), Self-concept (one lesson fragment) or Water (two lesson fragments), a week. This would cost them ± one and a half hours during four weeks. Students were free when and how to work through the program. After one week they received a reminder to subscribe. After eight weeks all students were sent a letter of thanks. Students who did not hand in the lesson plan were encouraged to so, and students who did hand it in received their ILS and the advisory guide.

Results

To trace the relation between student–computer interaction and students' learning style, correlations were calculated between frequencies of different student–computer interactions and the learning styles. In the first place students' learning styles were determined by interpreting the students' learning-style profiles (Fig. 2) according to the styles Vermunt (1992) identified. For that the ILS-scores of 12 students who completed the program were transformed to standard scores based on the scores of first-year university (psychology) students from the study of Vermunt (1992). Meaning-directed (two students; code 4), application-directed (three students; code 3), reproduction-directed undirected (five students; code 1) and strategy-directed (two students; code 2) learning styles could be identified. The last-mentioned style can be characterised as scoring high on deep, factual and concrete processing, scoring high on self-regulation, showing no differentiation between the motives but scoring low on ambivalence and a learning concept in which construction and use of knowledge are important. These learning styles were determined in consultation with Vermunt. The classification range from code 4 (meaning-directed) to code 1 (reproduction-directed undirected) correlated significantly with the ILS-scale scores Deep and Critical processing of information (r .74 and r .67). The more meaning-directed students were, the less they used the facilities Index video (r –.68) and Route map (r –.68) and the less time they spent on the Route map (r –.79). Both facilities were considered to be indicators of regulation behaviour.

Secondly, the learning profiles were classified again by emphasising the scale Regulation behaviour. Students' learning style profiles were classified into three categories: Self-regulated (6 students; code 3), Externally regulated (3 students; code 2) and Undirected (3 students; code 1). This classification (range 3 to 1) correlated significantly with the ILS-scale scores Relating (r .82), Critical (r .75), Deep (r .89) processing, Self-regulation process directed (r .68) and the scale Undirected (r –.66). There were also significant correlations with the number of times students make use of the program facilities Negotiating (r –.79), Index video (r –.70), Route map (r –.77). Furthermore, it correlated significantly with the time spent on Negotiating (r –.70), Index video (r –.71) and Route map (r –.67).

Another way of analysing the relation between learning styles and the use of the multi-media program was not by assigning students' standard scores to learning styles but by summarizing students' unstandardised scores of the ILS-subscales constituting each of the four styles Vermunt (1992) identified. Correlations were calculated between the program variables and these four styles (Meaning, Repro-duction, Application and an Undirected learning style). The higher the scores on the meaning-directed scale, the less use was made of the Index video (r –.69).

The scores on the Undirected scale were negatively correlated with the scores on the Meaning-directed scale (r –.67). The higher the scores on the Undirected scale, the more the card with points to pay attention to when making a lesson plan was visited (r .76). The self-concept diagnosis facility was more visited as well and more time was spent on the introduction to the diagnosis when scores were higher on the Undirected scale (r .70 and r .81). Also, when the scores were higher, the more the possibility to print information was used (r .66).

Some ANOVAs were carried out with the Directing, Reproduction, Application and Undirected scale as grouping variables. For that, the scale scores were split into two groups by the modus values. Dependent variables were the program variables. There were significant differences between low and high scoring groups only concerning the scales Reproduction and Undirected and the time variables. Concerning the scale reproduction the two groups differed in time spent on answering the questions (F(1,10)=8.4;P<0.02). The mean score for the high scoring group on the reproduction scale amounted to 8,096 seconds (sd 3,273) and for the low scoring group 4,053 seconds (sd 976). There was also a difference concerning the time spent on the overall `Learning goal' (F(1,10)=5.6;P<.05). The mean for the high scoring group amounted to 13 seconds (sd 4.8) and for the low scoring group to 7 seconds (sd 4.2). Concerning the scale Undirected the low and high scoring group differed only on the time spent watching the lessons (F(1,10)=4.9;P<0.05). The mean time spent by the low scoring group amounted to 1,955 seconds (sd 593) and for the high scoring group to 2,604 seconds (sd 704).

The last attempt to trace possible interferences between students' learning styles and the use of the multi-media program was done by calculating the correlations between aspects of the learning styles or the unstandardised ILS-subscales.

Concerning the dimension Information processing there were several negative relations between the deep-level processing subscale Relating and Structuring and the program facilities Negotiating (r −.78), Example video (r −.66) (orientation), Index video (r −.89) and Route map (r −.70) (both regulation). Furthermore, it correlated significantly with the time spent on Negotiating (r −.98) and Index video (r -.83) (regulation). Critical processing correlated negatively with the time spent on Route map (r −.72) (regulation). Surface-level processing subscale Memorising correlated with the number of times the general learning goal of the program was read (r .69) (orientation). The Stepwise analytical subscale correlated negatively with the number of times the introductions to the program part of analysing in pedagogical and didactical perspectives was read (r −.70) (orientation) and negatively with the number of times a lesson was watched (r −.67). The subscale Concrete processing did not correlate with any variable.

Concerning the dimension Regulation behaviour there was a negative correlation between the subscale Regulation of learning process and learning results with time spent on the Index video (r −.67), and on how many times students used the facilities Negotiating (r −.66) and Example lesson (r −.68) (orientation). The subscale Regulation of learning content correlated negatively with the time in which students answered the questions (−.68) (Testing). The Subscale Non-regulated correlated with the number of times students used the facilities Negotiating (r .69) and Points of attention (r .73) (orientation). It also correlated with the time spent on Negotiating (r .74), Example lesson (r .67), Index video (r .66) and Help concerning managing the program (r −.72).

Concerning the dimension Study motives the scale Test-directed correlated with the time spent on answering the questions (r .82), introductions to the lessons (r .78) (orientation) and consulting help about typing the answers (r −.71). The scale Personally interested correlated negatively with the time spent becoming acquainted with the 'fellow students' (r –.68) (orientation). The scale Ambivalence correlated significantly with the number of times students read the introduction to the analytical part of the program (r .73) (orientation) and calling in the Help facility (r .77). The scale scores also correlated with the time spent on the Help facility about typing (r .81) and about how to use the computer mouse (r .71).

Concerning the dimension Learning concept there was a negative correlation between the scores on the scale Knowledge construction and the program variable Index lesson plan (r –.67). There were also significant correlations between the scale Absorption of knowledge and the number of times students looked at the lesson plans of the video lessons (r .73) and the time spent on Index Literature (r .67). The scale Studying together correlated with the facility Diagnosis of your self-concept (r .73) and with the time spent on the introduction of this diagnosis (r .79) and the time spent on the diagnosis (r .72).

Discussion and Conclusions

First of all, it is striking that from all the students who followed the introduction lecture and saw the multi-media environment only one-third was willing to participate in the study in their spare time although study credits, study advice and professionalisation by working with the program were put forward as positive arguments. More striking is that out of the 34 students who said they wanted to participate only 13 really did. Perhaps multi-media (video, audio, text), real cases and open learning are not attractive enough to motivate students to allocate their energy and time to a learning activity besides the regular curriculum. Although people enjoy entertaining themselves by watching television, interaction with such an entertainment in a learning context is probably much more demanding and less motivating. However, from the comments of the students who did participate or let us know they were going to stop we concluded that students really enjoyed working with the program. Therefore, the cause of the drop-out may be the fact that the study was not embedded in the regular curriculum. Of course, students' first priority is to pass their tests and less to deepen their study via participating in this study. Students are probably only motivated to learn if enough study credits compensate their effort. If education wants to stimulate students' volitional, metacognitively guided employment of non-automatic, usually effort-demanding processes, in other words, students' mindfulness (Salomon and Globerson, 1987), hyper/multi-media learning environments have to be embedded in the curriculum, preferably a curriculum that can be characterised as a metacurriculum (Perkins, 1992) in which multi-media programs are used as tools to enhance knowledge construction. Even the most technology-enriched and knowledge-construction-directed environment cannot stimulate mindful learning if it is embedded in a curriculum in which only reproductive learning is reinforced by rewarding the ability to remember facts or the use of canned procedures to solve known problems.

Let us have a look at the correlational data. Instead of what we would expect, namely that deep-level processing, self-regulated, knowledge-construction-directed students would explore this thematic landscape learning environment, it seems that they just follow the linear route which is automatically controlled by the program. Meaning-directed students make less use and spend less time on indexes and route map to direct their own individual route through the program. The relations between the non-standard ILS-scores and the variables also show that meaning-directedness is strongly related to less use of indexes and to following the linear route controlled by the program not more than others reacting to the invitations by the program to explore the environment and the database. The concept that learning is construction of knowledge was also negatively related to the use of an index. Even the important aspect of this learning style, the preference for a self-regulated study behaviour, shows the same picture.

Despite this self-regulating preference and the related deep-level processing, students do not use or do not know how to use 'negotiating' as a knowledge construction tool, a tool which is very common and powerful in the learning practice outside school. They also spend less time on program parts in which the formulation of own opinions and argumentation can be supported by consulting Literature, opinions of `fellow students', children or supervisor, used lesson, plans, lessons, etc.

Strangely enough, more reproductive students spend twice the time on these parts of the program and also on reading the overall learning goal than students who are less reproduction directed. The test-directed aspect of this learning style is strongly related to time spent on these question/opinion parts and also to the introductions of the video lessons in which students were told what the lesson was about. Another important aspect of the reproductive learning style, the concept that learning is knowledge absorption, strongly related to viewing the example lesson plans the `fellow students' used and to using the Index Literature. The significant relations between undirected learning and spending more time on the diagnosis of the self-concept (subjective competence) probably reflects the ambivalent aspect of this learning style. The important aspect of this learning style, 'Studying together', was also strongly related to this diagnosis of the self-competence. Students probably have a strong tendency to have external feedback about their competence. They feel uncertain in the new environment. This might also be reflected in the relation between the scale Ambivalence, also a characteristic of this learning style, and making use of non-content help. Students who are more undirected also spend more time watching the video lessons and the facility of negotiating, probably because studying together is an important aspect of their learning concept.

Remarkable in the results is that the use of the different program parts and facilities and the time spent on them only seems to stand in relation with either the Meaning-directed learning style or the Reproductive or the Undirected learning style. The Application-directed, concrete-processing strategy-using learning style seems not to have any particular bias or constraint in the use of the program.

Summarizing conclusion

Although only few students completed the program and the learners had great freedom of choice, the results indicate that Meaning-directed students employ a strategy of a `low road of learning' (Salomon and Globerson, 1987) in such circumstances, a mentally undemanding way of learning as far as possible. They are not used to employ a mindful learning. They have to be stimulated to learn the volitional, metacognitively guided construction of knowledge by consulting and reflecting on different knowledge sources. In the study of Jacobson (1991) the criss-crossing and reflecting, too, was more demanded by the program than that it was a case of students' invention.

Students with Reproductive and Undirected learning styles seem to explore the environment by using the index facilities more, but other results expose this finding more as a reflection of their test-directed study behaviour or ambivalence about their subjective competence. That no relations are found with the Application-directed learning style might be due to the fact that the dramatized character of 'Rights in the mirror' is so concrete and easy to identify with for these students. This case-based, narrative and real-life problem-centred environment might suit their pragmatic attitude best.

The main finding is that a constructivist, technology-enriched learning environment does not automatically lead to more knowledge construction learning behaviour because of the less developed self-regulated behaviour and learning concept of students or because students are not used to being in control themselves.

Epilogue

Students do not fully exploit the facilities of an open constructivist learning environment. They would rather be nice guys in following the programmed route. Is this due to the fact that acquaintance of domain-specific knowledge prior to the use of certain domain-independent knowledge construction skills inhibits this use? Why not let students find out a lot of the domain-specific knowledge by using more domain-independent skills? For instance, landscape criss-crossing, situated conceptualisation, forming concepts in practice rather than in abstract learning environments seem to stimulate transfer of knowledge (Jacobson, 1991). The question remains if modelling and demonstrating as used by Jacobson and Spiro leads to volitional mindfulness in new situations or if other didactic principles are necessary, principles which exploit the possibilities electronic media offer much more and which are more directed towards construction and experiencing of cognitive skills rather than showing and telling about them. Not only knowledge but also students' development of cognitive skills might be indexed by experience. Maybe learning and teaching have to be liberated much more from sequentialism and reproductivism in order to engender cognitive flexibility and transfer.

References

Anderson, C. W. and Roth, K. J. (1989). Teaching for meaningful and self-regulated learning of science. *Advances in Research on Teaching*, 1, 265–309.

Bransford, J. D., Franks, J. J., Vye, N. J. and Sherwood, R. D. (1989). New approaches to instruction: because wisdom can't be told. In S. Vosniadou and A. Ortony (eds.), *Similarity and Analogical Reasoning*. Cambridge: Cambridge University Press.

Bransford, J. D., Sherwood, R. D., Hassselbring, T. S., Kinzer, C. K. and Williams, S. M. (1990). Anchored instruction: why we need it and how technology can help. In D. Nix and R. Spiro (eds.), Cognition, Education, Multimedia: *Exploring Ideas in High Technology*. Hillsdale, N J: Lawrence Erlbaum Associates.

Brown, A. L. and Palincsar, A. S. (1989). Guided, cooperative learning and individual knowledge acquisition. In Lauren B. Resnick (ed.), *Knowing, Learning, and Instruction. Essays in Honor of Robert Glaser*. Hillsdale, N J: Lawrence Erlbaum Associates.

Chi, M. T. H. and Basok (1989). Learning from examples via self-explanations. In Lauren B. Resnick (ed.), *Knowing, Learning, and Instruction. Essays in Honor of Robert Glaser*. Hillsdale, N J: Lawrence Erlbaum Associates.

Chi, M. T. H., Glaser, R. and Farr, M.J. (eds), (1988). *The Nature of Expertise*. Hillsdale, N J: Lawrence Erlbaum Associates.

Cunningham, D. J (1992). Beyond educational psychology: steps toward an educational semiotic. *Educational Psychology Review*, 4, 2, 165–194.

Cunningham, D. J (1992). Everything said is said by someone. *Educational Psychology Review*, 4, 2, 261–269.

Duffy, T. M. and Knuth, A. (1991). Hyper media and instruction: where is the match? In D. Jonassen & H. Mandl (eds), *Designing Hypermedia for Learning*. Heidelberg : Springer.

Honebein, P. C., Duffy, T. M. and Fishman, B. J. (1992). Constructivism and the design of learning environments: context and authentic activities for learning. In T. M. Duffy, J. Lowyck and D. Jonassen (eds), *Designing Environments for*

Constructive Learning. Hillsdale, N J: Lawrence Erlbaum Associates.

Jacobson, M. J. (1991). Knowledge acquisition, cognitive flexibility, and the instructional applications of hypertext: a comparison of contrasting designs for computer-enhanced learning environments. [Unpublished dissertation]. Urbana: University of Illinois at Urbana-Champaign.

Jacobson, M. J. and Spiro, R. J. (1991). Hypertext learning environments and cognitive flexibility: characteristics promoting the transfer of complex knowledge. In L. Birnbaum (ed.), *The International Conference on the Learning Sciences.* Proceedings of the 1991 conference. Evanston, IL: Northwestern University.

De Jong, F. P. C. M. (1992). *Zelfstandig leren. Regulatie van het leerproces en leren reguleren: een process benadering. [Independent learning. Regulation of the learning process and learning to regulate: a process approach].* Tilburg: De Jong.

Nolthuis, J. (1989). `Rights in the mirror': an interactive video drama programme about human rights education. In A.D.N. Edwards and S. Holland (eds), *Multmedia interface design in Education* [NATO ASI series]. Berlin: Springer.

Perkins, D. (1992). *Invited paper session,* San Francisco: AERA 1993.

Resnick, L. B. (1989). Introduction. In Lauren B. Resnick (ed.), *Knowing, Learning, and Instruction. Essays in Honor of Robert Glaser.* Hillsdale, N J: Lawrence Erlbaum Associates.

Salomon, G. and Globerson, T. (1987). Skill may not be enough: the role of mindfulness in learning and transfer. In E. de Corte (ed.), *Acquisition and transfer of Knowledge and Cognitive Skills International* Journal of Educational Research, 11, 6, 623–637.

Schmeck, R. R. (ed.), (1988). *Learning Strategies and Learning Styles.* New York: Plenum Press.

Simons, P. R. J. and De Jong, F. P. C. M. (1992). Metacognitive skills and computer-aided instruction [Special issue: An International Review]. *Applied Psychology.*

Spiro, R. J., Coulson, R. L., Feltovich, P. J. and Anderson, D. K. (1988). Cognitive flexibility theory: Advanced knowledge acquisition in ill-structured domains. In V. Patel (ed.), *Tenth Annual Conference of the Cognitive Science Society.* Hillsdale, N J: Lawrence Erlbaum Associates.

Spiro, R. J. and Jehng, J. (1990). Cognitive flexibility and hypertext: theory and technology for the nonlinear and multidimensional traversal of complex subject matter. In D. Nix and R. Spiro (eds), *Cognition, Education, Multimedia: Exploring Ideas in High Technology*. Hillsdale, N J: Lawrence Erlbaum Associates.

Vermunt, J. D. H. M. (1990). *Skilful Studying of Social Sciences. Part 2: Guide for Students*. [Revised version of F. van Rijswijk and J. Vermunt (1987), Skilful studying]. Tilburg: Tilburg University.

Vermunt, J. D. H.M. (1992). *Leerstijlen en sturen van leerprocessen in het hoger onderwijs: naar procesgerichte instructie in zelfstandig denken [Learning styles and regulation of learning in higher education: towards process-oriented instruction in autonomous thinking]*. Amsterdam: Swets & Zeitlinger.

Woods, P. (1989). Opportunities to learn and to teach: an interdisciplinary model. *International Journal of Educational Research,* 13, 597–606.

Fig. 1: Screendump of 'Rights in the mirror' showing the pedagogical question "What do you think of the children's reactions?", the memo field to type an answer, the information sources: Literature (text), Wim's rules of thumb (Mentor; text), opinions (pupil, fellow student Els and mentor Wim; audio); on Cor's lesson (fellow student; video) and the menu bar (Route, archive, lessons, index, stop, help, backward and forward.

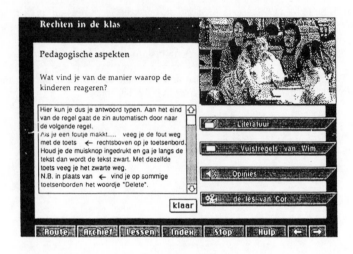

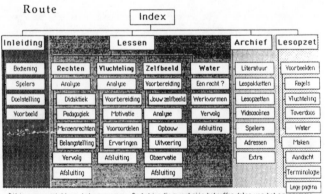

Dit is een overzicht van het programma. De hokjes die zwart zijn betreffen delen van het programma die je gedaan hebt. Wat wit is zou je dus nog kunnen doen. Het hokje dat knippert is het scherm waar je vandaan komt. Door ergens op te drukken ga je naar het betreffende scherm toe

Fig. 2: Meaning directed and undirected student.

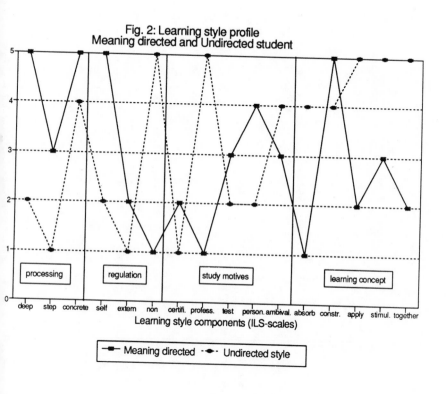

Fig. 2: Learning style profile
Meaning directed and Undirected student

Chapter 12 Experiential learning styles and student learning

Effects of Learning Styles and Context on Work-Based Learning

Cleminson, K. Putman and S. Bradford, Brunel University

Introduction

During the last decade two major trends have emerged in the education and training of professionals across a spectrum of occupational backgrounds. First, the move towards competency-based approaches of assessment and, secondly, a move towards a greater proportion of professional education to be based in the place of work, principles of which are articulated in Circular 9/92 (DFE, 1992) and the Council for Education and Training in Youth and Community Work (CETYCW, 1989). Central government has been influential in bringing about these changes either as a catalyst to change or, in the case of initial teacher education, as prime mover. In arguing that acquisition of practical skills rather than theoretical knowledge should be the principal aim of professional preparation, the "theory" of many courses has been marginalised or, indeed, eliminated. Thus there is a necessity for more time to be spent in the work-base learning skills and, hence, a need for those skills to be assessed in the workplace by a set of quantifiable measures.

At this point we should take note of Hirst's (1990) comment that all human action is, in some sense, necessarily theory laden. Thus the "theory–practice gap" that some perceive needs to be reconsidered by reconceptualising and making explicit the theory that underpins practice.

One of the major implications of these changes is the increasing involvement of practitioners themselves in the training of new recruits. The role of these practitioners is usually known as the "mentor", and is described by Wilkin (1992) as a crucial role in the development of the work-based learner. The purpose of this paper is to consider the role of the mentor in the work base. However, it is clear that the role is multi-faceted and that, as Everton and White (1992) conclude, any attempt to produce a definition or definitive description of the role is misleading and confuses what a mentor is with what a mentor should be. Thus Wilkin suggests that there will never be a model to which we can all subscribe. Clearly the role has become the focus of detailed analysis at this time (e.g., Vonk

1993) and this is reflected by the fact that in the decade between 1978 and 1988 the number of publications in the ERIC database which included "mentor" as a key word rose from 10 to 95 (Jacobi, 1991).

The analysis in this paper is based upon empirical data drawn from students and mentors involved in two courses in the Department of Education at Brunel University: the Postgraduate Certificate in Youth and Community Work, a two-year programme leading to initial professional qualification, and the Postgraduate Certificate in Education in Physics by Distance Learning, a two-year part-time course of initial teacher training.

The mentors on both courses were senior professionals with wide experience of their chosen profession and based in the mentee's workplace.

Structure of the Research

Employing a detailed research specification, which focussed on the perceptions of mentors and mentees in relation to the role of the mentor, the team drew up interview schedules designed to elicit information relating to the role as it is perceived and carried out in the work-base learning situation.

Two sets of schedules were prepared, one for mentees and one for mentors, although adjustments were made to accommodate differing occupational terminology. Each question was then identified in terms of the issues that were likely to be raised in response to interview questions and these were related to the major issues identified in the research specification. This provided a matrix framework for analysing the data for the interviews (Putman, Bradford and Cleminson, 1992) and the basis upon which the more detailed analysis in this paper was drawn.

Five mentor/mentee pairings were interviewed in each occupational group, providing a total of 20 interviews. All the interview material was tape recorded and interviews took place whenever possible in the workplace. With limited numbers to draw upon, the focus of this phase of the research was to seek qualitative data from deep-level interviews and analysis.

The preliminary findings drew attention to several key issues and these were then subject to further detailed analysis. This forms the basis of the work contained in this paper.

Mentoring

Calderhead and Lambert (1992) point out that in the school context it is simply not tenable to expect the learner to develop professional skills and knowledge through "unstructured experience and the occasional opportunity to talk over their practice with someone . . . ". As a consequence, the role of the mentor has developed to meet these needs, yet the role itself continues to be the subject of considerable debate and discussion. Andrews (1986) identifies five basic models for induction programmes, characterised by a "novice–mentor" relationship, which are helpful in the process of clarification. These are as follows:

1. The laissez-faire model – a largely self-propelled traditional model, based on a "sink or swim" approach.

2. A collegial model – where the mentee receives voluntary and informal supervision.

3. The formalised mentor/protégé model – with a structured contract between mentor and protégé.

4. The mandatory competency model – in which the probationary status of the learner is emphasised and participation is directed towards a performance-based competency outcome.

5. A self-directing professional model – which employs a self-directing contract and may include elements from 2 to 4 above.

Glickman (1990) has described four models of mentor behaviour. First, directive-control behaviour where the mentor is perceived to be the expert and prescribes how the student is to act. Second, directive-informational behaviour where the mentor acts as a resource person. Third, collaborative mentoring where the mentor and mentee are equal partners in the mentoring process. Finally, non-directive behaviour where the student knows best what changes need to be made and has the ability to think and act autonomously.

Vonk (1993) has argued that mentors adapt their mentoring approach to the needs of their students, and this was confirmed by our analysis. As one teacher mentor commented:

It would be impossible to enforce your pre-determined model of a mentor on the situation. You have to adapt to the mentee and his/her needs.

In practice the role emerges as a consequence of interaction between a series of determining factors. These may be summarised as follows:

i. Pre-conditional factors involving the recognition of the mentee, the appointment or identification of the mentor and the provision of training, support and guidance for the mentor.

ii. Central factors concerned with the formal institutional requirements of the role and the aims of student learning outcomes, the mentee and the nature of the learning environment or context.

The most significant of these factors were the mentee (in particular his/her learning style) and the context in which the mentoring role takes place. What is clear from our work is that, both in the case of the trainee teachers and the youth and community workers, the mentees are able to identify their needs and the mentors, in turn, are able to adopt mentoring styles to meet these needs. In practice the top-down model of mentor-led transfer of skills/knowledge as illustrated by Glickman's directive-control model does not work.

We needed therefore to investigate in further detail how and why these factors were so significant in determining the role of the mentor.

We have been concerned to analyse how learning took place in the work-based situation, relating that to the identified factors of learning style and context, with reference to relevant theory.

Socialisation into the Professional Culture

Using the strand matrix outlined above, a pattern was identified that suggested that the learning process was being influenced by social factors beyond the immediate mentee/mentor relationship.

J., a trainee teacher, referred to difficulties she had experienced with discipline in the classroom:

> I discussed this with other teachers in the department. It was pointed out to me that I was not fulfilling the "role" of the teacher as pupils might expect. B. told me to make the pupils wait outside the classroom in an orderly line before lessons, not to request pupils to do things, but to tell them what to do next . . . if they wanted help after the lesson to make them wait, or to make them come back later.

A., another mentee teacher, told us that after discussing training issues informally with colleagues in the staff room she had been strongly advised to:

> Forget all the theory; "discipline and control are what matters" . . . then they [the pupils] might learn something.

What began to emerge was a pattern that reflected the pressure of cultural values within the workplace that supplemented the values from the formal process, as personified by the mentor and the organising institution. This process was more subtle, although no less noticeable in the youth and community context. D., a 30-

year old youth and community worker from an inner London borough, reported:

> I found it very useful to discuss problems with other colleagues . . . I learned a lot from that sort of thing, in fact it influenced me more than other factors in the training process.

Both groups of mentees found these influences to be instructive and it was significant that there was little data to suggest that they found this aspect of the training process to be unhelpful. In fact closer consideration of the data reflected the value to mentees of this element in the process, as one youth and community worker concluded:

> The input from other professionals was important in "rounding off" my training and education.

This confirms what Zeichner and Gore (1990) suggest, that people entering a profession are greatly influenced by the established patterns and implicit beliefs that pervade the work-base. Calderhead and Lambert (1992) identify a range of different activities involved in this process, including "getting to know people . . . understanding protocol. . ." and becoming familiar with routines and facts about the school or context in which the work-based learning process is taking place.

What became clear was that the novice professional was required to negotiate and manoeuvre in a complex social system (Lacey, 1977), often composed of differing or competing professional cultures. Thus R., a 25-year-old youth and community worker from the south-west, told us:

> I became a bit confused at first, as I came into contact with a number of different professionals who seemed to be making different demands on my time and development as a trainee. However, I learned from those experiences to broaden my perspective and that being a youth and community worker involved more than learning just about my immediate professional studies.

Thus, the influence of socialisation into the professional culture was perhaps a little more significant than Calderhead and Lambert (1992) suggest, when they stated that regular contact with their peers assisted mentees in "getting to know their way round the system".

Mentees were being influenced by the professional culture/s they experienced and were responding to this in a positive and reflective way. However, the data from the initial investigation suggested that mentees in youth and community work were more positive and reflective about these influences than those in school. It appeared then that the context in which socialisation into the professional culture takes place has an important influence on the learning process for the mentee and ultimately on the role of the mentor.

Data from the initial analysis suggested that mentees in the youth and community context were more proactive and reflective than mentees in school. Mentees in school were clearly restricted in terms of meeting structures and feedback mechanisms due to their timetable commitments and demands. Most significantly mentees in school felt that they could not be seen to be failing by other professionals or by the children. As one teacher put it:

> . . . once you are seen being weak by the kids, the word gets around and you have all sorts of problems. You cannot afford to try too many things out.

In contrast, one youth and community mentee commented:

> I could always try things out and if it wasn't right no one minded. I thought about it, discussed it with my mentor and tried something different next time I had a chance.

The pressure to operate successfully, however, went beyond expediency. It was clear that different cultural values between professional groups were in operation and that the notion of a "reflective practitioner" (Schön, 1983) was in fact less well harnessed in the school context than in the youth and community context. Thus while Lacey's (1977) observation that college- and university-based courses tended to concentrate too much on what ought to be, they failed to meet the needs of the practitioner in terms of what actually was needed in practice. The reality is that the context may in fact reverse, or at least distort, this intention.

The danger is that the mentor or other professional cultural factors that come into play in the work-based learning context may produce a narrower or more biased view on experience and that the mentee will not be ideally prepared to meet the broader educational needs beyond the institutional context in which they are training.

Professional Knowledge and Skills

Context was again significant in another area of learning, although this was more relevant to mentees in the school.

Studies comparing experienced and novice practitioners have shown how the experienced practitioner usually has a much more sophisticated understanding of practice. Mentees have cognitive schema that are less elaborate, less accessible and less interconnected when brought to bear on professional practice (e.g., Livingstone and Borko, 1989). Thus, one mentee teacher commented that:

> I was going beyond any sort of learning I had experienced in school and

college, or even in the industrial situation I had worked in before coming into teaching. As a science technician working in a laboratory I applied knowledge to particular problems and I dealt with social relations on a separate level elsewhere. Here in school, knowledge was not enough in itself, you had to reapply and synthesise what you knew and deal with a whole range of social relations at the same time.

In the case of teachers, they are usually mentees with an elaborate academic background who may not expect to meet problems with subject matter. However, recent studies have shown that, for the purposes of teaching, novices have to relearn their subject matter (Vonk, 1993). As Borko, Livingstone, MacCaleb and Mauro (1988) note, all teachers need to reshape and revise their knowledge of subject content. In addition they have to develop what Shulman (1986) has called "pedagogical content knowledge" in order to translate academic knowledge into school knowledge. Thus a novice needs to develop both breadth and depth of knowledge: a comprehensive knowledge base with many interconnections representing a much deeper and thorough understanding than can be gained from academic learning. Yet it was clear from analysis of the data that differences existed in demands on the mentees to respond to this.

Initially the data suggested that professional knowledge and skill development was most significant for mentees teaching in schools with strong academic traditions and background. However, the kind of long-term deep learning referred to by Johnson (1983) and originally by Gibbs (1981) was to be found in those students working in a context where preparation demands were optimal and feedback from the mentor was immediate.

P., a part-time teacher from the home counties who worked in two different schools during the course of the two-year PGCE programme, summed up the differences as follows:

> In my first school there was little pressure to prepare lessons in detail, to reconsider subject knowledge or to evaluate in depth. In my second school, which was very tough, the head of department (my mentor) demanded thorough preparation. It was essential to retain the subject knowledge and to reapply that understanding. The difference was the situation in which I was operating . . . "

It was clear that, while the development of professional knowledge and skills is essential to the learner in the work-based learning situation, what affects the outcome is the context in which he/she learns.

The research team had anticipated that the personality and teaching style of the mentor would be a determining factor in the learning process, but we found that the mentee was in fact the key factor in shaping the relationship and the process of learning that took place (Putman, Bradford and Cleminson, 1992).

The Personal Dimension

There were two ways in which this personal dimension shaped the process: firstly in terms of personality or general disposition of the mentee and secondly in terms of the preferred learning styles of the mentee.

Part of the process of professional development involves the learner in becoming increasingly aware of their own personality and how others respond to that person. This awareness leads necessarily to a greater sense of control in dealing with others in the work-base. One youth and community worker commented:

> At first I had difficulty in dealing with two different superiors who were giving me conflicting instructions. Once I had learned that by arguing my case, using my verbal and analytical skills, I could avoid being pushed around, I just manoeuvred difficult situations to my advantage.

This view has implications for the types of mentor training activities that are developed. Mentoring itself must be a learning activity in order that mentors are able to develop the type of critical self-study that will enable them to respond to mentees in a way that is more than just a "sitting by Nelly" approach to training. In other words systematic and critical self-study on the part of mentor and mentee must form the basis for productive professional development (Nias, 1992).

The crucial factor here was the mentee, and in particular their own preferred learning style, and the context in which present learning takes place.

However, while it is clear that learning style is influential in shaping the process of learning, it was not possible to fit mentee learning styles to particular models. In applying out data to the extensive literature on the subject we found the model of learning style outlined by Honey and Mumford (1986) to be most helpful. They identified four distinct learning styles known as activities, reflections, theorists and pragmatists. Analysis of the data suggested that teaching mentees fell largely into the "pragmatist" category, while those from youth and community were more readily identifiable in terms of a reflective approach.

For example, thus, L., a youth and community mentee from a south-east county, described how:

> I considered what I needed to do, then evaluated and discussed practice with my mentor. Whenever possible I tried to analyse failures and successes and to use that information to develop as a professional.

In contrast, T., a school-based mentee, commented:

> The important thing was to perform well in the classroom and to use what I learned in the real situation. I wasn't too worried about theory or idealism, it was how it worked that mattered.

There were clear differences in the types of relationship that existed, according to personality and preferred learning style. However, what is important to note is that there are significant differences in the quality of the mentee–mentor relationship. This may relate to the knowledge of the mentor in terms of his/her understanding of how people learn (Vonk, 1993). However, the most significant factors in determining learning styles seemed to relate to context and to the professional culture in which learning took place.

Thus we were drawn to the conclusion that, while learning styles were important factors in shaping the role of the mentor, the context in which the learning occurs will be even more crucial.

Summary

We have set out to describe and analyse the role of the mentor in two occupational settings. In so doing we hope that we have arrived at a number of general principles that can be brought to bear on the mentor–mentee relationship. These can be summarised in the following way:

a) The mentee is central in determining the role of the mentor in the work-base. Top-down models of knowledge transfer are inappropriate, particularly when the mentees are autonomous learners who are able to identify their own training needs. The more self-confident and knowledgeable a novice is, the less effective directive mentor behaviour will be.

b) The mentor is most effective when he or she can respond and adapt to the needs of the mentee. For our samples this involved adopting a range of mentoring strategies that were non-directive, collaborative or directive-informational.

c) There are a range of different types of learning involved in professional education, including socialisation into the professional culture, development of knowledge and skills, and developing as a person coming to terms with the value system of the occupational culture.

d) While the working pattern of the work-base will obviously affect the frequency and timing of both formal and informal mentor interaction, at a deeper level the norms and values of different occupations will influence the dynamics and quality of the work-base learning of the mentee. The context of the work-base is central in shaping aspects of the mentor's role.

In addition it is suggested that:

e) Much of the mentor's knowledge about the professional will be tacit. Mentoring will be most effective if the mentor is able to make this knowledge explicit to the mentee so that it can be debated and considered. If this does not occur there will be conservation and narrowness of professional practice.

f) Mentoring will be most effective if the mentor becomes aware of the preferred learning style of the mentee. Thus effective mentoring is based not only on being aware of the job of meeting the needs of the mentee, but also being aware of the different ways in which the mentee is able to learn to develop as a professional.

Liston and Zeichner (1991), from a social reconstructionist standpoint, argue that influences on context interact on the levels of the individual, of the institution and of society. We believe that many of the descriptive models of mentoring presented are inherently conservative insofar as they relegate professional development of both mentor and mentee to an apprenticeship model of knowledge transfer so that only basic competencies are seen as important (and assessable). Thus while we have concentrated on the individual and institutional factors affecting work-base learning, the wider societal and political level of context in which mentoring is occurring should not be overlooked.

References

Andrews, I. H. (1986). *An Investigation of the Academic Paradigms Underlying Induction Programmes in Five Countries.* Paper presented at the Annual Meeting of the AERA, San Francisco.

Bentor, P. (ed.) (1990). *The Oxford Internship Scheme: Integration and Partnership in Initial Teacher Training.* Calaiste Gulbenkian Foundation.

Borko, H., Livingston, C., MacCaleb , J and Mauro, L. (1988). In J.Calderhead, *Teachers' Professional Knowledge.* London: Falmer Press.

Calderhead, J. (ed.) (1988). *Teachers' Professional Knowledge.* London: Falmer Press.

Calderhead, J. (1992). *Can the Complexities of Teaching be Accounted for in Terms of Competencies? Contrasting Reviews of Professional Practice from Stirling Research & Policy.* Paper presented at BERA Conference.

Calderhead, J. and Lambert, K. (1992). *The Induction of Newly Appointed Teachers: Recommendation for Good Practice.* NFER and TCI for England and Wales.

Council for Education and Training in Youth and Community Work (1989).

Guidelines to Endorsement. CETYW.

Department for Education Circular 9/92: *Initial Teacher Training (Secondary Phase)*. HMSO.

Everton, T. and White, S. (1992). Partnership in training: the University of Leicester's new model of school-based teacher education. *Cambridge Journal of Education*, 22, 2.

Gibbs, G. (1988). *Teaching Students to Learn: a Student Centred Approach*. Milton Keynes: Open University Press.

Glickman, C. D. (1990). *Supervision of Instruction: a Developmental Approach*. Hemel Hempstead: Allyn & Bacon.

Hirst, P. (1990). The theory–practice relationship in teacher training. In *Partnership in Initial Teacher Training*. London: Cassell.

Honey, P. and Mumford, A. (1986). *Using your Learning Styles* ,(2nd edn). P. Honey.

Honey, P. and Mumford, A. (1992). in E. Parsloe (ed.), *Coaching, Mentoring and Assessing: a Practical Guide to Developing Competence*. London: Kogan Page.

Jacobi, M. (1991). Mentoring and undergraduate academic success. In *Review of Educational Research*, 61, 4, 505-532.

Johnson, L. (1993). *Improving Student Learning* in Brief Introductions in Higher Education, The Enterprise Initiative Unit, Brunel University.

Lacey, C. (1977). *The Socialisation of Teachers: Contemporary Sociology of the School*. London: Methuen

Liston, D. P. and Zeichner, K. M. (1991). *Teacher Education and the Social Condition of Schooling*. London: Routledge.

Livingstone, C. and Borko, N. (1989). Expert–novice differences in teaching: a cognition analysis and implications for teacher education. *Journal of Teacher Education*, 40, 94, 36-42.

Nias, J. (1992). In C. Biott and J. Nias (eds), *Working and Learning Together for Change*. Oxford: Oxford University Press.

Parslow, E. (1992). *Coaching, Mentoring and Assessing: a practical guide to*

Developing Competence. London: Kogan Page.

Putman, K., Bradford, S. and Cleminson, A. (1993). In *Mentoring Partnership in Education,* 1, 1.

Schön, D. (1983) *The Reflective Practioner: How Professionals Think in Action.* London: Temple Smith.

Shulman, L. S. (1986). Those who understand: knowledge growth in teaching. *Education Research,* 15, 2, 4-14.

Vonk (1993). Mentoring the beginning teacher. *Mentoring,* 1, 1, 31-41.

Wilkin, M. (ed.) (1992). *Mentoring in Schools .* London: Kogan Page.

Zeichner, K. M. and Gore, J. M. (1990). In W. R. Houston (ed.), *Handbook of Research on Teacher Education.* New York: Macmillan.
Zeichner, K. M. and Teitelbaum, K. (1982). Personalised and inquiry-oriented teacher education. *Journal of Education for Teaching,* 8, 2, 95-117.

Course Design and Student Learning

Rev. Dr M. R. Seden, De Montfort University

---

1 Introduction to the Context of the Course

The construction industry is undergoing continuous evolution. Changing construction techniques and site management systems have modified the industry's professional roles, contracts and procedures. Its systems are facing new challenges and, in the next ten years, will be more critically compared with systems operating elsewhere, especially in the EC. The new perspectives offered by environmental considerations and information technology will substantially influence the range of roles within the industry. Construction values, information, communication and coordination in the life cycle of buildings, firms, sites and the built environment will be affected.

Professional roles are not as clearly differentiated as in former times and specialist work by designers and contractors has become a much more significant component of the average construction project. There have been many changes in management systems, logistic planning, construction coordination, etc. Thus, the industry is seeking graduates who, technically, are competent and selectively skilful but also have skills of problem solving in economic, financial and human resource areas. The BSc (Hons) Construction Technology and Management delivered by the Department of Building Studies, De Montfort University, has been designed to seek to meet this demand.

2 Aims of the Course

The principal aim of the course is to present an honours degree programme of studies which attracts suitably qualified and/or experienced students from a wide range of backgrounds and enables them to become broadly educated individuals, well prepared for careers in the construction industry.

In order to achieve the principal aim, the course seeks:

- to enable students to foster specialist interests and cooperative skills, so that they may aspire to a variety of roles within the construction industry, working for specialist clients, main contractors or sub-contractors (see figure 1);

- to give students the opportunity to develop a sound knowledge and understanding of the principles, processes and practices appropriate to a graduate working in the management of the construction process (see figure 2);

- to provide a stimulating environment within which the students are able to develop independent and challenging attitudes to conventional ideas and viewpoints (see figure 3);

- to present the students with a sound basis for understanding the structure of the construction industry and its associated professional inputs within the European and international contexts.

3 Criteria and Principles of Course Design: The Context of Learning

The course has been designed to make it as accessible as possible. It will normally be followed in one of two modes – sandwich and part-time. Therefore, each year group will contain a mix of students and experience and this will be drawn upon in seminar, tutorial and, especially, studio work to help develop a stimulating learning environment.

The studio in each study year is the focus of the course and consolidates and brings together the different subjects to help fulfil the principal course aim. It is the workshop of the course, and contains a series of carefully organised tasks which solve construction industry-related problems arranged around the studio theme of the year. Figure 3 shows the evolving integration of the programme of studio work. Elements of the studio work include collaborative projects with students of architecture and building surveying. Where possible, studio work is supported by visits.

The studio work is begun as speedily and as effectively as possible, early in years 1 and 3 by means of a block of "toolkit" activity. A spread of measurement, analytical and information skills are added to the previous mixed experience of the students to enhance their ability to solve problems and make decisions. This subject then runs through the year alongside the other subjects. It finishes in a final block of study to prepare the students for the next stage of the course.

In each year the main body of construction principles and knowledge is presented in the technical and managerial subjects, using lectures, seminars, tutorials, laboratories, computer-aided learning workshops and demonstration techniques. The subject of industrial context is studied in years 1 and 3 to provide a sound understanding of the processes, practices and professions within the construction industry, both in the UK and world-wide.

The industrial placement year is normally in 2 two of the course. This is so that re-entry into academic work is into the reasonably familiar learning experience of year 3. Thus the student can be better prepared for the more flexible form of year 4.

A particular course aim is to better equip the graduate to enter a range of specialist industry roles. In the final year of the course, the student specialises through the studio work by following two out of five studio elective routes. The possible combinations have already been shown in Figure 1, along with the industry roles closest to each pairing of studio elective routes. Subject support continues in four subjects, each containing an extension of the knowledge base developed in the technical and managerial subjects of the earlier years. Most of this subject support is concentrated in the first term.

The research project provides a sharply focussed study with depth and rigour and will terminate in a research report. This contrasts with the breadth of study in the rest of the final year.

4 Course Structure

4.1 Introduction

Figure 2 summarises the course structure.

The programme of studio activity in each study year integrates the technical and managerial subjects which support it. The studio is the most important learning context in each year of the student's studies. The "H" form of the "toolkit" subject indicates the dominance and intensity of the subject at the beginning and end of each of the first and third years.

4.2 Years 1 and 3

Subject support
Most of the subjects are established study areas in those aspects of technology and management applicable to construction. The study area of industrial context provides a basis for understanding the structure and practices of the construction industry. Subjects are presented in such a way that applications are encountered early in the year.

Toolkit
The first week or so, dedicated to the toolkit, gives the student basic skills in information technology, quantitative studies, report writing, information retrieval, etc., to establish a culture of productive problem solving. Information, IT and statistical studies continue throughout the year. The final week of the teaching year covers a field course on Surveying (year 1) or a final-year briefing (year 3).

Studio
The integrating studio leads and gathers together the year's work in a series of well defined selective activities, designed to achieve a sense of purpose

regarding the course. The year theme is developed in the studio around a specific site with a number of buildings largely predefined by academic staff. Aspects of the technology and management of the buildings' construction and performance are investigated.

4.3 Year 4

Introduction
The structure of the fourth year is different from years 1 and 3. The studio is dominant. The formally presented element of the course rapidly decreases term by term, while the studio work expands. Within the studio programme, students will specialise by selecting particular vocational areas to which their studio work is applied. A research project is pursued concurrently with the studios and taught courses.

Subject support
The main themes of the course are brought together in the four taught subject areas of construction systems, design and cost systems, engineering systems and management. During the first term, these key areas are consolidated and then developed further to support the needs of the studio electives. This development continues to a limited extent in term 2.

Studio
All students choose two of the five electives; each of these electives incorporates the themes of coordination, information technology and environmental concerns.

The form of the studio programme for the year is designed to encourage all students to take increasing responsibility for their own workloads. The studio assignments in each elective are subject to a decreasing amount of staff control as the year progresses. The brief for each of these assignments is clearly presented, while the outputs become less prescriptive. In this way, the course gives the students the opportunity to achieve their individual goals and prepare themselves for a variety of potential career paths, while ensuring that the course objectives are met. The policy is to provide the maximum flexibility for student development within a firm, but restrictive, course framework.

The content of the studio programme is practical and related to the problems and tasks that are symptomatic of the working environment represented by the chosen elective. Assistance is sought from industrial and professional partners in setting the briefs and in providing opportunities to visit and utilise live projects to complement the studio work.

Research project
This focussed and rigorous piece of work is an important counter-balance to the otherwise deliberately holistic approach to construction in the rest of the course in year 4.

4.4 The studio programme

The studio is the main workshop of the course, and is the focus for information gathering and team work. Real-life situations are assimilated through a progressive series of problem-solving exercises involving technical and managerial exploration and discussion. The challenge of identifying and debating data within groups aids the development of reasoned judgement and interpersonal skills.

The studios are structured, but not regimented, by staff. All the students contribute to the group work, while developing their own knowledge and skill base. A typical exercise brief contains clearly identified personal criteria to be met within a more flexible group challenge.

The studios in years 1 and 3 are construction technology led, with a strong supporting input from industrial context. The management input concentrates on identifying, planning and communication skills. As the students' technical knowledge base expands, so more specialist inputs are gradually absorbed into the main thrust of construction technology. Similarly, management skills are progressively absorbed into the main project.

By the end of year 3, the students have acquired a broad construction technology base. They capitalise on this through a rigorous study of specialised technical and management areas in year 4. In the year 4 studio, responsibilities of overall management are recognised and the balance of the studio reflects this.

5 Learning Styles and Strategies

Powell and Newland (1992) Honey and Mumford (1989) and Honey (1989) have identified complimentary sets of four learning styles. Powell describes them as dynamic learners, contemplative learners, rigorous learners and focussed learners. Honey describes them as activists, reflectors, theorists and pragmatists. Both may be related to the concept of the learning circle which every learner goes through from and within the context of an existing body of awareness, knowledge and skills. The learner has a learning experience (dynamic activist) then reviews it (contemplative reflector) and concludes it (rigorous theorist). Finally it is incorporated into the learner's developing body of awareness knowledge and skill (focussed pragmatist) to become part of their new personal context of learning, so closing the learning circle.

While such categorisations are inevitably provisional, they provide a valuable reference point in course design. This is especially so when considering Honey's claim that only 2% of learners have all four styles within their repertory, while 70% have only one or two. This implies that it is incumbent on course designers to provide a learning context where all four styles can be encouraged within the whole learning cycle to avoid discrimination against some learners. It could also help to minimise drop-out rates in the first year of courses. In addition, general human development theories(cf. Erikson, 1963; Rogers et al., 1983) often recognise the fluid way in which human beings develop and form as people (and learners). Earlier stages of growth, say as a child, may often be revisited by the adult and are usually referential in some way when considering current behaviour and learning. For example, the child-parent relationship lasts for life, well after the parent's death, as expressed in the child/adult's ongoing and developing life attitudes, feelings, decisions, actions and styles of learning. Such iterative, organic models provide a robust context to learning provision.

Clearly, different aspects of the learning cycle are most important to different people at different times, and many learning cycles are in motion for a person at any one time. Nevertheless, a person, whether student or staff, normally seems to tend towards one or two of these learning styles (cf. Honey, 1989).

This course and its learning strategies have been designed to allow for at least a fair experience of all four styles. Within this context, there are three main learning strategies, which are particularly important in providing full learning cycles, starting especially with the activist stage.

The toolkit block study weeks quickly introduce the learner to the skills needed for the active problem-solving culture of the course. The studio may then be speedily begun, and mini learning cycles developed.

The integrative studio continues to instil the problem-solving culture through a series of assignments designed to place each subject system in an overall context and to explore where they interact. It is here, in particular, that a sense of overall purpose and course identity is established, as space and time is given to allow the full learning cycle to be experienced time and again.

The final-year strategy is rather different to years 1 and 3. It is led by the studio work, but focussed on two electives chosen by each student from the five offered by the course. Four system-based, theoretical/reflective subject inputs support the wide-ranging studio work via lectures, etc., while a research project study begun at the end of the third year provides the opportunity to pursue a rigorous focussed research interest.

6 Course Design Features and Learning Issues

Two critical factors in encouraging learning have been discussed by Munns and Smith (1992), namely student motivation and course orientation.

Considering the whole course, it has been designed explicitly from the perceived career and personal aspirations of potential students. In particular, the final-year design has been crucial in providing the flexibility to enable learning which can respond to the changing environment of the construction industry, which can provide a significant range of career opportunities for the potential student, and which can develop transferable self-management communication and learning skills. Such a design feature provides a highly motivating context.

Within each year, the studio is the place where both subjects and learning cycles are integrated. If not addressed, this process happens implicitly, haphazardly and partially anyway. This explicit design feature seeks to maximise subject and learning cycle integration and make it as effective as possible. Therefore this course design feature in each year embodies the course orientation, namely the problem-solving ethos of the course. Active/dynamic learning is set in train from week 1 of the course in each year, with a range of small exercises reflecting the subject range, and based on one building site. The submission, feedback and debriefing of the exercises provides the review and conclusion modes of the learning cycle. The opportunity for all to resubmit for upgrading based on feedback and debriefing concludes the learning cycle. This has proved very popular with the students, and very effective.

In the subject delivery areas, lectures and tutorials predominate, apparently serving the theorist and reflector styles of learning best. Laboratories provide other opportunities for activist learning styles, while case-study work within all these delivery modes seems amenable to the pragmatist style of learning. However, it is in the studio that the total learning circle is most clearly experienced fully. The impression remains that it provides the touchstone for the other experiences of learning styles which are, in general, highly partial.

The toolkit merits special mention in that, apart from its remedial role, it tries above all to instil the activist problem-solving approach to learning. It seeks to emphasise the value placed in the course design on such a starting point in learning, and to prepare the student for the studio work which is central to each academic year and dominates the final year.

As in any sandwich course, the placement year is seen as very valuable. It is designed in as the second year of this course rather than the third, as is usual. This reflects the value placed on the activist problem-solving ethos and a desire to use the additional maturity arising out of placement year on as much of the course as possible. The ongoing touchstone of the learning cycle in the studio again is seen as providing a reference point for the learning experiences of the placement year.

The research project is an important component of the final year, as the subject support is a much smaller proportion of the year's learning experience. It provides an alternative rigorous focussed learning experience, and is the second form of the final year after the studio. The range of learners is still fully addressed, while the space and time for the complete learning cycle continues to be provided in the studio.

7 Conclusion

The first year of the course has run so far. Feedback from the students has indicated that the course design and implementation is motivating and inclusive. Experience has shown that effective course administration and shared course team commitment are both especially important in implementing course design features that facilitate the full learning circle. While course delivery will be improved in the light of ongoing experience and original design concepts, so far the course design appears basically authentic.

References

Erikson, E. H. (1963). *Childhood and Society.* Harmondsworth: Penguin.

Honey, P. (1989). *The Manual of Learning Styles / The Manual of Learning Opportunities.*

Honey, P. and Mumford, A. (1989). Trials and Tribulations. *The Guardian* 19 December.

Munns, A. K. and Smith F. W. (1992). *Spreadsheets on Tools to Examine Methods of Analysis.* Proceedings on the first Conference on Computer Based Training in Property and Construction, 39–48.

Powell, J. A. and Newland, P. (1992). *The Use of Interactive Multi-Media in Construction Based Training: Experimenting with an Experimental Approach.* Proceedings of the First Conference on Computer Based Training in Property and Construction, 67–80.

Rogers, C. et al. (1983). *Freedom to Learn for the 80's.* Merrill.

B SC (HONS) CONSTRUCTION TECHNOLOGY & MANAGEMENT

Final Year Studio Electives					SOME POTENTIAL CAREER OPPORTUNITIES
Building Engineering	Construction Contracting	Maintenance & Facilities Management	Project Evaluation	Construction Information Technology	
■					BUILDING SERVICES CO-ORDINATION
		■			TECHNICAL FACILITIES MANAGEMENT
	■	■			BUILDING MAINTENANCE CONTRACTING
	■		■		QUANTITY SURVEYING (CONTRACTING)
		■	■	■	STRATEGIC FACILITIES MANAGEMENT
■				■	PROJECT MANAGEMENT
	■				SPECIALIST ENGINEERING CONTRACTING
			■		BUILDING SERVICES QUANTITY SURVEYING
■			■	■	PROFESSIONAL QUANTITY SURVEYING (CLIENT BASED)
■				■	PUBLIC SECTOR MAINTENANCE
					PROJECT CONSULTANCY
	■			■	CONSTRUCTION PLANNING

Graduates also have the opportunity to persue research to Masters or Doctorate level

Figure 1: An indication of some possible initial career routes for graduates of the CTM course

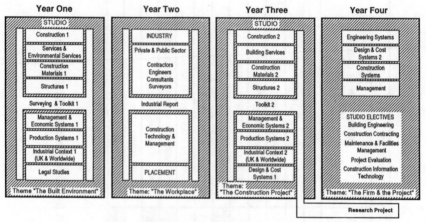

Figure 2: Outline Course Structure

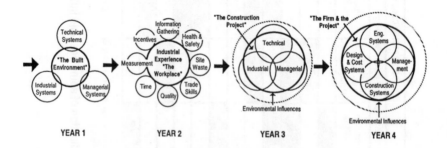

Figure 3: Course Concept   The Role of the Studio

Chapter 13 Reflection and student learning

Students Learning to Teach: a Report on a Foundation Teaching Studies Course for Students Intending to Become Primary School Teachers.

Susan Cox, Nottingham Trent University

An Outline of the Design of the Course

Factors influencing the creation of the course
The Foundation Teaching Studies course at Nottingham Trent University is a component of the Primary B Ed course. It has been in operation over a period of four years. The course was developed to fulfil a number of perceived needs in the training of teachers. Firstly there was the 'gap' which has always been apparent between theory and practice in teacher education and which has received a lot of attention from theorists themselves in recent years. We wanted to find ways of giving the course a school-based focus so that students could see the relevance of what they were doing in college to the activity they were interested in, which is teaching children. We wanted to move beyond the traditional idea of blocks of teaching practice interspersed with theoretical elements.

Secondly, we saw a need to demonstrate through our approaches to teaching and learning on the course the kinds of principles which we felt to be implicit in "good primary practice". A third consideration was the need to lay foundations for professional development. In the final year of their course students would be undertaking independent projects in school using an action research methodology, and it was seen to be important to establish critically reflective approaches from the start with an emphasis on autonomy and self-reliance. The promotion of what we see to be appropriate attitudes to learning commensurate with those of good primary practitioners' approaches to children's learning would establish appropriate attitudes to underpin students' development in later elements of the course.

It is important to point out that at the time we were introducing the course the 1988 Education Reform Act was influencing the direction in which our course was developing. The new Cate criteria had introduced a compulsory element of main subject study into all primary teacher education courses. On a four-year course students were to spend the equivalent of two years studying a specialist subject at their own level and the teaching of that subject and there were also new requirements for the length of time to be spent on studying the core subjects of the National Curriculum. All ten subjects of the National Curriculum needed to be covered in a way that reflected the new orders that were introduced from 1989 to 1992. This reduction in the time available for studying the full range of educational issues appropriate to primary teaching meant that there were pragmatic as well as philosophical reasons for designing a course which fully integrated work in school with college-based work.

In fulfilling these needs, the structure and processes of the course and its content are necessarily interlinked. The way the course is designed and the way it is taught carries important messages about educational processes to which we would want students to give attention. The content of the course to a large extent deals directly with ideas about the processes of learning and teaching.

Outline of the structure and content of the course
The course is based on a cyclical model. Experience in school is a key element, with regular periods of time (day and two-day visits) spent in the same classroom working with a teacher. There is a focus for each visit to school which is introduced to the students through sessions at the university. Following up the visit to school is a "School Group" meeting. A school group is a fairly small (12-15 members), stable group of students who work in the same schools. The tutor for the school group meetings has inside knowledge of the context within which the students are working, as we try to ensure a continued relationship between a tutor and particular schools over a number of years, and the tutor is allocated time to visit the students during the days they are in school. The school group meeting provides the forum for analysing the students' experience in school in terms of the focal issues currently being considered. It also functions reactively, taking up students' immediate concerns. Essentially the emphasis is on unpacking the students' own practice to reveal the underlying ideas, beliefs and values (or "theories") which have informed the students' actions, aiming to make what is tacit understanding more explicit. These understandings which are enacted on an interpersonal level are seen in relation to the wider social and cultural value systems within which they are constructed and which they help to construct – that is to say, the institutional framework of the school and the broader ideological context.

The students are encouraged to reflect critically upon their practice in the light of these contextual factors with a view to directly addressing and challenging their assumptions. Further decisions about their practice are made from a position that is more rigorously appraised and evaluated. The process continues in a cyclical manner, with students' growing awareness of the factors which influence their decisions about action enabling them to make considered changes and to develop the effectiveness of their own teaching.

There are a variety of features of the course, then, which support the student in this developmental process. The classroom teacher and the visiting tutor provide support on a one-to-one basis for the student in the classroom. The school group provides peer and tutor support. Apart from providing the necessary intellectually supportive context, this network of personal support is important in establishing and maintaining student confidence in making decisions and undertaking actions in the classroom. This is essential, as the course builds on students' existing knowledge and understanding and on their preparedness to engage in teaching activities in a way that they personally see to be appropriate at any particular time in the process of their development. Initially, students work mostly with small groups of children. Teaching the whole class in these early stages can lead to a preoccupation with control which means that the student has little opportunity to pay close attention to teaching and learning processes and to the individual child's responses. Students also keep a school log, in which they record their plans for action and their evaluations of their practice. This is seen as a developmental and interactive document - the class teacher and the tutor will offer feedback on the contents of a student's log, both verbal and written. The student is encouraged to respond to this, so a dialogue is often entered into, encouraging the student to reflect on specific aspects of their practice. The school group is also used as a study group for student-led seminars, in which students use learning packs prepared by the tutors.

The course structure creates a variety of contexts and relationships to facilitate learning. The more traditional input through a large group lecture, albeit one which usually includes student participation of some kind, is complemented by active learning through group work. The processes of group work are seen to be essential to the achievement of the aims of the course. Experience in school is analysed by the students themselves on an individual basis, in partnership with their class teacher and the visiting school-group tutor, in small groups of critical friends with their peers and sometimes in a group tutorial and in school groups with their peers and their tutor. Tutors encourage open communication in the school groups, and aim to create an atmosphere of cooperative learning. An active, investigative approach to learning is fostered.

In terms of the content of the course, there is currently a series of four cycles of learning. The first three have a specific focus within the broad theme of "Children Making Meaning". We look at children making meaning through play, through talk, through making marks and also through using mathematical systems. The fourth cycle focusses on the broad theme of "The Cultural Context for the Production of Meaning" and focusses on the way cultural factors influence how and what children learn and how we see children. Gender and race are used as specific examples to illustrate how meanings are constructed within an ideological framework and how they can be challenged. Permeated through these themes is an emphasis on getting to know and to understand children as individuals with their own perspective on the world and on looking critically at the way we make judgements of children. This takes in children with special needs and leads on to the important issue of assessment of children's learning. We also pay attention to the place of story in children's lives and in the curriculum, to the teaching of reading and to developing ways of planning teaching. To help students meet their perceived need for curriculum knowledge, we give a number of lectures and practical workshops which introduce them to the National Curriculum, and provide "survival guides" on different aspects of the curriculum, but detailed input on the curriculum areas is undertaken in later elements of the course. We maintain a holistic view of the primary curriculum and introduce students to teaching through topic. We also give some practical workshops on some of the practical skills they need to acquire, such as display and presentation.

(It is worth pointing out that the above represents a shortened version of the course, the duration of which is now one term rather than two owing to increasing difficulties with staffing and timetabling. Previously a whole term was spent on looking at "Contexts for Learning". The classroom context was looked at closely, studying issues such as classroom design, organisation and interaction. The whole primary curriculum was introduced through the medium of "topic"-based approaches.)

While these aspects of content are specifically intended to introduce students to areas of concern, for the intending teacher the structure and the processes of the course also comprise important areas of learning. It is intended that students will acquire a wide range of abilities in areas such as communication, making relationships and developing self-reliance and autonomy and will adopt reflective and analytical attitudes and investigative and enquiring approaches to learning. Fundamental values that are intrinsic to educational processes, such as respect for persons and fairness, are inherent in the course.

Rationale for the course
It should be clear that we see the student at the centre of the learning process. Our teaching role is conceived in terms of the setting up of situations and structures which are productive in facilitating learning, rather than in terms of the straightforward transmission of knowledge. We do not work on the premise that the college-based elements of the workshops and lectures will provide the students with fully worked-out solutions to the problems they will encounter, answers to questions about what they ought to do or a set of prescribed routines which they can act out in the classroom.

This reflects a particular view of professional practice and of the relationship of theory to that practice.

This view challenges the long-held conception of the division between research and practice within the professions, which Schön (1983) refers to and rejects as "Technical Rationality" ". . . research is institutionally separate from practice connected to it by carefully defined relationships of exchange. Researchers are supposed to provide the basic applied science from which to derive techniques for diagnosing and solving the problems of practice. Practitioners are supposed to furnish researchers with problems for study and with tests for the utility of research results. The researcher's role is distinct from and usually considered superior to the role of the practitioner". Research, then, on this view, is seen to provide the specialised, firmly bounded, scientific and standardised knowledge base for the professional to apply in practice.

For a long time this traditional conception has created tensions in the training of teachers, resulting in the view promulgated by the present government that the perceived need for relevance can be met only by a wholesale denial of the value of theory, and that the universities can no longer be seen to be necessary to the acquisition of teaching ability.

The ascendancy of this instrumental view of research and theoretical knowledge has its foundations in the predominance of positivist definitions of theory in which theories are essentially explanations of the way things are. This view of theory rests on the assumption that choices between different descriptions and explanations of phenomena can be determined by experiment and that generalisable empirical claims can be generated.

Although it is no longer held in scientific circles that theory is essentially value neutral, since all observations are theory laden, this positivist tradition could be seen to account for the division of labour which exists between researchers on the one hand and practitioners on the other.

This account of theoretical knowledge sits uncomfortably, however, with the practical knowledge of the practitioner - in this case the teacher. Firstly, a fundamental difficulty is that this model of the relationship between theory and practice is logically flawed, in that it must presuppose the desirability of ends. While the fruit of the labours of the researcher may help the practitioner to answer questions about the most effective way of achieving a particular outcome through empirical investigation,it cannot answer the questions about what these particular outcomes should be. The practitioner's knowledge is centrally concerned with these very complex, evaluative issues for the very reason that he or she is engaged in practical activity which requires decisions and choices about what to do. If these are considered choices, informed by reason and judgement, and are not made merely on the basis of opting for a particular path of action, then questions about values are necessarily incurred. To ask why one should do this rather than that is to ask for justification, and it is this which cannot be provided by explanations and description. To say that research shows that this is the most effective course of action begs the question of "effective in terms of what outcome?" Determination of both the outcome itself and the best – in terms of value, rather than efficiency – means of achieving that outcome must rest on further questions about what is desirable.

It might be argued that this is unproblematic in that the logical outcome of the teacher's activities is for learning to have taken place, and that if the researcher's work is concerned with the best ways of achieving that outcome then there is no logical difficulty in the instrumental model. If the teacher and the researcher are focussed on the same sphere of activity, in this case teaching, then the researcher's findings must be applicable to the teacher's practice in the same way as knowledge about what happens when you apply pressure to the pedals of a bicycle can be applied when riding a bike. However, bike riding is qualitatively different to teaching in that it is arguably a specific activity in a way that teaching is not. Teaching is not a single specific process but, to use Hirst and Peter's (1970) analysis, it is a family of activities, all contributing to the intended outcome of learning, and likewise learning is not a specific end-point in itself. ". . . Educating people suggests a family of processes whose principle of unity is the development of desirable qualities in them." Teaching covers a wide range of possible processes. While research may help to describe the best way of reaching a particular goal in terms of what works most effectively, it cannot prescribe what should be done - there may well be further educational and ethical considerations to be taken into account in deciding whether to take a particular course of action. There might be particular methods and processes which can be used to achieve a particular learning outcome in which further learning is implicit which may be more or less desirable. In this respect methods and processes become ends in themselves as well as means to an end. Likewise, what is to be taught is dependent upon decisions about what should be learnt - what desirable qualities should be acquired. If learning is to be educative then such decisions will take into account a variety of evaluative criteria.

Secondly, difficulties arise in applying the generalised findings of the research to the particularities of practice. Teachers teach children who are individuals in unique classroom settings, making the transposition of the categorisations of theory to practice problematic.

Thirdly, knowledge of the theory generated by research is neither a sufficient nor a necessary criterion for being able to teach. You cannot be said to have mastered the skills of bike-riding or teaching unless you can demonstrate them. No amount of theoretical knowledge will suffice. It is also logically coherent to say that one can acquire the skills of bike-riding and teaching through practising them without any knowledge of theory at all.

Is theory, then, an irrelevance? It might appear to be so, on this model of theory, for the teacher is faced with the real-life phenomena of the classroom. Judgements must be made in shifting contexts where a whole range of interconnecting circumstances and features of the situation must be taken into account. It is this practical knowledge which Schön refers to as "knowing in action" and which, he maintains, is the hallmark of the professional.

The dichotomy that appears to exist between theory and practice disappears, however, when the relationship between theory and practice is reinterpreted. A thorough-going positivist model implies that theory is non-practical and that practice is non-theoretical. If we leave the positivist baggage behind and take fully on board the fact that all so-called objective observation is theory laden a different relationship emerges. Theorising is itself a form of practice with its own forms of discourse and codes of conduct, which a theorist is inducted into in the same way as other practitioners are inducted into ways of behaving that are appropriate to their particular sphere of activity. It becomes less a question then of closing the gap between theory and practice than of recognising different forms of activity generating different bodies of knowledge. The instrumental and hierarchical view of the relationship between theory and practice arises from a conception of theory as distinct from and applicable to practice, whereas, in reality, the activities of both researchers and practitioners express principles and procedures that underpin their respective activities. As Carr and Kemmis (1986) put it: "Both are distinctive social activities conducted for distinctive purposes by means of specific procedures and skills and in the light of particular beliefs and values", and each mode of thought incorporates an interrelated set of concepts, beliefs assumptions and values that allow events and situations to be interpreted in ways that are appropriate to their respective concerns."

If theory is implicit, then, in all activities does this imply that theoretical knowledge is a precondition of action, that we cannot make a decision about what to do unless we have a clearly worked out set of guiding principles and ideas? This suggestion invokes a dualist account of mind and action in that thought is construed as logically prior to action. The case has been convincingly refuted by Ryle (1949). While one may think before one acts, this is a chronological relationship between thought and action, not a logical one. "Intelligent practice is not a step-child of theory." Ryle argues that there is a logical impasse in the suggestion that theory necessarily has priority over action. So the argument goes, if formulating a theory is itself an activity and if engaging in an activity is logically dependent on prior theory, we have a situation of "infinite regress", since the activity of formulating that theory requires a prior theory, and so on. He denies explicitly that intelligent actions are dependent on "some anterior internal operation of planning what to do".

"Intelligent" cannot be defined in terms of "intellectual"or "knowing how" in terms of "knowing that"; "thinking what I am doing" does not connote "both thinking what to do and doing it". When I do something intelligently, i.e., thinking what I am doing, I am doing one thing and not two. My performance has a special procedure or manner, not special antecedents.

It does not make sense, then, to say that a teacher cannot get on and do things in the classroom unless she or he has a theory to inform that action. It may well be desirable to do so but it is not a logical necessity. Rather, teachers' actions can be seen as embedded in social and cultural patterns of behaviour within an established framework of procedures and expectations. Appropriate courses of action are learnt by being part of the community, by learning its forms of language and discourse and the kinds of codes of practice that are followed. These are not unchanging or fixed but represent differing levels of consensus within particular social contexts.These codes of practice underpin all aspects of the teachers' professional concerns, from the institution of the school to forms of knowledge such as history and mathematics.

Carr and Kemmis 1986 argue that " 'Educational theory', on this view, is not an 'applied theory' that 'draws on theories of the social sciences'. Rather it refers to the whole enterprise of critically appraising the adequacy of the concepts, beliefs, assumptions and values incorporated in prevailing theories of educational practice." While it seems unnecessarily restrictive to claim as they do that this is the only coherent view of educational theory, it gives legitimacy to the theories which teachers already hold:

By subjecting the beliefs and justifications of existing and on-going traditions to rational re-consideration, theory informs and transforms practice by informing and transforming the ways in which practice is experienced and understood. The transition, therefore, is not from theory to practice as such but rather from irrationality to rationality, from ignorance and habit to knowledge and reflection. Furthermore, if educational theory is interpreted on this way, closing the gap between theory and practice is not a case of improving the practical effectiveness of the products of theoretical activities, but one of improving the practical effectiveness of the theories that teachers employ in conceptualising their own activities. (Carr and Kemmis, 1986)

To the extent that anyone can participate in an activity, then, they are following rules and procedures of which they may be aware to a greater or lesser degree, but which are implicit in the behaviours they adopt. In the case of student teachers, their previous life experience will have given them a level of "knowing in action" that enables them to take on the role of teacher. Their experience as a learner in the educational system will have given them some insight into the kinds of things which teachers do; they will know how to go about things even though they are unaware of having learnt how to do them. According to Schön's description of "knowing in action", if they have this level of ordinary practical knowledge they will be able to perform actions, recognitions and judgements spontaneously, without being aware of having learnt them, and will usually be unable to describe the knowing which their action reveals.

The knowledge which students bring to their first experience in school is the legitimate starting point for students' professional development on the FTS course. They are encouraged from the start to participate in teaching activities using their existing intuitive knowledge. Further learning about how to do things occurs in the company of others within the framework of beliefs, ideas and principles which give sense and meaning to the patterns and codes of practice. The structure and processes of FTS are designed to encourage students to articulate these to enable them to come to an understanding of their actions, the reasons for and consequences of what they do, and to evaluate them critically. The aim is that practical decision-making moves from the merely habitual or imitative to the more conscious, so that skill is informed by reflection.

Central to the whole process is the real-life experience of the school. The student engages in the series of cycles of learning which, as previously described, are intended to move the student progressively towards reflective practice. When students go into school they experience the complexity, uncertainty and conflicting values of the real-life situation. Whereas a traditional course, with an emphasis on applied theory, does not necessarily acknowledge this reality, FTS is designed to confront it and make sense of it. It is a central aspect of the subject matter of the course. The student faces the specificity and context-bound character of the decisions that need to be made and is asked to pay attention to the details of that context. They are encouraged to appreciate that if the "text-book" case is useful at all it must be reinterpreted in the light of the particular understandings that can be brought to bear on the particular situation. They are encouraged to "problematise" their teaching - to formulate the problems that are specific to their experience, their developing professional knowledge and understanding and their particular circumstances, and then to decide on appropriate courses of action to deal with them. On the view of educational theory I have presented, where ends and the means of achieving them are indeterminate, the nature of the problems that will be encountered is not predictable. The process of unpacking and appraising implicit values clarifies the kinds of problems that need to be solved. As Schön (1983) states: "In real world practice, problems do not present themselves to the practitioners as given. They must be constructed from the materials of problematic situations which are puzzling, troubling or uncertain. In order to convert a problematic situation to a problem, a practitioner must do a certain kind of work. He must make sense of a certain situation that initially makes no sense." It should be apparent, then, that a constructivist view of knowledge and learning underpins the Foundation Teaching Studies course. Learners are seen as becoming initiated into the complexities of culture, values and codes of conduct and are making sense of them by developing theories about what is going on. Through interaction with the language and forms of discourse of the social group, in this case that of educationists, they find out how to proceed. They make sense of things through actively constructing links with their existing knowledge. This they do by trying things out in practice and evaluating their strategies in the light of further experience and understanding in the company of others.

On the FTS course this model of learning informs the way we approach both student learning and children's learning and acknowledges the uniqueness of the individual's perspective and of the context within which learning is occurring and decisions about what to do are taken. The centrality of the social environment in the construction of meaning is acknowledged. Interaction with others through group work is intended to provide optimal conditions for learning. The course requires, on the part of the students, the acceptance of responsibility for their own learning, an acceptance of uncertainty and a readiness to question their own ideas and assumptions. The intellectual challenge of the course itself lies fundamentally in recognising that teaching is problematic, in developing understandings of implicit theory, critically evaluating these and appraising wider contextual factors which have shaped these ideas.

Development of the Course

The course has changed over the time it has been in operation in response to a number of factors. Some of these have been external requirements, such as government legislation (the need to accommodate the National Curriculum and the need to meet the new lecturers' contracts, for example), and logistical institutional factors, such as the unitisation and modularisation of courses and the increase in student numbers. Other changes have taken place in response to on-going clarification of the principles of its operation and in response to evaluation. The dynamics of reflective practice have in this respect influenced the development of the course itself. It would not be reasonable to present a complete account of this development, so I intend here to sketch inbriefly some of the sources and outcomes of this process and to focus on some key issues that have emerged.

A range of evaluative procedures have been used.

1. The identity of the teaching team with all members of the team being responsible for a school group, making regular visits into the same schools over a number of years and contributing to the other elements of the course, has facilitated a process of course development based on the common experiences of the members of staff. Regular team meetings have provided a forum for the exchange of ideas and observations and the clarification and development of the course ethos.

2. Members of the teaching team are in contact with the classroom teachers working with the students in school; thus there is a direct channel of communication with the practitioners, who to a large extent act as the role-models for the students.

3. More formal processes of obtaining student feedback and evaluation have been used each year. These have included regular staff student consultation through a committee of student and staff representatives and an evaluation carried out by a former member of the teaching team in the first year in

which the course operated. Comments and observations were collected from the heads and staff of four schools and 35 (out of approximately 80) students. A report was written in the form of fictional letters home written at different stages during the year and a fictional head teacher's report on the course. The the letters and the head teacher's report were read and 'validated' by the students themselves not involved in the original interviews and discussion. An evaluation took place in the second year where students were asked to respond to a range of comments that had been made at different times during the course by students, teachers and tutors. Evaluations in the third and fourth years involved students being asked to comment on a variety of aspects of the course. An inspection was carried out by HMI in the first year.

The qualitative data gathered in this way were used by the members of the team in formulating strengths and weaknesses of the course and informing action steps for the future.

Some problem areas emerged at an early stage, and these are important in relation to the aims of the course.

1. Students are preoccupied with survival in the classroom and their expectations are that they will be explicitly instructed in "how to" teach (tell me what to do and how to do it).

2. Students' existing attitudes to study tend not to allow them to accept uncertainty and tentativeness or to adopt enquiring approaches.

I would argue that these concerns and attitudes reflect existing conceptions of learning and teaching that tend to be simplistic. There is a tendency to see teaching as a technical enterprise concerned predominantly with the transmission of knowledge. This has to be seen also in the context of current educational policy, with government legislation putting the emphasis on "delivery" of the curriculum. The hold which the traditional "technical rationality" has had on the structures and practices of training institutions leads students to see a lack of connection between their college course and their experience in school and to see a division between the university and the schools in which they work. The expectation is that the onus is entirely on them to "put theory into practice" and to cope with this process must be seen to be straightforward in that the knowledge they acquire in college must be readily transferable to their activities in school. They look for ideas about what to teach and definitions of the problems they will encounter in how to teach with ready-made solutions to these. They see experiences of confusion and uncertainty as a sign of the inadequacy of the course in preparing them to teach. A lack of confidence in their own practical knowledge is the corollary of the expectation that the college course will provide what they need to know.

There is also a tendency to see "having no problems" as a goal. Rather than seeing the identification of problems as a way of developing their ability, they see it as a sign of weakness. This is of course a legitimate and reasonable starting point.

We needed to ask ourselves how successful we were being in getting students to challenge their assumptions and to address the complexities of teaching and how well we were implementing the "action research" approach. How effective were we in supporting students at the level of their existing practical knowledge and could we improve the strategies for helping them to a) accept situations and experiences which fall outside their expectations and b) find ways of constructively interpreting these in terms of problems to solve.

The following aims were considered:

1. To develop the processes that we were adopting, building on existing good practice, and to make these more explicit to the students, including the incorporation of activities within the course which help students to look directly at their conceptions of teaching and learning and to challenge their assumptions.

2. To improve and extend the student-centred, student-led aspects of FTS. This would help students to see the role of the professional peer group in clarification of aims and principles and in developing understandings. It would help students to see the role of the tutor as facilitator rather than knowledge provider.

3. To work on establishing partnership with the schools.

For 1991-92 a number of strategies were adopted, among which were:

1. Introducing activities and strategies across all school groups, aimed towards getting students to address directly their own conceptions of learning and their understanding of group work in facilitating learning.

2. Offering a structure to help students "problematise" their teaching by providing a pro forma for them to complete at intervals which they would have an opportunity to discuss with a tutor.

3. Paying attention to the quality of our own teaching processes, working to improve the support given to students in school to develop confidence and to make it clear to them that our role is that of facilitator rather than knowledge provider.

When asked to comment on the ways in which they thought they had developed as a result of the course, most students gave positive responses.

A common claim was that they had become more aware of the complexities and demands of teaching and learning. While it would be misleading to infer from this evidence any development in students' attitude towards "complexity" and their ability to "problematise" their practice, there is at least an indication that students are beginning to acknowledge that teaching is problematic. Moreover, some students did specifically identify development in their ability to analyse, evaluate and reflect.

Thirty-six students specifically identified "confidence" as an area of development. This was cited by students more frequently than any other area.

An analysis of the ways in which students see their conceptions of learning and teaching to have changed as a result of the course during 1991-92 provides evidence to suggest that most of the 112 students who responded found that their conceptions had changed.

> Almost a third found that there was more to teaching than they had previously thought; that it is harder work, is more complex or involves more planning and preparation than they had realised.

> Twenty-five respondents commented on the ways in which their understanding had grown of the variety of ways in which learning occurs (teaching as more open-ended, less teacher centred; more of a partnership; requiring the creation of good learning environments and good organisation and management; allowing children control; learning in groups; the importance of process; learning as an active process; the value of first-hand experience, etc.)

> Fourteen commented on their recognition that teachers are also learners.

> Eight commented on their understanding of the relationship between teaching and learning; that assumptions cannot be made about what has been learnt on the basis of what has been taught.

There is evidence here of the development of a deeper appreciation of the complexity of the learning process.

In 1992-93 a number of further changes were made with a view to giving students control of their own learning through group work.

1. The introduction of structured student-led seminars, for which learning packs were provided, giving students the opportunity to manage and develop group processes independently of the tutor. The context extends the

opportunities provided in school group sessions for student participation, since the students themselves control the discussion. Students' conceptions can be shared and evaluated more openly in the security of the peer group, the feedback gained from other students enabling them to elaborate and modify their ideas.

2. The introduction of group presentations based on students' analyses of aspects of their practice in school. The group of students working within each school were to take time out of the school day to discuss their practice with their peers and to develop theoretical perspectives. The material was to be jointly presented in the school group sessions back in college.

3. The introduction of Critical Friends Groups to support the processes of problematising and planning their practice (see Appendix 2).

In addition, the cycles of action and reflection were restructured so that the action research approach became more evident to students.

Changes for 1993-94 are being made to develop further the processes of reflection through "problematising".

We are to pilot a scheme whereby students will compile personal records of professional development. The intention is that these will record "critical incidents" in students' experience which occasion the kind of reflection we are seeking to foster. With the help of critical friends, students will examine the tacit understanding which they brought to bear on the situation and identify courses of further action to bring about change and to reconstruct their ideas. This will be an on-going record which will document more fully the path of the individual's learning during the course.

References

Carr, W. and Kemmis, S. (1986). *Becoming Critical*. London: Falmer Press.

Hirst P. H. and Peters R. S. (1970). *The Logic of Education*. London: Routledge & Kegan Paul.

Ryle, G. (1949). *The Concept of Mind*. London: Hutchinson.

Schön, D. (1983). *The Reflective Practitioner*. London: Temple Smith.

Appendix 1

Have your conceptions of teaching and learning changed during the course? Is so, give a brief statement as to how.

Respondents who said their conceptions had not changed, or not particularly: 9

The vast majority claimed that their conceptions had changed. Eight respondents said their conceptions had not fundamentally changed but had broadened, deepened, etc. Four said they had changed, becoming deeper, more focussed, etc. The rest identified the ways in which they had changed more specifically. The following areas were identified:

That there is more to it than previously thought; that it is harder work, is more complex, involves more planning/preparation, etc., than realised: 36

Understanding of the variety of ways in which learning occurs: teaching as more open ended, less teacher centred, more a partnership, requiring creation of good learning environments, good organisation and management, allowing children control, learning in groups, the importance of process, learning as an active process, the value of first-hand experience, etc.: 25

Recognising that teachers are also learners: 14

Understanding of the relationship between teaching and learning. One can't make assumptions about what has been learnt on the basis of what had been taught. Need to evaluate/assess what has been learnt: 8

Understanding the importance of planning. (This needs to be linked with the number of respondents who said that there was more planning involved than they had realised; see above: 8

Understanding the practical difficulties in teaching, e.g., number of children, resources, time, etc.: 4

Increased awareness of children and their learning: 3

Understanding the level of responsibility, commitment involved: 3

Understanding about individual differences and needs: 3

Experiencing teaching from teacher's point of view rather than, as previously, as a pupil: 2

Understanding the importance of personal experience of students in developing ideas: 2

Understanding about teaching methods: 2

Understanding that learning is about acquisition of skills as well as facts: 1

Some respondents interpreted the "how" in the question to mean "by what means?" Of these, six said their conceptions had changed as a result of school experience, one as a result of the experience in the Poly.

Comments not fully represented by the above:

I thought we would be told more about actual teaching methods e.g., "you have to do this". I realise you can't do this really.

I have changed my conceptions in so many areas - my interaction in the classroom, how children learn; pressures on teachers, etc., etc.

No change really, although I was surprised at how much five year olds knew and the speed at which they picked things up.

Difficult to evaluate learning and the permanency of it.

Yes, I've decided I don't want to be a teacher. Going into school made me realise this. To much planning and preparation involved.

Seeing FTS as a whole (school; workshops; school groups plus your own contribution; reading; teaching; participation in workshops; school group; school log; assignment, etc.), comment on the way you think you have developed as a result of the course.

Of the students who responded to this question,

positive comments: 80
mixed comments: 18
negative comments: 5

The following areas of development were identified:

Confidence: 36

Awareness of the complexities of teaching and learning/demands and expectations within teaching: 18

Awareness of the need for organisational ability, forward planning and

preparation, etc: 19
(Of these, 12 said that they had developed skill in this area.)

Understanding of children and learning: 12

Being able to analyse/reflect/evaluate: 9

Sense of professionalism and responsibility: 8

Skills in classroom management, teaching skills and strategies: 7

Awareness of individual children's needs and abilities: 6
(Of these, three said they had gained skills in this area.)

Ideas for teaching: 5

Personal attitude of learning: 4

Relationships with children. 4
Learning from the experience of others: 4

Independence: 3

Communication with others: 2

Understanding of topic: 2

Comments not fully represented by the above:

I feel I have developed enormously. I hardly recognise myself as the person who started school visits last autumn. I am conscious of so much more that is going on in the teaching/learning process.

The course has opened my eyes to how much there is to learn and the responsibility involved. The course has made me realise that there are many areas I need to concentrate on and analyse.

I have been able to identify and relate to problems more readily due to the experience the course has given us.

As a result of the course I now understand why certain things happen in schools and the importance of the whole community.

My thinking is more structured. Learning to use others' experience and ideas. I'm not on my own.

Tolerance.

I have realised what working hard is all about and it certainly makes me more determined.

More understanding better use of resources.

I have developed skills I never knew I had.

I have learned a lot more than I thought.
Become more committed to work as more involved than before.

Foundations for future T.P. have been learned.

Have learned to cope with stress.

Developed in reading stories.

The course has at times made me feel very negative towards teaching and particularly the National Curriculum. It would be helpful if the tutor could refrain from sarcasm and unnecessary comments and try to be more positive. However, school experience itself has counteracted the negativity picked up in college.
School experience a more valuable . . . Poly and school didn't always relate.

The input from college certainly makes you think of all the different aspects there are, but you can get bogged down with analysing . . . More continuous time in school needed.

More confidence in dealing with children. Not confident that I know exactly what I should/should not be teaching.

Appendix 2

Purposes of Critical Friends Groups

To give and receive support in a wide variety of ways, for example:

1. To identify and discuss issues that are seen by individuals and the group as a whole to be problematic.

2. Through discussion, to help each other discover the assumptions that we make that underlie the things we do and say, particularly in the classroom, working with children.

3. To help each other critically and reflectively examine these assumptions and to develop new ways of thinking and acting.

4. To provide a range of views to help each other to evaluate our personal interpretations and judgements and to test their validity.

6. To share ideas and specialist knowledge.

7. To provide critical feedback in helping each other to compile a personal record of professional development.

Reflection learning – the integrated use of theory and reflection as a route to improved learning

David Thompson, The Northern Regional Management Centre

Introduction

The Northern Regional Management Centre (NRMC) is an educational charity set up in 1980 by the then Polytechnics of Newcastle, Sunderland and Teesside. Its purpose is to research and develop new approaches to management development. It has played a significant role in linking the aims and requirements of employers with FE/HE through developing a suite of management programmes, from supervisor level through to MBA, which are:

* work based
* competence focussed
* certificated by an appropriate awarding body

All NRMC programmes aim to develop competence and therefore have a bias towards experience. They are for practising managers.

They key learning vehicle developed and used by NRMC is a form of experiential learning contract, called a Management Learning Contract (MLC). An MLC is an agreement between tutor, participant and employer's representative that defines:

* the participant's particular learning objectives over a set time span

* the targeted learning activities and theories to be addressed

* the evidence of learning to be produced and criteria

The principles of MLCs are well defined by Bóak (1990).

NRMC's use of MLCs reflect Kolb's (1984) learning cycle of action, reflection, theory and planning. They also follow the principles identified by Knowles (1973) as enhancing adult learning. In essence, these are participation by the learner in designing, delivering and assessing the learning actions, self-discovery, real consequences arising from learning actions, and relevance.

Outline of paper

The model of Kolb and Knowles have provided a powerful foundation for learning, and the development resulting from MLCs has been generally effective.

Evidence from the MBA suggests that deep learning at this level is strengthened if reflection does not occur at only one point in the learning cycle, but throughout. This in turn has led to a re-appraisal of the use of theory in the cycle.

This paper focuses on the use of reflection and theory and their relationship in MLCs in the NRMC MBA. It describes the three stages of learning seen in an MLC, showing how reflection and theory are used differently at each stage.

The stages of the MLC are:

- diagnosis and planning
- action
- evaluation

A contrast is seen between the nature of reflection using concise models and theories during the first stage of diagnosis and planning, and the reflection during the third stage of evaluation where reflection is on theory in a dynamic relationship with experience. It will be suggested that the latter reflection adds the critical dimension that enables deep learning to take place.

This paper is essentially a summary document of experiences from the MBA. The observations that are made reflect much that is already published on learning theories and processes, and on knowledge use and creation. The intention here is to outline an emerging approach to reflection and theory usage that appears to have strengthened the learning of participants, without ignoring some of the issues it raises, in the hope that it will encourage others to experiment with and evolve new practices.

Overview of the three MLC stages

Using the Boyatzis (1982) model of behaviours associated with effective managerial performance as a guide, NRMC MBA participants develop skills, behaviours and understanding through three MLCs over an eighteen month period. The three MLCs are in the areas of directing and developing subordinates, managing teams and lateral contacts, and finally in leading strategic change.

The approach to each MLC in the MBA that has evolved to the current format can be represented in a matrix:

Stage	Type of Reflection	Activities
1 Diagnosis and planning for action	Diagnostic	Recognition Context scanning Reading models Consciousness raising Benchmarking Incorporation of need

2 Action	Reflection on action	Learning activities eg.
		   experimentation, observation,
		   modelling, targeted reading etc.
		Log and note keeping
		Small learning cycles

3 Evaluation	Evaluative and conclusive	Dynamic use of theory and experience through questioning Report writing Oral presentation of learning

MLC Stage 1 – Diagnostic Reflection and Planning for Action

Diagnosis of learning needs is done through reflection on current competence. Boak and Thompson (1992) outline how participants can be effectively introduced in a collaborative setting to a framework of reflective actions, tools and concepts that provide the participant with a benchmark from which to proceed. This is used both to inform the planning of the subsequent learning actions and to encourage commitment in the participants to personal change. The framework for reflection is structured as follows:

Recognition – in line with Boyatzis' suggested starting point for development, participants start by looking for examples of good behaviour/management performance from their own world that is relevant to the MLC. This is partly a linguistic exercise as participants and tutors alike come to a common understanding of what the terms used to describe the experiences they bring to workshops actually mean. The articulation of events and the discipline of articulating events to others in question and answer settings aids the focus and depth of understanding.

Context scanning – participants explore the context in which good behaviour/management performance is set, to see the differences in contexts, and to see the links between various contexts and good behaviour/performance. Scanning is best started with simple description of the facts of the context as observed by the participant. These must be separated out from assumptions. This is often harder than it may seem, requiring the tutor and fellow participants to challenge all ungrounded assertions. The result of good scanning is a more objective and critical perspective of the jobs done and of the organisation in which they occur.

Reading – recognition and scanning of context are enhanced when the participant has something with which to compare his or her own setting. Sharing of contexts between participants provides opportunities to compare, as does reading theory. In this stage, reading tends to begin with visionary books. Visionary in this context is used to describe books and texts which are effective in engaging and enthusing the reader to look higher and wider at the world around, outside of his or her immediate context. They are readings that pull together the thinking and experiences of practitioners into an integrated perspective of management. In the management field, writers such as Kanter (1983) and Kotter (1982) both, incidentally, with strong academic backgrounds as well as wide practical experiences, provide an atmosphere of excitement and challenge to kick-start learning.

The better visionary books give an overview of the main themes of management and leadership that participants need to explore if they are to make progress. As Eraut (1985) suggests, visionary books tend to have experience derived know-how which professionals intuitively use. The know-how is usually provided in the form of models and at first glance are deceptively simple. A model from Kanter is provided here as a typical example. It is introduced to participants at the start of the MLC on leading change:

Power Tools in bringing about Change

Managers in large organisations who are effective in bringing about change have:

information - ranging from technical knowledge to political intelligence and expertise

resources - funds, materials, staff time and space

support - endorsement, the backing of other managers

In cases where they are not formally available, by virtue of position, they must be raised through a network of contacts in a process of coalition building. The process has a number of elements:

clearing the investment, which requires explaining the project to the boss and getting initial approval to explore further

preselling, often first to one's subordinates and to potential supporters elsewhere

horse trading of promises of benefits in exchange support or resources

securing blessings, from relevant higher managers with power, usually through formal presentations

formalising the coalition once promises of support and resources have been gained by presenting specific plans to the boss for implementation

---

Consciousness – in recognising good behaviour/performance and the context in which it is seen, participants need to recognise their own relative incompetence and learning needs of which they may be unconscious. Even if they appear to be conscious of them, their perception needs to be tested. Diagnostic reflection sees participants develop a more acute consciousness of their relative incompetence. Subsequent learning actions in the workplace then help the participant develop a level of conscious competence.

Sharing with fellow participants in workshops involves the participant exploring and surfacing areas of the self which for one reason or another may have been hidden, both from him or herself and from others. This is obviously a sensitive issue that requires counselling type skills in the tutor, and trust and openness between tutor and participants.

Consciousness raising is helped with the use of various information generating tools, for example the tools developed by Woodcock and Francis (1982) that unblock. Such tools for self-assessment of behaviour/performance, and feelings, need to be simple. They are typically rating questionnaires, derived from checklists of good practice or values on aspects of management performance which can be carried out by the participants. Consciousness raising requires feedback from people other than the tutor (who is a relative stranger) who have a stake in the participant's behaviour and performance.

More sophisticated tools, or at least those with more statistical credibility include Cattell's 16PF, or other related psychometric instruments such as the Myers-Briggs or OPQ that produce a personality profile for each participant. The NRMC MBA uses Cattell's 16PF. Apart from bringing to the participants' attention the strengths and limitations of such tools, it has proven useful firstly for each individual to have a normal and dispassionate view of his or her personality. And secondly, it underpins the notion that we are all unique individuals, with distinct profiles that are neither right nor wrong, and that development and the results of development will be different for each of us.

Development and thinking

Participants are introduced to two further models specifically to aid the self-management of learning:

The learning cycle – participants are introduced to the processes of learning that the MLC involves, including the learning cycle and all the issues connected with preferred learning styles. Honey and Mumford's (1986) Learning Styles Questionnaire (LSQ) is used. This further highlights to the participant during the diagnosis stage that learning, problem solving and change, which are in essence all related, can be approached in different ways. One approach though may not always be appropriate for all occasions and the targeted learning activities must take into account the need for the four stages of the learning cycle to be addressed. As such, the LSQ reinforces in the participant the concern for the process of learning as well as the objectives.

Intellectual competence – participants are introduced to various approaches to problem identification, analysis and solving the to enhance the quality of the process. The model of behaviours identified by Boyatzis includes a number of intellectual or cognitive competencies. Klemp and McLelland (1986) call these the behaviours of intelligent functioning:

- planning /causal thinking – essentially hypothesis generation because it involves seeing either the potential implications of events or the likely consequences of a situation based on what has happened in the past.

- diagnostic information thinking – is the natural outcome of planning/causal thinking, as manager seek to check the accuracy of conclusions drawn from cause and effect reasoning, and the natural precursor to conceptualisation/synthetic thinking;

- conceptualisation/synthetic thinking – essentially theory building to account for consistent patterns in recurring events or for connections between seemingly unrelated pieces of information

It is argued that these are behaviours that can be developed, perhaps like other behaviours. One would expect most programmes of academic credibility to develop them at least implicitly, though it appears that more programmes have modules developing study skills, problem-solving skills, research skills and the like. In the NRMC MBA, they are developed explicitly.

Planning for action

What has not happened in the first stage of the MLC is the accumulation of large amounts of theory. Diagnostic reflection does not require extensive reading of much theory. Nor does it require an attempt to make full sense of the context through overly detailed analysis. In this stage, that might be counter-productive. The use of general themes and relevant simple models aims to open the mind rather than to close it. They challenge the participants to look at how things are done, to stimulate ideas on how they might be done better, and to let go of current values and perceptions. The role of the tutor here is to identify such reading and point the participants to them, and to suggest specific ones if appropriate in the context.

Participants have so far been shaping their general pattern for development, but while a participant is conceptualising, he or she is less able to experience it. Eraut sees as important the need to experience with an open mind, unburdened by theories which risk turning into self-fulfilling prophecies. Additionally, over-emphasis on deconstructing events as they are may lead to paralysis by analysis.

Instead there are two positive outcomes from diagnostic reflection. The first is the recognition of need and commitment to change, and the second is a more informed planning process.

Need for change

During the phase of diagnostic reflection, it is possible to observe the four stages identified by Smith (1982) as the pattern of learning that leads to change:

1   conflict – ambivalence between the old and the new, as new information threatens present attitudes and behaviour;

2   defence – against the admission of personal limitations;

3   resolution of conflict – the original is examined objectively, and the decision to change is made when no one else insists on change, when he or she can express themselves freely, when he or she feels accepted regardless of attitude, and when not attacked;

4   incorporation – understanding and acceptance of the need for change. (This is aided by identification with others).

Unfortunately, on some occasions it has become apparent during the MLC or later that incorporation had not been achieved. On these occasions, the results of the MLC were less than satisfactory. Incorporation, while critical for learning and development, is not always easy to confirm until, that is, assessment takes place by which time it may be too late. At present, tutors seek to challenge all proposals for learning prior to commencement and look for signs that suggest defence mechanisms are protecting a fragile or defective self-image. It is an area however that needs further development.

Benchmarking

Earlier, the term benchmarking was used which implies that an objective level of ability or performance is set. Even with careful use of the above framework of reflection, all the diagnosis can realistically hope to achieve is a starting point that is anchored as well as possible, given the factors of time and resources. It would be possible to improve the diagnosis, for example with assessment centre methods, though inevitably at greater cost. There are probably other diagnostic tools available that could provide sharper diagnosis, though one should always be concerned about overly relying on them.

What has been found though, is that it is possible to combine the use of simple tools, feedback, with reflection by self of self in conjunction with others into a practical working package that is sufficient to enable effective and then deep learning to commence.

Planning

Participants produce a plan of learning activities, in effect the contract, including further focused study of the theories and models to be tested. These are integrated into the active experimentation. The plans lays out a schedule of actions that aims to generate relevant information on which the participant can reflect. This distinguishes the learning actions from more conventional ones which are often limited to the application of theory in action, putting knowledge into practice.

The plan specifies the learning objectives, justified with the findings of the reflective diagnosis. It specifies the intended learning activities and conceptual frameworks to be used to support the experimentation, focused on through the diagnostic reflection and, finally, it outlines the evidence of development to be produced along with relevant criteria. The evidence is always written up in a report for formal assessment.

The plan specifies the learning objectives, justified with the findings of the reflective diagnosis. It specifies the intended learning activities and conceptual frameworks to be used to support the experimentation, focused on through the diagnostic reflection and, finally, it outlines the evidence of development to be produced along with relevant criteria. The evidence is always written up in a report for formal assessment.

The plan therefore provides a structure for overall control of the learning. It is not however a straight-jacket. Boak points to the need to avoid learning actions that are dependent on matters outside the participant's control, and Mumford (1989) reminds us of the disorganised reality of a manager's life. Indeed, he encourages learning plans should take advantage of opportunities as they arise. The MLC plan therefore represents a reasonable balance between need for structure and the need to recognise other demands.

Ongoing management of the learning and new opportunities is done through reflection on action.

MLC Stage 2 – Learning activities and reflection on action

Participants carry out their targeted learning activities for each MLC over a period of three to four months before beginning to draw their learning together in their written report. Typically, participants spend ten hours plus a week. Activities depend on need and opportunity, and include targeted reading, observation, planning new behaviours, and action oriented ones such as modelling and, critically, experimentation.

In effect, the learning actions see the participant go round many smaller learning cycles. The action stage is therefore best represented as:

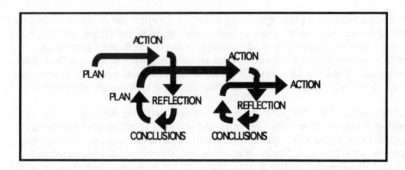

While this period of learning activities equates with Kolb's stage of action, it needs to be managed throughout. The management is done through a form of reflection.

The NRMC MBA has traditionally encouraged participants to keep a log of events as they happen. This is not formally assessed, nor necessarily seen by anyone except the participant. Some participants follow carefully the pattern of recording thoughts, actions (doing and saying) and feelings, often immediately after they occur. Others jot down the occasional note to trigger analysis at a later date. Honey (1991) has identified some of the problems associated with keeping personal logs from personal experience and observation. Participants on the NRMC MBA do tend to make notes as they go along, but there is no evidence however that the format of record helps or hinders their reflection and subsequent development.

Perhaps more important than the structure of recording events is the processing of the information generated. Guidance for reflection on actions is given in the form of a simple aide-memoire:

1	What did I do?	What did the other person do?
	What did I say?	What did the other person say?
	What did I feel?	What did I believe the other person felt and what led me to that conclusion?
2	What conclusions can I draw?	
	What could I have done differently and said differently?	
3	What will I try to do next time?	

This is not particularly sophisticated, but is effective. What is apparent is that the earlier phase of diagnostic reflection has developed skills and a greater willingness to the above simple tool. Participants report they take more time out to reflect before/after their actions and to explore alternatives before making decisions.

While the overall MLC process has largely worked, reflection on action is an area NRMC wishes to explore and develop further. The first stage diagnostic reflection works well, and we will see the third stage evaluative reflection is beginning to take shape into a powerful model. The middle stage of reflection on action is perhaps harder to identify because it is often private to the individual and happened "out there" where the action takes place. One attractive line NRMC aims to explore is the use of learning conversations, a form of dialogue with oneself, as described by Harri-Augstein and Thomas (1991). They propose a complete learning process in the humanistic tradition that has parallels with the processes described in this paper. Their approach to reflection on action is more systematic than that currently followed by NRMC MBA participants. It might be that it would enhance the process, though recognition must be given to the practical issues of time and and resources.

MLC Stage 3 – Evaluative Reflection

Towards the end of each MLC, participants begin to write up their learning in a report. There tends to be an overlap between writing preliminary chapters and the learning actions, but nevertheless, a point arrives when full evaluation and assessment has to take place.

Evaluative reflection takes place firstly in the writing of the final report for each MLC and secondly in an oral presentation of the learning to a panel of tutors and representatives of employers. Evaluative reflection aims to lead to a conclusion, in part for assessment purposes and also in recognition of the need for the participant to "stop the world, I want to get off". While personal growth is hopefully continuous, the evidence is that participants benefit from laying down significant marker posts of personal growth and achievement.

Evaluative reflection expects the participant to describe actions and thoughts and to explore them through questions that both challenge self-image and test assumptions. the process reflects the concept of double-loop learning identified by Argyris (1982) and others that expects the participants to go beyond the acquisition and application of methods and rules to the stage of questioning the basic assumptions that underpin them. Further than this, the process seeks to initiate triple-loop learning or a transformation of perceptions and values.

A general format of written report had evolved, and the guidance which is given to participants includes the framework for evaluative reflection. The guidance is:

<u>*Abstract*</u>

- *a summary of what is contained in the report*

<u>*Contents Page*</u>

- *showing headings, pagination and paragraph numbering*

<u>*Context setting*</u>

- *brief analysis of factors having influence over your effectiveness inthe MLC area, to include environment, job deamnds, self (perceived strengths and learning needs, and career aims), and also business factors*

- *original thinking at start of MLC, to include a justification for the choice of behaviours to develop (and why not others), what targeted behaviours might look like, the costs involved and the benefits hoped for*

Action taken

1 Pre-experimentation

• reading, and wider reading, to reflect longer term issues as well as nitty-gritty techniques. This should be a discussion (not regurgitation) of the relevant themes that can be seen in the MLC area, showing a clear understanding of the key thoeries/models /framework. This can best be done by discussing how they compare to practice to your organisation. At this stage forming too certain conclusions until they have personally experimented with them are to be avoided.

  make sure you reference properly the authors you quote.

• thinking/reflection/discussions/feedback from others to test your own perceptions

• planning, showing clearly your intentions, to include techniques to be applied and theories/models/frameworks to be tested, to be justified with a brief anlaysis of possible alternative strategies

2 Experimentation

• actions, thinking, feelings, to reflect both overall strategy and detailed events; good, flowing narrative can be very effective, covering who, how, what, why, when and where. Identify to yourself when you are narrating and when you passing comment.

  Many of the "products" (eg. logs, plans) produced during the MLC are best included in the Appendices. Your main report should reference the Appendices and fit out extracts when suitable.

• feedback you obtained during and after the experimentation, to show how you encouraged valid and relevant feedback (from others and from yourself), how you received it and what you did as a consequence

Learning achieved - evaluative reflection

• what worked and what didn't; why? What theories/models/frameworks/techniques stood up? How well? At all times? What were the influencing factors? Having tried them, where else would they work/not work? What are your own models/frameworks that you have generated against which you will not operate?

• what is different about yourself? What would an observer see different in you? How do you know what he/she might see? How fundamental is the change to your thinking and values, feelings and behaviour? Is it temporary or more permanent? What insights have you gained about yourself as a result of this MLC? How are you more able to handle a wider range of situations? How are you able to handle more critical/difficult situations? What has been/will be the impact of your change on the business?

  What evidence can you provide for any claims made here? How good is the evidence?

• What evidence can you provide for any claims made here? How good is the evidence?

• what will be done in the future, to be a reasonable extension of your learning showing how your thinking needs to develop, what feelings you need to manage better, and what behaviours you will aim to embed or change further. This should be both shorter term and therefore be supported with a working plan, and longer term and reflect your personal career aims.

Reference

• authors, titles, publications, publishers and dates

Appendices

• to contain all material produced in carrying out the MLC (questionnaires, feedback, notes, logs, plans, etc.) that would detract from the flow of the main report if presented there.

This outline is intentionally simple. It separates out the description of experimentation from the evaluation. Evaluative reflection consists mostly of answering questions that should add breadth and depth to the development of understanding. It would not be difficult to sharpen it up with more detailed questions nor to fill any perceived gaps, but perhaps at the risk of being prescriptive and narrowing. The outline is written for participants who are practising managers and who have not written, nor will need to write academic papers.

Complementing the written work is the oral presentation to tutors and employers. This is free-standing and assessable in its own right. It is used partly to develop and assess oral skills, themselves critical to effective management performance, and partly as Fleming (1991) describes as a way of encouraging a more self-conscious awareness of existing competence. This helps build a sound self-image. Additionally, the questions that follow the presentation enable any gap between the evidence provided and that deemed appropriate, often with an exploration of theories in other or hypothetical situations.

Evaluative reflection is done at the end of many programmes, particularly action oriented ones. The above guidance places emphasis in three areas:

- the requirement to integrate theory with experimentation;

- the need to produce evidence of personal change. (This aims to reduce the chance of the written report and supporting evidence being little more than a self-justification of an existing state of effectiveness rather than an evaluation of a changed and developed one. This is particularly valuable in assessing those who may not have incorporated the need for change during the diagnostic stage);

- the requirements evaluative feedback from others.

On this last point, Davies (1993), in reviewing the NRMC MBA, identified certain risks associated with the sole perspective of learning and development coming from the participants alone. The participant may be unwilling or unable to provide evidence of learning. He or she may not be aware of learning. If the learning activities took place in difficult circumstances, the results may appear to be a failure, when by other scales they may be a success. And fourthly, over concern with personal development may lead the participant not to relate it to the context in which he or she operates.

Observations

We have seen that reflection is needed in all three stages of the MLC, and that it takes a different form in each. It is clear that the different forms have a number of consequences for the use of theory and for the conventional view of the learning cycle. This impacts on the role of the tutor.

Use of theory

Eraut cites Oakenshott's distinction between technical knowledge, which can be coded as in a text book, and practical knowledge which can only be experienced in practice. He asserts that such practical knowledge is often uncodifiable, for example the non-verbal behaviours so critical to personal development.

Diagnostic reflection in the first stage uses theory less as codified knowledge but more to expand horizons and open opportunities, and as models of good practice for personal comparison. The choice of theory depends on its appropriateness. Canning (1992) has produced a helpful set of criteria:

* generality
* relevance
* consistency
* completeness
* testability
* centrality
* usability

In the third stage of the MLC, evaluative reflection aims for a dynamic evaluation of theory in light of experience, and experience in light of theory. The dynamic forms a dialogue or conversation that as Black and Sparkes (1982) say reflects that understanding is achieved by a continuous interaction between absorbing new information, trying to use it, and checking whether it was correctly used. This is not a smooth process but often a sequence of accidents.

Additionally, the dynamics encourage the generation of new knowledge. They reflect De Bono's (1990) concept of lateral thinking which is seen as generative, proactive and leading to jumps in understanding. Adair (1990) endorses the value of new (and indeed often unpredictable) information to the participant, but argues such "accidents" happen to those who "deserve" it by being prepared and sensitised, as are participants during diagnosis and planning.

The fact that this dynamic is helped through interaction with others has been noted. Throughout the programme, the benefits of a collaborative approach to development are clear. This reflects the concept of knowledge as a social construct and therefore, as suggested by Bruffee (1986), relative not absolute or fixed. It is constantly being created.

With reflective learning creating knowledge, participants legitimately come to develop their own rules for operating in their circumstances. This raises the interesting question as to whether there is a need for personal ethics to be more explicitly on the agenda of the programme.

The learning cycle is not a simple cycle

This paper has presented learning as a sequence which, while based on Kolb's learning cycle, has some significant variations. The observation one can make is that learning is deepened if a change is made from the four independent stages to one that is more complex. A revised model could be presented as:

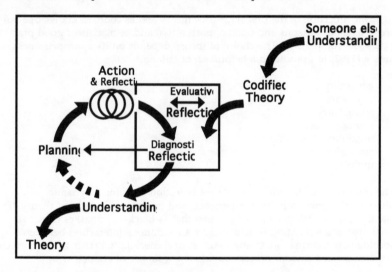

The revised model has three key changes to Kolb's original. Firstly, it distinguishes two outcomes of reflection, one a planning of action, the other the development of understanding, whilst it sees the value of reflection during the action. Secondly, the cycle now sees a dynamic, two-way link between theory and action. Thirdly, it emphasises the difference between theory and understanding, with understanding equating to deep learning.

Role of the tutor

Reflective learning has an impact on the role of the tutor. The tutor becomes a helper and guide, a facilitator. The tutor no longer has to be or is the sole expert. This is not to say that expertise is of no value, merely that the burden of expertise is shared between tutor, participant and employer. The tutor becomes more of a strategist. And the tutor becomes a learner as the participant provides insights to the tutor not seen before.

Since the participant is the initiator and executor of the learning, less energy has to be expended to motivate or set challenging exercises, without compromising the quality of learning.

The changed roles gives the tutor the opportunity to participate more directly in the learning, and therefore has provided an incentive for the learning to be good. Direct involvement in the heart of the action has also given more insights as to what works and what doesn't in ways that a more detached tutor role might not.

Conclusion

Reflective learning has considerably added value to the learning achieved by participants on the NRMC MBA. The strengths of reflective learning lie in the quality it can bring to learning for the participant, its creativity, its integration of theory and action, the location of expertise with those who use it, and its potential to develop a habit of lifelong learning through enabling the participant with learning skills. Crucially, reflective learning fosters real change in participants, both mental and behavioural.

References

Adair, J. (1990).*The Art of Creative Thinking.* Talbot.

Argyris, C. (1982).*Reasoning, Learning and Action* Jossey-Bass.

Black, P. and Sparkes, J. (1982). Teaching and learning; professionalism and flexibility in learning in Bligh. D, *Society for Research into H.E.*

Boak, G. (1990). Developing managerial competences; *The Management Learning Contract Approach.* Pitman.

Boak, G. and Thompson, D. (1992). Using a personal competency model for development and assessment of managers. *A Paper to the Bolton Business School Conference,* Reframing Competences.

Boyatzis, R. (1982). *The Competent Manager.* Wiley.

Bruffee, K. (1986). *Social Construction, Language and the Authority of Knowledge in College English.*

Canning, R. (1992). The missing element in training the trainers: *Integrating Theory with Practice in JEIT,* 16, 2.

Davies, J. (1990). To NRMC 1993 De bono, *Lateral thinking.* Penguin.

Eraut, M. (1985). *Knowledge Creation and Knowledge use in Professional Contexts.*

Fleming, D. (1991). *The Concept of Meta-Competence in Competence and Assessment Issue,* 16.

Harri-Augstein, S. and Thomas, L. (1991). *Learning Conversations* Routlege.

Honey, P. and Mumford, A. (1986). *Manual of Learning Styles,* Honey.

Honey, P. (1990). *Confessions of a Learner Inclined to Lapse in Training and Development.*

Huczynski, A. (1983). *An Encyclopaedia of Management Development Methods,* Gower.

Kanter, R. (1983). *The Change-Masters,* Unwin.

Klemp, G. and McClelland, D. (1986). Executive competence; what characterises intelligent functioning among senior managers. In R. Steinberg and R. Wagner, *Intelligence: Nature and Origins of Competence in Everyday World CUP.*

Knowles, M. (1973). *The Adult Learner; A Neglected Species.* Gulf.

Kolb, D. (1984). *Experiential Learning.* Prentice-Hall.

Kotter, J. (1982). *The General Manager.* Free Press.

Mumford, A. (1990). *Management Development: Strategies for Action.* IPM.

Revans, R. (1980). *Action Learning.* Blond and Briggs.

Smith, R. (1982). *Learning How to Learn: Applied Theory and Adults.* OpenUniversity.

Thompson D and Stephenson M Learning approaches for competent manager development NRMC 1991

Woodcock, M. and Francis, D. (1982). *The Unblocked Manager: A Practical Guide to Self-Development.* Gower.

Chapter 14 Learning on professional courses

Development of Professional Knowledge in Nursing Students

Jenny Spouse

Introduction

With the radical changes in health care provision and nurse education resulting from the development of hospital trusts and the introduction of a new (Project 2000) curriculum for nurse education, understanding of the nature of nursing students' learning and thinking becomes crucial to the success of nurse education programmes.

Until now, research into the education of nursing students has focused on the so-called theory-practice gap, and the influence of socialisation processes to which they may be exposed. How nursing students develop their professional thinking and skills (concepts of nursing and craft-knowledge); the learning activities and structures that help these developments has not yet been explored.

This paper discusses the research process used to identify such learning activities and offers some preliminary findings from a phenomenological study into the way a small group of students experience their first 2 years of learning to become nurses.

My interest is in how any individual who walks from the street into a college of nursing one day walks out 3 or 4 years later an accredited nurse able to fulfil the functions described in the Basic Principles of Nursing Care by the International Council of Nurses:

> "assist the individual, sick or well in the performance of those
> activities contributing to health or its recovery (or to a peaceful
> death) that he would perform unaided if he had the necessary
> strength, will or knowledge. And to do this in such a way as to
> help him to gain independence as rapidly as possible."
> (Virginia Henderson. 1960)

Developing the necessary skills and attitudes to achieve this function requires a major shift in perspective by the novice nursing student which goes beyond normal social behaviour.

Conventional learning theories address the nature of understanding factual information and its integration and use in written activities. Professional behaviour requires the student to use various types of knowledge in their day to day activities. They are confronted with sophisticated clinical situations to be interpreted and responded to. Frequently, such intellectual activities require a wide range of disparate factual information such as knowledge of anatomy, physiology, microbiology, pharmacology, law, psychology, sociology and management theory etc.; as well as a variety of esoteric understandings (ethics, interpersonal relationships, fear, grief, to name a few) which will influence the decision-making process. Traditionally, nursing has been taught along the technical rational model (Schön 1983), in which practitioners were taught the skills and knowledge of nursing and assessed on their ability to replicate them. In the clinical areas students were required to become competent in the use of specific procedures for patient care. The emphasis on task completion by a work force of differing levels of competency was designed to meet the workload needs of an under-resourced service. Inevitably the specific needs of individual patients were neglected (Hollingworth: 1985:13-63). The type of nurse described by Henderson required an approach to care based on humanistic rather than mechanistic ideologies: an overt shift from a technical rational model to that of the I-Thou relationship (Buber 1937:1958), in which each patient is seen as an individual sharing a number of problems similar to other people with the same disease but experiencing them in a manner which is unique to him. The aim of the nurse is to uncover those problems and to find effective ways of helping the patient resolve them. Providing the climate in which such skills can develop requires understanding of how nursing students live through their learning experiences.

The Research

To investigate how a small group of university students learn to become nurses , specifically:

1.   how they conceptualise nursing;

2.   how they develop the attributes of nurses;

3.   the way in which learning to nurse differs from other forms of learning in professional contexts;

4.   the factors that influence the process of becoming a nurse;

5.   the value of reflective practice to the development of understanding and knowledge;

The research approach:

I have used a phenomenological approach. I believe this approach allows me to learn about the meanings that their life experiences hold for them (Merleau Ponty, 1956; Van Manen 1990). In this activity the students share their perspective and allow me to see the world through their eyes, and feelings. Such an approach is intended to avoid the problems of imposing my own interpretations, which may not be those of the students.

The research participants are a group of 6 - 7 full time nursing students who commenced a B.A. (Hons.) Nursing degree in September 1991. They volunteered to participate following a written invitation to twenty students from my seminar group the previous term. On better acquaintance it transpired that six represented the spectrum of characteristics generally shared by nursing students. Their ages range from 18 -28 and they came to the course from differing social and educational backgrounds, intending to qualify for one of each of the four different parts of the professional register, i.e.: Sick Children's nurse, Mental Health nurse, Adult Health nurse. A male student was subsequently invited and agreed to join the group. I later discovered that he had commenced training for the Adult part of the Register some years previously, withdrawn, proceeded to qualify as a Registered Mental Nurse and was now planning to become an adult nurse.

The context - the course structure.

The course leads to a B.A. (Hons), in Nursing and runs over four academic years. It is structured as a modular programme, with each module worth 120 hours of student effort and students taking three or four modules a term. The first and second years are devoted to the Common Foundation Programme, followed by the specialist programme, leading to a specific professional registration in the third and fourth years. Throughout the course, clinical experience constitutes 50% of the total programme hours, with students studying full time, unlike most other nurse education courses in the UK, where students are required to be paid members of the clinical workforce for part of their course. During the Common Foundation Programme students undertake 18 Modules, five of which are based in practice: two in year 1 and three in year 2 (see Fig. 1.).

Figure 1. *Common Foundation Practice Modules : sequence and length of placement over one term:*

Practice Module no. and number of days Year 1.

10 Modules in total	P.1 (1008) : 5 days	P.2. (1009): 10 days

Year 2:

10 Modules in total	P.3 (1011):8 + 10+2	P.4.(1012):10+10	P.5. (10013:22

The philosophy of the course has been influenced by Schön's concept of the reflective practitioner (Schön: 1983), whereby professional knowledge is developed through critical analysis of practice experiences with the support of a clinical expert (known as a mentor). Students are required to organise their attendance in clinical practice around their academic timetable and their mentor. They have to demonstrate proficiency in a number of competencies which have been structured on Carper's Fundamental Patterns of Knowing in Nursing, which are identified as: Empirical, Aesthetic, Moral and Personal (Carper: 1975). Students are encouraged to internalise and integrate their learning through use of personal reflective journals and by presenting a document recording their achievement of competencies in each placement experience. This document is known as a Learning Contract and is assessed on the quality of critical analysis demonstrated.

The research commenced with the students in the second term of the Common Foundation Programme, when they were undertaking the first clinical practice module.

Owing to the logistical difficulties of getting an intake of 160 students through a limited number of placement experiences, the intake is divided into three groups and take the second year placement modules in different sequences. Inevitably the research participants were assigned to different groups and thus take the same modules at different times during the academic year. This made it organisationally difficult to see the students together as a group but allowed me to see how each student responded to their learning experiences.

The methodology.

I have tried to access the students' world partly through the medium of verbal expression and partly through art. Believing that to articulate complex and perhaps painful or difficult experiences requires a sophisticated level of verbal ability, insight and trust, I chose to use art as a second medium through which to gain insight into perhaps deeper and less tangible experiences. A third means of understanding the students experiences has been through observation of their working with their mentor in the clinical area and then meeting to discuss the experience afterwards.

The research has progressed in two phases. The first phase of five group (audio-recorded) interviews, took place over eight weeks in the second term of the first year of their course and gave us the opportunity to develop a relationship which I hoped would encourage the students to feel safe and valued and thus willing to be open about their good and bad experiences. I also envisaged that through sharing the dialogue and returning to the same topic areas over a period of 5 interviews each student would be able to unpeel the layers of their experiences and tap into those that were deep and meaningful. The topics we discussed were their understandings, anticipations and experiences of being seen in the role of a nurse and doing nursing work. Some of this original group had worked as care assistants in nursing homes or had helped to care for an elderly relative. One had, some years earlier, started to train as a nurse but had left after six months. Two of the students had no previous contact with nursing. Later I met four of the students on their own and we talked about their feelings about becoming nurses. These individual conversations contained much of what had arisen in the group but contained richer, fuller descriptions of their insights, expectations and understandings.

In the following year I met the students individually at least three times each term to hear their stories about their clinical placement experiences. These meetings were audio-taped and usually lasted about 50-70 minutes each. The student was asked to tell me about her/his placement experience, how it felt to be working there, whether s/he felt like a nurse and what experiences in the placement had been the most meaningful or significant. To obtain a clearer understanding I sometimes sought clarification or asked probing questions. At the end of term each student created an graphic image which summarised their lasting impression of the term's experiences. The meaning of this picture was then described by the student and discussed.

Seeing the student in practice:

Over the second and third terms I visited all but one of the students in their clinical placements and observed them working with their mentor. These observations lasted approximately 11/2 hours and were followed by an audio-taped interview with the student and her/his mentor together or sometimes separately. The intention of these interviews was to try to understand the thinking behind the actions observed and how the student was able to make use of the experience and whether it matched with the mentor's intention. It would be naive to assume that my presence had a neutral effect on the proceedings. Several of the students and mentors confessed to behaving differently from normal, particularly at the beginning of the observation. However these differences were so subtle that I was unaware of them, except in one instance where the student felt it had been so significant that it had enhanced her placement. As the focus of my attention was the meanings that students had derived from the learning experience during the observation, such changes did not affect the data collection.

The interviews

During the interviews students were invited to tell me what was happening for them on the placement. Depending upon the content of their story I might probe for clarification, or ask general questions about who they talked to about their experiences. As the students became more familiar with the interview process, so their accounts became more comprehensive and thus richer. At the end of each term each student would do a painting to represent her/his experiences as a nurse throughout the term after which s/he would discuss the images represented and their symbolism. During these discussions new aspects of the learning experiences would surface and contribute to their story.

The preliminary analysis:

Analysis of the datum is early and the results so far, tentative, using a modified grounded theory approach. Being familiar with some of the theoretical models for professional learning I was concerned not to allow them to influence my analysis of the transcripts. It was important to remain faithful to the principle of phenomenology and to continue with the process of bracketing off any pre-conceptions and to identify what each student was saying to me. The analysis consisted of carefully reading each transcript and identifying descriptors or themes for significant statements. Spidergrams of these descriptors and their location were developed under themes for each transcript. The next stage has been to re-read all the transcripts in order to check my understanding and to document fully the phrases or sentences that seemed to belong to each particular theme. Theme names were chosen to provide a statement that acted as a receptacle for the related descriptors. This activity has been completed for all the group interviews and for individual interviews of two of the students one more completely than the other. The transcripts from the latter student, Ruth have been broken down under eighteen themes of which four examples are given here.

Theme 1: "working with the mentor " which describes Ruth's experiences of working with her mentor.
Theme 2: "team member" includes her experiences of working with other members of the clinical team and how she feels about being a member of the team.
Theme 3 is labelled "relationships with patients" and applies to accounts of incidents with patients and Ruth's descriptions of her relationships with them.
A fourth theme is concerned Ruth's working knowledge of undertaking practical

tasks such as feeding a patient, how to talk to a patient with a mental disturbance or giving a patient a drug and has the label of "working on the wards".

I then wrote a preliminary case study of Ruth and gave it to her to read and verify. Following our discussion it was modified to correct factual detail rather than the sense making. From the preliminary work on the group transcripts and on Ruth's conversations it has been possible to explore how the themes fitted under the headings of Craft knowledge; Personal knowledge; use of Schema and Socialisation. These categories of professional learning have been derived from the work of the following writers who are mainly concerned with teacher education:

Schön. D. (1983);   Craft Knowledge
Brown, S & McIntyre, D (1993);

Connolly. F.M. & Clandinin. J. (1985); Personal Knowledge
Berliner.D.C. (1987);
Leinhardt. G; Greene. J.G. (1986);

Dreyfus. S; Dreyfus. H. (1980);   Use of a Schema
Benner. P. (1982);

Davis. F.(1975);   Socialisation to the culture of the profession
Zeichner.K; Tabachnick. B.R;Densmore. K. (1987).

Definitions of the four categories:

Craft knowledge: is derived from practical everyday experience rather than from knowledge of theory and is used to guide practitioner in her/his actions. Craft knowledge is often difficult to articulate because it is brought into use as a matter of course, unconsciously and spontaneously.

Personal Knowledge: a pattern of behaving and seeing the world that has been developed through childhood training and contact with cultural values.

Use of Schema: a set of rules or frameworks which can be applied to a given situation and used in the same manner that a recipe or a manual provides directions for cooking or car maintenance.

Socialisation: the adjustments made by the individual in order to become a recognised member of the group. These adjustments may depend upon the perceptions held by members of the new host society of what adjustments the incomer needs to make in order to be accepted. Adjustments that may be necessary order to be accepted are changes in language and vocabulary (Bourdieu:1991), customary behaviour and dress (Schutz:1970).

Writing the Case study of Ruth

In writing the case study of Ruth I have been influenced by the model provided by Bullough, Knowles and Crow (1991), where they have presented case studies of new teachers' experiences during their early days in teaching positions. In presenting Ruth's experiences of becoming a nurse, I have used the framework provided by the four categories of professional learning and have taken phrases and sentences from themes which seemed to match the definitions given above. As much as possible, I have used Ruth's own words to express key aspects of her learning experiences, but rather than bombard the reader with endless dialogue have mixed this with my paraphrasing of her conversations. In most instances this paraphrasing has been validated by Ruth.

Deciding to become a nurse.

The decision to embark upon any professional training which tends to be long and demanding, particularly after success in another field of employment, requires a great deal of courage and commitment. Ruth is a well qualified 26 year old who finished school with 11 '0' Levels and 3 Science 'A' Levels. On leaving school she entered an accountant's office and worked there successfully for five years, studying at night school and gaining Parts 1 & 2 of the Certificate in Accountancy. Ruth had considered becoming a nurse on finishing school but had rejected the idea in her wish to exert her independence by entering the business world. She became aware that her job was not giving her satisfaction and was concerned that the business world was too cut-throat and selfish for her liking. Both her parents had been career nurses and were delighted when she decided to enrol for a degree in nursing. She decided to do a degree rather than the more common certificate or diploma course, believing she would be in a better position to change her mind if nursing did not live up to her expectations and improve future employment prospects. She recognises the strong influence of her parents' experiences of nursing on her decision and her expectation of what she would be doing as a nurse.

Ruth's personal theories and images of nursing.

Memories of her mother nursing her through childhood illnesses and of childhood experiences of seeing patients on her parents' hospital wards provide images of the sort of nurse she would like to become :

> " So I could be a mum to somebody, even if he's a gentleman
> who's 20 years older than me. If I could still create that mumsy

environment that makes me feel secure and hopefully would
make someone else feel nice" (18.3.92: 6)

The vocational intention of achieving "fulfilment" (22.2.92: 3) and "personal
satisfaction rather than monetary gain" did not mislead Ruth into believing all
the glamorous images by which nursing is portrayed. She recognises that
nursing is hard and sometimes unpleasant and difficult work and that she will
have to give care to patients who may be dirty or have unusual social behaviour,
and have to face difficult moral and ethical questions about giving care to
patients who might normally die without expensive and heroic medical
treatment. The social penalties of having to work at times when friends may be
relaxing she recognised and considered to be a means "of protecting her from
getting into a rut" (17.3.92: 2-4). However, Ruth was not entering nursing with a
starry eyed view, her business experience had taught her that good will and
dedication can be exploited by 'the system'. Her perception of her father as a
caring but tough nurse supported this view and encouraged her to believe that
nurses need to be confident, self aware and assertive in order to protect
themselves (2.3.92:6.31 & 18.3.92: 7) and can be so, without losing the essence of
nursing in their care.

The public image of nurses is invariably of a female who is either a ministering
angel or an indefatigable tyrant. Government promotions of nursing as an
attractive job, suitable to the white middle class female, emphasises the caring
aspect which comes 'naturally to women' and thus by implication denies the
need for theoretical knowledge or technical skills. The advertising also implies
that although the pay is not remarkable, job satisfaction provides alternative
compensation (Smith: 1992: 2-19). In her conversations, Ruth said she believed
that she would gain sufficient personal fulfilment to compensate for the financial
loss caused by changing her job. She also believes that a good nurse requires more
than comforting skills:

" to be a good practical nurse, ... making every individual feel
unique .... who knows her stuff, ... to be emotionally responsive
to her patients, ... and to be willing to respond to developments in
the profession"(18.3.92 :9)

These personal theories that support her career decision and her ideas of how she
will be expected to function will affect Ruth's intellectual and social approach to
her learning to become a nurse and the sort of role she takes on (Liston & Zeichner
:1991:61). Throughout the early group interviews Ruth expressed concern and
confusion over the ethical and financial implications of current medical practices
and the role she may have to take (9.3.92: 4; 18.3.92: 8,10). This suggests that she was
already thinking about how she would fit into the overall pattern of care provision
and preparing herself for the ethical dilemmas she may have to face.

As already indicated Ruth has had a number of life experiences which may have prepared her for giving care to patients. Her strong memories of her own mother's approach when she was ill or through watching nurses working on her parents' wards and possibly, from the media, have provided Ruth with a repertory of images that she can use. Despite such knowledge, knowing how to treat patients for whom she has no social or emotional ties must be difficult. Invariably patients are dressed in night attire, which may be soiled or immodest through no fault of the patient or the student. The unpleasant task of cleaning patients or persuading them to take food and drink for which they have no desire but which are essential to their recovery, is a daunting task. No classroom experience can prepare a student, fresh in from the street, to manage her own feelings or the needs of such clients. Ruth's approach to helping such an elderly confused patient to eat breakfast comes from taking time to consider what she might normally do and to try it out:

> "I give her (the elderly confused patient) breakfast and just chat generally and try to do the things that I suppose I'd do for myself, like a couple of mouthfuls of food and then a bit of tea." (18.3.93:9).

The much publicised image of the smiling ever-sympathetic nurse imposes a heavy demand on individuals who may be on their feet providing care for long hours under tiring conditions, such as may be found in a busy ward full of elderly and demented patients or miserable, inconsolable children making their personal pain known to the world. Being pleasant to patients all the time is difficult but Ruth describes it as part of her routine approach:

> "I think it's part of your daily [job] being pleasant to people, at the right time, have a smile on your face and always be willing to have a laugh and a joke." (8.7.93:3)

These simple techniques of feeding a "difficult" patient, giving the appearance of maintaining a calm and pleasant image for the benefit of her patients, stem from Ruth's lived experience (Connolly & Clandinin: 1986; Tamir: 1991) and are used here as a set of practical solutions to practical problems. Such knowledge comes in the form of powerful images or recipes of how she can behave in specific situations, such as feeding patients or going about her daily business in the clinical area. On a higher level Ruth's notion of being a "mumsy person" provides an image of the sort of approach she hopes to be able to take with clients, the belief system that she believes informs her practice whatever the age of her patient.

This practical knowledge is derived from personal experience embedded in Ruth's own history rather than from observing the work of her mentor or by applying theoretical concepts to her practice.

Inevitably there are times when having an experienced practitioner to support her in practice would be useful:

Developing Craft Knowledge.

"I was bathing someone. I got myself in a bit of a pickle on lifting. I got her (the patient) onto a lift and into a bath, fine. She was very thin lady and she said it was really hurting her on the seat. So I said "right if you could raise your bottom, I'll stick a towel underneath. It seemed a great idea to me; and of course by lifting her bottom up, which I could only just do, she flattened out and I just wasn't happy about it. I think I should have gone to get someone and we should have stood her out, but I kept on going. It was probably one of those mornings when I've thought "Oh yes I can do that, I've done it before " and went swanning off. May be I should temper my enthusiasm. (18.3.93:14)

Feeling confident in her practical knowledge encouraged Ruth to embark upon the procedure, only to find that it was more complex than she had envisaged. Without the immediate presence of an experienced nurse she was caught in the dilemma of either stranding her patient on her own, in the hope of finding help immediately, or getting on with the situation. In this situation Ruth needed a different type of knowledge and technical skill; that of an experienced practitioner, who could demonstrate the procedure or guide Ruth through it. This sort of knowledge comes from what Schön calls craft knowledge, whereby the student is guided through the thinking and doing. Working with experts offers images that can be used in other situations:

"I liked a lot of the staff nurses who were mellow when dealing with people there. It was a gently, gently approach and I think you have to take that approach with some people." (18.3.93:12).

and:

"She (the mentor) listene. She would say (to the patient) 'Oh are you in pain? Do you want this?' whereas that wouldn't have occurred to me" (8.7.93: 6)

and :

"It helped because it was quite a technical placement, so we were doing things like the drugs, techniques and she would go through it all. This is the drug chart, this is the... this is what it means, and it struck me as a lot more a learning situation, whereas on V., I learned things but not in a structured way" (8.7.93: 10)

Competent practitioners in their everyday work are in a position to tap into a reservoir of knowledge, largely based on experiences and strategies previously used to manage similar problems. Selecting the appropriate strategies requires consideration of the problem (or framing). Selection of possible solutions depends upon the practitioners' discrimination and judgement, developed through experience. Schön calls such activity of problem identification reflection-in-action (Schön: 1983: 31). However for many practitioners such mental machinations would be difficult to articulate and thus to access (Berliner : 1986: 7). Consequently the student is left to her own conclusions and has to rely upon her limited judgement to manage situations such as the one mentioned above where Ruth was trying to figure out how to position her patient more comfortably and safely in the chair hoist for the bath .

These examples provide indications of two strategies Ruth was using to learn how to practice as a nurse. The first example showed her using personal knowledge to inform her actions when working on her own and the second illustrates learning from an experienced practitioner who offered models of practice, which she could then use later. Through such experiences she will develop her own repertoire of solutions. Initially these solutions may be derived mechanistically from a series of rules or models that have been applied to concrete situation. Dreyfus and Dreyfus identified a five-stage process of skill acquisition in which the learner progresses through five stages of increasing proficiency from novice to expert (Dreyfus and Dreyfus :1980). The novice relies heavily upon the procedural knowledge to guide action and is unable to cope with variations in the process or the situation in which the skill is practised; rather as the new skier may feel happy on the gentle nursery slopes and able to perform graceful snow plough skiing techniques, only to be paralysed with horror at the sight of a steep slope, pustulated with impassable moguls. With increased confidence and experience the practitioner is able to begin to experiment with new ways of behaving in different but controlled situations. To continue with the analogy of the skier, he can progress to trying to snow-plough down a steeper slope including a few bumps to be navigated. This leads on to trying increasingly more challenging situations in different contexts, starting with the gentle slope and graduating to ever more challenging terrain until a repertoire of successful and unsuccessful events has been accumulated. The technical aspects of weight distribution, body position and balance have become less predominating allowing the skier to concentrate on a new set of problems, turning, stopping, recognising and managing speed, managing the unexpected, noticing the texture of the snowy surface and judging the incline of the slope. With these under control, the distribution of weight and balance cease to be a conscious effort thus bringing an increase in confidence and a reduction in pre-occupation with the detail of the activity or the litany of the procedure. Throughout the process the learner is able to accumulate a number of differing solutions to a variety of problems in different contexts. Berliner (1988) believes the five stage acquisition of skill can be applied to teacher education and Benner's research has shown how it relates to the different stages through which newly qualified American nurses progress (Benner: 1984). As with the skier in the process of learning, the student progresses through the Novice stage of pre-occupation with rules, finding it difficult to transfer her knowledge to different situations. In the second stage of Advanced Beginner, the student remains deeply involved with her activity but can begin to recognise the similarities between contexts and thus the use of procedures in different contexts. At the stage of Competent the learner can now prepare for the activity by recognising the situation and what has previously been effective for managing it. The problem is adapted to the solution. In progressing through the stages of Proficient to Expert the practitioner continues to add to her repertoire of experiences and develops the ability to identify and evaluate each situation intuitively. This gives sufficient time to decide upon the best strategy for each specific problem, making the whole process seem effortless. Whilst Benner's findings apply to qualified nurses rather than to students it offers a useful model to explain some of Ruth's progress as the following quote indicates:

> "Something strikes you in particular that you might remember another time but then again, you're seeing so much, and so much looks routine, that you don't really make a mental note of it" (4.12.92:8)

and:

> "Being so new to me, it (doing an aseptic wound dressing) probably does feel pedantic, whereas once you're into it, you probably don't even think about what you are doing. .... but I have to accept at this stage that I'm more concerned with getting the technique right and being competent in that respect. I'm very aware that I must develop more talking to someone to reassure them during the process, but really at this stage I don't see I can cope with everything, and one of the things I put in my learning contract that one way to reassure people is to look as though you know what you are doing" (29.10.93: 4/5)

In the first quotation Ruth acknowledges that she is bombarded with so many new sights and learning experiences, that she is unable to discriminate which are the important ones, an experience typical for novices. A more experienced practitioner, Dreyfus and Dreyfus suggest one who has reached the proficient stage, would cease to be overwhelmed by all the potentially relevant elements and be able to identify those that are significant to the situation (Dreyfus and Dreyfus :1992: 6). In the second, she is recognising her need to follow a procedure carefully before she will becomes competent and this dominates all other considerations. In other situations, Ruth seems to have already developed a sense of what she should be doing and is able to recognise the quality of care that is being delivered, suggesting that she has a schema for some nursing activities but not others.

Using a Schema for care

> " When I'm with other people, because I'm not very good at
> saying we should be doing this, I go along with what they're
> doing and if they are lifting wrongly or whatever, I tend to go
> along with it rather than saying how we should be doing it. I
> don't feel proud of myself I must say" (21.1.93:2).

and:

> "The onus is on me to read texts on how it is done properly but
> I don't feel I was ever shown properly what to do. I felt I was
> competent enough on a helping standard, but whether I had the
> technical ability that a qualified nurse should have I don't
> know" (18.3.91:1).

and:

> ".. it bothers me that I'm being asked to question all these
> ethical issues of nursing, when to my mind I don't know the
> fundamentals. I don't think there is a right and a wrong. How
> can you come to a decision, at the end of the day, you just come
> to a compromise." (18.3.93: 6).

In the above situations, Ruth is learning through personal experience and
observation of others working in the practice area. Her conversations suggest an
ambivalence to theory. She seems to be saying that her nursing care could be
improved if she read the nursing texts but in the practical situation her need is
for practical help in the form of demonstration and supervision. Even then,
some of her role models do not appear to conform to the prescribed procedures,
thus presenting Ruth with a difficult dilemma. On the one hand she knows that
the procedure is unsafe for her and the patient, on the other, she is a very junior
student relying on the good will of the clinical staff to teach her and at the end of
the placement, to pass or fail her. To create a fuss by refusing to co-operate has
serious consequences. In such circumstances it would be understandable if she
allowed herself to be persuaded that the theory (and all those associated with it) is
wrong, thus reducing the personal conflict created by the dissonance in theory
and practice.

The importance of working with an experienced practitioner able to articulate her
practice in the way Schön describes as reflecting-in-action and reflecting-on-
action, provides Ruth with the opportunity to observe how things are done, to
test her understanding and to increase her theoretical knowledge. To achieve
such a perfect relationship requires confidence and interest on the part of the
expert and the student. The nature and organisation of patient care, where
frequently care can be given better by two nurses working together, provides the
ideal opportunity for a neophyte nurse to work with an expert practitioner.
Unfortunately this happens only rarely, due to complex influences of history and
social expectations as illustrated below:

"One of the staff nurses looked after me quite a few times, I think he was bemused as to what to hell I was supposed to be doing or learning" (18.3.93: 5).

and:

"She (the mentor) supervised me for the first two or three (days) and then said 'off you go'. Being given some responsibility, rightly or wrongly, it was what I really craved for - someone trusting me.

.... I actually felt I could walk into the side ward and I had a reason to be there on my own, not just my mentors' side kick. I'd actually gone in there to do something for myself. That felt good." (8.7.93: 9)

Socialisation to the culture of nursing.

The most important aspect of the supervisory relationship was, for Ruth, the quality of the relationship and the sense of recognition of worth and purpose. Her initial experience with the staff nurse who did not know what to do with her and did not appear to have considered discussing his dilemma with her, meant that neither gained from the encounter. In the second instance Ruth is longing to feel that she can do something constructive and useful. Fortunately this need has been recognised by her mentor who delegates activities which she knows Ruth is capable to carry out. Frequently in her conversations Ruth describes the draining sensation of having to follow staff around the wards whilst they go about their nursing care. She uses the metaphor of a "puppy dog, shadowing her mentor" to illustrate her willing eagerness to do something worthwhile, a painful experience for an adult. Throughout her second year Ruth was working in a variety of clinical situations, in the community and the hospital. She was frequently asked or was left to undertake a range of more or less simple tasks. On some occasions she wore uniform. Part of this process was to give her a wide understanding of the range of nursing activities before embarking upon her specialist experiences. It was also anticipated that she would begin to develop a self image of herself as a nurse:

"I felt more of a care assistant status, certainly not nursing wise." (24.3.93:3)

and:

"Wearing a uniform, it tells people who you are and in what capacity. I've got those old fashioned hang ups that nurses wear one" (8.7.93:3)

and:

"You're never really part of the team. I felt I got on with people OK. I don't think being called nurse made me feel part of the team. Just the other staff's attitude towards me and my attitude

and:
> to them." (8.7.93:3).

> "I don't really know what my role is as a student. I find it
> difficult to know exactly what to do. My bottom line was that if I
> can help a bit and learn a bit, then that's all I have to do. I felt
> that by the end of the process I'd done that." (18.3.93:13)

Davis identified six stages through which nurses progress in order toadjust
successfully to the requirements of the nurse role: initial innocence; labelled
recognition of incongruity; psyching out; role simulation; provisional
internalisation and stable internalisation (Davis :1975). Throughout this
discussion evidence has been presented of Ruth's ability to recognise incongruity
between practices and the given theories in some situations and also to "psyche
out" the requirements of her mentors, patients and the placement, which moves
beyond the stage theory offered by Davis. More recent research by Bradby found
that nursing students' successful socialisation to the profession depended upon
their ability to use external and internal support mechanisms (Bradby: 1990).
Ruth gains support and strength from confiding with her mother and two other
special friends:

> "My mother, bless her; if I've had a bad day, she's someone I
> could turn to. I had a bad day on Saturday and felt really down
> but I didn't phone anyone. I've got one or two girls at college,
> one in particular who I know I could phone up because I've
> done the same for her. I think just knowing that helps me to get
> through" (21.1.93: 4).

Without this support Ruth would clearly find the whole process of learning to
become a nurse a painful and lonely experience. Her relationship in the clinical
areas with her mentor becomes even more important, not only to help her adjust
to the strangeness of her new career but also to provide moral support and to
help her with her learning:

> "This mentor thing isn't easy and I'm aware that it's quite false
> at times, particularly when you question the way people
> behave.

> She was perfect for me. .... I felt 'S' was someone I could actually
> say what I thought, whereas others I would talk superficially to
> but I couldn't really open my heart. .... She had a nice manner
> about her, she would really listen, also a nice sense of humour
> which I really liked.

> ... On the whole she would answer, not terribly technical. There
> were younger staff nurses there who could probably have been

a lot more technical for me. I wasn't unduly worried about that,
she was good" (8.7.93: 9-11).

and:

"The more I do the course, the more I realise that it's you and
your mentor and that relationship really makes or breaks what
you get out of it. Talking to some of the girls on the course,
their mentor won't let them do things, so that hinders them,
even at third year level. .. My mentor's great ... She knows her
onion. She can tell me why she's doing things and her reasons.
... (she) has all the research at hand, but also she has all her
experience and the two come together" 29.10.93: 2)

In the clinical area Ruth's relationship with S offers security and support. Ruth
recognises that her own academic knowledge is not going to be advanced by S, but
feels this is compensated by her warmth and openness. Through such
relationships Ruth can relax and begin to take notice of what is happening in the
clinical area and begin to learn (Melia 1987) as is illustrated by the example with
the second mentor. One aspect of the mentor-student relationship is the way it
helps the student adjust to the expectations of the culture of the ward and of the
profession, whilst operating in a secure climate. This paradigm of Socialisation in
which not only adjustment to a new style of understanding values and
behaviours (Dilthey 1976; Husserl 1929: Schutz 1970): is required but also a new
field of language use (Bourdieu:1991) is often painful. During one placement
Ruth is rebuked for using terms of address that are frequently used in her own
social background.

"I'd like to think its' just my general way of dealing with
people. I accept that I often call people "love' and "dear'. You
shouldn't use patronising terms, but then I don't see it as
patronising. In the East End of London, where I come from you
get called that all the time." (18.3.93:7)

Being told that she should not call patients "love" or "dear", on the basis that it
could be interpreted as patronising was a puzzling experience but one with which
she was prepared to accept as part of getting used to the new cultural expectations
of the profession. Other experiences to which she was exposed, offered more
difficult dilemmas and caused her re-evaluate her expectations of the nursing
role critically:

" one lady was so pleased to see the community nurse, ... and I
really thought she was bringing her a breath of fresh air. I found it
quite sad. .... It struck me, it's a very long term thing (looking after
elderly chronically ill clients in the community) and in a way it's
quite cruel as it's just a job . But as a nurse you have to remember

your own sanity, that it's just a job because otherwise you could get sucked into doing the cooking for them (the clients), not in professional time, but in your private time, say, oh I'll come back this evening... I think that's quite a difficult decision" (28.10.92: 3).

Ruth's ability to articulate and write about her experiences is recognised as being very good. She consistently receives B+ grades for her Learning Contract, in which she has to discuss her clinical experiences. Generally she finds the preparatory reading and subsequent documentation laborious. Her art work illustrates how much she would prefer not to spend her time in the library but in clinical practice.

"I suppose they (Learning Contracts) do help somehow, but I still find them a bit of a paperwork exercise after the event that I've got to put together. .... may be they do subconsciously put a framework into your head about how you're going to do things, but I don't think, "today my strategy is to talk to this patient," that's not the way I do things" (8.7.93: 11)

These four models of professional learning provide a framework that is useful for presenting the case study of Ruth, but as the reader will recognise, there are some areas of professional knowledge development which are still to be addressed. The material that has been used for the case study, takes us up to just over half way through Ruth's professional preparation. She has five more terms before she finishes her course and so the record of Ruth's experiences are as yet, incomplete. It is possible that her experiences are different from those of the other research participants, and that with further data analysis new material will arise which may help to address the following questions about:-

1. the way in which learning to nurse differs from other forms of learning in professional contexts;
2. the way in which nursing students develop their knowledge and expertise;
3. the use and value of reflective practice in the development of understanding and knowledge.

References

Anderson W. (Ed) 1977. Therapy and the Arts: Tools of the Consciousness. New York. Harper Collophon Books.

Bendall E. (1976). Learning for Reality. Journal of Advanced Nursing. vol.1; 3-9.

Benner P. (1982). From Novice to Expert. American Journal of Nursing. March 1982. vol. 82;no. 3;402-407.

Benner, P. (1984). From Novice to Expert. Reading, U.S.A., Addison Wesley.

Berliner D.C. (1987) Ways of thinking about students and classrooms by more and less experienced teachers. in Calderhead J. (Ed) 1987. Exploring Teachers' Thinking. London. Cassell.

Bradby M. (1989). Self esteem and status passage. University of Exeter. unpublished PhD Thesis

Bourdieu, Pierre. (1991). Language & Symbolic Power. Oxford. Polity Press)

Buber Martin. (1937). I and Thou. English Translation, Second (revised) Edition 1958. Edinburgh. T and T Clark Ltd.

Bullough, R V. Knowles, JG. Crow, NA. (1991) Emerging as a teacher. London. Routledge.

Carper BA. 1978. Fundamental patterns of knowing in nursing. Advances in Nursing Science. 1978 Vol 1, pp. 13-23.

Connolly, F.M. & Clandinin. J (1985) Personal practical Knowledge and Modes of Knowing : Relevance for Teaching and Learning; in Eisner E (ed.) 1985; 84th Year Book of National Society for the Study of Education. Chicago. University of Chicago Press.

Cortazzi D; Roote S. (1973). Don't talk draw! the use of illustrations in learning from critical incidents in patient care. Nursing Times. August 30th 1973. vol. 69;no. 35;1134-1136.

Davis F. (1975). Professional Socialisation as subjective experience, the process of doctrinal conversion among student nurses; in Cox C and Mead A(Eds.) (1975) A Sociology of Medical Practice. London. Collier MacMillan. pp. 116-131.

Dreyfus S. and Dreyfus H. (1980). A five stage model of the mental activities involved in direct skill acquisition. (Supported by US Airforce Office of Scientific Research (AFSC) under contract (F49620-c-0063)with the University of California.

Dreyfus, H. L. &. D., S.E. (1986). Mind over Machine: the Power of Human Intuition & Expertise in the Era of the Computer. Oxford, Basil Blackwell.

Dreyfus, H. L., Dreyfus, Stuart E (1992). The Relationship of Theory and Practice in the Acquisition of Skill. Personal communication to the author.

Eraut M. (1985). Knowledge Creation and Knowledge Use in Professional Contexts. Studies in Higher Education. 1985. vol. 10; 117-133.

Henderson, Virginia, (1960)Basic Principles of Nursing Care. Geneva. International Council of Nurses; revised edition 1969

Leinhardt G, Greene J.G. (1986) The Cognitive Skill of Teaching. Journal of Educational Psychology. vol. 78; 75-79

Lincoln Yvonna S, Guba Egon G. (1985). Naturalistic Inquiry. Newbury Park, California. Sage Publications.

Liston, D. P. Zeichner, K. M. (1991). Teacher's Knowledge, Models of Inquiry and the Social Context of Schooling. Chapter 3 in Teacher Education and the Social Conditions of Schooling. New York, Routledge. 60-88.

McIntyre, Donald,. (1988) Designing a Teacher Education Curriculum. from Research and Theory on Teacher Knowledge in Calderhead, J Teachers' Professional Learning. Lewes. The Falmer Press.

Melia, K. (1987). Learning and Working : The occupational socialisation of nurses. London, Tavistock Publications.

Merleau Ponty, M. (1956) What is Phenomenology ? Cross Currents. vol. 6. pp. 59-70

Mezirow J. (1981). A critical theory of adult learning and education. Adult Education. Fall 1981. vol. 32;no. 1;3-24.

Oleson, V.L. & Whittaker, E.W.(1968). The Silent Dialogue: A study of the social psychology of professional socialisation. San Francisco. Jossey Bass.

Schön. D.A. (1983) The Reflective Practitioner : How Professionals Think in Action. New York Basic Books.

Schön D. (1987). Educating the Reflective Practitioner: Toward a New Design for

Teaching and Learning in the Professions. San Francisco. Jossey Bass.

Schutz, A. (1970) in :On Phenomenology and Social Relations: Selected Writings. Wagner, H R. (ed) Chicago. University of Chicago Press.

Smith, P. (1992). The Emotional Labour of Nursing. London, MacMillan.

Van Manen, M. (1990) Researching Lived Experience. The Faculty of Education, University of Toronto. The Althouse Press.

Wadeson H, Durkin J, Perach D. (Eds.) (1989). Advances in Art Therapy. New York. John Wiley and Sons.

Waller Diane and Gillroy Andrea (Eds.).(1992). Art Therapy A Handbook. Buckingham. Open University Press.

Wyatt, J.F.(1978). Sociological Perspectives on Socialisation into a Profession: A Study of Student Nurses and their Definition of Learning. British Journal of Educational Studies. Vol. XXVI; No.3; pp 263-276.

Zeichner K.M., Tabachnick B.R. and Densmore K. (1987). Individual, Institutional and Cultural Influences on the Development of Teachers' Craft Knowledge, in Calderhead J. (Ed) (1987). Exploring Teachers' Thinking. London. Cassell.

Reflection on Action: Supervising In-Service Lecturers' Professional Practice and Learning

Jonathan Simmons, Brunel College of Arts and Technology

---

1. Introduction

Visits to observe trainee lecturers during their Supervised Teaching Experience (STE), on courses like the in-service Certificate in Education, are intended to improve the professional practice of trainee lecturers. One possible way of improving this practice is via the conversation between the visiting tutor and the trainee lecturer which takes place after the observed class. These conversations can be considered as ideal examples of reflection on action; they are one significant arena in which reflective practices can be promoted on such courses (Calderhead and Gates, 1993). As the curriculum in the post-compulsory education sector moves further towards learner-led activities and activity (work)-based learning, such reflective dialogues will increase in importance for improving student learning.

There has been little research on what actually happens in such conversations (Zeichner and Tabachnick, 1982), despite the large body of writing on other aspects of STE (Boydell, 1986), including detailed accounts of how supervision should be undertaken (Handel and Lauvas, 1987) and organised (Turney, 1982a). The study reported here extends recent research by examining such post-observation conversations with trainee lecturers from the post-compulsory sector on an in-service Certificate in Education course at a large college in South London. This is a significantly different research population than those in previous studies, which have been mainly school teachers on pre-service courses, including work from America where the role of the supervisor is somewhat different from that in England (Stones, 1984a).

Previous research into STE (Boydell, 1986) has focussed on the question of whether visiting tutors were effective in improving trainee teachers' classroom practice. The results tended to indicate that visiting tutors had relatively little positive influence because of the large number of other variables which affected a trainee teacher's development. But this research had relied mainly on interviews and questionnaires, and "in several of the studies no attempt was made to examine even the overt behaviours of the supervisors" (Zeichner and Tabachnick, 1982, p. 39) in post-observation conversations. In other words, judgments were being made about whether STE visits were effective with little study of what actually went on in them.

The aim of the present research was to examine the nature of such discussions and how the visiting tutors attempted to achieve the course aim of encouraging the development of reflective practice. The study adopted a combination of qualitative and quantitative research methods in order to provide a fuller picture of the conversations and to examine the uses of quantification in research which was qualitative and interpretative in design (Silverman, 1986).

The quantitative model adopted in the present study was one which had been developed in similar research (Zeichner and Liston, 1985) and it was applied to tape recordings of the conversations made by the visiting tutors themselves. The qualitative analysis focused on the tactics adopted by visiting tutors in attempting to achieve the aims of the course. In addition, in recognition of the need to consider the meanings that the participants gave to their verbal behaviour, these methods were supplemented by interviews with participants after they had read the initial quantitative and qualitative analysis of their conversation. These interviews were intended partly to provide an interpersonal test of the validity and reliability of the analyses.

One key distinction of the present study is its focus on what actually happens in such conversations rather than on what ought to happen. This piece of research has lead me to raise some critical questions about theories of reflection and the reflective practitioner which are influential in curriculum development in the post compulsory sector (FEU, 1981) and particularly in teacher education (Grimmett and Erickson, 1988).

2. Research Context

The role of, and procedures for, STE post-observation conversations at the college fall within the scope of what is termed "clinical supervision", which has been defined as "the rationale and practice designed to improve the teacher's classroom performance. It takes as its principal data the events of the classroom. The analysis of these data and the relationship between supervisor and teacher form the basis of the programme, procedures and strategies designed to improve the students' learning by improving the teacher's classroom behaviour." (Cogan, 1973, p. 4). This is in contrast to the historically dominant emphasis in supervision on authoritarian modes of teacher evaluation which focussed on judging, rather than improving, a teacher's performance in the classroom.

The aims of the course for STE visits can be summarised as having an expressed emphasis on promoting personal, intellectual and practical aspects of reflective practice. Trainee lecturers are required to keep an STE file "to provide evidence of appropriate record keeping for and reflection on their teaching . . . Typically it contains examples of schemes of work, syllabi, class plans, evaluations of lessons, assessment of students, course evaluations etc." (course documentation). It provides one method which "fully integrates the STE process into the rest of the course" (course documentation).

The STE visit assessment form records the visiting tutor's observations under three sections covering planning and preparation, performance, social relationships and assessment, and negotiation of an action plan for future STE visits.

2.1. The visiting tutors

The visiting tutors (VT1 - 5) in the study were all five colleagues in the Education Studies Group (ESG) at the college. Each member of the group has responsibility for tutoring groups and for teaching units of the courses. The ESG meets regularly every week for team meetings and could be considered to have a strong collaborative and supportive culture with many shared implicit aims.

2.2. The trainee lecturers

Trainee lecturers in general come from a wide variety of backgrounds and subject areas, from accountancy to yoga. They are expected to have a relevant subject qualification as well as relevant work experience.

Trainee lecturers have many reasons for taking the course, from the purely instrumental person who is required by their employer to attend, to those who want to improve their teaching methods and learn more about the post-compulsory education system.

The five trainee lecturers in the study were on various stages of the Cert Ed and on different modes of attendance. They also taught very different subjects, so there was very little consistency between them as to their experience of the course and they cannot be considered as a representative sample. However, in terms of their experience of teaching and of the Cert Ed course they can be put in order from TL1, the most experienced, to TL2, the least experienced.

3. Data Collection and Analysis

The data collection was carried out by the five visiting tutors, who were asked to tape record any two post-observation conversations with trainee lecturers whom they were due to visit during the spring and summer terms 1991. Full cooperation was received from all the trainee lecturers.

Of the ten recordings made, following a small pilot, only seven were usable. Two of the recordings were so faint that they could not be transcribed, and one visiting tutor, through a variety of circumstances, managed to record only one conversation. The result was therefore a small sample which must act as a pilot study rather than a statistically random research sample.

However, two of the trainee lecturers were visited by two different sets of visiting tutors so that some comparison between different visiting tutors' approaches with the same trainee lecturer was possible: trainee lecturer TL1 was visited by visiting tutor VT1 and VT4, while trainee lecturer TL4 was visited by visiting lecturer VT3 and VT5. Two visiting tutors did visit two different trainee lecturers so comparisons were also possible between the same visiting tutors' approach with different trainee lecturers: VT2 visited TL2 and TL5, and VT5 visited TL3 and TL4.

The quantitative analysis adopted a procedure used in several other studies of this type (e.g., Zeichner and Liston, 1985 Weller, 1971). The basic unit of analysis was the "thought unit", which is defined as the smallest meaningful segment of verbal behaviour (Bales, 1951).

The resulting tapes averaged 195 thought units per transcript and ranged in length from 148 to 330. In contrast to the Zeichner and Liston approach, where "ten-minute segments (either from the first or the last 10 minutes) were abstracted . . . for the purposes of analysis" (Zeichner and Liston, 1985, p. 160), the whole of each transcript was analysed. The research sample was intended to allow analysis in depth rather than in breadth.

The quantitative model distinguished between the logical dimension of discourse, i.e., how ideas were expressed, and the substantive dimension, i.e., what was talked about. The logical dimension was divided between factual discourse, concerned with what has occurred, prudential discourse, concerned with suggestions or evaluations, justificatory discourse, concerned with reasons for alternative courses of action, and critical discourse, concerned with the adequacy of such reasoning. The substantive categories were aims, content and materials of lessons, teaching methods, lessons as a whole, students, context and other factors (Zeichner and Liston, 1985).

The statistics were looked at from two perspectives. The first showed the relative contribution of each speaker in each category and the second showed the relative role of each category in each speaker's contribution. The qualitative analysis consisted of identifying the tactics which the visiting tutors adopted in giving feedback to the trainee lecturers in relation to the overall course goals for STE. Participants were then interviewed after they had had time to reflect on the quantitative and qualitative analyses they had received. This analysis tried to illuminate the actors' meanings from the transcripts and tapes.

4. Quantitative Data

Analysis of the data showed a fair exchange of conversation between participants, with trainee lecturers contributing on average 41%, and visiting tutors 59%, of the thought units, ranging from 20% to 59% for trainee lecturers and from 41% to 80% for visiting tutors.

4.1. Logical categories

The most common types of statement in the conversations were informational in the factual category and evaluative in the prudential category. An example of the informational category is TL1 speaking about where his students sat: "That has been the pattern of seating for the last two or three sessions"; an example of the evaluative category came from VT1: "I think you had a pretty good spread of contributions from the group." When we break the statistics down between trainee lecturers and visiting tutors, we find that the most common types of statement from trainee lecturers were informational and pragmatic justification, whereas those from visiting tutors were descriptive, instructional and evaluative. For example, TL3 explaining the constraints of her course: "There isn't enough time. The course is too short. I've got 22 weeks, two and a half hours a week, and I'm trying to get them from not knowing anything about typing to passing an exam"; VT2 is commenting on VL5's use of a handout: "It's quite well worded, it's quite clear. When you introduced it, you said you were going to do an activity on group work; it might have been a good idea then to relate it to the work situation. You mentioned this later in the session but you could have mentioned it at the beginning."

The overall conclusion was that trainee lecturers tended to give information pertinent to, but not verifiable from, the observation of the specific lesson, and to justify their actions in pragmatic terms. They did this in response to the visiting tutors' descriptions of factors verifiable by observation of the specific lesson, their proposals of solutions to pedagogical problems, and their judgements on the trainee lecturers' work. This conclusion goes someway to support previous research which reported that trainee lecturers felt that visiting tutors did not understand the context in which they worked (Boydell, 1986). It also parallels the conclusions of Christensen's (1988) and Zeichner and Liston's (1985) work as regards the distribution of discourse between the categories.

4.2. Substantive categories

The most common topics in the conversations concerned procedures (i.e., methods used in planning, conducting and evaluating lessons) and students (i.e., their actions, thoughts or products). While comments on procedures tended to be evenly divided between references to specific procedures used in the observed lesson and references to procedures in general, the comments on students tended to be specific to the lesson rather than general. When we break this down between trainee lecturers and visiting tutors, we find that the most common topics from trainee lecturers were general references to procedures, specific references to students and comments on the context of their work, (e.g., classroom, college organisation, etc.). The most common topics from visiting tutors referred to procedures and to students specific to the observed lesson; these were followed by general references to procedures. Thus it appeared that the visiting tutors' descriptive, instructional and evaluative discourse tended to concern specific procedures and specific students, while the trainee lecturers' informational discourse and pragmatic justification tended to concern general procedures, specific students and the context of their work. This conclusion tends to confirm the impression, noted above, that trainee lecturers tended to explain and justify their actions in pragmatic and general terms in response to visiting tutors' specific suggestions and evaluations about procedures and students.

Comparisons with the work of Christensen indicate that, whereas participants in her study talked overwhelmingly in specific terms about teaching, in the present study they tended to be more evenly divided between specific and general terms. In her study visiting tutors tended to talk mostly in general terms, "making connections to general theory and principles involved in teaching" (Christensen, 1988, p. 281), while the visiting tutors in the present study tended to talk more in specific terms. Comparisons with the work of Zeichner and Liston (1985) indicate a similar distribution within the substantive categories, but since they do not report on the balance between specific and general references no other comparison was possible.

However, the low occurrence in the substantive category of goals in the conversations in Zeichner and Liston's study was replicated in the present study. Their conjectured explanation for this absence is that the goals of trainee lecturers' teaching are already set and so not open for discussion (Zeichner and Liston, 1985, p. 169). But it is difficult to draw any further conclusions because of a weakness in the analytical model. The category of procedures encompasses too wide a subject area. If it was broken down into separate categories for planning, conducting and assessing a lesson, then the role of goals in post-observation conversations might be more clearly visible.

It would also be useful, in any further study, to be able to determine the precise relationship between the logical and substantive categories. If the transcripts had been coded using appropriate computer software a more subtle analysis of the occurrence of a particular logical category in relation to the substantive categories would have been possible (Fielding and Lee, 1991).

5. Qualitative Analyses

One important concept which emerged from the transcripts of the conversations was that of barriers to change.

5.1. Barriers to change
Underlying the concept of barriers to change are a number of assumptions which need to be clarified. First, the concept assumes that all trainee lecturers resist change. While it is probably correct that most people are resistant to change in some areas, it should not be assumed from the following discussion that all trainee lecturers resist change all the time. In fact most trainee lecturers appear to be receptive to change and welcome an external view of their work which they rarely get from their own institutions.

445

Second, there is the assumption that if only the barriers could be removed then change would be possible. What this ignores is the fact that some aspects of the barriers may be impossible to remove. There may well be underlying differences which cannot be overcome simply by a better method of explanation or a better way of linking up with a trainee lecturers' way of thinking.

I identified eight barriers to change from these conversations, although they were not common to all the trainee lecturers.

The main source of barriers, as previous research had suggested, was that of visiting tutors not understanding the context in which trainee lecturers worked. TL3 and TL4's justification of their choice of teaching methods by the pressure of teaching to exams could be characterised in this way. The quantitative analyses confirm this point because of what they showed about the way in which trainee lecturers tended to talk about their work.

Connected to this factor was the second type of barrier, which stemmed from different perceptions of what had occurred in an observed lesson. For example, TL4 had used many questions to students in his lesson, as he saw it, to check on their learning. He concluded from their lack of answers that they had not learnt what he had intended, so he told them the answers. VT5 felt that TL4 answered his own questions too quickly and that by doing so TL4 was possibly undermining his students' confidence.

The underlying tension between the visiting tutors' assessment and counselling roles was the source of the third set of barriers. For the assessment function, visiting tutors are required to pass or fail trainee lecturers and the result forms a significant part of the overall assessment of the qualification. The counselling function of an STE conversation is intended to help trainee lecturers to develop themselves: to identify strengths and weaknesses and to build on strengths and improve on weaknesses. The former function can be viewed by both trainee lecturers and visiting tutors as threatening, such that it conflicts with the latter function, which is intended to be supportive and advisory. This tension was expressed explicitly by VT2 in her conversation with TL5, and all the participants acknowledged in interview that this tension created anxiety in the trainee lecturers which had to be taken account of.

Connected to this barrier was the fourth type, which stemmed from the participants' desire to avoid open disagreement. There were no explicit disagreements in the transcripts. All the visiting tutors said in interview that they avoided disagreements as far as possible because they found them unproductive. In interview, trainee lecturers talked about the ways in which they avoided disagreements either by not expressing their views or by not acting on advice given except, where it fitted their predispositions. There was an implicit recognition of the desire not to antagonise someone who holds the power to pass or fail them.

The next four barriers are linked to the participants' ideas about teaching.

A key set of barriers stemmed from differences in values. TL1 summed up this barrier when he commented, in interview, that there were suggestions that he listened to but did not take up. For example, in his case a profile of the students he taught had been recommended in all his STE conversations but he had never taken it up because he did not feel morally comfortable with it, even though VT4's argument for it had been very persuasive.

A sixth set of barriers stemmed from the way in which trainee lecturers thought about their work and their teaching style. For example, VT5 made several suggestions to TL4 about adopting more student-centred approaches such as the use of newspaper articles or case-studies. It was apparent from the transcript that, while TL4 could accommodate the use of newspaper articles relatively easily, the use of case studies would require a more radical reorientation in his whole approach to student learning.

This points to a seventh set of barriers stemming from the differing ideas which visiting tutors and trainee lecturers hold about what makes for good teaching. For example, VT2's specific suggestion to TL5 that he drew the principles of team work out of the group discussion after the activity rather than spelling them out himself beforehand implied a shift from deductive to inductive teaching strategies. TL5's response indicated that his priority was to make sure that his students got the point of the exercise.

Underlying many of the previous barriers, is the final and greatest barrier which concerns linking theory and practice. Traditionally theory is the area which for a variety of reasons has been regarded negatively in teacher training courses. One reason for this is that "when people start using a theory they tend to stop calling it a theory" (Eraut, 1989, p. 184). This is compounded by the inadequate ways in which theory has been linked to practice (Carr, 1980).

These reasons are clearly evident in the concrete terms in which TL3 explained her reasons for not showing alternative ways of typing up a given document:

> I did show one person something that somebody else had done in the lesson, because I said Tracy had squashed it up and it's very unusual because Tracy usually does very good work . . . and I showed her something somebody else had done and said don't you think this is a much better way of displaying it.

While it is possible to interpret these statements as implying references to theoretical concepts, TL3's use of such concrete cases was not extended to conceptual generalisations about teaching methods. This absence of links to theory was reinforced by the way the documentation of her lesson made assumptions about the use of methods which were not shared by her visiting tutors VT3 and VT5. It's not the case that she was not using theory, but that she was using it intuitively in utilitarian terms in ways which were endorsed by her work experience.

The tension between the ways in which visiting tutors and trainee lecturers view and express theory can lead to misunderstanding of what issues are being discussed and is a major barrier which has to be overcome in STE conversations (as well as in other parts of the course). This issue will be discussed further in a subsequent section.

5.2. Tactics to overcome barriers
The discussion of the assumptions underlying the concept of barriers to change in the previous section applies equally to a consideration of tactics to overcome barriers. The fact that the tactics are identified here does not mean that they are intrinsically effective in bringing about change, only that they have been adopted by the visiting tutors in these cases as possible ways around the barriers which they perceived. Their degree of success in actually moving trainee lecturers in the direction of the course goals has not been evaluated in the present study.

5.2.1. Setting the climate
Visiting tutors adopted two main tactics for starting STE conversations: open questions, such as "How do you feel that went ?", "If you were doing that session again, is there any way in which you would change it ?" and telling trainee lecturers whether they had passed or not. These were not discrete alternatives, since they were combined by some visiting tutors, but they can be considered as opposite tendencies.

The choice of opening depended on the visiting tutors' perception as to what would make trainee lecturers concentrate more during the following discussion and make them more receptive to suggestions. Informing some trainee lecturers of the result of the observation would relieve their anxiety and allow them to concentrate; for others starting with open questions would have the same effect. These tactics were one way of coping with the tension between assessment and counselling.

The use of initial open questions also had a number of other purposes. They were seen positively as a way of letting trainee lecturers talk about their work, encouraging confidence and autonomy in their own judgement as well as attempting to overcome a number of barriers. The barriers of visiting tutors' supposed lack of understanding of trainee lecturers' work context could be addressed by getting the trainee lecturers to identify the significant pressures on them; the barrier of trainee lecturers' thinking about their work could be addressed by visiting tutors connecting their suggestions to trainee lecturers' self-evaluations. The answers to these open questions could also reveal any differences in values.

The other tactic, which normally occurred near the start of the conversations, of establishing the typicality of the observed lesson, was adopted for similar reasons. For example, VT2 asked TL2 "Was that a standard morning's work ?" and was able to adapt her suggestions according to the answer.

The major difficulty with using the open questions arises if the visiting tutors' and trainee lecturers' view of the lesson conflicted. Tactics which visiting tutors adopted in order to avoid open disagreement are discussed in the next section.

5.2.2. Making suggestions

One key tactic was for visiting tutors to give positive feedback to trainee lecturers on their teaching performance before making suggestions for improvements. For example, VT2 compliments TL5 on his use of small group work:

> I thought you left them alone sufficiently but you did go up and
> eavesdrop and you did check their timing which was really
> important. One of the things about group activities is to jot down
> the things you overheard and bring them back at the end so that if
> they're not making the points you want you can prompt them.

This type of tactic was intended not only to boost trainee lecturers' confidence but also to allow the visiting tutors to approach trainee lecturers' weaknesses through their strengths. They argued that approaching weaknesses through strengths not only made trainee lecturers more receptive to suggestions but also provided practical ways in which trainee lecturers could transfer their learning or practice from one area to another. It was one way of attempting to overcome the barriers of trainee lecturers' thinking about their work, and of starting to link theory and practice.

Another tactic was to approach suggestions through factual questions in order to establish the
context within which suggestions had to operate:

> VT1: When they [students] present their assignment . . . do they have to
> give a verbal precis of the content ?

> TL1: They don't have to on this occasion, but certainly when they do the
> next one there will be a presentation.

> VT1: Will they have to defend what they have done ?

TL1: Yes.

VT1: I wonder how you saw them moving to that position. Obviously Paul will have no problem or Natalie, but how does Clare get to a position where she can do that ?

It is clear from the transcripts that both the participants saw such an approach as implying suggestions and evaluations in practical terms with which trainee lecturers would feel comfortable, but also as linking the suggestions to concepts developed on the course.

The tension between assessment and counselling clearly permeated the issue of making suggestions. Some suggestions were either phrased in "soft" terms, such as "I'll leave that one with you", or they were surrounded by so much positive feedback that they did not stand out clearly. These types of formulation prioritised the counselling function in that they recognised that visiting tutors cannot force trainee lecturers to take up practices, except where they are part of the course requirements.

But using course requirements, such as the STE commentary file, as a reason for adopting a practice has at least two attendant problems. First, it provides an extrinsic reason which may either not outlast trainee lecturers' attendance on the course or extend to their other work. Second, it resolves the tension between assessment and counselling in favour of assessment, which can raise more barriers than it lowers. However, the STE file can be used to ensure that issues are followed up by subsequent visiting tutors. This was clearly the case with TL3, where the issue of inadequate course documentation was addressed by VT3 as a result of his seeing the STE form from TL3's previous visit by VT5. On the other hand the case of VT1's continued resistance to the use of students profile, mentioned above, would have benefited from closer follow-up from visiting tutors.

Obviously there will be instances where there is no other option but to use course requirements to ensure that a suggestion is adopted. VT3 demonstrated how the use of the STE file as a course requirement could be made more acceptable by stressing its use as a way for TL3 to demonstrate fully her abilities. In general, however, both course requirements and other practices needed to be suggested on the basis of what is best practice.

An interesting tactic adopted by VT5 was posing alternative interpretations of trainee lecturers' actions to them as one way of overcoming several of the barriers to change. An example of this occurred when she addressed the issue of the way in which TL4 answered his own questions to students, mentioned earlier:
When you're asking questions and they didn't quite get it, was it as

a check on learning - did that signify to you that they didn't quite
get it, therefore I need to explain it again, or they didn't quite get it,
so I will tell them what they should know and carry on ?

VT5 said that she tried to pose the alternatives in such a way that both would
require something to be done, in this case either TL4 would be more supportive
or he would refrain from answering the questions for the students. She also tried
to pose the alternatives in such a way that, whichever alternative the trainee
lecturer chose, her initial evaluation of the incident was accepted as accurate. Her
exchanges with TL4 were significant and illuminating because they really
explored his thinking and reasoning in such a way that he considered the
purposes for his actions and the alternatives he could adopt.

One key to the way some visiting tutors made suggestions was the use of the STE
form, which was used for written feedback, on the observed lesson, to structure
feedback in that the STE form provided participants with an understanding

about each other's expectations and . . . [a] shared agreement about what
ought to be observed and analysed, [in such a way that] feedback will
have a chance to operate positively in the supervision cycle (Turney,
1982b, p. 165).

Whether the visiting tutors used it as a structure or not depended partly on
experience and partly on personal style. Those who did use it felt that it gave the
post-observation conversations validity and consistency and that it provided a
non-threatening, neutral and objective way of giving feedback and addressing
issues. They tended to use the form both as a prompt from which to work rather
than as the maximum of what they had to do and also as a way of ensuring that
they did not leave anything out. Those who did not use the form to structure
their feedback did use it as a prompt for ideas, as a way of giving both positive
and negative feedback, and as a written version of what was said. But they
preferred to focus on the specific aspects which they felt were relevant to the
particular lesson.

From the quantitative evidence, using the STE form gave a more balanced
coverage of the categories in the analytical model. From the qualitative evidence,
using the STE form gave more explicit links to theoretical concepts embedded in
the different sections of the form, but in the view of some visiting tutors its use
did not always get at the most relevant issue in each case. The issue of linking
theory to practice is the subject of the next section.

5.2.3. Linking theory and practice
There were many examples in the conversations of visiting tutors connecting
specific descriptions of what had occurred in a lesson with explicit references to

educational concepts. For example, in an extended commentary on TL2's cookery class for special needs students, VT2 said:

> One of the reasons it was messy as you called it was because you were trying to ensure that each student did a range of tasks . . . One of the reasons it was messy was because you were making demands on them so I certainly wouldn't knock that . . . I thought that there was a lot of planning and forethought that went into it that may not be immediately obvious . . . I thought the timing was good, I thought your sequencing was good and I liked the initial start with the picture of the pizza. I think having a summary of what it was going to look like at the end was a good thing to start with. And I thought it was good the way you revealed each of the ingredients rather than having them all on the page.

The concepts used in this passage are those inherent in lesson planning, the need to have a demanding but achievable goal for students and to break the lesson down into manageable chunks.

VT4's praise of TL1's lesson includes the following passage:

> The combination of content and method, as I said earlier, the goals and activities were very much integrated, so that matched very well. All the time you were getting them to talk about their own experiences. And you were obviously looking at where this fits in with what they've done before. So, obviously you were moving into a new area from the old one.

This clearly identifies a number of concepts developed on the Cert Ed concerning the relationship of content and method, working with student experiences, and linking a new area of study to knowledge learnt earlier on the course.

Another example was VT4 talking to TL1:

> On that point, I notice that your questions and answers form different functions. You had, for example, the recall checks "what do we call that mental attitude ?" . . and there were also things like "can you give me an example ?" or "how would you define it ?", which also gives you some insight into their understanding of the situation. So there was a good variety of questions there.

This seemed to be a valuable practice in that it explicitly identified concepts developed on the course and created links between them and the trainee lecturers' practice. However, it was mainly the visiting tutors who made such explicit links rather than the trainee lecturers.

There were also many examples of the participants making only implicit links to educational concepts, as can be seen from some of the quotes in previous sections. Other examples include TL2's account of using students to explain how they did things to each other, TL3's description of how she took account of the range of students' abilities, and TL4's identification of his own improvement in terms of how he had moved from a lecture format to one which involved students more in the lesson.

VT2's suggestions to TL5 that he should use some opening questions to get the group oriented towards the topic clearly implied the need to orientate learners to the aims of an activity. Other suggestions by her clearly implied that TL5 should shift from deductive to inductive teaching strategies.

There were also examples of trainee lecturers describing their work through metaphors which embodied theoretical assumptions. TL1 used the concept of "juggling" to identify the decisions involved in timing a lesson, which could be effected by factors such as the reaction of a group to the content of a lesson, or controlling student contributions. This was a concept that this trainee lecturer had imported from his subject area of management. It was not picked up by either of the visiting tutors, and despite that fact that it stood out in the detailed analysis of the transcripts it does point to the need for developing visiting tutors' abilities to identify such examples of trainee lecturers' personal constructs (Russell et al., 1988).

All these examples demonstrate that a high level of reflective practice was being encouraged and that visiting tutors did this by paying a great deal of attention to the specifics of the trainee lecturers' lessons and in the main by engaging in genuine dialogue with trainee lecturers about their work. However, there is an apparent contradiction between the conclusions of the quantitative data and that of the qualitative analyses, which will be considered in the final section.

6. Conclusions

Many of the extracts referenced or quoted in the previous section would have been coded under the factual and prudential categories of Zeichner and Liston's quantitative model which are concerned with description, suggestions and evaluation. It could be assumed from the quantitative data that the conversations were conducted in terms which would not normally be associated with a high level of reflection.

Despite statements to the contrary (Zeichner and Liston, 1985, p. 169), the quantitative model carried within it assumptions about the relative value of types of discourse. It assumed that if justificatory and critical discourse about goals was not in evidence then the discussion could not be considered to be developing reflective practice. It also assumed the opposite, that if justificatory and critical discourse about goals was being used then the conversation was considered to be more complex.

However, the context of a conversation could mean that passages which had been coded as mainly factual discourse were actually interpreted in the qualitative analyses as functioning in a reflective mode once the underlying movement of the conversation was taken account of. Another way in which apparently factual discourse could be interpreted as operating reflectively comes from the example quoted in Section 5.2.2. in which the combination of factual questions was recognised by both participants as implying underlying concepts. All the examples above of explicit and implicit theoretical concepts in the conversations support this argument.

My argument is that simply because a conversation was coded as justificatory and critical discourse did not mean that it was intrinsically more reflective, and that it was possible, from this evidence, to conduct a highly reflective discussion using very descriptive terms.

It is also the case that a fair degree of interpretation of the meaning of the thought units was required in order to code them; it was not simply a mechanical task. Re-reading the transcripts in order to write up this paper has lead me to reconsider some of the decisions I made almost two years ago. However, the value of such quantitative coding was that it did give an overall impression of the whole conversation, which can easily get lost in a purely interpretative research design. On the basis of this experience I would recommend further research could be carried out with a larger and more statistically random sample using a combination of research methods, while bearing in mind some of the limitations outlined here.

In order to promote reflective practice more explicit links to theory could have been made by the visiting tutors. Not only could they have made more explicit links between their suggestions and learning theory, but also they could have adopted the tactic of naming explicitly the concepts that trainee lecturers were using. They could also have attempted to identify the personal concepts which trainee lecturers were using, such as "juggling" used by TL1. These tactics would have had the double advantage not only of preventing theory appearing to be something separate from practice but also of demonstrating the sometimes not so obvious point that trainee lecturers naturally use theory to describe, explain and evaluate their work as well as to consider alternative strategies.

Linking theory and practice entails a complex process of reflection and should aim

> to help students interpret and criticise their observations and experiences . . . [while recognising] that students already have their

own implicit theories which underpin the way they perceive situations and think about their work; and that the process of reflection involves elucidating and modifying personal theories in the light of evidence, experience and alternative viewpoints, while at the same time personalising some of the public theories by integrating them into their thought and action. (Eraut, 1989, p. 176)

6.1. Implications for in-service training of visiting tutors

A general framework for training visiting tutors could be derived from existing programmes (Turney et al., 1982b) and other accounts of shorter training programme (Stones, 1984b; Sheal, 1989). Visiting tutors could also benefit from other more general training such as counselling or interview techniques.

The recommendations which arose from the present study are as follows:

* develop ways of understanding trainee lecturers' context of work and of convincing them that visiting tutors understand;

* develop ways of negotiating the tension between assessment and counselling;

* develop techniques of making suggestions which are to be followed up on subsequent visits or in other parts of the course;

* improve ways of making links between theory and practice;

* improve links between the reflection encouraged in post-observation discussions and that on other parts of the course;

* improve the linking of suggestions to trainee lecturers' ways of thinking about their work, e.g., via their metaphors.

7. Theoretical Afterword

The conclusions of this study raise some critical questions about two theories of reflection which are currently influential in the development of the curriculum for professional education: Kolb's experiential learning cycle and Schön's reflective practitioner.

7.1. Kolb's cycle of experiential learning

In Kolb's model (Kolb and Fry, 1975), learning is conceived of as a four-stage cycle: immediate concrete experience forms the basis for observations and reflections, which are assimilated into a theory, from which are derived new implications for action, and the cycle repeats itself with a new concrete experience

(Fig 1).

Concrete experiences
```
        / \
       /   \
      /     \
Testing implications of    Observations and
concepts in new situations    reflections
      \     /
       \   /
        \ /
   Formation of abstract
   concepts and generalisations
```

Figure 1

In my research the concrete experiences were the observed lessons. The post-observation conversations encompassed the stages of observation and reflection and formation of abstract concepts and generalisations.

What appears to be missing from this theory is any attention to two factors which were highly influential in the post-observation conversations. First, the trainee lecturers' prior knowledge, experience and attitudes influenced the types of observations and reflections they made. They may well have formed concepts from their reflections and observation, but they did so using pre-existing concepts to interpret their experience. Second, a whole range of those concepts already in the minds of learners are influenced by social ideas on education and by the body of received knowledge on education.

While many curricula claim to be based on Kolb's cycle, they also include consideration of learners' existing concepts and values, and attempt to challenge learners' existing ideas and to examine the body of received knowledge. In not emphasising such factors in his cycle, Kolb's theory can be used to support those practices which play down the significance of trainee lecturers questioning their personal concepts and of coming to grips with public theories (Bates and Rowland, 1988). I would question whether curricula which include reflection on both types of theory can get as much support for such practices from Kolb as is often assumed. To the extent that current curricula do include such reflection they do not appear to be based on his experiential learning cycle, even though they may claim to be, because on my reading of his theory there is a gap between the stages of "concrete experience" and of "observations and reflections".

7.2. Schön's reflective practitioner
The quantitative analyses demonstrated that visiting tutors paid a lot of attention to the specifics of the observed lessons and that trainee lecturers talked mainly in

pragmatic terms about the context of their work. This could be interpreted as the participants being locked into what Schön calls the technical rationality approach. According to Schön, technical rationality assumes that "professional activity consists in instrumental problem solving made rigorous by the application of scientific theory and technique" (Schön, 1983, p. 21). Technical rationality is characterised by Schön as a particular kind of theoretical thinking which separates knowing from doing, research from practice and means from ends. In contrast, Schön's model of the reflective practitioner depends upon a conception of professional work in which decision-making is conceived of as taking place in "indeterminate zones of practice" where there are many competing values and perspectives and no clearly right or wrong solutions. Reflective practitioners consider each decision in relation to their own repertoire of examples, images, understandings, possible responses, values, commitments and knowledge (Schön, 1987, p. 66).

The distinction between reflective practice and technical rationality is that "there is a high, hard ground where practitioners can make effective use of research-based theory and technique, and there is a swampy lowland where situations are confusing 'messes' incapable of technical solution" (Schön, 1983, p. 42). The swampy lowlands are where "complexity, uncertainty, instability, uniqueness, and value conflict" (Schön, 1983, p. 39) abound. There is an assumption that these two areas have distinct tests of rationality and that those methods used to examine the knowledge generated within technical rationality are qualitatively different from those used in the domain of reflective practice.

The question that this study raises for me about Schön's ideas is that of the nature of the connection between technical rationality and reflective practice. Schön assumes that there is a dichotomy between technical rationality and reflective practice. However, it should be clear that the reflective practice of identifying puzzles in the indeterminate zones of practice presupposes learners already knowing or expecting something in the first place (Selman, 1988). Reflective practice depends on learners already having worked within technical rationality and so learnt the basic technical skills of their profession. What visiting tutors are aiming to do is to develop trainee lecturers' ability to analyse and evaluate their own practice in the light of this knowledge.

One of the strengths of Schön's work has been to emphasise the way in which professional education has been based on the tenets of technical rationality, whereas the bulk of their work actually takes place in indeterminate zones of practice. His arguments have helped to render this often obscure aspect of teaching more apparent.

However, the danger is that the attention to reflective practice obscures its relationship to technical competence. On the basis of the evidence from this study, a reflective practitioner will demonstrate a constant mixture of thinking in the mode of technical rationality and of reflective practice. The curriculum for professional education must pay attention to the bridges which need to be built between technical rationality and reflective practice, especially the links between the underlying rationality of each (Schulman, 1988).

Many accounts of curricula for professional education start by using Schön's work as a rationale for their approach but also go on to include elements, identified in the previous paragraph, which Schön's approach does not really support. The curriculum for reflective practice requires surer theoretical foundations than the ones currently in use.

Notes

Zeichner and Liston's conceptual framework for analysing practical reasoning during supervisory conferences:
1. Logical categories

A. Factual discourse
what has or will occur in a teaching situation

A.1. Descriptive discourse
factors related to the specific observation, verifiable in terms of experience/observation

A.2. Informational discourse
information pertinent to the observation, but not verifiable by observation of the specific lesson

A.3. Hermeneutic discourse
meanings created by any of the participants in the lesson

A.4. Explanatory/hypothetical discourse
causal relationships operating in the lesson

B. Prudential discourse
suggestions about what to do or evaluations of what has been accomplished by the teacher

B.1. Instructional discourse
identifying and proposing a solution to a pedagogical problem

B.2. Advice/opinion
identifying and proposing two or more alternative solutions to a problem

B.3. Evaluation
a positive or negative judgment about the value, worth or quality of an action or factor related to an action

B.4. Support
empathetic response or emotive encouragement in relation to past, present or future action

C. Justificatory discourse
types of reasons or rationales underlying past, present or future actions

C.1. Pragmatic rationale
what is effective or efficient in a situation

C.2. Intrinsic rationale
based on claims about universal knowledge, universal values and student needs

C.3. Extrinsic rationale
based on criteria external to the situation and present action, e.g., need for enlightened citizenry, vocational needs of students

D. Critical discourse
assesses the adequacy of rationales offered for the justification of actions or assesses the values and assumptions embedded in the form and content of educational materials and practices

D.1. Pragmatic

D.2. Intrinsic

D.3. Extrinsic

D.4. Hidden curriculum

2. Substantive categories

1. Goals
lesson specific and not specific

2. Curriculum and materials
lesson specific and not specific

3. Procedures
   methods used in planning, conducting and evaluating; lesson specific
   and not specific

4. Lesson, general
   general statements about the lesson as a whole

5. Students
   actions, thoughts or products of students

6. Context
   e.g., classroom, college, community, students' home, supervisor's or
   student teacher's biography, student teaching seminars, educational
   research, co-operating teachers, supervisory process itself.

References

Bales, R. (1951). *Interaction Process Analysis.* Reading, MA: Addison-Wesley [quoted in Zeichner and Liston (1985)].

Bates, I. and Rowland, S. (1988). Is student-centred pedagogy "progressive" educational practice ?. *Journal of Further and Higher Education,* 12, 3, 7–20.

Boydell, D. (1986). Issues in teaching practice supervision research: a review of the literature. *Teaching and Teacher Education,* 2, 2, 115–125.

Calderhead, J. and Gates, P. (1993). *Conceptualising Reflection in Teacher Development.* London: Falmer Press

Carr, C. (1980). The gap between theory and practice. *Journal of Further and Higher Education,* 4, 1, 60-69

Christensen, P. S. (1988). The nature of feedback student teacher receive in post-observation conferences with the university supervisor: a comparison with O'Neal's study of co-operating teacher feedback. *Teaching and Teacher Education,* 4, 3, 275–86.

Cogan, M. (1973). *Clinical Supervision.* Boston: Houghton Mifflin.

Eraut, M. (1989). Initial teacher training and the NVQ model. In J. Burke (ed.), (1989). *Competency Based Education and Training.* Lewes: Falmer Press.

FEU (1981). *Experience, Reflection, Learning.* London: Further Education

Curriculum and Development Unit, Department of Education and Science, London

Fielding, N. G. and Lee, R. M. (1991). *Using Computers in Qualitative Research.* London: Sage.

Grimmett, P. P. and Erickson, G. L. (eds), (1988). *Reflection in Teacher Education.* Vancouver: Pacific Educational Press.

Handal, G. and Lauvas, P. (1987). *Promoting Reflective Teaching: Supervision in Action.* Milton Keynes: Society for Research into Higher Education and Open University Press.

Kolb, D. and Fry, R. (1975). Towards an applied theory of experiential learning. In Cooper (1975), *Theories of Group Processes.* London:John Wiley.

Russell, T., Munby, H., Spafford, C. and Johnston, P. (1988). Learning the professional knowledge of teaching: metaphors, puzzles and the theory-practice relationship. In P. P. Grimmett and G. L. Erickson (eds), *Reflection in Teacher Education.* Vancouver: Pacific Educational Press.

Schön, D. A. (1983). *The Reflective Practitioner.* New York: Basic Books.

Schön, D. A. (1987). *Educating the Reflective Practitioner.* San Francisco: Jossey-Bass.

Selman, M. (1988). Schön's gate is square: but is it art? In P. P. Grimmett and G. L. Erickson (1988), *Reflection in Teacher Education.* Vancouver: Pacific Educational Press.

Sheal, P. (1989). Classroom observation: training the observers. *English Language Teaching Journal, 43,* 2, 92–104.

Shulman, L. S. (1988). The dangers of dichotomous thinking in education. In P. P. Grimmett and G. L. Erickson (1988), *Reflection in Teacher Education.* Vancouver: Pacific Educational Press.

Silverman, D. (1986). *Qualitative Methodology and Sociology: Describing the Social World.* Aldershot: Gower Press.

Stones, E. (1984a). *Supervision in Teacher Education: a Counselling and Pedagogical Approach.* London: Methuen.

Stones, E. (1984b). An INSET course in the training of student teacher supervisors. *Journal of Further and Higher Education, 8,* 3, 3–14.

Turney, C. et al. (1982a). *The Practicum in Teacher Education: Research, Practice and Supervision.* Sydney: Sydney University Press.

Turney, C. et al. (1982b). *Supervisor Development Programmes: Role Handbook.* Sydney: Sydney University Press.

Zeichner, K. M. and Liston, D. (1985). Varieties of discourse in supervisory conferences. *Teaching and Teacher Education,* 1, 2, 155–74.

Zeichner, K.M. and Tabachnick, R. (1982). The belief systems of university supervisors in an elementary student-teacher programme. *Journal of Education for Teaching,* 8, 1, 34–54.

Chapter 15 Learning through discussion and projects

Learning without Knowing: Mastering Learning on a Part-Time MBA

Sean McCartney and Reva Berman Brown, University of Essex

"One can, perhaps, draw many parallels between the MBA course and the teaching of a Zen master . . . One of the central themes of Zen Buddhism is the impossibility of teaching enlightenment: the master, instead, having to guide the pupil into self-realisation."
(Second-year MBA student)

Introduction

This paper describes the University of Essex MBA programme, which has operated since 1991. It has been expressly designed to facilitate a deep learning experience for its students, in the belief that this is crucial to achieving the overarching goal of an MBA: making those on the programme more effective managers. In designing the course, we drew on research into ways of fostering deep learning (by which we mean understanding and applying knowledge) as distinct from surface learning (the memorisation of facts).

Research has raised issues about the utility of what might be termed 'the conventional classroom approach to learning' with its disproportionate emphasis on the student's ability to acquire and record knowledge (Stephenson and Weil, 1992). There has been considerable debate within management and business education on the role of action (Revans, 1971) and experiential learning (Kolb, 1984; Weil and McGill, 1989), though this has needed rethinking in the light of recent research into deep learning (Biggs, 1989; Boud and Felletti, 1991; Entwistle and Tait, 1990; Gibbs, 1992; Marton and Säljö, 1984, Perry, 1970; Ramsden, 1988).

Before 1991, a part-time MBA programme was offered by the University of Essex in collaboration with the Business School of Anglia Polytechnic University, teaching being provided by both institutions. For various reasons, this arrangement was terminated in 1991, and the two institutions now offer their own MBA programmes. Staff at the University of Essex decided to use the opportunity to design a new programme: an MBA as we think it should be.

We had two aims in writing this paper: to describe an innovative MBA, and to indicate how the MBA is explicitly driven by attempts to link the theory of deep learning to its practice. In that sense, the paper is a report of an empirical study, describing and interpreting the testing, by application, of a theoretical model. What has resulted from our MBA is confirmation of Kurt Lewin's aphorism: there is nothing as practical as a good theory.

The paper begins with the first aim, to describe the Essex MBA. The first section provides our educational rationale by considering what our MBA students need to know. Section 2 provides a model of the MBA and outlines the structure of the programme, its delivery and assessment. Section 3 looks at the concept of deep learning, describing the theory which the MBA puts into practice. We explain how our programme aims to facilitate deep learning by its participants and at the same time to counter attempts by the students to deal with the course by means of surface learning, discussing how the structure has adapted the concept of problem-based learning in the process. Section 4 provides a qualitative corroboration of our approach by looking at some participants' reflections on what the MBA learning experience has meant for them. And in Section 5 we reflect on our "results" - how sound our decision to base our MBA on the fostering of deep learning has been.

We assume that the underlying purpose of an MBA is largely practical, and is to make managers (the word is used advisedly) who participate in the programme better at their jobs. This, however, creates problems. There is little agreement on what constitutes effective management, and we have no way of directly measuring our students' effectiveness before and after their MBA experience, and thus of calculating the success of the programme. We therefore measure effectiveness indirectly by asking our students to tell us: throughout the course, they are required to reflect explicitly, in each piece of work submitted, on the impact the learning experience is having on them as managers and people.

1.   Our Educational Rationale: What Do our MBAs Need to Know?

An MBA such as ours at Essex is a paradox. It is a masters programme delivered in an institution of higher education, but it is pragmatic in purpose. Most masters programmes are specialist, building on what has been learnt at first degree level; the MBA is inherently generalist, and the student's first degree, if any, will typically be in a subject with little or even no relevance to management.

The strong relationship between the theoretical and practical aspects has two consequences: firstly, the students must be in employment, and secondly, they must already be managers, in order to have the status to get access to the level of information they will need for their term papers and dissertations. It has happened that, when students lose their jobs, they find it impossible to continue the course, and need to take time out until they find other employment in order to be able to complete their written assessed work. Essex MBA students, therefore, are quite experienced middle managers who have worked some way up the management ladder and are presumably effective managers; but it is quite likely that they have had no education in management beyond company training courses.

So what do our MBAs need to know? Several points should be made here:

(a)   The body of management knowledge is vast. Managers can only possibly know a fraction of it, but there is little consensus over what it is managers need to know.

(b)   In any case, the knowledge which managers need to have in order to be more effective differs from one manager to another. Each manager's needs are highly individual, if not unique.

(c)   As experienced managers, the students already know a great deal about management, albeit that knowledge might be largely intuitive, uninformed by theory.

In planning the Essex MBA, we rejected the idea that the programme should entail the students' absorbing a body of knowledge (a collection of syllabi and subjects) from their teachers (us) which we could then formally measure by examination. A student who has learnt techniques, such as capital budgeting or decision trees, as discrete pieces of knowledge divorced from the reality of his or her own managerial experience may, in fact, be in the position of Sawyer's deaf and dumb child learning to play the piano: learning an "imitation" of good management practice, rather than how to become a better manager (Ramsden, 1992, p. 38).

Instead, we planned an MBA which would introduce ideas, provoke discussion, foster deep learning, and help the students to apply to their work, in a focussed way, the theory they come across, and it is around this process that the course revolves.

2.   The Structure of the Essex MBA

The model of the Essex MBA

Set out in Table 1 is a diagrammatic representation of the MBA, illustrating the thematic construction of the programme. Two modules are undertaken in each term, and the summer term is devoted to the dissertation. Our major innovation is abolishing the core course/elective courses divide; there is no fixed core syllabus which is compulsory and which is examined before students can "progress" to electives. In a sense, all the modules are available as "electives".

A great deal of discussion has taken place in the quarter-century since the introduction of business schools in the UK about where the degree should fit along the generalist/specialist continuum and the topic/technique divide. A great many students enrol on an MBA expecting to be taught discrete subjects (marketing, operations management, international business) which will be built up like a jigsaw puzzle into a large picture. They also expect to receive practical know-how as well as the more theoretical know-about - the tools and techniques of management. As a result, MBA courses are composed of core subjects and electives, and knowledge is formally examined. This approach is consistent with surface learning and we make it clear to prospective students that the thematic Essex MBA does not satisfy this expectation.

Table 1:	THE MODEL OF THE ESSEX MBA	
YEAR 1		
Autumn term	**Spring term**	**Summer term**
Module 1	Module 3	
Module 2	Module 4	Dissertation
Module 1 Managing People		
Module 2 Managing Finance and Information		
Module 3 Managing (in) the External Environment		
Module 4 Managing Strategy		
YEAR 2		
Autumn term	**Spring term**	**Summer term**
Module 5	Module 7	
Module 6	Module 8	Dissertation
Module 5 Managing Corporate Finance		
Module 6 Managing Information Systems		
Module 7 Managing Decision-Making		
Module 8 Managing Organizational Development and Transformation		

Delivery

The programme lasts two academic years, with students attending one session (afternoon and evening) each week. One thematic area is covered in each of the two class-periods in the autumn term and there are a further two modules in the spring term. The modules are thematic rather than subject- or function-based. In the module "Managing the External Environment", for instance, topics will include marketing, business ethics, international business, theories about how the external environment impinges on organisations and vice versa. The content of a module is relatively flexible in that students may ask for an area to be included, or ask for one to be excluded, and this request is complied with if it seems educationally sensible. We try to provide them with what they need/want to learn about. At the end of each module, the students must submit a 4,000-word paper demonstrating the application to their own organisations of some of the ideas discussed in the classes. They are required to select the topic they wish to write about: as explained below, the element of self-selection is an important part of the deep learning experience. Considerable emphasis is placed on discussion of their ideas for papers by the students with the tutors, and, more importantly, with each other.

This leads to written proposals created in the second half of the term and handed in for confirmation of feasibility by the appropriate tutor. At the end of the term, a class will be devoted to group discussion of the individual projects: students come to the meeting with their problems (and successes) and can give assistance to others.

The resulting term paper must be submitted by the beginning of the following term for assessment. It is returned by the fifth week of the term, with a mark and written narrative feedback. It should be emphasised that papers are expected to display understanding of theory and familiarity with the literature in the area chosen by the student. The selected area may, however, have formed a small part of the module, and students are not expected to demonstrate any learning beyond what is relevant to their paper. A course text is recommended for each module, which students are required to read. What we expect from students is that they attend classes and participate in discussion, but the subject-based knowledge acquired is probably sketchy, and is not formally assessed. Thus students do not need, and are not expected, to know very much about large areas of the notional "syllabus". For example, in the module "Managing People", a student may submit a term paper on one of the theoretical areas, say motivation, in the student's own organisation. He or she will be expected, among other things, to demonstrate familiarity with the relevant literature on motivation, but may well have chosen to relegate knowing about, say group dynamics, to reading a chapter in the course text and attending a class where the concept was presented.

In the summer term, the students continue to attend, although there are no formal classes. They meet together informally and with their tutors if they choose to do so, or use the library facilities and develop their end-of year dissertation (8,000 words in Year 1, submitted at the end of the summer term; 15,000 words in Year 2, submitted at the beginning of September following the summer term).

At the end of each paper/dissertation, the students are required to articulate, in an appendix, the meaning which the learning experience involved in producing the paper has had for them. These reflections are the basis for our assessment of the success of the MBA, and are referred to in more detail later.

At the beginning of the course, the students are encouraged to form learning groups, which meet informally at times and places of their own choice. The groups form an important part of the course in that it is there that students are able to support and help each other. These learning groups are autonomous, self-selected and sometimes very fluid. There is no input from the tutors, nor any requirement from us that students should monitor and present to us what they do when they meet. They find these groups very effective in providing meaning and direction for their studies; in many of the term papers, acknowledgements include expressions of thanks – for example:

> My colleagues in my learning group provided invaluable advice on the format of the study and provided very welcome moral support during moments of high anxiety. (first-year term paper)

These learning groups form part of the process of reflection, which is discussed more fully in Section 4.

We make it clear to students what they are required to do, when undertaking their written, assessed work, and the standard for which they are to aim in two main ways:

(i)   The module outline lists what will be looked for in the term paper, e.g., a strategic or organisational level of "problem". For example,

> The course is assessed by means of a 4,000-word term paper, which is to be handed in on the first Thursday of the summer term. You are to select at least one major concept from the module and explain and explore an aspect of work behaviour with which you are familiar or with which you wish to become familiar, taken from your own work situation. The selection of the assignment is at your discretion.

Approval by the course tutor, of the suitability of the project, should be obtained by means of the submission of an abstract before work on the term paper is begun.

(ii) The course participants are provided with a copy of the pro forma which will be used to assess their work, with the aspects looked for listed. For example,

 * evidence that the relevant literature has been read and evaluated critically;
 * evidence of the integration of theory and practice in a work situation;
 * clarity of presentation of the problem and its analysis;
 * relevance of the conclusions reached/findings to the aims and process of the paper;
 * general comments.

The various pro formas which deal with each of the modules and the dissertations have been deliberately designed to guide an assessment that makes it impossible to use a surface approach; such an approach simply will not produce acceptable/pass-standard work.

Assessment
In designing the MBA, we made a deliberate decision to exclude exams, and formal assessment is purely on the basis of tutor assessment. The term papers and dissertations are blind double marked, and the final mark is correlated by discussion between the markers. The piece of work is then sent to an external examiner for validation. There is no requirement that the students demonstrate they have absorbed every aspect of a particular corpus of knowledge presented in a module.

3. Deep and Surface Learning

Studies have identified a number of concepts of learning, ranging from the most superficial to the most sophisticated, as seen by the learner. One of the more comprehensive schemes is given by Gibbs (1992). This is illustrated in Table 2.

TABLE 2:	CONCEPTS OF LEARNING
1	Learning as being given knowledge. The (active) teacher has the knowledge and transmits it the (passive) student.
2	Learning as memorising. The student is active, and may "take responsibility for his/her own learning", but the knowledge acquired is not transformed in any way, merely reproduced for assessment.
3	Learning as acquiring skills in eg applying algorithms to problems.
4	Learning as making sense. The student is trying to abstract meanings/concepts from the learning experience.
5	Learning as understanding reality. The learning experience enables the student to see the world differently.
Source: Gibbs, 1992	

Levels 1 to 3 are regarded as surface approaches to learning, and level 4 and 5 as deep learning approaches. We discuss how we have attempted to counter the application of surface learning on the part of our students towards the end of this section.

Contrasting deep and surface learning
In deep learning the intention is to understand, and the student maintains the structure of the task; in surface learning, the intention is only to complete the task requirements, and the student distorts the structure of the task (Ramsden, 1992, p. 46). Table 3 draws the contrasts between deep and surface learning.

TABLE 3: CONTRASTS BETWEEN DEEP AND SURFACE LEARNING
DEEP APPROACH TO LEARNING

1. The focus is on 'what is signified', for example the concepts applicable to solving the problem.
2. Relates previous knowledge to new knowledge.
3. Relates knowledge from different courses.
4. Relates theoretical ideas to everyday experience.
5. Relates and distinguishes evidence and argument.
6. Organises and structures content into a coherent whole.
7. The emphasis is internal and the impulse to learn comes from within the student.

SURFACE APPROACH TO LEARNING

1. The focus is on the 'signs', for example, the words and sentences of the text, or the formulae needed to solve the problem.
2. The focus is on unrelated parts of the task.
3. Information for assessment is simply memorised.
4. Facts and concepts are associated unreflectively.
5. Principles are not distinguished from examples.
6. The task is treated as an external imposition.
7. The emphasis is external and the impulse to learn comes from the demands of assessment.

Source: Ramsden, 1992

Obviously it could be argued that learning at any level will be beneficial to managers. Passively absorbing facts about, say, the workings of the foreign currency markets may help a manager become more effective, but a significant and lasting increase in effectiveness will come about only if the manager learns, as a result of the MBA, to perceive in a different light, if not the world, then at least his or her organisation and his or her own function within it.

Facilitating deep learning
A number of factors have been identified by writers as fostering deep learning. Biggs (1989) suggests four key elements of good tutoring which have this in mind. These are illustrated in Table 4.

TABLE 4:	FOSTERING DEEP LEARNING

1 A motivational context.
2 Active learning
3 A learning base which students can apply to new problems
4 Discussion (formal and informal)

Source: Biggs, 1992

We had these four factors in mind in designing the Essex MBA. Adults learn best what they need to learn in order to carry out tasks which matter to them. They therefore need to be involved in selecting what is to be learnt and in planning how the learning should take place. The flexibility of the "syllabus" answers that need, allowing our students to take 'ownership' of the programme, and sustaining the motivational context throughout the two years of the course.

Deep learning is associated with doing. Our students are part-time, and they are "doing" their learning at work in their organisations at the same time as they are doing it during the formal teaching sessions. Their learning activity is planned, reflected upon and processed, and related to abstract conceptions. (Gibbs, 1992, p. 11).

Discussion and interaction with others forms a large part of the formal teaching sessions. The course does not have conventional tutorials and seminars, and we place emphasis on peer tutoring and the formation of learning groups within the student cohort. We take care to bring students' existing knowledge and experience into the learning experience. During the teaching sessions, the subject matter to be learnt is well structured and integrated by the tutor; the content is taught in integrated wholes and we relate the knowledge to other knowledge. While what we do is not strictly interdisciplinary, it is multidisciplinary and very few topics are dealt with in discrete "chunks" isolated from the rest of the knowledge base.

A number of strategies have been put forward by which tutors can foster deep learning. Gibbs (1992) suggests eight, which are summarised in Table 5.

TABLE 5:	DEEP LEARNING STRATEGIES
1	Independent learning: negotiated between student and tutor
2	Personal development
3	Problem-based learning: learning takes place through tackling relevant problems
4	Explicit reflection by students on their learning
5	Independent group work
6	Learning by doing
7	Developing learning skills
8	Project work
Source: Gibbs, 1992	

Here too, the Essex MBA attempts to apply as many of these eight strategies as is feasible.

1. Independent learning: Not all of the programme is available for negotiation, but we can be and are persuaded to give less or more emphasis to (or even to omit) certain aspects. For instance, one of our cohorts wanted more input on research methods than we had originally intended to provide; another cohort asked for a change of emphasis during the delivery of "Managing Finance and Information" and the course was altered to take account of their needs. The students thus have a degree of autonomy and control over the choice of subject matter, but they have none over the assessment of their learning outcomes (the term papers and dissertations).

2. Personal development: The intention, by means of the accent on group work during the teaching sessions and the encouragement of the informal learning groups, is to enable students to "own" the course: to access their feelings and motivations in a learning atmosphere which is supportive and "safe", so that they feel comfortable about taking responsibility for their own learning.

3. Problem-based learning: We discuss this.

4. Reflection: We discuss this in Section 4 below.

5. Independent group work: We encourage interaction between students, both formally in class and informally in their learning groups which meet out of class times, in the belief that this is motivating and encourages a range of learning activity.

6. Learning by doing: This is done for us in that the students are already involved in practical work as managers in their organisations. We have no need of other aspects of learning by doing such as visits to organisations or business simulations, but we take the students on a week's residential study to a European city so that they can learn about non-British management first-hand.

7. Developing learning skills: Because the majority of our students have been away from formal study for a number of years, we take note of Gibbs's (1981) suggestion that it is possible to develop practical learning skills in the context of developing a sense of purpose, an awareness of task demands and flexibility in adapting to different demands. We provide them with practical information on how to undertake empirical research and how to write an academic term paper (in contrast to a business project).

8. Project work: The term papers and dissertations are variations of project work. They involve the application of prior knowledge to problems and involve direct personal experience. The students are working most independently when involved in these assessed aspects of the course.

The principal learning vehicles are the term papers and dissertations, on which most of the students' energy is expended. Each student therefore has a unique learning experience, based on issues/problems in their own organisations, to which their particular knowledge base can be applied, and on which they are required to reflect in each paper. A further point is that, since assessment is based entirely on the papers and dissertations, there is no divorce between the learning experience and the assessment of that experience. This also avoids fostering a surface learning approach through the assessment system. We would suggest that the way in which we assess the written work precludes the possibility of "staying in" a surface learning mode because it is impossible to produce acceptable term papers and dissertations using a surface approach.

In designing the MBA as we have done, we have made explicit to ourselves that we expected our students to arrive on the course with a predisposition to surface learning, because that is what they think learning is, as well as a presumption that the course will be operated in that mode, because this is how they have been taught in the past. These are, of course, assumptions on our part, and we did not wait for the arrival of our first students for confirmation of the assumptions before trying to design out such an approach from students.

We have attempted to counter the possibility of surface learning by making it difficult for students to apply the levels 1 to 3 of the conceptions of learning illustrated in Table 2: We don't "do" learning to them; they have to do it for (or to) themselves (level 1); we don't require memorising (level 2); we don't provide facts, formulae or procedures which students can apply to a similar situation at a later date (level 3).

Thus, because we have taken explicit steps in our programme design to counter the circumstances where surface learning applies, we have no firm evidence that, left to their own devices, our students would have chosen to concentrate on surface learning. We therefore don't claim to have "cured" our students of using surface learning; our claim is that our course is explicitly designed to inculcate and facilitate deep learning.

Problem-based learning
The generally accepted meaning of problem-based learning (PBL) is that it involves learning through tackling relevant problems. (This is not the same as learning how to solve problems.) Indeed, the problem on which the proposed learning is based may not be solvable because the aim of this method is for the student to learn rather than to achieve a problem-solution. It is through their confrontation with the problem that students discover what it is they need to learn about, and they then proceed to learn what is necessary in order to tackle the problem. Put simplistically, in PBL students start with problems and find out what they need to know (usually in teams) to make progress with that problem. In this sense, there is no "teaching". Gibbs (1992, p. 14) provides the main features of problem-based learning:

(i.) The problems presented are relevant. In professional courses such as engineering or management, it is possible to give students real-world problems to tackle. These problems are carefully designed to involve all the important parts of the syllabus or teaching programme. The Harvard Business School case-studies are examples of this approach and have been adopted and emulated wherever management is taught.

(ii.) A "need to know" is created. Motivation is generated because the students' learning is governed by what is necessary for them to tackle the problem.

(iii.) Knowledge is integrated. The selected real-world problems are interdisciplinary and strategic or large scale. Students are required to create combinations of knowledge/subject areas in order to deal with the problem.

(iv.) There is student interaction. Problem-based learning is designed in such a way as to require students to work in co operative groups, sharing their ideas, dividing up the learning and briefing each other as they proceed towards the problem-solution.

The Essex MBA is thus not strictly one of classical problem-based learning. While it contains the four features outlined above, there is a fundamental difference in the Essex approach. We have not reinvented the wheel in that we accept the value of PBL, as theory and practice, in a professional course such as ours. This is present in the underlying educational philosophy of the course, but PBL has required adaptation because the students are working managers, already involved in real (and not case-study) real-world problems.

(a) The basic point about the problems on the majority of PBL programmes is that these have been previously and carefully selected in order to provide material for students to cover the syllabus/topic in a manner conducive to self-learning. The Essex MBA does not have a fixed syllabus. The problem-based approach, often in the form of real-world case-studies, is used during the teaching sessions, but it is obvious to students that these are exemplars, providing the kind of problems that managers are confronted with in order to make connections between theory and practice.

(b) The requirement is that problems covered by the term papers and dissertations are generated by the students themselves. There is thus no opportunity on the part of the MBA tutors to design carefully or select problems for the students to consider in their term papers.

(c) Motivation is highly focussed expressly because the problems selected by the students are practically relevant to them and their organisations. They see the problem which they research and write about as relevant to both their studies and their careers.

(d) There is no need to simulate real-world problems for examination in the term papers and dissertations because these deal with real real-world problems.

(e) While the PBL which takes place during the teaching sessions will require co operative working and idea-sharing, the term papers and dissertations are individual pieces of work particular to the student, who has chosen the problem for personal and professional reasons. While the students discuss these during the teaching sessions and in their learning groups, accepting peer-group guidance, they are on their own in producing the piece of written work.

Thus, what the Essex MBA does is a variant of problem-based learning, but we don't have a name for it. The fundamental aspect of PBL - that students tackle problems in order to generate a need to find out - is present; what is conspicuously absent is the deliberate prior structure of the problems for term papers and dissertations in such a way as to clarify their learning needs for them. A large part of the problem is their problem of knowing what they need to know; the students have to work out the "question" as well as the "answer", thus determining their own syllabus. In fact, the approach uses all the above strategies, even independent group work; although the assessed written work results from individual effort, there is considerable collective discussion and interaction in their preparation, especially of the end-of-year dissertations.

4.   Student Reflections

Reflection on learning - both on content and process - provides many benefits, the chief of which is that it can help students move towards and then stay within a deep approach to learning. Reflection is particularly helpful in the context of professional courses as it can help to turn experience into learning. Reflection emphasises two of the four elements of fostering active learning (Table 2): (a) it involves learners in actively processing their learning and (b) it provides a learning base which students can apply to new problems and so makes their knowledge more apparent to them.

There are a number of methods which are held to encourage reflection. These include: learning diaries, reflection journals, portfolios of work, discussions of learning strategies, and the use of video, audio and observers in a learning context which involves the performance of behavioural skills (Gibbs, 1992, p. 14).

In Kolb's experiential learning model (1976), one of the four key learning abilities or processes is reflective observation. The learning cycle is said to move from new concrete experience, through reflective observation, which examines these experiences from different perspectives, to the formation of abstract concepts and generalisations, which in turn leads to theories that can be used for active experimentation in problem-solving and decision-making, which leads to new concrete experience and so on.

The term "reflection" as used by the MBA encompasses more than reflective observation. It contains elements of consideration of, or meditating upon, past knowledge or experience, and is synonymous with contemplation or serious thought or deliberation.

The use of reflection is a compulsory part of the MBA programme, taking the form of a non-assessed addition to each term paper and dissertation. We make no formal demands as to the shape or tone of the reflections. What we get ranges from the stilted to the verbose, from a few paragraphs to pages of insightful comment.

The benefits to the students of writing a reflection section is apparent in what they say. In theoretical terms, we have tapped into Kolb's model (1984) of experiential learning, and the process of reflection helps our students to move round the experiential learning cycle to foster critical reflection at crucial stages.

The benefits to us as designers and deliverers of the programme are also apparent: we have a regular and ongoing comment on how the students are reacting to the course; we know what we have done well and where they have gained in learning, self-knowledge and confidence; we can judge the effectiveness of our educational approach; we are made aware of weaknesses in the programme; and we can draw conclusions about the existence of a deep approach to learning in the students.

The first students on the Essex MBA are currently working on their final dissertations. Looking at the "reflections" on already submitted papers, it is striking, and very gratifying, to see how frequently students refer to changes in the way they tackle problems, the way they think about their organisation, even the kind of person they are.

. . . remembering my experiences at university, I was concerned that the MBA would be a process of learning, followed by the regurgitation of the required knowledge in an examination - rather than the acquisition of new ways of looking, of new ways of thinking, which in my case, I am pleased to see developing - if a little slowly and with much grinding of mental gears. (first-year term paper)

As a general point, the structure of the MBA course at Essex - which is focussed on the projects and dissertations produced by the students, is eminently suitable for a senior manager such as myself. Firstly, it is immediately relevant: by definition, the subject of the work has to relate to one's own organisation, and thus is of real benefit, both to the student, and to their company. Indeed, when I was first looking at MBA course, this factor was one that gave me some concern - I did not want to be working with case studies in industries that had no relevance to me, and be marked on work that was completely academic, and of little immediate practical use. (first-year dissertation)

This project, specifically, has firstly made me aware of the enormous quantity of literature available on the subject of quality. From the considerable amount of reading that I felt was necessary to give me a background before writing the project, I, of course, gained far more information than was strictly necessary to write this particular project. This excess information is, of course, not lost or wasted, but represents an excellent method of learning. (second-year term paper)

The qualitative decision-making has been very beneficial to me. As stated above, the quantitative part of the course I was already aware of, mainly due to my background as an engineer, and I subconsciously always approached decision-making from the quantitative perspective. I was always therefore looking for a maximising choice based on a computational strategy and I was uneasy if it was not possible to arrive at a choice in that way. The idea therefore that you can arrive at a "right" decision via a satisfying choice using a judgmental strategy is quite an eye opener. (second-year term paper)

As I have mentioned in a previous reflection, the design of the Essex MBA, in that projects must be based on examples from the students' own organisation, is of very real value, both to the student and the organisation. I have found that the research, and the writing of this paper, has completely changed the way I look at my company, and the way I hope to influence its future. (second-year term paper)

I have been forced to increase my knowledge without needing to memorise anything, or to accumulate recipes of procedures and techniques. To my surprise and pleasure, the project has led me to new ways of making sense of my working environment. You could say that I am beginning to form another way of understanding the reality of my professional world. (second-year term paper)

5. Our Reflections: Summary and Conclusions

We have two main areas about which we wish to draw conclusions: the linking of theory and practice, and the efficacy of this particular model of the MBA.

The link between theory and practice
What has resulted from the implementation of the Essex MBA is confirmation of the value of deep learning and evidence that the theory "works". In a sense, we took a risk in designing the programme. It is very different from the traditional MBA which is offered by the other higher education institutions in our catchment area. We could very easily have found ourselves floundering in sticky operational difficulties. The programme depends heavily on the intellectual and experiential quality of each student cohort. Trusting the theory about student learning has enabled us implement productive practice.

Of course, there have been hitches, setbacks and problems, but our reliance on the theory has enabled us to find solutions to the difficulties which have emerged. The biggest headache has, in fact, turned out to be deciding what to do when a student is made redundant, and cannot continue until he or she has found fresh employment, while the student obviously regards the MBA as an aid to finding it.

As the course proceeds, our students become aware of the ways in which the course links educational theory to practice as they make their own linkages between organisational theory and practice. We feel that we manage to change student conceptions of learning from the surface to the deep as they proceed towards the attainment of their MBA.

The efficacy of the Essex MBA

In order to have this particular MBA programme "work", a number of factors must exist:

(i)   The number of students needs to be small. We aim for classes of no more than 15. Currently, we have only one group per year and expansion could be accommodated within our approach only by running streams in parallel.

(ii) The students need the co operation of their organisations to enable them to pursue fruitful projects. Consequently, we cannot accept students unless they are employed and their employer is prepared to give them the necessary latitude.

(iii) The fact that papers and dissertations are grounded in the students' own organisations means the programme could not function if students were not able to access their organisations during the course. That is to say, the Essex MBA is not a part-time version of a (notional) full-time one, in which students are taken away from their organisation.

(iv) The students must be managers with some degree of seniority and experience, otherwise they lack the essential experiential knowledge base which students need to apply to problems and issues.

We think that our MBA has been successful in developing our students' potential to become better managers. They may not know very much in the factual sense, but they know what it is they know. More importantly, they know how to discover that which they do not know, as and when it is relevant to them.

As a result, by the end of the programme they do not know anything in particular, but they have learnt a great deal. The application of deep learning theory has provided a strong skeleton to support the flesh of practice. We would like to think that the Essex MBA is now an attractive body capable of effecting productive change.

A final word from the student of oriental philosophy quoted at the beginning of this paper, reflecting on what he has gained:

> I hope that by reflecting on the subjects studied I will have learnt more than just a collection of facts, and, at least, have achieved some understanding - enlightenment may be too much to hope for!

References

Biggs, J. B. (1989). Approaches to the enhancement of tertiary teaching. *Higher Education Research and Development*, 8, 7, 7–25.

Boud, D. and Felletti, G. (1991). *The Challenge of Problem Based Learning*. London: Croom Helm.

Boud, D., Keogh, R. and Walker, D. (eds), (1985). *Reflection: Turning Experience into Learning*. London: Kogan Page.

Entwistle, N. J. and Tait, H. (1990). Approaches to learning, evaluations of teaching, and preferences for contrasting academic environments. *Higher Education*, 19, 169–194.

Gibbs, Graham (1992). *Improving the Quality of Student Learning*. Bristol: Technical and Educational Services.

Kolb, D. A. (1976). Management and the learning process. *California Management Review*, 18, 3, 21–31.

Kolb, D. A. (1984). *Experiential Learning: Experience as the Source of Learning and Development*. Englewood Cliffs, NJ: Prentice-Hall.

Marton, F. and Säljö, R. (1984). Approaches to learning. In F. Marton, D. Hounsell and N. J. Entwistle (eds), *The Experience of Learning*. Edinburgh: Scottish Academic Press.

Perry, W. G. (1970). *Forms of Intellectual and Ethical Development in the College Years: A Scheme*. New York: Holt, Rinehart & Winston.

Ramsden, P. (1988). Studying learning: improving teaching. In P. Ramsden (ed.), *Improving Learning: New Perspectives*. London: Kogan Page.

Ramsden, P. (1992). *Learning to Teach in Higher Education*. London: Routledge.

Revans, R. (1971). *Developing Effective Managers*. Newark, NJ: Appleton Century Crofts.

Stephenson, John and Weil, Susan (eds) (1992). *Quality in Learning: A Capability Approach in Higher Education*. London: Kogan Page.

Weil, S. W. and McGill, I. (1989). *Making Sense of Experiential Learning*. Milton Keynes: SRHE/Open University Press.

Individual Project Work in Relation to Meaning and Reproducing Orientations within an Applied Social Studies Degree

Katherine Cuthbert, Manchester Metropolitan University

Introduction

The BA in Applied Social Studies by Independent Study at the Crewe+Alsager Faculty of the Manchester Metropolitan University is a modular, multi-disciplinary degree within which students are able to follow units in sociology, philosophy, psychology, health studies, special education, inquiry and communication skills and youth and community studies (although the latter will be not be available from the 1993 intake). The first two years of the degree are relatively conventional in character and have the aim of providing students with an understanding of core content in the disciplines which they are studying. By the end of their second year students must have completed at least four course units from each of two discipline or subject areas. They are required to pass ten such units altogether in order to complete successfully the first two years of the degree course.

The final year of the degree is rather less conventional and it is this part which makes it appropriate for the degree title to include the description by Independent Study. During this final year students are expected to complete an independent project which will constitute between 40% and 80% of their final-year programme. This project is quite likely to be inter-disciplinary in character and will frequently have an applied, problem orientation. Projects are composed of inter-related component essays and will be up to 37,000 words in length. They are likely to include practical work – for example, questionnaires, case-studies, correlational investigations, placements. Projects must obviously develop out of the discipline areas which students have studied in the first two years of the degree (see the diagramatic summary of the degree in Figure 1).

[For those not familiar with the general nature and ethos of independent study, probably the best summary description is provided by Forster (1972) and quoted in Candy (1991). She writes that

> Independent study is a process, a method and a philosophy of education: (1) in which a student acquires knowledge by his or her own efforts and develops the ability for inquiry and critical investigation; (2) it includes freedom of choice in determining those objectives, within the limits of a given project or program and with the aid of a faculty advisor; (3) it requires freedom of process to carry out the objectives; (4) it places increased educational responsibility on the student for the achieving of objectives and the value of the goals. (p. ii)]

Figure 1. Schematic Outline of the Course for the DipHE/BA (Hons) Applied Social Studies (by Independent Study)

Year 3 Optional units from psychology (change and wellbeing); sociology (sociological applications) and a range of college taught year 3/4 units (See Appendix 1).

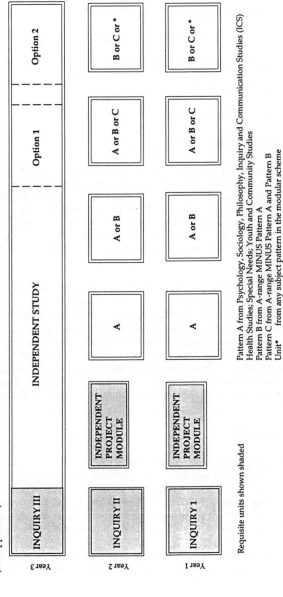

Requisite units shown shaded

Pattern A from Psychology, Sociology, Philosophy, Inquiry and Communication Studies (ICS) Health Studies; Special Needs; Youth and Community Studies
Pattern B from A-range MINUS Pattern A
Pattern C from A-range MINUS Pattern A and Pattern B
Unit* from any subject pattern in the modular scheme

A few examples of project titles will help to provide some indication of the kinds and range of topics students chose to investigate:

Transracial Adoption: Problems, Perspectives and the Policy Debate

Community Care of Schizophrenics

The Psychology of Adapting to Blindness

Fostering Children with Disabilities

Sociology and Politics of Black Rap Music.

This paper will be concerned primarily with this independent project work within our BA in Applied Social Studies degree but will focus on preparation for the project rather than its implementation in the third year. If project work of the kind very briefly described above is to be pursued successfully within an undergraduate degree, then students must be properly prepared for working in the ways which will be required. This preparation within our degree is provided within the first and particularly the second year, alongside the discipline-oriented course units.

The aim of this paper is two fold. Firstly, it will make some comment on the general rationale of the degree, particularly in relation to meaning and reproducing orientations to learning. Secondly, it will describe in some detail the way in which students are prepared for their third-year project work, particularly in the context of much increased student numbers. There will be a concern here to show how we have used the concept of a meaning-oriented approach to learning to try to develop appropriate practice. In addition there will be some very brief reference to the attempts we are beginning to make to carry out empirical research into student approaches to studying and performance within the degree.

Degree Rationale

The degree was initially validated by the CNAA in 1981. The underlying rationale for the degree was derived from a number of sources. Prominent among these was a concern to help students to learn how to learn and to provide them with an opportunity to commit themselves to work that was personally meaningful and relevant, with the expectation that this would lead to increased motivation (e.g., Decci, 1975; Rogers, 1969; Thomas and Harri-Augstein, 1977).

Since 1981, research and theory relating to student learning has been considerably extended. The work of Noel Entwistle in Edinburgh and Ference Marton in

Gothenburg and their various colleagues has been especially pre-eminent (e.g. Marton and Säljö 1976; Entwistle and Ramsden, 1983; Marton, Hounsell and Entwistle, 1984). The primary focus of their work has derived from the distinction between a deep, meaning-oriented approach to learning and one that is characterised as having a primarily surface, reproducing orientation. It is seen as desirable that students within higher education should be adopting a meaning-oriented approach to their learning, but there is evidence that it is all too easy for a reproducing orientation to become dominant (e.g., Gow and Kember, 1990; Ramsden, 1992; Gibbs, 1992). It is therefore of considerable importance to identify the kinds of teaching and learning conditions which are conducive to the development of a meaning-oriented approach (Entwistle and Ramsden, 1983; Gibbs, 1992).

Although the initial validation of our degree predates the full development of much of this work, it has now become influential on our own thinking about the rationale for the degree and our planning of changes in relation to teaching learning provisions. Brief comment on the nature of this rationale, drawing particularly on the work of Entwistle and Ramsden (1983) and Gibbs (1992) will be made here. More detailed comment on links with practice within the degree will then be made in the next section.

On the basis of their research into student perceptions of the departments within which they were studying, Entwistle and Ramsden (1983) suggest that freedom in learning (the amount of discretion possessed by students in choosing and organising academic work), good teaching, a workload that is not overwhelming and perceived interest and relevance act to promote deeper learning. Within the BA in Applied Social Studies it would be a reasonable expectation that freedom to learn and perceived interest and relevance would be supported within the third year at least.

In his approach to these issues Gibbs (1992) used case-studies of a number of teaching innovations designed to promote a deep approach to learning. On the basis of this action research project a number of strategies which could be expected to foster a deep approach to learning were identified. Briefly these may be summarised as follows:

> promoting independent learning and using project work;
> encouraging motivation through personal involvement in learning;
> making use of problem based-learning;
> emphasising reflective processes;
> promoting active and experientially based learning and developing student learning skills;
> using group work of various kinds.

The first two suggestions made here are clearly of particular relevance to our independent study degree and reinforce the features identified in relation to the work of Entwistle and Ramsden discussed briefly above. The further suggestions about the use of problem-based learning and emphasising reflective processes are also of relevance.

Biggs (1989) has also made comments on the kind of teaching approaches which might be expected to foster a meaning-oriented approach to learning. His suggestions about student motivation, learner activity and interaction with others are strongly compatible with those outlined above. He has, perhaps, placed more emphasis upon the importance of a well-structured knowledge base. Candy (1991) in his extensive discussion of self-directed learning has also argued that self directed learning must derive out of a strong and specific discipline base. Within our degree there has always been considerable emphasis on the necessity for providing an adequate base for the student's independent project work. It is expected that a student's project will be strongly rooted in the disciplines which they have studied, in a relatively conventional way, during the first two years of the degree programme.

The Degree in Practice: Project Preparation

The above comments suggest that there is a good case to be made for the project-oriented nature of the third year of our BA in Applied Social Studies being supportive of the development of a concern with meaning and understanding. However, this cannot, of course, be guaranteed and there will be various pressures within an independent study degree, as well as conventional degrees, which will be counter-productive to the development of appropriate approaches to study. In particular, possibilities might be too open ended for students to deal with - there might be too much freedom to learn - leading to anxiety and loss of direction. Ramsden (1976; summarised in Entwistle and Ramsden, 1983), in commenting on another independent study degree course, writes that "a perceived lack of any direction or helpful guidance by lecturers . . . led to the development of negative attitudes to learning".

From the original validation of the degree there has been a central emphasis on the proper preparation of students for their third year independent project work. However, our ability to provide suitable support and preparation has hopefully improved with experience. In this section I will describe the support mechanisms which have evolved to support second-year students in this preparatory process. It is also important to emphasise that, over the last year especially, we have had to cope with much increased student numbers and so it is essential that procedures are efficient in the use of staff time as well as providing appropriate support for students. Some of the procedures adopted have been more successful than others and so I intend to provide evaluative comment derived primarily from student feedback questionnaires.

The main part of the project development process extends from the end of a student's first year through to the end of the second year. A schematic summary of procedures and deadlines is provided in Figure 2. Preparation and support take place primarily within two half-unit modules called the Independent Learning Module and the Independent Project Module. The culmination of this preparation is for students to submit a formal, detailed proposal for their project to a registration board which is composed of the course team and a number of other representatives from inside and outside the university. The registration board can approve proposals or require further work and resubmission.

Figure 2 The Project Planning Sequence

This outline is intended to indicate the main components of the planning process, the major activities which are involved, and the course unit context within which they occur.

Year 1: May – June	Independent learning module	Students work on group-based project Students begin to discuss ideas, look at examples of completed project, etc.
Year 2: Oct – Feb	Inquiry II	Submit initial outline of ideas Discuss ideas with other students Make presentations to peers and tutors Feedback from peers and tutors Consult with tutors on individual basis Submit revised outline and receive feedback
Year 2: March	Independent project module	Individual consultations with tutors Detailed planning of provisional proposals Submission of provisional proposals
Year 2: April – May	Inquiry II (contd.)	Feedback on provisional proposal Revision as appropriate Submission of final proposal
Year 2: June	Registration board	Individual vivas Tutor comment and general discussion Decision of registration board

A brief overview of these preparatory procedures will first be provided and then certain aspects will be considered in greater detail in relation to the concern to support the development of a meaning-oriented approach to learning, and in relation to the more practical issue of managing the process with increased numbers of students.

Support for project preparation begins formally at the end of a student's first year. Within the Independent Learning Module students work in small groups to explore for themselves a particular topic area, so gaining their first experience of working relatively independently. During their second year students work on the process of developing their own individual projects. A number of strategies are used to provide a supportive framework. Firstly, students are provided with a series of quite lengthy handouts which explain the processes involved in project development and which are made available to students at intervals extending from the end of the first year and through the second year. Secondly, students are expected to develop their ideas through the submission of a series of increasingly detailed outlines of their project ideas. Thirdly, tutors provide feedback on these ideas through the use of structured pro formas. Finally, during the period immediately before the submission of provisional project proposals, there is a more intensive discussion of ideas on an individual basis, but with considerable emphasis being placed on making efficient use of tutor time.

First-Year Group-Based Project within the Independent Learning Module

The ILM was first implemented during the academic year 1985–86, and with some modifications has run every year since. I will describe the basic aims and structure of the unit, the kind of feedback we have received from students and the changes which have been made since its original introduction.

The module takes place at the end of the academic year, after the completion of course work and examinations for other course units. Students work full time on the module for a period of five weeks. They work in groups of around six to nine, with each group working to investigate a different topic area. During this time tutors are engaged in examination and project marking. From a practical point of view there is therefore a limit to the amount of time which can be devoted to active teaching on the module, but fortunately this is consistent with the aim of providing students with experience of working independently. The expectation is that tutors should have a primarily facilitative rather than a teaching role.

Two main aims were originally identified for the module. Firstly, this was to provide students with initial experience of working relatively independently (i.e., independently of tutors) to explore a given topic area, but having the supportive experience of working with other students. The second aim was to provide a context within which students could reflect upon and develop the learning skills required to work independently. These aims were described in the module outline as follows:

> The major aim of this module will be to increase the student's ability to work independently through a better understanding of the problem solving process and a reflective understanding of his/her own learning. The unit has been developed on the basis of recent research into student learning processes. While this research does not provide any simple or recognised formula for improving learning competence, it does suggest that such skills are most likely to be acquired through a process of active learning and reflective discussion. A major part of this module will therefore involve a group-based, problem-solving project within which students will compare and discuss the learning strategies which they use. Although a project report will be produced, the main concern will be with process rather than product.

To try to achieve these aims the module included a series of structured exercises to examine the processes involved in the reading of academic articles and essay writing in particular. These exercises drew upon the work of Gibbs (1981), and the intention was to integrate the exercises into the on-going project work being completed by the students (Martin and Ramsden, 1987; Ramsden, Beswick and Bowden, 1987). Performance on the module was assessed in three main ways which in each case were marked on a pass/fail basis. Firstly, students were required to make an individual contribution to the group report on the project area they were investigating and, secondly, they had to contribute to their group's oral presentation. The third part of the overall assessment was intended to encourage students to reflect upon their experience of learning within the module, and they were required to complete and submit a learning journal. Quite detailed guidelines were provided to help students appreciate the demands of this latter task.

In many ways the module has been successful and has now run for its seventh successive year. The great majority of students embark on the project work with some considerable enthusiasm. It is not unusual to have the comment that "this is the best thing that we have done all year". With appropriate tutor support, they are able to work to investigate their topic area largely for themselves and certainly gain useful experience of using library resources and searching out literature sources. There is also a considerable sense of achievement at the end of the module and an increase in the sense of confidence that students have in working in the ways required within the module, and which will provide a necessary base for working individually on their independent projects.

However, it is also important to emphasise that not all the original plans have been successful and to consider the reasons for the problems which have arisen. The least successful parts of the original module were those associated with the aim of supporting the explicit development of, and encouraging reflection upon, students' own learning skills. There was a tendency for students to find the exercises rather boring and a distraction from the more interesting project work. Although some students produced very interesting and thoughtful learning journals, these were more frequently mundanely descriptive rather than really reflective. An additional problem related to tutor expertise and time. Only a couple of tutors out of the total team of around half a dozen (there were variations in numbers and persons from year to year) were experienced in, and committed to, working to support the development of student learning skills, and so a particular onus was placed on them. A linked problem is that tutors have time-consuming responsibilities, principally in relation to the whole process of end-of-year assessment at the time that this module is taking place. So, particularly with considerably increased student numbers, there is a limit to the time input that can be made.

As a consequence of these problems, the explicit concern with student learning within the module has gradually declined. The exercises have been discontinued and students are no longer required to keep and submit a learning journal, although they are still encouraged to attempt the experience of keeping one. Although I am convinced that there is sufficient evidence to indicate the continued value of the group project component of the Independent Learning Module, it is something of a disappointment that the explicit emphasis upon the learning process has had to be reduced. I have used a journal approach more successfully in another context and, if circumstances change, and if I can build usefully on the experience of others in this field, it might become possible to reintroduce a greater emphasis upon the student learning process within the module.

Second-Year Project Planning: Use of Handouts, Planning Deadlines and Feedback Pro formas

In this section of the paper I will focus on the project-planning process in the second year, when students work on the development of their own individual projects. Although we have a number of concerns in supporting students through this process (e.g., increasing feelings of self-confidence, supporting self-management skills, helping them to make appropriate external contacts), one of our central aims is that students should be able to lay the foundation for a strong, in-depth, meaning-oriented understanding of their chosen topic area. I will describe some of the various component parts of the project-planning process identified briefly above and try to show how they might help to support the development of a meaning-oriented approach to students' project topic areas.

The purpose of the handouts about the project-planning process, which are made available to students from the end of the first year and through the course of the second year, is to try to show them what is involved in developing their project plans through from the initial ideas to the quite detailed provisional and final project proposals.

Some of the suggestions made are very much practically oriented, and in a sense quite mundane (e.g., finding out about the content of second-year course units, consulting the careers service, learning how to use bibliographic index cards efficiently), although still important. Others are more concerned with helping to give the student an appreciation of how they can most efficiently work with and develop their ideas and so are more closely linked with achieving a meaning-oriented approach to the problem area. Initially, there is an attempt to help students to understand where ideas for their projects might come from, with an emphasis upon their possible problem orientation and personal relevance (e.g., experience before college, particular life events, or possible future career plans). Later, the focus is rather more on the development of a coherent and meaningful structure for the project, with suggestions about working on an "ideas file", identifying the theoretical basis of the project, thinking about contrasting perspectives on the particular topic area, developing tentative structures or "trying things out" and beginning to develop their own, informed point of view within their topic area. These suggestions are, I think, very much inter-linked with having a meaning-oriented approach to a topic area, but they are not easy to explain clearly to students. The feedback evidence so far, though, is that they do find these handouts to be of considerable value. Just over 70% of students agreed that the handouts were useful in providing them with an understanding of what was involved in the project-planning process (the response rate was 68%).

The second important feature of the second-year project-planning process is that there is a series of planning deadlines, so that students have to submit increasingly detailed accounts of their ideas over the course of the year, extending, as indicated in Figure 1, from a brief initial outline of 200 to 300 words to the quite detailed provisional and final proposals. The purpose of having these successive deadlines is partly to support students in the development of their own self-management skills and to ensure that we don't have many students who reach the final project proposal submission deadline without having accomplished much preliminary work. However, there is another important purpose, which links in to our concerns to support the development of a meaning-oriented approach. We want to emphasise to students that a coherent understanding of a particular topic area cannot be produced at short notice. It is something which must be "worked at", refined over a period of time, and must clearly develop out of an appreciation of relevant literature in the area. Almost 71% of students agreed that it had been useful to have a series of project-related deadlines to work towards over the year.

The final crucial component of the project-planning process which was identified above is the provision of appropriate feedback and the use of structured pro formas for this purpose. These pro formas have been introduced for the first time during this last academic year, and in this case the stimulus of having much increased student numbers, has, I think, led to a wholly positive development. The intention is to provide detailed structured feedback to students, particularly in relation to the provisional project-planning stage, so that students can develop and refine their proposals for final submission.

There will be some aspects of the project proposal, e.g., relating to clarity of writing, use of proper grammar, etc., which are relatively objective and quite straightforward to assess, and we have chosen to do so using a simple rating scale, extending from excellent to inadequate. However, it is also essential that feedback is provided about the coherence and level of understanding which is demonstrated within the project proposal, and this is more relevant to our concerns with the extent to which a student seems able to demonstrate a meaning-oriented approach to the topic with which he or she is dealing. The difficulty is that assessing this kind of level of understanding, and providing appropriate feedback, is not an easy matter.

In order to ease the problem of dealing with relatively large numbers of students, and achieving standardisation between different tutors, we have retained the identification of specific criteria in conjunction with a simple rating scale for these more complex criteria. Of course the specification and actual description of these criteria then becomes crucial. The subset of criteria which are most relevant to the assessment of a meaning-oriented approach relate to the student's ability to develop a clear structure for the proposal and provide adequate explanatory accounts of the different component parts which make up the overall proposal. The overall project proposal is a reasonably complex document, but as part of the proposal students must briefly list its component parts, and write discursively but succinctly to explain their intentions for each of these components in a couple of paragraphs, probably up to around 500 words.

The most relevant criteria which derive from two sections of the full pro forma (sections on "overall structure" and "supporting component outlines") are as follows:

well-defined and coherent structure in terms of constituent components;

realistic appreciation of what may be accomplished within the project;

appropriate understanding of project topic area is shown;

perspectives, issues and content have been sensibly selected from the broader content of material relevant to that topic area;

relevant theoretical perspectives are suitably drawn upon to support the project;

each component has clear and unitary focus, rather than being a loose mixture of points;

individual components effectively relate or link together to provide a coherent overall treatment of project topic area.

We have aimed in the wording of these to be as clear and specific as possible, without too much over-simplification, with I'm sure varying degrees of success. One indicator of our success must be the practical value of the criteria and associated rating scale for both tutors and students. Reactions from both have been encouraging. Tutors found that the criteria provided them with a clearly organised basis for their assessment and that the scales were convenient to use. It should be emphasised that space was also provided for open-ended comment, and tutors were also free to make comment directly on the students' proposals if that seemed appropriate. A clear majority of students also indicated that the pro forma had provided them with useful written feedback on their project proposals (82.5% of respondents either agreed or strongly agreed that they had received useful written feedback; the response rate was 68%). The pro forma is also used to provide the basis for later face-to-face discussion, although in many cases it is possible for this to be quite brief.

Evaluation and Research

An important part of the evaluation of teaching innovations of the kind described in this paper must derive from student feedback and the experience and opinions of those closely in the day-to-day processes of managing the teaching–learning situation. However, as is emphasised within this conference, there are obviously more fundamental questions which need to be addressed. In the context of the BA in Applied Social Studies by Independent Study, there is the obvious question of whether this particular kind of degree programme is effective and successful in promoting a meaning-oriented approach to learning among its students. Is it any different in its effects as compared with a more conventional degree programme?

This is obviously a complex question and any answers must depend upon educational values as well as empirical evidence. Within the degree, we are only just beginning to address the challenge of researching into our practice. Currently, I am part way into the process of carrying out a longitudinal cohort study of students within the degree in relation to changes in scores obtained on the Approaches to Studying and Course Perceptions questionnaires. I do not have substantial results to report at this stage but can perhaps make some brief comment on the problems I have experienced in researching this area in this particular degree context:

- Using longitudinal or before and after designs requires repeated administration of questionnaires. I have the impression that students can become somewhat impatient with this and may well not give full attention to their completion. They certainly do not always read instructions properly.

- One reaction to this problem can be to use shortened versions of the questionnaires (e.g., Gibbs, 1992), but this has the disadvantage of limiting the available information (Richardson, 1992). Another possibility might be to develop alternative forms of the inventories.

- Items from the Approaches to Studying Inventory are not always relevant in the context of independent study (e.g., a poor first answer in an exam makes me panic). The new revised version looks more promising in this respect.

- The Approaches to Studying Inventory does not cover all aspects of studying which would seem relevant to the independent study context. The most obvious omission is in relation to self-management or self-regulatory skills (e.g., Zimmerman, 1990).

- Many of the researchers in this area have used qualitative and quantitative methods to complement each other (e.g., Entwistle, 1984) which I think is highly desirable. However, the effective practice of qualitative methods is quite time-consuming, which is possibly a problem for the small-scale researcher.

- Perhaps the most fundamental question which has arisen for me as I have tried to plan and think through possible research designs is the extent to which it is possible to be both teacher/facilitator and researcher. I have considerable sympathy with the action-research approach advocated, for example, by Carr and Kemmis (1986) and Winter (1989), but at the same time wonder at the extent to which it is ethically acceptable to invite students to comment on learning experiences and possible learning difficulties to researchers who will also be their assessors.

References

Biggs, J. B. (1989). Does learning about learning help teachers with teaching? Psychology and the tertiary teacher. Supplement to *The Gazette*, 26, 1. University of Hong Kong.

Candy, P. C. (1991). *Self-Direction for Lifelong Learning*. San Francisco: Jossey-Bass.

Carr, W. and Kemmis, S. (1986). *Becoming Critical*. Lewes: Falmer Press.

Deci, E. L. (1975). *Intrinsic Motivation*. New York: Plenum.

Entwistle, N. (1984). Contrasting perspectives onlLearning. In F. Marton, D. Hounsell and N. Entwistle (eds), *The Experience of Learning*. Edinburgh: Scottish Academic Press.

Entwistle, N. and Ramsden, P. (1983). *Understanding Student Learning*. London: Croom Helm.

Gibbs, G. (1981). *Teaching Students to Learn*. Milton Keynes: Open University Press.

Gibbs, G. (1992). *Improving the Quality of Student Learning:* Bristol: Technical & Educational Services.

Gow, L. and Kember, D. (1990). Does higher education promote independent learning? *Higher Education* 19, 307–322.

Ramsden, P. (1992). *Learning to Teach in Higher Education*. London: Routledge.

Richardson, J. T. E. (1992). A critical evaluation of a short form of the Approaches to Studying Inventory. *Psychology Teaching Review,* 1,1, 34–45.

Rogers, C. (1969). *Freedom to Learn*. Columbus: Merrill.

Zimmerman, B. J. (1990). Self regulating academic learning: the emergence of a social cognitive perspective. *Educational Psychology Review,* 2, 2, 173–201.

Chapter 16 Course design for improved student learning

Open Learning: the Route to Improved Learning?

Maureen A . Blackmore and Elaine Harries-Jenkins, Liverpool John Moores University

---

Introduction

Liverpool Polytechnic's origins can be traced back to the Liverpool Mechanics' and Apprentices' Library founded in 1823. Its colourful history spans more than a century and a half and recently culminated in incorporation, under the Further and Higher Education Act 1992, with the institution officially becoming Liverpool John Moores University (LJMU) on 1 September 1992. Like many other institutions LJMU has undergone internal restructuring in recent years which has had consequent knock-on effects for the programmes of study delivered. The institution has moved from a two-tier faculty/department structure prior to 1988 to a divisional structure, with schools clustered within some of the divisions. At present there are three academic divisions containing 17 schools. These internal changes must also be seen within changes in higher education at the national level. The white paper (Secretary of State for Education and Science) of May 1991 set out a new framework for higher education in the UK. At LJMU during the period 1989 to 1993 growth in student numbers has been rapid, resulting in a 49% increase in the total number of students. In the 1992–93 academic year approximately 19,000 students were enrolled (12,600 full time and sandwich, and 6,400 part time).

Integrated Credit Scheme
The major feature of the university's programme of course provision is the Integrated Credit Scheme (ICS), a modular credit accumulation and transfer scheme which is now the academic and administrative framework through which LJMU delivers its award programmes. The scheme was first introduced in selected areas in autumn 1990 and now all undergraduate degree programmes are within the ICS. This a modular structure built around differentiated levels of study (level 1, 2 and 3 correspond to the three years of a normal full-time undergraduate course, level M is for postgraduate study). Modules can be of different credit ratings and intensities depending upon the demand of the particular subject areas. The basic unit of credit within the scheme is defined as equivalent to 30 hours of student learning activity (a combination of formal

teaching, private study, course work preparation, etc.), a definition which allows for differing proportions of formal contact time across the range of subject disciplines within ICS. A normal workload for a full–time student would be 30 credit units per academic year (i.e., 90 for an honours degree). Basic award programme structures are either single subject (full programme) or joint subjects (half programmes). Each programme is defined at certain levels, core (compulsory) and optional modules, and, beyond these basic requirements, further specialist options or elective modules chosen from across the scheme. Normally, at least 80% of the content of each award programme is prescribed.

Undergraduate routes in the Business School
Within the Liverpool Business School there are five full–time degree routes:

- BA (Hons) Business Studies
- BA (Hons) Accounting and Finance
- BA (Hons) International Business Studies
- BA (Hons) Business Decision Analysis
- BSc (Hons) Business Information Systems.

In addition the Business School also offers some joint subject programmes: Business, Human Resource Management, Financial Management and Marketing and Information Systems for Business.

The first year of all these programmes is a joint foundation year. Thus all first-year students in the Liverpool Business School savour the same diet of subjects, most of which are offered as two credit modules. It is some of these modules which were chosen to be delivered in an open learning format in the second and third trimester of the 1992–93 academic year. This paper reports on the findings of an independent evaluation project during Trimester 2 (i.e., only halfway through the project).

Trimester 2 (January to March)
- Business Statistics Models
- Book-keeping and Financial Statements

Trimester 3 (April to June)
- Business Maths Models
- Financial Statements Interpretation

Materials which had been produced initially for a joint venture with a private university in Rome were modified to support the delivery of these modules. Both sets of materials conformed to a standard format including module aims and objectives, unit listings, details of both formal and informal assessments and further readings and references. The materials differed in length–for example, Book-keeping and Financial Statements at 314 pages compared with Business Statistics Models at 694 pages. The materials were desk-top published and distributed to the students prior to the start of the trimester. No attempt was made to evaluate the effectiveness of these materials as open learning materials.

Delivery of the modules
The academic year is structured around three trimesters (terms). Each ten-week trimester consists of nine teaching weeks. Assessment is carried out in week 10. For the open learning modules the nine teaching weeks were divided into three teaching blocks each of which was subdivided thus:

Week 1	mapping lecture	(1 hour)
Week 2	surgery	(2 hours)
Week 3	surgery	(2 hours)

(i.e., five hours of tuition available per student per study block).
In a mapping lecture the lecturer gave an overview of the next study block, provided a guide through the materials, highlighted key points and indicated where students should aim to be in the materials before the next study block. The format of surgeries differed in the two modules.

Business Statistics Models adopted a prescriptive approach, where students were given problems to work through in groups with tutor support. Book-keeping and Financial Statements advocated a "drop-in" approach, i.e., only students with problems were expected to attend. Since there were approximately 300 students to be taught, each mapping lecture was delivered twice in week 1.
Five surgeries were provided in both weeks 2 and 3 with two tutors in attendance. This pattern was then repeated for weeks 4 to 6 and 7 to 9 for each module.

Methods
Several methods have been used to collect data, including questionnaires, semi-structured interviews with both focus groups and individual students, and student diaries.

Questionnaires

Student learning intentions questionnaires
Questionnaires based on the work by Entwistle and Ramsden (1983) and refined by Gibbs (1992) were distributed to students when they entered Liverpool John Moores University in September 1992, at the start of the second trimester in January 1993 and again at the start of Trimester 3 in April 1993 in order to monitor any changes in students' learning patterns over the foundation year. Similar questionnaires had been distributed to first-year students in April 1992.

Module evaluation questionnaires (MEQ)
These were designed to monitor any differences in students' perceptions of modules delivered in an open learning format and those delivered by traditional

methods. The questionnaire consists of seven sections: (1) personal details (age, sex and course); (2) module organisation and assessment; (3) teaching staff and teaching styles; (4) teaching methods and student workloads; (5) self-development, e.g., reading outside the subject, debating with others, tackling new challenges, etc.; (6) library facilities; and (7) computer facilities. There was also a final section requesting comments. The questions were designed to provide not only information about module organisation, etc., but also satisfaction and importance ratings (Mazelan, Green, Brannigan and Tormey, 1993). On average students took between seven and ten minutes to complete the questionnaire. Data have been collected for two open learning modules (delivered by mapping lectures and surgeries) – Book-keeping and Financial Statements (Accounts), and Business Statistics Models (Statistics)–and two traditional modules (delivered by lectures and tutorials) – Macro Economics (Economics) and Introduction to Business Information Systems (BIS)–and subsequently analysed using SPSS (Statistical Package for Social Scientists).

Interviews

Students, 30 in all, volunteered to participate in semi-structured individual or group interviews. They were interviewed at the beginning, in the middle and at the end of Trimester 2 and also halfway through Trimester 3. Trigger questions were used to stimulate discussions. The sessions were taped and later transcribed. Responses were then grouped into categories for analysis.

Student Diaries

The 30 student volunteers were asked to keep a semi-prescriptive diary for four weeks during Trimester 2, i.e., weeks 4, 5, 6 and 7. The diary was chosen in an attempt to ascertain how much time students engaged in various activities and thus to help identify any constraints under which they were operating. In all only nine completed diaries were returned. Hence this anecdotal evidence should perhaps be viewed with caution.

Results

In order to put the results into context it should be noted that introduction of open learning into the Business School coincided with the introduction of the ICS. Hence the extent and pace of change was such that it was difficult to evaluate the impact of one component of that change. Tensions arose and compromises were necessary to transfer the foundation year into ICS. The academic year under ICS involved students in assessments at the end of each trimester compared with end-of-year examination as in the traditional course.

Questionnaires

Student learning intentions questionnaires

Table 1	Learning intentions questionnaires		
	Achieving (Stan.dev.)	Reproducing (Stan.dev.)	Meaning (Stan.dev.)
September 1992 (n=189)	16.24 (2.98)	15.11 (3.52)	16.35 (3.27)
January 1993 (n=228)	15.15 (3.25)	16.44 (3.47)	14.92 (3.29)
April 1993 (n=98)	14.31 (3.54)	17.07 (2.88)	14.56 (3.82)
National Norms	12.73 (4.26)	13.65 (4.40)	14.21 (4.51)
April 1992 (n=167)	13.83 (3.38)	15.93 (3.53)	12.51 (3.91)

The health warnings issues by Richardson at the conference should be heeded when considering the results, as should the following points:

i) the sample size did vary and therefore it cannot be guaranteed that the 98 students in April 1993 were in the 189 sample in September. Also the students attending the mapping lectures could be disproportionately of the reproducing category;

ii) the national norms quoted are for standard 18-year-old students. They do not contain data for mature or non-standard entry students;

iii) students had already received five modules in Trimester 1 in a traditional format.

Analysis of the questionnaires distributed in September 1992, January 1993 and April 1993 shows that students entering LJMU in September 1992 scored higher than the national norms for Social Sciences in all three categories. However, by January, when the students had received four modules in a traditional format, they had started to employ a more surface approach to learning, as evidenced by an increase in the reproducing score. By April 1993, when they had received two open learning modules and two traditional modules, they were engaged even more in a surface approach to learning, as witnessed by the reproducing score. However, it must be noted that the sample size had reduced during the year due to a fall in attendance at the mapping lectures. Nonetheless a trend is apparent. The score for the reproducing category was in fact higher in April 1993 than with students in April 1992. Again it must be remembered that this score was produced by a different cohort of students following a radically different course (i.e., a traditional self-contained degree programme) and hence a true comparison is not feasible. Both the achieving scores and meaning scores had fallen off during the year, but they were still higher than the national norms and higher than the 1992 scores. However, the trend was towards a decrease in the achieving and meaning categories but an increase in the reproducing category. The trimester system of nine weeks' teaching plus one week assessment could also act as a powerful disincentive for a deeper approach to learning.

Module evaluation questionnaires (MEQ)
The response rates to the questionnaires were: Accounts, 53%; Statistics, 49%; BIS, 53%; Economics, 45%. The sample represented a cross-section of the student population from all age groups and programmes of study. Student perceptions of the organisation and assessment of the modules indicated that the provision of adequate information concerning module organisation, syllabus, timetable, assessment procedures and course work was very important for their studies, but on the whole students were more dissatisfied with the information provided by the open learning modules than by the traditional ones, the dissatisfaction being greater with Statistics than with Accounts.

The ability to contact staff easily, the approachability of staff and their ability to appreciate what it was like to be a student were considered by students to be very important. They also considered it very important that staff should be well organised, teach clearly and at the right pace. On the whole students were fairly satisfied with the traditional modules yet fairly dissatisfied with the open learning modules. Again the rating for the Statistics module was less satisfactory than for Accounts.

Lectures were considered by all students to be a very important aspect of their studies. They were satisfied with the lectures delivered for BIS and Economics but were more dissatisfied with the lectures in the open learning modules.

The traditional modules were considered by students to be more satisfactory than the open learning modules in all instances of the provision of self-development opportunities, e.g., opportunities to discuss issues with others, tackle new challenges, etc.

The patterns of library use were the same for all four modules. However, students were only moderately satisfied with the ease of using computers and the opening hours of computer rooms for all modules and very dissatisfied with the availability/ease of obtaining a PC or terminal for all modules. They considered these factors to be a very important part of their studies. Hence, except for the computer issues, the traditional modules were more acceptable to the students than the open learning modules. Nonetheless it must be noted that for all modules there were disconcerting contrasts between the satisfaction and importance ratings in many areas. Hence there were many factors which students rated as very important to their studies yet they were not very satisfied with them. This was so for for all four modules. Thus even though the open learning modules were less acceptable than the traditional modules the latter, too, were found wanting in several areas.

The comments made by students at the end of the questionnaires (49% of respondents commented on Accounts, 56% on Statistics, 44% on BIS and 35% on Economics) indicated very forcefully that students expected to be taught. The tone of the comments regarding the open learning modules was more critical than for the traditional modules. Students wanted lectures and tutorials and did not expect to have to learn for themselves. However, some comments from the BIS and Economics questionnaires indicated that students were not too satisfied with traditional lectures and tutorials. This qualitative evidence points to the fact that many students came to the university with the expectation that they would receive lectures and tutorials. They were not aware of the purpose of surgeries and mapping lectures and hence could not benefit fully from them.

Interviews

These sessions have proved to be very informative and have highlighted several key issues:

- perceptions about open learning
- choice of modules
- written materials
- surgeries and mapping lectures
- support.

Student Diaries

Only nine completed diaries were returned – four female, five male. Of these nine, four were "A" Level entrants, three had BTec and two had no formal entry qualifications. This anecdotal evidence highlights timetabling problems, lack of personal support and a desire for help with time management.

Results of assessment

The qualitative evidence presented indicates that the level of student satisfaction with the open learning modules was low. Evidence from the Learning Intentions Questionnaires indicates that the students' learning experience was not enhanced by the introduction of open learning. However, the performance indicators that many people use to measure quality are the results of assessment. A comparison of 91–92 students with 92–93 students reveals some interesting findings. The results for 92–93 students were for "tracked" students–i.e., not the whole student population but those for whom entry requirements were known. It must be borne in mind that the 91–92 students had followed a traditional self-contained degree course with end-of-year assessment, whereas the 92–93 students followed an ICS course with assessment at the end of each trimester. The 92–93 results are for Trimester 2 only (i.e., only half the year). Hence there was both a quantitative and a qualitative difference in the assessments. Nonetheless examination of the results highlights some issues (see Table 2).

Table 2

	Accounts 91-92	Accounts 92-93	QT 91-92	Statistics 92-93
Pass Rate	89%	77%	74%	72%
Failures	11%	24%	27%	28%
Range of marks	6-88%	12-80%	2-87%	2-94%
Mean of marks	54.6%	49.2%	50.0%	50.0%
>70%	13%	7%	14%	17%
<40%	11%	24%	27%	28%
<30%	6%	8%	16%	16%

Thus the pass rate for Accounts was significantly less in 92–93 than in 91–92 (down by 12%) whereas it remained the same for Statistics. The total number of failures in Accounts had more than doubled, while those for Statistics remained more or less the same. There was no significant difference in the range of marks awarded but there was a difference between the Accounts mean marks in the two years.The Statistics mean marks showed no difference. The numbers of high achievers (i.e., over 70%) varied between the two subjects. The numbers fell by nearly half for Accounts but increased for Statistics. The numbers of students receiving less than 40% more than doubled for Accounts but remained the same for Statistics. Overall during 92–93 there has been an apparent increase in the failure rate in Accounts compared with Statistics over the previous year. Thus in spite of students' greater dislike of Statistics they performed better in assessment for that subject than for Accounts.

Discussion

In this complicated web of change and innovation it is difficult to tease out relevant strands. However, it must be remembered that any innovation requires time to bed down. The open learning project within the Liverpool Business School has not benefited from the luxury of time but has tried to innovate while coping with the sea of change.

Nonetheless the quality of the students' learning experience does appear to have suffered in that students have engaged in a surface approach to learning, where they concentrated on reducing what was to be learnt to the status of unconnected facts to be memorised and then reproduced at a later date (e.g., in an exam) rather than on developing a deeper approach to learning. However, it cannot be said that open learning has been the sole contributor to this. The introduction of open learning coincided with the introduction of the ICS into the Business School in September 1992. Many problems have arisen because courses had not been specifically designed to fit within the modular framework of nine-week modules. Most of the modules carried two credits, and since students must acquire 30 credits in one year this has been too much of a burden for many of them. The assessment pattern changed too under ICS such that students were assessed every ten weeks – yet another new system for them to cope with.

The sheer volume of Statistics materials also added to the problem. Too much material was given to students at once. There was no indication of what was and what was not important. There was also the added problem of students' preconceived notions. Many students were frightened by Statistics. This problem cannot be solved by giving students large volumes of materials. Something more needed to have been done to take away the panic. The materials for both modules were not easy to read; both modules involved numbers and contained too much jargon, and consequently they were not user-friendly. Overall students felt that they had been given a great bulk of materials from which they were unable to appreciate what was important.

Consequently they were confused and required additional help to map their way through the materials. Much more guidance was required. The choice of subject modules could also have been more helpful. Two quantitative subjects obviously posed problems for many of the learners. Also many students admitted that they had not read the materials during the study blocks and so were ill prepared to take full advantage of the surgeries.

Adequate preparation of both students and staff is essential when any innovatory change is introduced into a course. Although a brief induction period was provided for all new students it was obvious that the induction programme had not worked as planned. It was clear that more input was needed on study skills in order to encourage students to adopt more student–centred approaches to their studies. Staff too need help in transferring to this method of course delivery. Staff need to be trained to deliver in an open learning mode. It is a culture shock for many staff who are used to traditional didactic delivery mechanisms. Hence closing the circle with appropriate staff development is essential.

The provision of effective communication has also proved to be a problem. There were approximately 300 students in the foundation year in the Business School. The school has been creative in providing channels of communication, which included notice-boards – both individual course notice-boards and a special open learning project notice-board – videotext on large monitors around the Business School and electronic mail on the computer network. However, there were still students who did not know what was going on. The student grapevine worked if you were part of it but there were many students who were lonely individuals.

Although the picture painted so far does not appear too rosy, nonetheless this has been an evolutionary project and many positive things have surfaced to date including the reaction to student feedback. Staff did listen to the anxieties, etc., of students and responded accordingly both sympathetically and expeditiously. The Statistics course team took the issues on board. In week 7 of Trimester 2, due to pressure from student feedback, modifications were made to the format of the surgeries. Each surgery began with a 15-minute mini-lecture followed by group work. The session concluded with a brief summing up and a question and answer session. The team also modified the materials by providing a structured route through them in order to identify "core" areas and removed three units from the final assessment. They provided drop-in remedial sessions for individuals and rescheduled the examination to the next trimester. In addition a course work guidance session was provided and the time available to complete the course work was extended. Many students greatly appreciated this rapid response by the Business School and felt that they were partners in the project and had not been left to sink or swim. They realised that it was a learning process for staff and students alike.

Conclusions

Overall the conclusion must be that open learning did not necessarily enhance the student learning experience. The rate of change has been too much for the system to cope with at the moment. The concomitant introduction of ICS may have contributed to the problems along with other issues, but it has been too difficult a task to tease out the various individual strands contributing to the web. As with all evolutionary processes the learning can be painful. At Liverpool this has been true, but in typical Darwinian tradition the learning has been productive too. Many lessons have been and are being learnt which are feeding back into the developmental process, both from the point of view of the overall student experience and the staff experience. The Liverpool John Moores University in partnership with the Liverpool Business School is striving to encourage students to adopt more student-centred approaches to their learning so that they become life-long learners, not just surface learners.

References

Entwistle, N. and Ramsden, P. (1983). *Understanding Student Learning*. London: Croom and Helm.

Gibbs, G. (1992). *Improving the Quality of Student Learning*. Bristol: Technical & Educational Services.

Mazelan, P. M., Green, D. M., Brannigan, C. R. and Tormey, P. F. (1993). Student satisfaction and perceptions of quality. In *Aspects of Educational Training Technology*. M. Shaw and E. Roper (ed.), London: Kogan Page.

Secretary of State for Education and Science (1991). *Higher Education: A New Framework*. CM1541. HMSO.

Acknowledgements

The authors would like to express their thanks and appreciation to staff and foundation-year students within the Liverpool Business School for their co operation in this project. All have given of their time and thoughts so freely and frankly. Tribute is due to them all for sharing all the positive as well as the negative aspects of the project in a spirit of co operation.

Identifying and Working with Student Expectations of Learning

Allan Davies, Worcester College of Higher Education

Introduction

This paper is in two parts. The first part outlines the background to, and some of the main issues within, an action research project on reflection on a BA(Hons) graphic information design course at Falmouth School of Art and Design. The project was a case-study in the CNAA-funded 'Improving Student Learning' project and is written up by Graham Gibbs in his book *Improving the Quality of Student Learning* (1992). The second part looks at the impact that the research has had on the curriculum and identifies a promising area of enquiry for the future.

Improving Student Learning Project

The course
The BA(Hons) Graphic Information Design is a full-time, four-year sandwich course. It is concerned with the visual communication of information. This emphasis gives rise to a programme of study which distinguishes the course from general graphic design courses in three important ways:

- an over-riding concern for the communication of information, that is, "communication intended to reduce uncertainty", as a priority over persuasive or stylistic concerns;

- a primary concern for the end-user of information;

- an approach to design which recognises process and theoretical understanding as vital to successful communication, and which acknowledges the need for collaboration with specialists where and when possible.

The course prepares students to seek employment in a variety of situations, including publishing, in-house design units, specialist design groups and specialist computer graphics and audio/visual companies.

Background to the innovation

The brief
Traditionally, the dominant method of teaching design, particularly on graphics focussed courses, was that of the brief being written by the tutor and acted upon by the student; usually there was a time limit or 'deadline' involved. The beauty of the method was that it not only perpetuated the power relation between

teacher and pupil, as in secondary school, but it also simulated (to a certain extent) the professional practice of designers. There was no reason to challenge that which provided such a neat fit between education and work. However, graphic information design does not sit easily within this framework. It is a sufficiently new and developing subject not to have established within its methodology the entire traditional approach. One important ability of the information designer is that he or she can identify problems within visual information. That is, information designers are as much proactive about problems as they are reactive to set briefs. Hence, the final year of the course is one in which the students are responsible for identifying and acting upon what they feel to be genuine information design problems. They are responsible for writing their own briefs and solving them accordingly.

Since its inception the course has expected students in the final year to undertake such individual programmes of work, including a major project. This programme of work formed the largest component in the students' final assessment for the award of a degree.

The student was expected to establish project briefs individually and present them to the course team for approval. Following this, each student was allocated a tutor, and it was the students' responsibility to arrange contact with the tutor as they felt necessary. Other tutors with specialist subject knowledge could also be consulted by arrangement. This was, at the time, the only tutorial support which students received. There were no opportunities for students to interact together in an organised way.

Nevertheless, this handing over responsibility to the students has meant, for many of them, an important shift in their perception of what it is to be a graphic information designer. But, probably more importantly, it has provided a motivational context for a deeper kind of learning to take place.

However, it was the strongly motivated and well-organised students who tended to survive this situation with reasonable academic success; others did not do so well. While the emphasis on individual programmes of work was still considered appropriate, a number of problems were identified:

1. Tutorial support for students was often insufficient if the student did not, for whatever reasons, seek to organise it.

2. Tutorial advice, when given, often took the form of "handing over" knowledge from tutor to student. Students would tend to approach tutors for answers, hence perpetuating the passive mode of learning.

3. There was no opportunity to compare, contrast and debate differing views on project work or to extend thinking into broader design issues.

4. There were no opportunities to involve students in learning from their peers (or helping their peers to learn).

The circumstances were, therefore, that students in the earlier years of the course would experience assessment on a grand scale in somewhat intimidating circumstances, whereas the final-year experience was that of a one-to-one tutorial in which the tutor was perceived as the source of the knowledge. Neither approach was adequate in itself and there was no consistency of experience.

The report

Another important feature of the course programme in the final year is that students have to provide a written report on each of their projects. The report is intended to provide information about how the project came about, evidence of the depth of their research and their methodology and the conclusions reached - indeed, anything which could not be displayed in their final presentation.

In looking to ways in which these problems might be reduced, the course team were mindful of changes in the approach to teaching and learning which were beginning to be discussed in art and design education. Conferences on student-centred learning and a questioning of traditional teaching practices ("sitting with Nellie") provided a context in which change could be more actively sought, and also supplied an increasing amount of information about ways in which students' learning could be improved.

It is against this background that the innovation was introduced.

The innovation

Independent, solitary and unreflective final-year project work has been modified such that learning teams have been established to support independent work and encourage reflection.

What methods were used before the innovation was introduced, and what problems did this involve?
As has already been mentioned, the previous method of student support in the final year was that of the one-to-one tutorial with a member of staff. As the innovation has been in place for three years now, none of the present students has experienced the old approach, therefore there is little point in attempting to make any comparisons of students' perceptions of then and now. The experience most comparable is that which the present students had in the earlier years of their course, and it may be worth making some comment about this.

In the earlier years students would have received feedback on their work in the traditional way through the "crit", a meeting which all students would attend, and their work for that project, usually mounted on the studio wall, being "assessed" individually in front of the rest of the group. Of the drawbacks to this method, one student said

> It was all too late. If you were going to make mistakes then you had made
> them and missed them, and they showed up in your final work, then you
> were on to another project and you can't go back and rectify them or sort
> them out properly . . . It wasn't so bad for me to stand up in front of so
> many people but it really did frighten some people. It wasn't confidence
> building to make them go up there and do it, it was just making them
> worse' . . . 'it was alright if you were the first person in the group . . . but by
> the time you got to number 30 everyone was falling asleep and by the time
> you got to the eighth piece of work anyway, everything that was going to
> be said about nearly all the pieces of work had already been said and the
> tutor was just repeating himself.

What methods were introduced, and why?
A weekly group meeting of about 90minutes' duration was arranged for all
fourth year students. Each group would be about eight in number, large enough
for extended debate but not so large that some members would feel intimidated
by its size. Tutors were allocated to each group, although it was stressed that the
tutors should not play a dominant role in the group; indeed, the students
themselves were encouraged to determine their own rules and procedures.

The express purpose of these meetings, or tutorials as they became known, is to
enable students to discuss their work semi-informally among themselves. It is
believed that students would be more forthcoming about their strengths and
weaknesses in a more convivial atmosphere and therefore more able to reflect on
their achievements and mistakes. This is considered the most appropriate and
supportive context for students to engage in reflection on their own work and
provide support for their colleagues.

How does the innovation relate to the four key elements?
Essentially, the innovation is intended to fill a gap between the purpose of the
self-initiated brief and the purpose of the final project and report.

Of the key elements, *learner activity* is the most problematic for us since the
project work in which students engage in the final year is predominantly active -
simply identifying and then researching their main project entails students'
active participation. However, as the briefing paper points out, doing is not
sufficient for learning and, certainly, for us, separating out effective active
learning from ineffective active learning is no easy task. Nevertheless, active
learning is a key feature of the course and all students are expected to engage in
this form of learning.

It is felt that, in determining their own briefs, students are more likely to regard
the work as theirs and therefore be more inclined towards self-motivation in
realising their conclusions. This, then, could be seen as the major instrument in

determining the *motivational context.*

The report is intended to determine the understanding that the students have about the nature and purpose of their project and how well they understand the value of the exercise. In many ways this tests the *well-structured knowledge base,* although it doesn't necessarily foster it.

The purpose of the learning team, then, is to take advantage of the motivational context inspired by the self-initiated brief and to sustain that motivation throughout the period of the project by establishing an opportunity to *interact with others* on a regular basis. The interaction is intended to foster a deep approach to learning through the students having to explain to their colleagues the purpose of the project, how it is being planned, what reservations they have, how they might proceed, how they dealt with problems, and so on.

Also, the learning team meetings are a forum for sharing advice on skills and ideas. The team, at this stage in the course, represents a substantial learning resource - far greater possibly than any one tutor. This sharing of skills, knowledge and experience could well be regarded as underpinning and sometimes assessing students' well-structured knowledge base.

Examples of a deep approach to learning in graphic information design: an interview with Phillipa
Phillipa's major project was a teaching aid in physiotherapy. I asked her why she chose it.

> I was interested in exercise. I looked at different aspects of it and physiotherapy was perhaps the medical information side of it, putting exercise into appropriate use for people who really need it; stroke victims, amputees, sports injuries, it covers such a wide range.

I asked her if she had looked at the whole teaching programme.

> Yes, the whole teaching process, and I found that with all the subjects that they have got, there is physiology, pathology, anatomy, movement science, there is a wide range of subjects, but they are all inter-dependent on each other, so it obviously makes sense for them all to be viewed together in some way . . . so what I did was anatomy. You need to view that with pathology or movement science to work out where the muscles are and how they work, how you compare the exercises. And, basically, all they had were textbooks, so I thought the best thing to do was have a teaching aid, possibly inter-active that could involve the students. Also they did not have anything for open days or induction courses . . . they just have leaflets, so I thought something was needed to go with leaflets to interest people. So my target groups were prospective students and first-year students. I had to come up with something that solved problems in lots of different areas.

What we can see from this section of the interview is that Phillipa's motivation was strong because she elected to locate her major project in an area in which she had an interest. Her deciding to look at the whole teaching process is also evidence that she was concerned to develop a well-structured knowledge base in relation to her task. That is, she recognised that a successful outcome was dependent on her clear understanding of this new subject area.

Certain expressions that she uses seem to be evidence of a deep approach. Firstly, she makes a conceptual leap when, having recognised that the subjects in physiotherapy are inter-dependent, she says "so it obviously makes sense for them all to be viewed together." Her recognition of something obviously making sense is telling here. Secondly, she resolves the problem in the following words: "so I thought the best thing to do was have a teaching aid, possibly inter-active that could involve the students." Here the use of the personal pronoun suggests her "ownership" of the project, and the recognition that something inter-active . . . could involve the students is indicative of her understanding of ways of learning. Finally, she recognises at the end of this quote that her solution to one problem could be extended to solve one or two others that she had recognised.

2. Impact of the Research on the Curriculum

Formal outcomes
Since carrying out the research, and in the light of its outcomes, we have made certain modifications to the curriculum.

1. Learning teams, comprising about eight students, have been established in all four years of the course. They meet regularly, once a week for up to 90 minutes, with the express purpose of enabling students to reflect formally on what they have learnt during that week. The role of the tutor is that of facilitator allowing students to talk openly about their achievements in learning throughout the week.

   The concepts of deep and surface approaches and the criteria for identifying them are used explicitly during these sessions.

2. Briefings for major projects are more intense, with students working in small groups to share the nature of the problems presented to them. Students are invited to speculate at this stage as to what might constitute a deep approach to the project. Surface approaches are also considered.

3. Assessment is now more student focussed, with formal self- and peer assessment programmes built into the projects. Learning objectives and assessment criteria (based on Biggs's SOLO taxonomy) for the course are given to all students and are used at briefings and assessments.

4. The induction period for first-year students has been extended, with projects

being given which are specifically focussed on their approaches to learning

5. The "learning team" approach has been adopted for the contextual studies dissertation in the final year. Students now meet in small groups, with one-to-one tutorials kept to a minimum.

Evaluation of the modified curriculum

The modified curriculum has been in place for one academic year to date. No formal evaluation of the specific changes has yet been carried out, although other forms of evaluation on the student experience are very encouraging. The learning teams appear to be working well, with tutors reporting back positive observations about the ways in which students are becoming engaged in their projects. The self- and peer assessment programme has been taken up with enthusiasm. The termly student course evaluation has provided evidence of student support for the modifications.

One site of what transpired to be valuable information gathering about the modification of the curriculum was the first-year learning team meeting which I facilitated each week. The express intention of the early work on the course with the first year was to enable them to develop clear conceptions of their approaches to learning. The learning team was the opportunity for students to reflect on their week and identify and describe what they had learnt, how they had learnt it and whether they had taken a deep or surface approach. Identifying examples of deep and surface approaches during the early days of their course meant looking back at their previous school or foundation experience. Not surprisingly, many students could find numerous examples of a surface approach in their "A"-Level experience. Quite often a deep approach was related to the charismatic performance of a particular teacher. Students could recall with pleasure the desire to find out more because they felt that the teacher cared for both them and the subject. Identifying a deep approach which was entirely student motivated was not that easy. Even reference to student-centred approaches in GCSE work elicited far more examples of surface than deep approaches. Rick scoffed at his geography project when he said, "We were given a task to do: we went away, tore out some pages from a book or magazine and stuck them in our workbooks. I used to do quite well at that although I can't remember a thing about what I did."

Eventually, it occurred to me that if their immediate school experience was not coming up with useful examples then I should make references outside of them, and in particular to the hobbies that they might pursue or have pursued. What surprised me was the general astonishment on the students' part that the pursuit of hobbies could be equated with the learning they engage in at college. And when we did begin to elicit examples of a deep approach to learning in their recreational activities, many students began to devalue the concept of a deep approach. Indeed some students believed that learning at college was qualitatively different to that in their hobby pursuits.

It was listening to students grappling with their conceptions of learning that began to make me realise that the encouraging of a deep approach to learning was more problematic than I had thought. I had originally anticipated resistance from students in terms of their conception of learning and had believed that the task was merely to enable them to alter their conceptions. However, some of the students clearly identified their conception of learning with their expectation of what learning should be. Irrespective of whether these students could articulate the distinctions between deep and surface approaches, their view of what learning consisted in depended on certain structures and behaviours being evident in their college experience.

Through further discussions in this vein with students in other years, it became evident how profoundly their expectation of what learning their subject is and where it should be learnt played a part in their conception and approach. Some students saw no contradiction in recognising their capacity to take a deep approach in their non-scholastic lives while demanding structures from the curriculum and attitudes from the staff which clearly promoted a surface approach. Indeed, there was evidence from some discussions that some students had in fact taken a deep approach to a project but, because the outcome had not satisfied their expectations of what the outcome should be like, they were convinced that they had not learnt anything of value.

One formal evaluation that has taken place recently is the administering of the questionnaire to the second year and the comparing of the results with those recorded with the same group a year ago. It was the outcome of some of these individual results from the questionnaire, along with the informal observations outlined above, that prompted the present line of research into student learning.

The relationship between conception and expectation of learning
There is good evidence (see Gibbs, 1992, p. 6) to demonstrate that students' conceptions of learning have an impact on their approach to learning.

Students whose conception of learning is that of memorising or learning facts have difficulty in understanding what counts as a deep approach. Students whose conception of learning is that of making sense have the choice of either a deep or a surface approach depending on the circumstances. Also,

> the connection between these underlying conceptions of learning and the approach that students take to specific tasks is so strong that it is possible to predict the quality of outcomes directly from students' conceptions of learning. (p. 6)

There is, therefore, a strong relation between conception, approach and outcome.

Furthermore, there is a strong relationship between students' conception of learning and their conception of teaching. Students who take a surface approach usually have a "closed" conception of teaching in which "the teacher selects the content, presents it and tests whether it has stuck". Those taking a deep approach have an "open" conception of teaching in which "the learner functions independently with the facilitation of the teacher".

The task, therefore, is to design the curriculum as openly as possible, encouraging students to change their approach from surface to deep.This is the direction we took.

Many of the features that have been identified with the strategies for fostering a deep approach in students were present in the course, anyway. Problem-based learning, learning by doing and project work are characteristic of most practical design courses. The original innovation of the tutorial was seen as extending the range of strategies to include personal development, reflection and developing learning skills. As a peer-and self-assessment programme was also being introduced at the same time, we felt well equipped to promote a deep approach in graphic information design.

The results of the second questionnaire are more or less in line with the results of the case-study (see Appendix 1 for full results).

	Achieving	Reproducing	Meaning
1992	15	12	14.9
1993	13	10.19	15

26 students

The meaning orientation remains much the same, although in relation to arts undergraduates that is more or less normal. Encouragingly, the other two orientations have decreased.

What was of interest was certain individual scores. Despite the high profile given to the approaches to learning and the introduction of learning teams, one student's meaning orientation dipped dramatically. Surprisingly, several of the high reproducing scores recorded in the first test remained high after the second.

The growing belief that the innovations were not sufficient for these students to change their conception began to manifest itself. The question was, "What was it about these students' conceptions of learning that were so difficult to change?"

The discussions with the first-year learning teams suggested a possible line of enquiry. Could it be that, despite their ability to participate actively in the innovations, their original expectations of what and how they should be taught still remain.

Andrew H. was interviewed by Jeremy Tridgell:

Jeremy: Perhaps you could talk about any changes you have noticed in the way you've thought about your learning through learning teams . . . over the last year.

Andrew: The LTs have made quite a big difference, once a week, to be able to talk to people . . . not just briefly . . . to me to be able to alleviate problems, just to get other people's point of view . . . obviously ask questions . . . I think that's been the biggest change . . . in an academic change . . . essay writing . . . realising the importance of them. In the second year my attitudes changed quite a bit . . .

Andrew recorded only 6 on his meaning orientation this time against 13 previously.

Jeremy: When you started, how did you think you were going to be learning, how was the learning to take place?

Andrew: I don't know really. To go from taking information in the sixth form to foundation course where its all free, where its your choice . . . dunno really.

Jeremy: When you started out did you have an approach, did you feel you needed to know what the learning was going to be like . . .?

Andrew: . . . I just picked it up as I went along, I didn't anticipate . . . I didn't have a great knowledge of what it was about . . . I came away thinking it was a nice place.

Andrew's comments about the contrast between sixth form and foundation studies could be revealing here. Clearly, he has experienced two distinctly different course designs, and therefore may have at least some conception of alternative approaches. Who is he to trust? Why should the GID course be any better than any other course in meeting his needs?

Martin P's achieving orientation of 17 was very high in the first test but dropped to 12 in the second.

Allan: What were your expectations of learning when you came on the course?

Martin: When I applied I thought it was going to be more strict and structured . . . I suppose I was thinking more in terms of what I learned at school and on foundation course . . . in strict catagories, like typography. Also give you things to do and you have to do them, not like long briefs like we have now . . . . On this course it's up to the individual student as to what he wants to get out of it, which is good but it wasn't what I expected.

Allan: Did you expect to be told what to do and you go away and do it?

Martin: Up to a point, yes . . . I think it's taken me up to a year and a half to actually start working.

Allan: Is that anything to do with what you thought learning was?

Martin: Yes, I think it's not right that it's just up to the tutors to just read out of a book what is what; it's really up to you . . . I am thinking more about what the course is about.

It seems to have taken Martin 18 months to change his conception of learning from one of competing with others to that of needing to find out through personal interest. Why should it have taken him so long?

Martin is a politically active student who has played a substantial part in encouraging debating societies within the college. He is motivated, single-minded and articulate about these matters. However, he has not yet demonstrated this kind of commitment to his chosen degree subject - even though outside class he willingly talks about design matters. Could it be that, again, Martin is someone who takes a deep approach in his personal space but has had such entrenched expectations of what institutional learning is that he cannot dispense with them so easily?

The relation between learning in one's personal life and learning in an institution designed for learning seems, for some students, to be one of polar opposites. Paradoxically, it appears that students can have a conception of learning that is deep but are unable or unwilling to recognise that it is appropriate in a learning establishment.

If there is anything worthwhile in this view, and further work has to be carried out to substantiate it, it may enable us to understand why some apparently able and capable students find it difficult to make the best possible use of institutionalised learning. It might also be the case that we are doing a disservice to those students whose expectations of learning in higher education we haven't taken into account when we design our courses.

Reference

Gibbs, G. (1992). *Improving the Quality of Student Learning*. Bristol: Technical & Educational Services.

Appendix 1

June 93

Achieving

Reproducing

Meaning

June 92

Achieving

Reproducing

Meaning

Stuart B.

8

2

20

14

4

16

Matthew C.

9

1

21

12

9

16

519

David C.

18

15

16

20

17

18

Brett D.

20

13

15

17

15

16

Nicholas D.

11

8

16

15

13

12

520

Chris D.

14

13

15

11

10

12

Tim G.

16

8

23

17

7

23

Ian G.

10

9

14

9

11

13

521

Andrew H.

14

12

14

19

9

16

Andrew H.

13

16

6

15

16

13

Daryn H.

12

8

14

22

10

14

522

Michelle H.

16

8

19

14

12

14

Paul L.

10

14

13

13

12

16

Dean M.

9

7

11

10

11

19

523

Maria M.

12

10

12

12

16

16

Richard M.

18

7

16

20

10

18

Ceri P.

14

5

13

19

13

17

524

Martin P.

12

13

19

17

10

17

Kerry Q.

8

13

13

15

13

14

Peter S.

17

13

9

17

13

9

525

Chloe S.

14

12

12

14

15

14

Deborah S.

19

6

22

13

10

14

Phillip S.

11

17

14

10

14

10

526

Madeline T.

14

14

16

13

17

11

Alison W.

11

12

18

15

11

17

Helen Z.

8

9

10

18

14

14

527

Using a Standard Student Experience Questionnaire with Engineering Students: Initial Results

Roy Gregory, Lin Thorley, and Dr G. Harland, University of Hertfordshire

---

Background

The School of Engineering at the University of Hertfordshire runs degree and HND schemes in a variety of disciplines for over 2,000 students. The disciplines include Aerospace, Aerospace Systems, Building Services, Civil, Electrical and Electronic, Manufacturing Systems and Mechanical Engineering. It was decided by the school that a standard questionnaire would be given to all students as part of the annual monitoring and evaluation process, in order to monitor the student experience and give indications of areas for further investigation to improve quality. It was important, though, not to swamp the School Academic Committee with statistics! In order to start the procedures and gain experience quickly a trial was instituted using a standard already proven questionnaire.

This paper describes the process and early results of the questionnaire returns with comments on the implications and usefulness of the process. The work was carried out by scheme tutors as part of their normal monitoring and improvement procedures, within the working environment of the school and not as part of a special research project. The paper does not give a full or complete analysis, presenting the data in more or less their raw form. It includes initial data, experiences and tentative interpretations with a view to promoting a wider discussion.

The trial was a first for the School of Engineering and the biggest attempted in the university. It was conducted in consultation with Professor Graham Gibbs from the Oxford Centre for Staff Development. The questionnaire was administered in the week before and the two weeks after the Easter '93 vacation using, as far as possible, a published standard procedure. All the schemes involved had formal examinations in June or late May. The trial attempted to cover all the schemes of study in the school but in the short time scale not all were actually included. The responses were analysed mostly by an Optical Mark Reader but a few were processed manually. The manual analysis used a sample of at least 20% of the student year or a minimum, where possible, of 20.

A total of 674 replies were received from 20 schemes of study, out of a possible total of 997 students.

The Questionnaire

The trial was based on a standard Student Experience Questionnaire produced by Professor Paul Ramsden of Griffiths University for a project study and used with his permission Ramsden, 1990). It was originally designed for use in comparing institutions but was chosen for this study because it was readily available and had already been trailed and evaluated in Australia. It has "built-in" strategic level performance indicators and there are norm data from Ramsden's work available to make comparisons. These norm data cover 13 Australian institutions with 3372 undergraduate students across nine disciplines, of which engineering is one.

The 30 questions used in the questionnaire were taken from statements, both positive and negative, made by students about their experience of learning. The questionnaire is reproduced in *Learning to Teach in Higher Education* (Ramsden, 1991), which also describes the rationale behind it and the way the scores might be interpreted. The questionnaire also has the advantage of being based on a philosophy of teaching and learning which attempts to put into practice the current research findings of what constitutes good teaching.
This underlying philosophy encourages and assists interpretations of the data, which could make a positive contribution to improving the quality of student learning.

The questionnaire aims to provide performance parameters at a strategic level which can be used to identify areas of further investigation, in terms of both performance below norms which can be rectified and performance above norms which can be disseminated as good practice.

Scoring and Performance Indicators

The scoring is based on five elements generally recognised by researchers to be among the most significant for good student learning. The elements and the questions associated with these are scored such that "5" is a good score and "1" a poor score: a score of "5" represents a student strongly agreeing with a positive statement concerned with learning or strongly disagreeing with a negative statement. Scores are then averaged for a group of five to eight questions associated with each element. The elements are:

- good teaching
- clear goals and standards
- appropriate workload
- appropriate assessment
- emphasis on student independence.

These averaged scores are used as relative performance indicators to assess the students' learning experience on the the various schemes.

The performance indicators can then be used to identify priority areas for further investigation by, for example, sample student and staff interviews. It is useful to be able to compare across schemes and years. Where students perceive good practice and this is borne out by further detailed enquiry this can be shared across the school.

The Optical Mark Reader used to process the responses comes with its own software and can be used to produce all the data in Table 1. In the trial period a simple spreadsheet was used to translate the data from the questionnaire. The technology gave a quick and efficient way of analysing the results without consuming too much time, encouraging all scheme officers to use this type of approach.

Presentation of the Data

The data obtained is shown in Table 1 and in Figures 1 to 6. The table shows the scores in each of the elements ranging from "1" to "5", the higher values indicating a good score in that element. Table 1 also shows the type of scheme and the year related to the scheme number, the number of questionnaire replies and the total number of students in the year.

Norms (averages) are given for all the schemes analysed. The norms from the Ramsden work for engineering, natural sciences and humanities schemes are given for comparison. A factor is used to give an indication of relative performance which is plotted in Figures 1 to 6. This factor is calculated by dividing the actual score for a particular performance parameter, say "good teaching", by the average for "good teaching" for all the schemes. Above "1" this factor indicates a better than average score. The summation of these factors is shown in Figure 1 and in Table 1, giving an indication of the overall rating of the schemes based on the questionnaires.

Initial Discussion of the Data

There appears to be little difference between degree average scores and HND average scores for the various elements. In all these five aspects the HND/degree schemes are indistinguishable.

Figure 1 shows, however, clear differences in the students' overall learning experience on different schemes. Generally the first-year degree and HND schemes seem to do particularly well. Second-and third-year BEng schemes seem to do poorly and have particularly low 'appropriate workload' scores. The performance indicators could well be inter-related, with the students responding to the questionnaires influenced by the general feeling about the scheme at this point in time.

It could be useful from a strategic point of view to put effort into investigating the reasons for the significant differences between schemes 3, 2 and 9 and schemes 11, 19, 4, 13 and 10 (Figure 1). This could help both to improve the low scoring schemes and to raise the level of the majority (13 schemes) which cannot be separated in overall scoring.

It is interesting to note that first-year chemes also do better on "student independence" scores (Figure 6). There is a general trend for the perception of independence to decrease as the years progress. This could be related to a general sense of being "out of control", seen, for example, in the poor "appropriate workload" scores, or it could be a change in the students' expectation and perception of independence. There is no evidence that the degree schemes score any better than HND on "student independence". These are important areas for further investigation.

It is of concern that students generally seem to have a worsening experience of their education as they progress through a scheme.

From Table 1 it can be seen that in three areas ("clear goals", "appropriate assessment" and "student independence") there is remarkable agreement with the Ramsden figures for engineering. The Ramsden figures indicate that the norms are discipline dependent and that in many areas engineering scores are low compared with other disciplines. It would be useful to conduct a similar study in natural sciences to see whether the better scores for the discipline in "good teaching" and "clear goals" shown in Ramsden's figures would be obtained in the University of Hertfordshire. This would indicate the potential for looking at the reasons for these differences and the value this might have in improving learning. It is important for engineers to investigate why these differences exist.

The data show that the "good teaching" scores are higher than the Ramsden norms and that "appropriate workload" is lower. The reasons for this are not known.

The data do suggest that priority effort should be put into investigating the worst element score of "appropriate workload" to see whether there is transfer of good practice possible between the highest and lowest scoring schemes in that area. Figure 4 shows the schemes where much better than average "appropriate workload" scores are achieved. It is noticeable that these scores show the greatest difference among the schemes and hence have possibly a potential area for the most improvement by making use of 'in-house' good practice.

Tentative conclusions on a strategic level would be to put priority into investigating, monitoring and controlling workload. It might be that efforts to improve lecturing will be wasted unless and until this vital piece of scheme management is also put in place. This conclusion is supported by the frequency of student complaints on work scheduling and quantity of material presented

The MEng scheme scored particularly highly in the questionnaire but is in some senses a special case. Its orientation is towards management, business studies, European studies and human relations. Its contact hours are half that of most other schemes and there is a large proportion of essay work and in-course assessment.

There is also some evidence from the data that Manufacturing Systems schemes, which have a significant amount of content similar to the MEng, tend to score above average.

Since norms appear to be discipline related it is possible that in certain cases, such as the MEng, more appropriate norms for comparisons could be with disciplines which are generally in other schools. This supports the view that the scores are discipline dependent and that comparisons, even within engineering, must be made carefully.

The MEng scheme shows significantly higher than average scores in all but "clear goals". A detailed discussion with MEng students was carried out which indicated considerable anxiety at the freedom in the scheme, and this may have affected their feelings about "clear goals". There does not, however, appear to be any general correlation between high scores on "student independence" and low scores on "clear goals". Again the MEng may be a special case dealing with many personal development issues mostly new for engineering students.

A preliminary view of the data indicates that the scoring systems give a useful overview of quality across the school and the places for further investigation, as well as the type of concise information required by the Academic Committee in its overview role. This has the potential of providing rapid and understandable information which can be a useful monitoring tool. It can be used to make comparisons from scheme to scheme in similar discipline areas, although more experience is needed to determine how significant these comparisons are.

Reaction from Students and Scheme Tutors

Scheme tutors and students both expressed some reservations when they used the questionnaire. Both were focussed at a more detailed and individual course level and wanted to give or receive feedback at that level. There was a degree of frustration that at this tactical level their needs were not being met. This must be addressed by a more careful description of the use of the questionnaire and by staff development which looks at the importance of the use of the performance indicators for overall quality improvement.

The attitude of the staff and students to the questionnaire and the extent to which a standard procedure is followed in obtaining the answers from the students has an important effect on the results. It was not possible to monitor how far published guidelines were followed by tutors. Tutor practice in administering the questionnaire is likely to improve as the need for standard practice is appreciated by experience. It will, however, remain an issue that must be continually addressed.

The questionnaire needs to be supplemented, for monitoring and evaluation purposes, by data at scheme and course level for use by scheme committees and individual course tutors. This can be done by a more course specific questionnaire or by discussion between students and staff. It is apparent that there is a need for two levels of information which can then be used at two different levels of management, the strategic and the tactical, though how this is to be done without overloading students and staff has yet to be resolved.

A complete analysis has not yet been undertaken nor scheme tutor and director of studies views obtained. A detailed analysis has also yet to be made of the way individual questions were answered and what might be learnt from that. This may assist in understanding more specifically about students' attitudes on the particular schemes and also help in the development and improvement of the questionnaire - for this particular purpose.

There may need to be changes to the questionnaire to suit the application within the school and the UK educational system in general, but the initial results are encouraging. Discussions and investigations of the meaning of these figures will continue as part of the school's annual evaluation procedure and will play an important role in staff development.

Conclusions

- The questionnaire has provided a readily available and useful tool for a trial for standard questionnaires in the School of Engineering.

- It has provided the vehicle for developing a quick and "staff friendly" automatic system for handling questionnaires.

- It has provided performance parameters which have potential to give the strategic overview necessary to monitor quality and be able to prioritise on development and further investigations needed to improve quality.

- It has provided a useful staff development tool in promoting within the school the use of standard questionnaires, a debate on the educational meaning of the data and the need for a teaching and learning philosophy from which to offer an interpretation.

- It has demonstrated the importance of data for both strategic and tactical policy-making to improve overall scheme quality.
- It has raised important questions concerning the interpretation of

questionnaires and the way student perception scores must be related to norms derived from similar disciplines.

References

Ramsden, P. (1990). Higher Education Performance Indicators Project: *Report on Course Experience Questionnaire.*

Ramsden, P. (1991). *Learning to Teach in Higher Education.* London: Kogan Page.

Scheme No.	Description	Good Teaching	Clear Goals	Appropriate Workload	Appropriate Assessment	Student Independence	No. of Replies	No. of students on scheme
1	1st Year BEng 1	3.13	3.07	2.45	3.00	2.82	37	49
2	2nd Year BEng 1	3.04	2.90	2.04	3.08	2.36	54	55
3	4th Year BEng 1	2.84	2.77	2.05	2.85	2.33	20	69
4	1st Year HND 1	3.38	3.47	2.73	3.26	2.83	43	53
5	3rd Year HND 1	3.28	3.32	2.21	3.11	2.65	33	43
6	1st Year BEng 2	3.32	3.42	2.05	3.12	2.54	23	32
7	1st Year BEng 3	3.16	3.15	2.60	2.89	2.42	48	85
8	1st Year BEng 4	3.19	3.17	2.78	2.92	2.33	65	71
9	2nd Year BEng 3	3.10	2.87	2.29	2.83	2.25	105	144
10	MEng	3.47	3.03	3.54	3.62	2.94	18	21
11	1st Year HND 2	3.42	3.11	3.04	2.90	2.56	24	39
12	1st Year Part Time BEng	2.73	3.09	3.06	3.17	2.35	7	7
13	1st Year BEng 5	3.54	3.38	3.00	3.29	2.76	14	46
14	2nd Year BEng 5	3.30	3.16	2.67	3.02	2.37	20	63
15	4th Year BEng 5	2.94	3.02	2.72	3.46	2.55	20	97
16	1st Year HND 3	3.21	3.37	2.42	3.03	2.25	13	17
17	1st Year BSc	3.26	2.76	2.30	3.18	2.65	10	19
18	2nd Year BSc	3.08	2.86	2.69	3.11	2.45	13	32
19	1st Year HND 4	3.10	3.20	2.80	3.10	2.80	55	84
20	3rd Year HND 4	3.06	2.23	2.33	3.44	2.48	52	75
						total	674	997
	Average	3.19	3.13	2.62	3.10	2.54		
Norms	Engineering	2.79	3.18	2.86	3.05	2.56		
(Ref 1)	Natural Sciences	3.28	3.40	2.83	3.15	2.62		
	Humanities	3.57	3.51	3.17	3.74	3.05		

Results of Returned Questionnaires - Average Scores by Scheme

Table 1

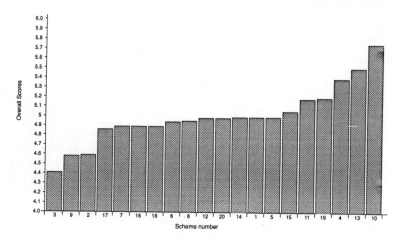

Figure 1

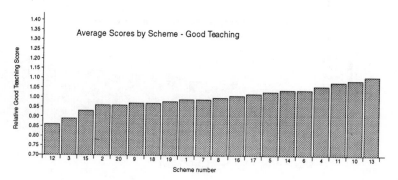

Figure 2

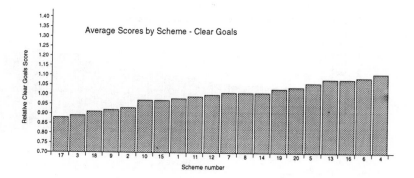

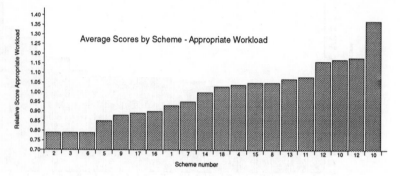

Figure 4

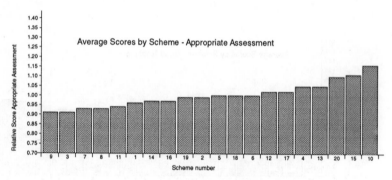

Figure 5

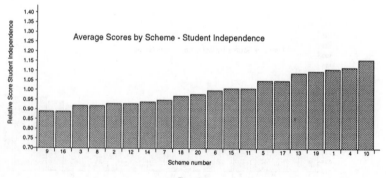

Figure 6